LOGIC

The Laws of Truth

LOGIC

The Laws of Truth

NICHOLAS J. J. SMITH

PRINCETON UNIVERSITY PRESS • PRINCETON AND OXFORD

Copyright © 2012 by Princeton University Press

Published by Princeton University Press, 41 William Street, Princeton, New Jersey 08540

In the United Kingdom: Princeton University Press, 6 Oxford Street, Woodstock,
Oxfordshire OX20 1TW

press.princeton.edu

Library of Congress Cataloging-in-Publication Data

Smith, Nicholas J. J. (Nicholas Jeremy Josef), 1972–
Logic : the laws of truth / Nicholas J.J. Smith.
pages   cm
Includes bibliographical references and index.
ISBN 978-0-691-15163-2 (hardcover : alk. paper)
1. Logic.   I. Title.
BC71.S616   2012
160—dc23   2011048269

British Library Cataloging-in-Publication Data is available

This book has been composed in Minion and Myriad Pro using ZzTEX
by Princeton Editorial Associates, Inc., Scottsdale, Arizona.

Printed on acid-free paper. ∞

Printed in the United States of America

1 3 5 7 9 10 8 6 4 2

For Cath, Jeremy and Oliver

CONTENTS

PREFACE

Over the years that I have been teaching logic, I have become convinced that to teach it effectively, one needs to convey two things: the how and the why of logic. For (to adapt a phrase from Kant) the why without the how is empty, and the how without the why is blind.

Conveying the how and the why of logic is the aim of this book. The book explains how to do logic: it presents the tools and techniques of modern logic in a clear and accessible way. It also explains why things are done the way they are in logic: the purpose of the tools and the rationales behind the techniques. In a nutshell, the why comes down to this: the aim of logic is to discern the laws of truth.

Coverage

The book is a thorough introduction to classical logic (also known as first-order logic with identity). Part I covers propositional logic, and Part II covers predicate logic and identity. Part III covers three topics: basic metatheory for the system of tree proofs used in Parts I and II (soundness and completeness results are proven; decidability and undecidability results are discussed but not proven), the major alternative systems of proof (axiomatic proofs, natural deduction, and sequent calculus), and basic notions from set theory. Some of these notions from set theory are employed earlier in the book, so the final chapter, in which these notions are explained, is more in the nature of an appendix: it can be read piecemeal, as and when necessary. (When an earlier section presupposes something explained in the final chapter, there is a reference forward at that point to the relevant section of the final chapter.)

Readership

When writing the book, I had two primary target audiences in mind. First, the book is designed for use as a textbook in a standard comprehensive introductory logic course—that is, a course that has no prerequisites and is open to students from all faculties and majors. Such courses are often taught by philosophy departments but attract students from across the humanities, natural sciences, social sciences, mathematics, engineering, computer science, law and health sciences.

Second, the book is intended to be suitable for independent study. In particular, students at the end of their undergraduate work or the beginning of their graduate studies—in philosophy, linguistics, and other subjects—often find that they need to know logic, but the opportunity has passed for them to take an undergraduate course in the subject. Others have learned some of the techniques of formal logic but want a better sense of how they relate to one another, or a deeper understanding of what these techniques amount to. This book should be well suited to such readers.

Parts of the book also constitute a contribution to the philosophy of logic and should be of interest even to specialists. Chapter 11 and §13.6.3 are the most obvious—but not the only—examples.

Choice of Proof Systems

The first question when introducing logic is: what system of proof should be used? The most popular choices are trees, or one or another flavor of natural deduction. In this book, logic is introduced via trees, in Parts I and II. Then in Part III—once the reader already has a good understanding of logic via trees—Chapter 15 presents all major forms of all other major proof systems: axiomatic, natural deduction, and sequent calculus. This broad exposure is, I believe, important, because after a proper introduction to logic, one should not find oneself in the position of picking up a different logic book and thinking "what on Earth is this?!"—a position students all too commonly find themselves in when they learn, say, trees and then encounter natural deduction (or vice versa), or even when they learn, say, Fitch-style natural deduction and then pick up a book that uses Gentzen-style natural deduction.

Selecting Material

The basic rationale behind the choice of material to cover was as follows. Studies in introductory logic lead naturally to further studies in many different areas, for example,

1. nonclassical logics (extensions of and alternatives to classical logic, e.g., modal, tense, intuitionist, relevance, many-valued, fuzzy, and free logics; as in Priest [2008], Burgess [2009]),

2. mathematical logic (more advanced metatheory, e.g., Löwenheim-Skolem and compactness theorems, undecidability of first-order logic,

Gödel's incompleteness theorems; as in Enderton [2001], Boolos et al. [2007]),

3. theory of computation (e.g., models of computation—automata of various kinds, Turing machines, register machines; computable and uncomputable functions; computational complexity; algorithmic complexity; as in Davis et al. [1994], Sipser [2006]),

4. philosophical logic (e.g., monism versus pluralism, normativity of logic, logic and reasoning, logic and ordinary language, theories of truth, analysis of logical consequence; as in Haack [1978], Hughes [1993]),

5. set theory (e.g., axiomatic set theories, consistency and independence, foundations of mathematics; as in Devlin [1993], Hrbacek and Jech [1999]), and

6. formal semantics (e.g., generalized quantifiers, theory of types, categorial grammar, intensional semantics, Montague grammar; as in Gamut [1991b], Heim and Kratzer [1998]).

The idea behind the present book was not to cover these further areas, but to cover introductory logic in sufficient detail to enable readers interested in any of these areas to see how they connect to introductory logic. At the same time, I wanted to cover the core of introductory logic in a way that will be useful and accessible to readers not intending to pursue logic any further.

The upshot of this approach is that there is more in the book than can be covered in a typical introductory logic course. The core material is as follows (excluding endnotes):

- Propositional logic: Chapter 1 (excluding §1.2.2), Chapter 2 (excluding §2.2.1, §2.5.4 after the first three paragraphs, §2.5.5, and §2.5.6), Chapter 3 (excluding §3.5), Chapter 4 (excluding §4.3.2 after the first paragraph) and Chapter 7.

- Predicate logic: Chapter 8 (excluding §8.3.3 after the first two paragraphs), Chapter 9, Chapter 10 (excluding §§10.3.3–10.3.7), and Chapter 12 (excluding §12.4 and §12.5).

- Identity: Chapter 13 (excluding §§13.5–13.7).

In these core parts of the book, the pace is gentle and the presentation maximally accessible. At the same time, the material is presented in proper detail (in contrast to texts that are gentle and reader friendly at the cost of presenting a simplified version of the material, e.g., a watered-down version of the model theory for first-order logic, or no model theory at all). When moving outside the core sections, readers may at times notice a slight increase in pace.

Those parts of the book not included in the above list of core material can be used in various ways. Independent readers and teachers with the requisite time available can cover one or more of them, according to time and interests. They can be used as material for extension classes. Students wishing to prepare for subsequent logic courses during the summer after introductory logic can read one or more of these parts. They can also be used as bridging material at the beginning of subsequent logic courses. To help readers work out which of the non-core parts they might like to cover, here is a rough indication of how these parts relate to the six areas of further study mentioned above. The numbers in boldface refer to the earlier list of six areas of study; **G** indicates general relevance: §1.2.2: **4, 6**. §2.2.1: **4, 6**. §2.5.4 after the first three paragraphs: **G**. §2.5.5: **G**. §2.5.6: **2, 3**. §3.5: **G**. §4.3.2 after the first paragraph: **G**. Chapter 5: **G**. Chapter 6 up to §6.6: **1, 4, 6**; §6.6: **G**. §8.3.3 after the first two paragraphs: **4, 6**. §§10.3.3–10.3.7: **2, 3**. Chapter 11 as a whole: **1, 4, 6**; §11.3: **2**. §12.4: **4, 6**. §12.5: **2**. §13.5: **G**. §13.6: **1, 4, 6**. §13.7: **2, 6**. Chapter 14 as a whole: **2**; §14.2, §14.3: **3**; §14.4: **1, 4, 6**. Chapter 15 as a whole: **1, 2, 4**; §15.1: **5**. Chapter 16: **G**.

Exercises and Solutions

Working out problems is crucial to learning logic, so the book contains numerous exercises. Being able to see whether one has done the exercises correctly is also crucial; hence, answers are available on the accompanying website (http://www.press.princeton.edu/titles/9727.html). Because the answers are online, the exercises cannot be used as take-home assessment tasks, but they could not be used for this purpose anyway: as soon as exercises are published, answers to them begin to circulate, either online or through personal networks within colleges and universities.

The exercise questions are also reproduced on the website. Additional exercises—and perhaps other resources—may be added in time. Any typographical errors or other mistakes in the exercises or answers will be corrected in the online version as I become aware of them.

ACKNOWLEDGMENTS

Many thanks to my research assistant, John Cusbert, for collaborating in the creation of the exercises and answers.

For very helpful discussions, comments, and support, I am extremely grateful to Samuel Baron, Max Cresswell, John Cusbert, Jennifer Duke-Yonge, Peter Evans, Daniel Haggard, Matthew Hammerton, Ed Mares, Michael McDermott, Stewart Shapiro, Michael Slezak, Sybille Smith, Vivian Smith, and Catherine Vidler.

Many thanks to Sybille Smith for advice on questions of German translation.

I thank Ian Malcolm, Rob Tempio, and the team at Princeton University Press and Princeton Editorial Associates for their help and guidance, and the anonymous readers for their useful comments.

I am grateful to the Australian Research Council for research support.

PART I

Propositional Logic

1

Propositions and Arguments

1.1 What Is Logic?

Somebody who wants to do a good job of measuring up a room for purposes of cutting and laying carpet needs to know some basic mathematics—but mathematics is not the science of room measuring or carpet cutting. In mathematics one talks about angles, lengths, areas, and so on, and one discusses the laws governing them: if this length is smaller than that one, then that angle must be bigger than this one, and so on. Walls and carpets are things that have lengths and areas, so knowing the general laws governing the latter is helpful when it comes to specific tasks such as cutting a roll of carpet in such a way as to minimize the number of cuts and amount of waste. Yet although knowing basic mathematics is essential to being able to measure carpets well, mathematics is not rightly seen as the science of carpet measuring. Rather, mathematics is an abstract science which gets applied to problems about carpet. While mathematics does indeed tell us deeply useful things about how to cut carpets, telling us these things is not essential to it: from the point of view of mathematics, it is enough that there be angles, lengths, and areas considered in the abstract; it does not matter if there are no carpets or floors.

Logic is often described as the study of *reasoning*.[1] Knowing basic logic is indeed essential to being able to reason well—yet it would be misleading to say that human reasoning is the primary subject matter of logic. Rather, logic stands to reasoning as mathematics stands to carpet cutting. Suppose you are looking for your keys, and you know they are either in your pocket, on the table, in the drawer, or in the car. You have checked the first three and the keys aren't there, so you reason that they must be in the car. This is a good way to reason. Why? Because reasoning this way cannot lead from true premises or starting points to a false conclusion or end point. As Charles Peirce put it in the nineteenth century, when modern logic was being developed:

> The object of reasoning is to find out, from the consideration of what we already know, something else which we do not know. Consequently, reasoning is good if it

be such as to give a true conclusion from true premises, and not otherwise. [Peirce, 1877, para. 365]

This is where logic comes in. Logic concerns itself with *propositions*—things that are true or false—and their components, and it seeks to discover laws governing the relationships between the truth or falsity of different propositions. One such law is that if a proposition offers a fixed number of alternatives (e.g., the keys are either (i) in your pocket, (ii) on the table, (iii) in the drawer, or (iv) in the car), and all but one of them are false, then the overall proposition cannot be true unless the remaining alternative is true. Such *general* laws about truth can usefully be applied in reasoning: it is because the general law holds that the particular piece of reasoning we imagined above is a good one. The law tells us that if the keys really are in one of the four spots, and are not in any of the first three, then they must be in the fourth; hence the reasoning cannot lead from a true starting point to a false conclusion.

Nevertheless, this does not mean that logic is itself the science of reasoning. Rather, logic is the science of *truth*. (Note that by "science" we mean simply *systematic study*.)[2] As Gottlob Frege, one of the pioneers of modern logic, put it:

> Just as "beautiful" points the ways for aesthetics and "good" for ethics, so do words like "true" for logic. All sciences have truth as their goal; but logic is also concerned with it in a quite different way: logic has much the same relation to truth as physics has to weight or heat. To discover truths is the task of all sciences; it falls to logic to discern the laws of truth. [Frege, 1918–19, 351]

One of the goals of a baker is to produce hot things (freshly baked loaves). It is not the goal of a baker to develop a full understanding of the laws of heat: that is the goal of the physicist. Similarly, the physicist wants to produce true things (true theories about the world)—but it is not the goal of physics to develop a full understanding of the laws of truth. That is the goal of the logician. The task in logic is to develop a framework in which we can give a detailed—yet fully general—representation of propositions (i.e., those things which are true or false) and their components, and identify the general laws governing the ways in which truth distributes itself across them.

Logic, then, is primarily concerned with truth, not with reasoning. Yet logic is very usefully applied to reasoning—for we want to avoid reasoning in ways that could lead us from true starting points to false conclusions. Furthermore, just as mathematics can be applied to many other things besides carpet cutting, logic can also be applied to many other things apart from human reasoning. For example, logic plays a fundamental role in computer science and computing technology, it has important applications to the study of natural and artificial languages, and it plays a central role in the theoretical foundations of mathematics itself.

1.2 Propositions

We said that logic is concerned with the laws of truth. Our primary objects of study in logic will therefore be those things which can be true or false—and so it will be convenient for us to have a word for such entities. We shall use the term "proposition" for this purpose. That is, *propositions* are those things which can be true or false. Now what sort of things are propositions, and what is involved in a proposition's being true or false? The fundamental idea is this: a proposition is a claim about how things are—it represents the world as being some way; it is true if the world is that way, and otherwise it is false. This idea goes back at least as far as Plato and Aristotle:

> SOCRATES: But how about truth, then? You would acknowledge that there is in words a true and a false?
> HERMOGENES: Certainly.
> S: And there are true and false propositions?
> H: To be sure.
> S: And a true proposition says that which is, and a false proposition says that which is not?
> H: Yes, what other answer is possible? [Plato, c. 360 BC]

> We define what the true and the false are. To say of what is that it is not, or of what is not that it is, is false, while to say of what is that it is, and of what is not that it is not, is true. [Aristotle, c. 350 BC-a, Book IV (Γ) §7]

In contrast, nonpropositions do not represent the world as being thus or so: they are not claims about how things are. Hence, nonpropositions cannot be said to be true or false. It cannot be said that the world is (or is not) the way a nonproposition represents it to be, because nonpropositions are not claims that the world is some way.[3]

Here are some examples of propositions:

1. Snow is white.

2. The piano is a multistringed instrument.

3. Snow is green.

4. Oranges are orange.

5. The highest speed reached by any polar bear on 11 January 2004 was 31.35 kilometers per hour.

6. I am hungry.

Note from these examples that a proposition need not be true (3), that a proposition might be so obviously true that we should never bother saying it was true (4), and that we might have no way of knowing whether a proposition is true or false (5). What these examples *do* all have in common is that they make claims about how things are: they represent the world as being some way. Therefore, it makes sense to speak of each of them as being true (i.e., the world is the way the proposition represents it to be) or false (things aren't that way)—even if we have no way of knowing which way things actually are.

Examples of nonpropositions include:

7. Ouch!

8. Stop it!

9. Hello.

10. Where are we?

11. Open the door!

12. Is the door open?

It might be appropriate or inappropriate in various ways to say "hello" (or "open the door!" etc.) in various situations—but doing so generally could not be said to be true or false. That is because when I say "hello," I do not make a claim about how the world is: I do not represent things as being thus or so.[4] Nonpropositions can be further subdivided into *questions* (10, 12), *commands* (8, 11), *exclamations* (7, 9), and so on. For our purposes these further classifications will not be important, as all nonpropositions lie outside our area of interest: they cannot be said to be true or false and hence lie outside the domain of the laws of truth.

1.2.1 Exercises

Classify the following as propositions or nonpropositions.

1. Los Angeles is a long way from New York.

2. Let's go to Los Angeles!

3. Los Angeles, whoopee!

4. Would that Los Angeles were not so far away.

5. I really wish Los Angeles were nearer to New York.

6. I think we should go to Los Angeles.

7. I hate Los Angeles.

8. Los Angeles is great!

9. If only Los Angeles were closer.

10. Go to Los Angeles!

1.2.2 Sentences, Contexts, and Propositions[5]

In the previous section we stated "here are some examples of propositions," followed by a list of sentences. We need to be more precise about this. The idea is not that each sentence (e.g., "I am hungry") is a proposition. Rather, the idea is that *what the sentence says* when uttered in a certain context—the claim it makes about the world—is a proposition.[6] To make this distinction clear, we first need to clarify the notion of a *sentence*—and to do that, we need to clarify the notion of a *word:* in particular, we need to explain the distinction between word *types* and word *tokens.*[7]

Consider a word, say, "leisure." Write it twice on a slip of paper, like so:

| leisure   leisure |

How many words are there on the paper? There are two word tokens on the paper, but only one word type is represented thereon, for both tokens are of the same type. A word token is a physical thing: a string of ink marks (a flat sculpture of pigments on the surface of the paper), a blast of sound waves, a string of pencil marks, chalk marks on a blackboard, an arrangement of paint molecules, a pattern of illuminated pixels on a computer screen—and so on, for all the other ways in which words can be physically reproduced, whether in visual, aural, or some other form. A word token has a location in space and time: a size and a duration (i.e., a lifespan: the period from when it comes into existence to when it goes out of existence). It is a physical object embedded in a wider physical context. A word type, in contrast, is an abstract object: it has no location in space or time—no size and no duration. Its *instances*—word tokens—each have a particular length, but the word type itself does not. (Tokens of the word type "leisure" on microfilm are very small; tokens on billboards are very large. The word type itself has no size.) Suppose that a teacher asks her pupils to take their pencils and write a word in their notebooks. She then looks at their notebooks and makes the following remarks:

1. Alice's word is smudged.

2. Bob and Carol wrote the same word.

3. Dave's word is in ink, not pencil.

4. Edwina's word is archaic.

In remark (1) "word" refers to the word token in Alice's book. The teacher is saying that this token is smudged, not that the word type of which it is a token is smudged (which would make no sense). In remark (2) "word" refers to the word type of which Bob and Carol both produced tokens in their books. The teacher is not saying that Bob and Carol collaborated in producing a single word token between them (say by writing one letter each until it was finished); she is saying that the two tokens that they produced are tokens of the one word type. In remark (3) "word" refers to the word token in Dave's book. The teacher is saying that this token is made of ink, not that the word type of which it is a token is made of ink (which, again, would make no sense). In remark (4) "word" refers to the word type of which Edwina produced a token in her book. The teacher is not saying that Edwina cut her word token from an old manuscript and pasted it into her book; she is saying that the word type of which Edwina produced a token is no longer in common use.

Turning from words to sentences, we can make an analogous distinction between sentence types and sentence tokens. Sentence types are abstract objects: they have no size, no location in space or time. Their instances—sentence tokens—do have sizes and locations. They are physical objects, embedded in physical contexts: arrangements of ink, bursts of sound waves, and so on. A sentence type is made up of word types in a certain sequence;[8] its tokens are made up of tokens of those word types, arranged in corresponding order. If I say that the first sentence of Captain Cook's log entry for 5 June 1768 covered one and a half pages of his logbook, I am talking about a sentence token. If I say that the third sentence of his log entry for 8 June is the very same sentence as the second sentence of his log entry for 9 June, I am talking about a sentence type (I am not saying of a particular sentence token that it figures in two separate log entries, because, e.g., he was writing on paper that was twisted and spliced in such a way that when we read the log, we read a certain sentence token once, and then later come to that very same token again).[9]

§

Now let us return to the distinction between sentences and propositions. Consider a sentence type (e.g., "I am hungry"). A speaker can make a claim about the world by uttering this sentence in a particular context. Doing so will involve producing a token of the sentence.[10] We do not wish to identify the proposition expressed—the claim about the world—with either the sentence type or this sentence token, for the reasons discussed below.

To begin, consider the following dialogue:

Alan: Lunch is ready. Who's hungry?
Bob: I'm hungry.
Carol: I'm hungry.
Dave: I'm not.

Bob and Carol produce different tokens (one each) of the same sentence type. They thereby make different claims about the world. Bob says that he is hungry; Carol says that she is hungry. What it takes for Bob's claim to be true is that Bob is hungry; what it takes for Carol's claim to be true is that Carol is hungry. So while Bob and Carol both utter the same sentence type ("I'm hungry") and both thereby express propositions (claims about the world), they do not express the same proposition. We can be sure that they express different propositions, because what Bob says could be true while what Carol says is false—if the world were such that Bob was hungry but Carol was not—or vice versa—if the world were such that Carol was hungry but Bob was not. It is a sure sign that we have two distinct propositions—as opposed to the same proposition expressed twice over—if there is a way things could be that would render one of them true and the other false.[11] So one sentence type can be used to express different propositions, depending on the context of utterance. Therefore, we cannot, in general, identify propositions with sentence types.[12]

Can we identify propositions with sentence tokens? That is, if a speaker makes a claim about the world by producing a sentence token in a particular context, can we identify the claim made—the proposition expressed—with that sentence token? We cannot. Suppose that Carol says "Bob is hungry," and Dave also says "Bob is hungry." They produce two different sentence tokens (one each); but (it seems obvious) they make the same claim about the world. Two different sentence tokens, one proposition: so we cannot identify the proposition with both sentence tokens.[13] We could identify it with just one of the tokens—say, Carol's—but this would be arbitrary, and it would also have the strange consequence that the claim Dave makes about the world is a burst of sound waves emanating from Carol. Thus, we cannot happily identify propositions with sentence tokens.

Let us recapitulate. A proposition is a claim about how things are: it represents the world as being some way. It is true if things are the way it represents them to be (saying it how it is) and otherwise it is false (saying it how it isn't). The main way in which we make claims about the world—that is, express propositions—is by uttering sentences in contexts. Nevertheless, we do not wish to identify propositions with sentences (types or tokens), because of the following observations:

- One sentence type can be used (in different contexts) to make distinct claims (the example of "I'm hungry," as said by Bob and Carol).

- The same claim can be made using distinct sentence types (the example of John and Johann's sentences in n. 12).

- The same claim can be made using distinct sentence tokens (the example of Carol's and Dave's tokens of "Bob is hungry").

It should be said that we have not discussed these issues in full detail.[14] We have, however, said enough to serve our present purposes. For we do not wish to deny vehemently and absolutely that propositions might (in the final analysis) turn out to be sentences of some sort. Rather, we simply wish to proceed without assuming that propositions—our main objects of study—can be reduced to something more familiar, such as sentences. In light of the problems involved in identifying propositions with sentences, our decision to refrain from making any such identification is well motivated.

So far so good, then. But now, if propositions are not sentences, then what are they? Propositions might start to seem rather mysterious entities. I can picture tokens of the sentence "I am hungry," and perhaps, in some sense, I can even picture the sentence type (even though it is an abstract object). But how do I picture the proposition that this sentence expresses (when a certain speaker utters it in a particular context)? It would be a mistake in methodology to try to answer this question in detail at this point. One of the tasks of logic—the science of truth—is to give us an understanding of propositions (the things that are true or false). What we need in advance of our study of logic—that is, what we need at the present point in this book—is a rough idea of what it is of which we are seeking a precise account. (Such a rough idea is needed to guide our search.) But we now have a rough idea of what propositions are: they are claims about the world; they are true if the world is as claimed and otherwise false; they are expressed by sentences uttered in context but are not identical with sentence types or with tokens thereof. The detailed positive account of propositions will come later (§11.4).

§

There is one more issue to be discussed before we close this section. We have seen that, to determine a proposition, we typically need not just a sentence type but also a context in which that sentence is uttered. For example, for the sentence type "I am hungry" to determine a proposition, it needs to be uttered by someone in a particular context. When Bob utters it, he then expresses the proposition that he (Bob) is hungry (that is how the world has to be for what he says to be true); when Carol utters it, she then expresses the proposition that she (Carol) is hungry (that is how the world has to be for what she says to be true); and so on. This general picture is widely accepted. However, exactly *how* it comes about that a particular proposition is expressed by uttering a certain sentence in a specific context is a topic of great controversy. Some of the factors that potentially play a role in this process are:

1. The meaning of the sentence type. (This is usually thought of as determined by the meanings of the sentence's component word types together with the syntax—the grammatical structure—of the sentence. The meaning of a word type is what a speaker has to know to understand that word; it is what a dictionary entry for that word aims to capture.)

2. Facts about the context of utterance. (Relevant facts include the time and place of the context, and the identity of the speaker.)

3. Facts about the speaker (e.g., what she intended to convey by uttering the sentence she uttered in the context).

Together, these facts—and perhaps more besides—determine what is said by the speaker in uttering a certain sentence in a certain context; that is, what claim she is making about the world—which proposition is expressed.[15] That much is widely agreed; the controversy enters when it comes to the question of exactly how the labor of determining a particular proposition is divided between the contributing factors mentioned above: what role each plays. We do not need to enter these controversies here, however: for in logic we are concerned with propositions themselves, not with how exactly they come to be expressed by uttering sentences in contexts.[16] This is not to say that in this book we shall be able to get by without sentences. On the contrary, our chief way of getting in touch with propositions is via the sentences that express them. The point to keep in mind is that our primary interest is in the propositions expressed: sentences are simply a route to these propositions.[17]

1.3 Arguments

We said that the laws of truth underwrite principles of good reasoning. Reasoning comes packaged in all sorts of different forms in ordinary speech, writing, and thought. To facilitate discussion of reasoning, it will be useful to introduce a *standard form* in which any ordinary piece of reasoning can be represented. For this purpose we introduce the notion of an *argument*. As was the case with the term "proposition," our usage of the term "argument" is a technical one that is abstracted from one of the ordinary meanings of the term. In our usage, an argument is a *sequence of propositions*. We call the last proposition in the argument the *conclusion*: intuitively, we think of it as the claim that we are trying to establish as true through our process of reasoning. The other propositions are *premises*: intuitively, we think of them as the basis on which we try to establish the conclusion. There may be any finite number of premises (even zero). We may present arguments in the following format:

Premise 1
Premise 2
_____

Conclusion

Here we use a horizontal line to separate the conclusion from the premises. The conclusion can also be marked by the term "Therefore" (often abbreviated as ∴):

Premise 1
Premise 2
Premise 3
∴ Conclusion

We may also present an argument in a linear fashion, with the premises separated by commas and the conclusion separated by a slash and the "therefore" symbol:

Premise 1, Premise 2, Premise 3, Premise 4 /∴ Conclusion

For example, consider the following piece of ordinary reasoning. I do not have a watch, and I am wondering what time it is. I notice that Sesame Street is just starting on television, and I know from my acquaintance with the timetable that this show starts at 8.30. I conclude that it is now 8.30. We can represent this piece of reasoning as the following argument:

If Sesame Street is starting, it is 8.30.
Sesame Street is starting.

∴ It is 8.30.

When looking at a piece of reasoning phrased in ordinary language with a view to representing it as an argument, we identify the conclusion as the proposition that the speaker is trying to establish—to give reasons for—and the premises as the reasons given in support of that conclusion. Phrases that commonly indicate conclusions in ordinary reasoning include "therefore," "hence," "thus," "so," and "it follows that;" phrases that commonly indicate premises include "because," "since," and "given that." However, these words are not always present, and even when they are they do not always indicate conclusions and premises, respectively. Hence there is no recipe we can follow mechanically when representing ordinary reasoning in the form of an argument: we must always think carefully about what is being said in the ordinary reasoning—about what it is that the reasoner is trying to establish (this will be the conclusion) and about what reasons are being given in support of this conclusion (these will be the premises). One point to note carefully is that when we represent a piece of reasoning as an argument in our technical sense—that is, a sequence of propositions—we always put the conclusion last. In ordinary English, however, the conclusion of a piece of reasoning is not always what is stated last.

Let's consider another example. When working out what to serve a guest for breakfast, someone might reason as follows: Mary must like marmalade, because she is English, and all English people like marmalade. Here the conclusion—the proposition that the reasoning is supposed to establish—is the thing said first: that Mary likes marmalade. The premises are the reasons given in support of this conclusion—that Mary is English, and that all English people like marmalade. So we represent this piece of reasoning as the following argument:

Mary is English.
All English people like marmalade.
Therefore, Mary likes marmalade.

Note that we count any sequence of one or more propositions as an argument. Thus we count as arguments things that do not correspond to anything we would ordinarily regard as a piece of reasoning. For example:

Snow is green.

It has been a wet winter.

This generosity when it comes to counting things as arguments, while it might initially seem silly, is in fact good, for the following reason. As we shall discuss in the next section, one of our aims is to develop an account that will enable us to determine of any piece of reasoning—no matter what its subject matter—whether it is *valid*. (We shall see what validity is, and why it is important, below.) The more things we count as arguments, the more widely applicable our account of validity will be. If we were more stringent about what counts as an argument, then there would be a worry that some piece of reasoning to which we want our account to apply cannot be represented as an argument (in the more restricted sense) and so would be left out of account. Our present approach avoids this worry. All we are assuming is that any piece of reasoning can be represented as a sequence of propositions (an argument), one of which (the conclusion) is what the piece of reasoning is intended to establish, and the rest of which (the premises) are intended to provide support for that conclusion. That is, every piece of reasoning can be represented as an argument. The fact that the opposite does not hold—that not every argument (in our technical sense) corresponds to an ordinary piece of reasoning—will not matter.

1.3.1 Exercises
Represent the following lines of reasoning as arguments.

1. If the stock market crashes, thousands of experienced investors will lose a lot of money. So the stock market won't crash.

2. Diamond is harder than topaz, topaz is harder than quartz, quartz is harder than calcite, and calcite is harder than talc, therefore diamond is harder than talc.

3. Any friend of yours is a friend of mine; and you're friends with everyone on the volleyball team. Hence, if Sally's on the volleyball team, she's a friend of mine.

4. When a politician engages in shady business dealings, it ends up on page one of the newspapers. No South Australian senator has ever appeared on page one of a newspaper. Thus, no South Australian senator engages in shady business dealings.

1.4 Logical Consequence

Consider the following argument:

1. The rabbit ran down the left path or the right path.
   The rabbit did not run down the left path.
   ∴ The rabbit ran down the right path.

It is said that dogs exhibit a grasp of logic by reasoning in this way.[18] Suppose a dog is chasing a rabbit through the forest, when it comes to a fork in the path. The dog does not know which way the rabbit has gone, but it knows (because the undergrowth is impenetrable) that it has gone left or right (first premise). The dog sniffs down one path—say, the left one—trying to pick up the scent. If it does not pick up the scent, then it knows the rabbit has not gone down the left path (second premise). In this case the dog simply runs down the right path, without stopping to pick up the scent. For the dog knows, purely on the basis of logic—that is, without having to determine so by sniffing—that the rabbit has gone right: it must have, because it had to go left or right, and it did not go left, so that leaves only the possibility that it went right.

The argument is a good one. What exactly is good about it? Well, two things. The first is that given that the premises are true, there is no possibility of the conclusion's not being true. We can put the point in various ways:

- The truth of the premises guarantees the truth of the conclusion.

- It is impossible for the premises all to be true and the conclusion not be true.

- There is no way for the premises all to be true without the conclusion being true.

We call this property—the property that an argument has when it is impossible for the premises to be true and the conclusion false—*necessary truth-preservation* (NTP), and we call an argument with this property *necessarily truth-preserving* (NTP).[19]

Consider another example:[20]

2. All kelpies are dogs.
   Maisie is a dog.
   ∴ Maisie is a kelpie.

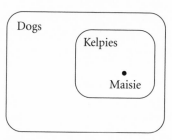

Figure 1.1. The argument is valid

Can we imagine a situation in which the premises are both true but the conclusion is false? Yes: suppose that (as in actual fact) all kelpies are dogs (so the first premise is true) and suppose that Maisie is a beagle (and hence a dog—so the second premise is true); in this case the conclusion is false. Hence argument (2) is not NTP.

Now consider a third example:

3. All kelpies are dogs.
   Maisie is a kelpie.
   ∴ Maisie is a dog.

Can we imagine a situation in which the premises are both true but the conclusion is false? No. Supposing the first premise to be true means supposing that (to represent the situation visually) a line drawn around all kelpies would never cross outside a line drawn around all dogs (Figure 1.1). Supposing the second premise to be true means supposing that Maisie is inside the line drawn around all kelpies. But then it is impossible for Maisie to be outside the line drawn around the dogs—that is, it is impossible for the conclusion to be false. So argument (3) is NTP.

There is a second good thing about argument (1), apart from its being NTP. Consider four more arguments:

4. Tangles is gray, and Maisie is furry.
   ∴ Maisie is furry.

5. Philosophy is interesting, and logic is rewarding.
   ∴ Logic is rewarding.

6. John is Susan's brother.
   ∴ Susan is John's sister.

7. The glass on the table contains water.
   ∴ The glass on the table contains H_2O.

All these arguments are NTP—but let's consider why each argument is NTP: what it is, in each case, that *underwrites* the fact that the premises cannot be true while the conclusion is false.

In the case of argument (4), it is the form or structure of the argument that makes it NTP.[21] The argument is a complex structure, built from propositions which themselves have parts. It is the particular way in which these parts are arranged to form the argument—that is, the form or structure of the argument—that ensures it is NTP. For the premise to be true, two things must be the case: that Tangles is gray, and that Maisie is furry. The conclusion claims that the second of these two things is the case: that Maisie is furry. Clearly, there is no way for the premise to be true without the conclusion being true. We can see this without knowing what Tangles and Maisie are (cats, dogs, hamsters—it doesn't matter). In fact, we do not even have to know what "gray" and "furry" mean. We can see that whatever Tangles and Maisie are and whatever properties "gray" and "furry" pick out, if it is true that Tangles is gray and Maisie is furry, then it must be true that Maisie is furry—for part of what it takes for "Tangles is gray, and Maisie is furry" to be true is that "Maisie is furry" is true.

The same can be said about argument (5). One does not have to know what philosophy and logic are—or what it takes for something to be interesting or rewarding—to see that if the premise is true, then the conclusion must be true, too: for part of what it takes for "philosophy is interesting and logic is rewarding" to be true is that "logic is rewarding" is true. Indeed it is clear that any argument will be valid if it has the following form, where A and B are propositions:

A and B

B

It doesn't matter what propositions we put in for A and B: we could go through the same reasoning as above (the conclusion's being true is part of what it takes for the premise to be true) and thereby convince ourselves that the argument is valid.

Contrast arguments (6) and (7). In the case of (6), to see that the premise cannot be true while the conclusion is false, we need specific knowledge of the meanings of the terms involved. We need to know that "Susan" is a girl's name,[22] and that the meanings of "brother" and "sister" are related in a particular way: if a person x is the brother of a female y, then y is the sister of x. Accordingly, if we replace these terms with terms having different particular meanings, then the resulting arguments need not be NTP. For example:

8. John is Susan's friend.
   ∴ Susan is John's aunt.

9. John is Bill's brother.
   ∴ Bill is John's sister.

Contrast argument (4), where we could replace "Tangles" and "Maisie" with any other names, and "gray" and "furry" with terms for any other properties, and the resulting argument would still be NTP. For example:

10. Bill is boring, and Ben is asleep.
    ∴ Ben is asleep.

11. Jill is snoring, and Jack is awake.
    ∴ Jack is awake.

In the case of (7), to see that the premise cannot be true while the conclusion is false, we need specific scientific knowledge: we need to know that the chemical composition of water is H_2O.[23] Accordingly, if we replace the term "water" with a term for a substance with different chemical properties—or the term "H_2O" with a term for a different chemical compound—then the resulting arguments need not be NTP. For example:

12. The glass on the table contains sand.
    ∴ The glass on the table contains H_2O.

13. The glass on the table contains water.
    ∴ The glass on the table contains N_2O.

So, some arguments that are NTP are so by virtue of their form or structure: simply given the way the argument is constructed, there is no way for the premises to be true and the conclusion false. Other arguments that are NTP are not so by virtue of their form or structure: the way in which the argument is constructed does not guarantee that there is no way for the premises to be true and the conclusion false. Rather, the fact that there is no such way is underwritten by specific facts either about the meanings of the particular terms in the argument (e.g., "Susan"—this has to be a girl's name), or about the particular things in the world that these terms pick out (e.g., water—its chemical composition is H_2O), or both.

If an argument is NTP by virtue of its form or structure, then we call it *valid*, and we say that the conclusion is a *logical consequence* of the premises. There are therefore two aspects to validity/logical consequence:

1. The premises cannot be true while the conclusion is false (NTP).

2. The form or structure of the argument guarantees that it is NTP.

An argument that is not valid is said to be *invalid*. An argument might be invalid because it is not NTP, or because, although it is NTP, this fact is not underwritten by the structure of the argument.

Note that the foregoing does not constitute a precise definition of validity: it is a statement of a fundamental intuitive idea. One of our goals is to come up with a precise analysis of validity or logical consequence.[24] The guiding idea that we have set out—according to which validity is NTP by virtue of form— can be found, for example, in Alfred Tarski's seminal discussion of logical consequence, where it is presented as the traditional, intuitive conception:[25]

> I emphasize . . . that the proposed treatment of the concept of consequence makes no very high claim to complete originality. The ideas involved in this treatment will certainly seem to be something well known. . . . Certain considerations of an intuitive nature will form our starting-point. Consider any class K of sentences and a sentence X which follows from the sentences of this class. From an intuitive standpoint it can never happen that both the class K consists only of true sentences and the sentence X is false.[26] Moreover, since we are concerned here with the concept of logical, i.e., *formal*, consequence, and thus with a relation which is to be uniquely determined by the form of the sentences between which it holds, this relation cannot be influenced in any way by empirical knowledge, and in particular by knowledge of the objects to which the sentence X or the sentences of the class K refer.[27] . . . The two circumstances just indicated[28] . . . seem to be very characteristic and essential for the proper concept of consequence. [Tarski, 1936, 414–15]

Indeed, the idea goes back to Aristotle [c. 350 BC-b, §1], who begins by stating: "A deduction is a discourse in which, certain things being stated, something other than what is stated follows of necessity from their being so." This is the idea of NTP. Then, when discussing arguments, Aristotle first presents an argument form in an abstract way, with schematic letters in place of particular terms, for example:

Every C is B.
No B is A.
Therefore no C is A.

He then derives specific arguments by putting particular terms in place of the letters, for example:

Every swan is white.
No white thing is a raven.
Therefore no swan is a raven.

The reasoning that shows the argument to be NTP is carried out at the level of the argument form (i.e., in terms of As, Bs and Cs; not ravens, white things, and swans): it is thus clear that Aristotle is interested in those arguments that are NTP by virtue of their form.

In this section, we have considered a number of examples of arguments and asked whether they are valid. We worked in an intuitive way, asking whether we could imagine situations in which the premises are true and the conclusion false. This approach is far from ideal. Suppose someone claims that she cannot imagine a situation in which the premises of argument (2) are true and the conclusion is false—or that someone claims that he can imagine a situation in which the premises of argument (3) are true and the conclusion is false. What are we to say in response? Can we show that these persons are mistaken? What we should like to have is a foolproof method of determining whether a given argument is valid: a method that establishes beyond doubt whether the argument is valid and that can be followed in a straightforward, routine way, without recourse to intuition or imagination. Think of the way you convince someone that $1{,}257 + 2{,}874 = 4{,}131$. You do not appeal to their imagination or intuition: you go through the mechanical process of long addition, first writing the numbers one above the other, then adding the units and carrying 1, then adding the tens, and so on, until the answer is attained. The task is thus broken up, in a specified way, into a sequence of small steps (adding numbers less than ten and carrying single digits), each of which is simple and routine. What we would like in the case of validity is something similar: a set of simple rules that we can apply in a specified order to a given argument, leading eventually to the correct verdict: valid or invalid.[29]

§

Recall the quotation from Peirce in §1.1 which ends "reasoning is good if it be such as to give a true conclusion from true premises, and not otherwise." The property of reasoning that Peirce mentions here—being such as to give a true conclusion from true premises—is NTP. In this passage, Peirce equates NTP with good reasoning. That view seems too strong—if "good reasoning" is taken to have its ordinary, intuitive meaning. For example, suppose that someone believes that there is water in the glass, but does not go on to conclude that there is H_2O in the glass. This does not necessarily mean that there is something wrong with her powers of reasoning: she may be fully rational, but simply not know that water is H_2O. Such a person could perhaps be criticized for not knowing basic science—but only if she could have been expected to know it (say, because she had completed high school)—but it would not be right to say that she had failed to reason well.

So we cannot equate good reasoning with NTP. Can we equate good reasoning with validity (i.e., NTP by virtue of form)? This suggestion might seem plausible at first sight. For example, if someone believes that Bill is boring and Ben is asleep, but he does not believe that Ben is asleep, then it seems that there is certainly something wrong with his powers of reasoning. Yet even the claim that reasoning is good if and only if it is valid (as opposed to simply NTP) would be too strong. As we shall see in §1.5, an argument can be valid without being a good argument (intuitively speaking). Conversely, many good pieces of reasoning (intuitively speaking) are not valid, for the truth of the premises does not guarantee the truth of the conclusion: it only makes the conclusion highly probable.

Reasoning in which validity is a prerequisite for goodness is often called *deductive* reasoning. Important subclasses of nondeductive reasoning are *inductive* reasoning—where one draws conclusions about future events based on past observations (e.g., the sun has risen on every morning that I have experienced, therefore it will rise tomorrow morning), or draws general conclusions based on observations of specific instances (e.g., every lump of sugar that I have put in tea dissolves, therefore all sugar is soluble)—and *abductive* reasoning, also known as (aka) "inference to the best explanation"—where one reasons from the data at hand to the best available explanation of that data (e.g., concluding that the butler did it, because this hypothesis best fits the available clues).[30] Whereas validity is a criterion of goodness for deductive arguments, the analogous criterion of goodness for nondeductive arguments is often called *inductive strength:* an argument is inductively strong just in case it is *improbable*—as opposed to *impossible,* in the case of validity—that its premises be true and its conclusion false.

The full story of the relationship between validity and good reasoning is evidently rather complex. It is not a story we shall try to tell here, for our topic is logic—and as we have noted, logic is the science of truth, not the science of reasoning. However, this much certainly seems true: if we are interested in reasoning—and in classifying it as good or bad—then one question of interest will always be "is the reasoning valid?" This is true regardless of whether we are considering deductive or nondeductive reasoning. The answer to the question "is the reasoning valid?" will not, in general, completely close the issue of whether the reasoning is good—but it will never be irrelevant to that issue. Therefore, if we are to apply logic—the laws of truth—to the study of reasoning, it will be useful to be able to determine of any argument—no matter what its subject matter—whether it is valid.

§

When it comes to validity, then, we now have two goals on the table. One is to find a precise analysis of validity. (Thus far we have given only a rough, guiding idea of what validity is: NTP guaranteed by form. As we noted, this does not amount to a precise analysis.) The other is to find a method of assessing arguments for validity that is both

1. foolproof: it can be followed in a straightforward, routine way, without recourse to intuition or imagination—and it always gives the right answer; and

2. general: it can be applied to any argument.

Note that there will be an intimate connection between the role of form in the definition of validity (an argument is valid if it is NTP by virtue of its form) and the goal of finding a method of assessing arguments for validity that can be applied to any argument, no matter what its subject matter. It is the fact that validity can be assessed on the basis of form, in abstraction from the specific content of the propositions involved in an argument (i.e., the specific claims made about the world—what ways, exactly, the propositions that make up the argument are representing the world to be), that will bring this goal within reach.

1.4.1 Exercises

State whether each of the following arguments is valid or invalid.

1. All dogs are mammals.
    All mammals are animals.

    _____

    All dogs are animals.

2. All dogs are mammals.
    All dogs are animals.

    _____

    All mammals are animals.

3. All dogs are mammals.
    No fish are mammals.

    _____

    No fish are dogs.

4. All fish are mammals.
    All mammals are robots.

    _____

    All fish are robots.

1.5 Soundness

Consider argument (4) in Exercises 1.4.1. It is valid, but there is still something wrong with it: it does not establish its conclusion as true—because its premises are not in fact true. It has the property that if its premises were both true, then its conclusion would have to be true—that is, it is NTP—but its premises are not in fact true, and so the argument does not establish the truth of its conclusion.

We say that an argument is *sound* if it is valid and, in addition, has premises that are all in fact true:

sound = valid + all premises true

A valid argument can have any combination of true and false premises and conclusion except true premises and a false conclusion. A sound argument has true premises and therefore—because it is valid—a true conclusion.

Logic has very little to say about soundness—because it has very little to say about the actual truth or falsity of particular propositions. Logic, as we have said, is concerned with the laws of truth—and the general laws of truth are very different from the mass of particular facts of truth, that is, the facts as to which propositions actually are true and which are false. There are countless propositions concerning all manner of different things: "two plus two equals four," "the mother of the driver of the bus I caught this morning was born in Cygnet," "the number of polar bears born in 1942 was 9,125," and so on. No science would hope to tell us whether every single one is true or false. This is not simply because there are too many of them: it is in the nature of science not to catalogue particular matters of fact but to look for interesting patterns and generalizations—for laws. Consider physics, which is concerned (in part) with motion. Physicists look for the general laws governing all motions: they do not seek to determine all the particular facts concerning what moves where, when, and at what speeds. Of course, given the general laws of motion and some particular facts (e.g., concerning the moon's orbit, the launch trajectory of a certain rocket, and a number of other facts) one can deduce other facts (e.g., that the rocket will reach the moon at such and such a time). The same thing happens in logic. Given the general laws of truth and some particular facts (e.g., that this proposition is true and that one is false) one can deduce other facts (e.g., that a third proposition is true). But just as it is not the job of the physicist to tell us where everything is at every moment and how fast it is moving, so too it is not the job of the logician to tell us whether every proposition is true or false. Therefore, questions of soundness—which require, for their answer, knowledge of whether certain premises are actually true—fall outside the scope of logic.[31]

Likewise, logic is not concerned with whether we know that the premises of an argument are true. We might have an argument that includes the premise "the highest speed reached by a polar bear on 11 January 2004 was 31.35 kilometres per hour." The argument might (as it happens) be sound, but that would not make it a convincing argument for its conclusion, because we could never know that all the premises were true.

So it takes more than validity to make a piece of (deductive) reasoning convincing. A really convincing argument will be not only valid but also sound, and furthermore have premises that can be known to be true. Some people have complained that logic—which tells us only about validity—does not provide a complete account of good reasoning. It is entirely true that logic does not provide a complete account of good reasoning, but this is cause for complaint only if one thinks that logic is the science of reasoning. From our perspective there is no problem here: logic is not the science of reasoning; it is the science of truth. Logic has important applications to reasoning—most notably in what it says about validity. However there is both more and less to good reasoning than validity (i.e., valid arguments are not always good, and good arguments are not always valid)—and hence (as already noted in §1.4) there is more to be said about reasoning than can be deduced from the laws of truth.

1.5.1 Exercises

1. Which of the arguments in Exercises 1.4.1 are sound?

2. Find an argument in Exercises 1.4.1 that has all true premises and a true conclusion but is not valid and hence not sound.

3. Find an argument in Exercises 1.4.1 that has false premises and a false conclusion but is valid.

1.6 Connectives

We have said that an argument is valid if its structure guarantees that it is NTP. It follows immediately that if validity is to be an interesting and useful concept, some propositions must have internal structure. For suppose that all propositions were simply "dots," with no structure. Then the only valid arguments would be ones where the conclusion is one of the premises. That would render the concept of validity virtually useless and deprive it of all interest. We are going to assume, then, that at least some propositions have internal structure—and of course this assumption is extremely natural. Consider our argument:

Tangles is gray, and Maisie is furry.
∴ Maisie is furry.

It seems obvious that the first premise—so far from being a featureless dot with no internal structure—is a proposition made up (in some way to be investigated) from two other propositions: "Tangles is gray" and "Maisie is furry."

Before we can say anything useful about the forms that arguments may take, then, our first step must be to investigate the internal structure of the things that make up arguments—that is, of propositions. We divide propositions into two kinds:

1. basic propositions: propositions having no parts that are themselves propositions; and

2. compound propositions: propositions made up from other propositions and *connectives*.

In Part I of this book—which concerns propositional logic—we look at the internal structure of compound propositions, that is, at the ways in which propositions may be combined with connectives to form larger propositions. It will not be until Part II—which concerns predicate logic—that we shall look at the internal structure of basic propositions.

A compound proposition is made up of component propositions and connectives. We now embark upon an investigation of connectives. Our investigation will be guided by our interest in the laws of truth. We saw that any argument of the form "A and B /∴ B" is valid (§1.4). The reason is that the premise is made up of two component propositions, A and B, put together by means of "and"—that is, in such a way that the compound proposition can be true only if both components are true—and the conclusion is one of those component propositions. Hence, the conclusion's being true is part of what it takes for the premise to be true. Thus, if the premise is true, the conclusion must be too: the laws of truth ensure, so to speak, that truth flows from premise to conclusion (if it is present in the premise in the first place). So the validity of the argument turns on the internal structure of the premise—in particular, on the way that the connective "and" works in relationship to truth and falsity.

Our search for connectives will be guided by the idea that we are interested only in those aspects of the internal structure of compound propositions that have an important relationship to truth and falsity. More specifically, we shall focus on a particular kind of relationship to truth and falsity: the kind where the truth or falsity of the compound proposition depends solely on the truth or falsity of its component propositions. A connective is *truth functional* if it has the property that the truth or falsity of a compound proposition formed from the connective and some other propositions is completely determined by the truth or falsity of those component propositions. Our focus, then, will be on truth-functional connectives.[32]

1.6.1 Negation

Consider the proposition "Maisie is not a rottweiler." Thinking in terms of truth and falsity, we can see this proposition as being made up of a component proposition ("Maisie is a rottweiler") and a connective (expressed by "not") that have the following relationship to one another: if "Maisie is a rottweiler" is true, then "Maisie is not a rottweiler" is false, and if "Maisie is a rottweiler" is false, then "Maisie is not a rottweiler" is true. We use the term "negation" for the connective which has this property: viz. it goes together with a proposition to make up a compound proposition that is true just in case the component proposition is false. Here is some terminology:

"Maisie is not a rottweiler" is the *negation* of "Maisie is a rottweiler."
"Maisie is a rottweiler" is the *negand* of "Maisie is not a rottweiler."

Note the double meaning of negation. On the one hand we use it to refer to the connective, which goes together with a proposition to make up a compound proposition. On the other hand we use it to refer to that compound proposition. This ambiguity is perhaps unfortunate, but it is so well entrenched in the literature that we shall not try to introduce new terms here. As long as we are on the lookout for this ambiguity, it should not cause us any problems.

Using our new terminology, we can express the key relationship between negation and truth this way:

If the negand is true, the negation is false, and if the negand is false, the negation is true.

Thus, negation is a truth-functional connective: to know whether a negation is true or false you need only know whether the negand is true or false: the truth or falsity of the negation is completely determined by the truth or falsity of the negand.

It is this particular relationship between negation and truth—rather than the presence of the word "not"—that is the defining feature of negation. Negation can also be expressed in other ways, for example:

- It is not the case that there is an elephant in the room.
- There is no elephant in the room.
- There is not an elephant in the room.

All these examples can be regarded as expressing the negation of "there is an elephant in the room."

Connectives can be applied to any proposition, basic or compound. Thus, we can negate "Bob is a good student" to get "Bob is not a good student," and we can also negate the latter to get "it is not the case that Bob is not a good student," which is sometimes referred to as the *double negation* of "Bob is a good student."

To get a complete proposition using the connective negation, we need to add the connective to one proposition (the negand). Thus negation is a *one-place* (aka *unary* or *monadic*) connective.

1.6.1.1 EXERCISES

1. What is the negand of:
   - (i) Bob is not a good student
   - (ii) I haven't decided not to go to the party.
   - (iii) Mars isn't the closest planet to the sun.
   - (iv) It is not the case that Alice is late.
   - (v) I don't like scrambled eggs.
   - (vi) Scrambled eggs aren't good for you.

2. If a proposition is true, its double negation is . . . ?

3. If a proposition's double negation is false, the proposition is . . . ?

1.6.2 Conjunction

Consider the proposition "Maisie is tired, and the road is long." Thinking in terms of truth and falsity, we can see this proposition as being made up of two component propositions ("Maisie is tired" and "the road is long") and a connective (expressed by "and"), which have the following relationship to one another: "Maisie is tired, and the road is long" is true just in case "Maisie is tired" and "the road is long" are both true. We use the term *conjunction* for the connective that has this property: it goes together with two propositions to make up a compound proposition that is true just in case both component propositions are true.[33] Here is some terminology:

> "Maisie is tired and the road is long" is the *conjunction* of "Maisie is tired" and "the road is long."
> "Maisie is tired" and "the road is long" are the *conjuncts* of "Maisie is tired and the road is long."

Again, "conjunction" is used in two senses: to pick out a connective and to pick out a compound proposition built up using this connective.

Using our new terminology, we can express the key relationship between conjunction and truth in this way:

The conjunction is true just in case both conjuncts are true.
If one or more of the conjuncts is false, the conjunction is false.

Thus, conjunction is a truth-functional connective: to know whether a conjunction is true or false you need only know whether the conjuncts are true or false: the truth or falsity of the conjunction is completely determined by the truth or falsity of the conjuncts.

It is this particular relationship between conjunction and truth—rather than the presence of the word "and"—that is the defining feature of conjunction. Conjunction can also be expressed in other ways, and not every use of "and" in English expresses truth-functional conjunction. For the moment, however, we shall continue with our preliminary examination of truth-functional connectives; we turn to a detailed discussion of the relationships among these connectives and expressions of English in Chapter 6. So keep in mind throughout the remainder of this chapter: we are here giving a first, brief introduction to truth-functional connectives via English words that typically, often, or sometimes express these connectives. In Chapters 2 and 3 we shall gain a much deeper understanding of these connectives via the study of a new symbolic language before returning to the subtleties of the relationships between these connectives and expressions of English in Chapter 6.

To obtain a complete proposition using the conjunction connective, we need to add the connective to two propositions (the conjuncts). Thus, conjunction is called a *two-place* (aka *binary* or *dyadic*) connective.

1.6.2.1 EXERCISES
What are the conjuncts of the following propositions?

1. The sun is shining, and I am happy.

2. Maisie and Rosie are my friends.

3. Sailing is fun, and snowboarding is too.

4. We watched the movie and ate popcorn.

5. Sue does not want the red bicycle, and she does not like the blue one.

6. The road to the campsite is long and uneven.

1.6.3 Disjunction

Consider the proposition "Frances had eggs for breakfast or for lunch." Thinking in terms of truth and falsity, we can see this proposition as being made up of two component propositions ("Frances had eggs for breakfast" and "Frances had eggs for lunch") and a connective (expressed by "or"), which have the following relationship to one another: "Frances had eggs for breakfast or for lunch" is true just in case at least one of "Frances had eggs for breakfast" and "Frances had eggs for lunch" are true. We use the term *disjunction* for the connective that has this property: it goes together with two propositions to make up a compound proposition that is true just in case at least one of those component propositions is true. Here is some terminology:

> "Frances had eggs for breakfast or for lunch" is the *disjunction* of "Frances had eggs for breakfast" and "Frances had eggs for lunch."
>
> "Frances had eggs for breakfast" and "Frances had eggs for lunch" are the *disjuncts* of "Frances had eggs for breakfast or for lunch."

Using this terminology, we can express the key relationship between disjunction and truth in this way:

 The disjunction is true just in case at least one of the disjuncts is true. If both the disjuncts are false, the disjunction is false.

Thus, disjunction is a truth-functional connective: to know whether a disjunction is true or false you need only know whether the disjuncts are true or false: the truth or falsity of the disjunction is completely determined by the truth or falsity of the disjuncts.

It is this relationship between disjunction and truth—rather than the use of the word "or" as in the example above—that is the defining feature of disjunction. Disjunction can also be expressed in other ways, for example:

- Either Frances had eggs for breakfast or she had eggs for lunch.

- Frances had eggs for breakfast and/or lunch.

- Frances had eggs for breakfast or lunch—or both.

To obtain a complete proposition using the disjunction connective, we need to add the connective to two propositions (the disjuncts). Thus, disjunction is a two-place connective.

1.6.4 *Conditional*

Imagine that we look out the window and see a haze; we are not sure whether it is smoke, fog, dust, or something else. Consider the proposition "if that is smoke, then there is a fire." A proposition of this form has two components, and claims that if one of them is true, then the other is true too. We call the former component the *antecedent*, the latter component the *consequent*, and the compound proposition a *conditional*. (Once again we also use the term "conditional" for the two-place connective used to form this compound proposition.) In the above example the conditional is "if that is smoke, then there is a fire," the antecedent is "that is smoke," and the consequent is "there is a fire."

Note that the antecedent is not always written first. The antecedent is the component proposition of which it is said that if it is true, then another proposition is true; the consequent is that other proposition. To put it another way: if the conditional is true, then one of its components might be true without the other component being true, but not vice versa. The consequent is the component that might be true even if the other component is not true; the antecedent is the component that cannot be true without the other component also being true (assuming the conditional as a whole is true). Thus, the relationship between the antecedent and the consequent is logical or *alethic* (having to do with truth), not temporal or spatial. If I say "there is a fire if that is smoke," the antecedent is "that is smoke," and the consequent is "there is a fire." In other words, this is just a different way of expressing the same conditional.

As well as being expressed by "if . . . then" and "if," conditionals can also be expressed using "only if." For example, suppose that I have just gotten off a mystery flight and am wondering where I am. Consider the proposition "I am in New York only if I am in America." This is a conditional in which the antecedent is "I am in New York," and the consequent is "I am in America:" it thus says the same thing as "if I am in New York, I am in America." The easiest way to see this is to think what it would take to make the latter claim false: I would have to be in New York without being in America. So "if I am in New York, I am in America" rules out the case in which I am in New York but am not in America. And that is exactly what "I am in New York only if I am in America" does: the claim is that it does not happen that I am in New York but not in America. In contrast, "I am in America only if I am in New York" says something quite different: it says the same thing as "if I am in America, then I am in New York." In general, "if P then Q" and "P only if Q" say the same thing.

1.6.4.1 EXERCISES

What are the (a) antecedents and (b) consequents of the following propositions?

1. If that's pistachio ice cream, it doesn't taste the way it should. $P \to \neg T$
2. That tastes the way it should only if it isn't pistachio ice cream.
3. If that is supposed to taste that way, then it isn't pistachio ice cream.
4. If you pressed the red button, then your cup contains coffee.
5. Your cup does not contain coffee if you pressed the green button. $G \to \neg C$
6. Your cup contains hot chocolate only if you pressed the green button.

1.6.5 Biconditional

Suppose the drink machine has unlabeled buttons, and you are wondering what is in your cup, which you have just removed from the machine. Consider the proposition "your cup contains coffee if and only if you pressed the red button." Someone who asserts this is committed to two claims:

> Your cup contains coffee if you pressed the red button.
> Your cup contains coffee only if you pressed the red button.

The first is a conditional with antecedent "you pressed the red button" and consequent "your cup contains coffee." The second is a conditional with antecedent "your cup contains coffee" and consequent "you pressed the red button." Now, under what conditions is the original proposition true? Suppose your cup contains coffee. Then, if the second conditional is to be true, it must be the case that you pressed the red button. Suppose your cup does not contain coffee. Then, if the first conditional is to be true, it must be the case that you did not press the red button. So the original proposition ("your cup contains coffee if and only if you pressed the red button") is true if your cup contains coffee and you pressed the red button, and true if your cup does not contain coffee and you did not press the red button, but it is false if your cup contains coffee and you did not press the red button, and it is false if your cup does not contain coffee and you did press the red button. In other words, it is true just in case its two component propositions ("your cup contains coffee" and "you pressed the red button") have the same truth value—that is, are both true, or both false.

We call the original claim a *biconditional.* Note that we are here regarding the proposition "your cup contains coffee if and only if you pressed the red button" as formed from two propositions ("your cup contains coffee" and "you pressed the red button") using the two-place connective "if and only if," that is, the biconditional. We regard this claim as equivalent to the conjunction of the two conditionals "your cup contains coffee if you pressed the red button" and "your cup contains coffee only if you pressed the red button"—but it is not the same proposition as "your cup contains coffee if you pressed the red button and your cup contains coffee only if you pressed the red button." The latter is a compound proposition built up using two basic propositions ("your cup contains coffee" and "you pressed the red button") and two different connectives (a conditional used twice and a conjunction). This idea of different propositions being equivalent—that is, true and false in the same situations—will be made clear in §4.3.[34]

Note that it is common to abbreviate "if and only if" as "iff," and that "just in case" is often used as a synonym for "if and only if" (e.g., "a conjunction is true just in case both its conjuncts are true" states the same thing as "a conjunction is true if and only if both its conjuncts are true").

1.6.6 Exercises

State what sort of compound proposition each of the following is, and identify its components. Do the same for the components.

1. If it is sunny and windy tomorrow, we shall go sailing or kite flying.

2. If it rains or snows tomorrow, we shall not go sailing or kite flying.

3. Either he'll stay here and we'll come back and collect him later, or he'll come with us and we'll all come back together.

4. Jane is a talented painter and a wonderful sculptor, and if she remains interested in art, her work will one day be of the highest quality.

5. It's not the case that the unemployment rate will both increase and decrease in the next quarter.

6. Your sunburn will get worse and become painful if you don't stop swimming during the daytime.

7. Either Steven won't get the job, or I'll leave and all my clients will leave.

8. The Tigers will not lose if and only if both Thompson and Thomson get injured.   *AND*

9. Fido will wag his tail if you give him dinner at 6 this evening, and if you don't, then he will bark.

10. It will rain or snow today—or else it won't.

2

The Language of Propositional Logic

2.1 Motivation

In this chapter we introduce a symbolic language PL (the language of Propositional Logic). Why do we need it? Why can't we continue to work in English (or some other natural language), as we did in the previous chapter when we looked at connectives? The main reason is that we are primarily interested in propositions. As noted in §1.2.2, English sentences provide a means of expressing propositions: we can make claims about the world by uttering sentences in contexts. However, from the point of view of someone interested in the propositions themselves—in particular, in their structure and the role it plays in determining their truth or falsity—English sentences are not the most useful route to propositions: for the structure of an English sentence does not always provide a good guide to the structure of the propositions that it can be used to express.[1] We shall see many illustrations of this point once we have our logical languages set up and begin to translate into them from English.[2] Our goal in introducing PL will be to have a language in which the structure of the sentences—or *formulas,* as they are usually called when formal symbolic languages, as opposed to natural languages, are under discussion—directly mirrors the structure of propositions: a language in which the ways of forming complex formulas from simpler components directly mirror the ways in which compound propositions can be formed from simpler propositions.

2.2 Basic Propositions of PL

Recall that in Part I of this book, we are not looking at the internal structure of basic propositions. We are looking at the internal structure only of compound propositions, which are built up from basic propositions and connectives. Accordingly, basic propositions will be represented in PL by simple capital letters (called "sentence letters," "propositional constants," or "propositional parameters"):

$$A, B, C, \ldots, P, Q, R, \ldots$$

The idea is that as basic propositions have (for the moment) no logically significant internal structure, we represent them using syntactically simple (as opposed to structured) symbols. (Recall the guiding idea that the structure—or lack thereof—of formulas of PL should directly mirror the structure—or lack thereof—of propositions.) There are only twenty-six letters of the alphabet, but we do not wish to restrict ourselves to just twenty-six basic propositions, so in case we ever need more we can add numerical subscripts to the letters:

$$A_2, A_3, \ldots, B_2, B_3, \ldots$$

We want to represent ordinary reasoning—carried out in English—in PL. To do this we require a *glossary*, such as the following:

A: Antelopes chew the cud
F: Your best friend is my worst enemy
N: Albany is the capital of New York

This glossary tells us what proposition each sentence letter of PL is supposed to represent.

2.2.1 Glossaries

For each sentence letter on the left-hand side, the glossary specifies which proposition it represents. Therefore, we need to put something on the right-hand side that determines a proposition. Generally speaking, we write an English sentence on the right-hand side of each entry—but given that the right-hand side needs to determine a proposition, this practice needs to be fully understood. It needs to be understood that when we write the sentence letter F opposite the sentence "your best friend is my worst enemy," we are saying that this sentence letter represents the proposition expressed by some particular utterance of the latter sentence in some particular context (for recall from §1.2.2 that different utterances of this sentence will generally express different propositions). Which utterance is relevant may be obvious from the context, or it may be specified by additional information in the glossary entry. Alternatively, it might not actually matter for the purposes at hand exactly which of various propositions F picks out: in such cases, while we are to understand that F does pick out a particular proposition that can be expressed by utterances of "your best friend is my worst enemy," we do not need to know precisely which of these propositions it is. In any case, the crucial point to keep in mind is that glossary entries pair sentence letters of PL with propositions. If we write a sentence letter of PL on the left-hand side of a glossary entry and a sentence of English on the right-hand side, it should not be thought that the sentence letter of PL stands for that *sentence* of English. Rather, the sentence of English that we put on the right-hand side is to be taken as a route to a particular proposition—and it is for this proposition that the sentence letter on the left-hand side is to stand.

Because glossary entries pair sentence letters of PL with particular propositions, PL is not context sensitive. That is, every token of F (or any other sentence letter) represents the same proposition: the one with which F is paired in the glossary entry. (If F was paired with the sentence type "your best friend is my worst enemy," then different tokens of F would, in general, express different propositions.) This is in stark contrast to English, where (as we saw in §1.2.2) different tokens of the same sentence type often express different propositions. This lack of context sensitivity is precisely one of the features that we want our formal symbolic language to have. We want a language that provides a transparent window onto propositions: when we see different sentence letters of PL, we know that we are dealing with different propositions,[3] and when we see multiple tokens of the same sentence letter, we know that we are dealing with just one proposition. One of the advantages of this approach is that we do not have to worry that an argument such as

P
If P then Q
$\therefore Q$

might not be valid because the different tokens of P and Q that occur in it might express different propositions. In contrast, this is a genuine worry in English. For example, consider the following sequence of sentences:

I am short.
If I am short, then I am not tall.
Therefore, I am not tall.

If Bob (who is short) reads the first two lines and Ben (who is tall) reads the last line, then the argument—sequence of propositions—that they express is not valid. Likewise, if Jane reads the first two lines when she is four (and short for her age) and then reads the last line when she is eighteen (and has become tall for her age) then the argument—sequence of propositions—that she expresses is not valid. When arguments are expressed in PL, however, it is always evident simply from the shape of the symbols used to represent them whether the same proposition appears twice or two different propositions appear.

One important qualification needs to be made when it comes to the context insensitivity of PL. We can give a certain glossary entry for F (e.g., the one above), operate with this glossary for a while, and then later, in a different context, abandon it and introduce a new glossary, in which we use the letter F again and pair it with a different proposition, for example,

F: Fred is tall

That is, we do not have to use the same glossary for ever. The key point is that as long as a given glossary is in play, the sentence letters in it are context insensitive.

We also need to make a clarification regarding the idea that the structure of formulas of PL should directly mirror the structure of propositions. What we mean is that PL should have the resources to mirror propositional structure: the ways of forming complex formulas in PL from simpler components should directly mirror those in which compound propositions can be formed from simpler propositions. We do not mean that every time we use PL to represent some propositions, it is mandatory that we represent their structure in all its detail. Sometimes it is useful to ignore some of the structure of certain propositions: we may be interested only in one part of the structure and wish to "black box" the rest, for example, with a glossary entry such as:

C: Antelopes do not chew the cud

Here we pair up a sentence letter of PL with a nonbasic proposition (a negation): some of the structure of this proposition (the fact that it is formed from another proposition using the negation connective) is not reflected in the formula of PL that represents it (which is a simple sentence letter, with no internal structure). In applications of logic, ignoring structure that is irrelevant for one's purposes can sometimes be useful. In this book, however—where we are introducing logic—we avoid glossary entries that pair sentence letters with nonbasic propositions. (In particular, in the exercises, we always look for glossaries that link sentence letters with basic propositions.)

Because the structure of PL formulas generally mirrors the structure of propositions, and because it should never be unclear which proposition a formula of PL is supposed to express, we can in many contexts afford to be casual about distinguishing between formulas of PL and propositions. For the sake of simplicity of presentation, we often therefore refer to formulas of PL as propositions (rather than as representations of propositions). We return to the issue of the precise relationship between formulas of the symbolic language and propositions in §11.4.

2.3 Connectives of PL

2.3.1 Negation

Negation is represented in PL by the symbol:

$$\neg$$

which is known as "neg." To form a compound proposition from the connective negation and another proposition, we place the neg before the other proposition. For example,

$$\neg P$$

is a negation, where P is the negand.[4]

2.3.2 Conjunction

Conjunction is represented in PL by the symbol:

$$\wedge$$

which is known as "caret." To form a compound proposition from the connective conjunction and two propositions, we place the caret between the propositions and place parentheses around them. For example,

$$(P \wedge Q)$$

is a conjunction, where P and Q are the conjuncts.[5]

2.3.3 Exercises

Using the glossary:

A: Aristotle was a philosopher
B: Paper burns
F: Fire is hot

translate the following from PL into English.

1. $\neg A$ 4. $(\neg F \wedge \neg B)$

2. $(A \wedge B)$ 5. $\neg (F \wedge B)$

3. $(A \wedge \neg B)$

It is not the case that (handwritten annotation)

2.3.4 Disjunction

Disjunction is represented in PL by the symbol:

$$\vee$$

which is known as "vel." To form a compound proposition from the connective disjunction and two propositions, we place the vel between the propositions and place parentheses around them. For example,

$(P \lor Q)$

is a disjunction, where P and Q are the disjuncts.

2.3.5 Exercises

Using the glossary of Exercises 2.3.3, translate the following from PL into English.

1. $((A \land B) \lor F)$

2. $(\neg A \lor \neg B)$

3. $((A \lor B) \land \neg(A \land B))$

4. $\neg(A \lor F)$

5. $(A \land (B \lor F))$

2.3.6 Conditional

The conditional is represented in PL by the symbol:

$\rightarrow$

which is known as "arrow." To form a compound proposition from this connective and two propositions, we place the arrow between the propositions—with the antecedent to the left and the consequent to the right—and place parentheses around them. For example,

$(P \rightarrow Q)$

is a conditional, where P is the antecedent and Q is the consequent.

2.3.7 Biconditional

The biconditional is represented in PL by the symbol:

$\leftrightarrow$

which is known as "double arrow." To form a compound proposition from this connective and two propositions, we place the double arrow between the propositions and place parentheses around them. For example,

$(P \leftrightarrow Q)$

is a biconditional with component propositions P (the left-hand expression) and Q (the right-hand expression).

2.3.8 Exercises

1. Using the glossary:

> B: The sky is blue
> G: Grass is green
> R: Roses are red
> W: Snow is white
> Y: Bananas are yellow

translate the following from PL into English.

(i) $(W \rightarrow B)$

(ii) $(W \leftrightarrow (W \land \neg R))$

(iii) $\neg(R \rightarrow \neg W)$

(iv) $((R \lor W) \rightarrow (R \land \neg W))$

(v) $((W \land W) \lor (R \land \neg B))$

(vi) $(G \lor (W \rightarrow R))$

(vii) $((Y \leftrightarrow Y) \land (\neg Y \leftrightarrow \neg Y))$

(viii) $((B \rightarrow W) \rightarrow (\neg W \rightarrow \neg B))$

(ix) $(((R \land W) \land B) \rightarrow (Y \lor G))$

(x) $\neg(\neg R \land (\neg W \lor G))$

even

2. Translate the following from English into PL.

(i) Only if the sky is blue is snow white.

(ii) The sky is blue if, and only if, snow is white and roses are not red.

(iii) It's not true that if roses are red, then snow is not white. $\neg (R \rightarrow \neg W)$

(iv) If snow and roses are red, then roses are red and/or snow isn't.

(v) Jim is tall if and only if Maisy is, and Maisy is tall only if Nora is not.

(vi) Jim is tall only if Nora or Maisy is.

(vii) If Jim is tall, then either Maisy is tall or Nora isn't.

(viii) Either snow is white and Maisy is tall, or snow is white and she isn't.

(ix) If Jim is tall and Jim is not tall, then the sky both is and is not blue.

(x) If Maisy is tall and the sky is blue, then Jim is tall and the sky is not blue.

3. Translate the following from English into PL.

(i) If it is snowing, we are not kite flying.

(ii) If it is sunny and it is windy, then we are sailing or kite flying.

(iii) Only if it is windy are we kite flying, and only if it is windy are we sailing.

(iv) We are sailing or kite flying—or skiing.

(v) If—and only if—it is windy, we are sailing.

(vi) We are skiing only if it is windy or snowing.

(vii) We are skiing only if it is both windy and snowing.

(viii) If it is sunny, then if it is windy, we are kite flying.

It's false that (if... then not...)

(ix) We are sailing only if it is sunny, windy, and not snowing.

(x) If it is sunny and windy, we're sailing, and if it is snowing and not windy, we're skiing.

2.3.9 Summary

Symbol in PL	Name of symbol	Expressed connective	Basic example
$\neg$	neg	Negation	$\neg P$
$\wedge$	caret	Conjunction	$(P \wedge Q)$
$\vee$	vel	Disjunction	$(P \vee Q)$
$\rightarrow$	arrow	Conditional	$(P \rightarrow Q)$
$\leftrightarrow$	double arrow	Biconditional	$(P \leftrightarrow Q)$

If you look at other logic books, you will find that other symbols are sometimes used for some of the connectives. Common alternatives include:[6]

Connective	Alternate symbols			
Negation	$\sim P$	$-P$	$\overline{P}$	NOT P
Conjunction	$P \,\&\, Q$	$P \cdot Q$	PQ	P AND Q
Disjunction				P OR Q
Conditional	$P \supset Q$	$P \Rightarrow Q$		
Biconditional	$P \equiv Q$	$P \Leftrightarrow Q$		

The choice of symbols has no deep significance. Making a choice is important: we must pick some basic symbols and then stick with them, so as to avoid ambiguity and unclarity. What choice we make is not nearly so important.[7] In this book we shall stick to the choices we have made and not consider the alternatives again.[8]

2.4 Wff Variables

For reasons that will become clear in the next section, we now want to introduce a device that enables us to talk in a general way about propositions of PL. Perhaps the easiest way to understand this new device is by analogy with *variables* in school mathematics. When we learn mathematics, we begin by noting particular facts, such as $3 + 2 = 5 = 2 + 3$, $7 + 9 = 16 = 9 + 7$—and then we move to the generalization $x + y = y + x$. The variables x and y allow us to state this generalization in a very compact way. Without them, we should have to say something long and potentially unclear, such as "when you have two numbers, if you add the first to the second (in that order), the result is the same as if you add the second to the first (in that order)."

Note that x and y are not new numbers: they are devices that enable us to talk in a general, nonspecific way about the ordinary old numbers 1, 2, 3, ... When we say "$x + y = y + x$," we mean *whatever number* (out of the usual numbers 1, 2, 3, . . .) x is taken to be, and *whatever number* (out of the usual numbers 1, 2, 3, . . .) y is taken to be, the result of adding x and y (in that order) is the same as the result of adding y and x (in that order).

We now want to do a similar thing with propositions of PL. We have encountered various specific propositions: A, B, $(A \lor B)$, $\neg(A \land B)$, and so on. (Think of these as analogous to specific numbers: 3, 5, $3 + 7$, $11 - 8$, and so on.) Now we want to introduce a device for talking in a general, nonspecific way about these propositions. (Think of this device as analogous to the variables x and y.) We shall use the lowercased Greek letters α (alpha), β (beta), γ (gamma), and δ (delta) for this purpose. (We shall also sometimes use these letters with subscripts, i.e., $\alpha_1, \alpha_2, \ldots, \alpha_n$, etc.) We call these letters *wff variables*. (The term "wff" is short for "well-formed formula;" it will be explained in the next section.) Just as x and y are not new numbers, so too α, β, γ, and δ are not new propositions of PL. Rather, they give us a general way of talking about the familiar old propositions—that is, propositions made up of the symbols A, B, C, . . . , $\neg$, $\land$, $\lor$, $\rightarrow$, $\leftrightarrow$, and left and right parentheses.

Using wff variables, we can say, for example,

If α is true, then $\neg\alpha$ is false.

This statement means: whatever proposition (out of the ones we are already familiar with: A, B, $(A \lor B)$, etc.) α is taken to be, if this proposition is true, then the proposition obtained from it by preceding it with a negation sign is false. This is analogous to the following:

If x is even, then $x + 1$ is odd.

This statement means: whatever number (out of the ones we are already familiar with: 1, 2, 3, . . .) x is taken to be, if this number is even, then the number obtained from it by adding 1 is odd.[9]

2.5 Syntax of PL

We now summarize in a compact and more formal way what we have said about the language PL. (It is not possible to do this in such a simple way without using wff variables; that is why we introduced them in the previous section.) Propositions of PL are made up by arranging the basic symbols of the language in certain ways, for example, placing a negation sign before a basic proposition. To describe the *syntax* of a language is to say (1) what the basic symbols of the language are, and (2) how these symbols can be combined to form the sentences of the language. The sentences of PL are called *wffs*.

1. The symbols of PL are:

   (i) basic propositions:

   $$A, A_2, A_3, \ldots, B, B_2, B_3, \ldots, C, C_2, C_3, \ldots, Z, Z_2, Z_3, \ldots$$

   (ii) connectives:

   $$\neg \quad \wedge \quad \vee \quad \rightarrow \quad \leftrightarrow$$

   (iii) punctuation symbols (parentheses):

   $$(\quad)$$

2. Wffs of PL are defined as follows:

   (i) Any basic proposition is a wff.
   (ii) If α and β are wffs, then so are:

   $\neg \alpha$
   $(\alpha \wedge \beta)$
   $(\alpha \vee \beta)$
   $(\alpha \rightarrow \beta)$
   $(\alpha \leftrightarrow \beta)$

   (iii) Nothing else is a wff.

That's it! We have here told the complete story of the syntax of PL. This is an example of a *recursive* definition (aka an *inductive* definition). Clause (2i) is known as the "base clause" and (2ii) as the "recursive clause." (We shall refer to the first line of clause (2ii), the one featuring $\neg$, as clause (2ii$\neg$); the second line, the one featuring $\wedge$, as clause (2ii$\wedge$); and so on.) "Recursive" means "characterized by recurrence or repetition" (as in "recur"). In only a small number of clauses, this definition characterizes an infinite number of strings of basic symbols as wffs. The key point is that the recursive clause may be applied repeatedly. Thus, for example, A is a wff, by clause (2i); so $\neg A$ is a wff, by clause (2ii$\neg$). But then given that $\neg A$ is a wff, $\neg \neg A$ is a wff, by clause (2ii$\neg$). (Note that in clause (2ii), α may be any wff: it does not have to be a basic proposition.) Likewise, $(A \vee \neg A)$ is a wff, by clause (2ii$\vee$), and so on. By plugging the products of the definition back into the recursive clause, we can generate more and more complex wffs, without limit. (Clause (2iii) is known as the "terminal clause": it makes explicit that only strings of symbols generated by the first two clauses are wffs.)

Note the use of wff variables in clause (2ii). The second line of this clause, for example, says that if α and β are wffs, then $(\alpha \wedge \beta)$ is a wff. This is a clear, compact way of saying: if you take any two wffs and add a conjunction symbol between them and parentheses around them, the result is a wff.

Some terminology: We have seen that in a negation $\neg \alpha$, the proposition α to which the negation connective is applied is called the "negand;" that in a conjunction $(\alpha \wedge \beta)$, the propositions α and β to which the conjunction connective is applied are called the "conjuncts;" and so on. Sometimes we want to speak about connectives and the propositions to which they apply in a general way (e.g., rather than talking specifically about negation or conjunction, we want to say something that applies to any connective): in this case we call those propositions the "arguments" of the connective.[10]

2.5.1 Exercises

1. State whether each of the following is a wff of PL.
   (i) $((A \rightarrow B))$ **NO**
   (ii) $(A \rightarrow \rightarrow B)$ **NO**
   (iii) $(A \rightarrow (A \rightarrow A))$ **YES**
   (iv) $A \rightarrow ((A \rightarrow A))$ **NO**
   (v) $((A \wedge B) \wedge) A$ **NO**
   (vi) $(A \vee (A \vee (A \vee (A \vee (A \vee (A \vee (A \vee A))))))$ ~~**YES**~~ **NO**
   (vii) $((AA \vee \wedge BC))$ **NO**
   (viii) $((A \vee A) \wedge BC))$ **NO**
   (ix) ABC **NO**
   (x) $((A \vee A) \wedge ((A \vee A) \wedge ((A \vee A) \wedge A)))$ **YES**

2. Give recursive definitions of the following.
   (i) The set of all odd numbers.
   (ii) The set of all numbers divisible by five.
   (iii) The set of all "words" (finite strings of letters) that use only (but not necessarily both of) the letters a and b.
   (iv) The set containing all of Bob's ancestors.
   (v) The set of all cackles: hah hah hah, hah hah hah hah, hah hah hah hah hah, and so on.

2.5.2 Logical and Nonlogical Vocabulary

In clause 1 in §2.5, we introduced the basic symbols of the language PL. These symbols fall into three categories:

- logical symbols,
- nonlogical symbols, and
- auxiliary symbols.

Every symbol is in exactly one of these categories. This division will hold for all the logical languages that we examine in this book. In the case of our first language—PL—the division is:

- the connectives are logical symbols,

- the basic propositions are nonlogical symbols, and

- the parentheses are auxiliary symbols.

We shall discuss the significance and implications of this division at various points below. For now, the rough idea is as follows. Logical symbols have fixed meanings, whereas the meanings of the nonlogical symbols have to be specified. That is why our glossaries specify translations for basic propositions of PL but do not specify translations for the connectives. (The auxiliary symbols have no meanings in themselves: they simply enable us to form meaningful compound propositions in an unambiguous way.)[11]

2.5.3 Constructing Wffs

If a given string of symbols is a wff, it must be constructible in accordance with the recursive definition given in §2.5. Sometimes it can be useful to trace through the construction of a wff. For example, consider the wff:

$$(\neg P \wedge (Q \vee R))$$

Here is how it can be constructed:

Step	Wff constructed at this step	From steps/by clause
1	P	/ (2i)
2	Q	/ (2i)
3	R	/ (2i)
4	$\neg P$	1 / (2ii¬)
5	$(Q \vee R)$	2, 3 / (2ii∨)
6	$(\neg P \wedge (Q \vee R))$	4, 5 / (2ii∧)

Note that at each step of the construction of our target wff, we have something that is itself a wff. We call these wffs the *subformulas* of the target wff. (A note on the terminology: the target wff is classified as a subformula of itself.)

In constructing the wff, we construct its subformulas from simplest to most complex. By "simpler" we mean "has fewer connectives." So we start with *basic* subformulas: ones with no connectives. This is phase 0 (steps 1–3 in the example). (Note that we are distinguishing phases from steps: in general, one phase may comprise several steps.) We next construct subformulas that add a connective to formulas constructed in phase 0: this is phase 1 (steps 4 and 5 in the example). We then construct subformulas that add a connective to formulas constructed in phase 0 or 1: this is phase 2 (step 6 in the above example). We can then construct subformulas that add a connective to formulas constructed in phase 0, 1, or 2: this is phase 3—and so on until we have constructed the target wff. (In the above example, we stop at phase 2, as the target wff is complete in that phase.)

As mentioned, each phase may involve several steps. That is, there may be more than one basic formula to be constructed in phase 0 (in the above example there are three: P, Q, and R), more than one formula to be constructed in phase 1 (in the example there are two: $\neg P$ and $(Q \vee R)$), and so on. Within a phase, it does not matter in which order the wffs are constructed (e.g., steps 4 and 5 above could be switched). It is crucial, however, that the phases be done in order: we cannot construct $(\neg P \wedge (Q \vee R))$ by putting $\wedge$ between $\neg P$ and $(Q \vee R)$ until we have the component wffs $\neg P$ and $(Q \vee R)$, constructed at an earlier phase.

Each nonbasic wff has a *main* connective: the one added last in the construction. Note that in the above construction, steps 1, 2, and 3 can be done in any order, and while step 4 must come after step 1, and step 5 must come after steps 2 and 3, it does not matter whether 4 comes before or after 5. Nevertheless, there is never a choice as to which step comes last—so there is never any uncertainty regarding which connective is the main one.[12]

We do not have to go through the construction of a wff to determine the main connective. If the wff has a negation outside all parentheses, that negation is the main connective. If not, then the main connective is the two-place connective with the least number of parentheses around it (i.e., only one set of parentheses).

2.5.3.1 EXERCISES

Write out a construction for each of the following wffs, and state the main connective.

1. $(\neg P \vee (Q \wedge R))$

2. $(\neg P \wedge (Q \vee R))$

3. $((\neg P \wedge \neg Q) \vee \neg R)$

4. $((P \to Q) \vee (R \to S))$

5. $(((P \leftrightarrow Q) \leftrightarrow R) \leftrightarrow S)$

6. $((\neg P \wedge \neg \neg P) \to (P \wedge \neg P))$

2.5.4 Abbreviations

Where it will cause no confusion, we may—for the sake of brevity and simplicity—omit outer parentheses. So we may sometimes write, say, $P \wedge Q$ instead of $(P \wedge Q)$. Strictly speaking, the former is not wellformed: clause (2ii$\wedge$) states that to construct a wff using $\wedge$, we must take two wffs and put $\wedge$ between them and parentheses around the outside. It is, however, a useful abbreviation, when no confusion can result from omitting the outer parentheses.[13]

Note that in clause (2ii) of the definition of wffs in §2.5, the wff variables α and β stand for wffs: that is, official wffs, with no parentheses omitted. If you have been working with (say) a conjunction, and you have omitted its outer parentheses—writing $\alpha \wedge \beta$—you must restore them before applying (say) clause (2ii¬). Otherwise—if you just stick on a negation symbol, without restoring the parentheses first—you will get $\neg\alpha \wedge \beta$. This is a legitimate abbreviation of $(\neg\alpha \wedge \beta)$, which is a wff—but this wff is not the negation of our original conjunction $\alpha \wedge \beta$. It is not a negation at all—it is a conjunction: of the negation of α, and β. To get the negation of $\alpha \wedge \beta$, you have to restore its outermost parentheses before applying clause (2ii¬). The result is then $\neg(\alpha \wedge \beta)$.

There is an additional unofficial convenience that we allow ourselves: where we have a formula with many parentheses in it, we may change the shape of some of them, to make the formula easier to read. For example, instead of:

$$((((A \rightarrow B) \wedge (B \rightarrow A)) \rightarrow (A \leftrightarrow B)) \wedge ((A \leftrightarrow B) \rightarrow ((A \wedge B) \vee \neg(A \vee B)))) \quad (2.1)$$

we may write:

$$\{[(A \rightarrow B) \wedge (B \rightarrow A)] \rightarrow (A \leftrightarrow B)\} \wedge \{(A \leftrightarrow B) \rightarrow [(A \wedge B) \vee \neg(A \vee B)]\} \quad (2.2)$$

We are not here augmenting the official syntax of PL with additional symbols [, {, and so on. Officially, (2.2) is not a wff. Rather, (2.2) is something that we allow ourselves to write in place of (2.1), in contexts where this format will cause no confusion, because (2.2) is easier to read. Only (2.1), however, is an official wff.

§

Some books also introduce conventions for omitting inner parentheses in an unambiguous way. In general we do not do this in this book (although we do allow the omission of internal parentheses in two special cases—see §4.3.2). Nevertheless, such conventions are worth mentioning here, if only because outside this book it is not uncommon to find expressions with no parentheses at all. On the face of it, an expression such as:

$$A \rightarrow B \wedge C \vee D$$

is multiply ambiguous. It could represent any of the following wffs:

1. $(((A \rightarrow B) \wedge C) \vee D)$ 4. $(A \rightarrow ((B \wedge C) \vee D))$

2. $((A \rightarrow B) \wedge (C \vee D))$ 5. $(A \rightarrow (B \wedge (C \vee D)))$

3. $((A \rightarrow (B \wedge C)) \vee D)$

We can pick out just one of these wffs as the intended reading of the original expression by introducing an *ordering* of the connectives and then stipulating that when restoring parentheses to an expression, we go through the connectives in the expression in the prescribed order, adding parentheses around each one in such a way that we always form the smallest possible subformula at each stage. For example, if we consider only the three connectives featured in the above expression, there are six possible ways of ordering them:

1. $\rightarrow, \wedge, \vee$
2. $\rightarrow, \vee, \wedge$
3. $\wedge, \rightarrow, \vee$

4. $\wedge, \vee, \rightarrow$
5. $\vee, \rightarrow, \wedge$
6. $\vee, \wedge, \rightarrow$

If we add parentheses to our original expression $A \rightarrow B \wedge C \vee D$ using the first ordering, we first add parentheses around the $\rightarrow$ in such a way as to make the smallest possible subformula containing $\rightarrow$:

$(A \rightarrow B) \wedge C \vee D$

We then add parentheses around the $\wedge$ in such a way as to make the smallest possible subformula containing $\wedge$:

$((A \rightarrow B) \wedge C) \vee D$

Finally we add parentheses around the $\vee$ in such a way as to make the smallest possible subformula containing $\vee$:

$(((A \rightarrow B) \wedge C) \vee D)$

The result is the first wff in our list of possible disambiguations of the original parenthesis-free expression.

What is going on here is analogous to disambiguation in school mathematics. We are taught that when we see the expression:

$20 + 2 \times 3$

we are to read it as $20 + (2 \times 3)$, not $(20 + 2) \times 3$. In other words, we are taught the convention that when restoring parentheses to an expression, $\times$ comes before $+$.

Conventions of this sort do not allow one to omit all inner parentheses. For example, they do not specify what to do with:

$A \rightarrow B \rightarrow C$

because they do not specify which $\rightarrow$ to treat first. We could stipulate that multiple instances of the same connective be treated in order from left to right (or alternatively from right to left). In that case, $A \rightarrow B \rightarrow C$ would represent the wff:

$((A \rightarrow B) \rightarrow C)$

However, if the wff we wanted to work with was actually:

$(A \rightarrow (B \rightarrow C))$

then the only parentheses we could leave off would be the outermost ones:

$$A \to (B \to C)$$

2.5.4.1 EXERCISE

1. For each of the remaining orderings (2–6) of the connectives $\to$, $\wedge$, and $\vee$ given in §2.5.4, state which disambiguation (1–5) results from restoring parentheses to our original expression in this order.

2.5.5 Polish Notation

There is another way of writing wffs, which allows us to do away with parentheses altogether. Instead of writing two-place connectives between the wffs, we write them in front:

- $(\alpha \wedge \beta)$ becomes $\wedge \alpha \beta$

- $(\alpha \vee \beta)$ becomes $\vee \alpha \beta$

- $(\alpha \to \beta)$ becomes $\to \alpha \beta$

- $(\alpha \leftrightarrow \beta)$ becomes $\leftrightarrow \alpha \beta$

When reading a formula in this notation, we take the argument of a one-place connective to be the well-formed expression immediately following it, and we take the two arguments of a two-place connective to be the two well-formed expressions immediately following it. (By "well-formed expression" here I mean well formed according to the new notation with the connectives out the front.) Thus,

- $(((A \to B) \wedge C) \vee D)$ becomes $\vee \wedge \to ABCD$

- $((A \to B) \wedge (C \vee D))$ becomes $\wedge \to AB \vee CD$

- $((A \to (B \wedge C)) \vee D)$ becomes $\vee \to A \wedge BCD$

and so on. Note that the main connective appears first.

This way of writing formulas was introduced by the Polish logician Jan Łukasiewicz; it is now known as "Polish notation."[14]

2.5.5.1 EXERCISES

1. Write the following in the notation of this book:

(i) $\vee \neg P \wedge QR$

(ii) $\neg \wedge \vee PQR$

(iii) $\wedge \neg \vee PQR$

(iv) $\vee \wedge \neg P \neg Q \neg R$

(v) $\leftrightarrow \leftrightarrow \leftrightarrow PQRS$

2. Write the following in Polish notation:

(i) $\neg(P \wedge (Q \vee R))$ (iv) $(P \rightarrow [(Q \vee R) \rightarrow S])$

(ii) $([P \rightarrow (Q \vee R)] \rightarrow S)$ (v) $[(\neg P \wedge \neg\neg P) \rightarrow (P \wedge \neg P)]$

(iii) $[(P \rightarrow Q) \vee (R \rightarrow S)]$

2.5.6 Finite Alphabets

According to our specification of the syntax of PL in §2.5, there are infinitely many symbols of PL: five connectives, two parentheses, and infinitely many basic propositions. In certain areas of logic, it is important that logical languages be generated from a finite set of basic symbols. (Such a set of symbols is often called an "alphabet.") It is therefore worth noting that PL can be seen as being generated from a finite alphabet of symbols. For each of the infinitely many basic propositions:

$A, A_2, A_3, \ldots, B, B_2, B_3, \ldots, C, C_2, C_3, \ldots, Z, Z_2, Z_3, \ldots$

is clearly made up in a specific way out of symbols from the following finite alphabet (which contains 36 symbols):

$A, B, C, D, E, F, G, H, I, J, K, L, M, N, O, P, Q, R, S, T, U, V, W, X, Y, Z$
$0, 1, 2, 3, 4, 5, 6, 7, 8, 9$

We can spell this out in the following definition of a basic proposition:

1. Any capital letter $A, \ldots, Z$ is a basic proposition.

2. If α is a capital letter and x is a finite string of the digits $0, \ldots, 9$ that does not begin with 0, then α_x is a basic proposition (except where x is the string 1).

3. Nothing else is a basic proposition.

Note that we can further specify exactly what we mean by "a finite string of the digits $0, \ldots, 9$ that does not begin with 0" (henceforth fsd for short) using a recursive definition:

1. Each of the single digits $1, \ldots, 9$ is an fsd.

2. If x is an fsd and y is one of the digits $0, \ldots, 9$ then xy is an fsd.[15]

3. Nothing else is an fsd.

3

Semantics of Propositional Logic

When we first introduced the notion of a connective in §1.6, we said that connectives are of interest to us because of their relationship to truth and falsity. More specifically, we said that we shall focus on a particular kind of relationship to truth and falsity: the kind where the truth or falsity of the compound proposition is determined by the truth or falsity of its component propositions (in a particular way characteristic of the given connective). In other words, our focus is on *truth-functional* connectives. In our discussion in the previous chapter of the connectives of PL, we described how they behave from a syntactic point of view—how they go together with wffs to form other wffs—but we have not yet said anything about their relationship to truth and falsity—about how the truth and falsity of the propositions made up using the connectives are related to the truth and falsity of their components. We turn to this task now.

We take it as a fundamental assumption that each proposition is either true or false (but not both). This assumption is known as *bivalence*. We call truth and falsity "truth values," and we symbolize them by T and F, respectively.[1]

3.1 Truth Tables for the Connectives

3.1.1 Negation

Recall that if a proposition is true, then its negation is false, and vice versa. We present this information in the form of a *truth table* for negation:

α	$\neg\alpha$
T	F
F	T

The table has a header row and then two rows beneath this. The first of these two rows depicts the possibility that α is true: this possibility is shown in the left cell of this row. The table tells us that in this situation, $\neg\alpha$ is false, as shown in the right cell of this row. The second of these two rows depicts the possibility that α is false: this possibility is shown in the left cell of this row. The table tells us that in this situation, $\neg\alpha$ is true, as shown in the right cell of this row.

That's all the possibilities there are: any wff α can only be true or false. The table tells us the truth value of $\neg\alpha$ in each of these situations. It thus tells us everything that we need to know—from the logical point of view, from the point of view of the laws of truth—about the meaning of negation.

Note the use made here of wff variables (§2.4). The table tells us that for any wff, if it is true, then its negation is false, and vice versa. If our table had, say, P in place of α, it would be telling us about the truth and falsity of just one particular wff $\neg P$: the negation of the particular basic wff P. The table we actually gave, however, tells us about the relationship between the truth and falsity of any wff whatsoever (α) and its negation ($\neg\alpha$).

3.1.2 Conjunction

Recall that a conjunction is true if both conjuncts are true; otherwise it is false. We present this information in the form of a truth table for conjunction:

α	β	$(\alpha \wedge \beta)$
T	T	T
T	F	F
F	T	F
F	F	F

Once again, the table covers all possibilities—all the different possible combinations of truth and falsity of the component propositions—and tells us the truth value of the compound proposition in each case. For negation—a one-place connective—there is one component, and hence two cases: the component can be either true or false. For conjunction—and all the other two-place connectives—there are two components; each of these can be true or false; and so in total there are four cases (both components true, first true and second false, first false and second true, or both false). The table has a row for each of these possible cases.

3.1.3 Disjunction

A disjunction is true just in case at least one disjunct is true:

α	β	$(\alpha \vee \beta)$
T	T	T
T	F	T
F	T	T
F	F	F

The fact that $(\alpha \vee \beta)$ is true when α and β are both true might strike you as a problem for the claim that $\vee$ corresponds to "or" and "either . . . or" in English. We discuss this issue in §6.4. For now we shall simply take the truth table of $\vee$ as given.

3.1.4 Conditional

Here is the truth table for the conditional connective $\rightarrow$:

α	β	$(\alpha \rightarrow \beta)$
T	T	T
T	F	F
F	T	T
F	F	T

Note that $(\alpha \rightarrow \beta)$ is automatically true if the antecedent α is false. That is, if the antecedent α is false, it does not matter whether the consequent is true (row 3) or false (row 4):[2] the conditional is true either way. Likewise, $(\alpha \rightarrow \beta)$ is automatically true if the consequent β is true. That is, if the consequent β is true, it does not matter whether the antecedent is true (row 1) or false (row 3): the conditional is true either way. Thus the only way to make the conditional false is to have the antecedent true and the consequent false (row 2).

The fact that $(\alpha \rightarrow \beta)$ is true when α is false or β is true (or both) might strike you as a problem for the claim that $\rightarrow$ corresponds to the English conditional "if . . . then." We discuss this issue in §6.3. For now we shall simply take the truth table of $\rightarrow$ as given.

3.1.5 Biconditional

A biconditional is true when both sides have the same truth value and is false otherwise:

α	β	$(\alpha \leftrightarrow \beta)$
T	T	T
T	F	F
F	T	F
F	F	T

3.2 Truth Values of Complex Propositions

Now that we have the truth tables for the connectives, we can work out the truth value of any proposition of PL, however complex, given the truth values of its basic components. For example, we can determine the truth value of $(\neg P \wedge (Q \vee R))$, given that P is T, Q is F, and R is F. We do this by tracing through the syntactic construction of the wff. At each step, we calculate the truth value of the subformula formed at that step, using the truth table for the connective added at that step:[3]

Step	wff constructed	From steps/by clause	tv	Origin of tv
1	P	/ (2i)	T	given
2	Q	/ (2i)	F	given
3	R	/ (2i)	F	given
4	$\neg P$	1 / (2ii¬)	F	1, tt for ¬
5	$(Q \vee R)$	2, 3 / (2ii∨)	F	2, 3, tt for ∨
6	$(\neg P \wedge (Q \vee R))$	4, 5 / (2ii∧)	F	4, 5, tt for ∧

The wff formed at step 4 is a negation, so in calculating its truth value, we look to the truth table for negation. In particular, we look to the row in which the negand is T, because we are adding the negation to P, and we see from step 1 that P is T. This row of the truth table tells us that the negation is F in this case, and so that is the truth value in step 4. Likewise, at step 5 the wff formed is a disjunction, so in calculating its truth value, we look to the truth table for ∨. In particular, we look to the row in which the first disjunct is F and the second disjunct is F, because we are adding the ∨ between Q and R, and we see from steps 2 and 3 that Q is F and R is F. This row of the truth table tells us that the disjunction is F in this case, and so that is the truth value in step 5; and so on. Note the parallelism between the third and fifth columns in the table: the syntactic construction of the subformulas and the assignment to each one of a truth value are perfectly synchronized.

We can also present the calculation of the truth value horizontally. We proceed in the same order as before, working through the subformulas from the simplest (the basic components) to the more complex, until finally we get to the target wff itself. First we write down the given truth values of the basic propositions beneath those propositions (phase 0):

$$(\neg P \wedge (Q \vee R))$$
$$\quad\; \text{T} \quad\;\; \text{F} \quad \text{F}$$

Then (phase 1) we move to subformulas constructed directly from one or more of the basic propositions. In this case, either of the subformulas $\neg P$ or $(Q \vee R)$ can be treated next. Let's start with $\neg P$. We know that P, the negand, is T, so $\neg P$ must be F. We write this in (under the main connective of this subformula $\neg P$, i.e., under the ¬) and cross out the truth value written under P, as it will not be needed any more, now that we have used it to calculate the value of $\neg P$:

$(\neg P \wedge (Q \vee R))$
F ~~T~~   F   F

Now we calculate the truth value of the subformula $(Q \vee R)$. We write value under the main connective of this subformula (i.e., the $\vee$), and again we cross out the values under the components of this subformula (the Q and the R), as they will no longer be needed:

$(\neg P \wedge (Q \vee R))$
F ~~T~~   ~~F~~ F ~~F~~

Finally (phase 2) we go through the same process for the entire formula, as we have now dealt with all its subformulas. We have a conjunction with two false conjuncts, so the whole conjunction is false:

$(\neg P \wedge (Q \vee R))$
~~F~~ ~~T~~ F   ~~F~~ ~~F~~ ~~F~~

3.2.1 Exercises

Determine the truth values of the following wffs, given the truth values for their basic components, which are written under those components.

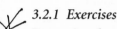

1. $(\neg P \wedge (Q \vee R))$
     T   T   F

2. $\neg(P \vee (Q \to R))$
     T   T   F

3. $(\neg\neg P \wedge (Q \to (R \vee P)))$
     F   T   T   F

4. $(\neg\neg P \wedge (Q \to (R \vee P)))$
     T   F   F   T

5. $((P \vee Q) \to (P \vee P))$
     F   T   F   F

6. $((P \vee Q) \to (P \vee P))$
     T   F   T   T

7. $(P \to (Q \to (R \to S)))$
     T   T   T   F

8. $(P \to (Q \to (R \to S)))$
     F   T   F   T

9. $\neg(((\neg P \leftrightarrow P) \leftrightarrow Q) \rightarrow R)$
         F   F   F   F

10. $\neg(((\neg P \leftrightarrow P) \leftrightarrow Q) \rightarrow R)$
         T   T   T   T

3.3 Truth Tables for Complex Propositions

We now show how to form a truth table for any wff, no matter how complex. A truth table lays out all possible combinations of truth and falsity of the basic propositions that make up a wff, and it shows the truth value of that wff in each of these cases. We saw how to lay out the cases—as rows in a truth table—when presenting the truth tables for the connectives in §3.1. In §3.2 we saw how to calculate the truth value of any wff, given an assignment of truth values to its basic components. So in this section we simply need to combine the techniques of the previous two sections.

Consider, for example, the wff $\neg(P \wedge \neg P)$. It has one basic component: P. So there are two possibilities to consider: P is true, or P is false. Our truth table has a header row, followed by one row for each possibility. On the left is one column for each basic component of our target wff. These columns constitute the *matrix* of the truth table. On the right is a column for the target wff itself. This column is the *body* of the truth table:

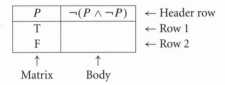

P	$\neg(P \wedge \neg P)$	
T		← Row 1
F		← Row 2

  ↑   ↑
Matrix   Body

All we need to do now is fill in the body of the table. That simply involves doing what we did in the previous section (i.e., calculating the truth value of a wff, given an assignment of truth values to its basic components) once for each row, that is, once for each possible assignment of truth values to the basic components of our proposition.

Rather than work out the truth value of the target wff in row 1, then in row 2, and so on, it is easier in practice to work on one subformula at a time, working out its truth value in each row, and then moving to another subformula and working out its truth value in each row, and so on. The order in which we treat the subformulas is the same as in §3.2: we start with the basic components (phase 0), then subformulas containing only one connective (phase 1), then subformulas constructed by adding one connective to subformulas treated at earlier phases (phase 2), and so on, until we reach our target wff.

So we begin by writing in the truth values of the basic components in each row. These are simply copied over from the matrix:

P	$\neg(P \wedge \neg P)$	
T	T	T
F	F	F

Then we work out the truth value of the subformula $\neg P$ in each row. As we work out the truth value of a subformula, we cross out the truth values of its components, so that they do not clutter up the table and confuse us later:

P	$\neg(P \wedge \neg P)$	
T	T	F T̸
F	F	T F̸

We do the same thing now for the subformula $(P \wedge \neg P)$:

P	$\neg(P \wedge \neg P)$	
T	T̸ F F̸ T̸	
F	F̸ F T̸ F̸	

And now finally we work out the truth value of the target wff in each row:

P	$\neg(P \wedge \neg P)$	
T	T T̸ F F̸ T̸	
F	T F̸ F T̸ F̸	

The more basic propositions occur in a wff, the greater will be the number of rows in its truth table. If there is one basic proposition, there are two possibilities to consider: that it is true, and that it is false. The truth table has a row for each possibility—so two rows. If there are two basic propositions, then as each of these can be true or false, there are four possibilities in total: both true, first true and second false, first false and second true, or both false. The truth table has a row for each possibility—so four rows. In general, the number of rows is calculated as in Figure 3.1. Why? Well, in assigning values to the components, there are two choices (T and F) for the first component, two choices (T and F) for the second, two for the third, and so on. These choices are independent of one another, so there are $2 \times 2 \times \ldots \times 2$ (n times) $= 2^n$ possible assignments in total—and we need a row for each possible assignment.

Number of basic components	Number of rows
1	2
2	4
3	8
4	16
$\vdots$	$\vdots$
n	2^n
$\vdots$	$\vdots$

Figure 3.1. The number of rows in a truth table

So consider, for example, the wff $(\neg P \land (Q \lor R))$. It has three basic components $(P, Q, \text{and } R)$, so its truth table has eight rows:

P	Q	R	$\neg P \land (Q \lor R)$
T	T	T	
T	T	F	
T	F	T	
T	F	F	
F	T	T	
F	T	F	
F	F	T	
F	F	F	

The matrix has a column for each basic component. Here is a trick for filling in the truth values in the matrix, to ensure that each possible combination of assignments of truth values to these basic propositions appears in exactly one row. Start at the rightmost column of the matrix and work down, alternating T, F, T, F, . . . to the bottom of the table. Move one column to the left and go down, alternating T, T, F, F, T, T, F, F, . . . to the bottom of the table (i.e., two Ts and then two Fs, and so on). Move one column to the left and go down, alternating T, T, T, T, F, F, F, F, . . . to the bottom of the table (i.e., four Ts and then four Fs, and so on). In general, as you move one column left, double the numbers of Ts and Fs written at each stage. Continue until the matrix is complete.

To complete the body of the table, we first calculate the truth value of the subformula $\neg P$ in each row (note that it is not necessary to copy over the values from the matrix and write them under the basic propositions in the body of the table):

P	Q	R	¬P ∧ (Q ∨ R)
T	T	T	F
T	T	F	F
T	F	T	F
T	F	F	F
F	T	T	T
F	T	F	T
F	F	T	T
F	F	F	T

Then the truth value of the subformula $(Q \vee R)$ in each row (or these two subformulas can be done in the opposite order: it does not matter, as each contains only one connective):

P	Q	R	¬P ∧ (Q ∨ R)	
T	T	T	F	T
T	T	F	F	T
T	F	T	F	T
T	F	F	F	F
F	T	T	T	T
F	T	F	T	T
F	F	T	T	T
F	F	F	T	F

And then the truth value of the target wff in each row can be written:

P	Q	R	¬P ∧ (Q ∨ R)		
T	T	T	~~F~~	F	~~T~~
T	T	F	~~F~~	F	~~T~~
T	F	T	~~F~~	F	~~T~~
T	F	F	~~F~~	F	~~F~~
F	T	T	~~T~~	T	~~T~~
F	T	F	~~T~~	T	~~T~~
F	F	T	~~T~~	T	~~T~~
F	F	F	~~T~~	F	~~F~~

3.3.1 Exercises

Draw up truth tables for the following propositions.

1. $((P \wedge Q) \vee P)$
2. $(P \wedge (P \vee P))$
3. $\neg(\neg P \wedge \neg Q)$
4. $(Q \to (Q \wedge \neg Q))$
5. $(P \to (Q \to R))$

6. $((P \vee Q) \leftrightarrow (P \wedge Q))$
7. $\neg((P \wedge Q) \leftrightarrow Q)$
8. $(((P \to \neg P) \to \neg P) \to \neg P)$
9. $\neg(P \wedge (Q \wedge R))$
10. $((\neg R \vee S) \wedge (S \vee \neg T))$

3.4 Truth Tables for Multiple Propositions

We can draw up a joint truth table for several wffs at once. The body of the table will then contain one column for each of these wffs, and the matrix will contain one column for each basic proposition that occurs in any of these wffs. For example, a truth table for $(P \to Q)$ and $\neg(P \wedge \neg P)$ looks like:

P	Q	$(P \to Q)$	$\neg(P \wedge \neg P)$
T	T	T	
T	F	F	
F	T	T	
F	F	T	

I have filled in the column for $(P \to Q)$. To fill in the column for $\neg(P \wedge \neg P)$, proceed just as before, working first on the subformula $\neg P$, then on the subformula $(P \wedge \neg P)$, and finally on the target wff itself.

We have already noted that it is unnecessary to copy over the values from the matrix and write them under the basic propositions in the body of the table if you do not want to. Indeed, you need not write in values for any of the subformulas: they all get crossed out in the end anyway. All you really need is the value for the target wff itself. However, in practice, unless you are exceptionally good at doing mental calculations, you will need to write in values for at least some of the subformulas—and then, of course, cross them out again later, leaving only the value for the target wff in each row. (If you do write only the truth value for the target wff, then it is not really necessary to write this value under the main connective: you can simply write it in the center of the column. However, for clarity, I generally write the value under the main connective, even when it is the only value in the column.)

3.4.1 Exercises

Draw up a joint truth table for each of the following groups of propositions.

1. $(P \rightarrow Q)$ and $(Q \rightarrow P)$
2. $\neg(P \leftrightarrow Q)$ and $((P \vee Q) \wedge \neg(P \wedge Q))$
3. $\neg(P \wedge \neg Q)$ and $\neg Q$
4. $((P \rightarrow Q) \wedge R)$ and $(P \vee (Q \vee R))$
5. $((P \wedge Q) \wedge (\neg R \wedge \neg S))$ and $((P \vee (R \rightarrow Q)) \wedge S)$
6. $(P \wedge \neg P)$ and $(Q \wedge \neg Q)$
7. $(P \vee (Q \leftrightarrow R))$ and $((Q \rightarrow P) \wedge Q)$
8. $\neg((P \wedge Q) \wedge R)$ and $((P \rightarrow Q) \leftrightarrow (P \rightarrow R))$
9. $(P \vee Q)$, $\neg P$ and $(Q \vee Q)$
10. $(P \rightarrow (Q \rightarrow (R \rightarrow S)))$ and $\neg S$

3.5 Connectives and Truth Functions

We have already noted (§1.6) that the terms "negation," "conjunction," "conditional," and so on can be used to refer to a connective or to a compound proposition. Thus, we say that the wff $\neg A$ is the *negation* of A, and we also say that the symbol $\neg$ in $\neg A$ is the *negation* connective. In this section we shall see that there is also a third kind of entity that these terms can be used to denote: *truth functions.*[4]

Consider the set of truth values: the set that contains T and F. Functions on this set—that is, functions whose inputs and outputs are truth values—are called "truth functions." Figure 3.2 shows two one-place and three two-place truth functions.[5] (In the names given to the functions—f_1^1, f_3^2, and so on—the superscript represents the number of places of the function, while the subscript is an index number to distinguish between different functions with the same number of places.) So f_1^1 and f_2^1 both send F to T, but while f_1^1 sends T to T, f_2^1 sends T to F. Similarly, f_1^2 and f_2^2 both send the pair (T, F) to F, but while f_1^2 sends the pair (T, T) to T, f_2^2 sends this pair to F; and so on.

Now look at f_2^1, for example. It might ring a bell—for it looks like the truth table for $\neg$:

α	$\neg \alpha$
T	F
F	T

Input	Output of function f_1^1	Output of function f_2^1
T	T	F
F	T	T

Input	Output of function f_1^2	Output of function f_2^2	Output of function f_3^2
(T, T)	T	F	T
(T, F)	F	F	T
(F, T)	F	T	T
(F, F)	T	F	F

Figure 3.2. Some examples of truth functions

This observation brings us to the point of this section. Presenting the truth table for ¬ as we did in §3.1.1 can be seen as doing two things at once:

1. defining a particular truth function (the one we labeled f_2^1 above), and

2. stating that this truth function is the meaning of the connective ¬.

We can separate these steps. The first step is to define the truth function f_2^1, as we did a moment ago (with no mention of any connectives—we just defined various functions on the truth values). The second step is to state, letting $[\alpha]$ represent the truth value of the proposition α:

$$[\neg\alpha] = f_2^1([\alpha])$$

Thus, to find the truth value of ¬α, we take the truth value of α and feed it as input to the function f_2^1; the output is the truth value of ¬α.

Similarly, look at f_3^2. It might also ring a bell—for it looks like the truth table for ∨:

α	β	$(\alpha \vee \beta)$
T	T	T
T	F	T
F	T	T
F	F	F

Presenting the truth table for ∨ as we did in §3.1.3 can be seen as doing two things at once:

1. defining a particular truth function (the one we labeled f_3^2 above), and

2. stating that this truth function is the meaning of the connective ∨.

Again, we can separate these steps. The first step is to define the truth function f_3^2, as we did a moment ago (with no mention of any connectives—we just defined various functions on the truth values). The second step is to state:

$$[(\alpha \vee \beta)] = f_3^2([\alpha], [\beta])$$

So to find the truth value of $(\alpha \vee \beta)$, we take the truth value of α and that of β, and feed them (in that order) as inputs to the function f_3^2; the output is the truth value of $(\alpha \vee \beta)$.

Similarly, presenting the truth table for $\leftrightarrow$ as we did in §3.1.5 can be seen as doing two things at once: defining the truth function labeled f_1^2 in Figure 3.2, and then stating:

$$[(\alpha \leftrightarrow \beta)] = f_1^2([\alpha], [\beta])$$

The same holds for the other connectives. We have not explicitly defined and labeled the truth functions that can be seen as the meanings of the remaining connectives, but it should now be obvious how to do so—for (as we have been saying) the information is implicit in their truth tables.[6]

So the third thing that "negation" ("disjunction," "biconditional," . . .) can mean—the first being the connective $\neg$ ($\vee$, $\leftrightarrow$, . . .) and the second being a compound proposition whose main connective is $\neg$ ($\vee$, $\leftrightarrow$, . . .)—is the truth function f_2^1 (f_3^2, f_1^2, . . .), which can be seen as the meaning of that connective.

We can now give an alternative characterization of a truth-functional connective: it is a connective whose meaning can be specified as a truth function. This definition encapsulates the idea that the connective is concerned only with the truth values of its arguments. When we say, for example, that:

$$[(\alpha \vee \beta)] = f_3^2([\alpha], [\beta])$$

(i.e., when we specify that the meaning of $\vee$ is given by the truth function f_3^2), we mean precisely that to determine the truth value of $(\alpha \vee \beta)$, we need look only at $[\alpha]$ and $[\beta]$: that is, at the truth values of α and β. Nothing else about α and β—apart from their truth values—is relevant to determining the truth value of the compound proposition $(\alpha \vee \beta)$: and that (according to our original characterization) is what it means for $\vee$ to be a truth-functional connective.

3.5.1 Exercises

1. Can the meaning of any of our two-place connectives ($\wedge$, $\vee$, $\rightarrow$, $\leftrightarrow$) be specified as the truth function f_2^2 defined in Figure 3.2?

2. Define truth functions f_4^2 and f_5^2 such that the meanings of $\wedge$ and $\rightarrow$ (respectively) can be specified as these truth functions.

3. Suppose we introduce a new one-place connective ⋆ and specify its meaning as the truth function f_1^1 defined in Figure 3.2. What is the truth value of ⋆A when A is T?

4. What truth values do you need to know to determine the truth value of ⋆$(A \rightarrow B)$?

   (i) The truth values of A and B.

   (ii) The truth value of A but not of B.

   (iii) The truth value of B but not of A.

   (iv) None.

5. Which of our connectives could have its meaning specified as the two-place function $g(x, y)$ defined as follows?

$$g(x, y) = f_3^2(f_2^1(x), y)$$

4

Uses of Truth Tables

4.1 Arguments

According to the intuitive conception laid out in §1.4, an argument is valid if it is NTP by virtue of its form: that is, if the structure of the argument guarantees that it is impossible for the premises to be true and the conclusion false. Let us focus just on the NTP part of the intuitive notion of validity for a moment and use it to motivate an analysis of validity in terms of truth tables. (We shall return to the issue of form in Chapter 5, where we shall see that this analysis also captures the "by virtue of form"/"guaranteed by structure" part of the intuitive conception.) The idea of NTP is that there is no way of making the premises true that does not also make the conclusion true—no possible scenario in which the premises are true and the conclusion false.[1] In the PL framework, an assignment of truth values to basic propositions determines the truth values of all compound propositions as well, via the truth tables for the connectives. So we can think of a possible scenario—a possible way of making propositions true or false—as an assignment of truth values to basic propositions. Now think about what a joint truth table for a collection of propositions does. In the matrix (see §3.3), it lays out all possible assignments of truth values to the basic components of those propositions. So it covers all possibilities regarding the truth and falsity of the propositions in our collection: one possibility per row. Therefore, to determine whether an argument is valid, we may proceed as follows:

- Translate the argument into PL (if the argument is in English and not already in PL.

- Produce a joint truth table with one column for each of the premises and one column for the conclusion.
  - If there is no row (i.e., no possible scenario) in which the premises are all true and the conclusion is false, then the argument is valid.

– If there is one (or more) row(s) in which the premises are all true and the conclusion is false, then the argument is invalid.

For example, consider the argument:

If Maisie is a kelpie, then Maisie is a dog.
Maisie is a kelpie.
∴ Maisie is a dog.

We translate the argument into PL as follows (the glossary is on the left, and the translation on the right):

K: Maisie is a kelpie $K \rightarrow D$
D: Maisie is a dog K
                  $\therefore D$

Here is the joint truth table for the premises and conclusion (note that the second premise and the conclusion are basic propositions and so appear already in the matrix: we do not need to repeat these columns in the body of the table):

K	D	$K \rightarrow D$
T	T	T
T	F	F
F	T	T
F	F	T

We now ask: is there any row of this table in which $K \rightarrow D$ and K are both true and D is false? The answer is no. There is only one row in which both premises are true—row 1—and in this row the conclusion is true also. So the argument is valid.

Consider another example:

Maisie is not a kelpie.
If Maisie is a kelpie, then Maisie is a dog.
∴ Maisie is not a dog.

Using the same glossary as in the previous case, we translate this argument as follows:

$\neg K$
$K \rightarrow D$
$\therefore \neg D$

Here is the joint truth table for the premises and conclusion:

K	D	¬K	K → D	¬D
T	T	F	T	F
T	F	F	F	T
F	T	T	T	F
F	F	T	T	T

We now ask: is there any row of this table in which $\neg K$ and $K \to D$ are both true and $\neg D$ is false? The answer is yes: row 3. So the argument is invalid: it is possible for its premises to be true while its conclusion is false.

Note that there is a row in which the premises and the conclusion are all true (row 4). This does not make the argument valid! The question is whether there is a row in which the premises are true and the conclusion false. There is such a row, so the argument is invalid, regardless of what is happening in other rows of the table.

4.1.1 Counterexamples

An argument is invalid if there is a possible scenario in which the premises are true and the conclusion false. A truth table tells us whether there is such a possible scenario—but it also does more: if there is, it specifies the scenario for us (and if there is more than one, it specifies them all). For a given argument, we term a scenario in which the premises are true and the conclusion is false a *counterexample* to the argument. So a truth table does not merely tell us whether an argument is invalid: if it is invalid, we can furthermore read off a counterexample to the argument from the truth table.

Remember that a possible scenario is characterized by an assignment of truth values to basic propositions. So a counterexample to an argument will be an assignment of truth values to the basic propositions that feature in the premises and conclusion that makes the premises true and the conclusion false. Look at the truth table above. In row 3, the premises are true and the conclusion false, as already noted. In this row, K is false, and D is true: we read this off from row 3 of the matrix. This is our counterexample. In a situation where K is false and D is true, the argument's premises are true and the conclusion is false.

4.1.2 Exercises

Use truth tables to determine whether each of the following arguments is valid. For any argument that is not valid, give a counterexample.

1. $A \lor B$
   $A \to C$
   $\therefore (B \to C) \to C$

2. $\neg A$
   $\therefore \neg((A \to B) \land (B \to C)) \lor C$

3. $(A \land \neg B) \to C$
   $\neg C$
   B
   $\therefore \neg A$

4. $(A \land B) \leftrightarrow C$
   A
   $\therefore C \to B$

5. $(\neg A \land \neg B) \leftrightarrow \neg C$
   $\neg(A \lor B)$
   $\therefore C \to \neg C$

6. $A \lor B$
   $\neg A \lor C$
   $B \to C$
   $\therefore C$

7. $\neg(A \lor B) \leftrightarrow \neg C$
   $\neg A \land \neg B$
   $\therefore C \land \neg C$

8. $\neg(A \land B) \to (C \lor A)$
   $\neg A \lor \neg B$
   A
   $\therefore \neg(C \lor \neg C)$

9. $A \to (B \land C)$
   $B \leftrightarrow \neg C$
   $\therefore \neg A$

10. $A \to B$
    $B \to C$
    $\neg C$
    $\therefore \neg A$

4.1.3 Soundness

Each row of the truth table represents a possible way of making propositions true or false. One of the rows (the *actual row*) represents the actual truth values of the propositions in question. Consider the argument:

> Snow is white.
> Grass is green.
> $\therefore$ Snow is white and grass is green.

Translating into PL we get:

> S: Snow is white S
> G: Grass is green G
> $\therefore (S \land G)$

Here is the truth table for this argument:

S	G	$(S \land G)$
T	T	T
T	F	F
F	T	F
F	F	F

Row 1 is the actual row. In this row, S and G are both true, which corresponds to the way things actually are.

An argument is valid if there is no row in which the premises are all true and the conclusion false. An argument is sound if it is valid and its premises are true: that is, actually true. In other words, an argument will be sound if it is valid and its premises are true in the actual row of its truth table.

Of course, we may not know which row is the actual row. So although truth tables give a foolproof test for validity, they do not give a foolproof test for soundness. A truth table lays out all the possibilities, and by looking at the table, we can see whether there is any row in which the premises are true and the conclusion false—that is, we can determine validity. The truth table does not, however, tell us which of its rows is the actual row—and unless we happen to know this information, we cannot determine whether the argument is sound. Note that there always is an actual row: the world really is some way or other, and the propositions in our argument say particular things about the world, and so these things are true or false; as the table represents all possible ways of making the propositions in our argument true or false, it must include among them the one representing the actual truth values of those propositions. The point is simply that we may not know what the actual situation is.

4.2 Single Propositions

If a proposition comes out true in every row of its truth table, it is a *tautology* or *logical truth*. Such a proposition can never come out false; it is true no matter what.

If a proposition comes out false in every row of its truth table, it is called a *contradiction, logical falsehood*, or *unsatisfiable*. Such a proposition can never come out true; it is false no matter what.

If a proposition is not a tautology (aka a logical truth) we call it a "non-tautology" or a "non-logicaltruth."[2]

A proposition that is not a contradiction is satisfiable: it is true in at least one row of its truth table. Note that the category of satisfiable propositions includes both tautologies and propositions that are true in some rows and false in others. The situation is summarized in Figure 4.1.

There are two notions sometimes applied to single propositions that (unlike the notions mentioned above) depend for their definitions on the notion of the actual row. (Thus, in just the way that truth tables provide a foolproof test for validity, but not for soundness, so too truth tables provide a foolproof test for the above notions, but not for the two about to be mentioned.) A proposition is said to be *contingently true* (or just *contingent*) if it is true (i.e., in the actual row) but is not a tautology (i.e., it is false in some other row(s)). A proposition is said to be *contingently false* if it is false (in the actual row) but

	Values in truth table	Type of proposition	
1	T in every row	**Tautology** aka **logical truth**	
2	F in every row	**Contradiction** aka **logical falsehood** aka **unsatisfiable**	
3	T in some or all rows	**Satisfiable**	= not 2
4	F in some or all rows	**Nontautology** aka **non-logicaltruth**	= not 1

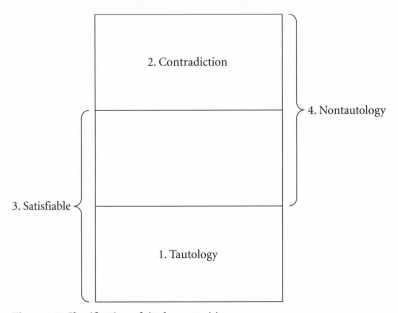

Figure 4.1. Classification of single propositions.

is not a contradiction (i.e., it is true in some other row(s)). In other words, a contingently true proposition is true but not logically so; a contingently false proposition is false but not logically so.[3]

4.2.1 Exercises

Write out truth tables for the following propositions, and state whether each is a tautology, a contradiction, or neither.

1. $((P \lor Q) \to P)$

2. $(\neg P \land (Q \lor R))$

3. $((\neg P \lor Q) \leftrightarrow (P \land \neg Q))$

4. $(P \to (Q \to (R \to P)))$

5. $(P \to ((P \to Q) \to Q))$ 8. $((P \to Q) \vee \neg(Q \wedge \neg P))$

6. $(P \to ((Q \to P) \to Q))$ 9. $((P \wedge Q) \leftrightarrow (Q \leftrightarrow P))$

7. $((P \to Q) \vee \neg(Q \wedge \neg Q))$ 10. $\neg((P \wedge Q) \to (Q \leftrightarrow P))$

4.3 Two Propositions

If two propositions have the same value in every row of their joint truth table (i.e., where one is T, the other is T, and where one is F, the other is F) they are said to be *equivalent* (or *logically* equivalent): they can never diverge in truth value—they have the same truth value, no matter what. (If two propositions are not equivalent, we say that they are *inequivalent*.)

If two propositions never both have the value T in any row in their joint table, they are said to be *jointly unsatisfiable*. Two propositions that are not jointly unsatisfiable are said to be *jointly satisfiable*. So two propositions are jointly satisfiable if they can both be true at the same time. Note that two propositions, each of which is satisfiable, need not be jointly satisfiable: consider, for example, P and $\neg P$.

If two propositions are jointly unsatisfiable, they never both take the value T at the same time. If they also never both take the value F at the same time, then they are *contradictory*: they always take opposite truth values. If they are not contradictory (but are jointly unsatisfiable) they are *contraries*: they can never both be true, but they can both be false.

Do not confuse the claim that two propositions are contradictory with the claim that a single proposition is a contradiction. Two contradictions are not contradictory (although they are jointly unsatisfiable, because each of them is unsatisfiable): they are equivalent, and they are contraries. The situation is summarized in Figure 4.2.

4.3.1 Exercises

Write out joint truth tables for the following pairs of propositions, and state in each case whether the two propositions are (a) jointly satisfiable, (b) equivalent, (c) contradictory, (d) contraries.

1. $(P \to Q)$ and $\neg(P \wedge \neg Q)$

2. $(P \wedge Q)$ and $(P \wedge \neg Q)$

3. $\neg(P \leftrightarrow Q)$ and
$\neg(P \to Q) \vee \neg(P \vee \neg Q)$

4. $(P \to (Q \to R))$ and
$((P \to Q) \to R)$

5. $(P \wedge (Q \wedge \neg Q))$ and
$\neg(Q \to \neg(R \wedge \neg Q))$

6. $(P \wedge \neg P)$ and $(R \vee \neg R)$

	Values in joint truth table	Type of propositions	
1	Same value in every row	**Equivalent**	
2	Some row in which both T	**Jointly satisfiable**	
3	No row in which both T	**Jointly unsatisfiable**	= not 2
4	Jointly unsatisfiable and no row in which both F	**Contradictory**	
5	Jointly unsatisfiable and some row in which both F	**Contraries**	

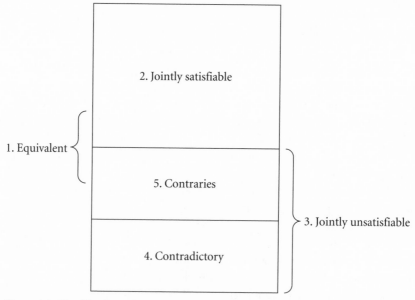

Figure 4.2. Classification of two propositions (joint truth table).

7. $(P \wedge \neg P)$ and $\neg(Q \rightarrow Q)$

8. $((P \rightarrow Q) \rightarrow R)$ and $\neg(P \vee \neg(Q \wedge \neg R))$

9. $(P \leftrightarrow Q)$ and $((P \wedge Q) \vee (\neg P \wedge \neg Q))$

10. $(P \leftrightarrow Q)$ and $((P \wedge Q) \vee (\neg P \wedge \neg Q))$

4.3.2 More Abbreviations

We said in §2.5.4 that we may omit outermost parentheses where this omission will cause no confusion. We also said that while some books introduce conventions for omitting inner parentheses in an unambiguous way, we do not do this in general in this book—although we do allow the omission of internal parentheses in two special cases. We come now to these special cases.

First, in the case of a wff involving multiple occurrences of $\wedge$ and no other connectives, we allow the omission of all parentheses: thus, we may write:

$$P \wedge Q \wedge R$$
$$P \wedge Q \wedge R \wedge S$$
$$P \wedge Q \wedge R \wedge S \wedge T$$

and so on. Second, in the case of a wff involving multiple occurrences of $\vee$ and no other connectives, we allow the omission of all parentheses: thus, we may write:

$$P \vee Q \vee R$$
$$P \vee Q \vee R \vee S$$
$$P \vee Q \vee R \vee S \vee T$$

and so on. Strictly speaking, the string of symbols $P \wedge Q \wedge R$ is not a wff—only the following two disambiguations of this string are wffs:

$$((P \wedge Q) \wedge R)$$
$$(P \wedge (Q \wedge R))$$

Likewise, the string of symbols $P \vee Q \vee R \vee S$ is not a wff—only the following five disambiguations of this string are wffs:

$$(((P \vee Q) \vee R) \vee S)$$
$$((P \vee Q) \vee (R \vee S))$$
$$((P \vee (Q \vee R)) \vee S)$$
$$(P \vee ((Q \vee R) \vee S))$$
$$(P \vee (Q \vee (R \vee S)))$$

However, it is easy to verify (using truth tables) that all wffs obtained from an unparenthesized string of $\wedge$s or $\vee$s by inserting parentheses are equivalent: the above two disambiguations of $P \wedge Q \wedge R$ are logically equivalent, every possible pair of the above five disambiguations of $P \vee Q \vee R \vee S$ is equivalent, and so on. So when we write, say, "$P \vee Q \vee R$," it is ambiguous which wff we mean: $(P \vee (Q \vee R))$ or $((P \vee Q) \vee R)$. However, these two wffs are equivalent, so the ambiguity is harmless.

§

The above applies only to $\wedge$ and $\vee$: we should not omit internal parentheses in straight strings of our other two-place connectives ($\rightarrow$ and $\leftrightarrow$). The reason in the case of $\rightarrow$ is straightforward: the string $P \rightarrow Q \rightarrow R$, for example, could be disambiguated in two ways:

$$((P \rightarrow Q) \rightarrow R)$$
$$(P \rightarrow (Q \rightarrow R))$$

and these two wffs are not logically equivalent (as can easily be verified using a truth table). The reason in the case of $\leftrightarrow$ is more subtle. For any straight string of $\leftrightarrow$s, the possible disambiguations of the string are all logically equivalent. For example (as can easily be verified using truth tables) the following are logically equivalent:

$$((P \leftrightarrow Q) \leftrightarrow R)$$
$$(P \leftrightarrow (Q \leftrightarrow R))$$

as are all of the following:

$$(((P \leftrightarrow Q) \leftrightarrow R) \leftrightarrow S)$$
$$((P \leftrightarrow Q) \leftrightarrow (R \leftrightarrow S))$$
$$((P \leftrightarrow (Q \leftrightarrow R)) \leftrightarrow S)$$
$$(P \leftrightarrow ((Q \leftrightarrow R) \leftrightarrow S))$$
$$(P \leftrightarrow (Q \leftrightarrow (R \leftrightarrow S)))$$

Nevertheless, we shall not write such strings as $P \leftrightarrow Q \leftrightarrow R$ and $P \leftrightarrow Q \leftrightarrow R \leftrightarrow S$. Doing so would (i) bring no apparent benefit and (ii) invite a certain sort of misinterpretation.

Regarding point (i), abbreviations are a convenience: we introduce one only when the benefit it brings outweighs any downside it may have. Writing straight strings of $\wedge$s or $\vee$s without parentheses does have a benefit: it makes for more convenient and natural translations. For example, consider the following propositions:

1. For breakfast I shall have scrambled eggs, baked beans on toast, pancakes, or cereal.

2. Today I shall give a lecture, attend a department meeting, and return some library books.

Using the following glossary:

> S: I shall have scrambled eggs for breakfast
> B: I shall have baked beans on toast for breakfast
> P: I shall have pancakes for breakfast
> C: I shall have cereal for breakfast
> T: Today I shall give a lecture
> M: Today I shall attend a department meeting
> L: Today I shall return some library books

it is natural to translate these propositions as follows:

1. $S \vee B \vee P \vee C$

2. $T \wedge M \wedge L$

That is, it is natural to translate them as *flat* lists of conjuncts/disjuncts—where each conjunct/disjunct is on the same level—rather than arbitrarily to choose a particular *nesting*, such as $(((S \vee B) \vee P) \vee C)$ (the first pair of disjuncts is the most deeply nested), $(S \vee ((B \vee P) \vee C))$ (the second pair of disjuncts is the most deeply nested), and so on. In other words, it is natural to treat the first proposition as having three equal main connectives and the second as having two equal main connectives, as opposed to one main connective. Although every wff of PL has a unique main connective (recall §2.5.3), we can simulate the effect of having several equal main connectives by writing such strings as $S \vee B \vee P \vee C$, which is ambiguous among all possible choices regarding which of the three connectives to take as the main one.

There is no corresponding benefit in writing such strings as $S \leftrightarrow B \leftrightarrow P \leftrightarrow C$ or $T \leftrightarrow M \leftrightarrow L$: they do not arise in a natural way as translations of common sorts of propositions.

Regarding point (ii), disambiguations of strings like $P \wedge Q \wedge R$ and $P \vee Q \vee R \vee S$ mean exactly what one naturally takes them to mean, whereas disambiguations of strings like $P \leftrightarrow Q \leftrightarrow R$ and $P \leftrightarrow Q \leftrightarrow R \leftrightarrow S$ mean something quite different from what one naturally takes them to mean. Writing strings of the latter sort would therefore invite confusion.

Consider first $\wedge$ and $\vee$. The proposition $(P \wedge Q)$ is true iff both P and Q are true. Generalizing in the natural way, one would assume that $P \wedge Q \wedge \ldots \wedge R$ is true iff P and Q and . . . and R are all true, which is indeed the case (i.e., all disambiguations of a straight string of $\wedge$s are true iff all basic propositions involved are true). Similarly, $(P \vee Q)$ is true iff at least one of P or Q is true. Generalizing in the natural way, one would assume that $P \vee Q \vee \ldots \vee R$ is true iff at least one of P or Q or . . . or R is true, which is indeed the case (i.e., all disambiguations of a straight string of $\vee$s are true iff at least one of the basic propositions involved is true).

Now consider $\leftrightarrow$. The proposition $(P \leftrightarrow Q)$ is true iff P and Q have the same truth value. Generalizing in the natural way, one would assume that $P \leftrightarrow Q \leftrightarrow \ldots \leftrightarrow R$ is true iff P, Q, . . . , R all have the same truth value—but this is not the case. For example, while all the possible disambiguations of $P \leftrightarrow Q \leftrightarrow R$ are true when P, Q, and R are all true, the disambiguations are all false when P, Q, and R are all false. Furthermore they are all true when exactly one (any one) of P, Q, and R is true (as easily seen by drawing up a truth table). To take another example, all possible disambiguations of $P \leftrightarrow Q \leftrightarrow R \leftrightarrow S$ are true when all of P, Q, R, and S are true, and they are true when all of P, Q, R, and S are false. But the disambiguations are also all true when exactly two (any two) of P, Q, R, and S are true (as easily seen by drawing up a truth table).

In sum, writing "$P \leftrightarrow Q \leftrightarrow R$," "$P \leftrightarrow Q \leftrightarrow R \leftrightarrow S$," and so on would bring no apparent benefit, while inviting confusion (it would tempt us to interpret these strings in a way that is at odds with their disambiguations). That is why I do not introduce an abbreviation that omits internal parentheses in straight strings of $\leftrightarrow$s, even though all disambiguations of such strings are indeed equivalent. We allow the omission of internal parentheses only in straight strings of $\wedge$s and $\vee$s.

4.4 Sets of Propositions

A *set* is a collection of objects; these objects are said to be the *members* of the set.[4] When the objects are propositions, we have a *set of propositions.* We write sets with braces (i.e., { and }) around the members. For example,

$$\{P, Q, R\}$$

is the set containing the three propositions P, Q, and R.

If there is no row of their joint truth table in which all propositions in a given set are true, the set of propositions is said to be *unsatisfiable.* A set of propositions that is not unsatisfiable is said to be *satisfiable,* so a satisfiable set of propositions is one in which the propositions in the set can all be true at the same time.

The earlier definitions of satisfiability for a single proposition and of joint satisfiability for two propositions are the special cases of this general definition where the set of propositions has one and two members, respectively. Note, however, the subtle shifts in terminology. If we have a set containing one proposition, and the set is satisfiable (by our current definition), then the proposition in the set is satisfiable (by our earlier definition). If we have a set containing two propositions, and the set is satisfiable (by our current definition), then the propositions in the set are jointly satisfiable (by our earlier definition).

Set of propositions (joint truth table)	
Some row in which all T	**Satisfiable** set
No row in which all T	**Unsatisfiable** set

4.4.1 Exercises

Write out a joint truth table for the propositions in each of the following sets, and state whether each set is satisfiable.

1. $\{(P \vee Q), \neg(P \wedge Q), P\}$

2. $\{\neg(P \to Q), (P \leftrightarrow Q), (\neg P \vee Q)\}$

3. $\{(P \to \neg P), (P \lor \neg P), (\neg P \to P)\}$

4. $\{((P \lor Q) \lor R), (\neg P \to \neg Q), (\neg Q \to \neg R), \neg P\}$

5. $\{(P \leftrightarrow Q), (Q \lor R), (R \to P)\}$

6. $\{(\neg P \to \neg Q), (P \leftrightarrow Q), P\}$

7. $\{\neg P, (P \to (P \to P)), (\neg P \leftrightarrow P)\}$

8. $\{(P \lor \neg Q), (P \to R), \neg R, (\neg R \to Q)\}$

9. $\{\neg R, \neg P, ((Q \to \neg Q) \to R)\}$

10. $\{(\neg P \lor \neg Q), \neg(P \land \neg Q), (P \lor \neg Q), \neg(\neg P \land \neg Q)\}$

4.5 More on Validity

4.5.1 Shortcuts

An argument is valid if it has no counterexamples—no rows in which the premises are true and the conclusion false. If you are testing an argument for validity, you can therefore sometimes take shortcuts in writing out the truth table. Start by filling in the column for the simplest proposition in the argument (i.e., the one with the least number of connectives):

- If it is the conclusion of the argument, then ignore any row in which it is true. That is, do not bother filling in the values of the premises in this row: just cross the row off. For a row cannot give us a counterexample unless the conclusion is false in that row.

- If it is a premise of the argument, then ignore any row in which it is false. That is, do not bother filling in the values of the other premises and the conclusion in this row: just cross the row off. For a row cannot give us a counterexample unless all premises are true in that row.

Now move to the next simplest proposition, and repeat the above process, and so on. If at any point you find a row in which the premises are all true and the conclusion is false, stop there: you have a counterexample, and so the argument is invalid. If you exhaust all rows (either by crossing them off or filling them in completely) and find no counterexample, then the argument is valid.

For example, consider the argument:

$(\neg P \lor Q)$
$((Q \to \neg R) \land (\neg R \to \neg P))$
$\therefore \neg P$

Here is its truth table, waiting to be filled in:

P	Q	R	$(\neg P \vee Q)$	$((Q \rightarrow \neg R) \wedge (\neg R \rightarrow \neg P))$	$\neg P$
T	T	T			
T	T	F			
T	F	T			
T	F	F			
F	T	T			
F	T	F			
F	F	T			
F	F	F			

The simplest proposition is $\neg P$, so we start with it, crossing off any rows in which it is true:

P	Q	R	$(\neg P \vee Q)$	$((Q \rightarrow \neg R) \wedge (\neg R \rightarrow \neg P))$	$\neg P$
T	T	T			F
T	T	F			F
T	F	T			F
T	F	F			F
F	T	T			T ×
F	T	F			T ×
F	F	T			T ×
F	F	F			T ×

The next simplest proposition is $(\neg P \vee Q)$, so we fill in its column next. We ignore any rows already crossed off, and we furthermore cross off any rows in which $(\neg P \vee Q)$ is false:

P	Q	R	$(\neg P \vee Q)$	$((Q \rightarrow \neg R) \wedge (\neg R \rightarrow \neg P))$	$\neg P$
T	T	T	T		F
T	T	F	T		F
T	F	T	F ×		F
T	F	F	F ×		F
F	T	T			T ×
F	T	F			T ×
F	F	T			T ×
F	F	F			T ×

As a result of our shortcuts, we only have to calculate the truth value of the long proposition $((Q \rightarrow \neg R) \wedge (\neg R \rightarrow \neg P))$ in two rows, not eight. In the first row, R is true, so $\neg R$ is false, and Q is true, so $(Q \rightarrow \neg R)$ is false—thus, the whole conjunction must be false,[5] and we can cross off this row. In the second row, R is false, so $\neg R$ is true, and P is true, so $\neg P$ is false, and so $(\neg R \to \neg P)$ is false—thus, the whole conjunction must be false, and we can cross off this row too. We have now dealt with all rows and seen that none of them provides a counterexample: a case in which the premises are true and the conclusion false. So the argument is valid.

4.5.2 Points to Note

We close this chapter with four important points about validity. First, valid arguments can have false premises and a false conclusion. Consider the following argument (using the glossary in §4.1.3) and its truth table:

		S	G	$\neg S$	$\neg G$	$\neg(S \lor G)$
$\neg S$						
$\neg G$		T	T	F	F	F
$\therefore \neg(S \lor G)$		T	F	F	T	F
		F	T	T	F	F
		F	F	T	T	T

The premises of this argument are both false in the actual row (row 1). But this does not matter for validity. What matters for validity is whether there is any row in which the premises are true and the conclusion false. There is no such row—the only row in which the premises are both true is row 4, and the conclusion is true there too—so the argument is valid.

Second, true premises and a true conclusion do not establish validity. Consider the following argument (using the glossary in §4.1.3) and its truth table:

		S	G	$(S \land G)$
S				
$\therefore (S \land G)$		T	T	T
		T	F	F
		F	T	F
		F	F	F

Its premise and conclusion are both true in the actual row (row 1). Nevertheless, the argument is invalid, because there is a row (row 2) in which the premise is true and the conclusion false. That is, it is possible to make the premise true and the conclusion false, even though in actual fact, the premise and the conclusion are both true.

Third, any argument whose conclusion is a tautology is valid. That might seem odd at first, but think of it this way: there cannot be a counterexample—a case where the premises are true and the conclusion is false—if there cannot be any case in which the conclusion is false. For example, consider the following argument (again using the glossary in §4.1.3) and its truth table:

	S	G	$(G \rightarrow G)$
S	T	T	T
$\therefore (G \rightarrow G)$	T	F	T
	F	T	T
	F	F	T

Recall our shortcuts. Here we can cross off every row, for the conclusion is true in all of them.

An argument whose conclusion is a tautology may or may not be sound. This example happens to be sound.

Fourth, any argument in which the premises form an unsatisfiable set is valid. (A special case of this is where there is only one premise, which is a contradiction.) Again, this point might seem odd at first, but think of it this way: there cannot be a counterexample—a case where the premises are all true and the conclusion false—if there cannot be any case in which the premises are all true. For example, consider the following argument and its truth table:

	S	G	$\neg S$
S	T	T	F
$\neg S$	T	F	F
$\therefore G$	F	T	T
	F	F	T

Recall our shortcuts. Here we can cross off the last two rows, because the first premise is false there, and we can cross off the first two rows, because the second premise is false there. In general, if the premises form an unsatisfiable set, there is no row in which they are all true; that is, at least one premise is false in each row. Thus, every row can be crossed off.

An argument in which the premises form an unsatisfiable set can never be sound: regardless of which row is the actual one, the premises cannot all be true in it, because they are not all true in any row.[6]

5

Logical Form

In §1.4 we presented the intuitive idea of validity, which comprises two aspects: (i) NTP (it is not possible for the premises to be true and the conclusion false), (ii) by virtue of form. In §4.1, we gave a precise definition of validity (for arguments in PL) in terms of truth tables: an argument is valid iff, in the joint truth table for the premises and conclusion, there is no row in which the premises are true and the conclusion false. As we discussed in §4.1, the precise definition captures the first part of the intuitive idea of validity (the NTP part). But what about the second part (the "by virtue of form" part)? In this chapter we show that the truth table definition of validity captures this idea too, by showing that if an argument is valid (according to the truth table definition), then so is every other argument that we can derive from it by replacing its component basic propositions with other propositions. Thus, the validity of the original argument does not depend on any features of the particular basic propositions that make it up: it depends only on the ways in which these propositions are arranged to make the argument—that is, on the form of the argument.

Apart from this theoretical upshot—that the truth table definition of validity captures the idea that validity is a matter of form—the considerations of this chapter also have a practical point. Consider the following argument:

Maisie is a kelpie.
If Maisie is a kelpie, then Maisie is a dog.
∴ Maisie is a dog.

To test whether it is valid, we translate into PL:

K: Maisie is a kelpie K
D: Maisie is a dog $K \rightarrow D$
                              $\therefore D$

and then do a truth table:

K	D	K → D
T	T	T
T	F	F
F	T	T
F	F	T

We then check whether there is any row in which the premises are both true and the conclusion false. There is no such row, so the argument is valid.

Now consider the following argument:

Rosie is a beagle.
If Rosie is a beagle, then Rosie is a dog.
∴ Rosie is a dog.

To test whether it is valid, we translate into PL:

B: Rosie is a beagle B
R: Rosie is a dog $B \rightarrow R$
                        $\therefore R$

and then do a truth table:

B	R	B → R
T	T	T
T	F	F
F	T	T
F	F	T

We then check whether there is any row in which the premises are both true and the conclusion false. There is no such row—the only row in which the premises are both true is row 1, and in that row the conclusion is true also—so the argument is valid.

It seems that we have done more work in the second case than needed. The two arguments, and their truth tables, differ only in the substitution of the letters B for K and R for D. It seems obvious, then, that the two arguments have the same form, and that if one is valid, then the other must be too. It would be nice not to have to go through the process of truth table construction to show that the second argument is valid, once we have recognized that it is of the same form as the first argument, which we already know to be valid. In this chapter—after making precise this idea of the *form* of an argument—we shall show a way of determining with only one use of a truth table whether all arguments of a given form are valid. This means that we shall not have to check the validity of every argument separately: provided we can see that an argument has the same form as one which we already know to be valid, we can be assured that this argument is valid without having to construct its truth table.

5.1 Abstracting from Content: From Propositions to Forms

Consider the proposition $(A \wedge B)$. It has a *content,* determined by the glossary entries for A and B and the truth table for $\wedge$. But forget about this content for a moment—about how the proposition represents the world to be—and consider its *form.* What is the form of this proposition? Well, it is a conjunction of two propositions. Wff variables (§2.4) come in handy here: they allow us to represent the form of this proposition—"a conjunction of two propositions"—as $(\alpha \wedge \beta)$. This form abstracts away from the particular propositions A and B in our original proposition, replacing them with placeholders (the variables α and β), in keeping with the idea that we wanted to abstract away from the content of the original proposition and just look at its form, that is, at the way it is put together.

Consider the proposition $\neg(A \wedge \neg B)$. What is its form? Well, if we think about it, we see that there is not just one answer to this question. The following answers are all correct:

1. It is a negation.

2. It is a negation of a conjunction.

3. It is a negation of a conjunction, the second conjunct of which is a negation.

We can thus give different answers to the question "what is the form of the proposition?" according to how deeply we look into its structure. Indeed, if we do not look into its structure at all, we can simply say:

4. It is a proposition.

Using wff variables, we can represent these four forms as follows:

1. $\neg\alpha$ 3. $\neg(\alpha \wedge \neg\beta)$

2. $\neg(\alpha \wedge \beta)$ 4. α

The forms arise from the original proposition by replacing one or more of its subformulas with a wff variable. In form 1, the variable α stands in place of the subformula $(A \wedge \neg B)$. In form 2, the variable α stands in place of the subformula A, and the variable β stands in place of the subformula $\neg B$. In form 3, the variable α stands in place of the subformula A, and the variable β

stands in place of the subformula B. In form 4, the variable α stands in place of the entire wff $\neg(A \wedge \neg B)$. The more complex the subformulas we "black box" as simply being propositions—that is, replace with wff variables—the coarser/less fine-grained is the resultant logical form. At one extreme, where we black box the entire original proposition, we end up with the form α, a proposition. At the other extreme, where we black box only basic propositions, we end up with the fine-grained form $\neg(\alpha \wedge \neg\beta)$.

5.1.1 Exercises

For each of the following propositions, give three correct answers to the question "what is the form of this proposition?"

1. $\neg(R \to (R \to Q))$ 3. $P \wedge (\neg P \to Q)$

2. $(R \vee P) \to (R \vee P)$ 4. $((\neg P \vee Q) \wedge P) \leftrightarrow R$

5.2 Instances: From Forms to Propositions

We have discussed how to get from a proposition to its (in general many) logical forms: we replace (i.e., black box) its subformulas with wff variables. We can also move in the opposite direction, starting with a logical form and then asking what propositions have—or as we shall also say, are instances of—this form. To be clear about this, we need to do two things: define what a logical form is, and describe how to get from a logical form to an instance of this form.

A logical form is simply something that looks just like a wff, except that in place of basic propositions, it has wff variables. So α, β, $\neg\alpha$, and $(\alpha \to (\beta \vee \gamma))$, for example, are logical forms, while the following are not: $(\alpha\vee)$ (it is not well-formed), $\neg P$ (it contains a basic proposition, not a wff variable), and $(\alpha \to B)$ (it contains a mixture of basic propositions and wff variables: logical forms contain no basic propositions, only wff variables).

Given a logical form, a proposition is an *instance* of this form if it can be obtained from the form by replacing the variables in the form with propositions, according to the rule:

all occurrences of the same variable must be replaced by the same proposition.

So given the form:

$$\neg(\alpha \to (\alpha \vee \beta)) \tag{5.1}$$

the following is an instance of this form:

$$\neg(A \to (A \vee B))$$

Here we have replaced α with A and β with B. Note that, in accordance with the rule, both occurrences of α were replaced by the same proposition, in this case A.

I have said that the wff variables may be regarded as placeholders for propositions. We can in fact think of them literally as boxes into which propositions may be put. Thus, form (5.1) can be thought of as:

$$\neg(\bigcirc \to (\bigcirc \vee \square))$$

Note that we represent distinct wff variables using different-shaped boxes (α becomes a circular box and β becomes a square box) to keep track of what propositions may be put into which boxes: the rule is that boxes with the same shape must receive the same proposition.

The following is not an instance of form (5.1):

$$\neg(A \to (B \vee C))$$

Here we have replaced the first occurrence of α (filled the first circular box) with A and the second occurrence (the second circular box) with a different proposition, B, thus violating our rule.

Note that different variables do not have to be replaced by different propositions. Thus, the following proposition is also an instance of form (5.1):

$$\neg(A \to (A \vee A))$$

Here we have replaced both α and β with A. In accordance with the rule, both occurrences of α must be replaced by the same proposition, in this case A, but it is perfectly all right also to replace a different variable, in this case β, with that same proposition.

Note also that, as long as the above rule is observed, a variable may be replaced by any proposition—not necessarily a basic one, as in the previous examples. Thus, the following proposition is also an instance of form (5.1):

$$\neg(A \to (A \vee (A \to B)))$$

Here we have replaced α with A (both times, as required) and β with the compound proposition $(A \to B)$. Likewise, the following proposition is also an instance of form (5.1):

$$\neg((A \vee B) \to ((A \vee B) \vee (A \to B)))$$

Here we have replaced α with $(A \vee B)$ and β with $(A \to B)$.

We say that two propositions share a particular form if they are both instances of it. Note that it does not make sense to say, in general, that two propositions are of the same form. This is because two propositions may both be instances of one form, while only one of them is an instance of another form. For example, the two propositions:

1. $(A \land (B \to C))$

2. $(A \land B)$

are both instances of the form:

$$(\alpha \land \beta)$$

(the first arises from this form by replacing α with A and β with $(B \to C)$; the second by replacing α with A and β with B), but only the first is an instance of the form:

$$(\alpha \land (\beta \to \gamma))$$

5.2.1 Exercises

1. The following propositions all have three logical forms in common. State what the three forms are, and in each case, show what replacements of variables by propositions are required to obtain the three propositions from the form.
   - (i) $\neg\neg C$
   - (ii) $\neg\neg(A \land B)$
   - (iii) $\neg\neg(C \land \neg D)$

2. State whether the given propositions are instances of the given form. If so, show what replacements of variables by propositions are required to obtain the proposition from the form.

   (i) Form: $\neg(\alpha \to \beta)$
   Propositions:
   - (a) $\neg(P \to Q)$
   - (b) $\neg(R \to Q)$
   - (c) $\neg(R \to (R \to Q))$

   (ii) Form: $\neg(\alpha \to (\alpha \to \beta))$
   Propositions:
   - (a) $\neg(P \to (P \to Q))$
   - (b) $\neg(P \to (P \to P))$
   - (c) $\neg(P \to (Q \to P))$

   (iii) Form: $(\alpha \lor \beta) \to (\alpha \land \beta)$
   Propositions:
   - (a) $(\neg P \lor Q) \to (\neg P \land Q)$
   - (b) $(P \lor \neg P) \to (P \land \neg P)$
   - (c) $\neg(R \lor S) \to \neg(R \land S)$

   (iv) Form: $\alpha \lor (\neg\beta \lor \alpha)$
   Propositions:
   - (a) $(P \lor Q) \lor (Q \lor (P \lor Q))$
   - (b) $Q \lor (\neg Q \lor (Q \land Q))$
   - (c) $\neg P \lor (\neg\neg P \lor \neg P)$

5.3 Argument Forms

Recall that a logical form is just like a proposition except that it has wff variables in place of basic propositions. Similarly, an *argument form* is just like an argument except that it has wff variables in place of basic propositions in the premises and conclusion. In other words, an argument form is just like an argument except that each premise and the conclusion is a logical form, not a proposition.

The transitions from arguments to argument forms and from argument forms to arguments are perfectly analogous to those already discussed from propositions to logical forms and the reverse.

Consider first the move from arguments to argument forms. If we are given the argument

$$P$$
$$(P \rightarrow R)$$
$$\therefore R$$

and asked "what is its form?" there are many correct answers. For example:

1. The argument has two premises and a conclusion. The first premise is a proposition, the second premise is a conditional, and the conclusion is a proposition.

    Expressing this using wff variables yields:

    $$\alpha$$
    $$(\beta \rightarrow \gamma)$$
    $$\therefore \delta$$

2. The argument has two premises and a conclusion. The first premise is a proposition, the second premise is conditional whose antecedent is the first premise, and the conclusion is the consequent of the second premise. This form captures more information about the structure of the argument.

    Expressing this using wff variables yields:

    $$\alpha$$
    $$(\alpha \rightarrow \beta)$$
    $$\therefore \beta$$

    Note that here we use *the same variable* for the first premise and the antecedent of the second premise, to represent the fact that they are the same proposition, and similarly we use the same variable for the consequent of the second premise and the conclusion.

3. The argument has two premises and a conclusion, all of which are propositions. This form is less fine grained than the first two.

Expressing this using wff variables yields:

α

β

$\therefore \gamma$

Consider next the transition from an argument form to arguments that are instances of this form. We proceed in the same manner as we did when moving from logical forms to propositions: we replace variables with propositions (not necessarily basic propositions), subject to the rule that multiple occurrences of the same variable must all be replaced by the same proposition (and not subject to a requirement that different variables be replaced by different propositions). Note that this rule now applies to all occurrences of a variable throughout the argument—not just within a particular premise or conclusion. So for example, given the argument form:

$\neg(\alpha \to (\alpha \to \beta))$

$\therefore (\alpha \vee \beta)$

the following arguments are instances of this form:

1. $\neg(P \to (P \to Q))$
   $\therefore (P \vee Q)$
   (here we have substituted P for α and Q for β).

2. $\neg(P \to (P \to P))$
   $\therefore (P \vee P)$
   (here we have substituted P for α and β).

3. $\neg(R \to (R \to (R \to Q)))$
   $\therefore (R \vee (R \to Q))$
   (here we have substituted R for α and $(R \to Q)$ for β).

but the following is not:

$\neg(P \to (P \to Q))$

$\therefore (Q \vee Q)$

for here we have substituted P for the first and second occurrences of α (in the premise) and a different proposition Q for the third occurrence of α (in the conclusion), thus violating our rule that all occurrences of the same variable throughout the argument must be replaced by the same proposition.

5.3.1 Exercises

For each of the following arguments, give four correct answers to the question "what is the form of this argument?" For each form, show what replacements of variables by propositions are required to obtain the argument from the form.

1. $\neg(R \rightarrow (R \rightarrow Q))$
   $\therefore R \vee (R \rightarrow Q)$

2. $(P \wedge Q) \rightarrow Q$
   $\neg Q$
   $\therefore \neg(P \wedge Q)$

3. $\neg Q \rightarrow (R \rightarrow S)$
   $\neg Q$
   $\therefore R \rightarrow S$

4. $(P \rightarrow \neg Q) \vee (\neg Q \rightarrow P)$
   $\neg(\neg Q \rightarrow P)$
   $\therefore P \rightarrow \neg Q$

5.4 Validity and Form

Having introduced the ideas of forms (of propositions and arguments) and of instances of forms, we can now put these ideas to work in the way we originally envisaged: showing in one fell swoop—that is, without having to do a truth table for each argument separately—that all arguments of a certain form are valid.

What we do first is apply our truth table test for validity to argument forms instead of arguments. We deem an argument form valid* if it passes the test (i.e., there is no row of its truth table in which the premises all have a T and the conclusion has an F) and invalid* if it fails the test (i.e., there is at least one row of its truth table in which the premises all have a T and the conclusion has an F).

For example, consider the form:

α
$(\alpha \rightarrow \beta)$
$\therefore \beta$

Here is its truth table:

α	β	$(\alpha \rightarrow \beta)$
T	T	T
T	F	F
F	T	T
F	F	T

We see that there is no row in which the premises (columns 1 and 3) both have a T and the conclusion has an F; so the argument form is valid*.

Now consider the argument form:

β
$(\alpha \rightarrow \beta)$
$\therefore \alpha$

Its truth table is the same as the one above. We see that there is a row in which the premises (columns 2 and 3 in this case) both have a T and the conclusion has an F (row 3), so the argument form is invalid*.

Note that calling an argument form valid* means something different from calling an argument valid (hence the use of the term "valid*"—as opposed to "valid"—for argument forms). The premises and conclusion of an argument are propositions—things that are true or false. To say that an argument is valid is to say that there is no way of making its premises true and its conclusion false. The premises and conclusion of an argument form are logical forms. These are not things that have content—that say something about the world— and they are not true or false. Rather, they are placeholders for things that have content and are true or false: they are placeholders for propositions. Thus, it does not make sense to speak of situations in which the premises of an argument form are true or its conclusion false—for it does not make sense to say that a logical form, which is what the premises and conclusion are, is true or false.[1]

So what *are* we doing when we apply the truth table test to an argument form—as opposed to an argument—if not checking all possible ways of making propositions true or false and seeing whether there are any cases in which the premises are true and the conclusion false? Well, what we are doing when we produce a truth table for an argument form, say:

$$\alpha$$
$$(\alpha \rightarrow \beta)$$
$$\therefore \beta$$

is seeing whether it is possible to assign truth values to any three propositions of the forms α, $(\alpha \rightarrow \beta)$, and β, respectively, in such a way that the first two propositions come out true and the third comes out false. The wff variables are placeholders for propositions. As we have said, they can be thought of as boxes, into which propositions can be put (subject to the rule that where the same box appears more than once, the same proposition must be put into it each time). These propositions will then have truth values (different ones in different possible cases). The truth table for the form shows us whether it is possible to put in propositions that can then be assigned truth values in such a way as to make the premises true and the conclusion false. Or—another way of thinking about the matter—we can conceive of the truth table test for the form as bypassing the stage of putting propositions in the boxes, and putting truth values in directly: it then shows us whether there is any way of putting truth values in the boxes in such a way as to make the premises come out T and the conclusion come out F.

This point about truth tables for argument forms underlies the key result we have been working toward:

Every instance of a valid* argument form is a valid argument.

The reason this result holds is as follows. If the truth table test of the form:

establishes that the form is valid*, that means—as we have just discussed—that it is not possible to assign truth values to any propositions of the forms $\alpha, \beta, \ldots, \gamma$, respectively, in such a way that $\alpha, \beta, \ldots$ come out true while γ comes out false. It then follows immediately that if we have an argument whose premises and conclusion are particular propositions that have the forms $\alpha, \beta, \ldots$ and γ respectively, it is not possible to assign truth values to these propositions in such a way that all but the last are true, while the last one is false. Hence our result: every instance of a valid* argument form is a valid argument.

Or think of it this way. If the truth table for the form shows it to be valid*, then there is no way of putting truth values in the boxes (thinking of the wff variables as boxes) in such a way as to make the premises all T and the conclusion F. Now when we substitute propositions for the variables to get an argument that is an instance of our form, we put propositions in the boxes. Now recall the process of filling in a truth table. First, we look at the truth values of basic propositions in each row; then we use these, and the truth tables for the connectives, to assign truth values to subformulas made up from basic propositions and one connective. We then use these truth values to assign truth values to more complex subformulas; and so on until we have determined the truth values of our target wffs—the premises and conclusion—in each row. At some point in this process, we put truth values in the boxes: the truth values of the propositions, which we put in the boxes earlier, when we were getting our particular argument as an instance of the argument form in question. Now if the truth table for the form has already shown us that there is no way of putting truth values in the boxes so that the premises are all T and the conclusion F, then we have a guarantee that this particular way—first putting certain propositions in the boxes, and then putting the truth values of these propositions in the boxes—will not make the premises true and the conclusion false. In other words, if there is no counterexample row in the truth table for the form, we have a guarantee that there can be no counterexample row in the truth table for any instance of the form. Hence, our result: every instance of a valid* argument form is a valid argument.

This result is very useful. Consider an argument form that we know to be valid, say:

α
$(\alpha \rightarrow \beta)$
$\therefore \beta$

It has two wff variables in it, so its truth table has four rows. An instance of this argument might have a truth table with any number of rows.[2] For example, if we substitute $(P \lor (Q \land R))$ for α and $(P \rightarrow S)$ for β, then the resulting argument features four basic propositions (P, Q, R, and S) and so its truth table has sixteen rows. But having seen that the form is valid, we do not need to do this sixteen-row truth table to see that the argument—which is an instance of this form—is valid.

But hang on! How can we know from having examined four possibilities that in none of sixteen possible cases will our premises be true while the conclusion is false? The key point is that ultimately each of these sixteen possible ways of assigning truth values to P, Q, R, and S can only lead to one of four possible ways of assigning truth values to $(P \lor (Q \land R))$ and $(P \rightarrow S)$—that is, to the formulas we substituted for α and β, respectively. The four possibilities are (i) both these formulas are true, (ii) the first is true and the second false, (iii) the first is false and the second true, and (iv) both are false. These are precisely the four possibilities that were covered in our truth table for the argument form—and that truth table showed that none of them yields a situation in which the premises are true and the conclusion false.

We are also now in a position to see that the truth table definition of validity captures the idea that validity is a matter of form: if an argument is valid (according to the truth table definition), this fact does not depend on the particular propositions that make it up, but only on the way in which those propositions are arranged—that is, on the form or structure of the argument. Suppose a certain argument is valid. Then it is an instance of at least one valid* form—namely, the form we obtain by replacing the basic propositions in the argument by wff variables in such a way that multiple occurrences of the same basic proposition are replaced by the same wff variable, while different basic propositions are replaced by different wff variables. For example, given the argument A, $A \rightarrow B / \therefore B$, we could arrive in this way at the form α, $\alpha \rightarrow \beta / \therefore \beta$. Obviously if the truth table test deems the former argument valid, it must also deem the latter argument valid*, for the truth table for the argument form differs from that for the argument only in having Greek letters in place of Roman letters. But now (as we have seen in this section) every other instance of this form is also valid. Thus, the validity of the original argument survives replacement of the particular basic propositions that make it up with any other propositions (provided that multiple occurrences of the same basic proposition are replaced by the same substitute proposition). Its validity, then, does not turn on its content—on the particular propositions that make it up. Rather, its validity turns on the form of the argument—on the way in which those propositions are put together.

5.4.1 Exercises

For each of the following arguments, (i) show that it is an instance of the form:

α
$\alpha \rightarrow \beta$
$\therefore \beta$

by stating what substitutions of propositions for variables have to be made to otbain the argument from the form, and (ii) show by producing a truth table for the argument that it is valid.

1. P
   $P \rightarrow Q$
   $\therefore Q$

2. $(A \wedge B)$
   $(A \wedge B) \rightarrow (B \vee C)$
   $\therefore (B \vee C)$

3. $(A \vee \neg A)$
   $(A \vee \neg A) \rightarrow (A \wedge \neg A)$
   $\therefore (A \wedge \neg A)$

4. $(P \rightarrow \neg P)$
   $(P \rightarrow \neg P) \rightarrow (P \rightarrow (Q \wedge \neg R))$
   $\therefore (P \rightarrow (Q \wedge \neg R))$

5.5 Invalidity and Form

It is not true in general that every instance of an invalid* argument form is an invalid argument. An argument form, say:

β
$(\alpha \rightarrow \beta)$
$\therefore \alpha$

is invalid* if it is possible to have three propositions of the forms β, $(\alpha \rightarrow \beta)$, and α, respectively, such that the first two are true and the third is false. But this does not mean that every set of three propositions of the forms β, $(\alpha \rightarrow \beta)$, and α, respectively, are such that the first two can be true while the third is false. Consider the following argument:

P
$(P \rightarrow P)$
$\therefore P$

It is an instance of the above invalid* form, but it is valid, as we can confirm by doing a truth table for this argument (see below). The three propositions P, $(P \rightarrow P)$, and P are of the forms β, $(\alpha \rightarrow \beta)$, and α, respectively, yet they are not such that the first two can be true while the third is false. That is quite compatible with the claim that the argument form

β
$(\alpha \rightarrow \beta)$
$\therefore \alpha$

is invalid*: for this claim to be true, there need only be some trio of propositions (not necessarily P, $(P \rightarrow P)$, and P) of the forms β, $(\alpha \rightarrow \beta)$, and α, respectively, such that the first two can be true while the third is false.

Recall that the truth table for the argument form

β
$(\alpha \rightarrow \beta)$
$\therefore \alpha$

looks like:

α	β	$(\alpha \rightarrow \beta)$
T	T	T
T	F	F
F	T	T
F	F	T

We see that there is a row in which the premises both have a T and the conclusion has an F—row 3—so the argument form is invalid*. Now look at the truth table for the argument

P
$(P \rightarrow P)$
$\therefore P$

which is an instance of the above form:

P	$(P \rightarrow P)$
T	T
F	T

There is no row in which the premises are both true and the conclusion false—because there is no row in which P, which is both a premise and a conclusion, is true and false—and so the argument is valid.

We noted near the end of §5.4 that while the truth table for an argument might not have the same number of rows as the truth table for an argument form of which the argument is an instance, each row will nevertheless ultimately be of one of the types covered in the truth table for the form (in a sense made clear in the earlier discussion). So no new row types will appear in the truth table for the argument that were not covered in the truth table for the form. However, some row types may disappear. That is what happens in the present case. Row 1 of the truth table for the argument—where P, which is what we substituted for both α and β in the form, is true—corresponds to row 1 of the truth table for the form, where α and β are both T. Row 2 of the truth table for the argument—where P, which is what we substituted for both α and β in the form, is false—corresponds to row 4 of the truth table for the form, where α and β are both F. There is thus no row in the truth table for the argument of the type of row 3 in the truth table for the form—that is, where α is F and β is T. But that was the row that rendered the form invalid*. Thus, the argument comes out valid, even though it is an instance of an invalid* form.

We have seen that every instance of a valid* argument form is a valid argument. Thus, if an argument is an instance of even one valid* form, then it is a valid argument: it does not matter if it is also an instance of various invalid* forms. In fact, it is certainly not the case that every form of a valid argument is valid*, because every argument (valid or invalid) is an instance of at least one invalid* argument form. Every one-premise argument is an instance of the invalid* form:

α
$\therefore \beta$

Every two-premise argument is an instance of the invalid* form:

α
β
$\therefore \gamma$

and so on. But if we can see that a given argument is an instance of just one valid* form, we know immediately that it is valid, without having to construct a truth table for the argument, for we know that every instance of any valid* form is a valid argument. This result is therefore very useful for recognizing valid arguments in practice.

Having clarified the differences among propositions, wff variables, and logical forms; arguments and argument forms; and what we are doing when we construct a truth table for an argument and when we construct one for an argument form, we shall henceforth (for the sake of simplicity) stop using the terms "valid*" and "invalid*" and simply apply the terms "valid" and "invalid" to both arguments and argument forms. It should always be kept in mind, however, that calling an argument form "valid" means something different from calling an argument "valid."

5.5.1 Exercises

1. (i) Show by producing a truth table for the following argument form that it is invalid:

$$\alpha$$
$$\therefore \beta$$

   (ii) Give an instance of the above argument form that is valid; show that it is valid by producing a truth table for the argument.

2. While it is not true in general that every instance of an invalid argument form is an invalid argument, there are some invalid argument forms whose instances are always invalid arguments. Give an example of such an argument form.

5.6 Notable Argument Forms

In this section we list some notable argument forms, the names by which they are commonly known, and whether they are valid or invalid (as can be verified by producing truth tables for the argument forms). Remember that all instances of the valid forms are valid arguments. (This is not an exhaustive list of valid argument forms! It is just a small sample.)

Argument form	Common name	Validity
$\alpha \to \beta$ α $\therefore \beta$	Modus ponens	Valid
$\alpha \to \beta$ $\neg \beta$ $\therefore \neg \alpha$	Modus tollens	Valid
$\alpha \to \beta$ β $\therefore \alpha$	Fallacy of affirming the consequent	Invalid
$\alpha \to \beta$ $\neg \alpha$ $\therefore \neg \beta$	Fallacy of denying the antecedent	Invalid
$\alpha \to \beta$ $\beta \to \gamma$ $\therefore \alpha \to \gamma$	Hypothetical syllogism	Valid

Argument form	Common name	Validity
$\alpha \to \beta$ $\gamma \to \delta$ $\alpha \lor \gamma$ $\therefore \beta \lor \delta$	Constructive dilemma	Valid
$\alpha \lor \beta$ $\neg\alpha$ $\therefore \beta$	Disjunctive syllogism	Valid

5.7 Other Logical Properties

In this chapter we have talked about validity and invalidity. Analogous comments apply to other central logical notions: tautology/nontautology, equivalence/inequivalence, and unsatisfiability/satisfiability. These notions were defined in Chapter 4.[3] From our present point of view, these properties fall into two categories: those whose presence can be established by citing a single truth table row (call these *s-properties*), and the rest (*a-properties*).[4] Here is how the properties divide up:

A-property	S-property
Validity	Invalidity
Tautology	Nontautology
Equivalence	Inequivalence
Unsatisfiability	Satisfiability

Note that in each row, the property on the left is just the property something has if it does *not* have the property on the right, and vice versa.

To show that an argument is invalid, it suffices to come up with a single truth table row in which the premises are true and the conclusion false, whereas no single truth table row can establish that an argument is valid. To show that a proposition is not a tautology, it suffices to come up with a single truth table row in which the proposition is false, whereas no single truth table row can establish that a proposition is a tautology. To show that two propositions are inequivalent, it suffices to come up with a single truth table row in which one of them is true and the other false, whereas no single truth table row can establish that two propositions are equivalent. And to show that a set of propositions is satisfiable, it suffices to come up with a single truth table row in which all the propositions in the set are true, whereas no single truth table row can establish that a set of propositions is unsatisfiable.

Now, returning to the issue of form: the a-properties are all analogous to validity, in the sense that if a form has the property, so does every instance of the form. For example, consider equivalence: two wffs are equivalent iff on every row of their joint truth table they have the same value. This notion applies to pairs of propositions—but we could also run the truth table test for equivalence on pairs of logical forms (in the way that, in §5.4, we applied the truth table test for validity to argument forms instead of arguments), deeming two logical forms equivalent* iff they have the same value in every row of their joint truth table. We could then show that given two equivalent* logical forms, if we take an instance of the first and an instance of the second (replacing the same variable by the same wff across both forms—just as, when going from an argument form to an instance of the form, we replace variables uniformly across all premises and the conclusion), the two resulting wffs must be equivalent. Or to take another example, consider the property of being a tautology: a wff is a tautology iff in every row of its truth table, it has the value T. This notion applies to propositions—but we could also run the truth table test for tautology on logical forms, deeming a form a tautology* iff it has the value T in every row of its truth table. We could then show that, given a logical form that is a tautology*, every instance of this form must be a tautology.

In contrast, the s-properties all behave like invalidity: that is, it does not follow that every instance of the form has the property if the form has that property. For example, consider satisfiability (of single wffs): a wff is satisfiable iff in some row of its truth table it has the value T. This notion applies to propositions—but we could also run the truth table test for satisfiability on logical forms, deeming a form satisfiable* iff it has the value T in some row of its truth table. We could then show that, given a satisfiable* logical form, it does not follow that every instance of this form must be satisfiable. For example, $\alpha \land \beta$ is a satisfiable* form, but its instance $A \land \neg A$ is not satisfiable.

The reason for the different behavior of a-properties and s-properties is that (as discussed in §5.4 and §5.5) no new row types appear in the truth table for the instance(s) that were not covered in the truth table for the form(s), but some row types may disappear. If the row type(s) that disappear are the row(s) that made the form have the s-property, then the instance will lack that s-property.

6

Connectives: Translation and Adequacy

In this chapter we examine two topics concerning connectives. First, in §§6.2–6.5, we take a closer look at issues surrounding translation from English into PL. More specifically, for each connective in PL, we have mentioned one or more words of English that typically express that connective—but we have noted that the correlations are not perfect: for example, "and" does not always express conjunction, and conversely, conjunction is often expressed using words other than "and." In these sections we engage in a more detailed discussion of the relationships between connectives of PL and expressions in English. Before discussing particular connectives, we introduce some essential background concepts in §6.1. In the final section of the chapter—§6.6—we look at a second issue associated with connectives: the issue of functional completeness (aka adequacy).

6.1 Assertibility and Implicature

Recall that a speaker can make a claim about the world by producing an utterance (i.e., a token—spoken, written, or otherwise—of some sentence) in a context. Let us consider the issue of assessing utterances for correctness: of judging whether an utterance is, in the circumstances in which it is produced, a good one; of judging whether the speaker said the right thing (or an acceptable thing) in the circumstances, or whether something else (or nothing at all) would have been better (in those circumstances). To the extent that an utterance of a certain sentence is correct in some context, we say that the sentence is *assertible* in that context.[1]

One way in which an utterance can be bad (wrong, incorrect) is if the proposition thereby expressed is false. There are, however, many other ways in which utterances can be bad. For example, even though you speak the truth, you may say the wrong thing if your utterance is rude, irrelevant to the discussion at hand, excessively long, unnecessarily complex and hard to follow, phrased in a language that your audience does not speak, too loud, or too soft. In a very influential study of these issues, Paul Grice introduced the Cooperative Principle:

> Make your conversational contribution such as is required, at the stage at which it occurs, by the accepted purpose or direction of the talk exchange in which you are engaged. [Grice, 1989, 26]

In general, other things being equal, utterances not conforming to the Cooperative Principle will be regarded as—to a greater or lesser extent—incorrect. But what exactly is involved in conforming to the Cooperative Principle? To help answer this question, Grice [1989, 26–27] laid out serveral more specific maxims:

- Maxims of Quantity:
  - Make your contribution as informative as required (for the current purposes of the exchange).
  - Do not make your contribution more informative than required.

- Maxim of Quality:
  - Try to make your contribution one that is true.
    - Do not say what you believe to be false.
    - Do not say something for which you lack adequate evidence.

- Maxim of Relation:
  - Be relevant.

- Maxim of Manner:
  - Be perspicuous.
    - Avoid obscurity of expression.
    - Avoid ambiguity.
    - Be brief (avoid unnecessary prolixity).
    - Be orderly.

In general, other things being equal, utterances not conforming to one or more of these maxims will be regarded as—to a greater or lesser extent—incorrect.

For example, suppose that we are all chatting about what we did on the weekend. If I say "I did some stuff," this will not be regarded as a cooperative contribution—I have not conformed to the first Maxim of Quantity: make your contribution as informative as is required. Likewise, if I launch into a lengthy description beginning with the complete thought process I went through in deciding what to have for breakfast, this will not be regarded as a good contribution—I have not conformed to the second Maxim of Quantity: do not make your contribution more informative than required. Or again, suppose I say:

We set up the camp on the beach. Before that we had lunch. That was after we sank the boat because we were sailing too fast. We hit a rock and then the bread was all soggy, so we had to dry it out before lunch. The boat builder says he will be able to fix the boat, but it will take ten days. We had to get her up from the bottom—but first we recovered the bread and the other things by diving for them. We got milk for lunch while the bread was drying and the farmer sang us a song. That was after we visited the boat builder. Before that we had to patch up the boat to get her across the lake.

Let's suppose that everything I say is true, and that I have provided an appropriate amount of information about my weekend. Nevertheless, my contribution leaves something to be desired—it is hard to follow. With much concentration—or pen and paper to construct a timeline—you can probably piece together the events, but my contribution to the exchange of information would be a better one if I told things in the order they happened—if I conformed to the last part of the Maxim of Manner: be orderly. Let's consider a final example. Suppose that we are in the middle of a discussion of some important matter, when I begin to describe what I did on the weekend. Let's suppose my description is entirely true—and orderly. Nevertheless, if I do not link it in some way with the discussion at hand, my contribution will be regarded as a bad one. For my comments to be regarded as a cooperative contribution to the conversation, I need to observe the Maxim of Relation: be relevant.

Grice regarded the above maxims as specific instances—that is, specific to the case of conversational exchanges—of more general principles governing any form of rational cooperative behavior. For example, if you are helping me to fix a car and I need four nuts, then I expect you to hand me four, not two or six (cf. the Maxims of Quantity); if you are helping me to make a cake and I need a spoon, then I expect you to hand me a real spoon, not a trick spoon made of rubber (cf. the Maxim of Quality) nor (at this point in the process) an oven cloth (cf. the Maxim of Relation) [Grice, 1989, 28].

Apart from these general principles governing all conversations, some utterances are also subject to further norms attached to particular words in those utterances. For example, consider the difference between describing an action as generous and describing it as magnanimous. There are situations in which the former is the right word to use and other situations in which the latter is the right word—but this difference cannot be traced to the above conversational maxims. In particular, consider the Maxim of Quality. The problem with describing an action as magnanimous, when "generous" would be the right word to use, is not that the former description is false while the latter is true. The difference is more subtle than that: roughly speaking, it is appropriate to call an act "magnanimous" only when the beneficiary of the act is less powerful than, or a rival of, the person who performs the act. This condition on the correctness of utterances featuring the term "magnanimous" is, then, separate from—and additional to—the general constraints governing all conversations: it is a condition attached in particular to the word "magnanimous." Many other words also have special conditions attached to them that dictate that some utterances involving these words, even though not false, are nevertheless incorrect. Think of a thesaurus, which gives a list of synonyms (e.g., "cheap," "inexpensive," and "low-cost"): substituting one of these words for another will not, in general, make a true statement into a false one, but it may well make an entirely appropriate statement into one that jars—that does not sound correct in the circumstances.

In light of the above, we can now—following Grice—group into three categories the information conveyed when one makes a claim by uttering a sentence in a context. First, there is *what is said*: the proposition expressed (by uttering that sentence in that context). This is what we aim to capture in translation from English into PL. That is, the wff of PL that we write down as the translation of an English utterance is supposed to be a perspicuous representation of the proposition expressed by that utterance.

Second, there is what is *implied*: the logical consequences of the proposition expressed. What is implied by an utterance are those propositions that follow logically from what is said (i.e., from the proposition expressed by the utterance). So suppose someone says something that we translate into PL as P. The speaker does not say $P \vee Q$, but she implies it. She does not say $P \vee Q$, because the latter proposition is true in a situation in which P is false and Q is true, whereas what she actually says—plain old P—is false in this situation. Nevertheless she implies $P \vee Q$, because $P \vee Q$ follows logically from P; that is, $P / \therefore P \vee Q$ is a valid argument. In general, where α is what is said by a certain utterance, every proposition β such that $\alpha / \therefore \beta$ is a valid argument is implied by that utterance.

Third, there is what is *implicated*—known as *implicatures*.[2] Roughly speaking, the implicatures of an utterance are those things that follow from the assumption that the utterance is correct.[3] Consider an example. A friend drops by, just as you are sitting down to lunch. "Would you like to join us?" you ask. "I've just eaten," she replies. Part of the information conveyed by this reply is that your friend would not like to join you for lunch—but this is not what is said, and it is not implied by what is said. Rather, it is an implicature. It follows from the assumption that your friend is speaking correctly—in particular, from the assumption that she is endeavoring to conform to the Cooperative Principle. You have just asked your friend a question, so the only way that she can make her conversational contribution as required (at this stage and by the accepted purpose of the exchange) is if she provides an answer (yes or no) to this question. Given that (at any point in time) the more recently one has eaten, the less likely one is to want to eat, it follows that the answer your friend wants to convey is no: she would not like to join you for lunch. Note that the information that your friend does not wish to join you for lunch follows only given the assumption that she is speaking correctly. If you do not assume that she is endeavoring to conform to the Cooperative Principle—in particular, if you do not assume that she is trying to say something relevant to the conversation at hand but leave it open that she is simply saying the first thing that pops into her head—then you cannot conclude that she is conveying the answer no to your question (she might not be trying to answer your question at all).

Recall that we distinguished between general norms of correctness (the Cooperative Principle, spelled out in the Maxims), which apply to all conversations, and specific norms, which apply to particular words (e.g., the norm governing correct use of the word "magnanimous" as opposed to "generous"). Grice calls implicatures that follow from the assumption that the speaker is conforming to the general norms *conversational implicatures* and implicatures that follow from the assumption that the speaker is conforming to the special norms governing one or more of the words used *conventional implicatures*. A key difference between the two kinds of implicatures is that conversational implicatures can be *cancelled,* whereas conventional implicatures cannot. For example, your friend might say "I've just eaten—but it looks so good, I'll have a second lunch, thanks." Here she explicitly cancels the implicature that would normally be carried by the first part of her utterance: her (extended) reply does not now convey the information that she would not like to join you for lunch; rather, it conveys the information that she would like to join you.[4] By contrast, consider the following claim:

> The prime minister's speech, in which she praised Senator Bellinghausen, was magnanimous—although I do not mean to suggest that there is any rivalry between the prime minister and the senator, nor that the prime minister is his superior.

This is just odd. If one refers to the prime minister's speech as magnanimous, then one does implicate a rivalry between the prime minister and Senator Bellinghausen or that the prime minister is his superior, and this implicature cannot then be retracted. If one does not think there is any such rivalry (etc.), then one should not use the word "magnanimous": one should simply describe the speech as "generous."

§

Before turning to particular connectives and the ways in which they may or may not be expressed in English, we make a general comment on our methodology. Suppose we are faced with an utterance of an English sentence that seems to express a proposition formed from a number of simpler propositions and a connective: that is, it is apparently of the form $*\alpha$ (where $*$ is some one-place connective) or $\alpha * \beta$ (where $*$ is some two-place connective). For example,

- "Necessarily, if James is a human being, then James is mortal" is apparently of the form $*\alpha$, where $*$ is the one-place connective "necessarily," and α is "if James is a human being, then James is mortal."[5]

- "I went to bed, because I was tired" is apparently of the form $\alpha * \beta$, where $*$ is the two-place connective "because," α is "I went to bed," and β is "I was tired."

- "I went to bed, even though I was not tired" is apparently of the form $\alpha * \beta$, where $*$ is the two-place connective "even though," α is "I went to bed," and β is "I was not tired."

- "I was tired, but I did not go to bed" is apparently of the form $\alpha * \beta$, where $*$ is "but," α is "I was tired," and β is "I did not go to bed."

How do we translate this utterance into PL? Our procedure is to draw up a truth table. That is, we ask, for each possible combination of truth values for α and β, whether $\alpha * \beta$ (or $*\alpha$, if we are dealing with a one-place connective) would be true or false if α and β had those values. For example: would "I went to bed, because I was tired" be true or false if "I went to bed" were false and "I was tired" were true? Would "I was tired, but I did not go to bed" be true or false if "I was tired" were true and "I did not go to bed" were false? And so on. At this point, one of two things might happen.

(1) It might happen that we succeed in constructing the truth table. In this case, we take as our translation of $*$ the connective of PL that has this same truth table.[6]

(2) It might happen that we cannot construct the truth table, because in one or more rows the answer to the question whether $\alpha * \beta$ (or $*\alpha$, if we are dealing with a one-place connective) would be true or false if α and β had the values specified in that row is: we do not know—more information is required. For example, is "I went to bed, because I was tired" true if "I went to bed" is true and "I was tired" is true? We do not know: the fact that both component propositions are true still leaves it open whether I went to bed *because* I was tired. To take another example: is "necessarily, John is human" true or false if "John is human" is true? We do not know: the fact that the component proposition is true does not determine whether it is necessarily true (i.e., could not be false). In this case, the connective $*$ is not truth functional: to determine the truth value of $\alpha * \beta$ (or $*\alpha$, if we are dealing with a one-place connective), it is not sufficient to know the truth values of α and β. Therefore, $*$ cannot be translated into PL: all the connectives in PL are truth functional. There are two ways of proceeding.

(2a) One option is to move beyond PL to a nonclassical logic that includes nontruth-functional connectives. (Such logics are beyond the scope of this book, which covers only classical logic.)

(2b) The other option is to revise the view that our original English utterance (e.g., "I went to bed, because I was tired," "necessarily, John is human") expresses a proposition of the form $\alpha * \beta$ (or $*\alpha$), instead offering a more complex translation. This translation will probably use a logical language more complex than PL: perhaps one of the languages of predicate logic (to be examined in Part II of this book), or perhaps the language of some nonclassical logic (which falls outside the scope of this book).

So much for laying out the possibilities in the abstract: in the following sections we shall encounter particular examples of all of them. One important general lesson that will emerge is this: when translating into PL, one should not focus solely on which English words are used (blindly translating "and" as $\wedge$, "if" as $\rightarrow$, etc.) but on what is being said—in particular, on the conditions under which the English utterance one is translating is supposed to be true or false.

6.2 Conjunction

6.2.1 Conjunction without "And"

Apart from "and," other expressions in English can also be used to express conjunction. For example, consider a typical utterance of the sentence "it was sunny, but it was cold." It would seem to express a proposition of the form $\alpha * \beta$, where $*$ is the two-place connective (expressed by) "but," α is (the proposition expressed by) "it was sunny," and β is (the proposition expressed by) "it was cold."[7] That is, here it seems that "but" expresses a two-place connective. Which one? In accordance with the procedure described above, we proceed to answer this question by trying to construct a truth table for "it was sunny, but it was cold." Using the glossary on the left, we construct the truth table on the right:

S: It was sunny
C: It was cold

S	C	S but C
T	T	T
T	F	F
F	T	F
F	F	F

We obtain the entry in the body of the table in row 1 by asking: would what I said (when I uttered "it was sunny, but it was cold") be true if "it was sunny" were true, and "it was cold" were true? Yes: hence there is a T in this row. For row 2 we ask: would what I said be true if "it was sunny" were true and "it was cold" were false? No: hence there is an F in this row, and so on. Now compare the above table with the following one:

S	C	$S \wedge C$
T	T	T
T	F	F
F	T	F
F	F	F

It has the same entries. So we translate "but" (in "it was sunny, but it was cold") as $\wedge$. In other words, "but" here expresses conjunction.

We thus translate "it was sunny, but it was cold" in the same way as we translate "it was sunny, and it was cold." In particular, here we translate both "and" and "but" as conjunction ($\wedge$). However, this does not mean that we are claiming that "but" and "and" have exactly the same meaning. The latter claim is clearly false. To take the traditional example, the following two statements convey different things:

1. He was poor and honest.

2. He was poor but honest.

As the only difference between the two is that the second uses "but" where the first uses "and," it would seem that these two words must have different meanings: otherwise, how could the two statements differ in what they convey? So let us agree that "and" and "but" do not mean exactly the same thing. This does not conflict with our claim that both should be translated as $\wedge$. Translating (1) and (2) in the same way—as $P \wedge H$ (using the glossary P: He was poor; H: He was honest)—commits us to this: in any situation in which (1) is true, (2) is true, and vice versa.[8] We do not, however, commit to the following: in any situation in which (1) is a good (appropriate, correct) thing to say, (2) is a good (appropriate, correct) thing to say, and vice versa. Therefore, we could say that the difference in meaning between "and" and "but" affects when it is appropriate to use these words but not whether the resulting utterances are true. More specifically, there is a condition on the correct use of "but" in "A but B": one must take there to be some contrast or opposition between A and B that makes it unlikely that they are both true. There is no such condition on the correct use of "and." Therefore, an utterance of the form "A but B" will have an implicature that "A and B" lacks. If someone says "A but B," and we assume that he is speaking correctly, then it follows that he takes there to be some contrast between A and B.[9] We can make no such inference if he says instead "A and B."

In sum, our claim is that "and" and "but" make the same contribution to the truth conditions of utterances in which they occur; however, they do not make the same contribution to assertibility conditions. In terms of our earlier example, when what is expressed by "it was sunny, but it was cold" is true, what is expressed by "it was sunny, and it was cold" is true too—and vice versa. However, it is not the case that when it is appropriate to say "it was sunny, and it was cold," it is appropriate to say "it was sunny, but it was cold"—and vice versa. Hence, we allow for the difference in meaning between "and" and "but" while maintaining that both express conjunction (i.e., that both should be translated as $\land$).

To make this approach more convincing (call it the *implicature approach*), we explore what seems to be the main alternative option: regarding "A but B" as saying the same thing as "A and B and it is unusual that A and B should both be true" (call this the *third conjunct approach*). Using the third conjunct approach, "it was sunny, but it was cold" would be translated into PL as $S \land C \land U$ (using the glossary S: It was sunny; C: It was cold; U: It is unusual for it to be cold and sunny at the same time). In contrast, "it was sunny, and it was cold" would be translated as $S \land C$. Consider the three pieces of information S, C, and U. Intuitively, an utterance of "it was sunny, but it was cold" conveys all three, while an utterance of "it was sunny, and it was cold" conveys only S and C. Both the implicature approach (whereby both are translated as $S \land C$, but "but" is subject to a norm of correct use to which "and" is not subject—and hence carries an additional implicature, in this case U) and the third conjunct approach capture this intuition. However, it is *also* intuitively the case (i) that the way in which U is conveyed by "it was sunny, but it was cold" is different from the way in which U is conveyed by "it was sunny, and it was cold, and it is unusual for it to be cold and sunny at the same time"—the latter comes straight out and says U, whereas the former conveys it in a more indirect fashion—and (ii) that one makes a stronger commitment to the truth of U when one says "it was sunny, and it was cold, and it is unusual for it to be cold and sunny at the same time" than when one says "it was sunny but it was cold." (Or—returning to our other example for a moment—consider the difference between saying "he was poor but honest" and saying "he was poor and honest, and most poor people are not honest." Either way conveys the opinion that most poor people are not honest, but the second comes straight out and says it, whereas the first insinuates it without directly saying it. As a consequence, it seems that you make a stronger commitment to the opinion that most poor people are not honest when you say "he was poor and honest, and most poor people are not honest" than when you say "he was poor but honest.") The third conjuct approach does not capture this further intuition: using this approach, an utterance of "it was sunny, but it was cold" commits you to the truth of U in the same way that an utterance of "it was sunny, and it was cold, and it is unusual for it to be cold and sunny at the same time" does. The implicature approach does capture the further intuition.

Using this approach, when you say "it was sunny, but it was cold," the truth of U is required for your statement to be correct but is not required for it to be true (i.e., U is an implicature), whereas when you say "it was sunny, and it was cold, and it is unusual for it to be cold and sunny at the same time," the truth of U is required for your statement to be true (i.e., U is implied).[10]

Before leaving the word "but," note that we are not saying that all uses of "but" should be translated as conjunction. What we have said applies only to uses of "but" like the one in "it was sunny, but it was cold." There are other uses of "but" that do not express conjunction. First, "but" has uses in which it does not express a connective at all—for example, in "I could not but laugh," "he had no choice but to leave town," and "who could have done it but him?" Second, there are cases where "but" (partially) expresses a connective other than conjunction. For example, in "it never rains but it pours," the claim is that if it rains, then it pours (i.e., it rains only if it pours)—so this statement is a conditional.[11]

§

Turning now to other words, the situation regarding "although . . . anyway" is very similar to that regarding "but." Consider the claim "although she was tired, she went out anyway." Using the glossary below, we can construct the truth table to its right by considering whether the claim in question would be true or false if she was tired and went out (row 1), was tired and did not go out (row 2), and so on:

		T	W	Although T, W anyway
T: She was tired		T	T	T
W: She went out		T	F	F
		F	T	F
		F	F	F

This truth table is the same as that for $T \wedge W$. So we translate "although . . . anyway" as $\wedge$. Similar considerations lead us to conclude that "although," "even though," "though," "despite the fact that," "in spite of the fact that," "notwithstanding," "however," "yet," "whereas," "nevertheless," "moreover," and the semicolon (as in "Tom left the house; Sarah stayed indoors") can all be used to express conjunction.

6.2.2 "And" without Conjunction

We have considered some words other than "and" that can be used to express conjunction. We turn now to cases in which "and" is not properly translated as conjunction. As in the case of "but," there are uses of "and" that do not express connectives at all, for example, "the weather just keeps getting hotter and hotter," "I ran and ran," "it will be years and years before the trees bear fruit," "two and two make four." There are also cases in which "and" does express a connective—but the conditional rather than conjunction. For example, in "study hard, and you will pass the exam," the claim is that if you study hard, then you will pass the exam.

It has been suggested that there are various other cases in which "and" is not properly translated as conjunction. We examine some of them now.

Consider the claims:

1. Albert took off his shoes and went inside.

2. Albert went inside and took off his shoes.

They would typically be taken to convey different things: (1) that Albert took off his shoes outside and then went in and (2) that Albert went in and then took off his shoes inside. Now what happens if we translate "and" here as conjunction? Using the glossary:

$S:$ Albert took off his shoes
$W:$ Albert went inside

the first claim comes out as $S \wedge W$ and the second as $W \wedge S$. These translations are logically equivalent. Both of them are true, provided S and W are both true—that is, provided Albert took off his shoes, and Albert went inside: it makes no difference which happened first. Do we have a problem here with the proposal to translate "and," as it occurs in these two utterances, as conjunction? Some have thought so—but the more common view is that we do not: the difference between the two utterances is not that they have different truth conditions—and so must express different propositions—but that they have different implicatures. If, in the course of recounting a series of events, someone says something of the form "A and B," then if we assume that she is obeying the conversational maxims (§6.1)—in particular, that she is being orderly—then we shall assume that she is telling things in the order in which they happened. "A and B" will then implicate that A happened before B.

We have just seen that "A and B" sometimes conveys the information that A happened before B. At other times, "A and B" conveys the information that B happened as a result of A. For example, consider the claims:

3. I had an overwhelming feeling that I could achieve anything, and I surged ahead and won the race.

4. I surged ahead and won the race, and I had an overwhelming feeling that I could achieve anything.

They would typically be taken to convey different things: (3) that the feeling caused me to surge ahead and win; (4) that surging ahead and winning caused me to have the feeling. Now if we translate "and" here as conjunction, then (using the glossary F: I had an overwhelming feeling that I could achieve anything; R: I surged ahead and won the race) (3) translates as $F \wedge R$ and (4) as $R \wedge F$. As before, these translations are logically equivalent. Both of them are true, provided F and R are both true—that is, provided I had an overwhelming feeling that I could achieve anything, and I surged ahead and won the race: it makes no difference which came first or whether one caused the other. Again, some have thought we have a problem here for the proposal to translate "and" as conjunction in these two utterances—but the more common view is that we do not: requiring that the second conjunct be true because the first conjunct is true is not a condition that must be satisfied for the claim to be true; it is, rather, an implicature.

The alternative to translating (1) as $S \wedge W$ (and treating the information that Albert took off his shoes before going in as an implicature rather than as part of the truth conditions of (1)) and (3) as $F \wedge R$ (and treating the information that the feeling caused the win as an implicature rather than as part of the truth conditions of (3)) is to regard "and" as *ambiguous* in the following way: in some contexts (e.g., "Albert bought bread and milk") it expresses conjunction (i.e., it is correctly translated as $\wedge$), in other contexts (e.g., (1)) it means the same as "and then" (and so cannot be translated as $\wedge$),[12] and in yet other contexts (e.g., (3)) it means the same as "and as a result of this" (and so again cannot be translated as $\wedge$). There is an influential argument against this alternative approach—an argument that has come to be known as "Grice's Razor."[13] Both the approach advocated above (the *implicature approach*) and the alternative approach just mentioned (the *ambiguity approach*) provide an account of the phenomena (i.e., of the fact that some uses of "A and B" convey simply that A and B are true; some also convey that A happened before B; and some also convey that B happened as a result of A), but the implicature approach does so in a more economical way. The implicature approach appeals to one meaning of "and" and to the conversational maxims, whereas the ambiguity approach appeals to three different meanings of "and." Now it is not as though we can do away with the conversational maxims altogether if we countenance two extra senses for "and": the maxims are completely general, and they do important work across the board (not just when explaining the phenomena associated with "and"). However, if we adopt the implicature approach, then we can do away with the extra senses of "and." In general, we should favor the simplest, most economical explanation: the one that captures the phenomena using the least resources. Hence, we should favor the implica-ture approach over the ambiguity approach.

§

Finally, let us turn to *phrasal* conjunction. In English, "and" can be used to join whole sentences (e.g., "Jack went shopping, and Jill went to the beach"), but it can also be used to join parts of sentences (phrases): verbs (e.g., "Jill swam and sunbathed"), adverbs (e.g., "Jack shopped quickly and efficiently"), and nouns in object position (e.g., "Jack bought milk and bread") and in subject position (e.g., "Jack and Jill are Swiss"). In many cases, a sentence involving phrasal conjunction is straightforwardly equivalent to a sentence involving sentential conjunction, which can be straightforwardly translated into PL using ∧. For example, "Jill swam and sunbathed" says the same thing as "Jill swam, and Jill sunbathed;" "Jack shopped quickly and efficiently" says the same thing as "Jack shopped quickly, and Jack shopped efficiently;" "Jack bought milk and bread" says the same thing as "Jack bought milk, and Jack bought bread;" and "Jack and Jill are Swiss" says the same thing as "Jack is Swiss, and Jill is Swiss." In other cases, however, the phrasal conjunction is not equivalent to any sentential conjunction—for example, "Jack and Jill are similar." (Note that "Jack is similar, and Jill is similar" is ungrammatical and makes no sense.) In yet other cases, the phrasal conjunction seems to admit two readings, one of which is equivalent to a sentential conjunction, and the other of which is not. For example:

1. Jack and Jill are married.

2. Jack is married, and Jill is married.

3. Bill and Ben are brothers.

4. Bill is a brother, and Ben is a brother.

5. Boris and Barbara walked to school.

6. Boris walked to school, and Barbara walked to school.

(1) could be read as saying simply that Jack is married (i.e., his marital status is "married") and Jill is married—in which case it says the same thing as (2)—or it could be read as saying that Jack and Jill are married to each other—in which case it does not say the same thing as (2). (3) could be read as saying simply that Bill is a brother (i.e., he has a sibling) and Ben is a brother—in which case it says the same thing as (4)—or it could be read as saying that Bill and Ben are brothers of each other—in which case it does not say the same thing as (4). (5) could be read as saying simply that Boris walked to school and Barbara walked to school—in which case it says the same thing as (6)—or

it could be read as saying that Boris and Barbara walked to school together—in which case it does not say the same thing as (6).

As already mentioned, phrasal conjunctions equivalent to sentential conjunctions are translated into PL using ∧. For example (using the glossary K: Jack is married; L: Jill is married), (2) is translated into PL as $K \wedge L$, and so is (1) on those occasions when it is deemed to be saying the same thing as (2). But what about phrasal conjunctions that are not equivalent to sentential conjunctions—for example, "Jack and Jill are similar," or (1) when it is taken to mean that Jack is married to Jill (and vice versa)? These have to be translated into PL as basic propositions, for example,

I: Jack and Jill are similar
M: Jack is married to Jill

When we discuss predicate logic (in particular, general predicate logic in Chapter 12), we shall see how to treat these claims in a more illuminating way.

6.3 Conditional and Biconditional

6.3.1 Indicative and Counterfactual Conditionals

In PL we have one conditional: →. We call → the *material conditional*. The material conditional $(P \rightarrow Q)$ is false if P is true and Q is false, and true otherwise, as the truth table for → shows. Thus, it is equivalent to $\neg(P \wedge \neg Q)$ and $(\neg P \vee Q)$ (do the truth tables and check). The proposition $(P \rightarrow Q)$ can therefore be read into English as "it is not the case both that P and that not Q" or "either not P, or Q."

In English, there are at least two different kinds of conditional.[14] Consider the following pair of English conditionals:

1. If humans did not build Stonehenge, nonhumans did.

2. If humans had not built Stonehenge, nonhumans would have.

Conditional (1) seems clearly true: Stonehenge is there; it was built by someone or something (that is, it is not a naturally occurring formation); so if it was not built by humans, it was built by nonhumans. Conditional (2) seems clearly false: it seems rather that if humans had not built Stonehenge, there would simply be no Stonehenge. There is no reason to think, for example, that if humans had not built it, aliens would have. So one of these propositions seems true and one false. Yet it is natural to regard each of them as composed of two component propositions—"humans did not build Stonehenge" and "nonhumans built Stonehenge"—using a two-place conditional connective. But then the conditional connective cannot be the same in both cases. For one compound is true and one false, and if—in the same situation—one connective yields a true compound from two propositions and another connective yields a false compound from the same two propositions, then the two connectives cannot be the same.

We call the conditional connective in (1) an *indicative* conditional. Here are some other examples of indicative conditionals:

3. If it rains tonight, we shall get wet.

4. If the roof leaked last night, there will be water on the kitchen floor.

5. If John is smoking out there, he is doing something very foolish.

We call the conditional connective in (2) a *subjunctive* or *counterfactual* conditional. Here are some other examples of subjunctive conditionals:

6. If it were to rain tonight, we would get wet.

7. If the roof had leaked last night, there would be water on the kitchen floor.

8. If John were smoking out there, he would be doing something very foolish.

One thing seems clear: the subjunctive conditional is not correctly translated into PL as →. This is because subjunctive conditionals are not truth functional. Consider the claim "if you had put your sandwich down, a dog would have eaten it." Suppose we regard this statement as a compound made up from the subjunctive conditional connective and the two propositions "you put your sandwich down" and "a dog ate your sandwich." In a situation in which you ate your sandwich quickly, without putting it down, while surrounded by hungry, unruly dogs, both components are false, and the subjunctive conditional is true. In a situation in which you ate your sandwich quickly, without putting it down, and there were no dogs for miles around, both components are again false, but the subjunctive conditional is false. So the subjunctive conditional is not a truth-functional connective. To know whether a subjunctive conditional is true in some situation, we need to know more than just the truth values of its components in that situation. To handle the semantics of subjunctives, we therefore need more machinery than we have so far: truth tables will not suffice.[15]

6.3.2 Indicative and Material Conditionals

We said in earlier chapters that "if . . . then" (and "if" and "only if") are translated into PL as →. We can now clarify that we meant uses of "if" (etc.) in indicative conditionals, not in counterfactuals. But even the claim that the indicative conditional is correctly translated as → is controversial. Before discussing objections to this translation, we give some reasons in its favor.

First, an uncontroversial point: if we take the indicative conditional to express a truth-functional connective, then that connective must be →. In other words, if the indicative conditional has a truth table at all, it is the truth table for →: no other truth table is a serious contender.[16] Recall the truth table for →:

α	β	$(\alpha \to \beta)$
T	T	T
T	F	F
F	T	T
F	F	T

Let us consider the four rows of the table. For a start, the F in row 2 is clearly correct: if a conditional has a true antecedent and a false consequent, it is false. Next, rows 1 and 4 must contain T, because a paradigm of a true indicative conditional is one in which the antecedent and the consequent are the same proposition. "If it is raining, it is raining" is undeniably true, whether it is raining or not.[17] Given our restriction to truth-functional connectives, if we are to make this conditional come out true both when its antecedent and consequent are both true and when they are both false, we must put T in both rows 1 and 4. Now consider row 3. We have a T in this row. The only other option is an F. But if we put F in row 3, we would end up with the truth table for the biconditional, whereas clearly conditionals and biconditionals say different things.

More significantly, there are arguments that seem to show—without any prior assumption that the indicative conditional is truth functional—that the indicative conditional "if A then B" has the same truth conditions as the material conditional $A \to B$: that is, (i) when "if A then B" is true, so is $A \to B$ and (ii) when $A \to B$ is true, so is "if A then B."[18] Condition (i) is uncontroversial. For suppose $A \to B$ is not true. Then (by the truth table for →) A is true, and B is false. But then the indicative conditional "if A then B" is certainly false. So when "if A then B" is true, $A \to B$ must be too. The real issue, then, is (ii). We want to show that if $A \to B$ is true, then "if A then B" is true. Here are two arguments for this conclusion:

1. The proposition $A \to B$ is equivalent to $\neg(A \wedge \neg B)$, so if $A \to B$ is true, $\neg(A \wedge \neg B)$ is true. But from $\neg(A \wedge \neg B)$, "if A then B" obviously follows. For given that it is not the case both that A and that $\neg B$, if A is the case, then $\neg B$ must not be the case—that is, B must be the case.

2. The proposition $A \to B$ is equivalent to $(\neg A \vee B)$, so if $A \to B$ is true, $(\neg A \vee B)$ is true. But from $(\neg A \vee B)$, "if A then B" obviously follows. For given that at least one of $\neg A$ and B is the case, if A is the case—that is, $\neg A$ is not the case—then B must be the case.

Jackson [1991, p. 2] gives an even simpler argument for the conclusion that the indicative conditional has the same truth conditions as the material conditional:

> Instead of saying "if it rains, then the match will be cancelled," one could have said, to much the same effect, "either it will not rain, or it will and the match will be cancelled;" and the latter is true if and only if either "it will rain" is false or "the match will be cancelled" is true; that is if and only if [the material conditional] is true.

So what's the problem with the proposal that we translate indicative conditionals using $\rightarrow$? Well, recall that $\alpha \rightarrow \beta$ is true when α is false or β is true (or both). However, the following conditionals all seem quite wrong, even though the first two have false antecedents and the second two have true consequents:

1. If this book is about pop music, it refers to the work of the logician Frege. (false antecedent, true consequent)

2. If this book is about pop music, it contains color photos of fruit and vegetables. (false antecedent, false consequent)

3. If this book is about logic, its author's surname starts with "S." (true antecedent, true consequent)

4. If this book is about naval architecture, its author's surname starts with "S." (false antecedent, true consequent)

Therefore, it might seem that we should not translate these propositions into PL using $\rightarrow$, because then we would translate English conditionals that seem clearly wrong into PL propositions that are straightforwardly true.[19]

What exactly is wrong with the conditionals just given? The problem seems to be that in each case the antecedent has nothing to do with the consequent: believing the antecedent to be true gives us no reason to think that the consequent is true. One might conclude that for an indicative conditional to be true, it is not enough simply for it not to be the case that both the antecedent is true and the consequent is false: there must also be some sort of connection between the two. If we pursue this line of thought, we shall be led to the view that the indicative conditional is not truth functional: whether "if A then B" is true will depend not just on whether A and B are true or false but on what they actually say—and in particular, on whether there is the right kind of connection between what A says and what B says.

The alternative is to defend the view that indicative conditionals have the same truth conditions as material conditionals, by treating the problematic examples in a way that should now be familiar: we explain why these conditionals seem wrong in a way that is compatible with their being true. So let us suppose, for the sake of argument, that indicative conditionals have the same truth conditions as material conditionals, and then see what follows from the conversational maxims about the conditions under which indicative conditionals are assertible. For it to be appropriate for one to assert a conditional "if A then B" (now thought of, for the sake of the argument, as having the same truth conditions as $A \to B$), one must believe it to be true (Maxim of Quality). That is, one must believe that the actual row is row 1, 3, or 4 in the following truth table:

A	B	$(A \to B)$
T	T	T
T	F	F
F	T	T
F	F	T

It must also be the case that one is not confident either way about the truth or falsity of A, and similarly about the truth or falsity of B. To see this, consider the cases in turn. Suppose you are confident that A is false; then (other things being equal) you are in a position to assert $\neg A$ (Maxim of Quality). But saying $\neg A$ is more informative than saying $A \to B$ (it further narrows down the possibilities: it tells us that the actual row is 3 or 4, whereas the conditional tells us only that the actual row is 1, 3, or 4)—so you should say $\neg A$, not $A \to B$ (Maxim of Quantity). Likewise, suppose you believe B to be true; then it would be more informative for you to say B than $A \to B$. Now suppose you believe A to be true; then, given that you also believe $A \to B$ to be true, you must (assuming you are minimally rational) believe B to be true; but then, as we have seen, it would be more informative for you to say B than $A \to B$. (In fact, you would be in a position to say something even more informative: $A \wedge B$.) Likewise, suppose you believe B to be false; then, given that you also believe $A \to B$ to be true, you must (assuming you are minimally rational) believe A to be false; but then, as we have seen, it would be more informative for you to say $\neg A$ than $A \to B$. (In fact, you would again be in a position to say something even more informative: $\neg A \wedge \neg B$.) Thus, if someone is to utter "if A then B" correctly, it follows that she is not confident that A is true, nor that it is false, and similarly for B. Yet she must be confident that "if A then B" is true—that is, that row 2 is not the actual row. The only way she can be in such a position is if there is some sort of connection between A and B: if A's being true would make it impossible, or very unlikely, for B to be false. Thus, if someone utters "if A then B," it will follow from the assumption that she is speaking correctly that she takes there to be some connection between A and B. On this view, then, the existence of such a connection is an implicature: it is not required for the truth of the conditional.

Now let us return to the problematic examples. They seem wrong because there is no connection between their antecedents and the consequents. Thus, we cannot imagine a situation in which any of them would be a good thing to say: if we knew the antecedent was false or the consequent true, it would be more informative to say that straight out, rather than uttering the conditional (Maxim of Quantity); if we did not know either of these things, then we would be in no position to think that the conditional is true (for there is no connection between the antecedent and consequent—hence no reason, if we do not know the truth values of either, to think we are not in a situation where the antecedent is true and the consequent false), and so again we should not say it (Maxim of Quality). We now have an explanation of why the conditionals seem wrong (i.e., we can imagine no situation in which we should want to utter them) that is compatible with their being true.[20]

6.3.3 Conditional and Biconditional without "If"

The statement "P unless Q" means that if Q is not true, P is true—so we translate it as $\neg Q \to P$. For example, using the glossary:

S: I'll come swimming tomorrow
R: It will be raining tomorrow

we translate "I'll come swimming tomorrow, unless it rains" as $\neg R \to S$. But hang on a minute—consider the truth table for $\neg R \to S$:

B	S	$(\neg R \to S)$
T	T	T
T	F	T
F	T	T
F	F	F

Note that it is true in row 1, where R and S are both true. But wouldn't you be surprised if it was raining and I turned up at the pool, after I had said "I'll come swimming, unless it rains?" Indeed—but this does not mean that what I said would be false in that situation. Rather, we take it to be an implicature of "P unless Q," as uttered in many contexts, that if Q is true, then P is false (i.e., $Q \to \neg P$), but we do not take this to be part of what is said. In our example, we take it that what I said is simply that nothing other than rain will stop me: as long as it is not raining, I shall be there. We take the further suggestion that rain will stop me as an implicature.

That "P unless Q" says (i.e., is properly translated as) $\neg Q \to P$ and (in many contexts) implicates $Q \to \neg P$—rather than saying $(\neg Q \to P) \wedge (Q \to \neg P)$—is suggested by the following two facts. First, one can cancel the suggestion that $Q \rightarrow \neg P$. For example, it would make perfect sense for me to say "I'll come swimming with you, unless it rains—and even that might not stop me" (or "and even then I might come anyway," or "and even if it rains, I still might come," etc.). If $R \rightarrow \neg S$ were part of what is said by "I'll come swimming with you, unless it rains," however, then this addition would make little sense: it would be akin to "P and Q—but Q might not be true." Second, it would also make perfect sense for me to say "I'll come swimming with you, unless it rains—in which case I won't come." This statement is properly translated as $(\neg R \rightarrow S) \wedge (R \rightarrow \neg S)$. However, if "I'll come swimming with you, unless it rains" were already properly translated as $(\neg R \rightarrow S) \wedge (R \rightarrow \neg S)$, then adding "in which case I won't come" would sound redundant: it would be akin to "P and Q—and Q."

Note that our translation of "I'll come swimming, unless it rains"—that is, $\neg R \rightarrow S$—is equivalent to $R \vee S$, whereas our translation of "I'll come swimming, unless it rains—in which case I won't come"—that is, $(\neg R \rightarrow S) \wedge (R \rightarrow \neg S)$—is equivalent to $\neg R \leftrightarrow S$, $R \leftrightarrow \neg S$, and $\neg (R \leftrightarrow S)$.

Instead of saying "I'll come swimming tomorrow, unless it rains" (or "I'll come swimming tomorrow, if it doesn't rain"), I could also say any of the following:

- I'll come swimming tomorrow, assuming it doesn't rain.
- I'll come swimming tomorrow, provided it's not raining.
- I'll come swimming tomorrow, as long as it isn't raining.
- I'll come swimming tomorrow, given it's not raining.

All these statements also translate as $\neg R \rightarrow S$. Hence, "assuming," "provided," and so on can be used (in certain contexts) to express the conditional.

6.3.4 "If" without Conditional

Consider the following claims:

1. There are biscuits on the sideboard, if you want them.

2. Harry's having a party, if you feel like going.

3. If you like, we can stop in at Claire's on the way home.

Claims of this sort are called "biscuit conditionals" (after claim (1), which is due to Austin [1970]) or "relevance conditionals." Evidently they are not properly translated as material conditionals, that is, using $\rightarrow$. Whether or not you want them is irrelevant to the truth of (1): claim (1) is true iff there are biscuits on the sideboard. Whether or not you feel like going is irrelevant to the truth of (2): claim (2) is true iff Harry's having a party. A similar point holds for claim (3). Thus, where "if A, C" is a biscuit conditional, the role of A is not to state a condition sufficient for the truth of C, and so the proper translation is not $A \to C$. Rather, the role of A is to state a condition sufficient for the listener to care whether or not C is true, and the claim as a whole says simply that C.

6.4 Disjunction

It is sometimes said that "or" in English is ambiguous: sometimes it expresses *inclusive disjunction* and sometimes *exclusive disjunction*. The difference between these is as follows:

- An inclusive disjunction "A or B" is true iff at least one—that is, one or both—of the disjuncts A and B is true.

- An exclusive disjunction "A or B" is true iff exactly one—that is, one or the other but not both—of the disjuncts A and B is true.

Inclusive disjunction is represented in PL by the connective $\lor$. Recall its truth table:

α	β	$(\alpha \lor \beta)$
T	T	T
T	F	T
F	T	T
F	F	F

Note that $\alpha \lor \beta$ is false in row 4—where α and β are both false—and true in all other rows—that is, where at least one of α and β is true. In some logic books, an additional two-place connective is introduced to represent exclusive conjunction—for example the symbol $\underline{\lor}$ might be used for this purpose.[21] (Note that we are not introducing this new symbol into PL; PL remains as defined in §2.5.) The truth table for this connective is then as follows:

α	β	$(\alpha \underline{\lor} \beta)$
T	T	F
T	F	T
F	T	T
F	F	F

The truth tables for $\lor$ and $\underline{\lor}$ differ only in the first row. In this row—where both α and β are true—the inclusive disjunction $\alpha \lor \beta$ (which states either α or β or both) is true, and the exclusive disjunction $\alpha \underline{\lor} \beta$ (which states either α or β but not both) is false.

In PL, we have no symbol for exclusive disjunction, and in this book we do not regard "or" as ambiguous: we always translate "*A* or *B*" as $A \lor B$. We now look at some of the reasons given in favor of translating certain uses of "or" as exclusive disjunction and indicate why they are not convincing. First, three preliminary points.

(1) Although PL does not have a special symbol for exclusive disjunction (e.g., $\underline{\lor}$), we can write a formula of PL having the truth conditions of an exclusive disjunction. For example, both $(A \lor B) \land \neg(A \land B)$ and $\neg(A \leftrightarrow B)$ have the same truth table as $A \underline{\lor} B$ (do the truth tables and check).

(2) There are certainly utterances of English that have the truth conditions of $A \underline{\lor} B$. For example, "*A* or *B*, but not both," "*A* unless *B*, in which case not *A*," "*A* if and only if not *B*," and "*B* if and only if not *A*." But none of these constitutes a case where "or" means something other than inclusive disjunction—that is, a case where "or" is not properly translated as $\lor$. The first example translates as $(A \lor B) \land \neg(A \land B)$, so here "or" translates as $\lor$.[22] The other examples do not involve "or" at all; they translate as $(\neg B \rightarrow A) \land (B \rightarrow \neg A)$, $A \leftrightarrow \neg B$, and $B \leftrightarrow \neg A$, respectively.

(3) Some writers claim that "*A* or *B*" in English always expresses inclusive disjunction, whereas "either *A* or *B*" always expresses exclusive disjunction (the difference here is simply that the second formulation contains "either"). However, many other writers have no such intuition: they hear "*A* or *B*" and "either *A* or *B*" as mere stylistic variants that have the same truth conditions— that say the same thing (i.e., express the same proposition). The Oxford English Dictionary does not help us decide the issue—it offers the noncommittal:

> The primary function of either, etc., is to emphasize the indifference of the two (or more) things or courses; e.g., "you may take either the medal or its value" = the medal and its value are equally at your option, you may take either; but a secondary function is to emphasize the mutual exclusiveness, = either of the two, but not both.[23]

Evidently, then, it would be unwise to assume of any given utterance of "either *A* or *B*" that it was supposed to express an exclusive disjunction—the speaker might be one of the many who regard "either . . . or" as a mere stylistic variant of "or," differing only in emphasis. In this book, at any rate, we take "either *A* or *B*" to say the same thing as "*A* or *B*."

§

With these preliminary points in mind, we turn now to cases in which "or" allegedly cannot be translated as $\lor$. Consider the following arguments:

1. James ate a sandwich.
   Therefore, James ate a sandwich or a hot dog.

2. James ate a sandwich and a hot dog.
   Therefore, James ate a sandwich or a hot dog.

If we translate "or" here as $\lor$, then these arguments translate as follows (using the glossary S: James ate a sandwich; H: James ate a hot dog):

$1'$. S
   $\therefore S \lor H$

$2'$. $S \land H$
   $\therefore S \lor H$

Both arguments $(1')$ and $(2')$ are valid (do the truth tables and check). Yet in English, both original arguments (1) and (2) seem quite wrong. One might see this as a reason to think that in these cases "or" should be translated in such a way that "he ate a sandwich or a hot dog" does not follow logically from "he ate a sandwich" or from "he ate a sandwich and a hot dog." Translating "or" as exclusive disjunction would yield these results. However, another response to the problem cases is possible: we explain why these arguments seem wrong in a way that is compatible with their being valid. Consider argument $(1')$. To be in a position to assert the premise, one needs to believe S (recall the Maxims of Quality in §6.1). But to be in a position to assert the conclusion, one must not believe S: for if one does believe S, then instead of asserting $S \lor H$, one should make the more informative claim S (recall the Maxims of Quantity).[24] Thus, someone in a position to assert the premise is in no position to assert the conclusion. The argument is then useless: we cannot imagine a situation in which it would be useful to reason in this way. That explains the intuitive incorrectness of the argument in a way that is perfectly compatible with its being valid. Similar comments apply to argument $(2')$.

We thus have two possible explanations of the intuitive incorrectness of arguments (1) and (2): (i) they are invalid (because "or" here expresses exclusive disjunction); (ii) although the arguments are both valid (because "or" here expresses inclusive disjunction), in each case there is (for reasons stemming from the conversational maxims) no situation in which one could assert the premise and the conclusion. Both explanations—(i) and (ii)—provide an account of the phenomena, but (ii) does so in a more economical way. Explanation (ii) appeals to one meaning of "or" together with the conversational maxims, which are needed in any case; (i) appeals to two different meanings of "or" (the exclusive meaning here, and the inclusive meaning in other contexts). Hence, by Grice's Razor (recall §6.2.2), we should favor explanation (ii).

§

A second kind of case that is sometimes thought (especially by beginners at logic) to involve exclusive disjunction in English is when the disjuncts are incompatible: that is, they cannot both occur. For example, suppose you are about to roll a die, and I say "you will roll 3 or 4." Obviously you cannot roll both 3 and 4—but this does not mean that my statement is an exclusive disjunction. To think it does is to confuse two issues:

1. The issue of whether both disjuncts can be true at the same time.

2. The issue of whether, in a situation in which both disjuncts are true, the disjunction is true.

When it comes to the question of whether a disjunction is inclusive or exclusive, it is the second question that matters. Our strategy for translating an utterance—say, "you will roll 3 or 4"—into PL is to consider in what situations what is said would be true, and in what situations what is said would be false, and then find a proposition of PL having these truth conditions. Now part of the assumption of the PL framework is that all combinations of assignments of truth values to basic propositions are possible. So we draw up a truth table covering all these possible assignments—one in each row:

You will roll 3	You will roll 4	You will roll 3 or 4
T	T	
T	F	
F	T	
F	F	

Then, on the basis of our intuitions (as competent speakers of English) about the truth or falsity in each possible scenario of what is said by our target utterance, we fill in each blank cell with T or F. The key row in this case is row 1: if it should contain a T, then our sentence will translate as an inclusive disjunction; if F, exclusive. In the present case, it is actually very difficult to imagine row 1: for it seems impossible that you should roll a 3 and a 4 (on the same throw). But our response to that fact should not be to say that the "or" in "you will roll 3 or 4" is exclusive. What should make us respond that way is if we consider row 1 and see that our target utterance is clearly false in such a scenario. This is not at all what happens in the present case: we have no clear idea what would be true or false in row 1—owing to the difficulty of conceiving such a scenario in the first place.

So the first point to note is that what should make us translate a disjunction as exclusive is not the fact that both its disjuncts cannot be true at the same time, but the fact that were its disjuncts both true, the disjunction would be false. Now, given that it is unclear what to say about the truth value of "you will roll 3 or 4" in the situation in which you roll a 3 and a 4, how should we go about translating this claim into PL? Well, a safe option is to translate it as inclusive disjunction, for the following reason. The inclusive disjunction makes a weaker claim than the exclusive disjunction: it conveys less information. It tells us only that we are in one of three out of four possible scenarios—that is, the three rows of the truth table in which it is true—whereas the exclusive disjunction rules out not only that we are in the bottom row but also that we are in the top row. Now consider what information I might want to convey to you when I say "you will roll 3 or 4." One of two cases is possible. The first is that I want to convey to you simply that we are not in a situation like row 4; that is, it is not the case that you will roll neither 3 nor 4. In that case, I should of course be interpreted as making an inclusive disjunctive claim. The second possibility is that I want to convey to you that we are not in a situation like row 4, nor in one like row 1: we are in a situation like row 2 or 3, that is, in which you roll exactly one of 3 or 4. But we already know that you will not roll a 3 and a 4—that is impossible—so I do not need to build the ruling out of this type of situation into the content of my claim. I can just utter the inclusive disjunction and rely on your background knowledge of the behavior of dice to fill in the missing information. So either way, I can be interpreted as uttering an inclusive disjunctive claim: in the first case because it carries exactly the information I want to convey; in the second case because, while it carries less information than I want to convey, I already know that you know the extra bit of information it does not convey, and so I do not need to say it explicitly.[25]

§

A final kind of alleged example of exclusive disjunction in English that one often encounters involves menu options. For example, one might be told at a diner that a certain fixed price meal includes tea or coffee. If it is somehow obvious in the context that this means one can have tea or coffee but not both—that is, it is obvious even though no explicit phrase, such as "one only of (tea or coffee)" or "(tea or coffee) but not both," is used—then it might seem to be a case of exclusive "or."

However, while it may certainly be the case that "you may have tea or coffee" conveys to us that we may have tea or coffee but not both, this is not a situation in which we have an utterance in English featuring "or" that is properly translated into PL using a connective other than ∨. The test of whether a disjunction is inclusive or exclusive is to consider the case in which both disjuncts are true and then ask whether the disjunctive claim is true or false in this case. If it is true, the disjunction is inclusive; if false, exclusive. Now suppose the menu (or waiter) says "you can have tea or coffee." Imagine a situation in which you help yourself to both. Is the waiter's claim false? No: what is going on here is that you have broken a rule or violated an order, which is quite different from making a proposition false. The waiter's utterance is not a factual statement but a setting out of the rules. It does not describe how the world is; it stipulates how the world should be. The same thing happens when the umpire says "players are to stay within the marked boundaries of the field at all times." When a player steps outside these boundaries, she breaks the rules—she does not make them false. The rules are not rendered false, because they are not propositions—things that can be true or false—in the first place. They are pronouncements or commands. Such things cannot be translated into PL at all—only propositions can be translated. So while a command or rule may stipulate taking exactly one, and not both, of two options, this is not a case in which we have a proposition that is properly translated into PL using a connective other than $\vee$.

Imagine a different case, in which the menu does express the proposition "all meals are served with tea or coffee." That is, this sentence in the menu is meant to function not as a rule about how things should happen, but as a simple statement of fact about what does happen in this particular establishment. Now suppose a meal is served with both tea and coffee. Is the statement on the menu false in this case? That is not at all obvious. Contrast the case where a meal comes out with neither tea nor coffee: the statement is obviously false in such a situation. But when the meal comes out with both beverages, something may well have happened that was not supposed to happen—a rule may have been violated in the kitchen—but it does not seem that the simple proposition "all meals are served with tea or coffee" has come out false. Indeed it seems perfectly true.

Thus, neither way of construing these menu-type examples—that is, as rules, or as propositions—results in a sentence of English featuring "or" that seems to translate into a proposition of PL featuring a connective other than $\vee$.[26]

6.5 Negation

"Ilsa is neither funny nor interesting" means that both the propositions:

F: Ilsa is funny
I: Ilsa is interesting

are false. So it translates as $\neg(F \vee I)$ or $(\neg F \wedge \neg I)$ (see the first two columns after the matrix in the truth table below).

F	I	$\neg(F \vee I)$	$(\neg F \wedge \neg I)$	$\neg(F \wedge I)$	$(\neg F \vee \neg I)$
T	T	F	F	F	F
T	F	F	F	T	T
F	T	F	F	T	T
F	F	T	T	T	T

"Ilsa is not both funny and interesting" means that it is not the case that both the propositions F and I are true: neither of them, or just one of them, may be true—but not both. So we translate this statement as $\neg(F \wedge I)$ or $(\neg F \vee \neg I)$ (see the last two columns in the truth table above). "Ilsa is both not funny and not interesting" says that F and I are both false. That is, it says the same thing as "neither F nor I." So we translate it as $\neg(F \vee I)$ or $(\neg F \wedge \neg I)$.

6.5.1 Exercises

Translate the following arguments into PL and then assess them for validity (you may use shortcuts in your truth tables).

1. Bob is happy if and only if it is raining. Either it is raining or the sun is shining. So Bob is happy only if the sun is not shining.

2. If I have neither money nor a card, I shall walk. If I walk, I shall get tired or have a rest. So if I have a rest, I have money.

3. Maisy is upset only if there is thunder. If there is thunder, then there is lightning. Therefore, either Maisy is not upset, or there is lightning.

4. The car started only if you turned the key and pressed the accelerator. If you turned the key but did not press the accelerator, then the car did not start. The car did not start—so either you pressed the accelerator but did not turn the key, or you neither turned the key nor pressed the accelerator.

5. Either Maisy isn't barking, or there is a robber outside. If there is a robber outside and Maisy is not barking, then she is either asleep or depressed. Maisy is neither asleep nor depressed. Hence Maisy is barking if and only if there is a robber outside.

6. If it isn't sunny, then either it is too windy or we are sailing. We are having fun if we are sailing. It is not sunny and it isn't too windy either—hence we are having fun.

7. Either you came through Singleton and Maitland, or you came through Newcastle. You didn't come through either Singleton or Maitland—you came through Cessnock. Therefore, you came through both Newcastle and Cessnock.

8. We shall have lobster for lunch, provided that the shop is open. Either the shop will be open, or it is Sunday. If it is Sunday, we shall go to a restaurant and have lobster for lunch. So we shall have lobster for lunch.

9. Catch Billy a fish, and you will feed him for a day. Teach him to fish, and you'll feed him for life. So either you won't feed Billy for life, or you will teach him to fish.

10. I'll be happy if the Tigers win. Moreover, they will win—or else they won't. However, assuming they don't, it will be a draw. Therefore, if it's not a draw, and they don't win, I'll be happy.

6.6 Functional Completeness

In §6.4, we mentioned that some logic books include a symbol—for example, $\underline{\vee}$—for exclusive disjunction, which has the following truth table:

α	β	$(\alpha \underline{\vee} \beta)$
T	T	F
T	F	T
F	T	T
F	F	F

We then remarked that even though we have no such connective in PL, we can form propositions in PL having these truth conditions—that is, having the same truth table as $\underline{\vee}$ (e.g., $(A \vee B) \wedge \neg(A \wedge B)$ or $\neg(A \leftrightarrow B)$). In this section we show something stronger: with its five connectives ($\neg$, $\vee$, $\wedge$, $\rightarrow$, and $\leftrightarrow$) PL has the resources to construct a formula with any truth conditions whatsoever. In other words, for any possible truth table you care to imagine, there is a formula of PL with that truth table. In fact, as we shall see, there are much smaller sets of connectives—sets containing just three, two, or even one connective, as opposed to the five in PL—that also have this property.

We call a set of connectives *functionally complete*—or *expressively complete* or *adequate*—if it has the property just mentioned: that is, if we can define all possible connectives from the connectives in that set. To clarify this notion, we need to explain two things: what it means to define one connective in terms of some others, and what we mean by "all possible connectives." First, some notation. We have symbols for specific connectives ($\wedge$, $\neg$, etc.), but we need a means of talking about connectives in a general way. For this purpose we shall use the symbols $*$ and $\dagger$. Each of these symbols stands to specific connectives ($\wedge$, $\neg$, etc.) in the way that each wff variable (α, β, etc.) stands to specific wffs (A, $(B \wedge \neg A)$, etc.). As in the case of wff variables, we may also use these symbols with subscripts (i.e., $*_1$, $*_2$, ..., $*_n$ and $\dagger_1$, $\dagger_2$, ..., $\dagger_n$).

6.6.1 Defining One Connective in Terms of Others

The basic idea behind defining one connective in terms of others is this: for any formula containing the former connective, we find a logically equivalent formula that does not contain that connective but does include the latter connectives. More precisely, we can define the connective $*$ in terms of the connectives $\dagger_1$, ..., $\dagger_n$ iff, for any formula γ containing (one or more) occurrences of $*$, there is a formula δ that contains no occurrences of $*$ but may contain occurrences of $\dagger_1, \ldots, \dagger_n$ (and contains no occurrence of any connective that neither occurs in γ nor is one of $\dagger_1, \ldots, \dagger_n$) and is equivalent to γ: that is, in their joint truth table, γ and δ have the same values on every row.

To show that $*$ can be defined in terms of $\dagger_1, \ldots, \dagger_n$, it is sufficient to show that for any formula γ in which $*$ occurs as the main connective, this occurrence of $*$ (i.e., the main connective) can be eliminated in favor of occurrences of $\dagger_1, \ldots, \dagger_n$. Let us see how this works via an example.

We can easily check that $(\alpha \to \beta)$ is equivalent to $(\neg\alpha \lor \beta)$: that is, they have the same truth table.[27] Thus, where we have a formula with $\to$ as the main connective—that is, a formula of the form $(\alpha \to \beta)$—we can find an equivalent formula—$(\neg\alpha \lor \beta)$—in which that occurrence of $\to$ has been omitted in favor of occurrences of $\neg$ and $\lor$. The claim now is that this fact suffices to show that $\to$ can be defined in terms of $\neg$ and $\lor$: that is, that for any formula γ containing occurrences of $\to$ (perhaps multiple occurrences—and even if there is only one, it need not be the main connective) there is a formula δ that contains no occurrences of $\to$ but may contain occurrences of $\neg$ and $\lor$ (and contains no occurrence of any connective that neither occurs in γ nor is one of $\neg$ and $\lor$), which is equivalent to γ. We illustrate this claim by using a particular case.

Consider the following wff:

$$(A \land (B \to (A \to C))) \tag{6.1}$$

Formula (6.1) contains two occurrences of $\to$. Neither is the main connective of (6.1): one is the main connective of the subformula $(A \to C)$, the other is the main connective of $(B \to (A \to C))$. We know that $(\alpha \to \beta)$ is equivalent to $(\neg\alpha \lor \beta)$. Applying this equivalence to the subformula $(A \to C)$, we know that $(A \to C)$ is equivalent to $(\neg A \lor C)$. Now consider the following subformula of (6.1):

$$(B \to (A \to C)) \tag{6.2}$$

In general, for any formula γ, if we replace a subformula α of γ with a formula β that is equivalent to α, the result will be equivalent to γ.[28] Let's apply this general principle to (6.2), replacing its subformula $(A \to C)$ with the equivalent $(\neg A \lor C)$:

$$(B \to (\neg A \lor C)) \tag{6.3}$$

By the general principle just stated, (6.3) is equivalent to (6.2). Next we apply our known equivalence between $(\alpha \to \beta)$ and $(\neg\alpha \lor \beta)$ to (6.3), yielding the result that the following is equivalent to (6.3):

$$(\neg B \lor (\neg A \lor C)) \tag{6.4}$$

Given that (6.4) is equivalent to (6.3), and (6.3) is equivalent to (6.2), it follows that (6.4) is equivalent to (6.2). Using the general principle again, if we replace (6.2) as it occurs as a subformula in (6.1) by the equivalent (6.4), the result:

$$(A \land (\neg B \lor (\neg A \lor C)))\qquad\qquad(6.5)$$

is equivalent to (6.1). Thus, (6.5) is equivalent to (6.1) and contains no occurrences of $\rightarrow$, all of them having been eliminated in favor of $\neg$ and $\lor$.

The general point illustrated by this particular case is as follows. Once we know that $(\alpha \rightarrow \beta)$ is equivalent to $(\neg\alpha \lor \beta)$, we know that occurrences of $\rightarrow$ as a main connective can be eliminated in favor of $\neg$ and $\lor$. Given a formula with multiple occurrences of $\rightarrow$, we work from the inside out, replacing each subformula in which $\rightarrow$ is the main connective by an equivalent subformula in which $\rightarrow$ is eliminated in favor of $\neg$ and $\lor$. When we have replaced all occurrences of $\rightarrow$ in this way, the result will be a formula equivalent to our original one, in which all occurrences of $\rightarrow$ have been eliminated in favor of $\neg$ and $\lor$.

By similar reasoning, the fact that $(\alpha \leftrightarrow \beta)$ is equivalent to $((\alpha \rightarrow \beta) \land (\beta \rightarrow \alpha))$ shows that we can define the connective $\leftrightarrow$ in terms of the connectives $\rightarrow$ and $\land$; that $(\alpha \rightarrow \beta)$ is equivalent to $\neg(\alpha \land \neg\beta)$ shows that we can define the connective $\rightarrow$ in terms of the connectives $\neg$ and $\land$; that $(\alpha \lor \beta)$ is equivalent to $\neg(\neg\alpha \land \neg\beta)$ shows that we can define the connective $\lor$ in terms of the connectives $\neg$ and $\land$; and so on.

6.6.2 The Range of Possible Connectives

Having clarified what it means to define one connective in terms of others, we now explain what we mean by "all possible connectives." Throughout this section, by "connectives" we mean truth-functional connectives (recall the discussion in §6.3). So how many possible (truth-functional) connectives are there? Well, consider first one-place connectives. A one-place connective $*$ has a two-row truth table:

α	$*\alpha$
T	
F	

We specify a one-place connective by putting T or F in each of the two blank spaces in this table. Two spaces; two possible fillings for each—so there are $2^2 = 4$ possible ways of filling in the blanks:

α				
T	T	T	F	F
F	T	F	T	F

Note that the order in which the columns appear here is arbitrary: all that matters is that each possible way of filling in each of the two blanks in our first table with a T or an F is represented by a column in the second table; we have to present these columns in some order, but the particular order we have chosen has no significance. Now, for each of the four columns just given, it will be convenient to have a symbol for a connective that has this column as its truth table. We already have a symbol for the third one: it is negation. For the other three, we introduce symbols as follows:

α	$①_1$	$①_2$	¬	$①_4$
T	T	T	F	F
F	T	F	T	F

In this symbolism, the circle represents the connective, the number inside the circle shows the number of places of the connective, and the subscript distinguishes different connectives with the same number of places. Thus, $①_1$ is the first one-place connective, $①_2$ is the second one-place connective, and so on.[29]

The connective $①_1$ yields a true proposition when the proposition to which it is applied is true and when that proposition is false. Connective $①_2$ yields a proposition whose truth value is the same as that of the proposition to which it is applied. The third connective—negation—yields a proposition whose truth value is the opposite of that of the proposition to which it is applied. Connective $①_4$ yields a false proposition when the proposition to which it is applied is true and when that proposition is false.

What about two-place connectives? A two-place connective $*$ has a four-row truth table:

α	β	$(α * β)$
T	T	
T	F	
F	T	
F	F	

We specify a two-place connective by putting T or F in each of the four blank spaces in this table. Four spaces; two possible fillings for each—that makes $2^4 = 16$ possible two-place connectives. Here are their truth tables:

α β	$②_1$	$\vee$	$②_3$	$②_4$	$\rightarrow$	$②_6$	$\leftrightarrow$	$\wedge$	$②_9$	$\underline{\vee}$	$②_{11}$	$②_{12}$	$②_{13}$	$②_{14}$	$②_{15}$	$②_{16}$
T T	T	T	T	T	T	T	T	T	F	F	F	F	F	F	F	F
T F	T	T	T	T	F	F	F	F	T	T	T	T	F	F	F	F
F T	T	T	F	F	T	T	F	F	T	T	F	F	T	T	F	F
F F	T	F	T	F	T	F	T	F	T	F	T	F	T	F	T	F

Again, note that the order in which the columns appear here is arbitrary: all that matters is that each possible way of filling in each of the four blanks in our previous table with a T or an F is represented by a column in the table just given. Now, having filled in the columns, it is convenient to have a symbol for each connective with one of the sixteen columns as its truth table. We already have symbols in PL for columns 2, 5, 7, and 8. We have previously seen a symbol for column 10 (exclusive disjunction). For the other columns, we use the circle symbolism again: the circle represents the connective, the number inside the circle shows the number of places of the connective, and the subscript distinguishes different connectives with the same number of places. Thus, $②_1$ is the first two-place connective, $②_3$ is the third two-place connective, and so on.

We have not talked about connectives with three or more places, but we could easily define them.[30] A three-place connective $*$ has an eight-row truth table:

α	β	γ	$*(\alpha, \beta, \gamma)$
T	T	T	
T	T	F	
T	F	T	
T	F	F	
F	T	T	
F	T	F	
F	F	T	
F	F	F	

We specify a three-place connective by putting T or F in each of the eight blank spaces in this table. Eight spaces; two possible fillings for each—that makes $2^8 = 256$ possible three-place connectives. Likewise, we can define four-place connectives (of which there are $2^{16} = 65{,}536$)—and so on for every positive finite number of places.

There is also such a thing as a zero-place connective. The truth table of a zero-place connective ∗ looks like:

where the blank is filled either with T or F. So there are two possible zero-place connectives; they are usually called the *verum* and the *falsum* and are symbolized by ⊤ and ⊥, respectively:

⊤	⊥
T	F

The idea of a zero-place connective seems rather odd at first, but it makes sense when we think about it. An n-place connective plus n propositions makes a proposition. So a zero-place connective all by itself—that is, with zero propositions added—forms a proposition. Being a proposition, this entity (i.e., the zero-place connective by itself) is either true or false. Note that ⊤ is always true, and ⊥ is always false: these propositions have no component propositions, so their truth values cannot vary with the truth values of their components.

Connectives ⊤ and ⊥ can feature in the definitions of other connectives. For example, ¬ can be defined in terms of → and ⊥, for as the following truth tables show, ¬α and $\alpha \rightarrow \bot$ are equivalent:

α	$\bot$	¬α	$\alpha \rightarrow \bot$
T	F	F	F
F	F	T	T

Note that ⊥ appears here as a component of the larger proposition $\alpha \rightarrow \bot$. This use is legitimate because a zero-place connective by itself—that is, with zero propositions added—is a wff.

§

We said that a set of connectives is functionally complete if we can define all possible connectives from the connectives in that set. We have just seen that there is an infinite number of possible connectives (a finite number of n-place connectives for each finite number n, but there is no upper bound on n)—so it may seem that no (small) set of connectives could possibly be functionally complete. But in fact the set {¬, ∨, ∧} is functionally complete; that is, we can define any connective ∗ in terms of ¬, ∨, and ∧. Here's how.

Suppose that $*$ (the connective to be defined in terms of $\neg$, $\vee$, and $\wedge$) is a zero-place connective. That is, $*$ is $\top$ or $\bot$. The connective $\top$ can be defined as $A \vee \neg A$, and $\bot$ can be defined as $A \wedge \neg A$:

A	$\top$	$A \vee \neg A$	$\bot$	$A \wedge \neg A$
T	T	T	F	F
F	T	T	F	F

Suppose now that $*$ is an n-place connective. We shall describe the method for defining $*$ in terms of $\neg$, $\vee$, and $\wedge$ by way of an example. In this example, $*$ is a two-place connective. However, as will be clear, the method used to define $*$ is quite general: it can be applied to n-place connectives for any positive finite n.

We start with the truth table for $*$. (This table is a given. Our aim is then to construct a formula containing only the connectives $\neg$, $\vee$, and $\wedge$ that has the same truth table as $*$.) For example,[31]

α	β	$(\alpha * \beta)$
T	T	T
T	F	F
F	T	T
F	F	F

It may happen that there are no rows in which $(\alpha * \beta)$ is true. In this case, $(\alpha * \beta)$ is equivalent to $(\alpha \wedge \neg\alpha)$. The latter is a formula that does not contain $*$, and does contain $\wedge$ and $\neg$, so this shows that $*$ can be defined in terms of $\wedge$ and $\neg$. A fortiori, it can be defined in terms of $\wedge$ and $\neg$ and $\vee$.[32]

The other possibility is that—as in our example—there is at least one row in which $(\alpha * \beta)$ is true. In this case, for each row in which $(\alpha * \beta)$ is true, we write a conjunction "describing" that row:

α	β	$(\alpha * \beta)$	row description
T	T	T	$(\alpha \wedge \beta)$
T	F	F	
F	T	T	$(\neg\alpha \wedge \beta)$
F	F	F	

The row description is read off from the matrix: in row 1, α is true and β is true, so the row description is $(\alpha \wedge \beta)$ (i.e., "α and β"); in row 3, α is false and β is true, so the row description is $(\neg\alpha \wedge \beta)$ (i.e., "not α, and β"). Note that each row description is true in the row it describes and false in all other rows.

We now form the disjunction of these row descriptions:

$$(\alpha \wedge \beta) \vee (\neg\alpha \wedge \beta) \tag{6.6}$$

The disjunction (6.6) uses only the connectives $\vee$, $\wedge$, and $\neg$, and it is true in exactly the rows in which $(\alpha * \beta)$ is true. For each row in which $(\alpha * \beta)$ is true, (6.6) has a disjunct that is true in that row—and in any row in which one of its disjuncts is true, a disjunction is true. In each row in which $(\alpha * \beta)$ is false, all disjuncts of (6.6) are false—recall that each row description is true only in the row it describes—and so the disjunction is false. Thus, $(\alpha * \beta)$ is equivalent to a formula (6.6), which involves only the connectives $\neg$, $\vee$, and $\wedge$. This establishes that $*$ is definable in terms of $\neg$, $\vee$, and $\wedge$.

Here's one more example to illustrate the method of defining an arbitrary connective $*$ in terms of $\neg$, $\vee$, and $\wedge$. Suppose $*$ has the following truth table:[33]

α	β	γ	$*(\alpha, \beta, \gamma)$
T	T	T	F
T	T	F	T
T	F	T	F
T	F	F	F
F	T	T	F
F	T	F	T
F	F	T	T
F	F	F	F

We form our row descriptions as follows:

α	β	γ	$*(\alpha, \beta, \gamma)$	row description
T	T	T	F	
T	T	F	T	$(\alpha \wedge \beta \wedge \neg\gamma)$
T	F	T	F	
T	F	F	F	
F	T	T	F	
F	T	F	T	$(\neg\alpha \wedge \beta \wedge \neg\gamma)$
F	F	T	T	$(\neg\alpha \wedge \neg\beta \wedge \gamma)$
F	F	F	F	

and then take their disjunction:

$$(\alpha \wedge \beta \wedge \neg\gamma) \vee (\neg\alpha \wedge \beta \wedge \neg\gamma) \vee (\neg\alpha \wedge \neg\beta \wedge \gamma) \tag{6.7}$$

Formula (6.7) uses only the connectives $\vee$, $\wedge$, and $\neg$, and it is equivalent to $*(\alpha, \beta, \gamma)$. Thus, $*$ is definable in terms of $\neg$, $\vee$, and $\wedge$.

So $\{\neg, \vee, \wedge\}$ is a functionally complete set of connectives. Furthermore, we can define $\wedge$ in terms of $\neg$ and $\vee$—$(\alpha \wedge \beta)$ is equivalent to $\neg(\neg\alpha \vee$

$\neg\beta)$—and we can define $\vee$ in terms of $\neg$ and $\wedge$—$(\alpha \vee \beta)$ is equivalent to $\neg(\neg\alpha \wedge \neg\beta)$. (These two equivalences are known as De Morgan's laws. Two n-place connectives $*$ and $\dagger$ are *duals* if $*(\alpha_1, \ldots, \alpha_n)$ is equivalent to $\neg\dagger(\neg\alpha_1, \ldots, \neg\alpha_n)$ and $\dagger(\alpha_1, \ldots, \alpha_n)$ is equivalent to $\neg*(\neg\alpha_1, \ldots, \neg\alpha_n)$. Hence, $\vee$ and $\wedge$ are duals.) So to show that some set of connectives is functionally complete, it suffices to show that $\neg$, and either $\vee$ or $\wedge$, can be defined using the members of that set.

We can now see that $\{②_9\}$ is a functionally complete set of connectives: every connective can be defined using just the single connective $②_9$. This connective is often symbolized by a vertical stroke | (the Sheffer stroke).[34] The following truth table shows that $\neg$ can be defined using only |:

α	$\neg\alpha$	$(\alpha \mid \alpha)$
T	F	F
F	T	T

and the following truth tables show that $\wedge$ and $\vee$ can each be defined using only |:

α	β	$(\alpha \wedge \beta)$	$((\alpha \mid \beta) \mid (\alpha \mid \beta))$	$(\alpha \vee \alpha)$	$((\alpha \mid \alpha) \mid (\beta \mid \beta))$
T	T	T	T	T	T
T	F	F	F	T	T
F	T	F	F	T	T
F	F	F	F	F	F

To show that a set of connectives is not functionally complete, we need to show that there is some connective that cannot be defined in terms of those in the set. For example, the set $\{\vee, \wedge\}$ is not functionally complete, because $\neg$ cannot be defined in terms of $\vee$ and $\wedge$. In the top row of their truth tables—where α and β are both true—both $(\alpha \vee \beta)$ and $(\alpha \wedge \beta)$ are true. Thus, however complex a formula we make up using the connectives $\vee$ and $\wedge$, it will always be true when its simple components are all true. But $\neg P$ is false when P is true. So no complex formula built up using $\vee$ and $\wedge$ will have the same truth table as $\neg P$: they will always differ in the top row. Hence, $\neg$ cannot be defined in terms of $\vee$ and $\wedge$.

6.6.3 Exercises

1. State whether each of the following is a functionally complete set of connectives. Justify your answers.

   (i) $\{\rightarrow, \neg\}$

   (ii) $\{\leftrightarrow, \underline{\vee}\}$

(iii) $\{②_{15}\}$ (The connective $②_{15}$ is often symbolized by $\downarrow$; another common symbol for this connective is NOR.)

(iv) $\{\rightarrow, \wedge\}$

(v) $\{\neg, ②_{12}\}$

(vi) $\{\vee, ②_4\}$

2. Give the truth table for each of the following propositions.

(i) $B \, ②_{14} \, A$

(ii) $(A \, ②_{11} \, B) \, ②_{15} \, B$

(iii) $\neg(A \vee (A \, ②_6 \, B))$

(iv) $A \leftrightarrow (A \, ②_3 \, \neg B)$

(v) $(A \, ②_{12} \, B) \, \underline{\vee} \, (B \, ②_{12} \, A)$

(vi) $(A \, ②_{12} \, B) \, \underline{\vee} \, (B \, ②_{16} \, A)$

3. Consider the three-place connectives $\sharp$ and $\natural$, whose truth tables are as follows:

α	β	γ	$\sharp(\alpha, \beta, \gamma)$	$\natural(\alpha, \beta, \gamma)$
T	T	T	T	F
T	T	F	F	F
T	F	T	T	T
T	F	F	T	T
F	T	T	T	T
F	T	F	F	T
F	F	T	T	F
F	F	F	T	F

(i) Define $\sharp$ using only (but not necessarily all of) the connectives $\vee$, $\wedge$, and $\neg$.

(ii) Do the same for $\natural$.

4. State a proposition involving only the connectives $\neg$ and $\wedge$ that is equivalent to the given proposition.

(i) $\neg(A \rightarrow B)$

(ii) $\neg(A \vee B)$

(iii) $\neg A \vee \neg B$

(iv) $\neg(\neg A \vee B)$

(v) $A \leftrightarrow B$

(vi) $(A \rightarrow B) \vee (B \rightarrow A)$

5. (i) What is the dual of $①_1$?

(ii) What is the dual of $\rightarrow$?

(iii) Which one-place connectives are their own duals?

(iv) Which two-place connectives are their own duals?

7

Trees for Propositional Logic

Using truth tables, we can frame a precise definition of validity (an argument $\alpha_1, \ldots, \alpha_n /\therefore \beta$ is valid iff there is no row in their joint truth table in which $\alpha_1, \ldots, \alpha_n$ are true and β is false), and we can also test whether a given argument is valid (we write out its truth table and check whether there is any such row). Similar remarks apply to the other central logical notions: using truth tables, we can both give precise definitions of these notions and test for their presence (a formula α is a tautology or logical truth iff it is true on every row of its truth table; two formulas α and β are logically equivalent iff they have the same value on every row of their joint truth table; a formula α is satisfiable iff it is true on some row of its truth table; etc.).

In this chapter, we look at a second method of testing for validity (tautology, equivalence, etc.): the method of *trees* (aka truth trees, semantic trees, and semantic tableaux). Given that truth tables already provide a foolproof test for each of these notions, why look at another method of testing for them? There are two main reasons.

First, trees provide a faster test for many cases we ordinarily encounter. If we have an argument featuring more than four basic propositions, its truth table will have at least 32 rows (recall §3.3), and so it will not be practical to write it out. Furthermore, even when our truth table has a manageable number of rows, the truth table test for validity often involves more work than necessary. We need to fill in every row (at least partially—recall §4.5.1) to determine whether there is any row in which the premises are all true and the conclusion is false. If we somehow had a way of targeting such a row directly (when such a row exists), we could proceed more quickly: we would not need to fill in all rows (even partially) and could focus on the kind of row we are looking for. This, in essence, is what trees do. We begin a tree by writing down some propositions that we suppose, for the sake of argument, are all true. We then work out what else—more specifically, what simpler propositions—must be true if these starting propositions are all true, and so on, until we work our way down to basic propositions or negations of basic propositions. We then see either that the starting propositions cannot all be true (because that would involve some proposition being both true and false), or else we see a particular scenario (i.e., assignment of truth values to basic propositions) in which they are all true. This particular scenario is the truth table row we seek. So where such a row exists, the tree takes us straight to it—and where no such row exists, the tree indicates as much.[1]

Second, truth tables play two roles in propositional logic:

1. Truth tables provide an analysis—a fundamental, precise definition—of each of our central logical notions (validity, equivalence, etc.). For example, recall that we started with an intuitive idea of validity (NTP by virtue of form), and truth tables then gave us a precise definition (no row in which the premises are true and the conclusion false) that captures this intuitive idea.

2. Truth tables provide a method of testing for the presence of each of the central logical notions. We can test whether an argument is valid, a proposition a tautology, and so on, by writing out the relevant truth table and examining it.

When we turn to predicate logic in Part II, we will (for reasons that will become clear) need to replace truth tables with something else: *models*. Models provide analyses of our central logical notions (validity, etc.), but they do not provide any tests for these notions. That is, in the context of predicate logic, models take over the first role of truth tables, but they do not fulfill the second role. So we will need something else to play this second role. There are various options (they are explored in Chapter 15), but the one we will adopt (at least initially, in Chapter 10) is the method of trees—and it will be easier to understand trees in the richer setting of predicate logic if we first familiarize ourselves with trees for propositional logic in this chapter.

§

In §7.1 and §7.2 we introduce the techniques for constructing trees. It will aid in the understanding of these techniques if we first have some idea of the purpose of trees; however, it is not possible to explain fully the point of trees without details about their construction. We therefore give a rough idea now of the purpose of trees and then return to this issue in §7.2.6.

The basic purpose of a tree is to tell us whether a given set of propositions is satisfiable: that is, whether all propositions in the set can be true. (This does not mean that trees cannot also be used to test for validity, equivalence, and so on: as we shall see in §7.3, trees can be used to test for all logical properties of interest.) We begin the tree by writing down these propositions. We then apply tree rules that determine further propositions to write down, given what we have already written. Each rule takes one proposition as input and gives one or more propositions as output. These rules have two essential features:

1. The output propositions are simpler than the input proposition; in particular, the main connective of the input is eliminated.[2]

2. The output propositions must be true, assuming that the input proposition is true.[3]

We continue applying rules—to the original propositions at the top of the tree and to the outputs of earlier applications of the rules—until we can apply them no more. Because (given property (1)) the output propositions are simpler than the inputs, eventually the process of writing down new propositions terminates: there are no more connectives to eliminate. At that point we have a group of relatively simple propositions—basic propositions and/or negations of basic propositions—that (given property (2)) we know must all be true, assuming that the original propositions at the top of the tree are all true.[4] We now look at these propositions. If we find among them both some basic proposition and its negation, we know that they cannot all be true—in which case the original propositions at the top of the tree are not satisfiable. If we find no such clash among the simple propositions, we can read off from them an assignment of truth values to basic propositions—a truth table row—in which the original propositions at the top of the tree are all true.

7.1 Tree Rules

When we construct a tree, we begin by writing some propositions at the top of the page. (In §7.3 we shall see how to choose these propositions, depending on what we want to show in a particular case—but for the moment, it is not important which propositions we begin with.) We then extend the tree by writing down things that must be true, assuming that the things we have already written are true. There are precise rules governing what we may write down, which we set out below; the justification for the rules comes from the truth tables for the connectives, as we shall see. Before setting out the rules, we note some preliminary points.

If we have written down α, then after we have written down everything that must be true given that α is true, we check off α, to remind us later that it has been fully dealt with (i.e., all consequences of the assumed truth of α have been written down).

Sometimes it follows from the assumption that some proposition is true that some other proposition is false. But trees offer no direct way of saying that a proposition is false: we write down some propositions, and then we write propositions that must be true, given the truth of what we have already written. The solution is simple: when a proposition is false, its negation is true; so if we want to indicate that a proposition α is false, we write down its negation, $\neg\alpha$. So although we cannot directly represent falsity in the tree framework, we can do something just as good, namely, consider the truth of negations.

Sometimes the truth of a proposition α implies the truth of several propositions, say, β and γ. In this case we write down both β and γ, one above the other:

$$\beta$$

$$\gamma$$

Sometimes it does not follow from the assumption that a proposition α is true that any particular proposition is definitely true: it follows only that either some proposition β is true, or some other proposition γ is true. In this case we introduce a branch into our tree, and write down β on one side of the branch and γ on the other:

Now we define the precise rules for generating our tree, given what has come before. The aim is, through repeated applications of the rules, to check off compound formulas in our tree, leaving us with basic propositions and/or negations of basic propositions. We thus have rules for each of our five connectives. For each connective, there are two cases to consider. We want to know what follows from the assumption that (i) a proposition whose main connective is this one is true and (ii) a proposition whose main connective is this one is false. The second case is handled by considering what follows from the assumption that the negation of the proposition is true. So we should expect to end up with ten rules (five connectives, two cases for each). In fact, for reasons we shall see, we have only one rule for negation, giving nine rules in total.

7.1.1 Disjunction

Recall the truth table for disjunction:

α	β	$(\alpha \lor \beta)$
T	T	T
T	F	T
F	T	T
F	F	F

We see here that if a disjunction $(\alpha \vee \beta)$ is true—that is, we are in rows 1, 2, or 3—then either α is true (rows 1 and 2) or β is true (rows 1 and 3). (If neither α nor β is true—row 4—then the disjunction is false.) Hence the rule:

$$(\alpha \vee \beta) \checkmark$$
$$\diagup \diagdown$$
$$\alpha \quad \beta$$

Note the check mark next to $(\alpha \vee \beta)$, which we add after writing in the branch with α on one side and β on the other.[5]

If a disjunction $(\alpha \vee \beta)$ is false, then both α and β are false. Equivalently, if $\neg(\alpha \vee \beta)$ is true, then both $\neg\alpha$ and $\neg\beta$ are true. Hence the rule:

$$\neg(\alpha \vee \beta) \checkmark$$
$$\neg\alpha$$
$$\neg\beta$$

7.1.2 Conjunction

Recall the truth table for conjunction:

α	β	$(\alpha \wedge \beta)$
T	T	T
T	F	F
F	T	F
F	F	F

If a conjunction $(\alpha \wedge \beta)$ is true—that is, we are in row 1—then both α and β are true. Hence the rule:

$$(\alpha \wedge \beta) \checkmark$$
$$\alpha$$
$$\beta$$

If $(\alpha \wedge \beta)$ is false—that is, we are in rows 2, 3, or 4—then either α is false (rows 3 and 4) or β is false (rows 2 and 4). Equivalently, if $\neg(\alpha \wedge \beta)$ is true, then either $\neg\alpha$ is true or $\neg\beta$ is true. Hence the rule:

$$\neg(\alpha \wedge \beta) \checkmark$$
$$\diagup \diagdown$$
$$\neg\alpha \quad \neg\beta$$

7.1.3 Conditional

If $(\alpha \rightarrow \beta)$ is true, then either α is false or β is true (for if α is true and β is false, then $(\alpha \rightarrow \beta)$ is false). Hence the rule:

$$(\alpha \rightarrow \beta) \; \checkmark$$

$$\diagup\!\!\diagdown$$
$$\neg\alpha \quad \beta$$

If $(\alpha \rightarrow \beta)$ is false, then α is true and β is false:

$$\neg(\alpha \rightarrow \beta) \; \checkmark$$
$$\alpha$$
$$\neg\beta$$

7.1.4 Biconditional

If $(\alpha \leftrightarrow \beta)$ is true, then α and β have the same truth value. In other words, if $(\alpha \leftrightarrow \beta)$ is true, then either both α and β are true, or both α and β are false (recall the truth table for $\leftrightarrow$). Hence the rule:

$$(\alpha \leftrightarrow \beta) \; \checkmark$$
$$\diagup\!\!\diagdown$$
$$\alpha \quad \neg\alpha$$
$$\beta \quad \neg\beta$$

If $(\alpha \leftrightarrow \beta)$ is false, then α and β have opposite truth values. That is, either α is true and β is false, or α is false and β is true:

$$\neg(\alpha \leftrightarrow \beta) \; \checkmark$$
$$\diagup\!\!\diagdown$$
$$\alpha \quad \neg\alpha$$
$$\neg\beta \quad \beta$$

7.1.5 Negation

If a negation $\neg\alpha$ is false, then α is true. Hence the rule:

$$\neg\neg\alpha \; \checkmark$$
$$\alpha$$

The other possibility—that a negation $\neg\alpha$ is true—gives us no useful rule. From the assumption that $\neg\alpha$ is true, it follows that α is false—that is, that $\neg\alpha$ is true. But that is precisely where we started. It yields the rule:

$$\neg\alpha \; \checkmark$$
$$\neg\alpha$$

This rule gets us nowhere, so we do not adopt it.[6] We therefore have only one rule for negation.

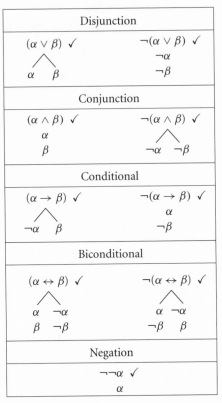

Disjunction	
$(\alpha \lor \beta)$ ✓	$\neg(\alpha \lor \beta)$ ✓
$\alpha \quad \beta$	$\neg\alpha$
	$\neg\beta$

Conjunction	
$(\alpha \land \beta)$ ✓	$\neg(\alpha \land \beta)$ ✓
α	
β	$\neg\alpha \quad \neg\beta$

Conditional	
$(\alpha \to \beta)$ ✓	$\neg(\alpha \to \beta)$ ✓
	α
$\neg\alpha \quad \beta$	$\neg\beta$

Biconditional	
$(\alpha \leftrightarrow \beta)$ ✓	$\neg(\alpha \leftrightarrow \beta)$ ✓
$\alpha \quad \neg\alpha$	$\alpha \quad \neg\alpha$
$\beta \quad \neg\beta$	$\neg\beta \quad \beta$

Negation
$\neg\neg\alpha$ ✓
α

Figure 7.1. Tree rules for PL.

The tree rules are summarized in Figure 7.1.

7.2 Applying the Rules

7.2.1 Not Digging Too Deep

The foregoing rules are presented using wff variables, which is to say that they apply to any propositions—however complex—that may be substituted for those variables. So, for example, suppose we have a tree containing the proposition

$$(\neg A \land \neg B)$$

The main connective here is a conjunction, so we apply the tree rule for (unnegated) conjunction—we write a column containing the first conjunct above the second conjunct:

$$(\neg A \wedge \neg B) \checkmark$$
$$\neg A$$
$$\neg B$$

To take another example, suppose we have a tree containing the proposition

$$\neg(\neg A \rightarrow \neg B)$$

The main connective here is a negation, and the main connective of its negand is a conditional, so we apply the rule for negated conditional—we write in a column containing the antecedent above the negation of the consequent:

$$\neg(\neg A \rightarrow \neg B) \checkmark$$
$$\neg A$$
$$\neg\neg B$$

When we apply a tree rule, we do not need to look inside the proposition of interest farther than its top one or two levels. That is to say, we need look only at its main connective where that is not negation—or, where the main connective is negation, we need look only at this negation and the main connective of its negand. So it can be useful, when learning to apply the rules, mentally to "black box" all structure of the proposition of interest below its outermost one or two connectives. Thus, in the first case above, the main connective is $\wedge$. So we apply the rule for unnegated $\wedge$. The fact that the conjuncts $\neg A$ and $\neg B$ have further internal structure (they are negations) is irrelevant at this point. So we can just think of the proposition to which we are to apply our rule as a conjunction of two formulas that are concealed in boxes, a circular box and a square box:

$$(\bigcirc \wedge \square)$$

The rule for conjunction tells us: write a column with the first conjunct (the content of the circular box) above the second conjunct (the content of the square box):

$$(\bigcirc \wedge \square) \checkmark$$
$$\bigcirc$$
$$\square$$

Now, having first conceived of the rule in this way—using black boxes—we copy in the contents of those boxes (the circular box contains $\neg A$ and the square box $\neg B$) to obtain our actual instance of the tree rule in question:

$$(\neg A \wedge \neg B) \checkmark$$
$$\neg A$$
$$\neg B$$

Thinking in terms of boxes helps avoid confusion about where negations come from: whether from the rule as applied to some boxes or from inside those boxes. In the case above, the negations in the outputs of our rule—in $\neg A$ and $\neg B$—did not come from the rule; they were there all along inside the boxes to which the rule was applied.

Now consider the second case discussed above:

$$\neg(\neg A \rightarrow \neg B)$$

Its main connective is a negation, so we need to look also at the main connective of its negand, which in this case is a conditional. We do not need to look any deeper into the structure of our proposition than this: we black box the antecedent and the consequent of this conditional:

$$\neg(\bigcirc \rightarrow \square)$$

So we are to apply the rule for negated conditional, which tells us to form a column with the antecedent (the content of the circular box) above the negation of the consequent (the content of the square box):

$$\neg(\bigcirc \rightarrow \square) \ \checkmark$$
$$\bigcirc$$
$$\neg\square$$

Now, having first conceived of the rule in this way—using boxes—we copy in the contents of those boxes (the circular box contains $\neg A$ and the square box $\neg B$) to obtain our actual instance of the tree rule in question:

$$\neg(\neg A \rightarrow \neg B) \ \checkmark$$
$$\neg A$$
$$\neg\neg B$$

Now we can see quite clearly where the negations in the outputs of our rule come from. The negation in $\neg A$ was not added by the rule: it was in the box. As for the two negations in $\neg\neg B$, the first was added by the rule, while the second was already in the box to which the rule was applied.

7.2.1.1 EXERCISES
Apply the appropriate tree rule to each of the following propositions.

1. $(\neg A \vee \neg B)$

2. $(\neg A \rightarrow B)$

3. $((A \rightarrow B) \wedge B)$

4. $((A \leftrightarrow B) \leftrightarrow B)$

5. $\neg(A \leftrightarrow \neg\neg A)$

6. $\neg(\neg A \vee B)$

7.2.2 Finishing What Is Started

A tree starts with one or more propositions. It is not finished until we have applied the appropriate rule to every proposition in the tree to which a rule can be applied (i.e., every proposition that is not basic or the negation of a basic proposition).[7] That includes not only the propositions we start with but also any other propositions generated by the tree rules along the way. For example, suppose we begin with the proposition:

$$(A \rightarrow (B \rightarrow A))$$

Applying the rule for unnegated conditional, we get:

$$(A \rightarrow (B \rightarrow A)) \checkmark$$
$$\neg A \quad (B \rightarrow A)$$

We now have a proposition $(B \rightarrow A)$ to which a rule—the rule for unnegated conditional—can be applied. Applying it yields:

$$(A \rightarrow (B \rightarrow A)) \checkmark$$
$$\neg A \quad (B \rightarrow A) \checkmark$$
$$\neg B \quad A$$

Our tree is now finished: all propositions other than basic propositions and negations of basic propositions have had the appropriate rule applied (as indicated by the check marks).

7.2.2.1 EXERCISES

Construct finished trees for each of the following propositions.

1. $((A \rightarrow B) \rightarrow B)$

2. $((A \rightarrow B) \lor (B \rightarrow A))$

3. $\neg(\neg A \rightarrow (A \lor B))$

4. $\neg\neg((A \land B) \lor (A \land \neg B))$

7.2.3 Closing Paths

A *path* (aka branch) through a tree is a complete route from the topmost proposition down until one can go no further. So in the tree:

$$(A \rightarrow (B \rightarrow A)) \checkmark$$
$$\neg A \quad (B \rightarrow A) \checkmark$$
$$\neg B \quad A$$

there are three paths:

1. $(A \to (B \to A)) \mapsto \neg A$

2. $(A \to (B \to A)) \mapsto (B \to A) \mapsto \neg B$

3. $(A \to (B \to A)) \mapsto (B \to A) \mapsto A$

When constructing a tree, if at any point we find that a path contains both a formula and its negation, we *close* the path with a cross. For example:

$$
\begin{array}{c}
((A \land \neg A) \lor B) \ \checkmark \\
\diagup \quad \diagdown \\
(A \land \neg A) \ \checkmark \qquad B \\
A \\
\neg A \\
\times
\end{array}
$$

In this tree there are two paths:

1. $((A \land \neg A) \lor B) \mapsto (A \land \neg A) \mapsto A \mapsto \neg A$

2. $((A \land \neg A) \lor B) \mapsto B$

The first path contains both a formula (in this case A) and its negation (in this case $\neg A$), so we close it with a cross ($\times$). The second path does not contain both a formula and its negation, so it is an *open* path.

7.2.3.1 EXERCISES
Construct finished trees for each of the following propositions; close paths as appropriate.

1. $\neg(A \to (B \to A))$

2. $((A \to B) \lor (\neg A \lor B))$

3. $\neg((A \to B) \lor (\neg A \lor B))$

4. $\neg\neg\neg(A \lor B)$

5. $\neg(A \land \neg A)$

6. $\neg(\neg(A \land B) \leftrightarrow (\neg A \lor \neg B))$

7.2.4 *Applying Rules on All Open—and No Closed—Paths*
It may happen at a certain stage of constructing a tree that the formula to which we are applying a rule is on more than one open path. For example, consider the following partially finished tree:

$$
\begin{array}{c}
((A \to B) \land (B \to A)) \ \checkmark \\
(A \to B) \ \checkmark \\
(B \to A) \\
\diagup \quad \diagdown \\
\neg A \quad B
\end{array}
$$

We need to apply the rule for unnegated conditional to $(B \to A)$. This formula is sitting on both of the following open paths:

1. $((A \to B) \wedge (B \to A)) \Mapsto (A \to B) \Mapsto (B \to A) \Mapsto \neg A$

2. $((A \to B) \wedge (B \to A)) \Mapsto (A \to B) \Mapsto (B \to A) \Mapsto B$

So we apply the rule twice: once at the end of each of these open paths. (In general, if the formula of interest is on n open paths, we apply the rule n times: once at the end of each open path.) The result is:

$$((A \to B) \wedge (B \to A)) \checkmark$$
$$(A \to B) \checkmark$$
$$(B \to A) \checkmark$$

In contrast, we never apply rules at the bottom of closed paths. Once a path has been closed with a cross, no more wffs can be added to it.

7.2.5 Order of Application of Rules; Checking Closure

There is no hard-and-fast requirement on the order in which one applies the tree rules. However, there are some useful rules of thumb. For convenience, it is useful to apply nonbranching rules before branching rules, if one has a choice. Applying branching rules first will not make the tree incorrect, but it will in general make it bigger. So, for example, if the tree begins with $(A \wedge B)$ and $(A \to B)$, one obtains a shorter tree by applying the rule for $\wedge$ to the first proposition and then applying the rule for $\to$ to the second proposition than by dealing with the propositions in the opposite order. In this particular case, the difference is not very large (do the two trees and see)—but in more complex trees, applying nonbranching rules first can make quite a significant difference to the size of the tree.

There is, however, one hard-and-fast requirement on the order in which one must do things when constructing a tree. One must check for closure each time wffs are added to the tree: after writing down the initial wffs in the tree, one must check whether the tree closes immediately. And each time a rule is applied, after writing down the results of applying that rule, one must check each path to which wffs were added to see whether it closes. If the check reveals that a path can close, then it must indeed be crossed off.[8]

7.2.6 The Underlying Idea

Now that we are familiar with the mechanics of trees, let us return to the basic idea behind them (discussed in a preliminary way in the second part of the opening section of this chapter). When constructing a tree, we begin by writing some proposition(s) at the top of the tree. The tree rules then determine what we may write next. The idea behind the rules is (roughly) this: we assume (for the sake of argument) that what we write at the top of the tree is true, and then the rules prescribe things to write that must be true, given that what we have already written is true. More precisely, as we apply rules and grow the tree, it may branch; what the rules ensure is not that everything on every branch is true (assuming the starting propositions are true), but rather that there is at least one path through the tree such that every proposition on that path is true (assuming that the propositions we started with are all true).[9]

Now recall that as we apply rules, we check off more complex propositions, until we end up with only basic propositions and negations of basic propositions. Recall also that if a negation of a basic proposition is true, then the basic proposition itself is false. So each path represents an alleged way for all propositions at the top of the tree to be true—an alleged possible assignment of truth values to basic propositions (true for the propositions that appear alone in the path, false for the ones that appear negated) under which the propositions at the top of the tree all come out true. I say "alleged" because some of these paths may not represent possible assignments at all. These are the closed paths: the ones featuring both a proposition and its negation, that is, which correspond to an assignment of truth values under which some proposition is both true and false. That is impossible: there are no such scenarios. So a closed path does not represent a possible assignment at all, whereas an open path represents a possible assignment in which all propositions at the top of the tree are true.[10]

Now suppose that all paths close in our tree. Then there is no scenario—no way of making propositions true or false, no assignment of truth values to basic propositions, no truth table row—in which all propositions at the top of the tree are true. Suppose, however, that one or more paths remain open when the tree is finished (i.e., when all possible rules have been applied on all open paths). In that case, it is possible for all propositions at the top of the tree to be true: an open path represents such a scenario.

7.3 Uses of Trees

We now consider how to use trees to find out things that we are interested in, such as whether a given argument is valid or whether two propositions are equivalent.

7.3.1 Validity

A tree will (directly) answer only one sort of question: whether all propositions at the top of the tree can be true (in the same scenario)—that is, whether the set containing those propositions is satisfiable. A tree will always give us an answer to a question of this type, but it cannot give a direct answer to other sorts of question, such as "can this proposition be false?" Such questions need to be rephrased in terms of the possibility of truth (i.e., satisfiability).

Now consider the question of whether an argument is valid. Can the premises all be true while the conclusion is false? If so, the argument is invalid; if not, it is valid. We cannot ask a tree this question directly—for a tree cannot tell us about falsity, only truth. So we have to rephrase the question: is it possible for all premises and the negation of the conclusion to be true at the same time? It is not hard to see that this is precisely the information we wanted—whether the premises can be true while the conclusion is false—just packaged in a different form.

So, to test whether an argument is valid, we write at the top of the tree the premise(s) and the negation of the conclusion. We then finish our tree. If all paths close, the argument is valid (it is not possible for the propositions at the top of the tree all to be true—i.e., it is not possible for the premises of our argument to be true while its conclusion is false). If one or more paths remain open (when the tree is finished), then the argument is invalid.

For example, consider the argument:

$(A \rightarrow B)$
$(B \rightarrow C)$
$\therefore (A \rightarrow C)$

We write out the two premises and the negation of the conclusion at the top of a tree, and then apply rules and close branches as appropriate until the tree is finished:

(We first apply the nonbranching rule for negated conditionals to $\neg(A \rightarrow C)$. Then we apply the rule for $(A \rightarrow B)$, at which point the path:

$(A \rightarrow B) \Mapsto (B \rightarrow C) \Mapsto \neg(A \rightarrow C) \Mapsto A \Mapsto \neg C \Mapsto \neg A$

closes (because it contains both A and $\neg A$). Thus, to decompose our final proposition ($B \rightarrow C$), we have to apply the rule only once: even though the formula is on two paths, at this point only one of those paths is still open.) All paths close, so the argument is valid.

Consider now the argument:

$(A \rightarrow C)$
$(B \rightarrow C)$
$\therefore (B \rightarrow A)$

Again we write out the two premises and the negation of the conclusion at the top of a tree, and then apply rules and close branches as appropriate until the tree is finished:

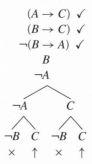

(We first apply the nonbranching rule for negated conditionals to $\neg(B \rightarrow A)$. Then we apply the rule for ($A \rightarrow C$), which causes the tree to branch. At this point, neither branch closes, so when we then apply the rule for ($B \rightarrow C$), we have to write the output of the rule—which is a branch with $\neg B$ on one side and C on the other side—twice: once at the bottom of each path. We now have four paths. Two of them close and two remain open.) There are two open paths (indicated by vertical arrows), so the argument is invalid.

As was the case with the truth table test for validity, when an argument is invalid, the test does not simply tell us this: it furthermore gives us a counterexample. We read off a counterexample from each open path in the tree. Looking down the left-hand open path in our tree, we see that B and C appear unnegated, while $\neg A$ appears negated. This path thus represents a scenario in which A is false, and B and C are true. This is our counterexample. We can confirm that in this scenario, the premises are true and the conclusion false by writing out the corresponding row of the truth table for our argument:

A	B	C	$(A \rightarrow C)$	$(B \rightarrow C)$	$(B \rightarrow A)$
F	T	T	T	T	F

(Remember that when doing truth tables we do not negate the conclusion!)

Thus, the tree test directly targets the truth table rows in which we are interested. We wanted to know whether there was any row in the truth table for our argument in which the premises are true and the conclusion false. Without having to search all eight of them, the tree test has given us a row of the type we were looking for. And when there are no such rows—as in the first argument considered above—the tree test demonstrates this, by having all its paths close.

Note that what the tree test tells us is this: if there is at least one open path, then there is at least one case in which all propositions at the top of the tree are true. There is no direct relationship between the number of open paths and the number of cases in which the propositions at the top of the tree are true. (Except in the case where that number is zero: if there are no open paths, then there are no such cases.) Look back at our most recent tree. The right-hand open path yields the same counterexample as the left-hand one (A false, B and C true). So here we have two open paths that yield one scenario in which the propositions at the top of the tree are true. In other cases, one path might yield more than one such scenario. For example, consider the argument:

A
$\therefore (\neg(A \wedge B) \wedge \neg((A \wedge B) \wedge C))$

Here is its tree:

Not all paths close, so the argument is invalid. The right-hand open path yields the counterexample: A true, B true, and C true. The left-hand open path contains A and B unnegated, but it does not contain C, either unnegated or negated. So what counterexample does it yield? Well, the point is that in a situation in which A is true and B is true, both propositions at the top of the tree are true. That is, as long as A and B are true, it does not matter whether C is true or false: the propositions at the top of the tree will be true either way. So this one open path yields two counterexamples: A true, B true, and C true; and A true, B true, and C false.

In general, when reading off a counterexample from an open path, we put in the value T for any basic proposition that appears unnegated in the path and the value F for any basic proposition that appears negated in the path. For basic propositions appearing in the propositions at the top of the tree that do not occur either by themselves or negated in the open path, we can put any value we like in the counterexample.

Note that although the number of open paths need not equal the number of truth table rows in which the premises are true and the conclusion is false, we can be assured that every such row can be read off some open path. That is, the tree will not overlook any counterexamples: it might have multiple counterexamples coming off the same open path, or the same counterexample coming off multiple open paths, but every counterexample will be there somewhere. This is because our tree rules all have the property that their outputs are jointly exhaustive:[11] if the input is true, then (in the case of a nonbranching rule) all outputs must be true and (in the case of a branching rule) either all outputs on the left branch must be true or all outputs on the right branch must be true. Thus, the tree covers all ways in which the propositions at the top of the tree could be true: no way is overlooked.

7.3.1.1 EXERCISES

Using trees, determine whether the following arguments are valid. For any arguments that are invalid, give a counterexample.

1. A
   $\therefore (A \lor B)$

2. $(A \lor B)$
   $\therefore B$

3. $(A \lor B)$
   $(A \to C)$
   $(B \to D)$
   $\therefore (C \lor D)$

4. $((A \lor \neg B) \to C)$
   $(B \to \neg D)$
   D
   $\therefore C$

5. B
   $(A \to B)$
   $\therefore A$

6. A
   $(A \to B)$
   $\therefore B$

7. $(A \lor (B \land C))$
   $(A \to B)$
   $(B \leftrightarrow D)$
   $\therefore (B \land D)$

8. $\neg(\neg A \to B)$
   $\neg(C \leftrightarrow A)$
   $(A \lor C)$
   $\neg(C \to B)$
   $\therefore \neg(A \to B)$

9. $(A \leftrightarrow B)$
   $(B \to C)$
   $(\neg B \to \neg C)$
   $(A \lor (B \land \neg B))$
   $\therefore C$

10. $(A \to B)$
    $(B \to C)$
    $(C \to D)$
    $(D \to E)$
    $\therefore \neg(A \land \neg E)$

7.3.2 Satisfiability

A proposition is satisfiable if there is at least one scenario in which it is true. A proposition is a contradiction if it is false in every scenario; that is, there is no scenario in which it is true (it is not satisfiable). A set of propositions is satisfiable if there is at least one scenario in which they are all true. Two propositions are jointly satisfiable iff the set containing them both is satisfiable; they are jointly unsatisfiable iff the set containing them both is unsatisfiable.

Satisfiability questions can be put directly to trees, without any need for reformulation: they are, at the outset, framed in terms that trees can handle. To test whether a single proposition is satisfiable, we write it at the top of our tree and then finish the tree: if all paths close, it is not satisfiable (i.e., it is a contradiction); if not all paths close, the proposition is satisfiable (i.e., it is not a contradiction), and we can read off from an open path a scenario in which it is true. To test whether a set of propositions is satisfiable, we write the propositions in the set at the top of our tree and then finish the tree: if all paths close, the set is unsatisfiable; if not all paths close, the set is satisfiable, and we can read off from an open path a scenario in which all formulas in the set are true.

7.3.2.1 EXERCISES

1. Using trees, test whether the following propositions are contradictions. For any proposition that is satisfiable, read off from an open path a scenario in which the proposition is true.
   (i) $A \land \neg A$
   (ii) $(A \lor B) \land \neg(A \lor B)$
   (iii) $(A \to B) \land \neg(A \lor B)$
   (iv) $(A \to \neg(A \lor B)) \land \neg(\neg(A \lor B) \lor B)$
   (v) $\neg((\neg B \lor C) \leftrightarrow (B \to C))$
   (vi) $(A \leftrightarrow \neg A) \lor (A \to \neg(B \lor C))$

2. Using trees, test whether the following sets of propositions are satisfiable. For any set that is satisfiable, read off from an open path a scenario in which all the propositions in the set are true.
   (i) $\{(A \lor B), \neg B, (A \to B)\}$
   (ii) $\{(A \lor B), (B \lor C), \neg(A \lor C)\}$
   (iii) $\{\neg(\neg A \to B), \neg(C \leftrightarrow A), (A \lor C), \neg(C \to B), (A \to B)\}$
   (iv) $\{(A \leftrightarrow B), \neg(A \to C), (C \to A), (A \land B) \lor (A \land C)\}$

7.3.3 Contraries and Contradictories

If two propositions are jointly unsatisfiable, they cannot both be true (in the same scenario). If, furthermore, they cannot both be false, then they are contradictories, whereas if they can both be false, they are contraries. To test whether two propositions can both be false, we need to test whether their negations can both be true. In other words, we need to test whether their negations are jointly satisfiable. So to find out whether two propositions are contraries or contradictories (or neither), we do two tests. First we test whether the set containing the two propositions is satisfiable. If it is, then the two propositions are not contraries or contradictories. If the set is unsatisfiable, then we test the set containing the negations of the two propositions for satisfiability. If this set is satisfiable (i.e., the two negations can both be true), then the original propositions can both be false—and so they are contraries. If the set containing the negations is unsatisfiable, then the original propositions cannot both be false—and so they are contradictories.

7.3.3.1 EXERCISES

Test whether the following pairs of propositions are contraries, contradictories, or jointly satisfiable.

1. $(\neg A \to B)$ and $(B \to A)$

2. $(A \to B)$ and $\neg(A \to (A \to B))$

3. $\neg(A \leftrightarrow \neg B)$ and $\neg(A \vee \neg B)$

4. $\neg(A \vee \neg B)$ and $(\neg A \to \neg B)$

5. $(\neg A \wedge (A \to B))$ and $\neg(\neg A \to (A \to B))$

6. $((A \to B) \leftrightarrow B)$ and $\neg(A \to B)$

7.3.4 Tautologies

To ask whether a proposition is a tautology is to ask whether it is true in every scenario. As this is a question about truth, can we not put it directly to a tree? No, we cannot. For trees can only answer questions about whether the proposition(s) at the top of the tree *can* be true—that is, whether there is at least one scenario in which the proposition(s) are true. But when we want to know whether a proposition α is a tautology, we want to know whether it is true in *all* scenarios. If we do a tree starting with α, and some path(s) remain open, this shows us only that α is satisfiable—that it can be true—not that it *must* be true.

So how do we determine the latter? Well, another way of putting the question is: can α be false? Now we are getting closer: we just need to change this talk of falsity to talk of truth of a negation, and we shall have a question we can put to a tree, namely, can $\neg\alpha$ be true? That is, is $\neg\alpha$ satisfiable? So, to test whether a proposition is a tautology, we write down its negation and then do a tree. If all paths close, the negation cannot be true—that is, our original proposition cannot be false and so is a tautology. If not all paths close, then the negation can be true—that is, our original proposition can be false and so is not a tautology. In this case we can read off from an open path a scenario in which the original proposition is false.

It is useful to think a bit further about why we cannot test whether α is a tautology by starting a tree with α itself (not its negation) and seeing whether all paths remain open. Here is a nontautology that would pass this test:

$$A$$

and here is a tautology that would fail it:

$$(A \wedge \neg A) \vee \neg(A \wedge \neg A)$$

(Do the trees and confirm these statements.) The problem with the proposed test is that it is based on the following mistaken line of thought: in a tree, there is one path per scenario (truth table row); an open path represents a truth table row in which the propositions at the top of the tree are true; a closed path represents a truth table row in which the propositions at the top of the tree are false. This line of thought involves two confusions about the nature of paths. First, a closed path does not represent a truth table row in which the propositions at the top of the tree are false: it does not represent a truth table row at all (for it involves some proposition being both true and false). A closed path is an impossible scenario, not a (possible) falsifying scenario. Second, a tree does not, in general, have a path corresponding to every truth table row: it is only guaranteed to represent those truth table rows in which the propositions at the top of the tree are true; truth table rows on which those propositions are false will not be represented at all. (Recall an advantage of trees: they target the cases we are interested in—if such exist—without our having to search through all possible cases.) So "all paths open" does not mean "true in all possible cases" (i.e., true in all truth table rows). Rather, it means just the same as "one path open." The only important distinction is between (i) all paths closed and (ii) not all paths closed (i.e., one or more paths open). One or more paths open means that there is some (one or more) possible scenario in which the propositions at the top of the tree are true.

7.3.4.1 EXERCISES
Test whether the following propositions are tautologies. (Remember to restore outermost parentheses before adding the negation symbol at the front—recall §2.5.4.) For any proposition that is not a tautology, read off from your tree a scenario in which it is false.

1. $A \rightarrow (B \rightarrow A)$

2. $A \rightarrow (A \rightarrow B)$

3. $((A \land B) \lor \lnot(A \rightarrow B)) \rightarrow (C \rightarrow A)$

4. $(A \land (B \lor C)) \leftrightarrow ((A \land B) \lor (A \land C))$

5. $\lnot A \lor \lnot(A \land B)$

6. $A \lor (\lnot A \land \lnot B)$

7. $(A \rightarrow B) \lor (A \land \lnot B)$

8. $(B \land \lnot A) \leftrightarrow (A \leftrightarrow B)$

9. $(A \lor (B \lor C)) \leftrightarrow ((A \lor B) \lor C)$

10. $(A \land (B \lor C)) \leftrightarrow ((A \lor B) \land C)$

7.3.5 Equivalence

The formula α is equivalent to β iff $(\alpha \leftrightarrow \beta)$ is a tautology. (Why? Well, $(\alpha \leftrightarrow \beta)$ is true in exactly those cases where α and β have the same truth value. The forumula α is equivalent to β just in case α and β have the same truth value in every case. So α is equivalent to β just in case $(\alpha \leftrightarrow \beta)$ is true in every case, i.e., is a tautology.) So to test whether α is equivalent to β using trees, we check whether $(\alpha \leftrightarrow \beta)$ is a tautology. That is, we start our tree with $\lnot(\alpha \leftrightarrow \beta)$. If every path closes, $(\alpha \leftrightarrow \beta)$ is a tautology, and so α is equivalent to β. If some path remains open, $(\alpha \leftrightarrow \beta)$ is not a tautology, and so α is not equivalent to β. In this case, we can read off from an open path a case in which $(\alpha \leftrightarrow \beta)$ is false—that is, a case in which α and β have different truth values.

For example, suppose we want to know whether P and $(P \lor P)$ are equivalent. We put a biconditional between them, a negation out the front of the result, and then finish the tree:

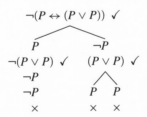

All paths close, so P and $(P \lor P)$ are equivalent.

There is an alternative way of phrasing the question of whether two propositions α and β are equivalent in such a way that trees can answer the question (i.e., an alternative to asking whether $(\alpha \leftrightarrow \beta)$ is a tautology). We want to know two things:

1. Can it ever be the case that α is true while β is false?

2. Can it ever be the case that α is false while β is true?

If the answer to both questions is no, then α and β must always have the same truth value—that is, they must be equivalent. Now we can answer the first question by doing a tree for α and $\neg\beta$, and we can answer the second question by doing a tree for $\neg\alpha$ and β. If all paths close on both trees, α and β are equivalent.

Note that the two trees drawn in our second method are simply the two main parts of the single tree drawn in our first method. The first method starts with $\neg(\alpha \leftrightarrow \beta)$ at the top of the tree. Applying the rule for negated biconditional, the tree then splits into two branches, with α and $\neg\beta$ on one side, and $\neg\alpha$ and β on the other side. In completing the left branch, we replicate the process of doing the first tree required by the second (two-tree) method for testing equivalence; in completing the right branch, we replicate the process of doing the second tree.

7.3.5.1 EXERCISES

Test whether the following are equivalent. Where the two propositions are not equivalent, read off from your tree a scenario in which they have different truth values.

1. P and $(P \wedge P)$

2. $(P \rightarrow (Q \vee \neg Q))$ and $(R \rightarrow R)$

3. $\neg(A \vee B)$ and $(\neg A \wedge \neg B)$

4. $\neg(A \vee B)$ and $(\neg A \vee \neg B)$

5. $\neg(A \wedge B)$ and $(\neg A \wedge \neg B)$

6. $\neg(A \wedge B)$ and $(\neg A \vee \neg B)$

7. A and $((A \wedge B) \vee (A \wedge \neg B))$

8. $\neg(P \leftrightarrow Q)$ and $((P \wedge \neg Q) \vee (\neg P \wedge Q))$

9. $((P \wedge Q) \rightarrow R)$ and $(P \rightarrow (\neg Q \vee R))$

10. $\neg(P \leftrightarrow Q)$ and $(Q \wedge \neg P)$

7.3.6 Summary

To test whether an argument is valid:

- Start the tree with the premises and the negation of the conclusion.

- If all paths close, the argument is valid.

- If a path remains open, the argument is invalid. Read off from an open path a scenario in which the premises are true and the conclusion false.

To test whether a proposition α is a tautology:

- Start the tree with the negation $\neg\alpha$.

- If all paths close, α is a tautology.

- If a path remains open, α is not a tautology. Read off from an open path a scenario in which α is false.

To test whether two propositions α and β are equivalent:

- Start the tree with the negated biconditional $\neg(\alpha \leftrightarrow \beta)$.

- If all paths close, α and β are equivalent.

- If a path remains open, α and β are not equivalent. Read off from an open path a scenario in which α and β have different truth values.

To test whether a proposition is satisfiable or a contradiction:

- Start the tree with the proposition.

- If all paths close, the proposition is a contradiction (i.e., not satisfiable).

- If a path remains open, the proposition is satisfiable (i.e., not a contradiction). Read off from an open path a scenario in which the proposition is true.

To test whether a set of propositions is satisfiable:

- Start the tree with the propositions in the set.

- If all paths close, the set is unsatisfiable.

- If a path remains open, the set is satisfiable. Read off from an open path a scenario in which all propositions in the set are true.

To test whether two jointly unsatisfiable propositions (as determined by the previous test for satisfiability, applied to the set containing the two propositions) are contraries or contradictories:

- Start the tree with the negations of the propositions.

- If all paths close, the propositions are contradictories.

- If a path remains open, the propositions are contraries. Read off from an open path a scenario in which both propositions are false.

7.4 Abbreviations

We said in §4.3.2 that we may, for convenience, omit internal parentheses in strings of straight $\wedge$s or straight $\vee$s. How do we handle such abbreviated propositions in trees? One way would be to introduce a convention for restoring parentheses to these expressions—for example, treat the multiple connectives in order from left to right (as discussed in §2.5.4)—and then proceed with the tree in the standard way. A second option is to introduce a method of handling the unparenthesized expressions directly in trees. We explain this second option now.

In the case of (unnegated) conjunction, we do the following:

$$\alpha_1 \wedge \alpha_2 \wedge \ldots \wedge \alpha_n \ \checkmark$$
$$\alpha_1$$
$$\alpha_2$$
$$\vdots$$
$$\alpha_n$$

When we write, say, $A \wedge B \wedge C$, this expression is ambiguous between the two equivalent wffs $(A \wedge (B \wedge C))$ and $((A \wedge B) \wedge C)$. The tree for the first of these wffs looks like:

$$(A \wedge (B \wedge C)) \ \checkmark$$
$$A$$
$$(B \wedge C) \ \checkmark$$
$$B$$
$$C$$

and the tree for the second looks like:

$$((A \wedge B) \wedge C) \ \checkmark$$
$$(A \wedge B) \ \checkmark$$
$$C$$
$$A$$
$$B$$

Both trees end with one column containing A, B, and C, plus some other checked-off wffs. So given $A \wedge B \wedge C$ as our starting point, we jump straight to checking this off and writing down A, B, and C below it:

$$A \wedge B \wedge C \ \checkmark$$
$$A$$
$$B$$
$$C$$

In the case of (unnegated) disjunction, we do the following:

$$\alpha_1 \vee \alpha_2 \vee \ldots \vee \alpha_n \ \checkmark$$

$$\alpha_1 \quad \alpha_2 \quad \ldots \quad \alpha_n$$

When we write, say, $A \vee B \vee C$, this expression is ambiguous between the two equivalent wffs $(A \vee (B \vee C))$ and $((A \vee B) \vee C)$. The tree for the first of these wffs looks like:

$$(A \vee (B \vee C)) \checkmark$$

$$A \qquad (B \vee C) \checkmark$$

$$B \quad C$$

The tree for the second looks like:

$$((A \vee B) \vee C) \checkmark$$

$$(A \vee B) \checkmark \qquad C$$

$$A \quad B$$

Both trees end with three branches, with A on one, B on another, and C on the other, plus some other checked-off wffs along the way. So given $A \vee B \vee C$ as our starting point, we jump straight to checking it off and writing down three branches, one with A on it, another with B on it, and the third with C on it:

$$A \vee B \vee C \checkmark$$

$$A \quad B \quad C$$

Negated conjunction and negated disjunction are handled in the obvious analogous ways:

$$\neg(\alpha_1 \wedge \alpha_2 \wedge \ldots \wedge \alpha_n) \checkmark$$

$$\neg\alpha_1 \ \neg\alpha_2 \ \ldots \ \neg\alpha_n$$

$$\neg(\alpha_1 \vee \alpha_2 \vee \ldots \vee \alpha_n) \checkmark$$

$$\neg\alpha_1$$
$$\neg\alpha_2$$
$$\vdots$$
$$\neg\alpha_n$$

Note that what we have just laid out are not extra tree rules: they are simply abbreviations. A tree with (say) $A \vee B \vee C$ in it and three branches coming off below this point is not strictly speaking a properly constructed tree. It is simply a convenience. We can always expand such a thing into a proper tree if we want to: first we would eliminate $A \vee B \vee C$—which (recall §4.3.2) is not a genuine wff but is likewise simply a convenience—in favor of a genuine wff (i.e., $(A \vee (B \vee C))$ or $((A \vee B) \vee C)$); then we would proceed to apply the official disjunction rule, which involves only two branches.

The distinction between proper or official trees and expressions of convenience is an important one. Suppose that you wish to know whether some argument is valid. At some point in your tree you find, say, the formula ($\neg A \to B$). The official way to proceed is as follows:

Obviously, however, you will not get the wrong result if you skip the $\neg\neg A$ on the left branch and go straight to A (i.e., if you do this step in your head, rather than writing it down). If you are just working something out (e.g., whether some argument is valid or some proposition a tautology) for your own purposes, this sort of abbreviation is fine: it won't lead you astray. But it is important to realize that it is an abbreviation and that what you have created is not an official tree. There are two sorts of reason this is important—why it is important to be aware of the difference between an official tree and one involving shortcuts or abbreviations. First, when we prove things about the system of tree proofs (e.g., that it is sound and complete; see Chapter 14), the only way we can prove things about all trees (of which there are infinitely many) is by referring to the rules that generate them (of which there are only finitely many). Our conclusions therefore apply only to trees generated in accordance with the rules: trees in which we have used ad hoc shortcuts will not be covered.[12] Second, in many contexts in logic, the notion of an *effective procedure* plays a crucial role. It is therefore important that the procedure of drawing up trees can be seen to be an effective one: all rules must be able to be applied mechanically, without any need for ingenuity or insight. In particular, we cannot have a rule that states "skip any steps that are obviously OK to skip." For further discussion of this point, see §14.2.

We should therefore always be aware of whether we are following the official rules or using insight and ingenuity to take shortcuts. In some contexts—for example, working out whether an argument is valid for one's own purposes—shortcuts ore OK. In other contexts, however, it is not just obtaining the right answer that matters: whether one gets it by the official rules is also crucial.

PART II

Predicate Logic

8

The Language of Monadic Predicate Logic

One of our aims is to come up with a method for determining whether any given argument is valid. In Part I we made a good start on this, but there are arguments that the account presented there cannot handle, because the propositions making up those arguments cannot be represented adequately in PL. In Part II of this book we therefore extend our logical language. We do this in three phases:

1. monadic predicate logic (Chapters 8–10),

2. general predicate logic (Chapter 12),

3. general predicate logic with identity (Chapter 13).

Within each phase we follow the same three-step process:

1. We introduce an extended language.

2. We introduce an account of the semantics of our new language. Just as the truth table semantics did for PL, the semantics for each new language specifies what a "possible way of making propositions true or false" is, and what is involved in a proposition being true or false in such a scenario.[1] This then allows us to frame precise analyses or definitions of key logical notions, such as validity (in every scenario in which the premises are true, the conclusion is true), equivalence (having the same truth value in every scenario), and so on.

3. We extend our system of tree rules to match the extended expressive resources of the new language. This enables us to use trees to test whether a given argument is valid, whether two given propositions are equivalent, and so on.

8.1 The Limitations of Propositional Logic

Before extending our existing language PL, let's discuss why we need to extend it. Consider the following argument:

> All kelpies are dogs.
> Maisie is a kelpie.
> ∴ Maisie is a dog.

In §1.4, this was one of our paradigms for an intuitively valid argument. Yet look what happens if we apply our truth table test for validity to this argument. First we translate into PL. The first premise is a basic proposition: it does not have any propositions as parts. Similarly for the second premise and the conclusion. And they are all different basic propositions. So the translation is:

K: All kelpies are dogs K
M: Maisie is a kelpie M
D: Maisie is a dog   ∴ D

A truth table for this argument consists simply of the matrix containing K, M, and D. So there is certainly a row on which K and M are true, and D is false. So the argument comes out as invalid, according to our existing test of validity.

Let's think about why the argument is valid (intuitively). The first premise describes a relationship between two properties—being a kelpie and being a dog: it states that if something has the property of being a kelpie, then it also has the property of being a dog. The second premise states that Maisie has the first of these properties (being a kelpie). The conclusion states that Maisie has the other property (being a dog). Visually, we can think of the situation as in Figure 8.1. We can picture a property as a line drawn around all the things that have that property—so the property of being a kelpie is pictured as a line drawn around all kelpies, and the property of being a dog is pictured as a line drawn around all dogs. Then if the first premise is true, the line around the kelpies never crosses outside the line drawn around the dogs (i.e., there is nothing inside the kelpie ring but outside the dog ring). If the second premise is true, then Maisie is to be found within the kelpie ring. But then if both premises are true, Maisie must be found within the dog ring—that is, the conclusion must be true. So the argument is NTP. Furthermore, it is so by virtue of its form. The foregoing reasoning does not depend on anything about Maisie in particular, or about kelpies or dogs. It is the structure of the argument that matters: it would go through just as well with any properties P and Q in place of the properties "being a kelpie" and "being a dog," and with any individual a in place of Maisie:

All *P*s are *Q*s.
a is a *P*.
∴ *a* is a *Q*.

As we can see from Figure 8.2, if it is true that *a* (whatever it is) is to be found in the region of the *P*s (whatever they are) and it is true that no *P* falls outside the region of the *Q*s (whatever they are), then it must be true that *a* is among the *Q*s.

Consider the following argument, which swaps around premise two and the conclusion of our original argument:

All kelpies are dogs.
Maisie is a dog.
∴ Maisie is a kelpie.

This argument is not valid—we can easily imagine a situation in which the premises are true and the conclusion is false (Figure 8.3). Premise 1 is the same as before: if it is true, then the line around the kelpies never crosses outside the line around the dogs. In a situation in which Maisie is, say, a beagle—so she is in the dog ring, but not in the kelpie ring—premise 2 is true. But in this

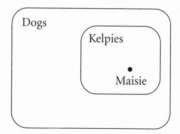

Figure 8.1. The argument is necessarily truth-preserving . . .

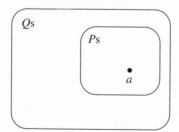

Figure 8.2. . . . in virtue of its form.

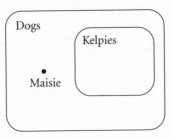

Figure 8.3. The argument is invalid.

situation the conclusion is false. The possibility of such a situation (even if in the actual situation, Maisie is a kelpie, and so the premises and conclusion are all true) shows the argument to be invalid.

In both arguments, the first premise has (at least) two components—a part that picks out the property of being a kelpie, and a part that picks out the property of being a dog—and whether the argument is valid depends on which of these two components figures in the second premise and which features in the conclusion. So the validity of the argument depends on the internal structure of the propositions that make it up. But as yet we have no handle on this internal structure: for the relevant parts of these propositions are not further propositions. From the point of view of propositional logic, these propositions are basic: they have no propositions as parts. But it is clear now that they do have logically important structure. So we need a richer language that does not simply translate each of these propositions as a simple, indivisible letter. Rather, it must bring out the fact that "all kelpies are dogs" has (at least) two parts, one of which shows up again in "Maisie is a kelpie" and the other of which shows up again in "Maisie is a dog."

8.1.1 Extending the Logical Language

We have seen that the internal structure of basic propositions can be logically important. We therefore no longer wish to regard a basic proposition such as "Maisie is a dog" as logically simple (i.e., as having no logically significant parts)—and so we do not want it to be represented in our logical language by a simple symbol (e.g., a capital letter, as in PL). Rather, we want to have symbols for its logically important parts—and the representation of the whole proposition "Maisie is a dog" should then be constructed out of these parts.[2] So we shall take the language PL, remove the symbols for basic propositions—the capital letters A, B, C, . . .—and in their place add symbols for the internal components of these propositions.[3] Note that we retain the five connectives.

We shall proceed as follows. We start with the simplest kind of basic proposition and distinguish its parts (a name and a predicate). We then see how far we can get representing further propositions using the connectives from propositional logic plus names and predicates. We soon find that we need more resources (quantifiers and variables). We then see how far we can get representing further propositions using connectives, names, predicates, quantifiers, and variables. We eventually find that we need even more resources—and so on. We thus proceed in stages, adding symbols to our logical language as we find a need for them. To keep things clear, rather than simply talking about "the logical language" and having to keep track of what resources it has at any given point, we introduce names for specific languages, each of which has a particular combination of resources: the language of monadic predicate logic (MPL), the language of general predicate logic (GPL), and the language of general predicate logic with identity (GPLI):

Part of book	Resource added	Language with resources
§8.2 §8.3	Names and predicates Quantifiers and variables	MPL
Chapter 12	Many-place predicates	GPL
Chapter 13	Identity predicate	GPLI

Note that the resources accumulate: MPL has the connectives of PL (but not the symbols for basic propositions) plus names, predicates, quantifiers, and variables; GPL has the resources of MPL plus many-place predicates; GPLI has the resources of GPL plus the identity predicate.[4]

8.2 MPL, Part I: Names and Predicates

We start with the simplest kind of basic proposition. Our aim is to determine its components. Consider the claim "Maisie is happy." What are its logically significant parts? Recall §1.6, where we first looked into the structure of compound propositions—that is, identified connectives. We said that our search for connectives was to be guided by an interest in those aspects of the internal structure of compound propositions that have an important relationship to truth and falsity—and hence to the laws of truth. The same point applies here: we are interested in those aspects of the internal structure of basic propositions that make a difference to truth and falsity. From this point of view, it seems clear that the proposition expressed by a typical utterance of "Maisie is happy" has two significant parts. When one makes a claim of the form "Maisie is happy," one says of some particular thing (in this case, Maisie) that it has some property (in this case, the property of being happy). So the proposition has two parts: a part that serves to pick out a particular individual (aka thing, object, entity) and a part that serves to pick out a particular property (aka attribute) that things may or may not possess. The proposition is true if the thing picked out does possess the property singled out (in this case, if Maisie is happy); it is false if the thing picked out does not possess the property (Maisie is not happy).

We thus represent the proposition expressed by "Maisie is happy" as having two parts. The part whose function is to pick out an object we call a *name* (aka singular term, referring term, individual constant). The part whose function is to pick out a property we call a *predicate*. Names will be symbolized in MPL by lowercased letters $a, b, c, \ldots, r, s, t$ (not including the last six letters in the alphabet, u, v, w, x, y, z—we reserve those for another purpose, to be discussed in §8.3). Predicates will be symbolized in MPL by uppercased letters: $A, B, C, \ldots, X, Y, Z$ (the entire alphabet may be used).[5]

When translating into MPL, the first step—as with PL—is to write a glossary. This time, however, a glossary pairs up names and predicates of MPL (as opposed to basic propositions, as in PL) with (utterances of) expressions of English, for example:

b: Brave New World[6]	*B:* is big
c: Caitlin	*E:* is exciting
d: Doug	*F:* is famous
e: Mount Everest	*G:* is gigantic
m: Maisie	*H:* is happy
n: New York	*I:* is interesting
	P: is pleasant

A proposition made up from one name and one predicate is called an *atomic proposition*. In MPL, we write an atomic proposition with the predicate immediately before the name, for example:

Fc
En
Ge

Using the glossary given above, these translate into English as:

Caitlin is famous.
New York is exciting.
Mount Everest is gigantic.

Going the other way, the following claims in English:

Maisie is happy.
Brave New World is interesting.
Mount Everest is famous.

translate into MPL as:

Hm
Ib
Fe

We retain all the connectives of PL in MPL. They work just as before: if α and β are wffs (of MPL), so are $(\alpha \rightarrow \beta)$, $\neg\alpha$, and so on. So far, the only wffs of MPL that we have encountered are atomic propositions made up of a predicate in front of a name. Using these as starting points, we can then construct wffs using connectives just as we did in PL. For example:

$(Fn \wedge Fe)$
$(In \vee \neg Hd)$
$(Bn \rightarrow Ge)$

Using the glossary given above, these translate into English as:

New York is famous and Mount Everest is famous.
Either New York is interesting or Doug isn't happy.
If New York is big then Mount Everest is gigantic.

Going the other way, the following claims in English:

Either Doug or Caitlin is famous.
If Mount Everest is big, it's pleasant.
Either Mount Everest is big and pleasant, or it's gigantic.

translate into MPL as:

$(Fd \vee Fc)$
$(Be \rightarrow Pe)$
$((Be \wedge Pe) \vee Ge)$

8.2.1 Exercises

Translate the following propositions from English into MPL:

1. The Pacific Ocean is beautiful.

2. New York is heavily populated.

3. Mary is nice.

4. John is grumpy. G_j

5. Seven is a prime number.

6. Pluto is a planet. P_p

7. Bill and Ben are gardeners

8. If Mary is sailing or Jenny is kite flying, then Bill and Ben are grumpy.

9. Mary is neither sailing nor kite flying.

10. Only if Mary is sailing is Jenny kite flying.

11. John is sailing or kite flying but not both.

12. If Mary isn't sailing, then unless he's kite flying, John is sailing.

13. Jenny is sailing only if both Mary and John are.

14. Jenny is sailing if either John or Mary is.

15. If—and only if—Mary is sailing, Jenny is kite flying.

16. If Steve is winning, Mary isn't happy.

17. Two is prime, but it is also even.

18. Canberra is small—but it's not tiny, and it's a capital city.

19. If Rover is kite flying, then two isn't prime.

20. Mary is happy if and only if Jenny isn't.

8.2.2 Names and Indexicals

Suppose that Bob says "I'm hungry." He is claiming of a particular individual (himself) that it (he) has a certain property (being hungry)—so we translate this into MPL as an atomic proposition. But we need to be careful. For suppose that Carol also says "I'm hungry." It would be a mistake to translate as follows:

i: I   Bob's claim: Hi
H: is hungry   Carol's claim: Hi

The problem here is that Bob and Carol are not making the same claim—they are not expressing the same proposition. (This is clear, because what one of them says could be true while what the other says is false.) Therefore, their two claims should receive different translations into MPL.

As discussed in §2.2.1, when writing a glossary for PL, we specify—for each sentence letter on the left-hand side—which proposition it represents.[7] If we write an English sentence on the right-hand side of the glossary, it is to be understood that the sentence letter on the left-hand side represents the proposition expressed by some particular utterance of this English sentence in some particular context. A similar point applies in the context of MPL. When we translate Bob's claim—"I'm hungry"—into MPL, the result is supposed to be a representation of the proposition Bob expressed. It is not supposed to be a representation of the sentence he used to express it. (That same sentence could be used to express different propositions: e.g., Carol makes a different claim—expresses a different proposition—using the same sentence.) In the present case, the crucial word is "I." When Bob says "I," he picks out himself; when Carol says it, she picks out someone different: herself. So their two utterances of "I" need to be translated as different names. There are various ways to phrase the glossary so as to make this clear:

> i: I (as uttered by Bob on this occasion)
> j: I (as uttered by Carol on this occasion)

or:

> i: I (Bob)
> j: I (Carol)

or simply:

> i: Bob
> j: Carol

Using any of these glossaries, our translations are then:

> Bob's claim: Hi
> Carol's claim: Hj

The translations are different—which is what we wanted.

What we have just said about translating claims involving "I" into MPL applies also to other singular pronouns—"me," "you" (singular), "he," "she," "him," "her," "it"—and to other indexical singular terms, such as "this" and "that" (accompanied by appropriate pointing gestures or other indications of which object is being picked out on a given occasion).[8] They are translated as names in MPL—but different occurrences of the same expression in English need to be translated using different names in MPL, if the different occurrences are used to pick out distinct objects.

The upshot is that MPL (like PL) is not context sensitive (which is a good thing, for the reasons discussed in §2.2.1). While a given glossary is in play, every token of Hi represents the same proposition—and similarly for Hj and every other atomic proposition whose components feature in that glossary.[9]

8.3 MPL, Part II: Variables and Quantifiers

We have seen how to translate a variety of claims into our augmented logical language—but there are also claims that we cannot translate. For example, consider Papa Bear's claim, "someone has been eating my porridge." As it happens, we know who has been eating his porridge: Goldilocks. But Papa Bear's claim is not the same as the claim "Goldilocks has been eating my porridge," because "someone" (unlike "Goldilocks") is not a singular term. To see this, note that there is no particular individual who has to have the property X to make the claim "someone is X" true. As it happens, Papa Bear's claim is true, because Goldilocks has the relevant property (she has been eating his porridge). But we can easily imagine a situation in which it is someone else who has been eating his porridge, and Goldilocks is not involved at all. In such a situation, Papa Bear's claim is still true. Thus, in the original situation the relationship between "someone" and Goldilocks is not the relationship of a singular term to the individual that it picks out. If Papa Bear had said "Goldilocks has been eating my porridge," then if someone else—not Goldilocks—had been eating his porridge, his claim would have been false. A singular term—such as "Goldilocks"—serves to pick out a unique individual, and unless that particular individual has the relevant property, an atomic proposition involving that singular term is false. With "someone," the situation is different. For Papa Bear's claim "someone has been eating my porridge" to be true, it is only required that someone—not necessarily Goldilocks or any other particular individual—has been eating his porridge.

The same point applies to other expressions, for example, "a man." Suppose Bob Wood comes to the door, and later I say "a man came to the door." My claim is true—thanks to Bob Wood. But the key point is that it would likewise have been true if it had been another man, say, Bill Smith, who came to the door. So "a man" (in "a man came to the door") is not a singular term: it does not serve to pick out a particular individual, who then has to have some attribute to make the claim true. Contrast "Bob Wood came to the door." Here I claim of a particular individual that he did something. If that particular individual did not do that thing, then the proposition is false. "Bob Wood came to the door" is true only if Bob Wood came to the door. Thus, the relationship between the singular term "Bob Wood"—as it figures in a claim of the form "Bob Wood did X"—and Bob Wood (i.e., the individual that the singular term serves to pick out) is very different from the relationship between "a man" (as it figures in a claim of the form "a man did X") and the man who (as it happens) did X (if there was such a man at all—i.e., if the claim is true).

Consider the claim "someone enjoys running." For the reasons given above, "someone" here is not a singular term: its function is not to pick out a particular individual, who must then enjoy running for the claim to be true. So what is its function? Well, what is required for the claim in question to be true is that someone or other enjoys running. Anyone will do—no particular person is required. As long as at least one person enjoys running, the proposition is true. So the function of "someone" is to specify how many people must like running for the proposition to be true. Thus, "someone" is a *quantifier*. In particular, it is an *existential quantifier:* in "someone enjoys running," it specifies that at least one—that is, one or more—persons must like running. Common ways of expressing existential quantification in English include:

- "some," as in "some dogs have fleas;"

- "at least one," as in "at least one adult must be present;"

- "someone," as in "someone has been using my toothbrush;" and

- "there is a(n)," as in "there is an elephant in the garden."

Note that we take "some" to mean at least one—that is, one or more—not exactly one.

Consider now the claim "everyone is eating porridge." Obviously, "everyone" here is not a singular term: the claim is certainly not that one particular individual is eating porridge, it is that all individuals are doing so. Nor is this an example of existential quantification: for the claim to be true, it is not enough that one or more persons is eating porridge; it must be the case that all persons are doing so. Rather, this is an example of *universal quantification:* in "everyone is eating porridge," "everyone" specifies that the quantity of persons who must be eating porridge (for the claim to be true) is all persons. Common ways of expressing universal quantification in English include:

- "all," as in "all dogs have fleas;"

- "every," as in "every cloud is grey;"

- "each," as in "each student shall receive a laptop computer;"

- "each and every," as in "each and every one of you is in trouble;"

- "everything," as in "everything you say is so funny;"

- "everyone," as in "everyone is special;"

- "everybody," as in "everybody laughs."

We turn now to the question of representing existential and universal quantification in our logical language. "Carl enjoys running" translates as follows:

c: Carl   *Lc*
L: enjoys running

Because "someone" and "everyone" are not singular terms, "someone enjoys running" and "everyone enjoys running" do not translate in an analogous way—that is, as:

s: someone Ls
e: everyone Le
L: enjoys running

We need to introduce some new resources into the logical language. In particular, we need symbols for universal and existential quantifiers—ways of saying "for all" and "there is an"—and as we shall see, to make these symbols work properly, we need something else as well: variables. Let's see how this works.

Consider the case of the universal quantifier first. Suppose that we wish to translate the following into MPL:

Everything is green.

We can rephrase this as follows:

Every thing is such that it is green.

In MPL, *individual variables*—or just "variables" for short—play the role played here by "thing" and "it." Variables are represented by lowercased letters from the end of the alphabet: u, v, w, x, y, z. So we obtain a partial translation into MPL as follows:

Every x is such that x is green.

Now using the glossary:

G: is green

this expression becomes:

Every x is such that Gx.

Now we just need a symbol in MPL that means "every x is such that." The symbol we use is:

$$\forall x$$

Now our full translation is:

$$\forall x G x$$

Note that $\forall$ is an upside-down A (for "all"). As well as "every x is such that," we can also read $\forall x$ as "for all x," "no matter which x you pick," "whichever x you pick," or "whatever x you pick."

Consider next the existential quantifier. Suppose that we wish to translate the following into MPL:

Something is green.

We can rephrase it as follows:

Some thing is such that it is green.

Using the variable x in place of "thing" and "it," as before, we obtain a partial translation into MPL:

Some x is such that x is green.

Using the same glossary as before, this expression becomes:

Some x is such that Gx.

Now we just need a symbol in MPL that means "some x is such that." The symbol we use is:

$$\exists x$$

Now our full translation is:

$$\exists x Gx$$

Note that $\exists$ is a back-to-front E (for "exists"). As well as "some x is such that," we can also read $\exists x$ as "there is some x such that," "there exists an x such that," or "you can pick an x such that."[10]

8.3.1 Examples

Here is a glossary:

Gx: x is green
Rx: x is red
Hx: x is heavy
Ex: x is expensive

Note that, now that we have introduced variables, we adopt the practice of writing in a variable next to the predicate in the glossary (i.e., instead of writing "G: is green," we write "Gx: x is green").

Now we can make the following translations into MPL:

Something is both red and green.
$\exists x(Rx \wedge Gx)$

Everything is either red or green.
$\forall x(Rx \vee Gx)$

All red things are heavy.
$\forall x(Rx \rightarrow Hx)$

Note that the correct translation in the last case is not $\forall x(Rx \wedge Hx)$. That expression states that everything is both red and heavy, whereas the original English states only that red things are heavy. One useful way to read the universal quantifier $\forall x$ is as "take anything at all" or "pick anything at all." On this reading, $\forall x(Rx \rightarrow Hx)$ states "take anything at all: if it is red, then it is heavy." That is another way of saying that all red things are heavy. In contrast, $\forall x(Rx \wedge Hx)$ states "take anything at all: it is red and it is heavy." That is not the same as saying that all red things are heavy: it states that everything is both red and heavy.

Some red thing(s) are heavy.
(There is at least one thing that is red and heavy.)
$\exists x(Rx \wedge Hx)$

Something is red but not heavy.
$\exists x(Rx \wedge \neg Hx)$

Something is neither red nor heavy.
$\exists x(\neg Rx \wedge \neg Hx)$ or $\exists x \neg(Rx \vee Hx)$

Something is red and heavy.
$\exists x(Rx \wedge Hx)$

only if _____
conseq.

If something is red, then it's heavy.
$\forall x(Rx \rightarrow Hx)$

The last example is tricky! Despite the appearance of the word "something," this statement is in fact a universal claim. It states: take anything at all: if it is red, then it is heavy.

Nothing is red.
(It is not the case that even one thing is red.)
(Everything is non-red.)
$\neg \exists x Rx$ or $\forall x \neg Rx$ $\neg \exists x$

No red things are heavy.
$\forall x(Rx \rightarrow \neg Hx)$ or $\neg \exists x(Rx \wedge Hx)$

Something isn't red.
(It is not the case that everything is red.)
$\exists x \neg Rx$ or $\neg \forall x Rx$

Something is red and something is heavy.
$\exists x Rx \wedge \exists x Hx$

Note that the correct translation in the last case is not $\exists x(Rx \wedge Hx)$. For the latter to be true, there must be some thing that is both red and heavy: it claims that there is some thing such that it is red and heavy. But the original English does not require there to be at least one thing that is both red and heavy: it requires only that there is some thing that is red and that there is some (possibly different) thing that is heavy.

8.3.2 Exercises
Translate the following from English into MPL.

1. If Independence Hall is red, then something is red.

2. If everything is red, then Independence Hall is red.

3. Nothing is both green and red.

4. It is not true that nothing is both green and red.

5. Red things aren't green.

6. All red things are heavy or expensive.

7. All red things that are not heavy are expensive.

8. All red things are heavy, but some green things aren't.

9. All red things are heavy, but not all heavy things are red.

10. Some red things are heavy, and furthermore some green things are heavy too.

11. Some red things are not heavy, and some heavy things are not red.

12. If Kermit is green and red, then it is not true that nothing is both green and red.

13. Oscar's piano is heavy, but it is neither red nor expensive.

14. If Spondulix is heavy and expensive, and all expensive things are red and all heavy things are green, then Spondulix is red and green.[11]

15. If Kermit is heavy, then something is green and heavy.

16. If everything is fun, then nothing is worthwhile.

17. Some things are fun and some things are worthwhile, but nothing is both. *"if not"*

18. Nothing is probable unless something is certain.

19. Some things are probable and some aren't, but nothing is certain.

20. If something is certain, then it's probable.

8.3.3 Restricted Quantification
Consider the claim "every person is special." The correct way to translate it is:

Sx: x is special $\forall x (Px \rightarrow Sx)$
Px: x is a person

Note that here the qualification or restriction on the quantification—that we are talking about all persons, not about everything whatsoever—comes in the form of a predicate Px, which is placed inside the scope of the quantifier.[12] In the case of an existential quantification—for example, "some people are special"—we similarly obtain:

$$\exists x(Px \wedge Sx)$$

(Recall that "all Ps are Ss" is translated with a conditional, whereas "some Ps are Ss" is translated with a conjunction.)

Sometimes we use such terms as "everyone" and "someone" (as opposed to "everything" and "something"). (i) "Everyone is special" states that every person is special (not that everything is special), and (ii) "someone is tall" says that some person is tall—so we translate these claims as follows:

Tx: x is tall   (i) $\forall x(Px \rightarrow Sx)$
Px: x is a person
Sx: x is special   (ii) $\exists x(Px \wedge Tx)$

§

Sometimes the information conveyed by utterances involving "everyone" and "someone" is more restricted, that is, restricted not only to persons but also to some particular group of persons. For example, suppose that a tour guide says to a group of people assembled in a hotel lobby, "everyone is ready—let's begin." Suppose also that an exam monitor says to a group of people sitting in a room, "everyone is ready—let's begin." Focus on the first part of what each says: "everyone is ready." The guide will typically be taken to be conveying the information that all persons who are on the tour are ready—not that all persons whatsoever (wherever in the world they may be) are ready. And the monitor will typically be taken to be conveying the information that all persons who are candidates for the exam are ready—not that all persons whatsoever (wherever in the world they may be) are ready. There are two ways to approach these cases.

According to the *pragmatic approach,* the proposition expressed by an utterance of "everyone is ready" is always the same: it is the proposition that all persons whatsoever are ready. The restricted claims—that everyone on the tour is ready, that all candidates are ready—are not what is said by the guide or the monitor: these claims are implicatures. To see how this story works, imagine that the proposition expressed by the guide is indeed that every person in the entire world is ready—and suppose also that she is conforming to the conversational maxims (§6.1): in particular, the Maxims of Quality. It will then follow that she is trying to make her contribution true. But it is obviously false (and obvious that she knows that it is false) that absolutely everyone in the whole world is ready—so we shall infer that the information she is actually trying to contribute is that some restricted set of persons is ready—say, the set of persons on the tour.[13] A similar story works for the monitor.[14]

According to the *semantic approach*, the proposition expressed by "everyone is ready" varies from context to context. Uttered by the tour guide, this sentence expresses the proposition that everyone on the tour is ready; uttered by the exam monitor, it expresses the proposition that every candidate for the exam is ready; and so on.

Following the pragmatic approach and applying the glossary:

Px: x is a person
Rx: x is ready

we translate both the tour guide's claim "everyone is ready" and the monitor's claim "everyone is ready" as $\forall x(Px \rightarrow Rx)$. On this approach, both speakers say the same thing—they express the same proposition (that all persons whatsoever are ready). However, because of their differing contexts, their claims have different implicatures (the guide's claim has the implicature that all persons on the tour are ready, the invigilator's that all persons who are taking the exam are ready). Following the semantic approach and applying the glossary:

Px: x is a person
Rx: x is ready
Tx: x is on the tour
Cx: x is a candidate for the exam

we translate the tour guide's claim "everyone is ready" as:

$$\forall x((Px \wedge Tx) \rightarrow Rx)$$

and the monitor's claim "everyone is ready" as:

$$\forall x((Px \wedge Cx) \rightarrow Rx)$$

On this approach, the two speakers express different propositions (using the same sentence).

The debate between pragmatic and semantic approaches to restricted quantification is an ongoing one. In this book, we take the pragmatic approach, largely because it makes translations from English into our logical language more straightforward, which is useful as we are getting the hang of the logical apparatus. Note, however, that the logical apparatus itself is perfectly compatible with both approaches. Regardless of whether you think that the proposition expressed by the tour guide is $\forall x(Px \rightarrow Rx)$ or $\forall x((Px \wedge Tx) \rightarrow Rx)$, both propositions can be represented perfectly well in MPL.

Note that if the tour guide says explicitly "everyone who is part of the tour is ready," we shall translate this as $\forall x((Px \land Tx) \rightarrow Rx)$. But if the tour guide says simply "everyone is ready," we translate this as $\forall x(Px \rightarrow Rx)$. That is, we add predicates to our translations to restrict the quantifiers only when expressions corresponding to these predicates are explicitly uttered in the English that we are translating.[15]

The issues we have been discussing do not affect just "everyone"—they also affect plain old "everything." For example, if a shopkeeper says "everything has been reduced," he will typically be taken to be conveying the information that every piece of merchandise in the shop has been reduced (not that absolutely everything in existence has been reduced—nor even that everything in the shop, including the sales assistants and the shoppers, has been reduced). In accordance with the pragmatic approach, using the glossary:

Rx: x has been reduced

we translate the shopkeeper's claim as $\forall x\, Rx$. That is, we take it that the proposition expressed by the shopkeeper is that absolutely everything has been reduced. We take the restricted claim—that every item of merchandise in the store has been reduced—to be an implicature, not what is said; hence it does not show up in the translation into MPL, which represents the proposition expressed. In contrast, following the semantic approach and applying the glossary:

Mx: x is an item of merchandise
Sx: x is in the shop
Rx: x has been reduced

the translation would be $\forall x((Mx \land Sx) \rightarrow Rx)$. In this book, however—where we adopt the pragmatic approach—we only give the latter translation when each of its constituents corresponds to some expression in the English claim that we are translating. Thus, we take this MPL expression to be the translation of "every piece of merchandise in the store has been reduced," whereas we take the translation of plain old "everything has been reduced" to be simply $\forall x\, Rx$.

8.3.4 Only; Necessary and Sufficient Conditions

Given the glossary:

Hx: x is a horse
Gx: x gallops

how do we translate "only horses gallop" into MPL? Recall that "all horses gallop" is translated as $\forall x(Hx \rightarrow Gx)$. That is, for anything whatsoever, if it is a horse, then it gallops. Similarly, "only horses gallop" states that for anything whatsoever, it gallops only if it is a horse. Remembering that "α only if β" is translated as $(\alpha \rightarrow \beta)$, we can see that "only horses gallop" will therefore be translated as $\forall x(Gx \rightarrow Hx)$. Now if we look at the latter wff, we see that it is also the translation of "all galloping things are horses." So "only horses gallop" and "all galloping things are horses" state the same thing. That may seem odd at first, but when we think about it, it is exactly right: if only horses gallop, then nothing but horses gallop—that is, everything that gallops is a horse; and conversely, if all galloping things are horses, then no nonhorse gallops—that is, only horses gallop.

What about "all and only horses gallop?" This states that all horses gallop and only horses gallop, so it translates as:

$$\forall x(Hx \rightarrow Gx) \wedge \forall x(Gx \rightarrow Hx)$$

We can also translate it as $\forall x(Hx \leftrightarrow Gx)$, that is, for anything whatsoever, it is a horse if and only if it gallops. In Chapter 10 we will be in a position to show that these two translations are logically equivalent.

What about the phrase "only some," as in "only some smokers get cancer?" Well, the claim here is that some smokers get cancer and some do not—in other words, some smokers get cancer, but not all of them do. So we translate as follows:

Sx: x is a smoker $\exists x(Sx \wedge Cx) \wedge \exists x(Sx \wedge \neg Cx)$ or
Cx: x gets cancer $\exists x(Sx \wedge Cx) \wedge \neg\forall x(Sx \rightarrow Cx)$

"P is a sufficient condition for Q" means that having the property P is enough for something to have the property Q; that is, if something is P, then it is Q. So we regard this statement as meaning the same thing as "all Ps are Qs," and we translate it as $\forall x(Px \rightarrow Qx)$. For example, "weighing more than a ton is sufficient for being heavy" says the same as "anything that weighs more than a ton is heavy." "P is a necessary condition for Q" means that something cannot possess the property Q if it does not possess the property P—in other words, something possesses the property Q only if it possesses the property P. So we regard this statement as meaning the same thing as "all Qs are Ps," and we translate it as $\forall x(Qx \rightarrow Px)$. For example, "weighing more than a pound is necessary for being heavy" says the same as "only things that weigh more than a pound are heavy" and as "anything that is heavy weighs more than a pound." Thus, "P is a necessary and sufficient condition for Q" says the same thing as "all Ps and only Ps are Qs," and translates as $\forall x(Px \rightarrow Qx) \wedge \forall x(Qx \rightarrow Px)$, or equivalently $\forall x(Px \leftrightarrow Qx)$.

8.3.5 *Exercises*

Translate the following propositions from English into MPL.

1. Everyone is happy.

2. Someone is sad.

3. No one is both happy and sad.

4. If someone is sad, then not everyone is happy.

5. No one who isn't happy is laughing.

6. If Gary is laughing, then someone is happy.

7. Whoever is laughing is happy.

8. Everyone is laughing if Gary is.

9. Someone is sad, but not everyone and not Gary.

10. Gary isn't happy unless everyone is sad.

11. All leaves are brown and the sky is gray.

12. Some but not all leaves are brown.

13. Only leaves are brown.

14. Only brown leaves can stay.

15. Everyone is in trouble unless Gary is happy.

16. Everyone who works at this company is in trouble unless Gary is happy.

17. If Stephanie is telling the truth, then someone is lying.

18. If no one is lying, then Stephanie is telling the truth.

19. Either Stephanie is lying, or no-one's telling the truth and everyone is in trouble.

20. If Gary is lying, then not everyone in this room is telling the truth.

8.4 Syntax of MPL

Having introduced the language of propositional logic in a relatively casual way earlier in Chapter 2, in §2.5 we gave a precise and compact account of the syntax of PL. Here we do the same for MPL.

1. The symbols of MPL are:

   (i) names:

   $a, b, c, \ldots, t$

   We use lowercased letters other than $u, v, w, x, y,$ and z, which are reserved for variables (see below). If we need more than twenty different name symbols, we use subscripts (i.e., $a_2, a_3, \ldots, b_2, b_3, \ldots$).

   (ii) variables:

   x, y, z, u, v, w

If we need more than six different variable symbols, we use subscripts (i.e., $x_2, x_3, \ldots, y_2, y_3, \ldots$).

(iii) predicates:

$A, B, C, \ldots X, Y, Z$

If we need more than twenty-six different predicate symbols, we use subscripts (i.e., $A_2, A_3, \ldots, B_2, B_3, \ldots$).

(iv) five connectives:

$\neg, \wedge, \vee, \rightarrow$, and $\leftrightarrow$

(v) two quantifier symbols:

$\forall$ and $\exists$

(vi) two punctuation symbols (parentheses):

(and)

Recall the distinction between logical and nonlogical vocabulary (§2.5.2). In the case of MPL, the logical symbols are the connectives, the quantifier symbols, and the variables; the nonlogical symbols are the names and predicates; and the parentheses are auxiliary symbols.

2. We define the notion of a *term* of MPL as follows:

  (i) A name is a term.

  (ii) A variable is a term.

  (iii) Nothing else is a term.

At this stage, then, the word "term" simply gives us a quick way of talking about names and/or variables.[16]

3. Wffs of MPL are defined as follows:[17]

  (i) Where $\underline{P}$ is a predicate and $\underline{t}$ is a term, the following is a wff:

$\underline{Pt}$

That is, a predicate followed by one name or variable is a wff. Wffs of this form are atomic wffs.

  (ii) Where α and β are wffs and $\underline{x}$ is a variable, the following are wffs:

$\neg \alpha$
$(\alpha \wedge \beta)$
$(\alpha \vee \beta)$
$(\alpha \rightarrow \beta)$
$(\alpha \leftrightarrow \beta)$
$\forall \underline{x} \alpha$
$\exists \underline{x} \alpha$

  (iii) Nothing else is a wff.

8.4.1 Terminology

We call the simple symbols ∀ and ∃ *quantifier symbols,* and reserve the term "quantifier" for complex symbols consisting of a quantifier symbol followed by a variable. So the following are quantifiers:

$$\forall x, \exists x, \forall y, \exists y, \ldots$$

It will be useful to have a single term that covers both connectives and quantifiers. We use *logical operator* (or sometimes just *operator*) for this purpose. So a logical operator is a connective or a quantifier.

8.4.2 Syntactic Variables

Wff variables (§2.4) allow us to make general statements about all wffs in a compact, clear way. Sometimes we need something that relates to specific symbols of a syntactic category other than wffs—for example names, predicates, or variables—in the way that a wff variable relates to specific wffs. Let us use *syntactic variable* as a general term here: so wff variables, name variables, predicate variables, and so on will all be called "syntactic variables." It is often useful to think of them as placeholders—boxes into which a specific item of syntax of the relevant sort (i.e., a wff, a name, or a predicate, as the case may be) may be put.

The recursive definition of a wff of MPL in §8.4 makes use of wff variables α and β. It also makes use of variables for predicates, terms, and variables. I have used underlining to represent these. So $\underline{P}$ is a predicate variable—a box into which any predicate may be put; and $\underline{t}$ is a term variable—a box into which any term (i.e., any name or predicate) may be put. Clause (3i) states that if we take any predicate of the language and place it before any term of the language (i.e., any name or variable), the result is a wff—for example, Pa, Px, Rb, or Gy. Likewise, $\underline{x}$ is a variable variable: a box into which any variable may be put. Clauses (3ii∀) and (3ii∃)[18] state that if we take any wff and stick on the front of it ∀ or ∃ followed by any variable, the result is a wff. For example:

- $\forall x\, Rx$
  Here the wff Rx takes the place of the wff placeholder α in clause (3ii∀), and the variable x takes the place of the variable placeholder $\underline{x}$.

- $\forall y\, Px$
  Here the wff Px takes the place of the wff placeholder α in clause (3ii∀), and the variable y takes the place of the variable placeholder $\underline{x}$.

- $\exists x((Pa \rightarrow Rb) \wedge Sx)$
  Here the wff $((Pa \rightarrow Rb) \wedge Sx)$ takes the place of the wff placeholder α in clause (3ii∃), and the variable x takes the place of the variable placeholder $\underline{x}$.

- $\forall y \exists x (Rx \land Py)$

  Here the wff $\exists x(Rx \land Py)$ takes the place of the wff placeholder α in clause (3ii∀), and the variable y takes the place of the variable placeholder $\underline{x}$.

In general in this book, I use the following typographical devices to indicate syntactic variables:

- Greek letters: variables for wffs, and

- underlining: variables for items of the same syntactic category as the underlined symbol.

So an item of vocabulary (a variable, a name, a predicate, etc.) with a line under it is a placeholder for any item of vocabulary of that sort (any variable, any name, any predicate, etc.) Think of the line as (the bottom of) a box, and the symbol above the line as telling you what sort of thing may go in the box: namely, something of the same syntactic category as that object above the line. So $\underline{a}$ is a syntactic variable for names: a box into which any name may be put. Likewise, $\underline{y}$ is a syntactic variable for variables: a box into which any variable may be put, and so on. The rules for filling these placeholders are the same as for wff variables (recall §5.2): where you see the same box twice, it must be filled with the same thing both times. So acceptable instances of $\underline{P}\underline{a} \to \underline{Q}\underline{a}$ include, for example, $Pa \to Qa$, $Pb \to Qb$, and $Rb \to Rb$—but not $Pa \to Qb$. For the rules for forming instances are that $\underline{P}$ must be filled with any predicate, that $\underline{Q}$ must be filled with any predicate, that $\underline{a}$ must be filled with any name, and that both occurrences of the placeholder $\underline{a}$ must be filled with the same name.[19]

8.4.3 Constructing Wffs

If a given string of symbols is a wff, it must be constructible in accordance with the recursive definition of §8.4. Sometimes it can be useful to trace through the construction of a wff. For example, consider the wff $\exists x(Fx \to Ga)$:

Step	Wff constructed at this step	From steps/by clause
1	Fx	/ (3i)
2	Ga	/ (3i)
3	$(Fx \to Ga)$	1, 2 / (3ii→)
4	$\exists x(Fx \to Ga)$	3 / (3ii∃)

Note that at each step of the construction of our target wff, we have something that is itself a wff. We call these wffs (including the last one, i.e., the target wff itself) the "subformulas" of the target wff.

Each nonatomic wff has a *main* operator. This is the one added last in the construction. So in our example above, the main operator is the existential quantifier ∃x.

Consider a second example: (∃x Fx → Ga):

Step	Wff constructed at this step	From steps/by clause
1	Fx	/ (3i)
2	Ga	/ (3i)
3	∃x Fx	1 / (3ii∃)
4	(∃x Fx → Ga)	2, 3 / (3ii→)

The main operator here is the →.

8.4.3.1 EXERCISES

Write out a construction for each of the following wffs, and state the main operator.

1. ∀x(Fx → Gx)

2. ∀x¬Gx

3. ¬∃x(Fx ∧ Gx)

4. (Fa ∧ ¬∃x¬Fx)

5. ∀x(Fx ∧ ∃y(Gx → Gy))

6. (∀x(Fx → Gx) ∧ Fa)

7. ((¬Fa ∧ ¬Fb) → ∀x¬Fx)

8. ∀x∀y((Fx ∧ Fy) → Gx)

9. ∀x(Fx → ∀yFy)

10. (∀x Fx → ∀yFy)

8.4.4 Quantifier Scope; Free and Bound Variables

We say that x is the variable *in* the quantifier ∀x, that y is the variable *in* the quantifier ∃y, and so on. Conversely, we say that the quantifier ∀x *contains* the variable x, that the quantifier ∃y *contains* the variable y, and so on.

If a wff has a quantifier in it, then it must have got there—in accordance with clause (3ii∀) or (3ii∃)—by being placed in front of some subformula α at some stage in the construction of the wff. For any quantifier appearing in a wff, we call this subformula α (i.e., the one to which the quantifier was prefixed during construction of the wff) the *scope* of the quantifier. So in our first example in the previous section, the scope of the quantifier ∃x is the wff (Fx → Ga). In our second example, the scope of the quantifier ∃x is the wff Fx.

Suppose a variable occurs somewhere in a wff. That occurrence of the variable is *bound* in that wff if (i) it is in a quantifier or (ii) it is in the scope of a quantifier that contains the same variable. An occurrence of a variable that is not bound in a wff is *free* in that wff. So, for example:

- The variable x is free in Rx.

- Both occurrences of x are bound in $\forall x\, Rx$.

- The variable x is free in $\forall y\, Rx$ (because although x is within the scope of the quantifier $\forall y$, that quantifier contains the variable y, not x).

- Both occurrences of x are bound in $(\forall x\, Rx \rightarrow Qa)$.

- All three occurrences of x are bound in $\forall x (Rx \rightarrow Qx)$.

- The first two occurrences of x are bound and the third is free in $(\forall x\, Rx \rightarrow Qx)$.[20]

Note that a variable can occur within the scope of more than one quantifier containing that variable. For example, in the wff $\forall x(Px \rightarrow \exists x\, Qx)$, the occurrence of x in Qx is within the scopes of both $\forall x$ and $\exists x$. Nevertheless, we do not say that this occurrence of x is bound "twice." Rather, for every bound occurrence of a variable $\underline{x}$ in a wff, we pick out exactly one quantifier in the wff that binds it: it is the quantifier $\forall \underline{x}$ or $\exists \underline{x}$, in whose scope the occurrence of $\underline{x}$ in question falls, that is added first in the construction of the wff. So in the above wff, the occurrence of x in Qx is bound by the quantifier $\exists x$, not by $\forall x$. Note carefully: the occurrence of x in Qx is indeed in the scope of $\forall x$, but it is not bound by that quantifier—because it is already bound (i.e., already in the process of constructing the wff) by the quantifier $\exists x$.

An occurrence of a quantifier $\forall \underline{x}$ or $\exists \underline{x}$ in a wff is *vacuous* if the variable $\underline{x}$ (i.e., the one in the quantifier) does not occur free in the scope of the quantifier (in that wff). For example, the quantifier $\forall x$ is vacuous in each of the following wffs, because in each case its scope does not contain any free occurrences of x:

- $\forall x\, Fa$

- $\forall x\, Fy$

- $\forall x \exists x\, Fx$ (Here the scope of $\forall x$ is $\exists x\, Fx$, which contains no free occurrences of x.)

For further discussion of vacuous quantifiers, see §10.1.7.

8.4.5 Open and Closed Wffs; Propositions

A wff with no free occurrences of variables is a *closed* wff. A wff with one (or more) free occurrences of variable(s) is an *open* wff.[21] Our syntax counts open and closed wffs as equally well formed. But note that open wffs are not propositions in the sense of things that can be true or false. Given the glossary:

Rx: x is red

the open formula *Rx* translates into English as "it is red." This does not express a proposition: it cannot be said to be true, or false, because "it" does not pick out anything in particular. Remember that "it" here is a variable, not a singular term. If I point to a billiard ball and say "it is red," then I do express a proposition. But in this case, "it" is a singular term, not a variable, and my statement translates into MPL as *Rb*, using the glossary:

b: that ball/the ball to which I pointed

This is quite different from the case in which "it" is the English translation of the free variable *x*: in this case "it" does not pick out some particular thing, and "it is red" cannot be said to be true or false.

The fact that open formulas are not propositions will be reflected in our semantics for MPL, to be introduced in the next chapter. The semantics will make precise the notion of a "way of making propositions true or false," and it will assign truth values only to each closed wff in each such scenario.

We could, if we wished, complicate our definition of the syntax of MPL in such a way as to make only closed formulas come out as well formed. However, as long as we remember that not every wff is a proposition (something that can be said to be true or false), it is simpler to do things the way we have here.

8.4.5.1 EXERCISES
Identify any free variables in the following formulas. State whether each formula is open or closed.

1. $Tx \land Fx$

2. $Tx \land Ty$

3. $\exists x Tx \land \exists x Fx$

4. $\exists x Tx \land \forall y Fx$

5. $\exists x Tx \land Fx$

6. $\exists x (Tx \land Fx)$

7. $\forall y \exists x Ty$

8. $\exists x (\forall x Tx \to \exists y Fx)$

9. $\exists y \forall x Tx \to \exists y Fx$

10. $\forall x (\exists x Tx \land Fx)$

11. $\forall x \exists x Tx \land Fx$

12. $\exists x Ty$

13. $\forall x Tx \to \exists x Fx$

14. $\exists x \forall y (Tx \lor Fy)$

15. $\forall x Fx \land Gx$

16. $\forall x \forall y Fx \to Gy$

17. $\forall x \forall y (Fx \to \forall x Gy)$

18. $\exists y Gb \land Gc$

19. $\exists y Gy \land \forall x (Fx \to Gy)$

20. $\forall x ((Fx \to \exists x Gx) \land Gx)$

9

Semantics of Monadic Predicate Logic

In this chapter we turn to the task of developing a semantics for our new language MPL. As mentioned at the beginning of Chapter 8, what our semantics needs to do is (i) give a precise account of what a "possible way of making propositions true or false" is, and (ii) tell us how the truth value of each proposition of MPL is determined in each such scenario. Once these tasks are done, we can then formulate precise accounts of our key logical notions, such as validity (in every possible scenario in which the premises are true, the conclusion is true) and equivalence (having the same truth value in every possible scenario).

At this point it will be useful to introduce some new terms. Propositions have truth values. Other expressions in a logical language—in particular, names and predicates—do not have truth values, but there are (as we shall see) entities that (roughly speaking) play the role for them that truth values play for propositions. It is useful to have an umbrella term for all these entities. We use the term "value" for this purpose. So the value of a proposition is its truth value; the value of a name—which is its *referent*—is what the name contributes to the determination of the truth value of a proposition in which it features; and the value of a predicate—which is its *extension*—is what the predicate contributes to the determination of the truth value of a proposition in which it features. We explain these concepts properly below—for now we are just introducing terms: "value" (a general term applying to different kinds of expressions), "referent" (the value of a name), and "extension" (the value of a predicate). (We already have the term "truth value" for the value of a proposition.)

We can now state the general principle governing all our systems of semantics—for propositional logic and for predicate logic. The guiding idea is that the values of nonlogical symbols are *unconstrained:* for any distribution of values to nonlogical expressions of the language, there is a possible scenario in which these expressions have those values. Propositions then have their truth values determined by the values of their nonlogical components, together with the laws of truth that govern their logical components.

In the case of PL, the nonlogical symbols are the basic propositions (represented in PL by capital letters), and the logical symbols are the connectives. A scenario is represented as a truth table row: an assignment of truth values to basic propositions. These assignments are completely unconstrained: for each basic proposition, there is a possible scenario in which it is true and a possible scenario in which it is false; furthermore, for any collection of basic propositions, any combination of assignments of truth values to these propositions is possible. Given an assignment of truth values to basic propositions, the truth value of each compound proposition is then determined via the truth tables for the connectives.

As discussed in §8.1, sets of such propositions as:

Maisie is a kelpie.
All kelpies are dogs.
Maisie is a dog.

pose a problem for the PL framework. Translated into PL, these propositions come out as simple nonlogical expressions, and so their truth values are unconstrained. Any assignment of truth values to them is possible. In particular, there is a possible scenario in which the first two are true and the third is false. Intuitively, that's not right: it seems clear that if the first two are true, the third cannot be false.

Now that we have enriched our logical language, a solution to this problem is within reach. Translated into MPL, these three propositions are no longer simple nonlogical expressions: each one is a wff made up of names, predicates, variables, and/or quantifiers. So there is now a possibility that although the assignment of values to nonlogical expressions (names and predicates) is unconstrained, nevertheless the laws of truth governing the logical expressions (and governing the truth of atomic wffs)—which determine the truth values of propositions given values for their nonlogical components—might rule out the possibility that "Maisie is a kelpie" and "all kelpies are dogs" are both true while "Maisie is a dog" is false. In fact, this is exactly what will happen.

So what we need to investigate are the following issues:

- What are the values of the nonlogical symbols of MPL? (A possible scenario will then simply be any assignment of values to nonlogical expressions.)

- What are the rules that determine the truth values of propositions of MPL on the basis of the values of their nonlogical components? (That is, how are the truth values of propositions of MPL determined in each possible scenario?)

Some of what we learned about propositional logic will carry over unchanged. For example, the way in which the truth value of a proposition whose main operator is one of our five connectives is determined by the truth values of its components will be just the same as before. Some of what we learn will be new. For example, we need to learn what the values of names and predicates are, and we need to see how the truth value of a proposition whose main operator is a quantifier is determined in a scenario.

9.1 Models; Truth and Falsity of Uncomplicated Propositions

Consider an atomic proposition, say, Pa. As just discussed, we no longer wish to view its truth value as simply given (i.e., a brute fact) in each possible scenario. Rather, now that atomic propositions are not represented by simple symbols (as they were in PL), we want their truth values to be determined by the values of their components: the name (in this case a) and the predicate (P). So what must the values of a and P be, in order that together, they determine a truth value for the atomic proposition Pa?

The answer flows straightforwardly from our discussion of atomic propositions in §8.2. An atomic proposition has two parts: a name and a predicate. The function of the name is to pick out a particular object. The function of the predicate is to single out a certain property. The atomic proposition is true if the object picked out by the name has the property singled out by the predicate; it is false if the object picked out by the name does not have the property singled out by the predicate.

So, we shall take the value of a name to be an object: this choice falls straight out of the story just told. As for predicates, the move that follows directly from the story just told is to take the value of a predicate to be a property. However, for reasons explained in §16.1.1, it is more convenient to work with sets than with properties. But we can easily rephrase the above story: instead of saying that Pa is true if the object picked out by a has the property picked out by P, we can say that Pa is true if the object picked out by a is a member of the set of objects that have the property picked out by P. We can now take the value of a predicate to be a set. Intuitively, it is the set of objects possessing the property that the predicate picks out; but all mention of properties is now confined to this intuitive gloss—the value of the predicate itself is simply a set of objects.

So the value of a name (e.g., a) is an object, and the value of a predicate (e.g., P) is a set of objects. As mentioned at the beginning of this chapter, we call the value of a name its "referent," and the value of a predicate its "extension." We now need to specify how these values determine a truth value for an atomic proposition (Pa). The answer is simple. The proposition Pa is true if the referent of the name a is a member of the extension of the predicate P (intuitive gloss: if the object picked out by the name is a member of the

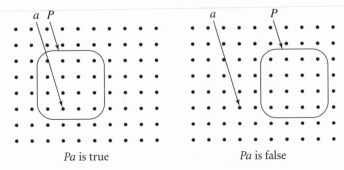

Figure 9.1. Truth and falsity of an atomic proposition Pa.

set of objects possessing the property singled out by the predicate). It is false if the referent of the name is not a member of the extension of the predicate (intuitive gloss: if the object picked out by the name is not a member of the set of objects possessing the property singled out by the predicate). Figure 9.1 represents these ideas in visual form. Objects are shown as dots. The arrow from the name a shows its referent: an object. The arrow from the predicate P shows its extension: a set of objects (represented as a ring drawn around the objects in the set). Proposition Pa is true if the referent of a is in the extension of P; it is false if the referent of a is not in the extension of P.

We now have an account of what the values of names and predicates are—objects, and sets of objects, respectively—which has the desired feature that the value of the name and the predicate in an atomic proposition together determine a truth value for that proposition.

§

Let's turn now to quantified propositions. The least complicated kind of proposition involving a (nonvacuous) universal quantifier is one of the form $\forall x\, Px$. Obviously, what it takes for $\forall x\, Px$ to be true is for everything to be in the extension of the predicate $\underline{P}$. But what is covered by "everything" here? Recall that we deem something a logical truth if it is true in every possible scenario—and when it comes to counting something as a possible scenario, we cast the net widely. In propositional logic, we take any assignment of truth values to basic propositions to constitute a possible scenario. Similarly, in predicate logic, we want to allow any assignment of referents to names and of extensions to predicates to count as a possible scenario (more on this below). In a similar vein, it seems that we should countenance all possibilities regarding what "everything" covers. It should not be sufficient to deem $\forall x\, Px$ logically true if it merely comes out true no matter what extension $\underline{P}$ is assigned: it should also be true no matter what "everything" covers. Thus, if logical truth is to be truth for all scenarios, a scenario needs to specify not just a referent for each name and an extension for each predicate but also what counts as "everything." We can make this idea more precise as follows. A scenario—or *model*, as we shall call it—comprises three things:[1]

1. A set of objects. This set of objects is the *domain* of the model. (Intuitively, the set specifies what counts as "everything" according to the model: "everything" covers all objects in the domain.)

2. A specification of a referent for each name.

3. A specification of an extension for each predicate.

Now that we have domains in the picture, we place a requirement on the specifications of referents and extensions: in a given model, the referent of each name must be an object in the domain of the model, and the extension of each predicate must be a subset of the domain of the model.[2] That is, an object cannot be the referent of a name in a model unless it is in the domain of the model, and an object cannot be in the extension of a predicate in a model unless it is in the domain of the model.

Let's return now to our least complicated kind of universally quantified proposition: $\forall x\, Px$. We can now say that it is true on a given model just in case the extension of P on that model includes the entire domain of the model: that is, just in case everything (according to that model) is in the extension of P (on that model). Similarly, the least complicated kind of proposition involving a (nonvacuous) existential quantifier is one of the form $\exists x\, Px$. It is true on a given model just in case the extension of P on that model includes at least one thing (from the domain of the model): that is, just in case something (according to that model) is in the extension of P (on that model).

§

A model comprises an assignment of values to names and predicates together with a domain of objects from which these values must be drawn (the value of a name must be a member of the domain; the value of a predicate must be a set of members of the domain). In keeping with the guiding idea set out at the beginning of this chapter, we regard any assignment of values to names and predicates as a possible scenario. That is, there are no constraints on the values of nonlogical symbols: for any name and any object you care to imagine, we countenance a model in which that name has that object as its referent; and for any predicate and any set of objects you care to imagine, we countenance a model in which that predicate has that set of objects as its extension.[3] However, there is one restriction on models: the domain must be a *nonempty* set—that is, it must contain at least one object. For we want each name to have a value in each model—after all, a model (a possible scenario) is just a free assignment of values to nonlogical symbols—and this value must be a member of the domain. So in all cases, the domain had better have at least one object in it.[4]

Note that the extension of a predicate may be the empty set: that is, the set—denoted ∅—that has no members. As explained in §16.1, the empty set is a perfectly good set: it is simply one with nothing in it. So a predicate assigned the empty set as its extension does have a value (i.e., its extension, the empty set): the point is simply that there are no objects in its extension. But why should we want to countenance predicates that apply to nothing? Well, if you think about it, such predicates are not all that strange. For example, consider the predicate "is 20 billion years old." It picks out a property that, plausibly, nothing possesses.[5]

We have said that a model assigns a referent to each name and an extension to each predicate. We now need to be a bit more precise. The full language MPL contains all those wffs that may be constructed in accordance with the clauses given in §8.4 from the symbols given in that section. Among those symbols there are infinitely many names and infinitely many predicates (recall the use of subscripts: $a_2, a_3, \ldots, b_2, b_3, \ldots$ and $P_2, P_3, \ldots, Q_2, Q_3, \ldots$). Suppose we restrict ourselves to a (possibly empty) subset of names and a (nonempty) subset of predicates, but we retain all the logical vocabulary of MPL. We may then construct wffs from this restricted base of symbols, using the same clauses as before. The result is a *fragment* of MPL.[6] We shall allow models of fragments—models that assign a referent to each name and an extension to each predicate in that fragment.[7]

Note the reason for requiring that a fragment contain at least one predicate, even though it may contain no names. A fragment containing just one predicate P, but no names, will include some propositions (i.e., closed wffs)—for example, $\forall x P x$. In contrast, a fragment containing no predicates will contain no wffs at all.[8]

Note also that when translating into MPL, we use a fragment of the full language: the one containing just those names and predicates featured in our glossary.[9] Note that as a matter of terminology, the full language MPL is counted as a fragment of itself (cf. the way that a wff is counted as a subformula of itself).

§

We now summarize. A *model* of a fragment of MPL consists of:

1. a domain (a set of objects);

2. a specification of a referent (an object) for each name in the fragment; and

3. a specification of an extension (a set of objects) for each predicate in the fragment.

The following properties are required:

- The domain must be nonempty.

- Every name and predicate in the fragment must be assigned a referent/extension.

- The referent of a name in a model must be an object in the domain of that model.

- An object can be in the extension of a predicate in a model only if it is in the domain of that model.

The following properties are allowed (but not required):

- The extension of a predicate may be the empty set.

- The extension of a predicate may be the entire domain.

- Different names may be assigned the same object as referent.

- Different predicates may be assigned the same set of objects as extension.

§

Suppose that we have a model $\mathfrak{M}$ of the fragment of MPL containing just the name a and the predicate P. Propositions of MPL that are not in this fragment are assigned no truth value in $\mathfrak{M}$. For example, Pb and Ra—which are propositions of the full language MPL but are not in this fragment— have no truth value assigned in $\mathfrak{M}$ (because the truth value of an atomic proposition in a model is True if the referent of the name is in the extension of the predicate and False if the referent is not in the extension; if there is no referent, or no extension, then the proposition is neither true nor false). This does not mean that we are abandoning bivalence (Chapter 3). On the contrary, it means that when we are dealing with a certain fragment of MPL, we are interested only in models of that fragment, and we ignore all models that do not assign referents/extensions to some names/predicates in the fragment. We may say, for the sake of simplicity, that (e.g.) a proposition α is logically true iff it is true on "all models," but what we really mean is: true on all models of any fragment of MPL that includes the proposition α—that is, true on all models that assign values to all nonlogical symbols occurring in α.

We have already seen how a model determines the truth value of an atomic proposition: $\underline{Pa}$ is true in a model $\mathfrak{M}$ iff the referent of $\underline{a}$ in that model is in the extension of $\underline{P}$ in that model. Note that we are talking here about atomic propositions—that is, closed atomic wffs. Formula Px is an atomic wff— but it is not a closed wff, for it contains the free variable x. So (§8.4.5) it is not a proposition: it is not something that can be said to be true or false.

Hence, a model does not determine a truth value for it: a model that assigns an extension to P does not determine a truth value for Px. The reason is that the variable x is not assigned a value. That is just the way things should be: the point of the distinction between variables and singular terms is that a singular term picks out a particular individual, whereas a variable does not. In a particular model, P gets an extension—but x does not get a referent (or any other value), and so Px is not assigend a truth value.[10]

9.1.1 Exercises

For each of the propositions:

  (i) Pa (ii) $\exists x\, Px$ (iii) $\forall x\, Px$

state whether it is true or false on each of the following models.

1. Domain: $\{1, 2, 3, \ldots\}$ [11]
   Referent of a: 1
   Extension of P: $\{1, 3, 5, \ldots\}$ [12]

2. Domain: $\{1, 2, 3, \ldots\}$
   Referent of a: 1
   Extension of P: $\{2, 4, 6, \ldots\}$ [13]

3. Domain: $\{1, 2, 3, \ldots\}$
   Referent of a: 2
   Extension of P: $\{1, 3, 5, \ldots\}$

4. Domain: $\{1, 2, 3, \ldots\}$
   Referent of a: 2
   Extension of P: $\{2, 4, 6, \ldots\}$

5. Domain: $\{1, 2, 3, \ldots\}$
   Referent of a: 1
   Extension of P: $\{1, 2, 3, \ldots\}$

6. Domain: $\{1, 2, 3, \ldots\}$
   Referent of a: 2
   Extension of P: $\varnothing$

9.2 Connectives

We said that some of what we learned about the semantics of propositional logic will carry over unchanged to the semantics of predicate logic—and that in particular, the way in which the truth value of a proposition whose main operator is one of our five connectives is determined by the truth values of its components will be just the same as before. Consider the truth table for negation:

α	$\neg\alpha$
T	F
F	T

We can now interpret this as follows. The first row tells us that in any model in which α is true, $\neg\alpha$ is false. The second row tells us that in any model in which α is false, $\neg\alpha$ is true. In other words, a formula $\neg\alpha$ is true in a model just in case its negand α is false in that model.

The same holds for the other truth tables, for example, the one for conjunction:

α	β	$(\alpha \wedge \beta)$
T	T	T
T	F	F
F	T	F
F	F	F

The first row tells us that in any model in which α and β are both true, $(\alpha \wedge \beta)$ is true. The second row tells us that in any model in which α is true and β is false, $(\alpha \wedge \beta)$ is false; and so on. (Note that all possibilities are covered: in any model that assigns values to α and β, either α and β are both true, or α is true and β is false, or α is false and β is true—row 3—or α and β are both false—row 4.) In other words, a formula $(\alpha \wedge \beta)$ is true in a model just in case both its conjuncts are true in that model.

In sum, where α and β are any propositions:

- $\neg\alpha$ is true in a model iff α is false in that model.

- $(\alpha \wedge \beta)$ is true in a model iff α and β are both true in that model.

- $(\alpha \vee \beta)$ is true in a model iff one or both of α and β is true in that model.

- $(\alpha \rightarrow \beta)$ is true in a model iff α is false in that model or β is true in that model (or both).

- $(\alpha \leftrightarrow \beta)$ is true in a model iff α and β are both true or both false in that model.

9.2.1 Exercises

State whether each of the following propositions is true or false in each of the six models given in Exercises 9.1.1.

(i) $(\neg Pa \wedge \neg Pa)$ (iv) $(\exists x Px \vee \neg Pa)$

(ii) $(\neg Pa \rightarrow Pa)$ (v) $\neg(\forall x Px \wedge \neg \exists x Px)$

(iii) $(Pa \leftrightarrow \exists x Px)$

9.3 Quantified Propositions: The General Case

Given a model, we know how to determine whether the simplest kinds of quantified propositions—those of the form $\forall \underline{x} P\underline{x}$ or $\exists \underline{x} P\underline{x}$—are true or false in that model. For example, consider the following model:

Domain: {Bill, Ben, Alice, Mary}
Extension of P: {Bill, Ben, Alice, Mary}

In this model, $\forall x\,Px$ is true (because everything in the model is indeed in the extension of P), and $\exists x\,Px$ is true too. In the following model:

Domain: {Bill, Ben, Alice, Mary}
Extension of P: {Bill, Ben, Alice}

$\forall x\,Px$ is false (not everything in the model is in the extension of P), but $\exists x\,Px$ is true (there is at least one thing in the domain of the model that is in the extension of P). In the following model:

Domain: {Bill, Ben, Alice, Mary}
Extension of P: $\emptyset$

$\forall x\,Px$ is false (not everything in the model is in the extension of P—indeed, nothing is), and $\exists x\,Px$ is false too (there is not even one thing in the domain of the model that is in the extension of P).

So far so good, but we also need to know how the truth values of more complex propositions whose main operator is a quantifier are determined. Consider, for example:

$\forall x(Px \rightarrow Rx)$
$\exists x(Px \wedge Rx)$
$\forall x(Px \leftrightarrow (Rx \vee Gx))$

Nothing we have said so far tells us how the truth values of these propositions are determined (relative to a given model).

Our strategy will be to trade in the question of the truth value of a quantified proposition in one given model for the question of the truth values of a non-quantified proposition in many models.[14] That may sound like a bad trade-off, but as we shall see, it is not, because we already know how the truth values of nonquantified propositions are determined. So we trade in one question we do not know how to answer for many questions we do know how to answer. Or, to put it more accurately, we derive an answer to the first question from the answers that we already have to the latter questions. Let us see how this is done.

First we define some new terminology. We have used Greek letters (α, β, ...) as wff variables. Where $\underline{x}$ is a variable, we shall use $\alpha(\underline{x})$ to stand for an arbitrary wff that has no free variables other than $\underline{x}$. Note that $\alpha(\underline{x})$ may have no free variables at all: the point is simply that it has no free variables other than $\underline{x}$. Then, where $\underline{a}$ is a name, we shall use $\alpha(\underline{a}/\underline{x})$ to stand for the wff that results from $\alpha(\underline{x})$ by replacing all free occurrences of $\underline{x}$ in $\alpha(\underline{x})$ with $\underline{a}$. So, for example, consider the wff $(Fx \vee Gx)$. It contains no free variables other than x, so we can represent it as $\alpha(x)$. Then $\alpha(a/x)$ is $(Fa \vee Ga)$ and $\alpha(b/x)$ is $(Fb \vee Gb)$.

9.3.1 Exercises

1. If $\alpha(x)$ is $(Fx \land Ga)$,
   what is
   (i) $\alpha(a/x)$
   (ii) $\alpha(b/x)$

2. If $\alpha(x)$ is $\forall y(Fx \to Gy)$,
   what is
   (i) $\alpha(a/x)$
   (ii) $\alpha(b/x)$

3. If $\alpha(x)$ is $\forall x(Fx \to Gx) \land Fx$,
   what is
   (i) $\alpha(a/x)$
   (ii) $\alpha(b/x)$

4. If $\alpha(x)$ is $\forall x(Fx \land Ga)$,
   what is
   (i) $\alpha(a/x)$
   (ii) $\alpha(b/x)$

5. If $\alpha(y)$ is $\exists x(Gx \to Gy)$,
   what is
   (i) $\alpha(a/y)$
   (ii) $\alpha(b/y)$

6. If $\alpha(x)$ is $\exists y(\forall x(Fx \to Fy) \lor Fx)$,
   what is
   (i) $\alpha(a/x)$
   (ii) $\alpha(b/x)$

Now we continue with the question of how the truth values of quantified propositions are determined. We are concerned to assign truth values only to propositions—that is, to closed wffs. Any proposition whose main operator is a quantifier must be of one of the following forms, where $\underline{x}$ is a variable:

$$\forall \underline{x}\alpha(\underline{x})$$
$$\exists \underline{x}\alpha(\underline{x})$$

That is, the scope of the quantifier must not contain any free variables other than the variable appearing in the quantifier itself—otherwise, placing the quantifier before this scope would not yield a closed wff. So, we want to know what the truth values of $\forall \underline{x}\alpha(\underline{x})$ and $\exists \underline{x}\alpha(\underline{x})$ are in some model $\mathfrak{M}$. What we do is introduce a new name $\underline{d}$—that is, one that is not assigned a referent on $\mathfrak{M}$. Then the truth values of $\forall \underline{x}\alpha(\underline{x})$ and $\exists \underline{x}\alpha(\underline{x})$ in $\mathfrak{M}$ are determined by the truth values of $\alpha(\underline{d}/\underline{x})$ on all those models exactly like $\mathfrak{M}$ except that they also assign a referent to $\underline{d}$. Specifically, $\forall \underline{x}\alpha(\underline{x})$ is true in $\mathfrak{M}$ if $\alpha(\underline{d}/\underline{x})$ is true in all these models, and $\exists \underline{x}\alpha(\underline{x})$ is true in $\mathfrak{M}$ if $\alpha(\underline{d}/\underline{x})$ is true in at least one of these models.

There is quite a lot of detail here, but the basic idea is intuitive. Consider the universal claim "everything is F." Now suppose we introduce a new name— say, "The Dude"—which does not yet refer to anyone. If the universal claim is true, then it must be that whoever we decide to call "The Dude," "The Dude is F" comes out true. For if there is even one thing in our domain that is not F, then we could make "The Dude is F" false by calling that thing "The Dude." Similarly, for "something is F" to be true, it must be that there is at least one thing such that if we called it "The Dude," then "The Dude is F"

would come out true. This is the essential idea behind our account of how the truth conditions of quantified claims are determined.

§

Let's work through some concrete examples to get the feel of this account. We start with a simple example—one that we already know how to handle—to illustrate the workings of our new account and see that it gives the right result in this simple case. Consider the proposition $\forall x\, Px$, and suppose we want to know whether it is true or false in the following model $\mathfrak{M}$:

> Domain: {Alice, Ben, Carol}
> Extension of P: {Alice}

What we do first is introduce a new name (i.e., a name to which $\mathfrak{M}$ does not assign any referent). In this case, $\mathfrak{M}$ assigns referents to no names—so we can use whatever name we please. Let's use a. Now we strip off the quantifier in $\forall x\, Px$, leaving Px, and then replace all free occurrences of x in this wff by a, yielding Pa. (What we are doing here is moving from $\forall x \alpha(x)$—where $\alpha(x)$ is Px in this particular case—to $\alpha(a/x)$, where a is a new name that is not assigned a referent in $\mathfrak{M}$.) We then consider whether this proposition Pa is true or false in each model that is just like $\mathfrak{M}$ except that it also assigns a referent to a. Each of these models must have the same domain as $\mathfrak{M}$ and must assign the same extensions to predicates as $\mathfrak{M}$ does. Now the referent of a name in a model can only be an object in the domain of that model. So the only possible referents of a we need to consider are the objects in the domain of $\mathfrak{M}$. Thus, there will be one such model for each object in the domain of $\mathfrak{M}$: one that is just like $\mathfrak{M}$ but assigns a *this* object in the domain, another that is just like $\mathfrak{M}$ but assigns a *that* object in the domain, and so on for all the objects in $\mathfrak{M}$'s domain. In the present case there are three objects in the domain of $\mathfrak{M}$: Alice, Ben, and Carol. So we need to consider the following three models:

$\mathfrak{M}_1$:
Domain: {Alice, Ben, Carol}
Extension of P: {Alice}
Referent of a: Alice

$\mathfrak{M}_2$:
Domain: {Alice, Ben, Carol}
Extension of P: {Alice}
Referent of a: Ben

$\mathfrak{M}_3$:
Domain: {Alice, Ben, Carol}
Extension of P: {Alice}
Referent of a: Carol

Note that they all have the same domain as $\mathfrak{M}$ and assign the same extension to P; they differ only by the referent of the new name a.

Now we ask whether our formula Pa is true or false in each of these models. Pa is true in $\mathfrak{M}_1$: the referent of a in that model is in the extension of P in that model. It is false in $\mathfrak{M}_2$: the referent of a is not in the extension of P in that model. And it is false in $\mathfrak{M}_3$. So our target formula $\forall x\, Px$ is false in our target model $\mathfrak{M}$: for it to be true, Pa would have to be true in all of $\mathfrak{M}_1$ through $\mathfrak{M}_3$.

§

Let's consider another example. We want to know whether $\exists x (Px \wedge Rx)$ is true or false in the following model $\mathfrak{M}$:

Domain: $\{1, 2, 3, 4, 5\}$
Extension of P: $\{2, 4\}$
Extension of R: $\{1, 2, 3\}$

So we introduce a new name—a will do in this case. We then strip off the initial quantifier and replace the subsequent free xs with this new name a, yielding $(Pa \wedge Ra)$. Now we ask whether this proposition is true or false in each model just like $\mathfrak{M}$ except that it assigns the new name a a referent. There are five objects in the domain of $\mathfrak{M}$ and so five models to consider:

$\mathfrak{M}_1$:
Domain: $\{1, 2, 3, 4, 5\}$
Extension of P: $\{2, 4\}$
Extension of R: $\{1, 2, 3\}$
Referent of a: 1

$\mathfrak{M}_2$:
Domain: $\{1, 2, 3, 4, 5\}$
Extension of P: $\{2, 4\}$
Extension of R: $\{1, 2, 3\}$
Referent of a: 2

$\mathfrak{M}_3$:
Domain: $\{1, 2, 3, 4, 5\}$
Extension of P: $\{2, 4\}$
Extension of R: $\{1, 2, 3\}$
Referent of a: 3

$\mathfrak{M}_4$:
Domain: $\{1, 2, 3, 4, 5\}$
Extension of P: $\{2, 4\}$
Extension of R: $\{1, 2, 3\}$
Referent of a: 4

$\mathfrak{M}_5$:
Domain: $\{1, 2, 3, 4, 5\}$
Extension of P: $\{2, 4\}$
Extension of R: $\{1, 2, 3\}$
Referent of a: 5

The sentence we are considering—$(Pa \wedge Ra)$—is a conjunction, so it is true in a model just in case both conjuncts are true in that model. In $\mathfrak{M}_1$ the referent of a is not in the extension of P, so the first conjunct Pa is false, and thus, the whole conjunction $(Pa \wedge Ra)$ is false. In $\mathfrak{M}_2$ the referent of a is in the extension of P, so the first conjunct Pa is true, and the referent of a is in the extension of R, so the second conjunct Ra is true, and thus, the whole conjunction $(Pa \land Ra)$ is true. Now all it takes for $\exists x(Px \land Rx)$ to be true in $\mathfrak{M}$ is for $(Pa \land Ra)$ to be true in even one model that is just like $\mathfrak{M}$ except that it assigns a referent to the new name a—so the fact that $(Pa \land Ra)$ is true in $\mathfrak{M}_2$ means that our target wff $\exists x(Px \land Rx)$ is true in our target model $\mathfrak{M}$. Put in more intuitive terms, it is true in $\mathfrak{M}$ that something is both P and R, because there is at least one object in the domain—in particular, 2—such that if the new name "The Dude" referred to that object (note that a refers to 2 in $\mathfrak{M}_2$), then "The Dude is both P and R" would be true.

§

Let's consider a third example. We want to know whether $(\forall x(Px \rightarrow Rx) \land Ra)$ is true or false in the following model $\mathfrak{M}$:

Domain: $\{1, 2, 3\}$
Extension of P: $\{1, 2\}$
Extension of R: $\{1\}$
Referent of a: 1

Our target wff is a conjunction, so it will be true in this model just in case both its conjuncts are true. Ra is true (because the referent of a is in the extension of R), so this leaves the other conjunct to consider: $\forall x(Px \rightarrow Rx)$. We strip off the quantifier, leaving $(Px \rightarrow Rx)$. We need to replace the free xs here with a new name: one that has not been assigned a referent in our target model. In this case a is already in use—so we take b as our new name, yielding $(Pb \rightarrow Rb)$. Now we need to ask whether the latter formula is true in each of the following models:

$\mathfrak{M}_1$:
Domain: $\{1, 2, 3\}$
Extension of P: $\{1, 2\}$
Extension of R: $\{1\}$
Referent of a: 1
Referent of b: 1

$\mathfrak{M}_2$:
Domain: $\{1, 2, 3\}$
Extension of P: $\{1, 2\}$
Extension of R: $\{1\}$
Referent of a: 1
Referent of b: 2

$\mathfrak{M}_3$:
Domain: $\{1, 2, 3\}$
Extension of P: $\{1, 2\}$
Extension of R: $\{1\}$
Referent of a: 1
Referent of b: 3

Note that each of these models is just the same as $\mathfrak{M}$ except that it assigns the new name b a referent, so each of them assigns the same extensions to P and R as $\mathfrak{M}$ does, and the same referent to the name a. They differ only by the referents they assign to the new name b. Now $(Pb \rightarrow Rb)$ is false in a model just in case Pb is true and Rb false. In $\mathfrak{M}_2$, Pb is true and Rb false, so $(Pb \to Rb)$ is false. That means our wff $\forall x(Px \to Rx)$ is false in our target model $\mathfrak{M}$: for it to be true in $\mathfrak{M}$, $(Pb \to Rb)$ has to be true in every model that differs from $\mathfrak{M}$ only in assigning a referent to b. So the first conjunct of our original wff $(\forall x(Px \to Rx) \land Ra)$ is false in $\mathfrak{M}$; hence this wff itself is false in $\mathfrak{M}$.[15]

9.3.2 Understanding Models

A key point about models is that a model specifies relations between symbols of the logical language and objects in the domain: it does not specify relations between symbols of the logical language and symbols of another language (say, English). People sometimes get confused over this point, because when presenting a model, we often describe it by something like:

Domain: {Alice, Ben, Carol}
Extension of F: {Alice, Carol}
Referent of b: Ben

Here we use the English names "Alice," "Ben," and "Carol" to specify the domain, and we use the English name "Ben" to specify the referent of b in this model. But this does not mean that the model consists (partly) of a relation between the two names b and "Ben." What the model (partly) consists of is a relation between the name b and the object Ben: the man Ben himself, not his English name "Ben." In general, the only practical way to describe a model is to say in English (or some other language) what the domain contains and what the referents of names and extensions of predicates are—but the model itself comprises a domain of objects (not their names),[16] together with relations between names and predicates of the logical language and objects and sets of objects in the domain. Thus, in the present example, the idea is that the domain contains three persons—the ones we happen to know by the names "Alice," "Ben," and "Carol"—not that it contains three names. The referent of b is then one of these persons (Bob)—not his name ("Bob").

As an analogy, consider the following. When you want a dog to fetch something—say, a newspaper—you typically point to the thing.[17] You do not go and touch or pick up the newspaper—if you were prepared to do that, you would not need to ask the dog to fetch it. The dog misunderstands if he then licks your finger: you wanted him to fetch the newspaper; holding your finger out and pointing was just a way of getting him to notice the newspaper. Those who think that, because models are typically presented in English, they give relations between symbols of the logical language and symbols of English, misunderstand in the same way. The English words used in describing the model are meant to pick out certain objects and sets: the model consists (partly) in relations between names and predicates of the logical language and these objects and sets of objects, not in relations between names and predicates of the logical language and the words of English we use to pick out these objects and sets.

9.4 Semantics of MPL: Summary

There are two steps to describing the semantics of a language:

1. Specify what constitutes a possible scenario (a possible way of making propositions true or false). (In general, it will be a free assignment of values to nonlogical symbols.)

2. Specify the rules that determine a truth value for each proposition (closed wff) in each scenario.

In the case of MPL, the two steps are as follows.

9.4.1 Step 1: Defining Models

A model of a fragment of MPL consists of:

1. a domain (a nonempty set of objects);

2. a specification of a referent (an object in the domain) for each name in the fragment; and

3. a specification of an extension (a subset of the domain) for each predicate in the fragment.

9.4.2 Step 2: Specifying How Truth Values Are Determined

There are eight types of closed wff (recall §8.4): atomic formulas, formulas whose main operator is one of the five connectives, and formulas whose main operator is one of the two quantifiers. So we have eight rules telling us how the truth values of closed wffs are determined relative to a given model—one rule for each type of wff:

1. $\underline{Pa}$ is true in $\mathfrak{M}$ iff the referent of $\underline{a}$ in $\mathfrak{M}$ is in the extension of $\underline{P}$ in $\mathfrak{M}$.

2. $\neg\alpha$ is true in $\mathfrak{M}$ iff α is false in $\mathfrak{M}$.

3. $(\alpha \wedge \beta)$ is true in $\mathfrak{M}$ iff α and β are both true in $\mathfrak{M}$.

4. $(\alpha \vee \beta)$ is true in $\mathfrak{M}$ iff one or both of α and β is true in $\mathfrak{M}$.

5. $(\alpha \rightarrow \beta)$ is true in $\mathfrak{M}$ iff α is false in $\mathfrak{M}$ or β is true in $\mathfrak{M}$ (or both).

6. $(\alpha \leftrightarrow \beta)$ is true in $\mathfrak{M}$ iff α and β are both true in $\mathfrak{M}$ or both false in $\mathfrak{M}$.

7. $\forall \underline{x} \alpha(\underline{x})$ is true in $\mathfrak{M}$ iff for every object o in the domain of $\mathfrak{M}$, $\alpha(\underline{a}/\underline{x})$ is true in $\mathfrak{M}_o^a$, where $\underline{a}$ is some name that is not assigned a referent in $\mathfrak{M}$, and $\mathfrak{M}_o^a$ is a model just like $\mathfrak{M}$ except that in it the name $\underline{a}$ is assigned the referent o.

8. $\exists \underline{x} \alpha(\underline{x})$ is true in $\mathfrak{M}$ iff there is at least one object o in the domain of $\mathfrak{M}$ such that $\alpha(\underline{a}/\underline{x})$ is true in $\mathfrak{M}_o^a$, where $\underline{a}$ is some name that is not assigned a referent in $\mathfrak{M}$, and $\mathfrak{M}_o^a$ is a model just like $\mathfrak{M}$ except that in it the name $\underline{a}$ is assigned the referent o.

9.4.3 Exercises

1. Here is a model:
   Domain: $\{1, 2, 3, 4\}$
   Extensions: $E: \{2, 4\}$ $O: \{1, 3\}$
   State whether each of the following propositions is true or false in this model.

   (i) $\forall x Ex$
   (ii) $\forall x (Ex \lor Ox)$
   (iii) $\exists x Ex$

   (iv) $\exists x (Ex \land Ox)$
   (v) $\forall x (\neg Ex \rightarrow Ox)$
   (vi) $\forall x Ex \lor \exists x \neg Ex$

2. State whether the given proposition is true or false in the given models.
   (i) $\forall x (Px \lor Rx)$
      (a) Domain: $\{1, 2, 3, 4, 5, 6, 7, 8, 9, 10\}$
          Extensions: $P: \{1, 2, 3\}$ $R: \{5, 6, 7, 8, 9, 10\}$
      (b) Domain: $\{1, 2, 3, 4, 5, 6, 7, 8, 9, 10\}$
          Extensions: $P: \{1, 2, 3, 4\}$ $R: \{4, 5, 6, 7, 8, 9, 10\}$
   (ii) $\exists x (\neg Px \leftrightarrow (Qx \land \neg Rx))$
      (a) Domain: $\{1, 2, 3, \ldots\}$
          Extensions: $P: \{2, 4, 6, \ldots\}$ $Q: \{1, 3, 5, \ldots\}$
                      $R: \{2, 4, 6, \ldots\}$
      (b) Domain: $\{1, 2, 3, \ldots\}$
          Extensions: $P: \{2, 4, 6, \ldots\}$ $Q: \{2, 4, 6, \ldots\}$
                      $R: \{1, 3, 5, \ldots\}$
   (iii) $\exists x Px \land Ra$
      (a) Domain: $\{1, 2, 3, \ldots\}$
          Referent of a: 7
          Extensions: $P: \{2, 3, 5, 7, 11, \ldots\}^{18}$ $R: \{1, 3, 5, \ldots\}$
      (b) Domain: $\{$Alice, Ben, Carol, Dave$\}$
          Referent of a: Alice
          Extensions: $P: \{$Alice, Ben$\}$ $R: \{$Carol, Dave$\}$

3. Here is a model:

   Domain: {Bill, Ben, Alison, Rachel}

   Referents: a: Alison r: Rachel

   Extensions: M: {Bill, Ben} F: {Alison, Rachel} J: {Bill, Alison}

   $\quad\quad\quad\quad\quad S$: {Ben, Rachel}

   State whether each of the following propositions is true or false in this model.

   (i) $(Ma \wedge Fr) \rightarrow \exists x(Mx \wedge Fx)$

   (ii) $\forall x \forall y(Mx \rightarrow My)$

   (iii) $(\neg Ma \vee \neg Jr) \rightarrow \exists x \exists y(Mx \wedge Fy)$

   (iv) $\forall x Mx \rightarrow \forall x Jx$

   (v) $\exists x \exists y(Mx \wedge Fy \wedge Sr)$

   (vi) $\exists x(Fx \wedge Sx) \rightarrow \forall x(Fx \rightarrow Sx)$

4. For each of the following propositions, describe (a) a model in which it is true, and (b) a model in which it is false. If there is no model of one of these types, explain why.

(i) $\forall x(Fx \rightarrow Gx)$	(xi) $\exists x Fx \rightarrow \exists x Gx$
(ii) $\forall x Fx \wedge \neg Fa$	(xii) $\exists x Fx \rightarrow \forall x Gx$
(iii) $\exists x Fx \wedge \neg Fa$	(xiii) $\forall x Fx \rightarrow Fa$
(iv) $\exists x(Fx \wedge Gx)$	(xiv) $\forall x(Fx \rightarrow Fa)$
(v) $\forall x(Fx \rightarrow Fx)$	(xv) $Fa \rightarrow Fb$
(vi) $\exists x Fx \wedge \exists x Gx$	(xvi) $\forall x(Fx \vee Gx)$
(vii) $\forall x Fx \rightarrow \exists x Fx$	(xvii) $\exists x(Fx \vee Gx)$
(viii) $\exists x(Fx \wedge \neg Fx)$	(xviii) $\forall x(Fx \wedge \neg Fx)$
(ix) $\exists x Fx \wedge \exists x \neg Fx$	(xix) $\forall x \exists y(Fx \rightarrow Gy)$
(x) $\exists x(Fx \rightarrow Fx)$	(xx) $\forall x(Fx \rightarrow \exists y Gy)$

5. (i) Is $\forall x(Fx \rightarrow Gx)$ true or false in a model in which the extension of F is the empty set?

   (ii) Is $\exists x(Fx \wedge Gx)$ true in every model in which $\forall x(Fx \rightarrow Gx)$ is true?

9.5 Analyses and Methods

We are now in a position to give precise definitions, in the context of predicate logic, of our key logical notions, such as satisfiability, validity, and equivalence. The definitions are exactly what one would expect, given that a model now plays the role that a truth table row played in propositional logic; that is, it represents a possible scenario, a possible way of making propositions true or false.

Concepts relating to arguments. An argument is valid iff there is no model in which the premises are true and the conclusion false. Equivalently, an argument is valid iff in every model (of the fragment of the language used to state the argument)[19] in which the premises are all true, the conclusion is true too. An argument is invalid iff there is a model in which the premises are all true and the conclusion false. Such a model is a *countermodel* (or counterexample) to the argument.

Concepts relating to single propositions. A proposition is a logical truth (aka logically true) iff there is no model in which it is false; or equivalently, iff it is true in every model (of the fragment of the language used to state the proposition).[20] A proposition is a logical falsehood (aka logically false, a contradiction) iff there is no model in which it is true; or equivalently, iff it is false in every model (of the fragment of the language used to state the proposition). A proposition is satisfiable iff there is at least one model in which it is true.

Concepts relating to pairs of propositions. Two propositions are equivalent iff there is no model in which one is true and the other false; or equivalently, iff they have the same truth value in every model (of the fragment of the language used to state the propositions). Two propositions are contradictory iff there is no model in which they have the same truth value; or equivalently, iff they have opposite truth values in every model (of the fragment of the language used to state the propositions). Two propositions are jointly satisfiable iff there is at least one model on which they are both true.

Concepts relating to sets of propositions. A set of propositions is satisfiable iff there is at least one model in which all propositions in the set are true.

In §1.4 we introduced the intuitive notion of validity and said that we want both a precise analysis of this notion and a method for determining whether a given argument is valid. Now recall the situation with regard to propositional logic. Truth tables kill two birds with one stone. They give us a precise analysis of validity (for arguments of PL): an argument is valid just in case there is no row of its truth table in which the premises are true and the conclusion false. Truth tables also constitute a method for determining validity (for any argument of PL): we write out the truth table for the argument and then check through the table line by line to see whether there is any row in which the premises are true and the conclusion false. (In practice the truth table may be too big for this method to be feasible—but in principle, the method is always available.) The situation is very different in predicate logic (as foreshadowed at the beginning of Chapter 7). We now have a precise analysis of validity: an argument is valid iff there is no model in which the premises are true and the conclusion false. Assuming that there is a fixed set of facts concerning what sets of objects exist (see §16.1.4), this analysis then fixes the facts about validity. However, it gives us no method for ascertaining these facts. Given any model and any closed wff (of MPL), our recursive specification in §9.4.2 of the truth conditions of closed wffs relative to a model fixes a fact as to whether that wff is true in that model. We have said that any nonempty set of objects as domain, together with an assignment of a referent for each name and an extension for each predicate, constitutes a model. So assuming there is some fact concerning what sets of objects exist—that is, what sets are available as domains—there is then a determinate totality of all models. So there is then a fact, concerning any argument, as to whether or not it is valid, because (i) for each model, and each proposition in the argument, there is a fact as to whether the proposition is true or false on that model, and (ii) there is a determinate totality of models. Thus, there is a fact as to whether there is any model in which the premises are true and the conclusion false.[21] But how can we ascertain whether a given argument is valid? Well, as yet we have no systematic way of finding out. Certainly, our analysis of validity does not yield any such method. First, there are infinitely many models; second, some of them have infinite domains. So, unlike in the propositional case, there is no way—even in principle—that we can lay out all possible scenarios and survey them to see whether a given proposition is true in each one (i.e., a logical truth) or whether some proposition (the conclusion of some argument) is true in every model in which the premises are all true (i.e., whether the argument is valid), and so on.

This is not to say that we can never answer such questions. Sometimes we can: by thinking things through in a more or less intuitive way. We proceed in such an intuitive way in the remainder of this section, to get a better feel for our new analyses of the fundamental logical concepts. But we will, eventually, want a systematic method for answering questions of interest to us (whether an argument is valid, whether a proposition is a logical truth, and so on). We turn to the task of developing such a method in Chapter 10.

For now, however—in the absence of a systematic method—let us work in a more informal way. Consider, for example, whether the following proposition is satisfiable:

$$(\forall x Fx \land \neg Fa)$$

Suppose it is true. It is a conjunction, so that means both conjuncts must be true. Making the left conjunct true requires making the extension of F include everything in the domain. Making the right conjunct true requires making Fa false—which requires making a refer to something in the domain that is not in the extension of F. Clearly these two things cannot both happen. So no model makes this proposition true: therefore, it is not satisfiable (i.e., it is a contradiction).

Consider, for another example, whether the following propositions are equivalent:

$$\forall x \neg F x$$
$$\neg \exists x F x$$

Suppose the first proposition is true in some model $\mathfrak{M}$. Then $\neg F a$ is true in every model that is just like $\mathfrak{M}$ except that it assigns a referent to a.[22] Thus, $F a$ is false in every such model—that is, the referent of a lies outside the extension of F. The only way this can happen in every such model is if nothing in the domain of $\mathfrak{M}$ is in the extension of F. So the models in which $\forall x \neg F x$ is true are those in which the extension of F is empty. Now consider the second proposition. It is true in a model $\mathfrak{M}$ just in case $\exists x F x$ is false in $\mathfrak{M}$. That is the case if there isn't even one model that is just like $\mathfrak{M}$—except that it assigns a referent to a—in which $F a$ is true. That is, $F a$ is false in every such model: the referent of a lies outside the extension of F. The only way this can happen in every such model is if nothing in the domain of $\mathfrak{M}$ is in the extension of F. So the models in which $\neg \exists x F x$ is true are those in which the extension of F is empty. Thus, the models in which $\forall x \neg F x$ is true are exactly those models in which $\neg \exists x F x$ is true—so these propositions are equivalent.

For a third example, consider whether the following argument is valid:

$$\forall x (F x \rightarrow G x)$$
$$F a$$
$$\therefore G a$$

The truth of the first premise in a model $\mathfrak{M}$ requires that $(F b \rightarrow G b)$ is true in every model that is just like $\mathfrak{M}$ except that it assigns a referent to b. Now for $(F b \rightarrow G b)$ to be true in a model, it must not be the case that $F b$ is true (i.e., the referent of b is in the extension of F) and $G b$ is false (i.e., the referent of b is not in the extension of G). So for $(F b \rightarrow G b)$ to be true on every model that is just like $\mathfrak{M}$ except that it assigns a referent to b, it must be that nothing in the domain of $\mathfrak{M}$ is both in the extension of F and not in the extension of G. Turning to the second premise, for it to be true in a model $\mathfrak{M}$, the referent of a must be in the extension of F. Now suppose that both premises are true in some model $\mathfrak{M}$: the referent of a is in the extension of F, and nothing in the domain is both in the extension of F and not in the extension of G. Then of course the referent of a must be in the extension of G—and so the conclusion will be true. So the argument is valid.

As a final example, consider whether the following argument is valid:

$$\forall x (F x \rightarrow G x)$$
$$G a$$
$$\therefore F a$$

By similar reasoning to that used in the previous example, a model in which both premises are true is one in which nothing in the domain is both in the extension of F and not in the extension of G, and the referent of a is in the extension of G. It need not be the case, in such a model, that the referent of a is in the extension of F: so the conclusion need not be true. Thus the argument is not valid. Countermodels are easy to imagine, for example:

Domain: {Maisie, Rover, Oscar}
Extensions: F: {Rover} G: {Maisie, Rover}
Referent of a: Maisie

9.5.1 Exercises

For each of the following arguments, either produce a countermodel (thereby showing that the argument is invalid) or explain why there cannot be a countermodel (in which case the argument is valid).

1. $\exists x F x \wedge \exists x G x$
   $\therefore \exists x (F x \wedge G x)$

2. $\exists x (F x \wedge G x)$
   $\therefore \exists x F x \wedge \exists x G x$

3. $\forall x (F x \vee G x)$
   $\neg \forall x F x$
   $\therefore \forall x G x$

4. $\forall x (F x \rightarrow G x)$
   $\forall x (G x \rightarrow H x)$
   $\therefore \forall x (F x \rightarrow H x)$

5. $\forall x (F x \rightarrow G x)$
   $\forall x (G x \rightarrow H x)$
   $\therefore \forall x (H x \rightarrow F x)$

10

Trees for Monadic Predicate Logic

As discussed in §9.5, we now have precise analyses of the notions of satisfiability, logical truth, validity, and so on (for propositions of MPL, arguments composed of such propositions, and the like)—but we do not yet have a systematic method of finding out the answers to questions framed in terms of these concepts, such as "Is this argument valid?" or "Is this proposition a logical truth?" In this chapter we extend the system of tree proofs (Chapter 7) to give us such a method.

The basic idea behind the tree method is just the same as it was for propositional logic. We begin by writing down some propositions at the top of our tree. (Note that they must be propositions, i.e., closed wffs.) We then apply rules with (roughly speaking—more on this below) the following property: assuming what we have already written is true, what we write down next will be true too. (That is why we can write down only propositions: things that can indeed be said to be true.) The basic idea behind the tree method is then as follows:

> A tree tells us whether it is possible for the propositions written at the top of the tree all to be true together. If this is possible, then the tree presents a scenario in which these propositions are all true.

In the case of propositional logic, where scenarios—ways of making propositions true or false—are truth table rows, this idea amounts to the following:

> A tree takes us directly to the truth table rows we are interested in—ones in which the formulas at the top of the tree are all true—if any such exist: we read off such a row from an open path. If no such rows exist, then the tree demonstrates this by showing all paths as closed.

In the case of predicate logic, where scenarios are models, the idea amounts to the following:

> A tree takes us directly to the models we are interested in—ones in which the formulas at the top of the tree are all true—if any such exist: we read off such a

model from an open path. If no such models exist, then the tree demonstrates this by showing all paths as closed.

It follows that the ways in which we use trees will be just the same as in propositional logic. To test a formula for being a logical truth, we start with the negation of the formula; if all paths close, then the negated formula cannot be true, and so the original formula is a logical truth. To test an argument for validity, we start with the premises and the negation of the conclusion; if all paths close, then the premises and the negation of the conclusion cannot all be true—that is, the conclusion cannot be false while the premises are all true— and so the argument is valid; and so on (see §7.3.6 for a summary of all the ways to use trees to answer questions of interest).

10.1 Tree Rules

What will change now that we have moved from propositional to predicate logic are the tree rules—or rather, the existing rules remain the same, but we need to add some new rules as well. For recall that we need two rules for each operator (except in the case of negation): one to apply to wffs where this operator is the main operator and one to apply to wffs where this operator is negated (i.e., where our wff is of the form $\neg\alpha$, and the operator we are interested in is the main operator of the negand α). So we need four new rules: two each for our two new operators, the universal quantifier and the existential quantifier.

Before introducing the new rules, it will be helpful to recall the general rationale behind tree rules, enabling us to appreciate the point of the new rules for quantified propositions. Stated roughly, the rationale is: the rules prescribe propositions that must be true, given that what we have already written down is true. Now let us give a more precise statement. Suppose we are applying some rule at the bottom of a path p. (Think of the path as a sequence of propositions: the ones on the path.) If we are applying a nonbranching rule, which will extend p to p′ (by adding some proposition(s) to the end of the sequence), then the rule should have this property:

> If there is a model in which every proposition on p is true, then there is a model in which every proposition on p′ is true.

If we are applying a branching rule, which will create two paths q and r (both of which share a common trunk p and then diverge), then the rule should have this property:

> If there is a model in which every proposition on p is true, then either there is a model in which every proposition on q is true, or there is a model in which every proposition on r is true, or both.

It is precisely because our rules all have this nature that trees can work the way they do. We start our tree by writing some propositions at the top, and we suppose—for the sake of argument—that there is a model in which these propositions are all true. The tree will then tell us one of two things:

1. There is in fact no such model (all paths close).

2. There is such a model (and we can read off such a model from an open path).

Note that our propositional rules all have the character just outlined. Consider the rule for negated ∨:

$$\neg(\alpha \vee \beta) \;\checkmark$$
$$\neg\alpha$$
$$\neg\beta$$

Suppose there is a model in which ¬(α ∨ β) is true. Then by rule (2) of §9.4.2, (α ∨ β) is false in this model. Then by rule (4), α and β are both false in this model. So by rule (2) again, both ¬α and ¬β are true in this model. Thus, the new rule has the property we wanted. Think of the proposition ¬(α ∨ β) to which we apply the rule as lying on some path p. Applying the rule extends p to p′, by adding ¬α and ¬β to the path. Now if there is a model in which every proposition on p is true—and hence in particular in which ¬(α ∨ β) is true—then there is a model (the same one, in fact) in which every proposition on p′ is true. For p′ differs from p only by the addition of ¬α and ¬β, and we have just seen that if ¬(α ∨ β) is true on some model, then so are ¬α and ¬β.

Consider now the branching rule for unnegated ∨:

$$(\alpha \vee \beta) \;\checkmark$$

$$\alpha \qquad \beta$$

Suppose there is a model in which (α ∨ β) is true. Then by rule (4) of §9.4.2, either α or β or both are true in this model. Thus, the rule has the property we wanted. Think of the proposition (α ∨ β) to which we apply the rule as lying on some path p. Applying the rule creates two paths, q and r: q contains everything on p plus α at the end; r contains everything on p plus β at the end. Now if there is a model in which every proposition on p is true—and hence in particular in which (α ∨ β) is true—then there is a model (the same one, in fact) in which every proposition on q is true, or there is a model (the same one, in fact) in which every proposition on r is true, or both. This reasoning holds because q differs from p only by the addition of α, and r differs from p only by the addition of β, and we have just seen that if (α ∨ β) is true in some model, then either α or β or both are true on that model.

Similar sorts of reasoning establish that the other tree rules for the connectives also have the character outlined above (see Exercises 14.1.2.1). We turn now to the new rules for the quantifiers—bearing in mind that they are designed precisely to share this basic characteristic.[1]

10.1.1 Negated Existential Quantifier

The rule for the negated existential quantifier is:

$$\neg\exists\underline{x}\alpha(\underline{x}) \ \checkmark$$
$$\forall\underline{x}\neg\alpha(\underline{x})$$

Note that the scope of the existential quantifier here is not just any wff α: it is a wff $\alpha(\underline{x})$ that does not contain any free variables other than $\underline{x}$. Otherwise, placing the quantifier before this scope would not yield a closed wff—and our trees are designed to handle only closed wffs (i.e., propositions).

This rule has the desired property outlined above. For suppose $\neg\exists\underline{x}\alpha(\underline{x})$ is true in some model $\mathfrak{M}$. Then by rule (2) of §9.4.2, $\exists\underline{x}\alpha(\underline{x})$ is false in $\mathfrak{M}$. Then (by rule (8)), there is no model that is just like $\mathfrak{M}$ except that it also assigns a referent to $\underline{a}$—where $\underline{a}$ is some name to which $\mathfrak{M}$ assigns no referent—in which $\alpha(\underline{a}/\underline{x})$ is true. That is, $\alpha(\underline{a}/\underline{x})$ is false in every model just like $\mathfrak{M}$ except that it also assigns a referent to $\underline{a}$. So by rule (2), $\neg\alpha(\underline{a}/\underline{x})$ is true in every such model. But by rule (7), that is precisely what it takes for $\forall\underline{x}\neg\alpha(\underline{x})$ to be true in $\mathfrak{M}$. So if the input of our rule is true in some model, so is the output.

10.1.2 Negated Universal Quantifier

The rule for the negated universal quantifier is:

$$\neg\forall\underline{x}\alpha(\underline{x}) \ \checkmark$$
$$\exists\underline{x}\neg\alpha(\underline{x})$$

This rule has the desired property outlined above. For suppose $\neg\forall\underline{x}\alpha(\underline{x})$ is true in some model $\mathfrak{M}$. Then by rule (2) of §9.4.2, $\forall\underline{x}\alpha(\underline{x})$ is false in $\mathfrak{M}$. Then by rule (7), there is some model just like $\mathfrak{M}$ except that it also assigns a referent to $\underline{a}$—where $\underline{a}$ is some name to which $\mathfrak{M}$ assigns no referent—in which $\alpha(\underline{a}/\underline{x})$ is false. So by rule (2), $\neg\alpha(\underline{a}/\underline{x})$ is then true in this model. But by rule (8), that is precisely what it takes for $\exists\underline{x}\neg\alpha(\underline{x})$ to be true in $\mathfrak{M}$. So if the input of our rule is true in some model, so is the output.

10.1.3 Existential Quantifier

The rule for the (unnegated) existential quantifier is:

$$\exists\underline{x}\alpha(\underline{x}) \ \checkmark \ \underline{a}$$
$$\alpha(\underline{a}/\underline{x})$$

where $\underline{a}$ is some name that is new to the path; that is, at the time of applying the rule at the bottom of some path, the name $\underline{a}$ used in applying the rule must be one that has not yet appeared anywhere—inside any wff—on that path. Note that when applying the rule and checking off the existentially quantified formula $\exists \underline{x}\alpha(\underline{x})$, we write the name $\underline{a}$ that we have used in applying the rule next to the check mark.

Here are some example applications and misapplications of this rule:

- $\exists x\, Fx \quad \checkmark a$
  Fa

- $\exists x\, Fx \quad \checkmark b$
  Fb

- $\exists x(Fx \to Gx) \quad \checkmark a$
  $Fa \to Ga$

- $\exists x(Fx \to Gx) \quad \checkmark a$
  $Fa \to Gx$
  Wrong! All occurrences of x that become free after the initial quantifier $\exists x$ is stripped away must be replaced with a.

- $\exists x(Fx \to Gb) \quad \checkmark a$
  $Fa \to Gb$

- $\exists x(Fx \to Gb) \quad \checkmark b$
  $Fb \to Gb$
  Wrong! The name used must be new to the path.

This rule has our desired property. For suppose there is a model $\mathfrak{M}$ in which $\exists \underline{x}\alpha(\underline{x})$ is true. Then by rule (8) of §9.4.2, there is at least one object o in the domain of $\mathfrak{M}$ such that $\alpha(\underline{a}/\underline{x})$ is true in $\mathfrak{M}_o^a$, where $\underline{a}$ is some name not assigned a referent in $\mathfrak{M}$, and $\mathfrak{M}_o^a$ is a model that is just like $\mathfrak{M}$ except that in it the name $\underline{a}$ is assigned the referent o. So if there is a model $\mathfrak{M}$ in which $\exists \underline{x}\alpha(\underline{x})$ is true, then there is a (different) model $\mathfrak{M}_o^a$ (differing from $\mathfrak{M}$ only in that it assigns a referent to the new name $\underline{a}$) in which $\alpha(\underline{a}/\underline{x})$ is true. We now need only observe that $\exists \underline{x}\alpha(\underline{x})$ is also true in this new model $\mathfrak{M}_o^a$ (because if we introduce another new name $\underline{b}$ to which $\mathfrak{M}_o^a$ assigns no referent, then $\alpha(\underline{b}/\underline{x})$ will be true on the model that is just like $\mathfrak{M}_o^a$ except that it assigns o as the referent of $\underline{b}$). So if there is a model in which the input to our rule is true, then there is a model (a different one in this case) in which both this input and the output of the rule are true—and that is the desired property for a nonbranching rule.

Let's consider why the name used in applying this rule has to be new to the path. Suppose we have a tree that starts with:

$$Fa$$
$$\exists x\, Gx$$

Then the assumption is that there is a model in which a is F and something is G. If we misapply the rule for the existential quantifier as follows, using the name a, which is not new to the path:

$$Fa$$
$$\exists x\, Gx \;\checkmark\; a$$
$$Ga$$

then the assumption is now that there is a model in which a is F and a is G: that is, the very same object that is F (namely a) is also G. But that clearly does not follow: from the fact that a is F and something is G, it does not follow that anything is both F and G.

Here's another example illustrating the trouble we get into if we do not choose a new name when applying the rule for the existential quantifier. Suppose we want to know whether $(\exists x\, Fx \wedge \exists x\, \neg Fx)$ is satisfiable. Clearly it is: it is true, for example, in the following model:

Domain: $\{1, 2\}$
Extension of F: $\{1\}$

Now we begin our tree as follows:

$$(\exists x\, Fx \wedge \exists x\, \neg Fx) \;\checkmark$$
$$\exists x\, Fx \;\checkmark\; a$$
$$\exists x\, \neg Fx$$
$$Fa$$

So far so good. But if we now misapply the rule for the remaining existentially quantified proposition—using the name a, rather than a new name—we obtain:

$$(\exists x\, Fx \wedge \exists x\, \neg Fx) \;\checkmark$$
$$\exists x\, Fx \;\checkmark\; a$$
$$\exists x\, \neg Fx \;\checkmark\; a$$
$$Fa$$
$$\neg Fa$$
$$\times$$

This tree tells us that our target wff is not satisfiable (for all paths close). As we have seen, however, this result is wrong.

The general point is that when we apply the rule for the existential quantifier, we reason as follows: something is F—so let's be specific and give this thing (or one such thing) a name.[2] Now that is fine, as long as all we assume about the thing we name is that it is F. If the name we use is not a new one, however, then we are not assuming only this: we are also assuming whatever else we have already said using this name. That is why the name used must be new. That way, when we transition from saying "something is F" to "a is F"— on the grounds that if something is F, we can give one such thing a name, say a—we are assured that all we are assuming about a is that it is F.

Note that the name used in applying the rule for the existential quantifier must be new to the path on which one is applying the rule: it need not be new to the entire tree. So the following tree is fine:

$$(\exists x Fx \vee \exists x Gx) \ \checkmark$$

$$\exists x Fx \ \checkmark a \qquad \exists x Gx \ \checkmark a$$
$$Fa \qquad\qquad Ga$$

Here we use the name a in applying the rule for the existential quantifier to $\exists x\, Fx$ on the left path, and we use the same name a in applying the rule for the existential quantifier to $\exists x Gx$ on the right path. That is fine: suppose we construct the left path first; then at the time of doing the right path, the name a has already been used somewhere else in the tree—but it has not been used anywhere else on the path on which we are applying the rule. This is all that matters, because we read off a model from each open path: not from the tree as a whole. When we introduce the name a in applying the rule for $\exists x\, Fx$, we are assuming there is a model in which $\exists x\, Fx$ is true—so we give (one of) the thing(s) that is F a name, a. We cannot assume that anything is true of a in this model except that a is F—that is why a must be new to this path. It does not matter, however, if in another model—drawn from a different path—we suppose that Ga is true.

10.1.4 Universal Quantifier

The rule for the (unnegated) universal quantifier is:

$$\forall \underline{x}\alpha(\underline{x}) \ \backslash \ \underline{a}$$
$$\alpha(\underline{a}/\underline{x})$$

Here $\underline{a}$ can be any name at all: it does not have to be new to the path. Note that when applying this rule, we write a backslash, not a check mark—and we write the name used in applying the rule next to the backslash. We use a backslash rather than a check mark because we can apply this rule repeatedly to the same formula: once each for different names $\underline{a}$, $\underline{b}$, $\underline{c}$, ... Each time the rule is applied, we write the name used next to the backslash.

Here are some example applications and misapplications of this rule:

- $\forall x\, Fx \;\backslash a$
  Fa

- $\forall x\, Fx \;\backslash b$
  Fb

- $\forall x\, Fx \;\backslash a\; b$
  Fa
  Fb
  Here we make two applications of the rule to the same formula, first using a and then using b.

- $\forall x(Fx \rightarrow Gx) \;\backslash a$
  $Fa \rightarrow Ga$

- $\forall x(Fx \rightarrow Gb) \;\backslash a$
  $Fa \rightarrow Gb$

- $\forall x(Fx \rightarrow Gb) \;\backslash b$
  $Fb \rightarrow Gb$
  This is correct: the name used does not have to be new to the path.

- $\forall x(Fx \rightarrow Gx) \;\backslash a$
  $Fa \rightarrow Gx$
  Wrong! All occurrences of x that become free after the initial quantifier $\forall x$ is stripped away must be replaced with a.

- $\forall x(Fx \rightarrow Gx) \;\backslash a\; b$
  $Fa \rightarrow Gb$
  Wrong! If we apply the rule twice to the same formula, once with a and once with b, then the first time we must replace all occurrences of x (that become free after the initial quantifier $\forall x$ is stripped away) with a, and the second time we must replace all such occurrences of x with b, as follows:

  $\forall x(Fx \rightarrow Gx) \;\backslash a\; b$
  $Fa \rightarrow Ga$
  $Fb \rightarrow Gb$

  The original example squashes these two correct applications of the rule into one misapplication.

- $Fa \rightarrow \forall x\, Fx \;\backslash b$
  $Fa \rightarrow Fb$
  Wrong! The universal quantifier is not the main operator. We need to apply the rule for the conditional first.

This rule has our desired property. Consider two cases in turn. Case (i): the name $\underline{a}$ used in applying the rule is new to the path. By rule (7) of §9.4.2, if there is a model $\mathfrak{M}$ in which $\forall \underline{x}\alpha(\underline{x})$ is true, then for every object o in the domain of $\mathfrak{M}$, $\alpha(\underline{a}/\underline{x})$ is true in $\mathfrak{M}_o^{\underline{a}}$, where $\underline{a}$ is our new name (which is not assigned a referent in $\mathfrak{M}$), and $\mathfrak{M}_o^{\underline{a}}$ is a model that is just like $\mathfrak{M}$ except that in it the name $\underline{a}$ is assigned the referent o. We now need only observe that $\forall \underline{x}\alpha(\underline{x})$ will also be true on this model $\mathfrak{M}_o^{\underline{a}}$. So if there is a model in which the input to our rule is true, then there is a model (a different one in this case) in which both this input and the output of the rule are true—and that is the desired property. Case (ii): the name $\underline{a}$ used in applying the rule is not new to the path. By rule (7) of §9.4.2, if there is a model $\mathfrak{M}$ in which $\forall \underline{x}\alpha(\underline{x})$ is true, then for every object o in the domain of $\mathfrak{M}$, $\alpha(\underline{d}/\underline{x})$ is true in $\mathfrak{M}_o^{\underline{d}}$, where $\underline{d}$ is a new name (which is not assigned a referent in $\mathfrak{M}$), and $\mathfrak{M}_o^{\underline{d}}$ is a model that is just like $\mathfrak{M}$ except that in it the name $\underline{d}$ is assigned the referent o. Now in this case, $\underline{a}$ *is* assigned a referent in $\mathfrak{M}$—say it is assigned the object k. We have just seen that $\alpha(\underline{d}/\underline{x})$ is true in every model just like $\mathfrak{M}$ except that it assigns a referent to $\underline{d}$ (remember that in the case we are considering now, $\mathfrak{M}$ assigns a referent to $\underline{a}$—the name we used in applying the rule for the universal quantifier, but it does not assign a referent to $\underline{d}$). So in particular, $\alpha(\underline{d}/\underline{x})$ is true in $\mathfrak{M}_k^{\underline{d}}$, the model that assigns as $\underline{d}$'s referent the object k. But then clearly $\alpha(\underline{a}/\underline{x})$ must be true in $\mathfrak{M}$, because in $\mathfrak{M}$, $\underline{a}$'s referent is that same object k (and the truth of a formula involving a name depends only on the name's referent, not on what name it is—and apart from assigning $\underline{d}$ the referent k, $\mathfrak{M}_k^{\underline{d}}$ is exactly like $\mathfrak{M}$).[3] So if there is a model in which the input to our rule is true, then there is a model (the same one in this case) in which both this input and the output of the rule are true—and that is the desired property.[4]

The tree rules are summarized in Figure 10.1 (the rules for the connectives are exactly the same as in PL).

10.1.5 Order of Application

It is desirable to apply the tree rules in the following order:

1. propositional logic rules—and among these, nonbranching rules first;

2. negated quantifier rules;

3. unnegated existential quantifier rule;

4. unnegated universal quantifier rule;

and then return to (1) and cycle through again, until no more rules can be applied. This is a heuristic—a rule of thumb. Our tree will not be incorrect if

Disjunction	
$(\alpha \lor \beta)$ ✓	$\neg(\alpha \lor \beta)$ ✓
$\overset{\displaystyle \wedge}{\alpha \quad \beta}$	$\begin{array}{c} \neg\alpha \\ \neg\beta \end{array}$

Conjunction	
$(\alpha \land \beta)$ ✓	$\neg(\alpha \land \beta)$ ✓
$\begin{array}{c} \alpha \\ \beta \end{array}$	$\overset{\displaystyle \wedge}{\neg\alpha \quad \neg\beta}$

Conditional	
$(\alpha \to \beta)$ ✓	$\neg(\alpha \to \beta)$ ✓
$\overset{\displaystyle \wedge}{\neg\alpha \quad \beta}$	$\begin{array}{c} \alpha \\ \neg\beta \end{array}$

Biconditional	
$(\alpha \leftrightarrow \beta)$ ✓	$\neg(\alpha \leftrightarrow \beta)$ ✓
$\begin{array}{cc} \alpha & \neg\alpha \\ \beta & \neg\beta \end{array}$	$\begin{array}{cc} \alpha & \neg\alpha \\ \neg\beta & \beta \end{array}$

Negation
$\neg\neg\alpha$ ✓
α

Existential quantifier	
$\exists\underline{x}\alpha(\underline{x})$ ✓$\underline{a}$ (new $\underline{a}$)	$\neg\exists\underline{x}\alpha(\underline{x})$ ✓
$\alpha(\underline{a}/\underline{x})$	$\forall\underline{x}\neg\alpha(\underline{x})$

Universal quantifier	
$\forall\underline{x}\alpha(\underline{x})$ \$\underline{a}$ (any $\underline{a}$)	$\neg\forall\underline{x}\alpha(\underline{x})$ ✓
$\alpha(\underline{a}/\underline{x})$	$\exists\underline{x}\neg\alpha(\underline{x})$

Figure 10.1. Tree rules for MPL.

we apply the rules in some other order—but it may be longer than necessary (in some cases much longer—see §10.3.1 for an example).

The requirement on checking closure still applies: when we add wffs to the tree, we must check all open paths, and if any of them can close, we must close them with a cross. Once a path is closed with a cross, no more wffs can be added to it. This procedure is not merely a heuristic: it is a hard-and-fast requirement.[5]

10.1.6 Saturated Paths and Finished Trees

We stop applying tree rules and draw a conclusion from our tree—for example, "valid: all paths close," or "invalid: some path remains open"—when the tree is *finished*. A tree is finished when each of its paths is either closed (with a cross) or *saturated*. Basically, a saturated path is one on which every applicable rule has been applied; a path such that every formula on it of a sort that figures as input to some tree rule—that is, every formula other than atomic formulas and negations of atomic formulas—has had the relevant rule applied to it. However, in light of the rule for the unnegated universal quantifier, we do not wish to define a saturated path in the simple way just stated, because we always can continue applying the rule for the universal quantifier, without limit, using a new name each time:

$$\forall x Gx \quad \backslash a\, b\, c \,\ldots$$
$$Ga$$
$$Gb$$
$$Gc$$
$$\vdots$$

but we do not want to mandate that any path containing a universally quantified formula must continue forever. So we define saturation as follows:

A path is saturated iff:

1. every formula on it—apart from atomic formulas, negations of atomic formulas, and formulas whose main operator is a universal quantifier—has had the relevant rule applied; and

2. every formula on it whose main operator is a universal quantifier
   (i) has had the universal quantifier rule applied to it at least once, and
   (ii) has had the rule applied to it once for each name that appears on the path (i.e., for any name appearing anywhere on the path—above or below the universal formula in question—the rule has been applied to that formula using that name).

Some examples will help to make this definition clear. The following tree is finished:

$$\exists x Fx \;\checkmark\; a$$
$$\forall x Gx \;\backslash\; a$$
$$Fa$$
$$Ga$$

There are no rules that can be applied to the atomic formulas Fa and Ga. The relevant rule has been applied to $\exists x Fx$. As for $\forall x Gx$, the universal rule has been applied to it at least once, and it has been applied once for every name appearing on the path (in this case, just the name a).

The following tree is not finished:

$$Fa$$
$$\exists x\, Fx \;\checkmark\; b$$
$$\forall x\, Gx \;\backslash\; a$$
$$Fb$$
$$Ga$$

To finish it, we need to apply the universal rule again to $\forall x\, Gx$, using the name b, because the name b occurs on this path. Once we do that, the tree is finished:

$$Fa$$
$$\exists x\, Fx \;\checkmark\; b$$
$$\forall x\, Gx \;\backslash\; a\, b$$
$$Fb$$
$$Ga$$
$$Gb$$

The following tree is not finished:

$$\forall x\, Gx$$

To finish it, we need to apply the universal rule at least once to $\forall x\, Gx$. As no names appear in the path, we may use any name we please when applying the rule. We choose a; now the tree is finished:

$$\forall x\, Gx \;\backslash\; a$$
$$Ga$$

10.1.7 Vacuous Quantifiers

Recall (§8.4.4) that an occurrence of a quantifier $\forall \underline{x}$ or $\exists \underline{x}$ in a wff is vacuous if the variable $\underline{x}$ (i.e., the one in the quantifier) has no free occurrences in the scope of the quantifier. The formulas $\forall \underline{x}\alpha$ and $\exists \underline{x}\alpha$ are each equivalent to α, when α does not contain free occurrences of $\underline{x}$—that is, when the quantifier is vacuous. These equivalences arise because $\forall \underline{x}\alpha$ ($\exists \underline{x}\alpha$) is true in a model $\mathfrak{M}$ just in case the wff resulting from α by replacing every free occurrence of $\underline{x}$ in it by some new name $\underline{a}$ is true on every (some) model just like $\mathfrak{M}$ except that it assigns a referent to $\underline{a}$. When α contains no free occurrences of $\underline{x}$, the wff resulting from α by replacing every free occurrence of $\underline{x}$ in it by some new name $\underline{a}$ is simply α itself. And because α contains no occurrences of $\underline{a}$ (remember $\underline{a}$ is a new name), it is true in any model just like $\mathfrak{M}$ except that it assigns a referent to $\underline{a}$ iff it is true on $\mathfrak{M}$ itself (because the truth value of a wff is fully determined by the values of its own components, together with the domain: it cannot be affected by the referents/extensions of names/predicates that do not occur in it). So what is required for $\forall \underline{x}\alpha$ or $\exists \underline{x}\alpha$ to be true in any model $\mathfrak{M}$ is simply that α be true in $\mathfrak{M}$. Hence $\forall \underline{x}\alpha$ and $\exists \underline{x}\alpha$ are each equivalent to α.

Note that in a wff such as $\forall x \exists x\, Fx$, it is the outer quantifier (in this case the universal one) that is vacuous. The scope of $\exists x$ here is Fx, which does contain a free x—so $\exists x$ is not vacuous. The scope of $\forall x$ is $\exists x\, Fx$, which contains no free x—so $\forall x$ is vacuous. Hence, $\forall x \exists x\, Fx$ is equivalent to $\exists x\, Fx$. Similarly, in $\forall x \exists x \forall x\, Fx$, the outer $\forall x$ and the $\exists x$ are both vacuous, so this wff is equivalent to $\forall x\, Fx$.

When we apply a tree rule to a vacuous quantifier, we simply strip off the quantifier: this action does not result in a wff with any free variables in it, and so there are no free variables to replace by names. We therefore simply write a check mark next to the formula (even in the case of the rule for the universal quantifier), with no name next to it. For example:

$\forall x \exists x\, Fx$ ✓ $\exists x \forall x\, Fx$ ✓
$\quad \exists x\, Fx$ $\quad \forall x\, Fx$

10.2 Using Trees

Let us now work through a couple of examples of using trees to answer questions of interest. First, let's test whether the following proposition is a logical truth:

$$([\exists x\, Fx \wedge \forall x(Fx \rightarrow Gx)] \rightarrow \exists x\, Gx)$$

We write the negation of this formula at the top of our tree and then finish the tree. Note that in the following tree, I number the wffs (on the left) and note where each step comes from (in braces on the right) to make it easier to keep track of what is going on:

1. $\neg([\exists x Fx \wedge \forall x(Fx \rightarrow Gx)] \rightarrow \exists x Gx)$ ✓
2. $\quad\quad [\exists x Fx \wedge \forall x(Fx \rightarrow Gx)]$ ✓   {1}
3. $\quad\quad\quad\quad \neg \exists x Gx$ ✓   {1}
4. $\quad\quad\quad\quad \exists x Fx$ ✓a {2}
5. $\quad\quad\quad \forall x(Fx \rightarrow Gx)$ \$a$ {2}
6. $\quad\quad\quad\quad \forall x \neg Gx$ \$a$ {3}
7. $\quad\quad\quad\quad\quad Fa$ {4}
8. $\quad\quad\quad\quad Fa \rightarrow Ga$ ✓   {5}

       9. $\neg Fa$ {8}   10. Ga {8}
           ×   {7, 9}   11. $\neg Ga$ {6}
                             ×   {10, 11}

All paths close, so the original formula is a logical truth.

Second, let's test whether the following argument is valid:

$\exists x F x$
$\exists x G x$
$\therefore \exists x (F x \wedge G x)$

We write the premises and the negation of the conclusion at the top of our tree and then finish the tree:

1.	$\exists x F x$ ✓ a		
2.	$\exists x G x$ ✓ b		
3.	$\neg \exists x (F x \wedge G x)$ ✓		
4.	$\forall x \neg (F x \wedge G x)$ \a b	{3}	
5.	Fa	{1}	
6.	Gb	{2}	
7.	$\neg (Fa \wedge Ga)$ ✓	{4, a}	

8. $\neg Fa$ {7}		9. $\neg Ga$ {7}
× {5, 8}		10. $\neg (Fb \wedge Gb)$ ✓ {4, b}

11. $\neg Fb$ {10}		12. $\neg Gb$ {10}
↑		× {6, 12}

After all rules have been applied—including applying the universal rule to wff (4) for every name on the open path—a path remains open, so the argument is invalid.

10.2.1 Reading off Models from Open Paths

We said earlier (§10.1) that where a path remains open, we can read off from it a model in which the formulas at the top of the tree are all true (indeed, in which every formula on the open path is true). Let us now see how to do this. To specify a model, we must specify three things:

1. a domain,

2. a referent for each name (in the relevant fragment of the language—i.e., each name that appears in the path), and

3. an extension for each predicate (in the relevant fragment—i.e., each predicate that appears in the path).

As our domain, we can take any set of objects we like: we must simply ensure that there is one member of the domain for each name appearing in the path. Where there are n names in the path, we write our domain as follows: $\{1, \ldots, n\}$. You can read this statement abstractly, as saying that the domain contains n distinct objects: a first one labeled "1," a second one labeled "2," and so on. Or you can read it concretely, as saying that the domain contains the first *n* positive integers; that is, the first object in the domain is the number 1, the second object is the number 2, and so on. It does not matter which way we read it—either way, we obtain a model in which every formula on the open path is true—so choose whichever way feels more comfortable.

We now need to specify the referents in our model of the names appearing on the open path. Because (in the previous step of specifying our model's domain) we put one object into the domain for each name in the path, we know at this stage that there will always be a separate object available to act as the referent of each name. All we need to do is match up names to objects in some way. One simple way of doing it—which we shall adopt in general—is:

> Referents: a: 1 b: 2 c: 3 . . .
> (for as many names as appear in the path)

That is, the first name in the path refers to the first object we put into our domain, the second name refers to the second object, and so on.[6]

Now we need to specify the extensions of predicates that appear on the open path. Remember that the guiding idea is that the model we construct is one in which every proposition on our path is true. What we do is look at the atomic propositions (if any) that occur as complete wffs (not as subformulas of some larger complete wff) on the open path. We then put into the extension of each predicate all and only the referents of those names that appear after the predicate in an atomic wff on the path. So suppose (for example) that we find Fa, Ga, and Gb (and no other atomic wffs) on our path. For Fa to come out true in the model we are constructing, the referent of a must be in the extension of F. For Ga to come out true, the referent of a must be in the extension of G. Likewise, for Gb to come out true, the referent of b must be in the extension of G. So we construct our extensions as follows:

> Extensions: F: {1} G: {1, 2}

Here we have put into the extension of F the referent of a on our model (i.e., the number 1), and we have put into the extension of G the referents of a and of b on our model (i.e., the numbers 1 and 2). And we have put nothing else into these extensions, because (in our example) the only atomic proposition on our path featuring the predicate F is Fa, and the only atomic propositions on our path featuring the predicate G are Ga and Gb.

Note that, following this method of constructing extensions, if we have a predicate $\underline{P}$ on our path but no atomic formula $\underline{Pa}$, for any name $\underline{a}$ (as a complete wff), then we make $\underline{P}$'s extension the empty set $\emptyset$. This case can easily happen; for example, the only predicate letter in a path might be P, and the only name a, and the path might contain $\neg Pa$. Here the atomic wff

Pa does not appear as a whole wff, only as a subformula in $\neg Pa$, and we are interested only in atomic formulas that occur as complete wffs.

§

We can now apply this method of constructing a model to the second example considered in the previous section. Our argument was invalid, so we can read off from the open path in our tree a countermodel: a model in which the premises are true and the conclusion false. Looking along the open path, we see that two names, a and b, occur. Hence we specify our domain and the referents of these two names as:

Domain: $\{1, 2\}$
Referents: a: 1 b: 2

We now look to see what atomic formulas occur on our path; we find Fa and Gb. (Note that Ga does not appear as a whole wff, only as a subformula in other wffs; similarly Fb does not appear as a whole wff, only as a subformula in other wffs. We are interested only in atomic formulas that occur as complete wffs.) So we specify the extensions as:

Extensions: F: $\{1\}$ G: $\{2\}$

Note that in this case, the names a and b appearing in our open path do not appear in the original argument:

$\exists x\, Fx$
$\exists x\, Gx$
$\therefore \exists x(Fx \wedge Gx)$

So if we simply want a countermodel to the argument—as opposed to a model in which every wff on the open path is true—then it does not matter if we leave out the assignment of referents to names from our model. That is, we could present the model as:

Domain: $\{1, 2\}$
Extensions: F: $\{1\}$ G: $\{2\}$

Note that it is crucial that everything else about this model (apart from the absence of a specification of referents for a and b) is the same as in the first model. In particular, we must include one object in the domain of the model for each of the names on our open path.

§

We must read off a model only from a saturated path. Consider the following argument:

$\exists x \forall y (Fx \wedge Gy)$
$\forall x Fx$
$\therefore \forall x \forall y (\neg Fx \vee \neg Gy)$

We begin its tree as follows:

1.	$\exists x \forall y (Fx \wedge Gy)$ ✓ a	
2.	$\forall x Fx$	
3.	$\neg \forall x \forall y (\neg Fx \vee \neg Gy)$ ✓	
4.	$\exists x \neg \forall y (\neg Fx \vee \neg Gy)$ ✓ b	{3}
5.	$\forall y (Fa \wedge Gy)$	{1}
6.	$\neg \forall y (\neg Fb \vee \neg Gy)$ ✓	{4}
7.	$\exists y \neg (\neg Fb \vee \neg Gy)$ ✓ c	{6}
8.	$\neg (\neg Fb \vee \neg Gc)$ ✓	{7}
9.	$\neg\neg Fb$ ✓	{8}
10.	$\neg\neg Gc$ ✓	{8}
11.	Fb	{9}
11.	Gc	{10}

At this point, the only formulas remaining to which rules can be applied are the universal quantifications (2) and (5). The names a, b, and c all appear in the path on which these formulas are located, so to saturate the path, we need to apply the universal rule three times to each of these formulas: using a, once again using b, and finally using c. We can see that eventually this yields the formulas Fa, Fb, Fc, Ga, Gb, and Gc on our path, and so the path will not close. Now if you just wanted to run a quick test to see whether the argument we started with is valid, you could stop here: evidently the path will not close, and so the argument is invalid. However if you actually want to read off a particular model in which the premises are true and the conclusion false, then you need first to saturate the path. Because if we read off a model from the unsaturated path in the above unfinished tree, we obtain the following:

Domain: $\{1, 2, 3\}$
Referents: a: 1 b: 2 c: 3
Extensions: F: $\{2\}$ G: $\{3\}$

This is not a model in which the premises are true and the conclusion false. For example, the second premise $\forall x Fx$ is clearly not true in this model, in which there are three objects in the domain, only one of which is F.

10.2.2 Exercises

1. Using trees, determine whether the following propositions are logical truths. For any proposition that is not a logical truth, read off from your tree a model in which it is false.

(i) $Fa \rightarrow \exists x Fx$

(ii) $\exists x Fx \rightarrow \neg\forall x \neg Fx$

(iii) $\forall x((Fx \wedge \neg Gx) \rightarrow \exists x Gx)$

(iv) $\forall x Fx \rightarrow \exists x Fx$

(v) $(Fa \wedge (Fb \wedge Fc)) \rightarrow \forall x Fx$

(vi) $\exists x Fx \wedge \exists x \neg Fx$

(vii) $\exists x(Fx \rightarrow \forall y Fy)$

(viii) $\forall x(Fx \rightarrow Gx) \rightarrow$
$(Fa \rightarrow Ga)$

(ix) $\neg\forall x(Fx \wedge Gx) \leftrightarrow$
$\exists x \neg(Fx \wedge Gx)$

(x) $\neg\exists x(Fx \wedge Gx) \leftrightarrow$
$\forall x(\neg Fx \wedge \neg Gx)$

2. Using trees, determine whether the following arguments are valid. For any argument that is not valid, read off from your tree a model in which the premises are true and the conclusion false.

(i) $\exists x Fx \wedge \exists x Gx$
$\therefore \exists x(Fx \wedge Gx)$

(ii) $\exists x \forall y(Fx \rightarrow Gy)$
$\therefore \forall y \exists x(Fx \rightarrow Gy)$

(iii) $Fa \rightarrow \forall x Gx$
$\therefore \forall x(Fa \rightarrow Gx)$

(iv) $Fa \rightarrow \forall x Gx$
$\therefore \exists x(Fa \rightarrow Gx)$

(v) $\forall x(Fx \vee Gx)$
$\neg\forall x Fx$
$\therefore \forall x Gx$

(vi) $\exists x(Fx \wedge Gx)$
$\therefore \exists x Fx \wedge \exists x Gx$

(vii) $\forall x(Fx \rightarrow Gx)$
Fa
$\therefore Ga$

(viii) $\neg\forall x(Fx \vee Gx)$
$\therefore \exists x(\neg Fx \wedge \neg Gx)$

(ix) $\forall x(Fx \rightarrow Gx)$
$\forall x(Gx \rightarrow Hx)$
$\therefore \neg\exists x(\neg Fx \wedge Hx)$

(x) $\forall x(Fx \vee Gx)$
$\therefore \neg\exists x(Fx \wedge Gx)$

10.3 Infinite Trees

Suppose we want to know whether the wff $\forall x \exists y(Fx \wedge Gy)$ is satisfiable. So we write this wff at the top of our tree. We first apply the rule for the universal quantifier: no names have yet been used, so we use a new name, a. Then we apply the rule for the existential quantifier, picking a new name b. Then we apply the rule for conjunction:

$$\forall x \exists y(Fx \wedge Gy) \setminus a$$
$$\exists y(Fa \wedge Gy) \checkmark b$$
$$(Fa \wedge Gb) \checkmark$$
$$Fa$$
$$Gb$$

Is the tree now finished? No, because the name b appears, as well as the name a, but the universal rule has only been applied using a. So we go back and apply the rule again using b. But this application then creates a new existentially quantified formula, and so we have to apply the rule for that, using a new name c. Then we apply the rule for conjunction:

$$\forall x \exists y (Fx \wedge Gy) \setminus a\, b$$
$$\exists y (Fa \wedge Gy) \checkmark b$$
$$(Fa \wedge Gb) \checkmark$$
$$Fa$$
$$Gb$$
$$\exists y (Fb \wedge Gy) \checkmark c$$
$$(Fb \wedge Gc) \checkmark$$
$$Fb$$
$$Gc$$

Is the tree now finished? No, because now the name c appears, as well as a and b, but the universal rule has only been applied using a and b. So we go back and apply the rule again using c. But this application then gives us a new existential formula—and applying the rule for that one gives us another new name d. So we have to go back and apply the universal rule for d, and so on. So this tree goes on forever.

10.3.1 Infinite Paths and Saturated Paths

The mere fact that a path continues infinitely—that we could write forever and not close the path—does not, in itself, mean that we can deem the initial formula to be satisfiable. We can reach that conclusion only if we have a saturated open path. So we need to ask the following question. If we applied every applicable rule to this path—including applying all universal rules for every name on the path—would the tree close, or would it still remain open? In the example just considered we can see that the tree would indeed remain open, no matter what we did. So we can conclude that our wff is satisfiable.

But consider a different example. We want to know whether the following wff is satisfiable:

$$(\forall x \exists y (Fx \wedge Gy) \wedge (Fa \wedge \neg Fa))$$

So we begin our tree as follows:

$$(\forall x \exists y (Fx \wedge Gy) \wedge (Fa \wedge \neg Fa)) \checkmark$$
$$\forall x \exists y (Fx \wedge Gy) \setminus a$$
$$(Fa \wedge \neg Fa)$$
$$\exists y (Fa \wedge Gy) \checkmark b$$
$$(Fa \wedge Gb) \checkmark$$
$$Fa$$
$$Gb$$

Here we have neglected to follow the heuristic that says to apply propositional rules first—but this procedure is only a rule of thumb. Ignoring it does not make our tree wrong—only (in general) longer than necessary. Now suppose we go back and apply the universal rule again for b, and then again for the new name c that results, and so on. We shall be writing forever: extending our tree in the same way as in the example discussed in §10.3. But although this tree will go on forever—when approached in this way—the resultant infinite path is not saturated, and so we cannot conclude that our wff is satisfiable. For there is a formula on the path—$(Fa \wedge \neg Fa)$—that could have a rule applied to it and is such that were this rule applied, the path would close straight away. So infinitude by itself shows nothing. What is significant—what does allow us to conclude that the formulas starting the tree can all be true—is when a path continues infinitely even if it is saturated.

The distinction between saturated and unsaturated infinite paths can be tricky to get one's head around at first, so it might be useful to consider an analogy. Consider the following infinite sequence of numbers:

$$1, 2, 3, 4, \ldots$$

It goes on forever—we cannot write out the whole thing. And yet we can see that the following is true: for any number in the sequence, there is another number in the sequence that is three times its size. Imagine the sequence as a path stretching into the infinite distance: you can see that as you walk down it, whatever number you get to (say 11, or 472), after some finite amount of further walking you will reach a number three times its size (in this case 33, or 1,416). So although we cannot actually write out the whole sequence, we can see that it is "complete with respect to multiplication by three." Contrast the sequence obtained from the first by removing the number 6:

$$1, 2, 3, 4, 5, 7, 8, 9, 10, 11, \ldots$$

It is also infinite: we cannot write out the whole thing. But we can still see that it is not complete with respect to multiplication by three: it contains the number 2, but it does not contain a number three times the size (i.e., 6).

The distinction between an infinite path that is saturated and one that is not is just like the distinction between an infinite sequence of numbers that is complete with respect to multiplication by three and one that is not. So given an infinite path in a tree, imagine walking down the path, starting at the top. We need to ask ourselves: for every wff we pass that should have a rule applied, is there—some finite distance down the path—a point at which that rule is applied (including applying the universal rule once for every name appearing anywhere down the path)? If so, the path is saturated.

10.3.2 Reading off Models

Let's go back to the example in §10.3, where we could conclude that the infinite path is saturated and so concluded that the wff at the top of the tree is satisfiable. We can read off from our open path a model in which the wff is true in the same way as before, only this time the domain will be infinite. Our saturated infinite path contains infinitely many names, so the domain must contain infinitely many objects:

Domain: $\{1, 2, 3, \ldots\}$
Referents: a: 1 b: 2 c: 3 …

Remember from the end of §10.2.1 that we must read off a model only from a saturated path. So in this case we read off our model from the entire (imagined) saturated path, not simply from the small initial section of this path that we have actually written down. What about the extensions of predicates? Two predicates appear in the open path: F and G. If we look at the pattern emerging in our tree (extend the tree a bit more if you can't see the pattern yet), we see that for every new name $\underline{d}$ that is introduced, $F\underline{d}$ appears on the path, and although Ga does not appear on the path, for every new name $\underline{d}$ introduced after a, $G\underline{d}$ does appear on the path. So our extensions are:

Extensions: F: $\{1, 2, 3, \ldots\}$ G: $\{2, 3, \ldots\}$

10.3.3 Finite and Infinite Models

So the model we read off from the open path has an infinite domain. But note that the tree is not telling us that the wff at the top of the tree is true only in models with infinite domains. A tree tells us whether there is any model in which the wff(s) at the top are true, and if so, it specifies at least one such model. (If a tree has more than one open path, it supplies one model for each open path—but they need not be different models.) So all we know at this stage is that $\forall x \exists y (Fx \wedge Gy)$ is satisfiable—there is at least one model in which it is true—and furthermore we have one such model: the one just constructed. We cannot conclude from this that all models in which it is true also have an infinite domain. In fact they do not—the wff is also true in the following model:

Domain: $\{1\}$
Extensions: F: $\{1\}$ G: $\{1\}$

How did I devise the latter model? Not from a tree, nor by following some other systematic method. I came up with it ad hoc—by looking at the formula $\forall x \exists y (Fx \wedge Gy)$ and trying to think of a model with a finite domain in which it is true. (Recall question (4) in Exercises 9.4.3.) But there is in fact a variant of the tree method that always finds a finite model of the propositions at the top of the tree, if such a model exists.[7] Given any group of propositions with which we might begin a tree, there are two possibilities, the second of which divides into two further possibilities:

1. the set is unsatisfiable, or

2. the set is satisfiable
   (i) there is a model with a finite domain in which every proposition in the set is true, or
   (ii) there is a model with an infinite domain in which every proposition in the set is true but no model with a finite domain in which every proposition in the set is true.

In case (1), all paths in the tree will close. In case (2), some path in the tree will remain open. Our tree method makes no distinction between cases (2i) and (2ii): even if there is a model of the starting propositions with a finite domain, our tree method may yield a model with an infinite domain. This is what happened in the example considered above. In contrast, the variant method does distinguish these two cases: in case (2i) it yields a finite model, whereas in case (2ii) it yields an infinite one.

10.3.4 *Extending the Initial Section*

We said that when reading off extensions for predicates from an infinite saturated path—of which, of course, we have actually written down only a finite initial section—we have to look at the pattern emerging in the initial section. Sometimes there are different ways of extending the initial section, which lead to different infinite paths and so yield different models. In such cases, before we can see a pattern emerging, we have to decide how the initial section is to be extended. An example will make this clear.

Suppose we want to test whether the two wffs $\forall x \exists y (Fx \land Gy)$ and $\forall x \exists y (Fx \land \neg Gy)$ are jointly satisfiable. So we write these wffs at the top of our tree and begin applying rules:

1. $\forall x \exists y (Fx \land Gy)$
2. $\forall x \exists y (Fx \land \neg Gy)$

Given our experience with the first example in this section, we know that this tree will go forever: we have to apply the universal quantifier rule to line 1 for infinitely many names $a, b, c, \ldots$, and likewise for line 2. However, there are different ways that the tree might progress. Or, to put the point more accurately, there are different infinite finished trees that begin this way.

1. $\forall x \exists y(Fx \wedge Gy) \setminus a\ b\ldots$
2. $\forall x \exists y(Fx \wedge \neg Gy) \setminus a\ b\ldots$
3. $\quad \exists y(Fa \wedge Gy) \checkmark b$ $\qquad \{1, a\}$
4. $\quad\quad (Fa \wedge Gb) \checkmark$ $\qquad \{3\}$
5. $\quad\quad\quad Fa$ $\qquad\qquad \{4\}$
6. $\quad\quad\quad Gb$ $\qquad\qquad \{4\}$
7. $\quad \exists y(Fa \wedge \neg Gy) \checkmark c$ $\qquad \{2, a\}$
8. $\quad\quad (Fa \wedge \neg Gc) \checkmark$ $\qquad \{7\}$
9. $\quad\quad\quad Fa$ $\qquad\qquad \{8\}$
10. $\quad\quad\quad \neg Gc$ $\qquad\qquad \{8\}$
11. $\quad \exists y(Fb \wedge Gy) \checkmark d$ $\qquad \{1, b\}$
12. $\quad\quad (Fb \wedge Gd) \checkmark$ $\qquad \{11\}$
13. $\quad\quad\quad Fb$ $\qquad\qquad \{12\}$
14. $\quad\quad\quad Gd$ $\qquad\qquad \{12\}$
15. $\quad \exists y(Fb \wedge \neg Gy) \checkmark e$ $\qquad \{2, b\}$
16. $\quad\quad (Fb \wedge \neg Ge) \checkmark$ $\qquad \{15\}$
17. $\quad\quad\quad Fb$ $\qquad\qquad \{16\}$
18. $\quad\quad\quad \neg Ge$ $\qquad\qquad \{16\}$
$$\vdots$$

Domain: $\{1, 2, 3, \ldots\}$
Referents: a: 1 b: 2 c: 3 $\ldots$
Extensions: F: $\{1, 2, 3, \ldots\}$ G: $\{2, 4, 6, \ldots\}$

Figure 10.2. An infinite tree and the model read off from it.

For simplicity, let's use "1a" to mean "apply the universal quantifier rule to line (1) using the name a," "2b" to mean "apply the universal quantifier rule to line (2) using the name b," and so on. Suppose we decide to extend the tree in accordance with the following pattern:

$$1a, 2a, 1b, 2b, 1c, 2c, \ldots$$

(It is to be understood here that after we do 1a, we then carry out all steps that can be done as a result of that action before doing 2a, after which we do all steps that can be done as a result of *that* action before doing 1b, etc.) Then the tree, and the model read off from it, will be as in Figure 10.2. If, however, we decide to extend the tree in accordance with the following pattern:

$$2a, 1a, 2b, 1b, 2c, 1c, \ldots$$

then the tree, and the model read off from it, will be as in Figure 10.3. Note that the extensions of G are different in these two models.

1. $\forall x \exists y (Fx \wedge Gy) \ \backslash a \ b \dots$
2. $\forall x \exists y (Fx \wedge \neg Gy) \ \backslash a \ b \dots$
3. $\quad \exists y (Fa \wedge \neg Gy) \ \checkmark \ b$ $\{2, a\}$
4. $\quad\quad (Fa \wedge \neg Gb) \ \checkmark$ $\{3\}$
5. $\quad\quad\quad Fa$ $\{4\}$
6. $\quad\quad\quad \neg Gb$ $\{4\}$
7. $\quad \exists y (Fa \wedge Gy) \ \checkmark \ c$ $\{1, a\}$
8. $\quad\quad (Fa \wedge Gc) \ \checkmark$ $\{7\}$
9. $\quad\quad\quad Fa$ $\{8\}$
10. $\quad\quad\quad Gc$ $\{8\}$
11. $\quad \exists y (Fb \wedge \neg Gy) \ \checkmark \ d$ $\{2, b\}$
12. $\quad\quad (Fb \wedge \neg Gd) \ \checkmark$ $\{11\}$
13. $\quad\quad\quad Fb$ $\{12\}$
14. $\quad\quad\quad \neg Gd$ $\{12\}$
15. $\quad \exists y (Fb \wedge Gy) \ \checkmark \ e$ $\{1, b\}$
16. $\quad\quad (Fb \wedge Ge) \ \checkmark$ $\{15\}$
17. $\quad\quad\quad Fb$ $\{16\}$
18. $\quad\quad\quad Ge$ $\{16\}$
$$\vdots$$

Domain: $\{1, 2, 3, \dots\}$
Referents: $a\!:1 \ b\!:2 \ c\!:3 \ \dots$
Extensions: $F\!: \{1, 2, 3, \dots\} \ \ G\!: \{3, 5, 7, \dots\}$

Figure 10.3. Another infinite tree and the model read off from it.

Of course there are also infinitely many other ways in which we could grow the tree, for example:

$$1a, \ 1b, \ 2a, \ 2b, \ 1c, \ 1d, \ 2c, \ 2d, \dots$$
$$1a, \ 1b, \ 1c, \ 2a, \ 2b, \ 2c, \ 1d, \ 1e, \ 1f, \ 2d, \ 2e, \ 2f, \dots$$
$$1a, \ 2a, \ 1b, \ 1c, \ 2b, \ 2c, \ 1d, \ 1e, \ 1f, \ 2d, \ 2e, \ 2f, \dots$$

Note that these ways all ensure that the path will become saturated. Other methods for extending the tree forever do not result in a saturated path, for example: $1a, \ 1b, \ 1c, \ \dots$. Here, although the tree continues forever, the universal rule never gets applied to line 2, so the path is not saturated.

Thus, looking at the initial section of a tree and "seeing a pattern emerging" in general entails the following: decide on a strategy for extending the initial section, and make sure that it will result in a finished tree; follow this strategy for a while; and then look for a pattern emerging in the extensions of predicates.

This procedure raises two issues, both of which require further consideration. First, how do we ensure that our strategy for extending the initial section will result in a finished tree? Second, how do we find the pattern that emerges from a given strategy? We discuss these issues in the following two subsections.

10.3.5 Ensuring that Trees Are Finished

We can give a single strategy for extending any initial section to a finished tree (one in which every path is either closed or saturated). Before we present the strategy, we introduce the idea of giving an *address* to each proposition in a tree. Our addresses will be like street addresses in (parts of) Manhattan (e.g., 156 West 48th Street, or 901 Sixth Avenue) in the sense that knowing the address enables you to find your way there (count up the streets [or avenues] until you reach the street you want, then count up the buildings until you reach the desired one). We specify an address for every proposition in a tree recursively, as follows:

1. The first proposition at the top of the tree has address 1.

2. Any proposition α in the tree (apart from the first) is in one of the following positions:

   (i) immediately below another proposition (whose address is n). In this case α's address is $n1$:

   $$\vdots$$
   $$n$$
   $$n1$$

   (ii) on the left side of a branch that begins under another proposition (whose address is n). In this case α's address is $n1$:

   $$\vdots$$
   $$n$$

   $$n1$$

   (iii) on the right side of a branch that begins under another proposition (whose address is n). In this case α's address is $n2$:

   $$\vdots$$
   $$n$$

   $$n2$$

Note that by assigning the topmost proposition address 1 and then working down recursively, this procedure specifies an address for every proposition in any tree. Figure 10.4 gives an example (the propositions in this tree are not shown: only their addresses). Note also that the address of an entry tells you how to get there. For example, take address 1212. The first digit specifies the start (at address 1: the top of the tree). The next digit (2) directs us to go right

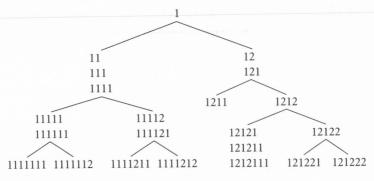

Figure 10.4. Assigning addresses to the propositions in a tree.

(at this point we are at address 12). The next digit (1) says to go left (if there is a branch) or straight down (if there is not). In this case there is no branch, so we go straight down (at this point we are at address 121). The next digit (2) says to go right. Now all the digits of our address are exhausted—and we are at the address we wanted: 1212. The address 1212 is thus like a starting point (1) followed by three directions: right (2); left (1), where "left" means "straight ahead" in case there is no branch; and right (2).

Now, given any finite tree, our procedure for extending it is as follows:

1. Go through every proposition in the tree in order of address (i.e., go to α before β if α's address is a smaller number than β's address). For each proposition α you visit:

   (i) If α lies on no open path, or α is an atomic proposition or a negated atomic proposition, or α has been checked off, do nothing and move to the next proposition.

   Otherwise stay on α and go to step (ii).

   (ii) If α can have a propositional rule[8] or a negated quantifier rule[9] applied to it, apply the relevant rule at the bottom of every open path on which α lies, and check α off.

   If α can have the unnegated existential quantifier rule applied to it,[10] apply this rule at the bottom of every open path on which α lies, and check α off. When applying the rule at the bottom of a path, use the alphabetically first name that does not occur on that path.[11]

   If α can have the unnegated universal quantifier rule applied to it,[12] apply this rule at the bottom of every open path on which α lies (do not check α off). When applying the rule at the bottom of a path, do so once for each name that appears on that path—but in each case, apply the rule using that name only if this results in writing down a formula not already on the path.[13] If no names appear on the path, apply the rule using the name a.

   In all cases, when you write something at the bottom of an open path, check the path for closure, and close it with a cross if you can do so.

When you have visited the last proposition in the tree and dealt with it in accordance with the above instructions, go to step (2).[14]

2. If the tree has changed (in any way: you have added a proposition, closed a path, checked off a formula, etc.) since you last began step (1), go back to the beginning of step (1).[15]

   If the tree has not changed since you last began step (1), stop.

Let's think about what happens when you apply this procedure to a given finite tree. If the tree is already finished, nothing happens: you go through step (1) without changing the tree in any way, and then step (2) tells you to stop. If the tree is not already finished, one of two things might happen:

1. You go through step (1) a number of times, adding to the tree. Eventually there are no more additions, and step (2) tells you to stop. The result is a finished finite tree.

2. You keep going through step (1), adding to the tree forever. The result (after an infinite amount of time, so to speak) is an infinite tree. But note the crucial point: this infinite tree is finished.[16]

10.3.6 Finding the Pattern

In the previous section, we solved one of our two problems: coming up with a strategy for extending a finite initial section of a tree in a way that ensures a finished tree. Now to the second problem: how do we detect what pattern emerges from this strategy, so that we can read off a model? Here the news is not so good. We have given an effective procedure for extending any finite segment of a tree to a finished tree. But there is no effective procedure that when applied to a finite segment of tree, will tell us whether—when finished— the tree will have an infinite path. It is not just that no one has come up with such a procedure: it has been shown that there cannot be such a procedure.[17] Of course, in simple cases, a pattern does emerge clearly. For example, there is no doubt that the tree discussed in §10.3 will never close, even when saturated, and the pattern emerging in the extensions of F and G is easy to discern. Hence, we can safely conclude that the proposition at the top of the tree is satisfiable and read off a model in which it is true (as we did in §10.3.2). However, the point is that although we can do this sort of thing in individual cases, there is no single, effective procedure that can be applied to any finite tree and that will give a correct answer as to whether, when finished, that tree will be infinite. We return to this issue in §14.2. In the meantime, we confine ourselves to examples that are simple enough that—using insight and ingenuity, rather than following a mechanical procedure—it is possible to tell, from an examination of an initial section of the tree, whether the finished tree will be infinite.

10.3.7 What Infinite Trees Do Not Look Like

We conclude our discussion of infinite trees by noting two features we can be sure we shall never see. (The fact that we can never see these things will be important in §14.1, when we prove the soundness and completeness of the tree method.)

First, no tree has a path that looks like:

$$\alpha$$
$$\beta$$
$$\gamma$$
$$\vdots$$
$$\times$$

(The three dots with no proposition below them indicate that the sequence of propositions beginning with α, β and γ goes on infinitely.) That is, no tree has an infinite path with a cross at the bottom: an infinite closed path, that is, an infinite path that contains both some wff and its negation. The reason we never see this form of path is because of our closure-checking requirement (§10.1.5). If a path contains both some wff δ and its negation $\neg\delta$, then one of them must come before the other. Suppose, without loss of generality, that δ comes first.[18] Then, as soon as $\neg\delta$ is entered, the path must close:

$$\alpha$$
$$\beta$$
$$\gamma$$
$$\vdots$$
$$\delta$$
$$\vdots$$
$$\neg\delta$$
$$\times$$

Thus, the path cannot be infinitely long, because wffs are never added below a cross. That is, we cannot get a path like:

$$\alpha$$
$$\beta$$
$$\gamma$$
$$\vdots$$
$$\delta$$
$$\vdots$$
$$\neg\delta$$
$$\vdots$$
$$\times$$

In sum, if a path is infinitely long, it is open. Equivalently, if a path closes, it does so after some finite amount of time; a path cannot stay open through all finite stages of constructing a tree but then close at infinity.

So the first feature we never see is an infinite closed path. The second is an infinite tree (that is, a tree with infinitely many propositions in it) in which every path is finite. If the procedure for building a tree never terminates—that is, the tree grows forever—then the finished tree (after an infinite amount of time, so to speak) has an infinite path. That is, the tree cannot grow only side-ways, with new paths forever being added, but every path eventually ending (either because it closes or becomes saturated). Thus, an infinite tree might look like:

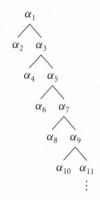

but will never look like:

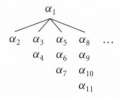

The reason is that our branching rules have only two branches—whereas to obtain an infinite tree with no infinite path (i.e., an infinite tree with infinitely many finite paths) starting from a finite set of initial propositions and applying tree rules, one would need rules with infinitely many branches.

Before showing this, let's introduce some terminology. For any two entries α and β in some tree, we say that β is a *descendant* of α (in that tree) iff we can get from α to β by moving down a path (i.e., iff there is a path that contains both α and β, and β is lower down that path than α is). We say that β is an *immediate descendant* of α iff it is a descendant of α, and there are no entries in between α and β (i.e., iff there is a path that contains both α and β, and β is the wff immediately after α on this path). If an entry in a tree has infinitely many descendants, it will be said to be *ID*; if an entry has only finitely many descendants, it will be said to be *FD*.

Now let us show that if one of our trees is infinite, it must have an infinitely long path. For each entry in one of our trees, the number of immediate descendants that it has is either zero, one, or two. Thus, if an entry α is ID, it must have at least one immediate descendant that is also ID. (Because if α has no immediate descendants, then it is not ID. So suppose α has one or two immediate descendants. If they are both FD, then so is α: an entry cannot be a descendant of α without being a descendant of one of α's immediate descendants, and a finite number of finite numbers adds up to a finite number. Thus, if α is ID, it must have at least one immediate descendant that is also ID.) Now suppose we have an infinite tree, that is, a tree with infinitely many entries.[19] Every entry in the tree is a descendant of the topmost entry, so the topmost entry (call it "1") is ID. Thus, 1 must have at least one immediate descendant which is ID: call this entry "2." (If there are two such entries, call the first of them—the one with the lower address—2.) Being ID, 2 must have at least one immediate descendant that is ID: call this entry "3." (If there are two such entries, call the first of them "3.") We can go on in this way forever, specifying an infinite series of ID entries: 1, 2, 3, ... But this series of entries constitutes an infinite path! So we have shown that our infinite tree must have an infinite path.[20]

10.3.8 Exercises

Translate the following arguments into MPL, and then test for validity using trees. For any argument that is not valid, read off from your tree a model in which the premise(s) are true and the conclusion false.

1. All dogs are mammals. All mammals are animals. Therefore, all dogs are animals.

2. If everything is frozen, then everything is cold. So everything frozen is cold.

3. If a thing is conscious, then either there is a divine being, or that thing has a sonic screwdriver. Nothing has a sonic screwdriver. Thus, not everything is conscious.

4. All cows are scientists, no scientist can fly, so no cow can fly.

5. Someone here is not smoking. Therefore, not everyone here is smoking.

6. If Superman rocks up, all cowards will shake. Catwoman is not a coward. So Catwoman will not shake.

7. Each car is either red or blue. All the red cars are defective, but some of the blue cars aren't. Thus, there are some defective cars and some nondefective cars.

8. For each thing, it swims only if there is a fish. Therefore, some things don't swim.

9. All robots built before 1970 run on kerosene. Autovac 23E was built before 1970, but it doesn't run on kerosene. So it's not a robot.

10. Everyone who is tall is either an athlete or an intellectual. Some people are athletes and intellectuals, but none of them is tall. Graham is a person. Therefore, if he's an athlete, then either he's not an intellectual, or he isn't tall.

11

Models, Propositions, and Ways the World Could Be

In this chapter we pause the development of the machinery of predicate logic to reflect on the significance of the machinery now in hand. In particular, we wish to investigate how the logical apparatus relates to the guiding ideas set out in Chapter 1:

- Logic is the science of truth.

- Our primary objects of study in logic are those things that can be true or false: propositions.

- A proposition is a claim about how things are—it represents the world as being some way; it is true if the world is that way, and otherwise it is false.

Among our technical apparatus we have closed wffs, and we have models. Relative to a given model, each closed wff is either true or false. How do the technical definitions of closed wffs (§8.4 and §8.4.5) and of truth and falsity relative to a model (§9.4.2) relate to the above ideas? In other words, which bit of the logical apparatus is supposed to be the precise version of the intuitive idea of a proposition, which bit is supposed to represent the world (or a way the world could be), and so on?

One answer that might spring to mind is this: closed wffs represent propositions; different models represent different ways the world could be; a wff being true in a model represents a way the world could be being the way a proposition says the world is; and a wff being false in a model represents a way the world could be not being the way a proposition says the world is. However, this idea does not withstand close scrutiny. One immediate problem concerns the idea that a closed wff by itself represents a proposition. A wff is a sequence of symbols. These symbols are simply objects: in themselves, they do not have meanings, and they do not pick out anything. They have no more content than do rocks or pieces of wood. A sequence of such symbols—a wff—likewise has no content (when considered simply as it is, in and of itself): it does not make a claim; it does not represent things as being thus or so. How then can such a thing—an *uninterpreted* wff, as it is called—be an adequate representative of the intuitive notion of a proposition?

But wait a minute: we have been in the habit of referring to closed wffs as propositions—are we now saying that this was a mistake? No, we are not. As noted at the end of §2.2.1, we spoke of wffs in these terms for the sake of simplicity of presentation, because talking in this way is convenient and harmless in most contexts. We now need to engage in a proper analysis of the matter, to determine which bit of our logical machinery can be regarded as the precise version of the intuitive notion of a proposition. There is a prima facie problem with regarding uninterpreted wffs as propositions, noted in the previous paragraph. But we should not expect to find that it is entirely incorrect, in every context, to think of closed wffs in these terms: if that were the case, we should never have called them "propositions" in the first place. Evidently, the full story is going to be somewhat complex. There are various legitimate candidates for the role of precise representative of the intuitive idea of a proposition. One candidate (in spite of the prima facie problem noted in the previous paragraph) is closed wffs, but there are others too. To ward off potential confusion, we shall, for the time being, refrain from calling closed wffs "propositions": we temporarily reserve this term for the intuitive notion introduced in Chapter 1 (and summarized in the third bullet point above).

As noted, an uninterpreted wff has no content of any sort: it does not say anything; it does not make any claim; it cannot (considered by itself, without reference to something else, such as a model) be said to be true or false. A useful way into our topic is to consider ways in which uninterpreted wffs can be given content. Although we did not reflect on this explicitly at the time (that is what we are doing now), we have already seen two different ways of giving content to wffs: *translation* and (as we shall call it) *valuation*. There is also a third way, which we have not hitherto encountered: *axiomatization*. We explore these processes in subsequent sections. It will be important to understand in detail how each works—and also to see that they are quite different.[1]

11.1 Translation

Recall how we translate a claim expressed in English into MPL. Take, for example, the claim "Mount Everest is tall." We set up a glossary:

m: Mount Everest
Tx: x is tall

and then translate the English as Tm. The idea is that Tm represents the proposition expressed by some utterance of the sentence "Mount Everest is tall." Of course, it is not the bare wff Tm that does this: it is the wff in conjunction with the glossary; or as we shall say, the wff *under* this particular glossary. The wff Tm could represent countless other propositions. For example, under the glossary:

m: Marcel Marceau
$Tx: x$ is talkative

it represents the proposition that Marcel Marceau is talkative.

So what does a glossary contribute that makes a bare, uninterpreted wff—which (considered by itself) says nothing—into a representation of a particular proposition (a particular claim about the world)? The short answer is that the glossary gives m and T contents that determine that Tm has the same content as the proposition expressed by some utterance of "Mount Everest is tall," but this answer requires unpacking and explanation.

Recall the guiding idea: a proposition is a claim about the world—it represents things as being thus and so. It is true if the world is the way the proposition represents the world to be—if things are thus and so—and otherwise it is false. Implicit in this picture are the ideas that there are (in principle) different ways the world could be (or could have been), and that a proposition gets a truth value when confronted with (or considered relative to) such a way. For example, the thing we call "Mount Everest" is tall, so given the way the world actually is, the proposition expressed by "Mount Everest is tall" is true; but that thing could have been much lower—if, for example, there had been millions of years of heavy rain causing extensive erosion—and relative to *that* way things could have been, the proposition expressed by "Mount Everest is tall" is false.[2] Because we will be talking about them quite a lot, it will be useful to have a short term for a "way the world could be." We use "ww" for this purpose.[3]

So, whatever exactly the content of the proposition expressed by "Mount Everest is tall" is, it must at least have this feature: it determines whether the proposition would be true or false, relative to each way the world could be. In other words, the content of a proposition determines a function from wws to truth values.[4]

Now, what are the contents of T and m? Well, they are what they need to be to determine a content for Tm[5]—and the content of Tm is to be the same as the content of the proposition expressed by "Mount Everest is tall." As we have said, this content must, at a minimum, determine a truth value for the proposition relative to each ww. To obtain a truth value for Tm, we need a referent for m (an object) and an extension for T (a set of objects). So the content of T must, at a minimum, determine a function from wws to sets of objects, and the content of m must, at a minimum, determine a function from wws to objects.

We have defined the notion of a value for certain kinds of expressions in the logical language: names, whose values are objects; predicates, whose values are sets of objects; and closed wffs, whose values are truth values. We now define the notion of an *intension* for these kinds of expressions. An intension is a function from wws to values.[6] Thus, the intension of a name is a function from wws to objects, the intension of a predicate is a function from wws to sets of objects, and the intension of a closed wff is a function from wws to truth values.[7] In these terms, we can express the above points as follows. The content of a name must at least determine an intension for it, the content of a predicate must at least determine an intension for it, and the intension of a name m and a predicate T together determine an intension for the closed wff Tm.[8]

Recapping, and putting the pieces together, the content of a proposition is that which determines that it is true relative to some wws and false relative to others. (This notion of the content of a proposition is implicit in the original picture, according to which a proposition represents the world as being some way and is true if the world is that way and false if the world is not.) For simplicity, we henceforth take this content just to be a function from wws to truth values.[9] Now, a glossary assigns contents to T and m (in the case of the example given above—but the point is general), which together ensure that Tm has the same content as the proposition expressed by some utterance of "Mount Everest is tall." Given that the content of this proposition is a function from wws to truth values, the content of Tm must be an intension: a function from wws to truth values. Hence, the contents of T and m—conferred on them by the glossary—must likewise be intensions:[10] a function from wws to objects in the case of the name m, and a function from wws to sets of objects in the case of the predicate T.

§

Glossaries, then, endow nonlogical symbols with intensions. How do we get from intensions to truth values? In other words, how do we get from intensions to values—to models? (Recall that a model is an assignment of values to nonlogical symbols.) By supplying a ww. An intension determines a value relative to each ww (that is just what an intension is). So to obtain a particular value from an intension, we plug in a particular ww. For example, consider the two wws mentioned above: the one corresponding to the way the world really is (the actual ww) and the imagined one, in which there has been severe erosion. The intension of T is a function from wws to sets of objects; the intension of m is a function from wws to objects. Applying these functions to the

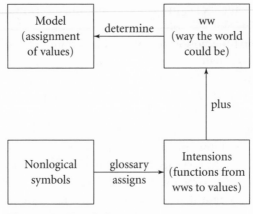

Figure 11.1. Translation.

first ww, we obtain an extension for T and a referent for m—this is the model generated by the given intensions of T and m and the first ww; likewise, applying these functions to the second ww, we get an extension for T and a referent for m—this is the model generated by the given intensions of T and m and the second ww. These ideas are represented in Figure 11.1. The bottom two boxes and the arrow between them represent what is involved in the process of translation itself; the remaining boxes and arrows show how to obtain models.

Well, actually we don't quite have models yet: we have an extension for T and a referent for m, but to obtain a model of the fragment of MPL containing T and m we also need a domain. We may take the domain of a model generated by a ww (together with some intensions) to be all the objects that exist, according to that ww. We can imagine the world containing more or fewer individuals—for example, imagine that your parents had more, or fewer, children. As part of specifying a way the world could be (or could have been), a ww specifies which things would exist (were the world that way). These are the things that go into the domain of any model generated by that ww (i.e., by that ww together with any intensions).[11]

§

Note that in the picture just presented—the picture of how uninterpreted wffs gain content via translation—models and wws are quite different kinds of things. A model is an assignment of values to nonlogical symbols (which then determine an assignment of truth values to closed wffs). A ww is a way the world could be. A ww does not in itself involve assigning values to expressions. Rather, the value of an expression (name, predicate, or closed wff) is determined by its content (an intension) together with a ww. We obtain a value for an expression at, or relative to, a ww by combining its content with the facts according to that ww. A ww plus contents for some items of nonlogical vocabulary determines an assignment of values to those items—that is, a model:

ww + contents ↦ model

A closed wff is true or false only in a model—that is, given an assignment of values to its nonlogical components. A wff cannot be true or false outside of any model—that would amount to the wff being assigned a value (a truth value) without its components getting values (recall that a model just is an assignment of values to the nonlogical components of wffs). And that cannot happen: now that we have moved beyond propositional logic, the truth value of a closed wff is never a brute fact—it is always determined by the values of the nonlogical components of the proposition. Thus, if we say that a wff is true at, or relative to, a ww, this is just a convenient manner of speaking. What we really mean is that the wff is true in the model determined by that ww together with certain contents.

Given some nonlogical symbols endowed (via a glossary) with contents, we have many models of the fragment of MPL containing those symbols: one model for each ww.[12] One of these models has a special status. We call it the *actual* model. It is the one generated by (the given contents and) the *actual* ww (i.e., that ww which—out of all the possible ways the world could be—represents the way the world really is). When we speak of soundness as involving validity plus truth of premises, what we mean is truth on the actual model.[13] So an argument is sound just in case there is no model at all in which the premises are true and the conclusion false (i.e., it is valid), and in the actual model the premises are true.

Note that it makes no sense to speak of the actual model of a fragment of MPL in abstraction from an assignment of intensions to the nonlogical symbols in the fragment (i.e., a glossary): although there is just one actual ww, the actual model is the one generated by applying certain intensions to this ww. Hence, without intensions, we still have an actual ww, but we have no actual model. In other words, there is not just one model that is the actual model, once and for all. Rather, for any intensions for the nonlogical symbols in a fragment, there is an actual model of the fragment together with those intensions.

11.2 Valuation

In the previous section we examined one way of giving content to bare wffs: translation. In this section we look at a second way: valuation. Like translation, valuation is something we have already encountered in earlier chapters. Recall that in Chapter 9, we would sometimes present a model, for example,

Domain: $\{1, 2, 3, \ldots\}$
Extensions: $E: \{2, 4, 6, \ldots\}$ $O: \{1, 3, 5, \ldots\}$

and then ask, of various closed wffs, for example,

1. $\forall x E x$ 3. $\forall x (E x \lor O x)$

2. $\exists x O x$ 4. $\exists x (E x \land O x)$

whether each of them is true or false in the given model. Call the process of specifying a particular model for some wffs—of specifying values for their nonlogical components—*valuation*. It seems very natural to say that in the context of valuation, closed wffs take on a kind of content; they say something, and hence can be assessed for truth or falsity. In the abstract, wffs have many models, in some of which they are true and in others false, but once we fix on a particular model, it is natural to think of a wff as saying something about the things in the domain of this model and as being simply true if it is true relative to the chosen model.

Note that the kind of content that wffs take on in valuation—that is, when we pick out a specific model—is quite different from the kind they take on in translation. In translation, nonlogical symbols are assigned intensions via a glossary, and intensions, together with a ww, determine a model. So in translation, there is an indirect relationship between the kind of content assigned to wffs (i.e., intensions) and models. To obtain a model, given intensions, we also need a ww; different wws will yield different models from the same intensions. In contrast, valuation does not involve a glossary, and there are no intensions. There is a direct relationship between the kind of content assigned and models. The contents assigned are just values: a content is assigned by picking out a model, and a model is just an assignment of values to nonlogical symbols (together with a domain from which these values are drawn).

Recall Figure 11.1: using translation, we reach a model (i.e., an assignment of values to the nonlogical symbols) by going around three sides of a square. Contrast this process to that shown in Figure 11.2: using valuation, a model is simply specified (out of nowhere, so to speak). Intensions and wws play no role here as intermediaries between the nonlogical symbols and their values; rather, the values are assigned directly.

The model assigned in the process of valuation is often called the *intended model* of (the relevant fragment of) the logical language. A fragment has infinitely many different models, in some of which it is true and in others, false.[14]

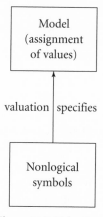

Model
(assignment
of values)

valuation | specifies

Nonlogical
symbols

Figure 11.2. Valuation.

Once one of them has been singled out as the intended model, it is then natural to speak of a wff as simply "true" (as opposed to "true in such and such a model") if it is true in the intended model. Note that the intended model cannot be equated with the actual model. The notion of an actual model makes sense only when symbols have intensions (it is defined as the model determined by those intensions and the actual ww—the ww corresponding to the way the world really is)—and using valuation, we do not give symbols intensions; we only give them values.

To appreciate fully the difference between translation and valuation, we have to be very clear on the issue discussed in §9.3.2. When we engage in valuation—when we assign a model directly to a fragment of the logical language—we often use English to do so. For example, suppose we introduce a model as follows:

Domain: the set of persons alive in the world on 11 June 2011 at 11:44:00 a.m.
Referents: a: Angela Merkel b: Barack Obama
Extensions: F: females M: males

Relative to this model, Fa is true, $\forall x Fx$ is false, $\exists x Fx \land \exists x Mx$ is true, and so on. It is easy to confuse what is going on here with a case where we translate the propositions:

1. Angela Merkel is female.

2. Everyone is a woman.

3. There is at least one woman and there is at least one man.

a: Angela Merkel
b: Barack Obama
Fx: x is female
Mx: x is male

However, the two processes—valuation and translation—are completely different.

In the example of valuation just given, one particular model is specified of the fragment of MPL containing the names a and b and the predicates F and M. I specify a set of objects as the domain, two objects as referents of a and b, and two sets of objects as extensions of F and M. To make these specifications, I rely on your grasp of English expressions such as "persons," "the world," "11 June 2011," and "Angela Merkel." But as discussed in §9.3.2, these expressions are just a route to certain objects and sets. I could (in principle) specify the very same model in other ways. For example, if we had a completely accurate database of the entire population of the world, updated in real time, I could specify the domain as the set containing everyone in the database as of 11 June 2011 at 11:44:00 a.m., the referent of a as the person numbered 165,465,464 (or whatever) in the database, the extension of F as the set containing persons numbered 165,465,464, 654,684, 465,464, . . . and 65,464 (or whatever), and so on.

In contrast, in the example of translation the expressions a, b, F, and M are not assigned values: no particular model is specified. Hence, no particular truth value is determined for Fa—the translation of "Angela Merkel is female"—or for any other closed wff. Rather, the expressions a, b, F, and M are assigned intensions. Together with a ww, they determine a model (an assignment of values), but no particular ww is singled out by the process of translation. Relative to some wws, Fa—taken under the given glossary—comes out false; relative to others, it comes out true.

Thus, when it comes to truth values, translation gives us both less and more than valuation. Less, in that by itself, translation gives us no truth values whatsoever. More, in that it gives us something—intensions—that determines truth values relative to every ww. (That is, given just one intension for each nonlogical symbol—provided by a glossary—we get a truth value for each closed wff relative to any ww.) In contrast, valuation yields one truth value for each closed wff (in the fragment assigned values by the specified model). It gives us values directly—nothing else (e.g., a ww) is required for truth values to be forthcoming. However, valuation just specifies one model: it has no implications for other truth values that closed wffs might have in other models.

11.3 Axiomatization

We have looked at two ways of giving content to uninterpreted wffs: translation (in which the contents are intensions, given by a glossary) and valuation (in which the contents are values, given by direct stipulation of a model). We now look at a third way: axiomatization. Using axiomatization, we supply content to some nonlogical symbols—and hence to wffs formed from them—by specifying a group of wffs containing these symbols. These wffs are called *axioms* (or *postulates*). The most obvious and prominent examples of axiom systems (e.g., the axioms for Peano arithmetic; various axiom systems for set theory; axiomatizations of geometry; axiom systems in algebra, including those for groups, rings, and fields) employ logical resources we have not yet introduced: many-place predicates (Chapter 12), identity (Chapter 13), and often function symbols (§13.7). We therefore use a toy example here, but it illustrates the basic idea perfectly well. Consider the predicates A, B, and C, and suppose we lay down the following axioms governing these predicates:

1. $\forall x (Ax \lor Bx)$

2. $\neg \exists x (Ax \land Bx)$

3. $\forall x (Cx \rightarrow Ax)$

This set of axioms does not fix particular values (extensions) for A, B, and C. However, it does constrain their extensions: if the axioms are all to come out true in a model, certain relationships must hold among the extensions of A, B, and C in that model. For axiom (3) to be true, the extension of C must be a subset of the extension of A; for axiom (2) to be true, the extensions of A and B must not overlap; and for axiom (1) to be true, the extensions of A and B must together exhaust the entire domain. Here are some models that make all the axioms true:

1. Domain: $\{1\}$
   Extensions: $A: \{1\}$ $B: \emptyset$ $C: \{1\}$

2. Domain: $\{1, 2\}$
   Extensions: $A: \{1, 2\}$ $B: \emptyset$ $C: \{2\}$

3. Domain: $\{1, 2\}$
   Extensions: $A: \{1\}$ $B: \{2\}$ $C: \{1\}$

4. Domain: $\{1, 2, 3\}$
   Extensions: $A: \{1, 2\}$ $B: \{3\}$ $C: \{2\}$

and here are some models that make at least one of the axioms false:

5. Domain: $\{1\}$
   Extensions: $A: \{1\}$ $B: \{1\}$ $C: \{1\}$

6. Domain: {1, 2}
   Extensions: A: {1} B: ∅ C: {2}

7. Domain: {1, 2}
   Extensions: A: {1} B: {2} C: {1, 2}

8. Domain: {1, 2, 3}
   Extensions: A: {1} B: {2} C: {1}

In general, the more axioms we add, the greater the constraints will be on the values of the nonlogical symbols featured in the axioms. Note, however, that we can never determine a unique model by adding more axioms. This follows from the isomorphism lemma (Chapter 9, n. 3): if we have a model that makes all our axioms true, we can always define a different model that still makes them all true by switching all objects in the domain for new objects (without making any other changes; i.e., if x is in the extension of a certain predicate or is the referent of a certain name before the switch, then its replacement is in the extension of that predicate or is the referent of that name after the switch). Therefore, the most that a set of axioms can do is fix a model "up to isomorphism." Note that not all axiom systems fix their models up to isomorphism.[15] For example, we listed four models that make true all the axioms in our example system, but none of these models can be derived from any of the others just by switching objects in the domain (while holding referents and extensions fixed—relatively speaking—in the way discussed above). In other words, no two of these four models are isomorphic.[16]

So axiomatization does not fix intensions for nonlogical symbols, nor does it fix particular values for them (i.e., particular objects, or particular sets of objects). It does, however, constrain the possible values of nonlogical symbols, and to this extent, it gives them a kind of content. The point is often put this way: what are As, Bs, and Cs, according to the above axiom system? Or to put it another way, what are the contents of the predicates A, B, and C? The answer is: whatever they need to be to make the axioms true. They could be anything at all—provided they have the right relationships to one another to make the axioms true. So the axioms transform A, B, and C from being empty symbols—which have infinitely many different possible extensions, one in each model of the language—to having some sort of content. This content determines that some assignments of values to them are now acceptable (those made by models in which the axioms are true) while other assignments are not acceptable.

If we consider bare, uninterpreted closed wffs, we can say that they are true in some models and false in others, but we cannot say that they are simply true or false without qualification. Both translation and valuation yield (different) unqualified notions of truth: translation involves the notion of truth in the actual model; valuation involves the notion of truth in the intended model. Axiomatization does not yield an unqualified notion of truth. Rather, the notion that emerges naturally in this context is that of a *theorem*: a wff that is true in every model that makes all the axioms true. In other words, a theorem is a logical consequence of the axioms. A set of wffs that is closed under logical consequence—that is, one for which every wff that is a logical consequence of some wffs in the set is also in the set—is a *theory*. A set of axioms generates a theory: the set of all wffs that are true in every model in which all the axioms are true. A theorem of an axiomatic system is a wff that is a member of the theory generated by the axioms. For example, in our example above, $\neg\exists x (Cx \land Bx)$ is a theorem of the system: it follows logically from axioms (2) and (3).

11.4 Propositions

At the beginning of this chapter, we asked which bit of the logical apparatus is supposed to be the precise version of the intuitive idea of a proposition. We are now in a position to return to this question. One answer emerges from the process of translation; another comes from the process of valuation. In addition, there are at least five other reasonable answers to the question. We examine these seven answers now.

(1) The notion of a proposition that emerges naturally from a consideration of translation is: a proposition is a closed wff together with intensions for its nonlogical components. In other words—given that a glossary assigns intensions to nonlogical symbols—a proposition is a closed wff under a glossary. This notion meshes perfectly with the intuitive idea of a proposition as a claim about how the world is, which is true if the world is that way, and false if it is not.

(2) The notion of a proposition that emerges naturally from a consideration of valuation is: a proposition is a closed wff together with a model (which assigns values to the nonlogical components of the wff). This notion meshes perfectly with the intuitive idea of propositions as things that are true or false.

Consideration of axiomatization does not lead naturally to any notion of proposition. This is to be expected, given the close intuitive link between propositions and truth/falsity, together with the fact (noted in §11.3) that axiomatization does not yield an unqualified notion of truth.

We now have two models for propositions on the table: a closed wff plus intensions for its nonlogical components (provided by a glossary) and a closed wff plus a model (which assigns values to its nonlogical components). We can picture propositions, in these two senses, as closed wffs with the nonlogical vocabulary tagged with additional material—either intensions or values (provided by the model):

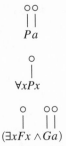

If we think of the circles here as intensions, we have images of propositions in the first sense; if we think of the circles as values, we have images of propositions in the second sense. (Note, however, that a proposition in the second sense is a closed wff plus a model. A model assigns values to nonlogical symbols, but there is more to a model: there is also a domain. The domain is not explicitly represented in these pictures.)

(3) There are other models of propositions worthy of our attention. Most obviously, there is the notion of a closed wff by itself. Note that the core logical notions—validity, logical truth, equivalence, and so on—are defined with reference to all models: no reference is made to any particular special model (e.g., an actual model, or an intended model). Whether a wff is a logical truth is a matter of whether it is true on all models whatsoever. Thus, it does not depend on whether content has been assigned to the nonlogical symbols in the wff by translation, valuation, axiomatization, or some other process. Likewise, the validity of an argument depends on whether there is any model in which the premises are true and the conclusion false. Thus, when considering validity, any content that wffs may have been assigned—content that makes some models more salient than others (e.g., the actual model, the intended model, or the models that make the axioms true)—is ignored, and all models are treated equally. (Remember that validity is supposed to depend only on form or structure—on the way in which an argument is composed out of wffs, and the ways in which these wffs are composed out of smaller components—not on any specific contents that these components may have.) Similar comments apply to the other core logical notions (satisfiability, equivalence, and so on). From a purely logical point of view, then, all we care about is the wffs themselves. It is therefore natural, in contexts where we are considering purely logical properties (validity, equivalence, and so on), to refer to a closed wff by itself as a proposition. This line of thought explains why we spoke of closed wffs in these terms in earlier chapters.

Recall that in §2.1 we said that our goal in introducing PL (and the point carried over to subsequent logical languages) was to have a language in which the structure of the wffs directly mirrors the structure of propositions. For the three notions of proposition just examined, we go further: we take wffs (either alone, or together with something else—intensions or models) to *be* propositions. Thus, we no longer say simply that the structure of wffs directly mirrors the structure of propositions; we say that the structure of wffs is the structure of propositions. This identification is theoretically economical: it avoids an unnecessary duplication of entities (i.e., wffs, and the things whose structure they represent: propositions). It is also elucidatory: the question of what propositions really are reduces at least partially to the question of what wffs are, and that question (as we shall see in §16.7) is quite tractable.

We have now mentioned three notions of proposition that arise naturally from processes examined earlier in the book: translation, valuation, and consideration of logical properties (e.g., validity, satisfiability). There are other reasonable notions of a proposition that arise naturally in other contexts. The next two notions to be discussed can be regarded as two different ways of unpacking one basic idea: two claims (one made by person X and one by person Y) have the same content—or in other words, X and Y express the same proposition—iff these claims are true and false in exactly the same situations. The two unpackings differ in their conceptions of a "situation": the first way takes it to be a ww; the second takes it to be a model.

(4) The notion of proposition emerging from the basic idea considered in the previous paragraph when a "situation" is taken to be a ww is: a proposition is a function from wws to truth values.[17] Recall our first notion of proposition: a closed wff together with intensions for its nonlogical components (provided by a glossary). These intensions, together with the structure of the wff, determine an intension for the entire closed wff. The notion of proposition currently under discussion takes this latter intension itself (without the closed wff) to be a proposition.

Here's an intuitive way of thinking about propositions in this sense. Think of the space of all wws: all the ways the world could be. Suppose someone makes a claim. In one sense of "content," we could regard the content of her claim as the information it conveys about how things are: about the way the world is. This information consists of a division of the wws into those compatible with the claim (those relative to which it is true) and those incompatible with it (those relative to which it is false). A function from wws to truth values is precisely such a division: it divides the space of wws into two groups: those mapped to True (intuitively, the ones compatible with the claim) and those mapped to False (intuitively, the ones incompatible with the claim). In this picture, two people make the same claim—express the same proposition—iff they divide the wws in exactly the same way.

(5) To explain the notion of proposition that emerges from the basic idea considered three paragraphs ago when a "situation" is taken to be a model, we

need some background notions. Consider the relation of *logical equivalence* among closed wffs: a wff α stands in this relation to a wff β iff they have the same truth value in every model (of any fragment of the language containing all nonlogical symbols that occur in α or β). It is easy to see that this relation is: *reflexive*—any proposition α is logically equivalent to itself; *symmetric*—if α is logically equivalent to β, then β is logically equivalent to α; and *transitive*—if α is logically equivalent to β and β is logically equivalent to γ, then α is logically equivalent to γ. Hence, it is an equivalence relation.[18] Thus, it divides the set of all closed wffs into equivalence classes: nonoverlapping groups that between them cover all the closed wffs, such that each wff in a given group is logically equivalent to every other wff in that group, and no wff in a group is logically equivalent to any wff not in that group. Given a closed wff α, we use $|\alpha|$ to denote the equivalence class containing α. Note that if α and β are logically equivalent, then $|\alpha|$ and $|\beta|$ denote the same equivalence class. Now we can state the fifth notion of proposition: the propositions are the equivalence classes of closed wffs just considered.

(6, 7) We have now considered five notions of proposition. We mention two more. Recall our pictures of propositions in the first two senses: closed wffs with the nonlogical vocabulary tagged by circles (representing intensions in the first case and values in the second). To form pictures of propositions in our last two senses, imagine that the circles move down and replace the nonlogical symbols to which they are attached. More precisely, a closed wff is a sequence of symbols. For any such sequence, generate a new sequence by replacing nonlogical symbols in it by intensions or by values (of the sort appropriate to each kind of symbol). The result will be a proposition in the sixth or seventh sense, respectively.[19]

11.4.1 Pluralism with Regard to Propositions

We asked which bit of the logical apparatus is supposed to be the precise version of the intuitive idea of a proposition, and got seven different answers. We should not, I think, press the question as to which one of these is *the* formal analogue of the intuitive notion. The seven candidates are not like presidential candidates, only one of whom can win: it is not to be expected that an intuitive idea (e.g., the idea of a proposition sketched in Chapter 1) should necessarily have sufficiently determinate content to fix just one formal notion as its correct counterpart. Rather, all seven are perfectly good notions: each has its pros and cons; some are useful in one context, some in another. Let us briefly mention a couple of differentiating factors, which lead to some notions being more useful than others in certain contexts.

First, only three of the notions make use solely of the logical machinery developed so far: closed wffs, closed wffs plus models, and equivalence classes of closed wffs under the relation of logical equivalence. Three of the other notions make mention of intensions and/or wws, but these are part of the background picture (which we use, for example, to make sense of translation), not part of the logical machinery itself. There are extensions of classical logic—known as *intensional logics*—in which wws and intensions are brought into the (expanded) logical fold. We have been somewhat vague about what wws are: they are ways the world could be—the things relative to which propositions are true or false.[20] There are various ways of making this notion more precise. We could take a ww to be a complete way the world could be—throughout its entire history and across its entire spatial extent—down to the finest detail;[21] or we could take a ww to be a way the world could be at some particular moment of time, or in some particular place at some particular time, and so on. All that really matters is that intensions and wws be made for each other: whatever exactly a ww is taken to be, an intension (of some expression in the logical language) must be a function from one of these things to values (of the sort appropriate to that kind of expression: truth values for closed wffs, objects for names, and so on).[22]

Second, some of the notions are more coarse-grained than others. That is to say, if we group utterances according to which ones express the same proposition, then for some notions of proposition (the more coarse-grained ones) the groups will be larger, and for others (the more fine-grained ones) the groups will be smaller. For example, the view of propositions as closed wffs is rather fine-grained, whereas the views of propositions as sets of wws, or as equivalence classes of wffs are rather coarse-grained. Also, the sixth and seventh notions are less fine-grained than the first and second. For example, we might represent two utterances as expressing different propositions in the first sense—different because P and Q are different nonlogical symbols, although the attached intension is the same in both cases:

If we consider the corresponding propositions in the sixth sense—where the attached intension takes the place of the nonlogical symbol—then the two utterances will be regarded as expressing the same proposition.

11.5 Logical Consequence and NTP

Consider the following argument:

The sun is hot.
Therefore, the sun is not cold.

Translating into MPL yields:

> s: the sun Hs
> Hx: x is hot $\therefore \neg Cs$
> Cx: x is cold

This argument is invalid. Here is a model in which the premise is true and the conclusion false:

> Domain: {Plato, Aristotle, Socrates}
> Referent of s: Plato
> Extensions: H: {Plato, Aristotle} C: {Plato}

This is an example of an argument that is NTP—after all, it is obviously impossible for the sun to be both hot and cold—but not so by virtue of its form; hence, it is not valid. In light of our discussions earlier in this chapter, we can now shed more light on cases of this sort.

Note that the countermodel to the argument we gave above cannot be reached by taking the intensions assigned to the nonlogical symbols by the glossary given above and applying them to some ww. For one thing, the intension of "the sun" does not determine Plato as referent relative to any ww. In other words, Plato could not be the sun (no matter how different things were). In addition, the intensions of "hot" and "cold" do not determine overlapping extensions relative to any ww: nothing could be hot and cold (no matter how different things were).

Given intensions for the nonlogical symbols in a fragment of the logical language, I will call a model of that fragment a *ww-model* iff it can be generated by taking those intensions and applying them to some ww. Recall that a glossary assigns intensions to nonlogical symbols, and that intensions for the nonlogical symbols in a fragment of the logical language, together with a ww, determine a model of the fragment. Consider Figure 11.3. Given a glossary G for some fragment of the logical language, some models of the fragment can be generated from the intensions assigned by that glossary, together with some ww. These are the ww-models (of the fragment under G). Other models cannot be generated in this way: there is no ww that, together with the intensions assigned by G, generates such a model.

Given the notion of a ww-model, we can then say that an argument is NTP iff there is no ww-model in which the premises are true and the conclusion false. Another term for this concept is *entailment*: when an argument is NTP, the premises *entail* the conclusion. (Obviously this definition makes sense only for arguments—sequences of closed wffs—whose nonlogical symbols have been endowed with intensions. Without intensions—given just some closed wffs—we cannot distinguish ww-models of those wffs from other models:

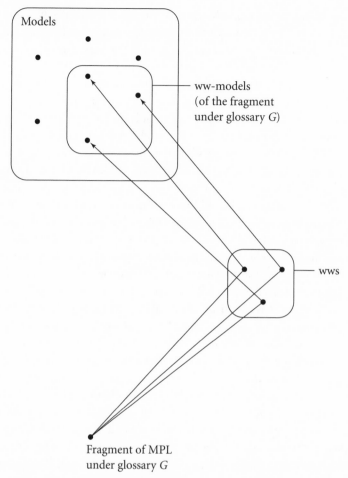

Models

ww-models
(of the fragment
under glossary *G*)

wws

Fragment of MPL
under glossary *G*

Figure 11.3. Models and ww-models.

the notion of a ww-model is defined relative to some given intensions.) In contrast, an argument is valid iff there is no model at all (ww-model or other) in which the premises are true and the conclusion false. (This notion is defined for arguments—sequences of closed wffs—by themselves: intensions are not needed.) Clearly, if an argument is valid, it is NTP relative to any assignment of intensions to its nonlogical vocabulary. If there is no model at all in which the premises are true and the conclusion false, then a fortiori there is no ww-model in which the premises are true and the conclusion false, no matter how we pick out the ww-models (i.e., no matter what set of intensions we use to generate a set of ww-models).[23] The converse does not hold: an argument can be NTP but not valid. The argument given at the beginning of this section provides an example.

The definition of NTP is obtained from that of logical consequence by replacing "model" with "ww-model." Other logical notions have counterparts obtained in an analogous manner. For example, a logical truth is a wff that is true in every model. A *necessary truth* is a wff (together with intensions for its nonlogical components) that is true in every ww-model (relative to those intensions). Dual to the notion of logical truth is the notion of satisfiability: a logical truth is a proposition (closed wff) that is true in all models; a satisfiable proposition is one that is true in some model. Likewise, dual to the notion of necessity is the notion of possibility: a proposition (closed wff under a glossary) is necessarily true if it is true in all ww-models; a proposition is possibly true if it is true in some ww-model.[24]

In logic we are interested in validity, logical truth, satisfiability and so on—the notions defined in terms of models. One of our goals is to come up with a general procedure for testing for each of these properties. To illustrate the idea with the example of logical truth (analogous comments apply to validity and the other notions), we want a single procedure we can apply to any proposition whatsoever that will tell us whether that proposition is logically true. The two procedures we have seen are: construct a truth table and see whether the proposition is true in every row, or construct a tree for the negation of the proposition and see whether all paths close.

Turning from the notions defined in terms of models to those defined in terms of ww-models, there can be no general science of the latter notions: nothing analogous to logic; nothing which stands to these notions as logic stands to the former notions. There is no hope of a single procedure that can be applied to any proposition and will tell us whether it is necessarily true. (Again, analogous comments apply to entailment and the other notions defined in terms of ww-models.) To see why, consider, for example, the following claim:

All jibs are headsails.

Does it express a logical truth? To find out, we need only discern the structure of the proposition. Our procedure is to translate into MPL—say, as follows:

Jx: x is a jib $\forall x(Jx \to Hx)$
Hx: x is a headsail

When we then test for logical truth—by doing a tree starting with $\neg \forall x(Jx \to Hx)$—the glossary is irrelevant: all that matters is the bare wff itself. Thus, we do not need to know anything about jibs or headsails to determine whether this proposition is logically true.[25]

The situation is very different when it comes to necessary truth. Here the glossary cannot be cast aside. We want to know: is there any ww-model in which this proposition is false? In other words, is there any model that can be reached by taking the intensions assigned to J and H by the glossary and applying them to some ww, in which $\forall x(Jx \to Hx)$ is false? Obviously we cannot answer this question without knowing about the intensions in question and about the space of wws (i.e., about which facts are represented there— which supposed possibilities are genuine ways the world could be, and which are really impossible). Thus, a science of *necessity*—if it were able to yield an answer for any proposition as to whether that proposition is a necessary truth—would need to include a complete account both of the contents of every expression and of how the world could and could not be. If such a science were possible at all, it would certainly look nothing like logic: the rules of logic can be written down in a few pages, but the rules of necessity would fill countless libraries of dictionaries and encyclopedias.[26]

11.6 Postulates

Consider the argument from the beginning of §11.5:

The sun is hot.
Therefore, the sun is not cold.

It is not valid. Intuitively, it is NTP. As discussed in §11.5, there is no hope for a general science of NTP (as opposed to validity). Nevertheless, there is a way of bringing arguments of this sort into the fold of logic. Recall Figure 11.3. Our argument is NTP iff in every ww-model in which the premises are true, the conclusion is true. The ww-models, relative to a given glossary, are those generated by the intensions assigned by that glossary together with some ww. But although the ww-models are defined in this way, it does not mean that the only way to pick them out is (so to speak) to bounce the intensions off the wws. Given a set M of models (e.g., the set of ww-models of some fragment under some glossary), it may be possible to pick out that set of models via axiomatization, that is, by stating some wffs such that the models in which all of those wffs are true are precisely the models in M.[27] Let a *postulate* for a glossary (which, recall, assigns intensions to the nonlogical symbols in some fragment of the logical language) be a closed wff that is true in all ww-models (relative to that glossary) of the fragment. A *complete* set of postulates for a given glossary is an axiomatization of its ww-models: a set of closed wffs such that a model makes all these wffs true iff it is a ww-model (relative to that glossary). We shall say that a glossary is *axiomatizable* iff there is a complete set of postulates for that glossary. There is no reason to think that every glossary should be axiomatizable, but this does not always matter: often a partial set of postulates is all we need. For example, recall our glossary for the argument given above:

s: the sun
Hx: x is hot
Cx: x is cold

The only aspect of the intensions assigned by this glossary that is relevant to the fact that the argument is NTP is that there is no ww relative to which the intensions of H and C pick out extensions that overlap. We can capture this aspect of the glossary via the following axiom:

$$\forall x(Hx \rightarrow \neg Cx)$$

(or anything logically equivalent to it, e.g., $\forall x(Cx \rightarrow \neg Hx)$ or $\neg \exists x(Hx \wedge Cx)$). Now consider the following argument—which is our earlier argument, with the postulate added as an extra premise:

Hs
$\forall x(Hx \rightarrow \neg Cx)$
$\therefore \neg Cs$

This argument is valid. Remember, to determine whether an argument is valid, we need only look at the wffs that make it up: any contents these wffs may have is irrelevant. Thus, once we have postulates, we can throw away the glossary: we just work with the *wffs*—their intensions are beside the point. Provided that we can supply the relevant postulates, we can then tackle the question of whether an argument is NTP via the question of whether an associated argument—with the relevant postulates added as extra premises— is valid. The latter question is one we can handle using purely logical techniques.

Similar comments apply to other notions: necessary truth, possible truth, and so on. For example, if a proposition (a closed wff under a glossary) is necessarily true, then—provided we can capture, in postulates, the aspects of the intensions assigned by the glossary that render it necessarily true—we can get a handle on the fact that it is necessarily true in this way: the proposition (closed wff under a glossary) is necessarily true iff the proposition (closed wff—now the intensions become irrelevant) is true in every model in which the postulates (closed wffs—their intensions are also irrelevant) are true— that is, iff the proposition is a logical consequence of the postulates. The latter question is one that can be addressed using purely logical techniques. For example, "no kelpie is a cat" is, intuitively, a necessary truth: because a kelpie is one specific kind of dog, and nothing can be both a dog and a cat. If we translate into the logical language using the glossary:

Kx: x is a kelpie
Cx: x is a cat
Dx: x is a dog

then the result:

$$\neg\exists x(Kx \wedge Cx) \tag{11.1}$$

is not a logical truth: there are models in which (11.1) is false. However, if we also introduce as postulates $\forall x(Kx \rightarrow Dx)$ and $\neg\exists x(Dx \wedge Cx)$, then (11.1) does follow logically from these two postulates: there is no model in which the postulates are true and (11.1) is false. Thus, provided that the relevant postulates are forthcoming, the validity of an argument with the postulates as premises and a proposition α as conclusion gives us a means—within formal logic—to determine whether the proposition α is necessarily true.

12

General Predicate Logic

12.1 The Language of General Predicate Logic

We said in §8.1.1 that our development of predicate logic would proceed as follows: we start with the simplest kind of basic proposition and distinguish its parts—a name and a predicate; we then see how far we can get representing further propositions using the connectives from propositional logic plus names and predicates; we find that we need more resources—quantifiers and variables; we then see how far we can get representing further propositions using connectives, names, predicates, quantifiers, and variables; we eventually find that we need even more resources, and so on. We come now to the point where, to represent the propositions expressed by some common kinds of utterance, we need more resources than we have so far. Consider the claims:

Brutus was Caesar's friend.
Brutus betrayed Caesar.
Brutus betrayed one of his friends.

None of these can be translated adequately into MPL; that is, the propositions they express cannot be represented adequately in MPL. Each claim involves a *relation*—betraying, being friends with—and we have no means of expressing relations in MPL. We can say that Caesar is ambitious, that Brutus is honorable, and so on—that is, we can attribute properties to individuals—but we cannot express the idea that a relation holds between two individuals.

The claim "Brutus betrayed Caesar" involves two singular terms, "Brutus" and "Caesar," and the predicate "betrayed." The latter predicate is, then, a *two-place* (or dyadic) predicate "x betrayed y": a predicate that yields a proposition when two names are plugged into its two argument places. (These two argument places are represented by x and y in "x betrayed y.") But MPL contains only one-place (or monadic) predicates, such as "x is ambitious," "x is honorable." In this chapter we extend our logical language to include two-place (and indeed three- and more-place) predicates, taking us from monadic to general (*polyadic*, i.e., many-place) predicate logic. This change is the only one we make to our language. So, for example, what we have already said about quantifiers remains unchanged. However, when we combine quantifiers with many-place predicates, new richness and complexity emerges, so we shall spend some time exploring the new possibilities arising from the interaction of our existing quantifiers and the new predicates.

12.1.1 Many-Place Predicates

Consider the following claims:

1. Alice is interesting.   4. Bob is next to Carol.

2. Bob is pleasant.   5. Alice is opposite Bob.

3. Alice is taller than Bob.   6. Carol is standing between Alice and Bob.

To translate them into our logical language, we need glossary entries for the singular terms they contain:

a: Alice
b: Bob
c: Carol

Claims (1) and (2) are handled in the familiar way. We introduce glossary entries for the predicates they contain—the only difference is that we now add a superscript 1 to indicate explicitly that these are one-place predicates:

I^1x: x is interesting
P^1x: x is pleasant

We can now translate claims (1) and (2) as follows:

I^1a
P^1b

Claims (3), (4) and (5) contain two-place predicates: "is taller than," "is next to," and "is opposite." In English, if we want to add singular terms to such a predicate to yield a statement, we need two such terms: "Alice is taller than" is not a grammatical or meaningful statement; neither is "is taller than Bob." But "Alice is taller than Bob" is. In our logical language, we use capital letters for two-place predicates, as for one-place predicates: the difference is that they have a superscript 2 to indicate that they have two argument places:

T^2xy: x is taller than y
N^2xy: x is next to y
O^2xy: x is opposite y

We can now translate claims (3), (4), and (5) as follows:

T^2ab
N^2bc
O^2ab

Claim (6) contains a three-place predicate: "is standing between . . . and." In English, if we want to add singular terms to such a predicate to yield a statement, we need three such terms: "Carol is standing between Alice and" is not a grammatical or meaningful statement; neither are "Carol is standing between and Bob" or "is standing between Alice and Bob." But "Carol is standing between Alice and Bob" is. In our logical language, we use capital letters for three-place predicates, as for one- and two-place predicates: the difference is that they have a superscript 3 to indicate that they have three argument places:

S^3xyz: x is standing between y and z

We can now translate claim (6) as follows:

S^3cab

In general, we allow predicates with any positive finite number n of argument places. An n-place predicate is represented by a capital letter with the superscript n. In practice, however, we rarely deal with predicates of more than two places in this book and never with predicates of more than three places.

Some terminology: a one-place predicate picks out a property of objects. The many-place analogue of a property is called a "relation." Thus, a two-place predicate picks out a two-place relation between objects, a three-place predicate picks out a three-place relation between objects, and so on.

12.1.2 Atomic Wffs

Recall that when we give the official syntax of a logical language (§2.5 for PL and §8.4 for MPL), we first list the basic symbols and then explain how to construct wffs using these symbols. We have now added some basic symbols to the language of MPL: n-place predicates for n greater than 1. So now we need to explain how to make wffs using two-, three-, and in general n-place predicates. In our syntax for MPL, the only point in the definition of a wff where predicates played a role directly was clause (3i): the definition of an atomic wff. So this clause is the only one we need to modify. The modification is straightforward: the old clause states that to make a wff from a one-place predicate, one follows it with one name or variable. The new clause will simply generalize this: to make a wff from an n-place predicate, one follows it with n

names and/or variables. (The complete syntax is presented in §12.1.3.) So, for example, the following are well formed:

$$T^2ab \qquad T^2ax \qquad T^2xy \qquad T^2zc$$

while the following are not:

$$T^2a \qquad T^2x \qquad T^2abc \qquad T^2xyz$$

The key thing is that the number of terms (where a term is a name or a variable) after the predicate must be the same as the superscript of the predicate: so the two-place predicate T^2 must have two terms after it.[1]

The distinction (§8.4.5) between wffs and propositions (i.e., closed wffs) remains: T^2xy and T^2ax are just as well formed as T^2ab, but only the last is a proposition, because the first two contain free variables (and so are not closed wffs).

12.1.3 Syntax of GPL

Here we present in one place the full syntax of GPL: the language of General Predicate Logic. As remarked in the previous section, the only differences from the syntax of MPL in §8.4 are clause (1iii) covering predicates, in the section on symbols, which now allows n-place predicates for any positive finite n; and the corresponding generalization of clause (3i) covering atomic wffs, in the section on well-formed formulas.

1. The symbols of GPL are:

   (i) names:

   $$a, b, c, \ldots t$$

   We use lowercased letters other than u, v, w, x, y, and z, which are reserved for variables. If we need more than twenty different name symbols, we use subscripts (i.e., $a_2, a_3, \ldots, b_2, b_3, \ldots$).

   (ii) variables:

   $$x, y, z, u, v, w$$

   If we need more than six different variable symbols, we use subscripts (i.e., $x_2, x_3, \ldots, y_2, y_3, \ldots$).

   (iii) predicates:

   $$A^1, B^1, C^1, \ldots, A^2, B^2, C^2, \ldots$$

   We use uppercased letters from anywhere in the alphabet (with one exception:[2] the letter "I" is not used for a two-place predicate, so that I^2 is not a predicate symbol of the language, although I^1, I^3, I^4 and so on are), with a superscript indicating the number of argument places. If we need more than twenty-six different n-place predicate symbols for any n (or more than twenty-five in the case $n = 2$), we use subscripts (i.e., $A_2^1, A_3^1, \ldots, A_2^2, A_3^2, \ldots$).

   (iv) five connectives:

   $$\neg, \wedge, \vee, \rightarrow, \text{ and } \leftrightarrow$$

(v) two quantifier symbols:

$\forall$ and $\exists$

(vi) two punctuation symbols (parentheses):

(and)

The logical symbols are the connectives, the quantifier symbols, and the variables; the nonlogical symbols are the names and predicates; and the parentheses are auxiliary symbols.

2. We define the notion of a *term* of GPL as follows:

(i) A name is a term.

(ii) A variable is a term.

(iii) Nothing else is a term.

3. Wffs of GPL are defined as follows:

(i) Where $\underline{P^n}$ is any n-place predicate and $\underline{t_1} \ldots \underline{t_n}$ are any terms, the following is a wff:

$$\underline{P^n}\underline{t_1} \ldots \underline{t_n}$$

That is, an n-place predicate followed by any mixture of n names and/or variables is a well-formed formula. Wffs of this form are atomic wffs.

(ii) Where α and β are wffs and $\underline{x}$ is a variable, the following are wffs:

$\neg\alpha$

$(\alpha \wedge \beta)$

$(\alpha \vee \beta)$

$(\alpha \rightarrow \beta)$

$(\alpha \leftrightarrow \beta)$

$\forall\underline{x}\alpha$

$\exists\underline{x}\alpha$

(iii) Nothing else is a wff.

12.1.3.1 EXERCISES

State whether each of the following is a wff of GPL.

1. $\forall x F^1 y$

2. $\forall x \exists y F^1 y$

3. $\forall x R^2 xy$

4. $\forall x \exists x R^2 yy$

5. $R^2 x$

6. $\forall x R^2 x$

7. $\forall x (F^1 x \rightarrow R^2 x)$

8. $\forall x \exists y (F^1 x \rightarrow R^2 xy)$

9. $\forall x \exists y (F^1 xy \rightarrow R^2 y)$

10. $\forall x \exists y \forall x \exists y R^2 xy$

12.1.3.2 ABBREVIATIONS

We may leave the numerical superscript off a predicate letter when it is clear how many places the predicate has. For example, if I write the following glossary entry:

Hxy: x heard *y*

then it is perfectly clear—from the fact that two variables x and y follow the letter H in the glossary—that H is a two-place predicate. So no confusion results from omitting the superscript 2 on the H.

12.1.4 Order of Arguments

Consider the following two propositions:

Tab
Tba

Both contain the same two-place predicate T (i.e., T^2, but where we have omitted the superscript 2, in line with §12.1.3.2) and the same two names. They differ with respect to the order in which these two names appear after the predicate. This order is significant. Given the glossary entry:

Txy: x is taller than y

(together with the glosary entries for a and b in §12.1.1) the two propositions do not say the same thing. Tab says that Alice is taller than Bob, whereas Tba says that Bob is taller than Alice. Similarly, given the glossary entry:

$Sxyz$: x is standing between y and z

$Sabc$ says that Alice is standing between Bob and Carol, whereas $Sbac$ says something quite different: that Bob is standing between Alice and Carol.

We can set up our glossary however we please. So, for example, the above entry for $Sxyz$ is fine, but the following entry would also have been fine:

$Sxyz$: y is standing between x and z

(One might prefer to set up the glossary in the latter way, because it looks like what it means: here the middle argument is the one corresponding to the person who is standing between the other two.) What really matters is:

1. We must have only one entry for each predicate in a given glossary.

2. We must translate correctly given the glossary chosen.

So (1) we cannot have both the above entries for $Sxyz$: we must choose one or the other, and (2) given that we have adopted the first glossary entry for $Sxyz$, we must translate "Bob is standing between Alice and Carol" as $Sbac$. Sure, relative to the second glossary, $Sbac$ says that Alice is standing between Bob and Carol, but relative to the first glossary, it says that Bob is standing between Alice and Carol. So given that the first is indeed our chosen glossary, it would be incorrect to translate "Bob is standing between Alice and Carol" as $Sabc$: we must translate it as $Sbac$.

Thus, you can choose your glossary freely, but once it is chosen, you cannot choose freely how to translate given claims: you must translate them in accordance with your chosen glossary.[3]

12.1.5 Number of Arguments

Consider the following piece of reasoning:

Alice is taller than Bob.
Bob is tall.
∴ Alice is tall.

We must translate it using two predicates:

T^1x: x is tall
T^2xy: x is taller than y

We cannot employ a single predicate that somehow has one argument place in its occurrences in the second premise and the conclusion, and two argument places in its occurrence in the first premise. That sort of thing is not allowed in GPL: each predicate has a fixed number of places, indicated by its numerical superscript. Unless the predicate appears with exactly that number of terms after it, the result is not a well-formed formula. So absolutes (tall, short, heavy, etc.) need to be translated by one-place predicates, whereas their associated comparatives (taller, shorter, heavier, etc.) need to be translated by (different) two-place predicates.[4]

12.1.6 Exercises

Translate the following into GPL.

1. Bill heard Alice.

2. Bill did not hear Alice.

3. Bill heard Alice, but Alice did not hear Bill.

4. If Bill heard Alice, then Alice heard Bill.

5. Bill heard Alice if and only if Alice heard Alice.

6. Bill heard Alice, or Alice heard Bill.

7. Clare is taller than Dave, but she's not taller than Edward.

8. Mary prefers Alice to Clare.

9. Mary doesn't prefer Dave to Clare; nor does she prefer Clare to Dave.

10. Edward is taller than Clare, but he's not tall.

11. The Eiffel tower is taller than both Clare and Dave.

12. If Dave is taller than the Eiffel tower, then he's tall.

13. Although the Eiffel tower is taller, Clare prefers Dave.

14. If Alice is taller than Dave, then he prefers himself to her.

15. Dave prefers Edward to Clare only if Edward is taller than the Eiffel tower.

16. Dave prefers Edward to Clare only if she's not tall.

17. Mary has read *Fiesta,* and she likes it.

18. Dave doesn't like *Fiesta,* but he hasn't read it.

19. If Dave doesn't like *The Bell Jar,* then he hasn't read it.

20. Dave prefers *The Bell Jar* to *Fiesta,* even though he hasn't read either.

12.1.7 *Multiple Quantifiers*

Consider the following open wff:

$$Lxy$$

It is made up of a two-place predicate L (i.e., L^2) with two different variables, x and y, plugged into its argument places. So it takes two quantifiers out the front—one containing the variable x and one containing the variable y—to make a closed wff (a proposition). Each of these quantifiers can be either existential or universal, and the quantifier containing x might come first—with the quantifier containing y then coming second—or vice versa. This results in eight options to consider (note that throughout, we do not change the original wff Lxy—i.e., in this wff, we keep x and y in the same order):

1. $\forall x \forall y Lxy$
2. $\forall y \forall x Lxy$
3. $\exists x \exists y Lxy$
4. $\exists y \exists x Lxy$
5. $\forall x \exists y Lxy$
6. $\exists y \forall x Lxy$
7. $\forall y \exists x Lxy$
8. $\exists x \forall y Lxy$

Let us go through these options in turn. It will make the formulas easier to think about if we give L a specific content—say, via the glossary $Lxy: x$ likes y.

Proposition (1): $\forall x \forall y Lxy$. This says (relative to our glossary) "for every x and every y, x likes y" or "no matter which thing you pick first (call it x) and no matter which thing you pick second (call it y), x likes y." (Note that when we talk of a second selection we do not necessarily mean that you must pick a different thing the second time: picking the same thing twice is allowed.) In other words, everything likes everything.

Proposition (2): $\forall y \forall x Lxy$. This says "for every y and every x, x likes y" or "no matter which thing you pick first (call it y) and no matter which thing you pick second (call it x), x likes y." (Note that we read the quantifiers from left to

Figure 12.1. $\forall x \exists y L x y$.

right, not according to the alphabetical ordering of the variables they contain.) In other words, everything likes everything.

Thus, propositions (1) and (2) are equivalent.

Proposition (3): $\exists x \exists y L x y$. This says "you can choose a thing (call it x), and you can choose a thing (call it y) such that x likes y." In other words, something likes something.

Proposition (4): $\exists y \exists x L x y$. This says "you can choose a thing (call it y), and you can choose a thing (call it x) such that x likes y." In other words, something likes something.

Thus, propositions (3) and (4) are equivalent.

Proposition (5): $\forall x \exists y L x y$. This says "no matter what thing you pick first (call it x), you can pick a thing second (call it y) such that x likes y." That is, for every thing, there is some thing that it likes. (For different things x and y, the thing that x likes need not be the same as the thing that y likes.) Figure 12.1 gives a visual form to this idea—picturing "x likes y" as an arrow going from x to y. The only essential point in the picture is that every object sends out an arrow. Note that different things may send their arrows to different places: there is no requirement that all arrows go to the same place. There is also no requirement that each thing send out exactly one arrow—just that each thing send out at least one arrow.

Proposition (6): $\exists y \forall x L x y$. This says "you can pick a thing first (call it y) such that no matter what you pick second (call it x), x likes y." That is, there is something that everything likes. Figure 12.2 gives a visual form to this idea. The only essential point in the picture is that there is one particular thing that

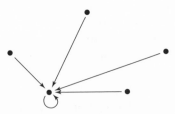

Figure 12.2. $\exists y \forall x L x y$.

Chapter 12 General Predicate Logic

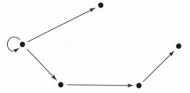

Figure 12.3. $\forall y \exists x \, Lxy$.

receives an arrow from everything in the domain. It is not required that there be exactly one such thing, only that there be at least one.

Propositions (5) and (6) are not equivalent: proposition (5) could be true without proposition (6) being true. If each thing sends an arrow somewhere, it does not follow that there is one particular thing to which everything sends an arrow. However, proposition (6) logically implies proposition (5): it could not be true without proposition (5) being true. If everything sends an arrow to one particular thing, then a fortiori everything sends an arrow somewhere.

Proposition (7): $\forall y \exists x \, Lxy$. This says "no matter what thing you pick first (call it y), you can pick a thing second (call it x) such that x likes y." That is, for every thing, there is some thing that likes it. (For different things x and y, the thing that likes x need not be the same as the thing that likes y.) Figure 12.3 gives a visual form to this idea. The only essential point in the picture is that everything receives an arrow. Note that different things may receive their arrows from different places: there is no requirement that all arrows come from the same place. There is also no requirement that each thing receive exactly one arrow—just that each thing receive at least one arrow.

Proposition (8): $\exists x \forall y \, Lxy$. This says "you can pick a thing first (call it x) such that no matter what you pick second (call it y), x likes y." That is, there is something that likes everything. Figure 12.4 gives a visual form to this idea. The only essential point in the picture is that there is one particular thing that sends an arrow to everything in the domain (including itself). It is not required that there be exactly one such thing: only that there be at least one.

Propositions (7) and (8) are not equivalent: proposition (7) could be true without proposition (8) being true. If each thing receives an arrow from

Figure 12.4. $\exists x \forall y \, Lxy$.

somewhere, it does not follow that there is one particular thing that sends an arrow to everything. However, proposition (8) logically implies proposition (7): it could not be true without proposition (7) being true. If there is one particular thing that sends an arrow to everything, then a fortiori each thing receives an arrow from somewhere.

We have now examined eight different propositions that can be derived from the open formula Lxy by adding two quantifiers: one to bind the x and the other to bind the y. Note that we did not need to make any additions or alterations to the parts of our syntax that deal with quantifiers to generate this variety of propositions. Our syntax already stipulates that when α is any wff, $\forall \underline{x}\alpha$ and $\exists \underline{x}\alpha$ are wffs. So as soon as we introduce two-place predicates and allow Lxy as a wff, we automatically allow that $\forall x Lxy$, $\forall y Lxy$, $\exists x Lxy$, and $\exists y Lxy$ are wffs; then given that they are wffs, so are $\forall y \forall x Lxy$, $\exists y \forall x Lxy$, and so on.

Of course, if we have an atomic wff $Rxyz$ involving a three-place predicate, we need three quantifiers in front to make a proposition: one containing x, one containing y, and one containing z, so we have even more complexity. And so on for n-place predicates for any finite n.

12.1.8 Uniform Change of Variables

Something that always results in an equivalent proposition is the uniform substitution of variables. For example, the following propositions are all equivalent:

1. $\exists x \forall y Lxy$

2. $\exists z \forall y Lzy$
   Here x in proposition (1) has been uniformly replaced by z. (By "uniformly" we mean that every occurrence of x has been replaced by z.)[5]

3. $\exists x \forall w Lxw$
   Here y in proposition (1) has been uniformly replaced by w.

4. $\exists y \forall x Lyx$
   Here x in proposition (1) has been uniformly replaced by y, and y in that proposition has been uniformly replaced by x.[6]

These propositions are all equivalent—think about what they say (relative to our glossary Lxy: x likes y):

1. You can pick a thing first (call it x) such that no matter what you pick second (call it y), x likes y.

2. You can pick a thing first (call it z) such that no matter what you pick second (call it y), z likes y. (It makes no difference whether we tag the first-picked thing as x or as z: we are still saying the same thing.)

3. You can pick a thing first (call it x) such that no matter what you pick second (call it w), x likes w. (It makes no difference whether we tag the second-picked thing as y or as w: we are still saying the same thing.)

4. You can pick a thing first (call it y) such that no matter what you pick second (call it x), y likes x. (It makes no difference whether we tag the first-picked thing as x and the second-picked as y, or vice versa: we are still saying the same thing.)

Note that in going from proposition (1) to (4), we uniformly change the variables—that is, we change all xs to ys, and vice versa. So the x and the y are switched inside Lxy as well. This action is different from what we did in §12.1.7, when we saw that $\exists x \forall y Lxy$ does not say the same thing as $\exists y \forall x Lxy$: in the latter case we have only switched the x and y in the quantifiers but left them in the original order inside Lxy.

Let's introduce some new notation. Where α is a wff and y is a variable that does not occur in α, $\alpha(y/x)$ is the result of replacing all free occurrences of x in α by occurrences of y. (If there are no free occurrences of x in α, then $\alpha(y/x)$ is just α.) Now we can say, quite generally, that:

$$\forall x \alpha \quad \text{is equivalent to} \quad \forall y \alpha(y/x)$$
$$\exists x \alpha \quad \text{is equivalent to} \quad \exists y \alpha(y/x)$$

12.1.9 Exercises

Translate the following into GPL.

1. (i) Something is bigger than everything.
    (ii) Something is such that everything is bigger than it.
    (iii) If Alice is bigger than Bill, then something is bigger than Bill.
    (iv) If everything is bigger than Bill, then Alice is bigger than Bill.
    (v) If something is bigger than everything, then something is bigger than itself.
    (vi) If Alice is bigger than Bill and Bill is bigger than Alice, then everything is bigger than itself.
    (vii) There is something that is bigger than anything that Alice is bigger than.
    (viii) Anything that is bigger than Alice is bigger than everything that Alice is bigger than.
    (ix) Every room contains at least one chair.
    (x) In some rooms some of the chairs are broken; in some rooms all of the chairs are broken; in no room is every chair unbroken.

2. (i) Every person owns a dog.
    (ii) For every dog, there is a person who owns that dog.

   (iii) There is a beagle that owns a chihuahua.

   (iv) No beagle owns itself.

   (v) No chihuahua is bigger than any beagle.

   (vi) Some chihuahuas are bigger than some beagles.

   (vii) Some dogs are happier than any person.

  (viii) People who own dogs are happier than those who don't.

   (ix) The bigger the dog, the happier it is.

   (x) There is a beagle that is bigger than every chihuahua and smaller than every person.

3.   (i) Alice is a timid dog, and some cats are bigger than her.

   (ii) Every dog that is bigger than Alice is bigger than Bill.

   (iii) Bill is a timid cat, and every dog is bigger than him.

   (iv) Every timid dog growls at some gray cat.

   (v) Every dog growls at every timid cat.

   (vi) Some timid dog growls at every gray cat.

   (vii) No timid dog growls at any gray cat.

  (viii) Alice wants to buy something from Woolworths, but Bill doesn't.

   (ix) Alice wants to buy something from Woolworths that Bill doesn't.

   (x) Bill growls at anything that Alice wants to buy from Woolworths.

4.   (i) Dave admires everyone.

   (ii) No one admires Dave.

   (iii) Dave doesn't admire himself.

   (iv) No one admires himself.[7]

   (v) Dave admires anyone who doesn't admire himself.[8]

   (vi) Every self-admiring person admires Dave.

   (vii) Frank admires Elvis but he prefers the Rolling Stones.

  (viii) Frank prefers any song recorded by the Rolling Stones to any song recorded by Elvis.

   (ix) The Rolling Stones recorded a top-twenty song, but Elvis didn't.

   (x) Elvis prefers any top-twenty song that the Rolling Stones recorded to any song that he himself recorded.

12.2 Semantics of GPL

The semantics for MPL (Chapter 9) told us two things:

1. What the values are of the nonlogical symbols of MPL. (A possible scenario or model is then simply any assignment of values to nonlogical symbols—together with a domain from which these values are drawn.)

2. What the rules are that determine the truth values of propositions (closed wffs) of MPL on the basis of the values of their nonlogical components.

Regarding point (1), in moving from monadic to general predicate logic, all we have done is add some new nonlogical symbols: many-place predicates. So we now need to define the value of a many-place predicate. Regarding point (2), our statements about the truth values of atomic propositions formed from one-place predicates, and of nonatomic propositions, will carry over unchanged from MPL to GPL. All we need to add is an account of how the truth value of an atomic proposition formed from a many-place predicate is determined by the values of the names and the many-place predicate that make it up.

So, what is the value of a many-place predicate? Consider, for example, the two-place predicate T. Its value must be something that, together with values for a and b, determines a truth value for Tab and Tba (and, for that matter, for Taa and Tbb). Now think about these propositions. Each has three parts: two names (or two occurrences of one name) and a predicate. The function of each name is to single out a particular object; the function of the predicate is to pick out a certain relation. At this point, we might think of saying the following:

> If these two objects (the one picked out by a and the one picked out by b) stand in this relation (the one picked out by T), then the proposition is true; the proposition is false if the objects picked out by the names do not stand in the relation picked out by the predicate.

But this prescription won't do: it obscures a crucial distinction. Suppose the relation picked out by T is the relation "taller than." Suppose a picks out Alice and b picks out Bob. Then we cannot simply talk about "Alice and Bob standing in the 'taller than' relation": it might be that they stand in the relation when taken in one order (Alice is taller than Bob) but not when taken in the other order (Bob is not taller than Alice). In other words, it might be that Tab is true and Tba is false. So we have to say something like this:

> An atomic proposition formed from two names and a two-place predicate is true if the objects picked out by the names, when taken in the order in which their names feature in the proposition, stand in the relation picked out by the predicate; it is false if those objects, when taken in the order in which their names feature in the proposition, do not stand in the relation picked out by the predicate.

Thus, Tab is true if Alice and Bob taken in that order stand in the "taller than" relation—that is, if Alice is taller than Bob; Tab is false if Alice and Bob taken in that order do not stand in the "taller than" relation—that is, if Alice is not taller than Bob.

So the value of a two-place predicate, such as T, must be something that, together with values for a and b, determines truth values for Tab and for Tba—and not necessarily the same truth value for both. That is, it should not be built into the semantics that Tab and Tba always have the same truth value, given the same values for T, a, and b. One simple proposal that does the job is that the value of T is a set of *ordered pairs*. The ordered pair containing Alice and Bob in that order—that is, Alice first and Bob second—is written ⟨Alice, Bob⟩.[9] The ordered pair containing Bob and Alice in that order—that is, Bob first and Alice second—is written ⟨Bob, Alice⟩. These are different ordered pairs: both contain the same two individuals, but in different orders. Note that ⟨Alice, Alice⟩ and ⟨Bob, Bob⟩ are perfectly good ordered pairs: the first contains Alice in positions one and two; the second contains Bob in positions one and two. Thus, we should not think of an ordered pair as two objects standing in a line, one behind the other—for Alice cannot stand behind herself. Rather, we should think of an ordered pair as an abstract ranking or ordering: a stipulation of a first object and a second object. There is no reason (in general) why Alice (or any other individual) should not be ranked first and second.[10]

Recall the truth conditions for atomic propositions involving one-place predicates: $P\underline{a}$ is true in a model $\mathfrak{M}$ iff the referent of $\underline{a}$ in that model is in the extension of $\underline{P}$ in that model, where the extension of $\underline{P}$ is a set of objects from the domain. Given that the value of a two-place predicate is a set of ordered pairs (of objects drawn from the domain), the story about how truth values are determined for atomic propositions containing two-place predicates is now as follows: $R\underline{ab}$ is true in a model $\mathfrak{M}$ iff the ordered pair consisting of the referent of $\underline{a}$ in that model followed by the referent of $\underline{b}$ in that model is in the extension of $\underline{R}$ in that model, where the extension of $\underline{R}$ is a set of ordered pairs of objects from the domain. (Note that the case where $\underline{a}$ and $\underline{b}$ are the same name is covered here: Raa, for example, will be true just in case the ordered pair consisting of the referent of a in positions one and two is in the extension of R.)

Let's consider an example. Here is a model $\mathfrak{M}$ of the fragment of GPL containing the names a, c, g, and r and the two-place predicate R:

Domain: {Alice, Charles, Roger, Susan, *The Catcher in the Rye*, *The Great Gatsby*, *The Wind in the Willows*, *The Lord of the Rings*}

Referents: a: Alice c: Charles g: *The Great Gatsby* r: *The Catcher in the Rye*

Extension of R: {⟨Alice, *The Great Gatsby*⟩, ⟨Charles, *The Great Gatsby*⟩, ⟨Susan, *The Wind in the Willows*⟩}

On this model, Rag is true: the ordered pair consisting of the referent of a followed by the referent of g—that is, ⟨Alice, *The Great Gatsby*⟩—is in the extension of R. Likewise, Rcg is true, because the ordered pair consisting of the referent of c followed by the referent of g—that is, ⟨Charles, *The Great Gatsby*⟩—is also in the extension of R. In contrast, Rar is false in this model: the ordered pair consisting of the referent of a followed by the referent of r— that is, ⟨Alice, *The Catcher in the Rye*⟩—is not in the extension of R.

More complex propositions are handled in just the same way as in monadic predicate logic. Consider the proposition $\forall x \exists y Rxy$. It is of the form $\forall x \alpha(x)$, where $\alpha(x)$ is $\exists y Rxy$. Its truth value is determined by rule (7) of §9.4.2: it is true on our model $\mathfrak{M}$ iff $\exists y Rby$ is true in every model just like $\mathfrak{M}$ except that it also assigns a referent to the new name b. Now this formula $\exists y Rby$ has its truth value determined by rule (8) of §9.4.2: it is true on one of the models just considered iff Rbd is true on some model just like that model except that it also assigns a referent to the new name d. So our original formula is not true in $\mathfrak{M}$: if we let b denote Roger, then there is nothing d can denote such that Rbd will be true—for there is no ordered pair in the extension of R with Roger in its first position.

So far we have discussed two-place predicates. The extension to three-, four-, and in general n-place predicates is straightforward. The extension of a three-place predicate is a set of ordered *triples* of objects from the domain. The proposition $\underline{Sabc}$ is then true in a model $\mathfrak{M}$ iff the ordered triple consisting of the referent of $\underline{a}$ in that model followed by the referent of $\underline{b}$ in that model followed by the referent of $\underline{c}$ in the model is in the extension of $\underline{S}$ in the model. For example, consider the following model:

Domain: {Alice, Bob, Carol, David, Edwina, Frank}
Referents: a: Alice b: Bob c: Carol e: Edwina
Extension of B: {⟨Alice, Bob, Carol⟩, ⟨Carol, Alice, Edwina⟩,
                ⟨Edwina, Carol, Frank⟩, ⟨Frank, Edwina, David⟩}

$Babc$ is true in this model, because ⟨Alice, Bob, Carol⟩ is in the extension of B; $Bbac$ is false, because ⟨Bob, Alice, Carol⟩ is not in the extension of B; $Bcae$ is true, because ⟨Carol, Alice, Edwina⟩ is in the extension of B; and so on.

In general, the extension of an n-place predicate is a set of ordered n-tuples of members of the domain. An ordered n-tuple comprises some things given in a particular order: first, second . . . nth.[11] You can think of an ordered n-tuple $\langle x, y, z, \ldots, w \rangle$ as a *list:* x first, y second, z third, and so on down to w in nth position.[12] Then (where $\underline{P^n}$ is any n-place predicate and $a_1 \cdots a_n$ are any names) the atomic proposition $\underline{P^n} a_1 \ldots a_n$ is true in a model iff the ordered n-tuple consisting of the referents of a_1 through a_n in that model (taken in that order) is in the extension of $\underline{P^n}$ in that model.

12.2.1 Summary

Here we summarize the semantics of GPL.

12.2.1.1 MODELS

A model of a fragment of GPL comprises:

1. a domain (a nonempty set of objects);

2. a specification of a referent for each name in the fragment:
   - the referent of a name is an object in the domain;

3. a specification of an extension for each predicate in the fragment:
   - the extension of a one-place predicate is a set of objects from the domain;
   - the extension of an n-place predicate (for any finite n greater than 1) is a set of n-tuples of objects drawn from the domain.

12.2.1.2 TRUTH CONDITIONS

There are eight types of propositions of GPL (see clause (3) of the syntax for GPL in §12.1.3):[13] atomic propositions, propositions whose main operator is one of the five connectives, and propositions whose main operator is one of the two quantifiers. So we have one rule for each type of proposition, which states how its truth value is determined relative to a given model $\mathfrak{M}$. The only new type of proposition that emerged when we moved from MPL to GPL was atomic propositions with many-place predicates. Accordingly, the only difference between the following truth conditions for propositions of GPL and those for MPL given in §9.4.2 concerns the first rule: the one for atomic propositions. This rule is now generalized to cover atomic propositions formed from predicates with any positive finite number of places (the rule for MPL covered only one-place predicates). The remaining clauses are reproduced here simply for the sake of having the complete semantics of GPL stated in one place for ready reference:

1. $\underline{P^n} a_1 \ldots a_n$ is true in $\mathfrak{M}$ iff the ordered n-tuple consisting of the referents in $\mathfrak{M}$ of $\underline{a_1}$ through $\underline{a_n}$ in that order is in the extension in $\mathfrak{M}$ of $\underline{P^n}$.

2. $\neg\alpha$ is true in $\mathfrak{M}$ iff α is false in $\mathfrak{M}$.

3. $(\alpha \wedge \beta)$ is true in $\mathfrak{M}$ iff α and β are both true in $\mathfrak{M}$.

4. $(\alpha \vee \beta)$ is true in $\mathfrak{M}$ iff one or both of α and β is true in $\mathfrak{M}$.

5. $(\alpha \rightarrow \beta)$ is true in $\mathfrak{M}$ iff α is false in $\mathfrak{M}$ or β is true in $\mathfrak{M}$ (or both).

6. $(\alpha \leftrightarrow \beta)$ is true in $\mathfrak{M}$ iff α and β are both true in $\mathfrak{M}$ or both false in $\mathfrak{M}$.

7. $\forall \underline{x} \alpha(\underline{x})$ is true in $\mathfrak{M}$ iff for every object o in the domain of $\mathfrak{M}$, $\alpha(\underline{a}/\underline{x})$ is true in $\mathfrak{M}_o^a$, where $\underline{a}$ is some name not assigned a referent in $\mathfrak{M}$, and $\mathfrak{M}_o^a$ is a model just like $\mathfrak{M}$ except that in it the name $\underline{a}$ is assigned the referent o.

8. $\exists \underline{x} \alpha(\underline{x})$ is true in $\mathfrak{M}$ iff there is at least one object o in the domain of $\mathfrak{M}$ such that $\alpha(\underline{a}/\underline{x})$ is true in $\mathfrak{M}_o^a$, where $\underline{a}$ is some name not assigned a referent in $\mathfrak{M}$, and $\mathfrak{M}_o^a$ is a model just like $\mathfrak{M}$ except that in it the name $\underline{a}$ is assigned the referent o.

12.2.2 Exercises

1. Here is a model:

Domain: {1, 2, 3, ...}
Referents: a: 1 b: 2 c: 3
Extensions: E: {2, 4, 6, ...} P: {2, 3, 5, 7, 11, ...}[14]
L: {⟨1, 2⟩, ⟨1, 3⟩, ⟨1, 4⟩, ..., ⟨2, 3⟩, ⟨2, 4⟩, ..., ⟨3, 4⟩, ...}[15]

State whether each of the following propositions is true or false in this model.

(i) Lba F
(ii) $Lab \lor Lba$ T
(iii) Laa F
(iv) $\exists x Lxb$
(v) $\exists x Lxa$
(vi) $\exists x Lxx$
(vii) $\forall x \exists y Lxy$
(viii) $\forall x \exists y Lyx$
(ix) $\exists x (Px \land Lxb)$
(x) $\exists x (Px \land Lcx)$

(xi) $\forall x \exists y (Ey \land Lxy)$
(xii) $\forall x \exists y (Py \land Lxy)$
(xiii) $\forall x (Lcx \rightarrow Ex)$
(xiv) $\forall x ((Lax \land Lxc) \rightarrow Ex)$
(xv) $\forall x \forall y (Lxy \lor Lyx)$
(xvi) $\exists x \exists y \exists z (Ex \land Py \land Ez \land Pz \land Lxy \land Lyz)$
(xvii) $\exists x \exists y \exists z (Lxy \land Lyz \land Lzx)$
(xviii) $\forall x \forall y \forall z ((Lxy \land Lyz) \rightarrow Lxz)$

2. Here is a model:

Domain: {1, 2, 3}
Referents: a: 1 b: 2 c: 3
Extensions: F: {1, 2} G: {2, 3} R: {⟨1, 2⟩, ⟨2, 1⟩, ⟨2, 3⟩} S: {⟨1, 2, 3⟩}

State whether each of the following propositions is true or false in this model.

(i) $\forall x \forall y (Rxy \rightarrow Ryx)$
(ii) $\forall x \forall y (Ryx \rightarrow Rxy)$
(iii) $\forall x \exists y (Gy \land Rxy)$
(iv) $\forall x (Fx \rightarrow \exists y (Gy \land Rxy))$
(v) $\exists x \exists y \exists z Sxyz$

(vi) $\exists x \exists y Sxay$
(vii) $\exists x \exists y Sxby$
(viii) $\exists x Sxxx$
(ix) $\exists x \exists y (Fx \land Fy \land Sxby)$
(x) $\exists x \exists y (Fx \land Gy \land Sxby)$

3. Here is a model:

Domain: {Alice, Bob, Carol, Dave, Edwina, Frank}
Referents: a: Alice b: Bob c: Carol d: Dave e: Edwina f: Frank
Extensions: M: {Bob, Dave, Frank} F: {Alice, Carol, Edwina}
L: {⟨Alice, Carol⟩, ⟨Alice, Dave⟩, ⟨Alice, Alice⟩, ⟨Dave, Carol⟩, ⟨Edwina, Dave⟩, ⟨Frank, Bob⟩}
S: {⟨Alice, Bob⟩, ⟨Alice, Dave⟩, ⟨Bob, Alice⟩, ⟨Bob, Dave⟩, ⟨Dave, Bob⟩, ⟨Dave, Alice⟩}

State whether each of the following propositions is true or false in this model.

(i) $\forall x \forall y (Lxy \rightarrow Lyx)$

(ii) $\exists x Lxx$

(iii) $\neg \exists x Sxx$

(iv) $\forall x \forall y (Sxy \rightarrow Syx)$

(v) $\forall x \forall y \forall z ((Sxy \land Syz) \rightarrow Sxz)$

(vi) $\forall x (Mx \rightarrow \exists y Lyx)$

(vii) $\forall x (Fx \rightarrow \exists y Lyx)$

(viii) $\forall x (Fx \rightarrow \exists y Lxy)$

(ix) $\exists x \exists y (Lax \land Lyb)$

(x) $\forall x ((Lxd \lor Ldx) \lor Mx)$

4. For each of the following propositions, describe (a) a model in which it is true and (b) a model in which it is false. If there is no model of one of these types, explain why.

(i) $\forall x Fxx$

(ii) $\forall x \forall y (Fxy \rightarrow Fyx)$

(iii) $\forall x \forall y (Fxy \leftrightarrow Fyx)$

(iv) $\exists x \forall y Fxy$

(v) $\forall x \exists y Fxy$

(vi) $\exists x \exists y Fxy$

(vii) $\forall x \forall y Fxy$

(viii) $\exists x \exists y Fxy \land \neg Faa$

(ix) $\forall x \forall y Fxy \land \neg Faa$

(x) $\forall x \forall y (Fxy \leftrightarrow Fyx) \land Fab \land \neg Fba$

12.3 Trees for General Predicate Logic

In moving from trees for propositional logic to trees for monadic predicate logic, we said (at the beginning of Chapter 10) that the basic idea remained the same: a tree tells us whether it is possible for the propositions written at the top of the tree all to be true together; if this is possible, then the tree presents a scenario in which these propositions are all true. Hence, the ways we use trees remained the same too. For example, to test a formula for being a logical truth, we start with the negation of the formula; if all paths close, this negation cannot be true, and so the original (unnegated) formula is a logical truth; and so on for testing for validity, satisfiability, and the other logical properties. What did change was that we added new rules for the new operators: the quantifiers. Furthermore, in line with the change in the semantics for our logical language from representing "ways of making propositions true or false" (i.e., scenarios) as truth table rows to representing them as models, we introduced a method for reading off a model from an open path of a tree.

In moving from monadic to general predicate logic, the basic idea behind trees once again stays the same—hence, the ways we can use trees remain the same too. We have not added any new logical operators—only some new predicates—so there are no new tree rules. The only change we have made to our language is adding new many-place predicates. The corresponding change in the semantics was that we assigned such predicates sets of n-tuples of members of the domain as extensions, not sets of members of the domain (as in the case of one-place predicates). The corresponding question that we need to discuss in the case of trees—the only new issue we need to discuss in relation to trees when moving from MPL to GPL—is how to read off the extensions of many-place predicates from open paths.

The procedure is a simple generalization of the procedure for one-place predicates. Given an open path, we put into the extension of a *one*-place predicate $\underline{F}$ the referent of any name $\underline{a}$ which appears after $\underline{F}$ in a standalone atomic wff $\underline{Fa}$ in our path. (By "standalone" I mean that the atomic wff $\underline{Fa}$ appears in the path as a complete wff, not simply as a subformula of a larger wff.) For an n-place predicate $\underline{F^n}$, we put into the extension of this predicate the ordered n-tuple consisting of the referents of the names a_1 through a_n (in that order), for any (occurrences of) names a_1 through a_n appearing after $\underline{F^n}$ (in that order) in a standalone atomic wff $\underline{F^n a_1} \ldots a_n$ in our path. So, to take a concrete example, suppose we are dealing with the three-place predicate R and that the only standalone atomic wffs involving R that appear in our path are $Raba$ and $Rbac$. Assume the referents of the names a, b, and c are the objects 1, 2, and 3, respectively. Then we form the extension of R as follows:

$$R : \{\langle 1, 2, 1 \rangle, \langle 2, 1, 3 \rangle\}$$

The idea is that the model we are constructing must be one in which every wff on our open path is true. For $Raba$ to be true, the n-tuple consisting of the referents of a, b, and a, in that order, must be in the extension of R. Hence, we put $\langle 1, 2, 1 \rangle$ into the extension of R. Likewise, we put $\langle 2, 1, 3 \rangle$ into the extension to make $Rbac$ true.

Let's consider some examples. First, let's test whether the following argument is valid:

$\forall x (Fx \to \exists y Rxy)$
Fa
$\therefore \exists x Rax$

We construct the tree as follows:

1.	$\forall x (Fx \to \exists y Rxy)$ \a		
2.	Fa		
3.	$\neg \exists x Rax$ ✓		
4.	$\forall x \neg Rax$ \b	{3}	
5.	$Fa \to \exists y Ray$ ✓	{1}	

6.	$\neg Fa$	{5}	7.	$\exists y Ray$ ✓ b	{5}
	×	{2, 6}	8.	Rab	{7}
			9.	$\neg Rab$	{4}
				×	{8, 9}

All paths close, so the argument is valid.

For a second example, let's test whether the following proposition is a logical truth:

$$(\exists x \forall y Rxy \rightarrow \forall x \exists y Rxy)$$

We construct the tree as follows:

1.	$\neg(\exists x \forall y Rxy \rightarrow \forall x \exists y Rxy)$ ✓	
2.	$\exists x \forall y Rxy$ ✓ a	{1}
3.	$\neg\forall x \exists y Rxy$ ✓	{1}
4.	$\exists x \neg \exists y Rxy$ ✓ b	{3}
5.	$\forall y Ray$ \ $a\,b$	{2}
6.	$\neg\exists y Rby$ ✓	{4}
7.	$\forall y \neg Rby$ \ $a\,b$	{6}
8.	Raa	{5, a}
9.	Rab	{5, b}
10.	$\neg Rba$	{7, a}
11.	$\neg Rbb$	{7, b}
	↑	

There is only one path in this tree: it is saturated and open. So we can read off a model in which the wff at the top of the tree is true—that is, in which the original wff $(\exists x \forall y Rxy \rightarrow \forall x \exists y Rxy)$ is false. The names appearing on the path are a and b, so our domain and referents are:

Domain: $\{1, 2\}$
Referents: a: 1 b: 2

The only predicate on the path is R. To get its extension, we look for stand-alone atomic wffs featuring R that occur in our path. We find two: Raa and Rab. So we set the extension of R as follows:

Extension of R: $\{\langle 1, 1 \rangle, \langle 1, 2 \rangle\}$

12.3.1 Exercises

1. Using trees, determine whether the following propositions are logical truths. For any proposition that is not a logical truth, read off from your tree a model in which it is false.

(i) $\forall x (Rxx \rightarrow \exists y Rxy)$

(ii) $\forall x (\exists y Rxy \rightarrow \exists z Rzx)$

(iii) $\forall x Rax \rightarrow \forall x \exists y Ryx$

(iv) $\forall x \exists y \exists z Ryxz \rightarrow \exists x \exists y Rxay$

(v) $\neg\forall x \exists y Rxy$

(vi) $\forall x \forall y \forall z ((Rxy \wedge Ryz) \rightarrow Rxz)$

(vii) $\exists x \forall y Rxy \rightarrow \forall x \exists y Rxy$

(viii) $\exists y \forall x Rxy \rightarrow \forall x \exists y Rxy$

(ix) $\exists x \forall y Rxy \rightarrow \exists x \exists y Rxy$

(x) $\forall x \forall y \exists z Rxyz \vee \forall x \forall y \forall z \neg Rxyz$

2. Using trees, determine whether the following arguments are valid. For any argument that is not valid, read off from your tree a model in which the premises are true and the conclusion false.

(i) $\forall x \forall y \forall z((Rxy \land Ryz) \rightarrow Rxz)$
  Rab
  Rba
  $\therefore \exists x Rxx$

(ii) $\forall x Fxa \rightarrow \exists x Fax$
  $\exists x Fxa$
  $\therefore \exists x Fax$

(iii) $\exists x \exists y \exists z (Rxy \land Rzy)$
  $\therefore \exists x Rxx$

(iv) $\forall x \forall y (Rxy \rightarrow Ryx)$
  $\exists x Rxa$
  $\therefore \exists x Rax$

(v) $\forall x \forall y (\neg Rxy \rightarrow Ryx)$
  $\therefore \forall x \exists y Ryx$

(vi) $\forall x \forall y (Rxy \rightarrow (Fx \land Gy))$
  $\therefore \neg \exists x Rxx$

(vii) $\forall x (Fx \rightarrow (\forall y Rxy \lor \neg \exists y Rxy))$
  Fa
  $\neg Rab$
  $\therefore \neg Raa$

(viii) $\forall x \forall y (\exists z (Rzx \land Rzy) \rightarrow Rxy)$
  $\forall x Rax$
  $\therefore \forall x \forall y Rxy$

(ix) $\forall x \exists y Rxy$
  $\therefore \exists x Rxb$

(x) $\exists x \forall y (Fy \rightarrow Rxy)$
  $\exists x \forall y \neg Ryx$
  $\therefore \exists x \neg Fx$

3. Translate the following arguments into GPL and then test for validity using trees. For any argument that is not valid, read off from your tree a model in which the premises are true and the conclusion false.

(i) Alice is older than Bill, and Bill is older than Carol, so Alice must be older than Carol.

(ii) Alice is older than Bill. Bill is older than Carol. Anyone older than someone is older than everyone who that someone is older than. It follows that Alice is older than Carol.

(iii) I trust everything you trust. You trust all bankers. Dave is a banker. Thus, I trust Dave.

(iv) Everybody loves somebody, so everybody is loved by somebody.

(v) Nancy is a restaurateur. She can afford to feed all and only those restaurateurs who can't afford to feed themselves. So Nancy is very wealthy.

(vi) Everything in Paris is more beautiful than anything in Canberra. The Eiffel tower is in Paris, and Lake Burley Griffin is in Canberra. Therefore, the Eiffel tower is more beautiful than Lake Burley Griffin.

(vii) Politicians only talk to politicians. No journalist is a politician. So no politician talks to any journalist.

(viii) There is no object that is smaller than all objects; therefore, there is no object such that every object is smaller than it.

(ix) Either a movie isn't commercially successful or both Margaret and David like it. There aren't any French movies that Margaret and David both like. So there aren't any commercially successful French movies.

(x) There's something that causes everything. Thus, there's nothing that is caused by everything.

12.4 Postulates

Consider the following piece of reasoning:

Alice is taller than Bob.
Carol is shorter than Bob.
∴ Alice is taller than Carol.

We translate as follows:

a:	Alice	*Tab*
b:	Bob	*Scb*
c:	Carol	∴ *Tac*
Txy:	*x* is taller than *y*	
Sxy:	*x* is shorter than *y*	

The result is not valid. This should not be a surprise, in light of §11.5. The glossary endows the predicates T and S with intensions that are related in the following ways:[16]

1. For every ww, if the intension of T determines that $\langle x, y \rangle$ is in the extension of T relative to that ww, then the intension of S determines that $\langle y, x \rangle$ is in the extension of S relative to that ww. (In other words, necessarily, for any x and y, if x is taller than y, then y is shorter than x.)

2. For every ww, if the intension of S determines that $\langle x, y \rangle$ is in the extension of S relative to that ww, then the intension of T determines that $\langle y, x \rangle$ is in the extension of T relative to that ww. (In other words, necessarily, for any x and y, if x is shorter than y, then y is taller than x.)

3. For every ww, if the intension of T determines that $\langle x, y \rangle$ and $\langle y, z \rangle$ are in the extension of T relative to that ww, then it also determines that $\langle x, z \rangle$ is in the extension of T relative to that ww. (In other words, necessarily, for any x, y, and z, if x is taller than y and y is taller than z, then x is taller than z.)

4. For every ww, if the intension of S determines that $\langle x, y \rangle$ and $\langle y, z \rangle$ are in the extension of S relative to that ww, then it also determines that $\langle x, z \rangle$ is in the extension of S relative to that ww. (In other words, necessarily,

for any x, y, and z, if x is shorter than y and y is shorter than z, then x is shorter than z.)

Thus, there is no ww-model (relative to the given glossary) in which the premises are true and the conclusion false. In other words, the argument is NTP. If Carol is shorter than Bob (second premise) then by point (2), Bob is taller than Carol. From this and the first premise (Alice is taller than Bob) the conclusion (Alice is taller than Carol) follows by point (3). However, when it comes to validity (and other logical properties, e.g., equivalence, satisfiability), glossaries—and the intensions they confer—fall by the wayside. Validity is NTP by virtue of form. When determining validity, we use a glossary to translate into GPL, but then we apply the tree test to the argument (the sequence of closed wffs): any content conferred on these wffs in the process of translation is ignored. We consider all models—not just ww-models (which are no longer meaningfully defined, once the intensions are out of the picture). That is why the argument under consideration comes out invalid: although there are no ww-models in which the premises are true and the conclusion false, there are models in which the premises are true and the conclusion false.

To obtain a valid argument, we need to take the restrictions on models (which rule out some models as not being ww-models) embodied in the intensions and embody them in further wffs, which we then add as premises. (Because, as we have been saying, only wffs themselves affect validity: any intensions these wffs may have been given, via some glossary, are irrelevant when assessing validity.) The idea behind these further wffs is that at least one of them is false in any countermodel to the original argument. These further wffs are postulates (§11.6). In the present case, the conclusion can be derived from the premises via points (2) and (3). So we embody these points in the following postulates:

$$\forall x \forall y (Sxy \to Tyx)$$
$$\forall x \forall y \forall z ((Txy \land Tyz) \to Txz)$$

and then add them as premises to our argument:

Tab
Scb
$\forall x \forall y (Sxy \to Tyx)$
$\forall x \forall y \forall z ((Txy \land Tyz) \to Txz)$
$\therefore Tac$

This argument is valid (as can easily be confirmed by producing a tree).[17]
Let's consider another example:

Mary likes everyone, so Mary likes Bob.

We translate as follows:

b: Bob $\forall x(Px \to Lmx)$
m: Mary $\therefore Lmb$
Px: x is a person
Lxy: x likes y

The result is invalid. To obtain a valid argument, we need to add Pb (Bob is a person) as a postulate.

Note that it is not always necessary to add postulates to make a valid argument. For example, consider the argument:

Mary likes everything, so Mary likes Bob.

Using the above glossary, this translates as:

$\forall x\, Lmx$
$\therefore Lmb$

which is valid as it stands.

Let's consider a different sort of example:

Mary likes everyone Bob likes.
Bob likes a pilot.
Hence, Mary likes a pilot.

Adding "Tx: x is a pilot" to the above glossary, this translates as:

$\forall x((Px \wedge Lbx) \to Lmx)$
$\exists x(Tx \wedge Lbx)$
$\therefore \exists x(Tx \wedge Lmx)$

which is invalid (do the tree and confirm this). To obtain a valid argument, we need to add the postulate $\forall x(Tx \to Px)$ (all pilots are persons). (Look at the countermodel derived from your tree for the original argument: note that it turns on having some object x in the extension of T but not in the extension of P, such that ⟨the referent of b, x⟩ is in the extension of L and ⟨the referent of m, x⟩ is not in the extension of L.) This example is different, because the original argument is not NTP, and the postulate—when taken under the given glossary—is not necessarily true (presumably it is possible for there to be pilots that are not persons—e.g., robot pilots). Rather, the postulate is simply supposed to be true (i.e., when taken under the given glossary, it comes out true relative to the actual ww). The original argument is an example of an *enthymeme*: an argument in which a premise is not explicitly stated. Examples of this sort commonly occur when the suppressed premise (e.g., "all pilots are persons") is so obviously true that one does not bother saying it. In such cases, the role of the postulate is simply to make explicit the suppressed premise.

12.4.1 Exercises

For each of the following arguments, first translate into GPL and show that the argument is invalid using a tree. Then formulate suitable postulates and show, using a tree, that the argument with these postulates added as extra premises is valid.

1. Roger will eat any food; therefore, Roger will eat that egg.

2. Bill weighs 180 pounds. Ben weighs 170 pounds. So Bill is heavier than Ben.

3. John ran 5 miles; Nancy ran 10 miles; hence, Nancy ran farther than John.

4. Sophie enjoys every novel by Thomas Mann, so she enjoys *Buddenbrooks*.

5. Chris enjoys novels and nothing else; therefore, he does not enjoy anything by Borges.

12.4.2 Translation

Consider the two claims, "Alice is taller than Bob" and "Bob is shorter than Alice." We translate as follows:

a:	Alice	*Tab*
b:	Bob	*Sba*

Txy: x is taller than y
Sxy: x is shorter than y

Neither of these formulas of GPL is a logical consequence of the other, but each is a logical consequence of the other together with the postulate $\forall x \forall y (Sxy \leftrightarrow Tyx)$.

A second option would be to bypass the postulate and simply translate both claims using one two-place predicate. If we use T, both will translate as Tab; if we use S, both will come out as Sba. Either way, as both claims are translated as the same wff, they are (trivially) logically equivalent.

Which way of translating is the right one? The question comes down to this: are the two claims, "Alice is taller than Bob" and "Bob is shorter than Alice" different ways of expressing the same proposition (in which case the second way is right), or are they expressions of two different propositions that necessarily have the same truth value (i.e., are true/false relative to the same wws—in which case the first way is right)? There is no general answer to this kind of question. We said in the last part of §1.2.2 that which proposition a speaker expresses on a given occasion is determined by the meaning of the sentence type she utters, facts about the context of utterance, and facts about the speaker—and perhaps more besides. Thus, whether some particular utterance of the sentence "Alice is taller than Bob" and some particular utterance of

"Bob is shorter than Alice" express the same proposition is not something we can answer in the abstract: we need to know many specific details—apart from simply which sentences were uttered—and even then the issues are highly controversial. Suffice it to say here that we have the logical resources to take either approach: if we translate some particular utterance of the sentence "Alice is taller than Bob" as Tab, then it is open to us to translate a given utterance of "Bob is shorter than Alice" as Sba or as Tab.

The more we tend toward translating utterances of different sentences as expressing the same propositions (i.e., the second way above), the less postulates we need to obtain valid arguments. For example, if "Alice is taller than Bob" and "Bob is shorter than Alice" are translated in the same way (as Tab, or alternatively as Sba), then the argument "Alice is taller than Bob, so Bob is shorter than Alice" comes out as valid (trivially so, because the premise and the conclusion are the same wff). Conversely, the more we tend toward translating utterances of different sentences as expressing different propositions (i.e., the first way above), the more situations we can regard as making sense from a purely logical point of view. For example, suppose we make the natural assumption that someone who assents to an utterance of a sentence believes the proposition expressed by that utterance, and that someone who dissents from an utterance of a sentence does not believe the proposition expressed by that utterance.[18] Then, if we want to translate "Alice is taller than Bob" and "Bob is shorter than Alice" in the same way, we cannot make sense of a situation in which someone assents to "Alice is taller than Bob" but dissents from "Bob is shorter than Alice": that would mean that the person both believes a certain proposition and does not believe the same proposition, which is simply impossible. In contrast, the situation does make sense if "Alice is taller than Bob" and "Bob is shorter than Alice" express different propositions.

Consider another example: active versus passive constructions. "Alice shouted at Carol" is said to be in the *active* voice, while "Carol was shouted at by Alice" is in the *passive* voice. Suppose we translate an utterance of "Alice shouted at Carol" as Sac, using the glossary:

a: Alice
c: Carol
Sxy: x shouted at y

Should we now translate an utterance of "Carol was shouted at by Alice" as Sac, or should we introduce a new predicate:

Hxy: x was shouted at by y

and then translate as Hca? Again, there is no general answer to this question. If you translate in the former way, you are supposing that the particular utterances of "Alice shouted at Carol" and "Carol was shouted at by Alice" express the same proposition (just as two different utterances of "Alice shouted at Carol" might express the same proposition). If you translate in the latter way, you are supposing that the two utterances express different propositions. The former supposition carries with it the feature that postulates (e.g., $\forall x \forall y (Sxy \leftrightarrow Hyx)$) are not required to make certain arguments valid (e.g., "Alice shouted at Carol, so Carol was shouted at by Alice"): their validity is ensured by the method of translation. The latter supposition carries with it the feature that more situations can be regarded as making sense from a purely logical point of view (e.g., someone assenting to "Alice shouted at Carol" but dissenting from "Carol was shouted at by Alice"). Which (if either) of these features is *advantageous* will depend on the situation—on why we are translating into GPL and what we hope to achieve thereby.

The sort of issue we have just been discussing arises virtually every time we are translating into a logical language. For example, suppose you hear someone say "Bob is tall, so Bob is tall." This reasoning may sound like the most trivial case of logical consequence, but the hypothesis remains open that the two tokens of "Bob" refer to different people, in which case the correct translation yields an invalid argument:

a: Bob Smith Ta
b: Bob Jones $\therefore Tb$
$Tx:$ x is tall

In this case, it may be that to capture the reasoning being expressed as a valid argument, we need to add extra premises: Bob Jones is taller than Bob Smith (T^2ba, using the glossary entry T^2xy: x is taller than y); if something is tall, then anything taller than it is tall ($\forall x \forall y ((Tx \wedge T^2yx) \rightarrow Ty)$).[19]

A translation is a hypothesis about the propositions expressed by certain utterances. Generally, there will not be conclusive evidence in favor of one translation over all other possible translations. What we can be sure about, however, are such assertions as: if the correct translation is so and so, then the argument is valid; if the correct translation is such and such, then the proposition expressed is logically true.

12.4.3 Complex Predicates
Consider the following claims:

1. Alice is walking.

2. Bob is walking slowly.

3. Constance is walking quickly.

4. Doug is reading.

5. Ed is reading slowly.

6. Frances is reading quickly.

We translate them into GPL as follows:

a: Alice	*Wx*: *x* is walking	1. *Wa*
b: Bob	*Sx*: *x* is walking slowly	2. *Sb*
c: Constance	*Qx*: *x* is walking quickly	3. *Qc*
d: Doug	*Rx*: *x* is reading	4. *Rd*
e: Ed	*Lx*: *x* is reading slowly	5. *Le*
f: Frances	*Ux*: *x* is reading quickly	6. *Uf*

In English, the predicates are expressed using four words (apart from "is"): "walking," "reading," "slowly," and "quickly." The sentence "Bob is walking slowly" has something (the word "walking") in common with "Alice is walking" and something (the word "slowly") in common with "Ed is reading slowly;" similarly for others of these sentences. In contrast, in GPL we have six different predicates. The translation of "Bob is walking slowly" has nothing in common with the translation of "Alice is walking," nor with the translation of "Ed is reading slowly;" indeed, none of the translations has any symbol in common with any of the other translations.

This may seem odd at first, but we need to remember that the translation into GPL of an utterance of a sentence, such as "Bob is walking slowly," is supposed to be a representation of the proposition expressed by the utterance—not a representation of the sentence uttered. English, like other natural languages, has the following useful feature: learning a relatively small number of words and a relatively small number of grammatical rules enables us to produce and understand a relatively large (in fact, a potentially unlimited) number of meaningful sentences. For example, if I have learned the meanings of the adverbs "slowly" and "quickly," then for any new verb *X* I learn ("read," "walk," "write," "run," "eat," . . .), I can work out the meaning of "*X* slowly" and "*X* quickly": I do not have to learn the meanings of the latter separately. This feature is all well and good, but it does not automatically follow from it that the proposition I express by uttering "Bob is walking slowly" must have a component in common with any proposition that I express by uttering a sentence that has a word in common with "Bob is walking slowly" (e.g., "Constance is walking quickly," "Ed is reading slowly"). Learning a few words allows us to express a lot of propositions; it does not follow that the propositions themselves must, so to speak, carry a trace of the means by which we express them. That is, the propositions expressed by "Bob is walking slowly" and "Constance is walking quickly" might have no component in common. That is precisely the view we arrive at if we take GPL as our logical language.[20]

Note that, when translated into GPL, the following argument comes out as invalid:

Alice is walking slowly, so Alice is walking.

To get a valid argument, we need to add the postulate $\forall x (Sx \rightarrow Wx)$.

Consider the following claims:

1. Bones is a gray dog.
2. Ernest is a gray elephant.

3. Bones is a small dog.
4. Ernest is a small elephant.

In accordance with the foregoing discussion, we translate them as follows:

b: Bones	Sx: x is small	1. Rb
e: Ernest	Mx: x is a small dog	2. Le
Dx: x is a dog	Rx: x is a gray dog	3. Mb
Ex: x is an elephant	Ax: x is a small elephant	4. Ae
Gx: x is gray	Lx: x is a gray elephant	

Note that we can, if needed, introduce the following wffs as postulates:

$\forall x(Mx \rightarrow Dx)$ $\forall x(Ax \rightarrow Ex)$
$\forall x(Rx \rightarrow Gx)$ $\forall x(Lx \rightarrow Gx)$
$\forall x(Rx \rightarrow Dx)$ $\forall x(Lx \rightarrow Ex)$

but not the following:

$\forall x(Mx \nrightarrow Sx)$ $\forall x(Ax \nrightarrow Sx)$

For necessarily, if Bones is a gray dog and Ernest is a gray elephant, then Bones and Ernest are both gray; but if Bones is a small dog and Ernest is a small elephant, it does not necessarily follow that Bones and Ernest are both small.

Thus, we do not have the option of translating claims (3) and (4) as follows:

$Sb \wedge Db$ $Se \wedge Ee$

but we do have the option of translating claims (1) and (2) this way:

$Gb \wedge Db$ $Ge \wedge Ee$

Taking the latter option is like translating "Alice is taller than Bob" and "Bob is shorter than Alice" as the same wff (§12.4.2): we build the postulates into the translation.

12.5 Moving Quantifiers

If you have a two-place connective (other than $\leftrightarrow$, which is discussed separately in §12.5.1) with a quantifier attached to one side, you can move that quantifier to the front, and the result will be equivalent to the original formula—except in one case: when we move a quantifier attached to the antecedent of a conditional to the front of the entire conditional, we must change it to the other kind of quantifier to obtain a formula equivalent to the original one. More precisely, where β contains no free occurrences of $\underline{x}$:

$\wedge$: $(\forall \underline{x}\alpha \wedge \beta)$ is equivalent to $\forall \underline{x}(\alpha \wedge \beta)$
       $(\exists \underline{x}\alpha \wedge \beta)$ is equivalent to $\exists \underline{x}(\alpha \wedge \beta)$
       $(\beta \wedge \forall \underline{x}\alpha)$ is equivalent to $\forall \underline{x}(\beta \wedge \alpha)$
       $(\beta \wedge \exists \underline{x}\alpha)$ is equivalent to $\exists \underline{x}(\beta \wedge \alpha)$
$\vee$: $(\forall \underline{x}\alpha \vee \beta)$ is equivalent to $\forall \underline{x}(\alpha \vee \beta)$
       $(\exists \underline{x}\alpha \vee \beta)$ is equivalent to $\exists \underline{x}(\alpha \vee \beta)$
       $(\beta \vee \forall \underline{x}\alpha)$ is equivalent to $\forall \underline{x}(\beta \vee \alpha)$
       $(\beta \vee \exists \underline{x}\alpha)$ is equivalent to $\exists \underline{x}(\beta \vee \alpha)$
$\rightarrow$: $(\forall \underline{x}\alpha \rightarrow \beta)$ is equivalent to $\exists \underline{x}(\alpha \rightarrow \beta)$
       $(\exists \underline{x}\alpha \rightarrow \beta)$ is equivalent to $\forall \underline{x}(\alpha \rightarrow \beta)$
       $(\beta \rightarrow \forall \underline{x}\alpha)$ is equivalent to $\forall \underline{x}(\beta \rightarrow \alpha)$
       $(\beta \rightarrow \exists \underline{x}\alpha)$ is equivalent to $\exists \underline{x}(\beta \rightarrow \alpha)$

Let's consider why these equivalences hold. (In the following reasoning we assume that α contains no free occurrence of any variable other than $\underline{x}$—and so we write it as $\alpha(\underline{x})$—and that β contains no free occurrence of any variable.) Take the first one. The left-hand formula $(\forall \underline{x}\alpha(\underline{x}) \wedge \beta)$ is true in a model $\mathfrak{M}$ just in case (a) in every model just like $\mathfrak{M}$ except that it also assigns a referent to $\underline{a}$—where $\underline{a}$ is some name to which $\mathfrak{M}$ assigns no referent—$\alpha(\underline{a}/\underline{x})$ is true, and (b) β is true in $\mathfrak{M}$. The right-hand formula $\forall \underline{x}(\alpha(\underline{x}) \wedge \beta)$ is true in $\mathfrak{M}$ just in case in every model just like $\mathfrak{M}$ except that it also assigns a referent to $\underline{a}$, $\alpha(\underline{a}/\underline{x})$ is true and β is true. But β does not involve the name $\underline{a}$ (remember that $\underline{a}$ was a new name brought in to replace free occurrences of $\underline{x}$, and β contains no free occurrences of $\underline{x}$), so "β is true in every model just like $\mathfrak{M}$ except that it also assigns a referent to $\underline{a}$" holds just in case "β is true in $\mathfrak{M}$" holds. So the conditions required for the left-hand formula to be true in a model are exactly those required for the right-hand formula to be true; hence, the equivalence holds.

Consider a second example: $(\forall \underline{x}\alpha(\underline{x}) \rightarrow \beta)$ is equivalent to $\exists \underline{x}(\alpha(\underline{x}) \rightarrow \beta)$. The left-hand formula $(\forall \underline{x}\alpha(\underline{x}) \rightarrow \beta)$ is true in a model $\mathfrak{M}$ just in case either (a) in some model just like $\mathfrak{M}$ except that it also assigns a referent to $\underline{a}$—where $\underline{a}$ is some name to which $\mathfrak{M}$ assigns no referent—$\alpha(\underline{a}/\underline{x})$ is false, or (b) β is true in $\mathfrak{M}$. The right-hand formula $\exists \underline{x}(\alpha(\underline{x}) \rightarrow \beta)$ is true in $\mathfrak{M}$ just in case there is some model just like $\mathfrak{M}$ except that it also assigns a referent to $\underline{a}$, in which $\alpha(\underline{a}/\underline{x})$ is false or β is true. But β does not involve the name $\underline{a}$, so "there is some model just like $\mathfrak{M}$ except that it also assigns a referent to $\underline{a}$ in which β is true" holds just in case "β is true in $\mathfrak{M}$" holds. So the conditions required for the left-hand formula to be true in a model are exactly those required for the right-hand formula to be true; hence, the equivalence holds.

Similar reasoning establishes the other equivalences. A useful way to remember that it is only when we move a quantifier to or from the antecedent of a conditional that we need to change it to the other type of quantifier to maintain equivalence is to keep in mind that $(\alpha \rightarrow \beta)$ is equivalent to $(\neg\alpha \vee \beta)$. It is the negation here that leads to the need to change the quantifier. For example, $(\forall \underline{x}\alpha \rightarrow \beta)$ is equivalent to $(\neg\forall \underline{x}\alpha \vee \beta)$, which is equivalent to $(\exists \underline{x}\neg\alpha \vee \beta)$ (there's the change of quantifier, as we pass the negation across it; see §12.5.3), which is equivalent to $\exists x(\neg\alpha \vee \beta)$, which is equivalent to $\exists \underline{x}(\alpha \rightarrow \beta)$.

Note that there is an important implication here for how we translate into our logical language. Given the glossary:

r: Rosie
Bx: x is a beagle
Dx: x is a dog

we translate "all beagles are dogs" as $\forall x(Bx \rightarrow Dx)$ and "if everything is a beagle, then Rosie is a dog" as $(\forall x\,Bx \rightarrow Dr)$, not as $\forall x(Bx \rightarrow Dr)$. By the equivalences presented above, the latter is equivalent to $(\exists x\,Bx \rightarrow Dr)$, which does not say "if everything is a beagle, then Rosie is a dog," but "if even one thing is a beagle, then Rosie is a dog."

12.5.1 Biconditional

The case of the biconditional is more complex. In general, $(\forall \underline{x}\alpha \leftrightarrow \beta)$ is equivalent to neither $\forall \underline{x}(\alpha \leftrightarrow \beta)$ nor $\exists \underline{x}(\alpha \leftrightarrow \beta)$, and $(\exists \underline{x}\alpha \leftrightarrow \beta)$ is equivalent to neither $\exists \underline{x}(\alpha \leftrightarrow \beta)$ nor $\forall \underline{x}(\alpha \leftrightarrow \beta)$. Consider, for example

$$(\forall x\alpha \leftrightarrow \beta) \tag{12.1}$$

(where β contains no free occurrences of x). Formula (12.1) is equivalent to

$$(\forall x\alpha \rightarrow \beta) \wedge (\beta \rightarrow \forall x\alpha) \tag{12.2}$$

From §12.5, (12.2)'s left conjunct is equivalent to $\exists x(\alpha \rightarrow \beta)$, and its right conjunct is equivalent to $\forall x(\beta \rightarrow \alpha)$, so[21] (12.2) is equivalent to

$$\exists x(\alpha \rightarrow \beta) \wedge \forall x(\beta \rightarrow \alpha) \tag{12.3}$$

From §12.5, (12.3) is equivalent to

$$\exists x[(\alpha \rightarrow \beta) \wedge \forall x(\beta \rightarrow \alpha)] \tag{12.4}$$

Now consider the scope of the initial existential quantifier here:

$$[(\alpha \rightarrow \beta) \wedge \forall x(\beta \rightarrow \alpha)] \tag{12.5}$$

One might think that from §12.5, (12.5) is equivalent to

$$\forall x[(\alpha \rightarrow \beta) \wedge (\beta \rightarrow \alpha)] \tag{12.6}$$

But one would be wrong, because $(\alpha \to \beta)$ might contain free occurrences of x.[22] However, using the first of the two equivalences at the end of §12.1.8, the right conjunct of (12.5) is equivalent to $\forall w(\beta \to \alpha(w/x))$, where w is a new variable that does not occur in α or β, so (12.5) is equivalent to

$$[(\alpha \to \beta) \wedge \forall w(\beta \to \alpha(w/x))] \tag{12.7}$$

Now we can make the move we wanted to make earlier and conclude that (12.7) is equivalent to

$$\forall w[(\alpha \to \beta) \wedge (\beta \to \alpha(w/x))] \tag{12.8}$$

and hence[23] that (12.4) is equivalent to

$$\exists x \forall w[(\alpha \to \beta) \wedge (\beta \to \alpha(w/x))] \tag{12.9}$$

So (12.1) is equivalent to (12.9).

12.5.2 Other Implications and Nonimplications

In what follows, $\alpha \vDash \beta$ or $\beta \dashv \alpha$ means that α implies β; that is, the argument with α as premise and β as conclusion is valid. When we write $\alpha \nvDash \beta$ or $\beta \not\dashv \alpha$, we mean that α does not imply β; that is, the argument with α as premise and β as conclusion is invalid. If α implies β and vice versa, then α and β are equivalent.

$\wedge$: $(\forall \underline{x}\alpha \wedge \forall \underline{x}\beta) \vDash \dashv \forall \underline{x}(\alpha \wedge \beta)$

         $(\exists \underline{x}\alpha \wedge \exists \underline{x}\beta) \nvDash \dashv \exists \underline{x}(\alpha \wedge \beta)$

$\vee$: $(\forall \underline{x}\alpha \vee \forall \underline{x}\beta) \vDash \not\dashv \forall \underline{x}(\alpha \vee \beta)$

         $(\exists \underline{x}\alpha \vee \exists \underline{x}\beta) \vDash \dashv \exists \underline{x}(\alpha \vee \beta)$

$\to$: $(\forall \underline{x}\alpha \to \exists \underline{x}\beta) \vDash \dashv \exists \underline{x}(\alpha \to \beta)$

         $(\exists \underline{x}\alpha \to \forall \underline{x}\beta) \vDash \not\dashv \forall \underline{x}(\alpha \to \beta)$

These relations can be established by reasoning similar to that used in §12.5. Note that for all the other possible combinations of types of wff not listed here—for example $(\forall \underline{x}\alpha \to \forall \underline{x}\beta)$ and $\forall \underline{x}(\alpha \to \beta)$, or $(\forall \underline{x}\alpha \to \forall \underline{x}\beta)$ and $\exists \underline{x}(\alpha \to \beta)$—neither formula implies the other.

12.5.3 Prenex Normal Form

A wff is said to be in *prenex normal form* if it has all its quantifiers (if any) in front, and then everything else (atomic wffs and connectives) follows after that. For any wff of GPL, there is a wff in prenex normal form equivalent to it. To find such a prenex equivalent of a given formula, we proceed as in the example of $(\forall x\alpha \leftrightarrow \beta)$ in §12.5.1. That is, we replace any biconditionals with equivalent combinations of conjunctions and conditionals, and apply the equivalences of §12.5 to move quantifiers to the front of subformulas. To move quantifiers to the left of negations, we also need to appeal to the following equivalences, which are established by the kind of reasoning given in §10.1.1 and §10.1.2 in relation to the tree rules for negated existential and universal quantifications:

$$\neg\exists \underline{x}\alpha \quad \text{is equivalent to} \quad \forall \underline{x}\neg\alpha$$
$$\neg\forall \underline{x}\alpha \quad \text{is equivalent to} \quad \exists \underline{x}\neg\alpha$$

As we saw in §12.5.1, it may also be necessary at times to replace variables uniformly with other variables, using the equivalences at the end of §12.1.8. Finally, at each stage of the process we make use of the fact that substitution of equivalent subformulas maintains equivalence of the whole formula (where "equivalence" here is understood in the sense of n. 22):

If α_1 is equivalent to α_2, and α_1 is a subformula of β_1, then β_1 is equivalent to β_2, where β_2 arises from β_1 by replacing an occurrence of α_1 with an occurrence of α_2.

In the example in §12.5.1, we appealed to particular instances of this fact in nn. 21 and 23.

12.5.4 Exercises

For each of the following wffs, find an equivalent wff in prenex normal form.

1. $(\forall x\,Px \lor \forall x\,Qx)$

2. $(\exists x\,Px \lor \exists x\,Qx)$

3. $(\forall x\,Px \rightarrow \forall x\,Px)$

4. $(\forall x\,Px \leftrightarrow \forall x\,Px)$

5. $\neg\forall x(Sx \land (\exists y\,Ty \rightarrow \exists z\,Uxz))$

13

Identity

We said in §8.1.1 that our development of predicate logic would proceed as follows. We start with the simplest kind of basic proposition and distinguish its parts—a name and a predicate; we then see how far we can go representing further propositions using the connectives from propositional logic plus names and predicates. We find that we need more resources—quantifiers and variables; we then see how far we can go representing further propositions using connectives, names, predicates, quantifiers, and variables. We eventually find that we need even more resources—many-place predicates; we then see how far we can go representing still further propositions using connectives, names, predicates of any number of places, quantifiers, and variables. We eventually find that we need one more resource—the identity predicate. We are at this final stage now. To represent the propositions expressed by some common kinds of utterance, we need more resources than we have so far.

Consider the claims:

Alice is the tallest person.
Mark Twain is Samuel Langhorne Clemens.
Mark Twain isn't Mary Ann Evans.
There are two dogs.
There are between ten and twenty dogs.

None of these can be translated adequately into GPL; that is, the propositions they express cannot be represented adequately in GPL. We can translate "Alice is taller than Bob" and "Alice is not taller than herself," but not "Alice is the tallest person." For the claim in the latter case is that Alice is taller than everyone else—everyone other than herself, everyone who is not Alice—and we have no way of expressing this in GPL. Again, we can translate "Mark Twain is a novelist," but not "Mark Twain is Samuel Langhorne Clemens"— the claim that Mark Twain and Samuel Langhorne Clemens are one and the same individual—or "Mark Twain isn't Mary Ann Evans"—the claim that

Mark Twain and Mary Ann Evans are not one and the same individual (i.e., they are two separate individuals). Likewise, we can translate "there aren't any dogs," "there is at least one dog," and "everything is a dog"—but not "there are two dogs" or "there are between ten and twenty dogs."

In this chapter, we introduce a single new two-place predicate into our logical language: the *identity* predicate, written I^2. With its aid, we will be able to express all the claims just considered.

Recall that in clause (1iii) of the syntax for GPL in §12.1.3, we said that we use uppercased letters from anywhere in the alphabet as predicates, with one exception: the letter "I" is not used for a two-place predicate; that is, I^2 is not a predicate symbol of the language GPL (although I^1, I^3, I^4, and so on are predicate symbols of GPL). What we are doing now is extending GPL to a new language GPLI—the language of General Predicate Logic with Identity—which has the new symbol I^2, in addition to all the symbols of GPL.

From the syntactic point of view, I^2 functions just like all other two-place predicates. So the full syntax of GPLI is exactly like that of GPL minus the qualification in clause (1iii), which says that I^2 is not a predicate. From the semantic point of view, however, I^2 will not be treated just like any other two-place predicate: it will be given special treatment. This is because—unlike all other predicates in GPLI—the identity predicate is part of the logical vocabulary. In particular, its extension will not be allowed to vary freely from model to model. Rather, in every model it will pick out the identity relation (on the domain of that model). So before we see how to use the new identity predicate in translations from English into GPLI, it will be helpful to clarify the identity relation.

13.1 The Identity Relation

In English, we often use the word "identical" to mean "exactly the same in all respects," "similar in every detail," or "exactly alike." For example, we speak of identical twins, of a very good forgery being identical to the original, of two persons wearing identical dresses, and so on. Figure 13.1 shows a way of picturing this relation of "exact similarity." In this picture, a and b are exactly alike (they have the same size and shape—and as size and shape are the only properties pictured, they are exactly the same in all respects), whereas c and d are not exactly alike (e.g., they have different sizes). In logic, however, we use the word "identical" in a different way. In our sense, to be *identical* to something is to be the very same thing as that thing. You are identical to yourself and to no one else, I am identical to myself and to no-one else, and so on for every object: each object is identical to itself and to nothing else. So *two* objects are never identical to one another (in the sense of "identity" used in logic), because they are two different things, not one and the same thing.

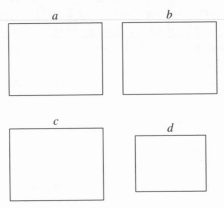

Figure 13.1. Exact similarity and lack of exact similarity.

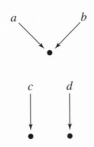

Figure 13.2. Identity and lack of identity.

An object *a* is identical to an object *b* only if they are in fact the same object—that is, there is just one object with two names, "*a*" and "*b*." So in the sense that we shall use "identity," we should picture identity and nonidentity as in Figure 13.2. In this picture *a* and *b* are identical (the names "*a*" and "*b*" pick out the same object), whereas *c* and *d* are nonidentical (the names "*c*" and "*d*" pick out different objects).

Some authors use the term "*qualitative* identity" to mean "exact similarity," and "*numerical* identity" to mean "being the very same thing."[1] However, in this book the simple term "identity" will be used for the relation of "being the very same thing" (and never for the relation of "being exactly alike").

If we have a set of objects, we can picture a two-place relation among these objects as a collection of arrows: we draw an arrow from one object to another if the first object stands in the relation in question to the second object. For example, suppose that Alice (*a*) is 5'8" in height, Bill (*b*) and Carol (*c*) are both 5′10″ in height, and Diana (*d*) is 6′ in height. Then we can picture the relation "*x* is taller than *y*" among these four persons as:

We can picture the relation "*x* is the same height as *y*" as:

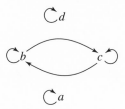

And we can picture the relation "*x* is identical to *y*" as:

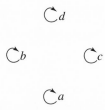

Whatever set of objects we are dealing with, the identity relation among the members of this set will always look like this, when pictured as a collection of arrows; that is, it will have an arrow from each object to itself and no other arrows.

Another way to picture a two-place relation among some objects is as a set of ordered pairs. We put the ordered pair ⟨*x*, *y*⟩ in the set representing the relation just in case *x* bears the relation to *y* (i.e., just in case there is an arrow from *x* to *y*, in the previous way of picturing relations). So the relation "*x* is taller than *y*" among our four persons is the set of ordered pairs:

$$\{\langle b, a\rangle, \langle c, a\rangle, \langle d, a\rangle, \langle d, b\rangle, \langle d, c\rangle\}$$

The relation "*x* is the same height as *y*" is:

$$\{\langle a, a\rangle, \langle b, b\rangle, \langle b, c\rangle, \langle c, b\rangle, \langle c, c\rangle, \langle d, d\rangle\}$$

And the relation "*x* is identical to *y*" is

$$\{\langle a, a\rangle, \langle b, b\rangle, \langle c, c\rangle, \langle d, d\rangle\}$$

a

c

d

b d c a

Figure 13.3. Horizontal and vertical axes . . .

∘(b, a) ∘(d, a) ∘(c, a) ∘(a, a)

∘(b, c) ∘(d, c) ∘(c, c) ∘(a, c)

∘(b, d) ∘(d, d) ∘(c, d) ∘(a, d)

∘(b, b) ∘(d, b) ∘(c, b) ∘(a, b)

Figure 13.4. . . . and the plane they determine.

Whatever objects we are dealing with, the identity relation among these objects will always look like this, when represented as a set of ordered pairs. That is, for each object, there will be a pair with that object in both first and second place and there will be no other pairs.

A third way of picturing a two-place relation among some objects is as a *graph*. Imagine lining up all objects in the set in some order (it does not matter which order) along a horizontal axis and lining up copies of them in the same order along a vertical axis. The first object (in the chosen ordering) should appear on both axes (i.e., the axes meet at this point). Thus, given our set of four persons—and choosing, arbitrarily, to order them b, d, c, a—we create axes as in Figure 13.3. This gives us a plane—a set of points whose coordinates are of the form (x, y), where x is some object on the horizontal axis, and y is some object on the vertical axis (Figure 13.4). We can now picture a relation this way: we fill in the point (x, y) just in case x bears the relation to y (i.e., iff the ordered pair $\langle x, y \rangle$ is in the set representing the relation in the second way of picturing relations, or iff there is an arrow from x to y in the first way of picturing relations). Figure 13.5 shows the relation "x is taller than y" among our four persons (when the axes are set up as in Figure 13.3); Figure 13.6 shows the relation "x is the same height as y;" Figure 13.7 shows the relation "x is identical to y." The identity relation will always look like Figure 13.7 when

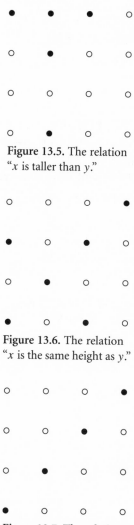

Figure 13.5. The relation
"x is taller than y."

Figure 13.6. The relation
"x is the same height as y."

Figure 13.7. The relation
"x is identical to y."

represented as a graph (whatever order the objects are put in along the axes, as long as they are in the same order on both axes): a diagonal line starting at the bottom left (where the horizontal and vertical axes meet) and going up to the right.

13.2 The Identity Predicate

Our new predicate I^2 is meant to express the relation of identity in the sense of being one and the same thing, explained in the previous section. With this in mind, let's return to some of the claims considered at the beginning of the chapter.[2]

1. Mark Twain is a novelist.

2. Mark Twain is Samuel Langhorne Clemens.

3. Mark Twain isn't Mary Ann Evans.

Note the different functions of "is" here. In claim (1), we have what is called the "is" of predication: it is simply part of the predicate "is a novelist." In claim (2), we have what is called the "is" of identity: the claim here is that Mark Twain and Samuel Langhorne Clemens are identical—they are one and the same person (i.e., he had two names). Likewise claim (3) uses the "is" of identity: the claim here is that Mark Twain and Mary Ann Evans are not identical—they are not one and the same person. So we translate as follows:

m:	Mary Ann Evans	1. Nt
s:	Samuel Langhorne Clemens	2. I^2ts
t:	Mark Twain	3. $\neg I^2tm$
Nx: x is a novelist		

Note that, as the new identity predicate I^2 is part of the logical vocabulary, we do not put an entry for it in our glossary.

Next, consider:

4. Alice is taller than Bob.

5. Alice is not taller than herself.

6. Alice is the tallest person.

We translate as follows:

a:	Alice	4. Tab
b:	Bob	5. $\neg Taa$
Px: x is a person		6. $\forall x((Px \land \neg I^2xa) \to Tax)$
Txy: x is taller than y		

Note that we need the new identity predicate to translate claim (6). The claim is that Alice is taller than everyone else, that is, than every person who is not identical to Alice.

Let's consider some further examples:

7. Mark Twain is taller than some other novelist.[3]
   $\exists x((Nx \land \neg I^2xt) \land Ttx)$

8. Samuel Langhorne Clemens is taller than someone other than Mary Ann Evans.
   $\exists x((Px \land \neg I^2xm) \land Tsx)$

9. Mark Twain is taller than everyone except Samuel Langhorne Clemens.[4]
   $\forall x((Px \land \neg I^2xs) \to Tmx)$

10. Some novelist other than Mark Twain is taller than Mary Ann Evans.
$\exists x((Nx \land \neg I^2 xt) \land Txm)$

11. Mary Ann Evans is taller than every novelist apart from herself.
$\forall x((Nx \land \neg I^2 xm) \rightarrow Tmx)$

We have seen that "is" sometimes translates as the identity predicate (the "is" of identity) and sometimes as part of some other predicate (the "is" of predication). Another word to watch carefully is "same." If I say "Alice and Mary's dresses are exactly the same," this is not an identity claim: I am not saying they have just one dress between them; I am saying that their (two) dresses are exactly alike in all respects. But if I add "they bought them at the same shop," this is an identity claim: I am saying that the shop at which Alice bought her dress is one and the same shop as the one at which Mary bought her dress; that is, there is one single shop at which they both bought their dresses. Finally, such words as "identity" and "is identical to" need to be treated carefully: as we have seen, typical uses of these words in English (e.g., "the forgery and the original were identical") do not translate as the identity predicate, because they are claims about exact similarity, not about identity in our sense.

13.2.1 Abbreviations

We allow ourselves to write $I^2 t_1 t_2$ (where t_1 and t_2 are any terms, i.e., names or variables) as $t_1 = t_2$. That is, we may write I^2 as $=$ and put this symbol between its two argument places, rather than out the front. We then also abbreviate $\neg t_1 = t_2$ as $t_1 \neq t_2$. Thus, when fully unpacked, $t_1 \neq t_2$ is an abbreviation of $\neg I^2 t_1 t_2$. Note that $=$ and $\neq$ are not new symbols of the language GPLI: they are not part of the official syntax at all. They are informal abbreviations that we permit ourselves for reasons of convenience—on a par with omitting outermost parentheses or superscripts on predicates.[5]

13.2.2 Exercises

Translate the following into GPLI.

1. Chris is larger than everything (except himself).

2. All dogs are beagles—except Chris, who is a chihuahua.

3. Ben is happy if he has any dog other than Chris by his side.

4. Chris is happy if he is by anyone's side but Jonathan's.

5. Jonathan is larger than any dog.

6. Everything that Mary wants is owned by someone else.

7. Mary owns something that someone else wants.

8. Mary owns something she doesn't want.

9. If Mary owns a beagle, then no one else does.

10. No one other than Mary owns anything that Mary wants.

11. Everyone prefers *Seinfeld* to *Family Guy*.

12. *Seinfeld* is Adam's most preferred television show.

13. *Family Guy* is Adam's least preferred television show.

14. Jonathon watches *Family Guy*, but he doesn't watch any other television shows.

15. Jonathon is the only person who watches *Family Guy*.

16. Diane is the tallest woman.

17. Edward is the only man who is taller than Diane.

18. Diane isn't the only woman Edward is taller than.

19. No one whom Diane's taller than is taller than Edward.

20. Edward and Diane aren't the only people.

21. You're the only one who knows Ben.

22. I know people other than Ben.

23. Everyone Ben knows (not including Chris and me) is happy.

24. The only happy person I know is Ben.

25. Ben is the tallest happy person I know.

26. Jindabyne is the coldest town between Sydney and Melbourne.

27. There's a colder town than Canberra between Sydney and Melbourne.

28. For every town except Jindabyne, there is a colder town.

29. No town between Sydney and Melbourne is larger than Canberra or colder than Jindabyne.

30. Jindabyne is my most preferred town between Sydney and Melbourne.

13.3 Semantics of Identity

Because I^2 is a two-place predicate, its value in a model should be a set of ordered pairs. Then the semantics of GPL (§12.2) will carry over to GPLI: once we have an extension for I^2, everything else proceeds as before. The story we tell about the truth values of closed wffs involving I^2—given a set of ordered pairs as the extension of I^2—will be the same as the story about the truth values of closed wffs involving any two-place predicate $\underline{R}^2$—given a set of ordered pairs as the extension of $\underline{R}^2$. For example, $\forall x \exists y I^2 xy$ will be true in a model just in case for every object x in the domain, the extension of I^2 in that model contains an ordered pair with x in first position (this is just a new instance of the familiar story about the truth of $\forall x \exists y \underline{R}^2 xy$, for any two-place predicate $\underline{R}^2$); $\exists x (Rx \wedge I^2 xx)$ will be true in a model just in case the extension of I^2 contains a pair $\langle x, x \rangle$ for some object x that is in the extension of R (again, this is just a new instance of the familiar story about the truth of $\exists x (Rx \wedge \underline{R}^2 xx)$, for any two-place predicate $\underline{R}^2$); and so on.

However, because I^2 is part of the logical vocabulary, we shall not treat it in exactly the same way as any other two-place predicate. In particular, its extension should not be allowed to vary freely from model to model. There should not be two models that differ only in the extension of I^2—whereas for any other two-place predicate R^2, there are two models that differ only in the extensions they assign to R^2.

So the extension of I^2 in a model should be a set of ordered pairs of objects drawn from the domain of that model, and this extension should already be fixed once the rest of the model (the domain, the referents of names, and the extensions of all other predicates) is in place. Given that we said that I^2 is supposed to pick out the identity relation, the way to proceed is clear. Once a domain (a set of objects) is specified, the identity relation on that domain is fixed, in the way discussed in §13.1: it is the collection of arrows such that each object in the domain has an arrow pointing to itself (and there are no other arrows); it is the set of ordered pairs containing one pair $\langle x, x \rangle$ for each object x in the domain (and no other ordered pairs); it is the diagonal graph. Now we can simply say that the extension of I^2 in a model is the identity relation on the domain of that model (thinking of the identity relation as a set of ordered pairs). Thus, in a model whose domain is $\{1, 2, 3\}$, the extension of I^2 is the following set of ordered pairs:

$$\{\langle 1, 1 \rangle, \langle 2, 2 \rangle, \langle 3, 3 \rangle\}$$

In a model whose domain is $\{1, 2, 3, 4, 5\}$, the extension of I^2 is the following set of ordered pairs:

$$\{\langle 1, 1 \rangle, \langle 2, 2 \rangle, \langle 3, 3 \rangle, \langle 4, 4 \rangle, \langle 5, 5 \rangle\}$$

In a model whose domain is $\{Alice, Bob, Carol, Dave\}$, the extension of I^2 will be the following set of ordered pairs:

$$\{\langle Alice, Alice \rangle, \langle Bob, Bob \rangle, \langle Carol, Carol \rangle, \langle Dave, Dave \rangle\}$$

and so on. In general, whatever the domain is, the extension of I^2 contains exactly one ordered pair for each object in the domain: the pair containing that object in both first and second place.

Note that the extension of the identity predicate is not exactly the same in all models (e.g., in the first example above it contains three ordered pairs, in the second example, five; in the second example it includes the ordered pair $\langle 4, 4 \rangle$, in the first it does not). However, unlike all other predicates, its extension is not allowed to vary freely from model to model: it always contains all and only those pairs $\langle x, y \rangle$ such that x and y are members of the domain in question and x is identical to y; or in other words, it always contains all and only those pairs $\langle x, x \rangle$ such that x is a member of the domain in question.

Now that we know the extension of the identity predicate in any given model, we can (as foreshadowed at the beginning of this section) work out the truth value in that model of a given formula involving this predicate as in §12.2. For formulas of the form $\underline{a} = \underline{b}$—that is, formulas involving the identity predicate with both its argument places filled by names—there is another way of thinking that can also be useful. Consider the formula $a = b$, that is, I^2ab. Officially, for this claim to be true in a model, it must be that the pair consisting of the referent of a followed by the referent of b is in the extension of I^2. But we know that the only pairs in the extension of I^2 are those with the same object in both first and second place. So for $a = b$ to be true in a model, it must be that the two names a and b have the same referent in that model.

§

To both gain practice in determining the truth values of claims involving identity and gain a better understanding of the identity relation, let us see why the following formulas must be true in every model—that is, why they are logically true:

1. Reflexivity of identity:
   $\forall x\, x = x$

2. Symmetry of identity:
   $\forall x \forall y (x = y \rightarrow y = x)$

3. Transitivity of identity:
   $\forall x \forall y \forall z ((x = y \wedge y = z) \rightarrow x = z)$

4. Leibniz's Law (simple version):
   $\forall x \forall y ((\underline{P}x \wedge x = y) \rightarrow \underline{P}y)$

Formula (1) states that every object is identical to itself. For it to be true in a model $\mathfrak{M}$, it must be the case that $a = a$ is true in every model like $\mathfrak{M}$ except that it assigns a referent to a (where a is a name not assigned a referent in $\mathfrak{M}$). But $a = a$ is true in every model that assigns a referent to a: for it to be true, it is required that the referent of a be the same as the referent of a, and this is automatically the case in any model that assigns a referent to a. So $\forall x\, x = x$ is indeed true on any model $\mathfrak{M}$.

Formula (2) states that for any first-picked object and any second-picked object, if the first picked is identical to the second picked, then the second picked is identical to the first picked. For it to be true in a model $\mathfrak{M}$, it must be the case that $a = b \to b = a$ is true in every model just like $\mathfrak{M}$ except that it assigns referents to a and b (where a and b are names not assigned referents in $\mathfrak{M}$). But $a = b \to b = a$ is true in every model that assigns referents to a and b. If a and b are assigned different referents, then the antecedent of the conditional is false, and so the conditional is true. If a and b are assigned the same object as referent, then the antecedent of the conditional is true, but so is the consequent, and so the conditional is true. So $\forall x \forall y (x = y \to y = x)$ is indeed true in any model $\mathfrak{M}$.

Formula (3) states that for any first-picked object, any second-picked object, and any third-picked object, if the first picked is identical to the second picked and the second picked identical to the third picked, then the first picked is identical to the third. For this statement to be true in a model $\mathfrak{M}$, it must be the case that $(a = b \land b = c) \to a = c$ is true in every model just like $\mathfrak{M}$ except that it assigns referents to a, b, and c (where a, b, and c are names not assigned referents on $\mathfrak{M}$). But $(a = b \land b = c) \to a = c$ is true in every model that assigns referents to a, b, and c. If a and b are assigned different referents, then the left conjunct of the antecedent is false, so the antecedent is false, and so the conditional is true. If b and c are assigned different referents, then the right conjunct of the antecedent is false, so the antecedent is false, and so the conditional is true. If a and b are assigned the same referent, and b and c are assigned the same referent, then the antecedent is true; but in this case a and c are assigned the same referent, and so the consequent is true too, and so the conditional is true. So $\forall x \forall y \forall z ((x = y \land y = z) \to x = z)$ is indeed true in any model $\mathfrak{M}$.

Formula (4) involves the syntactic variable $\underline{P}$. When we say that it is true in every model, what we mean is that every instance of it—obtained by replacing $\underline{P}$ with any one-place predicate—is true in every model. Consider such an instance:

$$\forall x \forall y ((Px \land x = y) \to Py) \tag{13.1}$$

Proposition (13.1) states that for any first-picked object and any second-picked object, if the first picked has the property P, and the first picked is identical to the second picked, then the second picked has the property P. For (13.1) to be true in a model $\mathfrak{M}$, it must be the case that $(Pa \land a = b) \to Pb$ is true in every model just like $\mathfrak{M}$ except that it assigns referents to a and b (where a and b are names not assigned referents in $\mathfrak{M}$). But $(Pa \land a = b) \to Pb$ is true in every model that assigns referents to a and b. If a and b are assigned different referents, then the right conjunct of the antecedent is false, so the antecedent is false, and so the conditional is true. So suppose a and b are assigned the same object as referent. If this referent is not in the extension of P, then the left conjunct of the antecedent is false, so the antecedent is false, and so the conditional is true. If this referent is in the extension of P, then the antecedent is true, but the consequent is true too, and so the conditional is true. So (13.1) is indeed true in any model $\mathfrak{M}$.

We can obtain a more general version of Leibniz's Law by replacing $\underline{P}x$ with any formula $\alpha(x)$ (no matter how complex) that has no free occurrence of any variable other than x, and $\underline{P}y$ with the result of replacing some or all free occurrences of x in $\alpha(x)$ by occurrences of y, where y is a variable that is free for x in $\alpha(x)$.[6] We'll see the reasoning that shows that every instance of this more general form of Leibniz's Law is true in every model—packaged in a slightly different form—in connection with the second tree rule for identity (the rule of Substitution of Identicals) to be introduced in §13.4.

13.3.1 Exercises

1. Here is a model:

   > Domain: {Clark, Bruce, Peter}
   > Referents: a: Clark b: Clark e: Peter f: Peter
   > Extensions: F: {Bruce, Peter}
   > R: {⟨Clark, Bruce⟩, ⟨Clark, Peter⟩, ⟨Bruce, Bruce⟩, ⟨Peter, Peter⟩}

   State whether each of the following propositions is true or false in this model.

   (i) $\forall x(\neg Fx \to x = a)$
   (ii) $\forall x(x = a \to \forall y Rxy)$
   (iii) $\exists x(x \neq f \land Ff \land Rxf)$
   (iv) $\forall x(x \neq b \to Rax)$
   (v) $\exists x(x \neq a \land \forall y(Fy \to Rxy))$
   (vi) $\exists x(x \neq e \land Rxx)$

2. Here is a model:

   > Domain: {1, 2, 3, ...}
   > Referents: a: 1 b: 1 c: 2 e: 4
   > Extensions: F: {1, 2, 3} G: {1, 3, 5, ...}
   > R: {⟨1, 2⟩, ⟨2, 3⟩, ⟨3, 4⟩, ⟨4, 5⟩, ...}

   State whether each of the following propositions is true or false in this model.

   (i) $\exists x(Rax \land \neg Rbx)$
   (ii) $\forall x((Fx \land \neg Gx) \to x = c)$
   (iii) $\forall x(x \neq a \to \exists y Ryx)$
   (iv) $\forall x(Gx \to \exists y \exists z(Rxy \land Ryz \land Gz))$

(v) $\forall x((x = a \lor x = b) \rightarrow x \neq c)$

(vi) $\exists x(\neg Fx \land x \neq e \land \exists y(Fy \land Ryx))$

3. For each of the following propositions, describe (a) a model in which it is true and (b) a model in which it is false. If there is no model of one of these types, explain why.

  (i) $\forall x(Fx \rightarrow x = a)$

  (ii) $\exists x(x = a \land x = b)$

  (iii) $\exists x \forall y(x \neq y \rightarrow Rxy)$

  (iv) $\forall x \forall y(Rxy \rightarrow x = y)$

  (v) $\forall x \forall y(x \neq y \rightarrow \exists z Rxyz)$

  (vi) $\exists x(x = a \land a \neq x)$

  (vii) $\forall x \forall y((Fx \land Fy) \rightarrow x = y)$

  (viii) $\exists x(Fx \land \forall y(Gy \rightarrow x = y))$

  (ix) $\forall x(Fx \rightarrow \exists y(x \neq y \land Rxy))$

  (x) $\forall x((Fx \land Rax) \rightarrow x \neq a)$

  (xi) $\exists x \exists y \exists z(x \neq y \land y \neq z \land x \neq z \land Rxyz)$

  (xii) $\forall x \forall y \forall z(Rxyz \rightarrow (x \neq y \land y \neq z \land x \neq z))$

  (xiii) $\forall x \forall y(x \neq y \rightarrow (Fx \lor Fy))$

  (xiv) $\exists x(Fx \land \forall y((Fy \land x \neq y) \rightarrow Rxy))$

  (xv) $\forall x \forall y \forall z(Rxyz \rightarrow (Rxxx \land Ryyy \land Rzzz))$

  (xvi) $\forall x(Rxx \rightarrow \forall y(x = y \rightarrow Rxy))$

  (xvii) $(Fa \land Fb) \land \forall x \forall y((Fx \land Fy) \rightarrow x = y)$

  (xviii) $\exists x \exists y(Fx \land Fy \land \forall z[Fz \rightarrow (x = z \lor y = z)])$

13.4 Trees for General Predicate Logic with Identity

The identity predicate is part of the logical vocabulary, and therefore our system of tree proofs must be extended to accommodate the introduction of this new predicate into the language. We extend the system with two new tree rules. The first rule gives us a new way of closing a path:

$$\vdots$$

$$\neg I^2 \underline{a}\underline{a}$$

$$\times$$

That is, we close any path that contains a formula of the form $\neg I^2 \underline{a}\underline{a}$: the negation of a formula consisting of the identity predicate with both argument places filled by the same name. In looking for situations in which this rule may be applied, don't forget that $\neg I^2 \underline{a}\underline{a}$ may also be written as $\neg \underline{a} = \underline{a}$ or as $\underline{a} \neq \underline{a}$.

The rationale behind the rule is as follows. We close a path when there cannot be a model in which all the formulas on that path are true. (Remember, a closed path is one corresponding to *no* model—not one corresponding to a model in which the formulas at the top of the path are false.) Any formula of the form $\underline{a} = \underline{a}$ is true in every model, so there is no model in which its negation $\underline{a} \neq \underline{a}$ is true.

To state the second rule, we need some new terminology. Recall (§9.3) that we use $\alpha(\underline{x})$ to stand for an arbitrary wff with no free occurrence of any variable other than $\underline{x}$, and $\alpha(\underline{a}/\underline{x})$ to stand for the wff resulting from $\alpha(\underline{x})$ by replacing all free occurrences of $\underline{x}$ in $\alpha(\underline{x})$ with the name $\underline{a}$. We now also introduce the following terminology. We use $\alpha(\underline{a})$ to stand for an arbitrary wff in which the name $\underline{a}$ occurs (one or more times). We then use $\alpha(\underline{b}//\underline{a})$ to stand for any wff resulting from $\alpha(\underline{a})$ by replacing some (i.e., one or more—maybe all, but maybe not) occurrences of $\underline{a}$ in $\alpha(\underline{a})$ with the name $\underline{b}$. So, for example, if $\alpha(a)$ is Fa, then $\alpha(b//a)$ is Fb and $\alpha(c//a)$ is Fc. If $\alpha(b)$ is $(Rab \wedge Rbc)$, then we may replace the placeholder $\alpha(d//b)$ with any of the wffs $(Rad \wedge Rbc)$, $(Rab \wedge Rdc)$, or $(Rad \wedge Rdc)$. If $\alpha(c)$ is $((Rab \rightarrow Rbc) \vee a = c)$, then we may replace the placeholder $\alpha(a//c)$ with any of the wffs $((Rab \rightarrow Rba) \vee a = c)$, $((Rab \rightarrow Rbc) \vee a = a)$, or $((Rab \rightarrow Rba) \vee a = a)$, and so on.

We can now state our second new tree rule—the rule of *Substitution of Identicals* (SI):

$$\alpha(\underline{a})$$
$$I^2\underline{ab} \qquad \text{(or } I^2\underline{ba})$$
$$\alpha(\underline{b}//\underline{a})$$

Note the following points. (i) The two inputs to the rule—$\alpha(\underline{a})$ and either $I^2\underline{ab}$ or $I^2\underline{ba}$—may come in either order on the path on which the rule is being applied. (ii) When applying this rule, we do not check off any formulas. (iii) We do not apply this rule using a formula $\alpha(\underline{a})$ as input if $\alpha(\underline{a})$ has been checked off. (iv) In looking for situations in which this rule may be applied, don't forget that $I^2\underline{ab}$ may also be written as $\underline{a} = \underline{b}$ and that $I^2\underline{ba}$ may also be written as $\underline{b} = \underline{a}$.

Suppose we are applying this rule at the bottom of a path p (which has on it $\alpha(\underline{a})$, and $I^2\underline{ab}$ or $I^2\underline{ba}$). Applying the rule extends p to p' (which differs from p by also having $\alpha(\underline{b}//\underline{a})$ on it). The desired property that our rule should have is (recall §10.1):

If there is a model in which every proposition on p is true, then there is a model in which every proposition on p' is true.

Let's check that our new rule SI has this property. Path p contains $I^2\underline{ab}$ or $I^2\underline{ba}$. A model in which either of these is true is one in which $\underline{a}$ and $\underline{b}$ have the same referent. Path p also contains $\alpha(\underline{a})$. A model in which this is true is one in which the *referent* of $\underline{a}$ has certain features.[7] Now a model in which $\alpha(\underline{b}//\underline{a})$ is true is one in which either the referent of $\underline{a}$ or the referent of $\underline{b}$ has those very same features.[8] But the referent of $\underline{a}$ just is the referent of $\underline{b}$, so

1.	$\neg\forall x\forall y\forall z((x=y \land y\neq z) \to x\neq z)$ ✓	
2.	$\exists x\neg\forall y\forall z((x=y \land y\neq z) \to x\neq z)$ ✓ a	{1}
3.	$\neg\forall y\forall z((a=y \land y\neq z) \to a\neq z)$ ✓	{2}
4.	$\exists y\neg\forall z((a=y \land y\neq z) \to a\neq z)$ ✓ b	{3}
5.	$\neg\forall z((a=b \land b\neq z) \to a\neq z)$ ✓	{4}
6.	$\exists z\neg((a=b \land b\neq z) \to a\neq z)$ ✓ c	{5}
7.	$\neg((a=b \land b\neq c) \to a\neq c)$ ✓	{6}
8.	$(a=b \land b\neq c)$ ✓	{7}
9.	$\neg a\neq c$ ✓	{7}
10.	$a=b$	{8}
11.	$b\neq c$	{8}
12.	$a=c$	{9}
13.	$b=c$	{10, 12 (SI)}[9]
	×	{11, 13}

Figure 13.8. A GPLI tree.

our characterization of a model in which $\alpha(\underline{b}//\underline{a})$ is true (one in which either the referent of $\underline{a}$ or the referent of $\underline{b}$ has certain features) is equivalent to our characterization of a model in which $\alpha(\underline{a})$ is true (one in which the referent of $\underline{a}$ has certain features). So our rule does indeed have the desired property.

As an example, let's test whether the following proposition is a logical truth:

$$\forall x\forall y\forall z((x=y \land y\neq z) \to x\neq z)$$

We write down the negation of this formula, and then finish the tree (Figure 13.8). All paths close, so the proposition is indeed a logical truth. As a second example, let's test whether the following proposition is a logical truth:

$$\forall x\forall y\forall z(((Rxy \land Ryz) \land x=z) \to Ryy)$$

We write the negation of this formula at the top of a tree and then finish the tree (Figure 13.9). A path remains open, so the proposition is not a logical truth.

The tree rules are summarized in Figure 13.10 (the rules for the connectives and the quantifiers are the same as before).

13.4.1 Saturated Paths

Recall (§10.1.6) that we stop applying tree rules and draw a conclusion from our tree—for example, "valid: all paths close" or "invalid: some path remains open"—when the tree is finished, and that a tree is finished when each of its paths is either closed (with a cross) or saturated. The basic idea of a saturated ʲpath is one on which every rule that can be applied has been applied. But as we saw in §10.1.6, we need to be a bit more specific than this in the case

1.	$\neg\forall x\forall y\forall z(((Rxy \land Ryz) \land x = z) \to Ryy)$ ✓	
2.	$\exists x\neg\forall y\forall z(((Rxy \land Ryz) \land x = z) \to Ryy)$ ✓ a	{1}
3.	$\neg\forall y\forall z(((Ray \land Ryz) \land a = z) \to Ryy)$ ✓	{2}
4.	$\exists y\neg\forall z(((Ray \land Ryz) \land a = z) \to Ryy)$ ✓ b	{3}
5.	$\neg\forall z(((Rab \land Rbz) \land a = z) \to Rbb)$ ✓	{4}
6.	$\exists z\neg(((Rab \land Rbz) \land a = z) \to Rbb)$ ✓ c	{5}
7.	$\neg(((Rab \land Rbc) \land a = c) \to Rbb)$ ✓	{6}
8.	$((Rab \land Rbc) \land a = c)$ ✓	{7}
9.	$\neg Rbb$	{7}
10.	$(Rab \land Rbc)$ ✓	{8}
11.	$a = c$	{8}
12.	Rab	{10}
13.	Rbc	{10}
14.	Rcb	{11, 12 (SI)}
15.	Rba	{11, 13 (SI)}
	$\uparrow$	

Figure 13.9. A second GPLI tree.

of formulas whose main operator is a universal quantifier. We said that a condition on a path being saturated is that every formula on it whose main operator is a universal quantifier:

1. has had the universal quantifier rule applied to it at least once, and

2. has had the rule applied to it once for each name that appears on the path.

We also need to add a further qualification with regards to SI. For suppose we simply said that this rule must be applied wherever it can be applied, before a path can be deemed saturated. Then we would encounter some problems. For example, suppose that $a = b$ and Fa appear on our path. Then we can apply SI to get Fb. But now we can apply SI to $a = b$ and Fb to obtain another occurrence of Fa—and then we can apply SI to $a = b$ and this new formula Fa to get yet another occurrence of Fb, and so on forever, extending our path with repetitions of formulas already on it. For another example, suppose that our path contains $a = b$ and $b = a$. Then, whatever applications of SI we can make using $a = b$, we can also make duplicate applications using $b = a$. But this just makes our path longer, to no purpose: again, we are extending our path with repetitions of formulas already on it. So we add the following condition on saturation:

a path is not saturated unless every application of SI that could be made on that path and that would result in the addition to the path of a formula that does not already appear on it has been made.

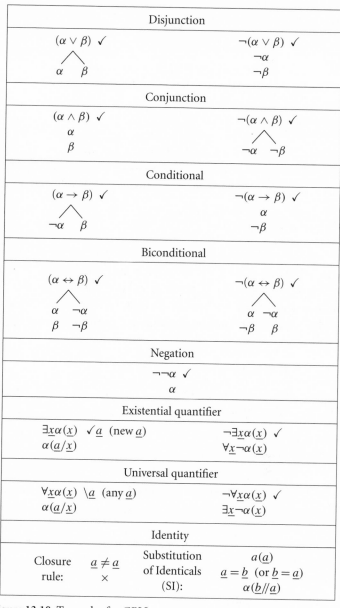

Disjunction	
$(\alpha \vee \beta)$ ✓	$\neg(\alpha \vee \beta)$ ✓
⟨α β⟩	$\neg\alpha$
	$\neg\beta$

Conjunction	
$(\alpha \wedge \beta)$ ✓	$\neg(\alpha \wedge \beta)$ ✓
α	
β	⟨$\neg\alpha$ $\neg\beta$⟩

Conditional	
$(\alpha \rightarrow \beta)$ ✓	$\neg(\alpha \rightarrow \beta)$ ✓
⟨$\neg\alpha$ β⟩	α
	$\neg\beta$

Biconditional	
$(\alpha \leftrightarrow \beta)$ ✓	$\neg(\alpha \leftrightarrow \beta)$ ✓
⟨α $\neg\alpha$⟩	⟨α $\neg\alpha$⟩
β $\neg\beta$	$\neg\beta$ β

Negation
$\neg\neg\alpha$ ✓
α

Existential quantifier	
$\exists \underline{x}\alpha(\underline{x})$ ✓$\underline{a}$ (new $\underline{a}$)	$\neg\exists \underline{x}\alpha(\underline{x})$ ✓
$\alpha(\underline{a}/\underline{x})$	$\forall \underline{x}\neg\alpha(\underline{x})$

Universal quantifier	
$\forall \underline{x}\alpha(\underline{x})$ \$\underline{a}$ (any $\underline{a}$)	$\neg\forall \underline{x}\alpha(\underline{x})$ ✓
$\alpha(\underline{a}/\underline{x})$	$\exists \underline{x}\neg\alpha(\underline{x})$

Identity			
Closure rule:	$\underline{a} \neq \underline{a}$ ✕	Substitution of Identicals (SI):	$a(\underline{a})$ $\underline{a}=\underline{b}$ (or $\underline{b}=\underline{a}$) $\alpha(\underline{b}//\underline{a})$

Figure 13.10. Tree rules for GPLI.

Consider an example:

1. $a = b$
2. $Saba$
3. $Sbba$ $\{1, 2 \, (\text{SI})\}$

This tree is not finished: it can be extended as follows:

4. $Sabb$ $\{1, 2 \, (\text{SI})\}$
5. $Sbbb$ $\{1, 2 \, (\text{SI})\}$

because if $Saba$ is represented as $\alpha(a)$, then all of $Sbba$, $Sabb$, and $Sbbb$ may be represented as $\alpha(b // a)$—and hence as legitimate outputs of the rule SI, applied to $a = b$ and $Saba$. The tree is still not finished: it can be extended as follows:

6. $Saaa$ $\{1, 2 \, (\text{SI})\}$

because $Saba$ can be represented as $\alpha(b)$ (as well as $\alpha(a)$), and then $Saaa$ can be represented as $\alpha(a // b)$—and hence as a legitimate output of the rule SI, applied to $a = b$ and $Saba$. The tree is still not finished: the new formula $Saaa$ can be represented as $\alpha(a)$, and hence all the following formulas can be represented as $\alpha(b // a)$, and hence as legitimate outputs of the rule SI, applied to $a = b$ and $Saaa$:

$$Sbaa, Saba, Saab, Sbba, Sbab, Sabb, Sbbb$$

Now some of these already appear in our tree, so we do not need to write them in. Writing in the new ones yields:

7. $Sbaa$ $\{1, 6 \, (\text{SI})\}$
8. $Saab$ $\{1, 6 \, (\text{SI})\}$
9. $Sbab$ $\{1, 6 \, (\text{SI})\}$

Now the tree is finished. We have only applied SI to rows 1 and 2, and rows 1 and 6, but all of rows 3–5 and 7–9 can be represented as $\alpha(a)$, $\alpha(b)$, or both, so there are many more applications of SI that could be made. However, none of them would result in the addition of a new formula to the path.

13.4.2 Reading off Models

Given a saturated open path, we can read off a model in which the propositions at the top of the tree are true. The process involves three stages:

1. Construct a provisional domain and assignment of referents to names.

2. Trim the domain and assignment of referents to names to obtain a final domain and assignment of referents to names.

3. Assign extensions to predicates.

Steps 1 and 3 are exactly as in the case of trees for predicate logic without identity; only step 2 is new.

Step 1. Here we follow the procedure described in §10.2.1. We put one object into the domain for each name appearing in our path and then assign the first of these objects as the referent of the first name, the second as the referent of the second name, and so on. To take a concrete example, look at the open path in the tree in Figure 13.9. We find three names on this path: a, b, and c. So our provisional domain and referents are:

Domain: $\{1, 2, 3\}$
Referents: a: 1 b: 2 c: 3

Step 2. Now we trim our provisional domain and referents, in light of any identity statements $\underline{a} = \underline{b}$ appearing on our path. Remember that the idea is to construct a model in which every formula on our open path is true. The proposition $\underline{a} = \underline{b}$ is true only if the referents of $\underline{a}$ and $\underline{b}$ are the same, so we need to make them so, and then we strike from the domain any object no longer used as the referent of any name. To return to our concrete example, our open path contains the identity statement $a = c$. So the referents of a and c—which, in our provisional assignment, are different objects (1 and 3, respectively)—must be made the same. What we do is leave the referent of a (the alphabetically first name in our identity statement) as it is and change the referent of c to be the same object (in this case 1). And now we strike out object 3 from our domain, as it is no longer the referent of any name.[10] So our final domain and referents are:

Domain: $\{1, 2\}$
Referents: a: 1 b: 2 c: 1

Step 3. Now we assign extensions to the predicates appearing on our path, following the procedure described in §12.3: for every standalone atomic wff $\underline{F}^n \underline{a_1} \ldots \underline{a_n}$ appearing on our path, we put into the extension of the n-place predicate $\underline{F}^n$ the ordered n-tuple consisting of the referents of the names $\underline{a_1}$ through $\underline{a_n}$ (in that order), and we put no other n-tuples into the extension of $\underline{F}^n$. In our present example, Rab, Rbc, Rcb, and Rba appear (as standalone atomic wffs—i.e., not simply as subformulas in some more complex wff). So we need to put into the extension of R the following pairs:

- the referent of a followed by the referent of b (to make Rab true in the model we are constructing),

- the referent of b followed by the referent of c (to make Rbc true),

- the referent of c followed by the referent of b (to make Rcb true), and

- the referent of b followed by the referent of a (to make Rba true).

So our extension is:

R: $\{\langle 1, 2\rangle, \langle 2, 1\rangle, \langle 1, 2\rangle, \langle 2, 1\rangle\}$

As this is a set of ordered pairs, there is no point writing the same pair twice when we describe the set.[11] So we may write our extension more compactly as:

R: $\{\langle 1, 2\rangle, \langle 2, 1\rangle\}$

Note that what we are doing in moving from writing the extension of R as $\{\langle 1, 2\rangle, \langle 2, 1\rangle, \langle 1, 2\rangle, \langle 2, 1\rangle\}$ to writing it as $\{\langle 1, 2\rangle, \langle 2, 1\rangle\}$ is crucially different from what we did in step 2. Sets $\{\langle 1, 2\rangle, \langle 2, 1\rangle, \langle 1, 2\rangle, \langle 2, 1\rangle\}$ and $\{\langle 1, 2\rangle, \langle 2, 1\rangle\}$ are (two ways of writing) the same set (a set containing the two ordered pairs $\langle 1, 2\rangle$ and $\langle 2, 1\rangle$), so when we go from describing the extension of R in the first way to describing it in the second way, we are not changing our model: we are simply describing the same model in a more compact fashion. This is convenient but not essential: there is nothing incorrect about describing the extension of R as $\{\langle 1, 2\rangle, \langle 2, 1\rangle, \langle 1, 2\rangle, \langle 2, 1\rangle\}$. However, it is incorrect to assign a and c different referents: in a model in which a refers to 1 and c refers to 3, $a = c$ is false. That is why we must trim our domain and referent assignments in light of any identity statements on our path. Doing so is not a mere convenience: not doing so makes our model incorrect. What we achieve in step 2 is not a shorter description of the same model we had in step 1: it is (in general) a different model. Crucially, it is a model that—unlike the provisional model obtained in step 1—makes the identity statements on our path true.

Let's work through another example: testing whether the following set of propositions is satisfiable:

$$\{\forall x(Rxb \wedge x = a), \exists x\,Rxb, a = b\}$$

We write down the three propositions and then finish the tree (Figure 13.11). The path is now saturated: the universal rule has been applied to line 1 for every name appearing in the path, and anything we could obtain by applying SI to lines on the path is already on the path. The path is open, so the set of propositions we started with is satisfiable.

Let's read off a model from this open path (a model in which all three propositions in the original set are true). Three names—a, b, and c—appear on the path, so we start with the following provisional domain and assignment of referents:

Domain: $\{1, 2, 3\}$
Referents: a: 1 b: 2 c: 3

We now trim this in light of any identity statements appearing on our path. The proposition $a = b$ appears on line 3, so we set the referent of b to be the

1.	$\forall x (Rxb \wedge x = a)$ \ $a\,b\,c$	
2.	$\exists x\, Rxb$ ✓ c	
3.	$a = b$	
4.	Rcb	$\{2\}$
5.	$(Rab \wedge a = a)$ ✓	$\{1, a\}$
6.	Rab	$\{5\}$
7.	$a = a$	$\{5\}$
8.	$(Rbb \wedge b = a)$ ✓	$\{1, b\}$
9.	Rbb	$\{8\}$
10.	$b = a$	$\{8\}$
11.	$(Rcb \wedge c = a)$ ✓	$\{1, c\}$
12.	Rcb	$\{11\}$
13.	$c = a$	$\{11\}$
14.	Rca	$\{3, 4\ (\mathrm{SI})\}$
15.	Raa	$\{3, 6\ (\mathrm{SI})\}$
16.	Rba	$\{3, 9\ (\mathrm{SI})\}$
17.	Rcc	$\{13, 14\ (\mathrm{SI})\}$
18.	Rac	$\{13, 15\ (\mathrm{SI})\}$
19.	Rbc	$\{13, 16\ (\mathrm{SI})\}$
20.	$a = c$	$\{7, 13\ (\mathrm{SI})\}$
21.	$b = b$	$\{3, 10\ (\mathrm{SI})\}$
22.	$b = c$	$\{10, 13\ (\mathrm{SI})\}$
23.	$c = b$	$\{21, 22\ (\mathrm{SI})\}$
24.	$c = c$	$\{22, 23\ (\mathrm{SI})\}$

$\uparrow$

Figure 13.11. A third GPLI tree

same as the referent of a—object 1—and remove object 2 (the former referent of b) from the domain:

Domain: $\{1, 3\}$
Referents: a: 1 b: 1 c: 3

There is more trimming to be done. The proposition $c = a$ appears on line 13, so we set the referent of c to be the same as the referent of a—object 1—and remove object 3 (the former referent of c) from the domain:

Domain: $\{1\}$
Referents: a: 1 b: 1 c: 1

No more trimming is possible. We now need to specify the extension of R. Rcb appears on line 4, so we put the ordered pair consisting of the referent of c (object 1) followed by the referent of b (object 1) into the extension of R:

R: $\{\langle 1, 1 \rangle\}$

Given that 1 is the only object in the domain, R now contains every possible ordered pair of objects from the domain. (There is only one such pair when the domain contains just one object.) We are therefore finished: nothing more can be added to the extension of R. (There are plenty more atomic formulas involving R in the tree, but they all lead to the same ordered pair. For example, Rab appears on line 6, so we need to have the ordered pair consisting of the referent of a followed by the referent of b in the extension of R—but we already do: it is just the pair $\langle 1, 1 \rangle$ again.)

13.4.3 Exercises

1. Using trees, determine whether the following sets of propositions are satisfiable. For any set that is satisfiable, read off from your tree a model in which all propositions in the set are true.

   (i) $\{Rab \rightarrow \neg Rba,\ Rab,\ a = b\}$

   (ii) $\{Rab,\ \neg Rbc,\ a = b\}$

   (iii) $\{\forall x(Fx \rightarrow x = a),\ Fa,\ a \neq b\}$

   (iv) $\{\forall x(Fx \rightarrow Gx),\ \exists x Fx,\ \neg Ga,\ a = b\}$

   (v) $\{\forall x(x \neq a \rightarrow Rax),\ \forall x\neg Rxb,\ a \neq b\}$

   (vi) $\{\exists x \forall y(Fy \rightarrow x = y),\ Fa,\ Fb\}$

   (vii) $\{\forall x \forall y(Rxy \rightarrow x = y),\ Rab,\ a \neq b\}$

   (viii) $\{\forall x((Fx \wedge Rxa) \rightarrow x \neq a),\ Fb \wedge Rba,\ a = b\}$

   (ix) $\{\exists x \exists y \exists z Rxyz,\ \forall x(x = x \rightarrow x = a)\}$

   (x) $\{\forall x\neg Rxx,\ \forall x \forall y x = y,\ \exists x Rax\}$

2. Using trees, determine whether the following arguments are valid. For any argument that is not valid, read off from your tree a model in which the premises are true and the conclusion false.

   (i) $\exists x Fx$
       $\exists y Gy$
       $\forall x \forall y x = y$
       $\therefore \exists x(Fx \wedge Gx)$

   (ii) $\exists x \exists y(Fx \wedge Gy \wedge \forall z(z = x \vee z = y))$
        $\therefore \exists x(Fx \wedge Gx)$

   (iii) Rab
         $\therefore \forall x \forall y \forall z(((Rxy \wedge Ryz) \wedge x = z) \rightarrow Ryy)$

   (iv) $\forall x \forall y(Rxy \rightarrow Ryx)$
        $\exists x(Rax \wedge x \neq b)$
        $\therefore \exists x(Rxa \wedge x \neq b)$

   (v) $\forall x \forall y x = y$
       $\therefore \forall x \forall y(Rxy \rightarrow Ryx)$

(vi) $\forall x \forall y \forall z((Rxy \wedge Rxz) \rightarrow y = z)$
$Rab \wedge Rcd$
$b \neq d$
$\therefore a \neq c$

(vii) $\exists x \exists y (Rxy \wedge x = y)$
$\therefore \neg \forall x Rxx$

(viii) $\forall x (x = a \vee x = b)$
$\therefore \forall x x = a$

(ix) $\forall x Rax$
$\neg \forall x \forall y x = y$
$\therefore \exists x \exists y \exists z (Rxy \wedge Rxz \wedge y \neq z)$

(x) $\forall x x = a$
$\therefore \forall x x = b$

3. Translate the following propositions into GPLI and then test whether they are logical truths using trees. For any proposition that is not a logical truth, read off from your tree a model in which it is false.

(i) If Stan is the only firefighter, then no one else is a firefighter.

(ii) If Julius Caesar is left-handed but Lewis Carroll isn't, then Lewis Carroll isn't Julius Caesar.

(iii) If the sun is warming all and only things other than itself, then the sun is warming Apollo.

(iv) If Kevin Bacon isn't Kevin Bacon, then he's Michael J. Fox.

(v) If no one who isn't Twain is a witty author, and Clemens is an author, then Clemens is not witty.

(vi) No spy trusts any other spy.

(vii) Either everything is identical to this ant, or nothing is.

(viii) If Doug is afraid of everything but Santa Claus, then either he's afraid of himself, or else he's Santa Claus.

(ix) If Mark respects Samuel and only Samuel, then Mark doesn't respect himself.

(x) Either I am a physical body, or I am identical to something that's not a physical body.

13.5 Numerical Quantifiers

At the beginning of this chapter we gave some examples of claims that cannot be translated adequately into GPL: to translate these claims, we need the identity predicate. We return now to the final two examples: "there are two dogs" and "there are between ten and twenty dogs." Using the glossary:

Dx: x is a dog

we translate "there aren't any dogs" as $\neg \exists x\, Dx$, "there is at least one dog" as $\exists x\, Dx$, and "everything is a dog" as $\forall x\, Dx$. Now what about "there are two dogs" (i.e., exactly two: no more, no less)? Well, let's start with a weaker claim: "there are at least two dogs." Note that we cannot translate this as:

$$\exists x\, Dx \land \exists y\, Dy \tag{13.2}$$

Formula (13.2) says (under our glossary) "you can pick an object that is a dog, and you can pick an object that is a dog." This would be true if there were only one dog: you could pick it both times. Nor can we translate "there are at least two dogs" as $\exists x \exists y (Dx \land Dy)$: this formula is equivalent to (13.2) (recall §12.5). What we need to say is "you can pick an object that is a dog, and you can pick another object—a different object from the first one—that is a dog." Translating this statement requires the identity predicate. Our translation is:

$$\exists x \exists y (Dx \land Dy \land x \neq y)$$

Similarly, "there are at least three dogs" translates as:

$$\exists x \exists y \exists z (Dx \land Dy \land Dz \land x \neq y \land x \neq z \land y \neq z) \tag{13.3}$$

Formula (13.3) says (under our glossary) "you can pick an object that is a dog, and you can pick an object different from the first one that is a dog, and you can pick an object different from both the first one and the second one that is a dog." Note that there are three nonidentity statements here ($x \neq y$, $x \neq z$, and $y \neq z$)—that is, one for every possible (nonordered) pairing of the variables appearing in our initial three quantifiers.[12] The following would not do:

$$\exists x \exists y \exists z (Dx \land Dy \land Dz \land x \neq y \land y \neq z) \tag{13.4}$$

Formula (13.4) says (under our glossary) "you can pick an object that is a dog, and you can pick an object different from the first one that is a dog, and you can pick an object different from the second one that is a dog." This statement would be true if there were only two dogs, say, Rosie and Maisie: you could pick Rosie first and third, and Maisie second. The translation strategy generalizes. "There are at least four dogs" translates as:

$$\exists x \exists y \exists z \exists w (Dx \land Dy \land Dz \land Dw \land$$
$$x \neq y \land x \neq z \land x \neq w \land y \neq z \land y \neq w \land z \neq w)$$

and so on. Note that the translation of "there are at least n dogs" has n existential quantifiers in front, each containing a different variable $\underline{x}$; it then has one wff $D\underline{x}$ for each of these variables. And then, for each nonordered pairing of these variables, it has one nonidentity statement involving this pair of variables (it does not matter which variable in the pair appears on the left side of the nonidentity sign and which appears on the right).[13]

$$\S$$

So much for saying that there are at least n dogs, that is, n or more. How do we say that there are at most n dogs, that is, n or less? Well, "there is at most one dog" translates as:

$$\forall x \forall y ((Dx \land Dy) \to x = y) \tag{13.5}$$

Formula (13.5) says (under our glossary) that if you make two choices and get a dog each time, you must have chosen the same thing both times. "There are at most two dogs" translates as:

$$\forall x \forall y \forall z ((Dx \land Dy \land Dz) \to (x = y \lor x = z \lor y = z)) \tag{13.6}$$

Formula (13.6) says (under our glossary) that if you make three choices and get a dog each time, you must have chosen the same thing on at least two of your picks (the first and second, the first and third, or the second and third). Similarly, "there are at most three dogs" translates as:

$$\forall x \forall y \forall z \forall w ((Dx \land Dy \land Dz \land Dw) \to$$
$$(x = y \lor x = z \lor x = w \lor y = z \lor y = w \lor z = w)) \tag{13.7}$$

Formula (13.7) says (under our glossary) that if you make four choices and get a dog each time, you must have chosen the same thing on at least two of your picks (the first and second, the first and third, the first and fourth, the second and third, the second and fourth, or the third and fourth). The translation strategy extends to "there are at most four dogs," "there are at most five dogs," and so on.

Note that the translation of "there are at most n dogs" has $n + 1$ universal quantifiers in front, each containing a different variable $\underline{x}$. It then has one wff $D\underline{x}$ for each of these variables and then, for each nonordered pairing of these variables, it has one identity statement involving this pair of variables (it does not matter which variable in the pair appears on the left side of the identity sign and which appears on the right).[14]

$$\S$$

Now that we can say "there are at least n dogs" and "there are at most n dogs," we can say that there are exactly n dogs by taking the conjunction of these two claims. (The first conjunct rules out the possibility that there are less than n dogs; the second conjunct rules out the possibility that there are more than n dogs; the only possibility left is that there are exactly n dogs.) So "there is (exactly) one dog" translates as:

$$\exists x Dx \land \forall x \forall y ((Dx \land Dy) \to x = y)$$

"There are (exactly) two dogs" translates as:

$$\exists x \exists y (Dx \wedge Dy \wedge x \neq y) \wedge$$
$$\forall x \forall y \forall z ((Dx \wedge Dy \wedge Dz) \rightarrow (x = y \vee x = z \vee y = z))$$

"There are (exactly) three dogs" translates as:

$$\exists x \exists y \exists z (Dx \wedge Dy \wedge Dz \wedge x \neq y \wedge x \neq z \wedge y \neq z) \wedge$$
$$\forall x \forall y \forall z \forall w ((Dx \wedge Dy \wedge Dz \wedge Dw) \rightarrow ,$$
$$(x = y \vee x = z \vee x = w \vee y = z \vee y = w \vee z = w))$$

and so on. Furthermore, we can say "there are between ten and twenty dogs" (inclusive) by conjoining "there are at least ten dogs" and "there are at most twenty dogs" (and if we mean it noninclusively—that is, that that there are strictly more than ten and strictly less than twenty—then we can conjoin "there are at least eleven dogs" and "there are at most nineteen dogs").

§

Instead of translating "there are exactly n dogs" as literally the conjunction of "there are at least n dogs" and "there are at most n dogs," we can also translate such statements in a different, but ultimately equivalent, way. (This alternative translation strategy has the advantage that it yields shorter formulas in GPLI.) "There is (exactly) one dog" is rendered as:

$$\exists x \forall y (Dy \leftrightarrow y = x) \tag{13.8}$$

Note how (13.8) says two things (under our glossary). It says that there is a dog (i.e., at least one): there is an x such that for every y, if $y = x$, then y is a dog (this claim is the right-to-left direction of the embedded biconditional), or in other words x is a dog. It also says that every dog is identical to this x: for every y, if y is a dog then $y = x$ (this claim is the left-to-right direction of the embedded biconditional). Putting these two statements together, the wff says that there is exactly one dog.

"There are (exactly) two dogs" is rendered as:

$$\exists x \exists y (x \neq y \wedge \forall z (Dz \leftrightarrow (z = x \vee z = y))) \tag{13.9}$$

Formula (13.9) likewise says two things. It says that there are (at least) two dogs: there is an x and a different y (this is the first conjunct, $x \neq y$) such that for every z, if $z = x$ or $z = y$, then z is a dog (this claim is the right-to-left direction of the embedded biconditional), or in other words, x and y are dogs. It also says that every dog is identical to this x or this y: for every z, if z is a dog then $z = x$ or $z = y$ (the left-to-right direction of the embedded biconditional). Putting these two things together, the wff says that there are exactly two dogs.

In similar fashion, "there are (exactly) three dogs" is rendered as:

$$\exists x \exists y \exists z(x \neq y \wedge x \neq z \wedge y \neq z \wedge \forall w(Dw \leftrightarrow (w = x \vee w = y \vee w = z)))$$

"There are (exactly) four dogs" is rendered as:

$$\exists x \exists y \exists z \exists w(x \neq y \wedge x \neq z \wedge x \neq w \wedge y \neq z \wedge y \neq w \wedge z \neq w \wedge$$
$$\forall v(Dv \leftrightarrow (v = x \vee v = y \vee v = z \vee v = w)))$$

and so on. Note that the translation of "there are exactly n dogs" has n existential quantifiers in front, each containing a different variable $\underline{x}$. It then has one nonidentity statement for each nonordered pairing of these variables;[15] then one universal quantifier involving a new variable y; then the single wff $D\underline{y}$; and then a series of n identity statements, each of which has y on one side and one of the n variables $\underline{x}$ on the other side.

Sometimes it is useful to have an abbreviation for (13.8)—"there is exactly one dog"—and formulas like it. The symbol $\exists!$ is often used for this purpose. Thus, $\exists! x\, Dx$ abbreviates $\exists x \forall y(Dy \leftrightarrow y = x)$ (or any formula equivalent to it in which y is uniformly replaced by some other variable, apart from x), $\exists! y Cy$ abbreviates $\exists y \forall z(Cz \leftrightarrow z = y)$ (or any formula equivalent to this in which z is uniformly replaced by some other variable, apart from y), and so on. More generally, where $\alpha(\underline{x})$ is a formula that has no free occurrence of any variable other than $\underline{x}$, y is a variable that is free for $\underline{x}$ in $\alpha(\underline{x})$,[16] and $\alpha(y/\underline{x})$ is the result of replacing all free occurrences of $\underline{x}$ in $\alpha(\underline{x})$ by occurrences of y, $\exists! \underline{x} \alpha(\underline{x})$ abbreviates $\exists \underline{x} \forall y(\alpha(y/\underline{x}) \leftrightarrow y = \underline{x})$. We read "$\exists x \ldots$" as "there is an $x \ldots$" (i.e., "there is at least one $x \ldots$"), whereas we read "$\exists! x \ldots$" as "there is exactly one $x \ldots$." Note that neither $\exists!$ nor $!$ are new symbols of the logical language: $\exists!$ is simply an abbreviation—something we may write for the sake of convenience (like $=$ and $\neq$). (We shall not in fact be using this abbreviation in this book. In particular, do not use it in your answers to the following set of exercises.)

13.5.1 Exercises

1. Translate the following propositions into GPLI and then test whether they are logical truths using trees. For any proposition that is not a logical truth, read off from your tree a model in which it is false.
   (i) There are at most two gremlins.
   (ii) There are at least three Beatles.
   (iii) There is exactly one thing that is identical to Kevin Bacon.
   (iv) If there are at least two oceans, then there is an ocean.
   (v) Take any two distinct dogs, the first of which is larger than the second; then the second is not larger than the first.
   (vi) If there is exactly one apple, then there is at least one apple.

(vii) It's not the case both that there are at least two apples and that there is at most one apple.

(viii) Either there are no snakes, or there are at least two snakes.

2. Translate the following arguments into GPLI and then test for validity using trees. For any argument that is not valid, read off from your tree a model in which the premises are true and the conclusion false.

(i) There are at least three things in the room. It follows that there are at least two things in the room.

(ii) There are at least two bears in Canada, so there are at most two bears in Canada.

(iii) There is at most one barber. So either every barber cuts his own hair, or no barber cuts any barber's hair.

(iv) There are at most two things. If you pick a first thing and then pick a second thing (which may or may not be a different object from the first thing), then one of them is heavier than the other. So everything is either the heaviest or the lightest thing.

(v) Some football players are athletes. Some golfers are athletes. Thus, there are at least two athletes.

(vi) Everything is a part of itself. So everything has at least two parts.

(vii) There are at least two things that are identical to the Eiffel tower. Therefore, there is no Eiffel tower.

(viii) I'm afraid of Jemima and the chief of police. So either Jemima is the chief of police, or I'm afraid of at least two things.

13.6 Definite Descriptions

Consider the following claims:

1. Someone is jogging.

2. Bill Clinton is jogging.

3. The forty-second president of the United States of America is jogging.

As we have already discussed (§8.3), claims (1) and (2) have very different translations into the logical language: claim (2) is translated using a singular term, whereas claim (1) is translated using a quantifier:

b: Bill Clinton	1. $\exists x(Px \land Jx)$
Jx: x is jogging	2. Jb
Px: x is a person	

What about claim (3)? The English sentence used to make claim (3) features a *definite description*: "the forty-second president of the United States of America." Definite descriptions are expressions of the form "the so-and-so." For example,

- the prime minister of New Zealand,
- the inventor of Post-it notes,
- the third mayor of Newcastle,
- the tallest person in this room, and
- the first man on the moon.

It is a commonplace that when we use a definite description "the X," we assume that there is exactly one X. If we thought that Buzz Aldrin and Neil Armstrong stepped onto the moon simultaneously, we would not talk about "the first man on the moon;" if we thought that New Zealand's system of government involved a president and no prime minister, we would not talk about "the prime minister of New Zealand;" and so on. Let's call this assumption the *uniqueness assumption*. It plays a role in all theories of definite descriptions, although it gets cashed out in different ways in different theories.

It is a point of controversy whether claims made using sentences involving definite descriptions should be classed with claim (1) (quantifications of some sort) or with claim (2) (involving a singular term in the logical language, corresponding to the definite description in English). We shall explore versions of both approaches.

13.6.1 Russellian Descriptions in GPLI

Bertrand Russell argued that claims made using sentences involving definite descriptions should be translated into the logical language as quantified formulas of a certain sort: formulas in which there is no singular term corresponding to the definite description in the original English.[17] Russell's idea was that the uniqueness assumption is something that we actually state when we use a definite description. This statement shows up when the claim is translated into the logical language. Consider, for example, the claim "the inventor of Post-it notes is rich." We translate as follows (using Russell's approach):

Ix: x invented Post-it notes $\exists x(\forall y(Iy \leftrightarrow y = x) \land Rx)$
Rx: x is rich

Note how the first part of the translation (the part preceding the conjunction symbol) says that there is exactly one inventor of Post-it notes. (Recall formula (13.8): our second way of translating "there is exactly one dog" is $\exists x \forall y(Dy \leftrightarrow y = x)$. The first part of the present translation is just like this, except that it has the predicate I in place of the predicate D.) The second part then says that this thing (i.e., x) is rich.[18] Thus, the translation of "the inventor of Post-it notes is rich" is the same as the translation of "there is exactly one inventor of Post-it notes, and that individual is rich." Note that the translation is a quantified formula, and it does not include any symbol corresponding directly to the English expression "the inventor of Post-it notes." Using Russell's approach, we do not have glossary entries for definite descriptions. In the present example, we do not have a glossary entry with "the inventor of Post-it notes" on the right-hand side. Rather, we have an entry for the predicate "invented Post-it notes," and then we translate the whole claim "the inventor of Post-it notes is rich" using this predicate and quantifiers (and the predicate "rich"). Note also that the predicate Ix ("x invented Post-it notes") involves no assumption of uniqueness: there would be nothing amiss about using this predicate in the propositions Ia, Ib, Ic, and so on, where a, b, and c denote distinct individuals. Rather, using Russell's approach, the uniqueness assumption is embodied in the first part of the translation: the part saying that there is exactly one inventor of Post-it notes (i.e., exactly one x such that Ix).

Let's consider some further examples of claims made using sentences involving definite descriptions and see how they translate into GPLI using Russell's approach.

(i) "The queen of England is rich." Let's start by translating "there is exactly one queen of England" (i.e., the relevant uniqueness assumption):

$e:$ England $\exists x \forall y (Qye \leftrightarrow y = x)$
$Qxy:$ x is queen of y

Now we just have to add "and this individual (i.e., the one and only individual who is queen of England, or x in the above wff) is rich":

$$\exists x (\forall y (Qye \leftrightarrow y = x) \land Rx)$$

Note that "$\land Rx$" is added within the scope of the initial quantifier $\exists x$—that is, we do not add it on at the end, like so: $\exists x \forall y (Qye \leftrightarrow y = x) \land Rx$. The latter is not a closed wff, because the final occurrence of x is free.

(ii) "The queen of England is Elizabeth Windsor." We start with our translation of "there is exactly one queen of England," and then we conjoin "and this individual is Elizabeth Windsor" (using the additional glossary entry l: Elizabeth Windsor):

$$\exists x (\forall y (Qye \leftrightarrow y = x) \land x = l)$$

(iii) "The queen of England is the inventor of Post-it notes." Here we have two definite descriptions: "the queen of England" and "the inventor of Post-it notes." We start by translating the two uniqueness assumptions: "there is exactly one queen of England" and "there is exactly one inventor of Post-it notes":

$$\exists x \forall y (Qye \leftrightarrow y = x) \quad \text{and} \quad \exists z \forall y (Iy \leftrightarrow y = z)$$

Note that we use a different variable (z, not x) for the second claim, as we need to put these two claims together, and we do not want the variables to clash. Now we just need to add that the former individual (x: the one and only individual who is queen of England) and the latter individual (z: the one and only individual who invented Post-it notes) are identical:

$$\exists x (\forall y (Qye \leftrightarrow y = x) \wedge \exists z (\forall y (Iy \leftrightarrow y = z) \wedge x = z)) \qquad (13.10)$$

Note that the second uniqueness claim is placed inside the scope of the existential quantifier in the first uniqueness claim. This is because the final identity claim $x = z$ needs to be in the scope of both existential quantifiers (otherwise one or both of x or z in $x = z$ would be free, and we would then not have a closed wff). Note that the following is equivalent to (13.10)—it results from that formula by moving the quantifier $\exists z$ to the front (recall §12.5):

$$\exists x \exists z (\forall y (Qye \leftrightarrow y = x) \wedge \forall y (Iy \leftrightarrow y = z) \wedge x = z) \qquad (13.11)$$

If you find (13.11) easier to parse, you can just as well use it—rather than (13.10)—as the translation of "the queen of England is the inventor of Post-it notes."

(iv) "The father of Elizabeth Windsor is rich." We start by translating the uniqueness assumption "Elizabeth Windsor has exactly one father" (using the additional glossary entry Fxy: x is father of y):

$$\exists x \forall y (Fyl \leftrightarrow y = x)$$

Now we just have to add: "and this individual (i.e., the one and only individual who is father of Elizabeth Windsor, or x in the above wff) is rich":

$$\exists x (\forall y (Fyl \leftrightarrow y = x) \wedge Rx)$$

(v) "The father of the queen of England is rich." Here the definite description—"the father of the queen of England"—rides piggy-back, as it were, on the definite description "the queen of England." It involves two uniqueness assumptions: that there is exactly one queen of England and that this individual has exactly one father. We first translate these assumptions:

$$\exists x (\forall y (Qye \leftrightarrow y = x) \wedge \exists z \forall y (Fyx \leftrightarrow y = z))$$

Note that the second uniqueness condition involves x—the subject of the first uniqueness condition; thus, it must fall within the scope of the existential quantifier in the first uniqueness condition. Now we just have to add that the individual z—the subject of the second uniqueness condition—is rich:

$$\exists x (\forall y (Qye \leftrightarrow y = x) \land \exists z (\forall y (Fyx \leftrightarrow y = z) \land Rz))$$

Again, this formula is equivalent to the following, which is an equally good translation of "the father of the queen of England is rich":

$$\exists x \exists z (\forall y (Qye \leftrightarrow y = x) \land \forall y (Fyx \leftrightarrow y = z) \land Rz)$$

Using Russell's approach, then, a claim such as "the inventor of Post-it notes is rich" turns out to involve two parts: a part claiming that there is a unique inventor of Post-it notes and a part claiming that this individual is rich.[19] Therefore, if we deny such a claim, we could be interpreted in two ways: as denying the uniqueness assumption (as in "not so: there was no inventor of Post-it notes—they were developed by a team") or as accepting the uniqueness assumption but denying the further claim that this individual is rich (as in "not so: he made no money at all from the invention"). The first kind of denial of $\exists x (\forall y (Iy \leftrightarrow y = x) \land Rx)$ (our original translation of "the inventor of Post-it notes is rich") comes out as:

$$\neg \exists x (\forall y (Iy \leftrightarrow y = x) \land Rx)$$

Here the negation is placed in front of the entire formula. The second kind of denial comes out as:

$$\exists x (\forall y (Iy \leftrightarrow y = x) \land \neg Rx)$$

Here the uniqueness assumption is still asserted; the negation applies only to the subformula Rx.

13.6.1.1 EXERCISES
Translate the following into GPLI, using Russell's approach to definite descriptions.

1. Joseph Conrad is the author of *The Shadow Line*.

2. The author of *The Shadow Line* authored *Lord Jim*.

3. The author of *The Shadow Line* is the author of *Lord Jim*.

4. Vance reads everything authored by the author of *Lord Jim*.

5. Joseph Conrad authored *The Inheritors,* but it's not the case that he is the author of *The Inheritors*.

6. The author of *The Shadow Line* is taller than any author of *Lord Jim*.

7. There is something taller than the author of *The Shadow Line*.

8. The author of *The Shadow Line* is taller than Joseph Conrad, who is taller than the author of *Lord Jim*.

9. The father of the author of *The Shadow Line* is taller than Joseph Conrad.

10. The father of the author of *The Shadow Line* is taller than the author of *The Shadow Line*.

13.6.2 Descriptions as Singular Terms in an Extension of GPLI

An alternative approach to claims made using sentences involving definite descriptions is to translate using a wff that features a singular term corresponding to the definite description. In GPLI, our only singular terms are the simple expressions $a, b, c, \ldots$. If we translate using such a singular term, the claim "the inventor of Post-it notes is rich" comes out as:

> *a:* the inventor of Post-it notes Ra
> *Rx:* x is rich

The prevailing view is that this sort of translation will not do, because certain arguments that intuitively should be valid turn out to be invalid when translated this way. For example,

> Art Fry invented Post-it notes.
> No one else invented Post-it notes.
> Therefore, the inventor of Post-it notes is Art Fry.

translates as follows (adding the entry f: Art Fry, to our previous glossary):

$$If$$
$$\forall x (Ix \rightarrow x = f)$$
$$\therefore a = f$$

The latter argument is invalid (as can easily be seen by producing a tree). Likewise, the argument:

> Art Fry is the inventor of Post-it notes.
> Therefore, Art Fry, and no one else, invented Post-it notes.

translates as:

$$f = a$$
$$\therefore \forall x (Ix \leftrightarrow x = f)$$

which is invalid (as can easily be seen by constructing a tree).

I am not convinced by this objection; we return to the idea of translating definite descriptions as names in §13.6.3 and see that it is quite viable (when done in the right way). In the meantime, however, let's look at what we might do if we want to translate definite descriptions as singular terms but are convinced that they cannot be translated as simple names (i.e., as a, b, c, and so on). We need to introduce a new kind of singular term into the logical language. We call the language GPLI enriched with this new kind of singular term the language of General Predicate Logic with Identity and Descriptions (GPLID). In addition to all the symbols of GPLI, GPLID contains the symbol $\imath$. This is an upside-down Greek letter iota (ι); we refer to it as the *definite description operator*.[20] It is part of the logical vocabulary.

The syntax of GPLID is interesting, because it involves a new two-way interaction between the categories of *term* and *wff*. A term is something that, from the syntactic point of view, behaves like a name or a variable: putting n (occurrences of) terms after an n-place predicate yields a wff. In GPLI, the only terms are names and variables—simple symbols. In GPLID, however, we can use the new definite description operator $\imath$ to form *complex* terms. For example, suppose we have a wff with one free variable, say, Fx. We can form the term $\imath x Fx$ from this wff by adding the definite description operator followed by an occurrence of the variable x in front of the wff. We read this term as "the F" (or "the one and only x that is F," or "the unique x such that Fx," etc.). Now we can make a wff by putting this new term anywhere that a name or variable can go. For example, we can put x after G to make the wff Gx— but instead of the variable x, we could also put our new term $\imath x Fx$ after G to make the wff $G\imath x Fx$: "the F is G." Or again, we can put the variables x and y after the two-place predicate R to make the wff Rxy—but instead of the variable x, we could also put our new term $\imath x Fx$ (and then the variable y) after R to make the wff $R\imath x Fxy$: "the F bears the relation R to y." And now we can create a new term from this wff by placing $\imath y$ before it. The result is $\imath y R\imath x Fxy$: "the thing to which the F bears the relation R" (or "the thing y such that the F bears the relation R to y"). And so on. Thus, we cannot—as we have up until now—first define the terms of the language and then define the wffs on this basis, because we can create new terms from wffs (by applying the definite description operator to them) and then make new wffs from these terms, and so on. Thus, we have to define the terms and wffs of GPLID simultaneously:

1. A name (a, b, c, . . .) is a term.

2. A variable (x, y, z, . . .) is a term.

3. Where $\underline{P^n}$ is any n-place predicate and $\underline{t_1} \ldots \underline{t_n}$ are any terms, $\underline{P^n}\underline{t_1} \ldots \underline{t_n}$ is a wff.

4. Where α and β are wffs and $\underline{x}$ is a variable, the following are wffs:

$$\neg\alpha \quad (\alpha \wedge \beta) \quad (\alpha \vee \beta) \quad (\alpha \rightarrow \beta) \quad (\alpha \leftrightarrow \beta) \quad \forall\underline{x}\alpha \quad \exists\underline{x}\alpha$$

5. Where α is a wff and $\underline{x}$ is a variable, $\imath\underline{x}\alpha$ is a term.

6. Nothing else is a term or wff.

Clause (5) is new: it specifies how we can make terms from wffs using the definite description operator (and a variable). Clauses (1), (2), and (4) are exactly as in §12.1.3. (But note the absence here of clause (2iii) in §12.1.3, which said that only names and variables are terms. In GPLID, names and variables are terms—according to clauses (1) and (2)—but they are not the only kinds of terms.) Clause (3) is phrased in the same way as clause (3i) in §12.1.3, but because—thanks to clause (5)—more things now count as terms, clause (3) now generates new wffs. Note the loop generated by clauses (3) and (5): clause (3) generates wffs from terms; clause (5) generates terms from wffs.
Here is a glossary:

b:	Martin Van Buren	Px:	x is a person
s:	the United States of America	Rxy:	x respects y
Cx:	x is a country	Sxy:	x is president of y
Fxy:	x is father of y	Zxy:	x is a citizen of y

The following are some examples of terms and wffs of GPLID generated by the foregoing recursive definition—together with their readings in English, given the above glossary:

1. $\imath x\, Sxs$
   term: the president of the United States of America

2. $\imath x(Cx \wedge Sbx)$
   term: the country of which Martin Van Buren is president

3. $b = \imath x\, Sxs$
   wff: Martin Van Buren is the president of the United States of America.

4. $\imath x\, Fxb$
   term: Martin Van Buren's father

5. $\imath y\, Fy\imath x\, Sxs$
   term: the father of the president of the United States of America

6. $\imath y\, Sy\imath x(Cx \wedge Sbx) = \imath x\, Sxs$
   wff: The president of the country of which Martin Van Buren is president is the president of the United States of America.

7. $\forall x\forall y((Cy \wedge Zxy) \rightarrow Rx\imath zSzy)$
   wff: Every citizen of every country respects the president of that country.

8. $\imath x(Px \wedge \forall y(Py \rightarrow Ryx))$
   term: the person everyone respects

9. $\imath x(Cx \land \forall y(Py \to Ryx))$

   term: the country everyone respects

10. $Z\imath x(Px \land \forall y(Py \to Ryx))\imath x(Cx \land \forall y(Py \to Ryx))$

    wff: The person everyone respects is a citizen of the country everyone respects.

§

The definite description operator $\imath$—like the quantifiers $\forall$ and $\exists$—binds variables. We call $\imath$ the "definite description operator." Let us refer to $\imath x$, $\imath y$, and so on—that is, the definite description operator plus a variable—as a *definition description prefix*. We say that x is the variable in the definition description prefix $\imath x$, that y is the variable in the definition description prefix $\imath y$, and so on. Conversely, we say that the definition description prefix $\imath x$ contains the variable x, that the definition description prefix $\imath y$ contains the variable y, and so on. If a wff has an occurrence of a definition description prefix $\underline{\imath x}$ in it, then it must—in accordance with clause (5) above—have been placed in front of some wff α; we call this formula α the *scope* of that occurrence of that definition description prefix; we call the entire expression $\imath x \alpha$ a *definite description*. Now suppose a variable occurs somewhere in a term or wff. That occurrence of the variable is *bound* in that term or wff if (i) it is in a quantifier or a definition description prefix or (ii) it is in the *scope* of a quantifier or a definition description prefix that contains the same variable. An occurrence of a variable that is not bound in a term or wff is said to be *free* in that term or wff. We can now extend our "open" and "closed" terminology from wffs to terms: a term that contains a free occurrence of a variable is an open term; a term that contains no free occurrence of any variable is a closed term. Note that if α contains no free occurrence of any variable other than $\underline{x}$—in which case we can write α as $\alpha(\underline{x})$—then the definite description $\imath x \alpha(\underline{x})$ is a closed term (aka a closed definite description). In contrast, if α contains a free occurrence of a variable other than $\underline{x}$, then the definite description $\imath x \alpha$ is an open term (aka an open definite description). Here are some examples:

- The term $\imath x Px$ is closed (a closed definite description), because both occurrences of x are bound.

- The term $\imath x Rxy$ is open (an open definite description), because even though both occurrences of x are bound, the occurrence of y is free.

- The term a is closed (a name).

- The term x is open (a variable).

- The wff $R\imath x Rxyz$ is open, because even though both occurrences of x are bound, the occurrences of y and z are free.

- The wff $\forall y \exists z R\imath x Rxyz$ is closed.

§

So much for the syntax of GPLID. Because $\imath$ is part of the logical vocabulary, we need to extend the semantics to deal with it.[21] Recall the guiding idea: a model is a free assignment of values to nonlogical symbols; each model should determine a truth value for each closed wff. Now consider a closed wff formed using a definite description, for example, $Z\imath x Sxss$ ("the president of the United States of America is a citizen of the United States of America," given our earlier glossary). To assign a truth value to this wff, we need referents for $\imath x Sxs$ ("the president of the United States of America") and for s. (The wff is then true if the ordered pair comprising the referent of $\imath x Sxs$ followed by the referent of s is in the extension of Z; it is false if this ordered pair is not in the extension of Z.) So closed complex terms, such as $\imath x Sxs$, require referents. In this respect they are like names. However, they are unlike names in that their referents should not be given freely (i.e., in an unconstrained way): they should be determined by the values assigned to the nonlogical symbols (in this case S and s) together with a general rule governing the behavior of the logical symbol $\imath$ in all models. The obvious candidate for the rule governing $\imath$ is: the value of $\imath x \alpha(\underline{x})$ in a model should be the unique object in the domain that satisfies the formula α.[22] So the referent of $\imath x Fx$ is the one and only object in the extension of F; the referent of $\imath x Sxs$ is the one and only object that bears the relation S to s;[23] and so on.

We now face a problem, however. The values of nonlogical symbols—F, S, and s in the examples just given—are unconstrained. For any combination of values for these symbols, there is a model that assigns those values to the symbols. Thus, there are models in which there is no unique thing in the extension of F (F could have the empty set as its extension, or it could have more than one object in its extension) or no unique object that bears the relation S to s (S might not have any ordered pair in its extension with the referent of s in second position, or it might have more than one such ordered pair). In general, there are models in which there is no unique object in the domain that satisfies the formula α (in some models there is no such object; in others there is more than one). In such models, the rule given above does not determine a value for $\imath x \alpha(\underline{x})$.

At this point, two routes lie open. First, we can extend the rule so that it determines a referent for $\imath x \alpha(\underline{x})$ in all models. This was Frege's approach.[24] The basic idea is to supplement the above rule with a specification of a referent for $\imath x \alpha(\underline{x})$ in those cases where the domain does not contain a unique object satisfying α. There are several options. For example, one could specify some other object in the domain (bearing in mind that there is no single object guaranteed to be in every domain); or one could say that every model has, in addition to the domain, an extra entity, which is to be the referent of every closed term $\imath x\alpha(\underline{x})$ where the domain does not contain a unique object satisfying α. Second, one could allow that $\imath x\alpha(\underline{x})$ simply lacks a referent in some models. Again, there are several options here. For example, one could say that every expression of which $\imath x\alpha(\underline{x})$ is a subexpression lacks a value when $\imath x\alpha(\underline{x})$ lacks a value (in just the way that every formula of which the name a or the predicate P is a part lacks a value in models of fragments that do not include a and P). Alternatively, one could alter the rest of the semantics to allow (for example) some closed wffs to have truth values even though they contain terms that do not have referents.

Both routes take us outside standard classical logic (some farther outside than others) and hence are beyond the scope of this book. So at this point we leave this strand of the discussion of definite descriptions and turn to the prospects for translating definite descriptions as singular terms in (unaugmented) GPLI.

13.6.2.1 EXERCISES
Translate the claims in Exercises 13.6.1.1 into GPLID, using the definite description operator to translate definite descriptions.

13.6.3 Descriptions as Singular Terms in GPLI

I propose the following way of treating definite descriptions as singular terms in GPLI:[25] we translate definite descriptions as names, and we formulate the uniqueness assumptions associated with them as postulates.[26] For example, consider the first example in §13.6.1: "the inventor of Post-it notes is rich." We translate as follows:

a:	the inventor of Post-it notes	translation: Ra
Ix:	x invented Post-it notes	uniqueness postulate:
Rx:	x is rich	$\forall x(Ix \leftrightarrow x = a)$

Note that the predicate I ("invented Post-it notes") does not appear in the translation Ra: it appears only in the postulate $\forall x(Ix \leftrightarrow x = a)$ (i.e., "a—and no one else—invented Post-it notes").

Compare this translation to the Russellian translation $\exists x(\forall y(Iy \leftrightarrow y = x) \wedge Rx)$. As noted in §13.6.1, there are two parts to the Russellian translation: the uniqueness assumption—"there is one and only one x such that x invented Post-it notes" (i.e., $\exists x(\forall y(Iy \leftrightarrow y = x))$)—and the claim that this individual x is rich (i.e., $\wedge Rx$)). Under the present method of handling descriptions, the translation proper of "the inventor of Post-it notes is rich" is just the second of these two, with the name a in place of the variable x. The first part of the Russellian translation turns up as the associated postulate, again, with the name a in place of the variable x.[27]

Recall that the translation into the logical language of a claim made in English is supposed to represent the proposition expressed in that claim. In the Russellian view, the uniqueness claim is part of the proposition expressed when one utters "the inventor of Post-it notes is rich." In the present approach, the proposition expressed is simply Ra, and the uniqueness claim is a separate assumption. The idea is that when we make a claim using a definite description "the X," the proposition expressed has a name (a simple singular term) in it corresponding to this definite description (in the above example, the name a). However, in this view, when we use a description "the X" to pick out an object, we are also assuming that this object is the one and only thing that is X. This assumption is embodied in the postulate (in the above example, $\forall x (Ix \leftrightarrow x = a)$). This postulate is not (contra the Russellian view) part of what is claimed to be true when one makes a claim using a definite description: it is simply something that one assumes to be true.

Now let's return to the arguments mentioned in §13.6.2, which were supposed to pose a problem for the view that definite descriptions can be represented in GPLI as names:

1. Art Fry invented Post-it notes.
   No one else invented Post-it notes.
   Therefore, the inventor of Post-it notes is Art Fry.

2. Art Fry is the inventor of Post-it notes.
   Therefore, Art Fry, and no one else, invented Post-it notes.

From the present point of view, they are enthymemes (arguments in which a premise is not explicitly stated—recall §12.4). Translated simply as they stand, they come out as invalid (adding the entry f: Art Fry, to our previous glossary):

1. *If*
   $\forall x (Ix \rightarrow x = f)$
   $\therefore a = f$

2. $f = a$
   $\therefore \forall x (Ix \leftrightarrow x = f)$

However, if we add the uniqueness assumption associated with the description "the inventor of Post-it notes" (which we are translating as the name a)—that is, $\forall x (Ix \leftrightarrow x = a)$—as an extra premise in each argument, then the resulting arguments are valid:

1. *If*
   $\forall x (Ix \rightarrow x = f)$
   $\forall x (Ix \leftrightarrow x = a)$
   $\therefore a = f$

2. $f = a$
   $\forall x (Ix \leftrightarrow x = a)$
   $\therefore \forall x (Ix \leftrightarrow x = f)$

Let's consider the remaining examples in §13.6.1 of claims made using expressions involving definite descriptions and see how they translate into GPLI using the present approach. In each case, if you compare the new translation to the Russellian translation in §13.6.1, you will see that the new translation corresponds to the second part of the Russellian translation, whereas the first part of the Russellian translation (representing the uniqueness claim) shows up as the associated postulate. We use the following glossary:

e: England	q: the queen of England
f: the father of Elizabeth Windsor	Fxy: x is father of y
g: the father of the queen of England	Qxy: x is queen of y
i: the inventor of Post-it notes	Rx: x is rich
l: Elizabeth Windsor	

(i) The queen of England is rich:

translation: Rq
uniqueness postulate: $\forall x (Qxe \leftrightarrow x = q)$

(ii) The queen of England is Elizabeth Windsor:

translation: $q = l$
uniqueness postulate: $\forall x (Qxe \leftrightarrow x = q)$

The uniqueness postulate is the same in (ii) as in (i), because the same definite description—"the queen of England"—features in both claims. The idea is that each definite description "the X" is represented as a name $\underline{a}$, and that when we use such a name, we furthermore assume (although we do not actually state this in every case) that $\underline{a}$ is the one and only one thing that is X.

(iii) The queen of England is the inventor of Post-it notes:

translation: $q = i$
uniqueness postulate for q (the queen of England):
   $\forall x (Qxe \leftrightarrow x = q)$
uniqueness postulate for i (the inventor of Post-it notes):
   $\forall x (Ix \leftrightarrow x = i)$

(iv) The father of Elizabeth Windsor is rich:

translation: Rf
uniqueness postulate for f (the father of Elizabeth Windsor):
   $\forall x (Fxl \leftrightarrow x = f)$

(v) The father of the queen of England is rich:

translation: Rg
uniqueness postulate for g (the father of the queen of England):
$\forall x(Fxq \leftrightarrow x = g)$
uniqueness postulate for q (the queen of England):
$\forall x(Qxe \leftrightarrow x = q)$

There is only one definite description here: "the father of the queen of England" (g). However, its uniqueness postulate involves another definite description—"the queen of England" (q)—which in turn requires its own uniqueness postulate.

Recall that in Russell's approach, a claim such as "the inventor of Post-it notes is rich" involves two parts: a part claiming that there is a unique inventor of Post-it notes and a part claiming that this individual is rich. Therefore, if we deny such a claim, we could be interpreted in two ways: as denying the uniqueness assumption (as in "not so: there was no inventor of Post-it notes—they were developed by a team"); or as accepting the uniqueness assumption but denying the further claim that this individual is rich (as in "not so: he made no money at all from the invention"). Something similar happens in the present proposal. Recall that "the inventor of Post-it notes is rich" is translated as Ra, with the associated uniqueness postulate $\forall x(Ix \leftrightarrow x = a)$. The second kind of denial of "the inventor of Post-it notes is rich" is represented as $\neg Ra$, together with the uniqueness postulate $\forall x(Ix \leftrightarrow x = a)$. (The denial is represented as $\neg Ra$, which involves a. Because a is being used, the associated uniqueness claim is assumed to be true, hence the presence of the postulate.) The first kind of denial of "the inventor of Post-it notes is rich" is the denial of the uniqueness assumption. However, we do not represent it simply as $\neg\forall x(Ix \leftrightarrow x = a)$—that is, as the negation of the uniqueness postulate. The uniqueness postulate features the name a—the translation of the definite description "the inventor of Post-it notes"—and the idea is that any time one makes a claim using a definite description, one assumes the truth of the associated uniqueness claim (in this case $\forall x(Ix \leftrightarrow x = a)$). So instead, we represent the first kind of denial as $\neg\exists x\forall y(Iy \leftrightarrow y = x)$: it is not the case that there is one and only one inventor of Post-it notes.[28]

§

Using the present approach to definite descriptions, we have glossary entries such as:

f: the father of Elizabeth Windsor
i: the inventor of Post-it notes
q: the queen of England

We said in §11.1 that a glossary entry assigns an intension to a nonlogical symbol: a function from wws to values of the appropriate kind for that symbol. In the present case, the symbols are names, so the relevant kind of value is an object. Glossary entries of the sort shown above, then, assign functions from wws to objects to the singular terms that feature in them. What are these intensions like? Take a specific example, say,

q: the queen of England

Consider a ww: a way the world could have been. To find the object to which the intension of "the queen of England" (which the above glossary entry assigns as the intension of q) sends this ww—that is, to find the object that "the queen of England" picks out relative to this ww—we find the thing that, had the world been this way, would have been England (note that England might have been bigger, or smaller, or located somewhere else entirely, had things been different), and we find the pairs of things that, had the world been this way, would have been such that the first was a queen of the second (note that things apart from countries might have had queens, and things apart from persons might have been queens, had things been different). The thing picked out by "the queen of England," relative to this ww, is then the unique thing that is the queen of England (according to this way the world could have been). In general, the referent of "the X" relative to any ww is the unique thing that would have been X had the world been that way.

If these claims about intensions are right—and they seem undeniably so—then the intensions of (most) definite descriptions are *partial* functions. For there are certainly ways the world could have been such that England did not exist at all, such that England did exist but was not a monarchy, such that England had two queens, and so on. Relative to each of these wws, "the queen of England" fails to pick out an individual. This is reminiscent of the situation in GPLID surrounding terms of the form $\imath x \alpha$ relative to models in which there is no unique object in the domain satisfying the wff α. But this time the situation is very different: now we do not need to change our logical apparatus in any way at all. The name q—our translation of "the queen of England"—is assigned a referent in every model (of the relevant fragment of GPLI), because it is part of the definition of a model (of this fragment) that it must assign a value to every nonlogical symbol in the fragment. All that is going on in the present case is that the intensions assigned to nonlogical symbols by our glossary, together with certain wws, do not determine models at all. Recall Figure 11.3. That picture suggests that every ww, together with the intensions assigned to a fragment by some glossary, determines a model of the fragment. We now see that this is not the case when the glos-

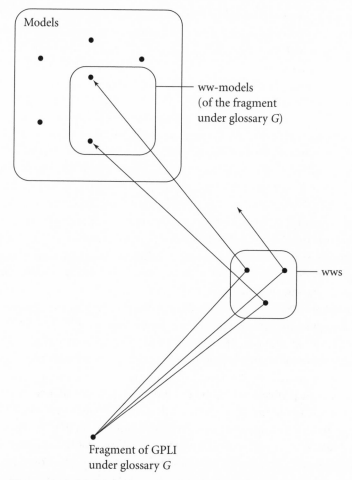

Models

ww-models
(of the fragment
under glossary G)

wws

Fragment of GPLI
under glossary G

Figure 13.12. Models and ww-models with partial intensions.

sary in question assigns to a name in the logical language the intension of a typical definite description. In such cases, the relevant picture is Figure 13.12, which shows a ww and a set of intensions for the fragment such that applying those intensions to that ww does not lead to any model at all. This situation does not require any modification of our logical apparatus (the definitions of models of GPLI, and of such logical notions as validity in terms of these models), because logic does not discriminate ww-models from the other models: as discussed in §11.4, such logical notions as validity and tautology are defined with respect to all models; whether some of these models can be generated by applying intensions to wws—and if so, which ones—is irrelevant.

There is, however, one notion that is potentially affected by the fact that the intensions of definite descriptions are (in general) partial: the notion of truth in the actual model (which figures in the definition of soundness of an argument—recall §11.1). Suppose that we have a definite description— for example, "the (present) king of France" (Russell's [1905, p. 479] famous example)—where one of the wws sent to no model at all (by the intension of this definite description) is the *actual* ww: the one corresponding to the way the world really is. In this case, we cannot say whether a claim made using such a definite description—for example, "the (present) king of France is bald"—is true or false: what we mean by "true" here is true in the actual model (the one determined by the intensions of the expressions involved and the actual ww), and here there is no actual model. For every model of (the relevant fragment of) GPLI, we can state whether the translation of "the (present) king of France is bald" is true or false in this model (and we can do the same for the associated uniqueness postulate). However, as none of these is the actual model—because the actual ww does not determine any model at all—we cannot say that this claim is simply true, nor that it is simply false.

It cannot be stressed too much that this problem is not a logical one: it does not require any adjustments to our system of model theory. The models are all in order as they are. It is, rather, a practical problem: our practice of assessing claims based on whether they are true (in the actual model) or false (in the actual model) breaks down when no model is the actual model. One response to this problem would be to adjust our practice of assessing claims based on their truth and falsity so that it can be applied even when there is no actual model. But if we think carefully about the matter, it is clear that this approach is wrong. The solution to this practical problem is simply not to use definite descriptions (e.g., "the present king of France") whose intensions send the actual ww to no referent. That is, we should try to make sure that the uniqueness assumption associated with a given description is actually true before using that description to make claims.[29] Sometimes, of course, we will make a mistake. The point is that when we do make a mistake (and find out about it) we should stop using the definite description in question[30]—rather than adjusting our practice of assessing claims based on whether they are true (in the actual model) or false (in the actual model) so that it can be applied even when there is no actual model.

Note the crucial difference here from the situation in GPLID surrounding terms of the form $\imath x \alpha$ relative to models in which there is no unique object in the domain satisfying the wff α. In that context, it would miss the point completely to say "do not use such terms." Whether we use them or not, the logical problem remains. However, in the present case there is no logical problem, only a practical one—and this problem does go away if we refrain from using definite descriptions whose associated uniqueness assumptions are actually false.

§

In sum, we have examined three ways of handling definite descriptions: in GPLI using Russell's approach (which does not view definite descriptions as singular terms); in GPLID using the new definite description operator (which does view descriptions as singular terms but requires new logical apparatus: syntactic, semantic, and proof-theoretic); and in GPLI, treating descriptions as simple names, with the uniqueness assumption as an associated postulate (rather than part of the proposition expressed, as in Russell's approach). The great advantage shared by Russell's approach and the approach developed in the present section is that they require no new logical machinery beyond that already available in GPLI. Thus, for these two approaches, once we have translated claims using definite descriptions into GPLI, we can then proceed to use trees to test for satisfiability, validity, and so on, just as we did in §13.4. Just remember that, when treating definite descriptions in the way developed in the present section, the question we are most interested in may not be "is this argument—as literally stated—valid?" (or "is this proposition—as literally stated—a logical truth?," and so on) but "is this argument, along with the uniqueness assumptions associated with any definite descriptions that feature in it added as extra premises, valid?" (or "is this proposition true in every model in which the uniqueness assumptions associated with any definite descriptions that feature in it are all true?," and so on).

13.6.3.1 EXERCISES

Translate the claims in Exercises 13.6.1.1 into GPLI, treating definite descriptions as names and stating appropriate uniqueness assumptions as postulates.

13.7 Function Symbols

Consider the following claims:

1. $5 + 7 = 12$
2. $4 \times (5 + 7) = 48$
3. $3^2 = 9$

4. $x \times y$ is even, unless x and y are both odd
5. $x \times (y + z) = (x \times y) + (x \times z)$

They all involve *function symbols*. A function symbol is like a predicate in that it has a fixed number of argument places, each of which may be filled by a term; but unlike a predicate, when those argument places are filled with terms, the result is a term—whereas when we fill the argument places of a predicate with terms, the result is a wff.[31] For example, consider the expression

"5 + 7." It is formed from the names (numerals) "5" and "7," together with the two-place function symbol $+$. When we fill the two argument places of this function symbol with two names—as in "5 + 7," or "2 + 2," and so on— the result is a name: of the number 12 (i.e., the number also known by the name "12"), or the number 4, and so on. Note that complex names such as "5 + 7"—names formed from function symbols and other names (in this case the simple names "5" and "7")—can themselves be plugged into the argument positions of function symbols, as in example (2) above: here the complex name "4 × (5 + 7)"—which denotes 48 (i.e., the number also known by the simple name "48")—is formed from the two-place function symbol $\times$ with its first argument place filled by the simple name "4" and its second argument place filled by the complex name "5 + 7." Function symbols can have their argument places filled with variables, as well as names, as in example (4). They can also have their argument places filled with complex terms formed from function symbols, variables and/or names, as in example (5).

Our logical language GPLI does not contain function symbols: the only terms it contains are the simple names $a, b, c, \ldots$ and the simple variables $x, y, z, \ldots$. This is not to say that such claims as (1)–(5) cannot be represented in GPLI: in fact they can, by a roundabout route, as we shall see in §13.7.3. But first, let's look at what happens if we expand GPLI by adding function symbols to the language, giving us the language of General Predicate Logic with Identity and Function Symbols (GPLIF).

13.7.1 Syntax of GPLIF

Recall that the syntax of GPLI is just like that of GPL (§12.1.3), except that I^2 is a predicate symbol of GPLI (it is the identity predicate, also represented as $=$). The syntax of GPLIF is like that of GPLI except for the following two additions.

First, we add function symbols to the stock of basic symbols of the language:

$$f^1, g^1, h^1, \ldots, f^2, g^2, h^2, \ldots$$

We use lowercased letters from anywhere in the alphabet, with a superscript indicating the number of argument places. (There will be no confusion with the use of lowercased letters as names and variables, because the latter do not have superscripts.) If we ever need more than twenty-six different n-place function symbols for any n, we use subscripts: $f_2^1, f_3^1, \ldots, f_2^2, f_3^2, \ldots$. The function symbols are nonlogical symbols.[32]

Second, we add a clause to the definition of terms:

Where $\underline{f^n}$ is any n-place function symbol and $t_1 \ldots t_n$ are any terms, $\underline{f^n t_1} \ldots t_n$ is a term.

So, for example, the following are all terms:

$$f^1a \quad g^2aa \quad g^2xa \quad g^2xy \quad f^1g^2aa \quad g^2f^1ax \quad g^2g^2aag^2xy$$

We can make these expressions easier to read in two ways: by adding parentheses around the arguments of a function and commas between them, and by omitting the superscripts on functions. (It is the added parentheses that now ensure there will be no confusion between function symbols, and names and variables.) Then the above terms are written as:

$$f(a) \quad g(a,a) \quad g(x,a) \quad g(x,y) \quad f(g(a,a)) \quad g(f(a),x) \quad g(g(a,a),g(x,y))$$

(The latter expressions are allowed for the sake of convenience—like $a = b$ instead of I^2ab, $Fa \wedge Gb$ instead of $(F^1a \wedge G^1b)$, and so on; only the former are official expressions of GPLIF.) Note the way in which terms formed using function symbols can themselves be plugged into the argument places of function symbols to form new terms. Thus, if we start, for example, with just one function symbol and one name, we get infinitely many terms:

$$f(a) \quad f(f(a)) \quad f(f(f(a))) \quad \ldots$$

The definition of wffs is the same as in GPLI, but note that because more expressions now count as terms, the following clause—which is unchanged from clause (3i) in §12.1.3—now generates new wffs:

Where $\underline{P^n}$ is any n-place predicate and $t_1 \ldots t_n$ are any terms, $\underline{P^n}t_1 \ldots t_n$ is a wff.

For example, the following are all wffs:

$$P^1f^1a \quad P^1g^2aa \quad Q^2yg^2xa \quad Q^2ag^2xy \quad P^1f^1g^2aa$$
$$Q^2g^2f^1axg^2aa \quad P^1g^2g^2aag^2xy$$

These may also be written as follows:

$$Pf(a) \quad Pg(a,a) \quad Qyg(x,a) \quad Qag(x,y) \quad Pf(g(a,a))$$
$$Qg(f(a),x)g(a,a) \quad Pg(g(a,a),g(x,y))$$

Let's now translate the claims at the beginning of §13.7 into GPLIF. As always, we need to begin with a glossary. For a start, we need names corresponding to the numerals "5," "7," and so on. Rather than writing separate glossary entries for each one (i.e., a_5: 5, a_7: 7, and so on) we use the following shorthand:

a_n: n

Because function symbols are part of the nonlogical vocabulary, they require glossary entries. Here are entries for the sum and product functions:

$s(x, y)$: $x + y$
$p(x, y)$: $x \times y$

In claim (3), we find the expression "3^2." We could think of this as the one-place function "x squared" with 3 as argument, or we could think of it as the two-place function "x to the power y" with 3 as first argument and 2 as second argument. Simply to give us practice with a one-place function symbol, let's think of it in the first way:

$q(x)$: x squared

We also require glossary entries for the predicates:

Ex: x is even
Ox: x is odd

Now we translate the claims as follows:

1. $s(a_5, a_7) = a_{12}$
2. $p(a_4, s(a_5, a_7)) = a_{48}$
3. $q(a_3) = a_9$
4. $\forall x \forall y (\neg(Ox \land Oy) \rightarrow Ep(x, y))$
5. $\forall x \forall y \forall z p(x, s(y, z)) = s(p(x, y), p(x, z))$

Note the universal quantifiers in translations (4) and (5). When a mathematics book, for example, says "$x \times y = y \times x$," although no quantifiers are used explicitly, what is usually meant is that the statement holds for any x and y; that is, the initial universal quantifiers are left implicit. When we represent such claims in GPLIF, we make the quantifiers explicit.

13.7.2 Semantics of GPLIF

Let's turn now to the semantics of GPLIF. Because function symbols are part of the nonlogical vocabulary, they need to be assigned values by models. Thus, we need to augment our notion of a model: as well as assigning values to names and predicates, a model must also assign values to function symbols. What is the value of a function symbol? Well, it must have the following feature. The value of f^n, together with the values of the predicate P^1 and the names $a_1, \ldots, a_n$, must determine a truth value for the closed wff $P^1 f^1 a_1, \ldots, a_n$. The value of P^1 is a set of objects. Thus, the value of $f^1 a_1, \ldots, a_n$ must be an object (then $P^1 f^1 a_1, \ldots, a_n$ will be true if that object is in the extension of P^1, and it will be false if that object is not in the extension of P^1). The values of the names $a_1, \ldots, a_n$ are objects. Thus, the value of f^n must be something that takes us from n objects (the values of the names $a_1, \ldots, a_n$) to a single object (the value of $f^1 a_1, \ldots, a_n$). We shall, then, take the value of f^n to be an n-place function on the domain: something that sends every n-tuple of members of the domain (taken as input to the function) to an object in the domain (the output of the function, for that input). It will be convenient to represent this function as a set of $(n + 1)$-tuples of members of the domain that contains exactly one $(n + 1)$-tuple x' for each n-tuple x of members of the domain: the first n entries of x' constitute x and represent a possible input to the function; the last entry of x' represents the output of the function for input x.

For example, here is a model of the fragment of GPLIF used in our earlier translations:

Domain: $\{1, 2, 3, \ldots\}$
Referents: a_1: 1 a_2: 2 a_3: 3   ...
Extensions: E: $\{2, 4, 6, \ldots\}$ O: $\{1, 3, 5, \ldots\}$
Values of function symbols: q: $\{\langle 1, 1 \rangle, \langle 2, 4 \rangle, \langle 3, 9 \rangle, \langle 4, 16 \rangle, \ldots\}$
   s: $\{\langle 1, 1, 2 \rangle, \langle 2, 1, 3 \rangle, \langle 2, 2, 4 \rangle, \langle 1, 2, 3 \rangle, \langle 3, 1, 4 \rangle, \langle 3, 2, 5 \rangle, \langle 3, 3, 6 \rangle, \langle 2, 3, 5 \rangle,$
     $\langle 1, 3, 4 \rangle, \langle 4, 1, 5 \rangle, \ldots\}$
   p: $\{\langle 1, 1, 1 \rangle, \langle 2, 1, 2 \rangle, \langle 2, 2, 4 \rangle, \langle 1, 2, 2 \rangle, \langle 3, 1, 3 \rangle, \langle 3, 2, 6 \rangle, \langle 3, 3, 9 \rangle, \langle 2, 3, 6 \rangle,$
     $\langle 1, 3, 3 \rangle, \langle 4, 1, 4 \rangle, \ldots\}$

Note that the value of q—a one-place function symbol—is a set of ordered pairs, containing exactly one pair beginning with x for each object x in the domain. The second member of the pair whose first member is x is the value of the function picked out by q for input x. The value of s (and similarly for p)—a two-place function symbol—is a set of ordered triples, containing exactly one triple beginning with x, y for each ordered pair of objects $\langle x, y \rangle$ in the domain. The last member of the triple whose first members are x and y (in that order) is the value of the function picked out by s for input $\langle x, y \rangle$.

The model given above is just one of infinitely many models of the fragment of GPLIF used in our earlier translations. As always, a model is a free (i.e., unconstrained) assignment of values to nonlogical symbols. Thus, any assignment of a set of ordered pairs (containing exactly one pair beginning with x for each object x in the domain) to q would be legitimate, as would any assignments of sets of ordered triples (containing exactly one triple beginning with x, y for each ordered pair of objects $\langle x, y \rangle$ in the domain) to s and p.

Note that the value of an n-place function is similar to the value of an $(n + 1)$-place relation, but is not exactly the same. The value of an $(n + 1)$-place relation can be any set of ordered $(n + 1)$-tuples of members of the domain. The value of an n-place function, in contrast, cannot be just any set of ordered $(n + 1)$-tuples of members of the domain: it must be one that contains exactly one $(n + 1)$-tuple x' for each n-tuple x of members of the domain, where the first n entries of x' constitute x. We shall return to this relationship between n-place functions and $(n + 1)$-place relations in §13.7.3.

Mathematical discourse is a rich source of claims made using function symbols. Arguably, such claims can also be found in nonmathematical talk. Consider, for example:

1. Everyone loves his/her first car.

2. Everyone loves his/her mother and father.

3. No one's mother loves his/her first car.

We could translate these as follows:

$c(x)$: x's first car   1. $\forall x[Px \rightarrow Lxc(x)]$
$f(x)$: x's father   2. $\forall x(Px \rightarrow [Lxf(x) \wedge Lxm(x)])$
$m(x)$: x's mother   3. $\neg \exists x[Px \wedge Lm(x)c(x)]$
Px: x is a person
Lxy: x loves y

We need to be mindful, however. The natural thing to say about the intension assigned to c by this glossary entry is that, relative to the actual ww, it picks out a function that sends each individual to his or her first car. But this is a partial function: some people have never had a car, so this function does not send them to any object at all. As we have seen, however, the value of a one-place function symbol in a model is a set of ordered pairs containing exactly one pair beginning with x for every object x in the domain. In other words, it is built into the semantics that function symbols pick out total functions.[33] Thus, the intension assigned to c by this glossary entry, together with the actual ww, do not determine a value for c. So there is no actual model of the fragment of GPLIF in question, relative to this glossary. As we saw in §13.6.3, this is a practical problem, not a logical one. In any case, it is something to keep in mind.[34]

13.7.3 Simulating Functions in GPLI

Given a closed wff in GPLIF, how can we test whether it is a logical truth (i.e., true in all GPLIF models)? Given an argument in GPLIF, how can we test whether it is valid (i.e., the conclusion is true in all GPLIF models in which the premises are true)? Similar questions apply to equivalence, satisfiability, and so on. One approach would be to adjust the tree method for GPLI to handle function symbols. This extension is perfectly feasible: only relatively minor adjustments are necessary.[35] We shall, however, take a different approach, because it involves a point of independent interest: that there is a sense in which we can do without function symbols and work instead in GPLI. More precisely:

(S) Given any finite set Γ of closed wffs of GPLIF, there is a finite set Γ' of closed wffs of GPLI, such that Γ is satisfiable iff Γ' is satisfiable.

Note that "Γ is satisfiable" means there is some model of GPLIF in which all wffs in Γ are true; "Γ' is satisfiable" means there is some model of GPLI in which all wffs in Γ' are true.

We shall establish (S) shortly. For now, its significance in relation to tree tests in GPLIF is as follows. Note that, when we use a tree to test for the presence or absence of some logical property (validity, logical truth, and so on), we are always—whether or not it is our primary intention—testing whether the initial set of formulas written at the top of the tree is satisfiable (i.e., whether they can all be true together): if all paths close, this set is not satisfiable; if there is a saturated open path, the set is satisfiable. We then extract whatever further information we want from this result about satisfiability—for example, an argument is valid iff the set containing its premises and the negation of the conclusion is unsatisfiable, or a proposition is a logical truth iff its negation is unsatisfiable. Now, given (S), instead of running a tree test in GPLIF beginning with an initial set Γ of wffs, we can instead run the tree test for GPLI on the corresponding set Γ': (S) ensures that the verdict of the tree test will be transferable.

Now to establish (S).[36] Given a set $\Gamma = \{\gamma_1, \ldots, \gamma_n\}$, we first show how to generate the corresponding set Γ', and we then show that Γ is satisfiable iff Γ' is satisfiable. The key to the proof is the close relationship—touched on in §13.7.2—between n-place functions and $(n + 1)$-place relations.

First we show how to generate the set Γ' from a given set Γ.[37] We illustrate the method for generating Γ'—which is fully general (i.e., it applies to any finite set Γ of closed wffs of GPLIF)—using a particular example. Let γ be the formula:

$$\forall x(Px \rightarrow [Lxf(x) \wedge Lm(a, x)c(a, b, x)])$$

and let Γ be the set containing just γ. (If we have a set Γ with multiple formulas in it, we handle each of them in turn as we do γ.)

Step 1. We find a formula γ^* equivalent to γ in which the only place that any function symbol occurs is at the front of a term immediately to the left of an identity sign, to the right of which is a variable, for example,

$$f(x) = y \qquad m(a, x) = z \qquad c(a, b, x) = w$$

We do this by successively replacing each subformula $\alpha(\underline{t})$ of γ containing a term $\underline{t}$ that contains a function symbol by the equivalent formula $\exists \underline{x}(\underline{t} = \underline{x} \wedge \alpha(\underline{x}/\underline{t}))$, where $\underline{x}$ is a new variable, and $\alpha(\underline{x}/\underline{t})$ is the result of replacing all occurrences of $\underline{t}$ in $\alpha(\underline{t})$ by occurrences of $\underline{x}$.[38] In our example we have the following sequence of replacements. First we replace $f(x)$ in the subformula

$Lxf(x)$ of γ:

$$\forall x(Px \rightarrow [\exists y(f(x) = y \land Lxy) \land Lm(a, x)c(a, b, x)]) \qquad (13.12)$$

Next we replace $m(a, x)$ in the subformula $Lm(a, x)c(a, b, x)$ of (13.12):

$$\forall x(Px \rightarrow [\exists y(f(x) = y \land Lxy) \land \exists z(m(a, x) = z \land Lzc(a, b, x))]) \quad (13.13)$$

Finally we replace $c(a, b, x)$ in the subformula $Lzc(a, b, x)$ of (13.13):

$$\forall x(Px \rightarrow [\exists y(f(x) = y \land Lxy) \land \exists z(m(a, x) = z \land \exists w(c(a, b, x) = w \land Lzw))])$$

This last formula is γ^*: it is equivalent to γ (because it arises from it by replacing subformulas with equivalent formulas—recall §12.5.3) and the only place that any function symbol occurs in it is at the front of a term that is immediately to the left of an identity sign, to the right of which is a variable.

Step 2. For each n-place function symbol $\underline{f}$ that appears in γ^*, we introduce a new $(n + 1)$-place predicate $\underline{R}$. We now work through γ^*, replacing each subformula of the form:

$$\underline{f}(\underline{t_1}, \ldots, \underline{t_n}) = \underline{x}$$

by the formula:

$$\underline{Rt_1} \cdots \underline{t_n}\underline{x}$$

Note that, from the way γ^* was constructed: (i) all terms $t_1, \ldots, t_n$ here are names or variables (i.e., none of them contains function symbols); (ii) once we have made these replacements, the resulting formula—call it γ^{**}—contains no function symbols. In our example, we have three function symbols: f, m, and c. Their new corresponding predicates shall be F, M, and C. (These are, as required, new predicate letters.) Because f is a one-place function symbol, F is a two-place predicate; because m is a two-place function symbol, M is a three-place predicate; and because c is a three-place function symbol, C is a four-place predicate. Taking γ^* and replacing subformulas involving function symbols with formulas involving relations in this way results in:

$$\forall x(Px \rightarrow [\exists y(Fxy \land Lxy) \land \exists z(Maxz \land \exists w(Cabxw \land Lzw))])$$

This is our γ^{**}.

Step 3. For each new $(n + 1)$-place predicate $\underline{R}$ introduced in Step 2, we now formulate a postulate of the following form:

$$\forall x_1 \ldots \forall x_n \exists y \forall z(Rx_1 \ldots x_n z \leftrightarrow z = y)$$

This proposition says that for each n-tuple of objects $x_1 \ldots x_n$, there is exactly one object y such that $Rx_1 \ldots x_n y$ holds. In other words, R behaves like an

n-place *function*. In the case of our three new predicates F, M, and C, the postulates are as follows:

- $\forall x \exists y \forall z (Fxz \leftrightarrow z = y)$

- $\forall x_1 \forall x_2 \exists y \forall z (Mx_1x_2z \leftrightarrow z = y)$

- $\forall x_1 \forall x_2 \forall x_3 \exists y \forall z (Cx_1x_2x_3z \leftrightarrow z = y)$

We now specify Γ': it contains γ^{**} plus all postulates for the new predicates that appear in γ^{**}. So in our case Γ' contains the following wffs:

- $\forall x (Px \rightarrow [\exists y (Fxy \wedge Lxy) \wedge \exists z (Maxz \wedge \exists w (Cabxw \wedge Lzw))])$

- $\forall x \exists y \forall z (Fxz \leftrightarrow z = y)$

- $\forall x_1 \forall x_2 \exists y \forall z (Mx_1x_2z \leftrightarrow z = y)$

- $\forall x_1 \forall x_2 \forall x_3 \exists y \forall z (Cx_1x_2x_3z \leftrightarrow z = y)$

It remains to show that Γ' (constructed in the way just discussed) is satisfiable iff Γ is satisfiable.

Suppose Γ is satisfiable—that is, there is a model $\mathfrak{M}$ of GPLIF in which each wff γ in Γ is true. Then each γ^* is true in $\mathfrak{M}$, because each γ is equivalent to its corresponding γ^*. Now we can construct a model $\mathfrak{M}'$ of GPLI (not GPLIF) in which everything in Γ' is true—that is, each γ^{**} and its associated postulates. What we do is set the extension of each new $(n + 1)$-place predicate $\underline{R}$ to be the same as the value of its associated function symbol $\underline{f}$. We then strike out the assignments of values to function symbols from the model (leaving a model of GPLI). That the extensions of these predicates arise from functions in this way ensures that their associated postulates are true in $\mathfrak{M}'$. As for each γ^{**}, it is true in $\mathfrak{M}'$, because it differs from the corresponding γ^* (which is true in $\mathfrak{M}$) only by having $\underline{R}t_1 \ldots t_n\underline{x}$ where the former has $\underline{f}(t_1, \ldots, t_n) = \underline{x}$—and the way that the extension of $\underline{R}$ is derived from the value of $\underline{f}$ guarantees that $\underline{f}(t_1, \ldots, t_n) = \underline{x}$ is true in $\mathfrak{M}$ iff $\underline{R}t_1 \ldots t_n\underline{x}$ is true in $\mathfrak{M}'$.[39]

Suppose Γ' is satisfiable—that is, there is a model $\mathfrak{M}'$ of GPLI in which every γ^{**} and its associated postulates are true. Now we can construct a model $\mathfrak{M}$ of GPLIF in which each corresponding γ is true. What we do is set the value of each function symbol $\underline{f}$ to be the same as the extension of its associated predicate $\underline{R}$. The reasoning showing that each γ is true in $\mathfrak{M}$ is then much the same as above. The only new point is that this time the role of the postulates is as follows: the truth in $\mathfrak{M}'$ of the postulate for $\underline{R}$ guarantees that $\underline{R}$'s extension in $\mathfrak{M}'$ is the right kind of set of $(n + 1)$-tuples to be the value in $\mathfrak{M}$ of the function $\underline{f}$.[40]

13.7.4 Exercises

1. Translate the following into GPLIF.
    (i) $2 + 2 = 4$
    (ii) $2 \times 2 = 4$
    (iii) $2 + 2 = 2 \times 2$
    (iv) $2^2 = 2 \times 2$
    (v) $(x + y)^2 = (x + y)(x + y)$
    (vi) $(x + y)^2 = x^2 + 2xy + y^2$
    (vii) Whether x is even or odd, $2x$ is even.
    (viii) Tripling an odd number results in an odd number; tripling an even number results in an even number.
    (ix) $5x < 6x$
    (x) If $x < y$, then $3x < 4y$

2. Here is a model:

> Domain: {Alison, Bruce, Calvin, Delilah}
> Referents: a: Alison b: Bruce c: Calvin d: Delilah
> Extensions: F: {Alison, Delilah} M: {Bruce, Calvin}
> S: {⟨Alison, Bruce⟩, ⟨Alison, Calvin⟩, ⟨Alison, Delilah⟩,
>   ⟨Bruce, Calvin⟩, ⟨Bruce, Delilah⟩, ⟨Calvin, Delilah⟩}
> Values of function symbols: f: {⟨Alison, Bruce⟩, ⟨Bruce, Calvin⟩,
>   ⟨Calvin, Bruce⟩, ⟨Delilah, Calvin⟩}
> m: {⟨Alison, Delilah⟩, ⟨Bruce, Alison⟩,
>   ⟨Calvin, Delilah⟩, ⟨Delilah, Alison⟩}
> s: {⟨Alison, Alison, Bruce⟩, ⟨Alison, Bruce, Calvin⟩,
>   ⟨Alison, Calvin, Delilah⟩, ⟨Alison, Delilah, Alison⟩,
>   ⟨Bruce, Alison, Calvin⟩, ⟨Bruce, Bruce, Calvin⟩,
>   ⟨Bruce, Calvin, Delilah⟩, ⟨Bruce, Delilah, Alison⟩,
>   ⟨Calvin, Alison, Delilah⟩, ⟨Calvin, Bruce, Delilah⟩,
>   ⟨Calvin, Calvin, Delilah⟩, ⟨Calvin, Delilah, Alison⟩,
>   ⟨Delilah, Alison, Alison⟩, ⟨Delilah, Bruce, Alison⟩,
>   ⟨Delilah, Calvin, Alison⟩, ⟨Delilah, Delilah, Alison⟩}

State whether each of the following propositions is true or false in this model.
    (i) $\forall x\, M f(x)$
    (ii) $\exists x\, M m(x)$
    (iii) $s(c, b) = d$
    (iv) $s(a, a) = f(c)$
    (v) $F f(b) \rightarrow M f(b)$
    (vi) $\forall x \forall y \exists z \forall w (s(x, y) = w \leftrightarrow w = z)$

(vii) $\exists x \exists y \exists z \exists w(s(x, y) = z \land s(x, y) = w \land z \neq w)$

(viii) $s(s(b, a), s(d, a)) = s(b, c)$

(ix) $\exists x \exists y s(x, y) = m(y)$

(x) $\forall x \exists y s(y, x) = x$

3. Here is a model:

Domain: $\{1, 2, 3, \ldots\}$
Referents: a_1: 1 a_2: 2 a_3: 3 $\ldots$
Extensions: E: $\{2, 4, 6, \ldots\}$ O: $\{1, 2, 3, \ldots\}$
L: $\{\langle x, y \rangle : x < y\}$[41]
Values of function symbols: q: $\{\langle x, y \rangle : y = x^2\}$[42]
s: $\{\langle x, y, z \rangle : z = x + y\}$[43]
p: $\{\langle x, y, z \rangle : z = x \times y\}$[44]

State whether each of the following propositions is true or false in this model.

(i) $s(a_2, a_2) = a_5$

(ii) $p(a_2, a_2) = a_3$

(iii) $s(a_2, a_2) = p(a_2, a_2)$

(iv) $q(a_2) = p(a_1, a_2)$

(v) $\forall x \forall y q(s(x, y)) = p(s(x, y), s(x, y))$

(vi) $\forall x \forall y q(s(x, y)) = s(s(q(x), p(a_2, p(x, y))), q(y))$

(vii) $\forall x E p(a_2, x)$

(viii) $\forall x((Ox \to Op(a_3, x)) \land (Ex \to Ep(a_3, x)))$

(ix) $\exists x L p(a_5, x) p(a_5, x)$

(x) $\forall x \forall y (Lyx \to Lp(a_3, x) p(a_4, y))$

4. For each of the following propositions, describe (a) a model in which it is true and (b) a model in which it is false. If there is no model of one of these types, explain why.

(i) $f(a) = f(b)$

(ii) $f(a) \neq f(b)$

(iii) $f(a) \neq f(a)$

(iv) $\forall x \exists y f(x) = y$

(v) $\exists x \forall y f(x) = y$

(vi) $\forall x \forall y s(x, y) = s(y, x)$

(vii) $\forall x \forall y f(s(x, y)) = s(f(x), f(y))$

(viii) $\exists x \exists y s(x, y) = f(x) \to \exists x \exists y s(x, y) = f(y)$

(ix) $\exists x \exists y s(x, y) = f(x) \to \exists x \exists y f(s(x, y)) = f(x)$

(x) $\forall x \forall y \exists z \forall w(s(x, y) = w \leftrightarrow w = z)$

PART III

Foundations and Variations

14

Metatheory

At the end of §1.4, we said that one of our goals was to find a method of assessing arguments for validity that is both:

1. foolproof: it can be followed in a straightforward, routine way, without recourse to intuition or imagination—and it always gives the right answer; and

2. general: it can be applied to any argument.

In this chapter we consider the extent to which this goal has been achieved. It turns out that there is an essential tension between the desiderata: generally speaking, the more general a system of logic is—the greater its expressive power—the less foolproof it will be. In our case, when we moved from MPL to GPL we crossed a watershed, with greater foolproofness on one side (the MPL side) and greater expressive power on the other.

Before proceeding, let us comment on the title of the chapter. In propositional logic, we looked at two methods of determining validity: truth tables and trees. Once we moved to predicate logic, we had just one method: trees. (We look at further methods of proof for both propositional and predicate logic in Chapter 15.) In this chapter we focus on the tree method. Given a system of proof—say, the tree method for GPLI—we call propositions that can be proven using that method "theorems" of that system. So, for example, $(Pa \lor \neg Pa)$ is a theorem of our system of tree proofs for GPLI, because we can prove, using a GPLI tree, that $(Pa \lor \neg Pa)$ is a logical truth. In this chapter we switch from using trees to establish results about particular propositions and arguments to considering the system of tree proofs itself and establishing (or in some cases mentioning, without proving) results about this system. These results about a proof system—or about proof systems in general—are called "metatheorems;" the activity of proving metatheorems is called "metatheory" or "metalogic."

In §§14.1–14.3 we discuss metatheorems related to the issue of whether the tree method of assessing arguments for validity is foolproof. In §14.4 we discuss the issue of whether our method is general.

14.1 Soundness and Completeness

The idea that our method of assessing arguments for validity should be foolproof encompasses two parts: the method should be mechanical (able to be followed in a straightforward, routine way, without recourse to intuition or imagination), and it should always give the right answer. In this section we partially address the second part: we show that, in one particular sense, the tree method for GPLI never goes wrong with respect to validity (when the rules are followed correctly; of course, wrong answers may emerge if we misapply a rule, for example, using an old name in the rule for the existential quantifier). More specifically, we establish two results:

(S)   If all paths close in a tree that starts from certain propositions, then there is no model in which those propositions are all true.

(C)   If there is no model in which certain propositions are all true, then all paths close in every finished tree that starts from those propositions.

Given (S), if the tree method tells you that an argument is valid (by having all paths close when you build a tree starting from the premises and the negation of the conclusion), then the argument really is valid (there is no model in which the premises and the negation of the conclusion are all true; that is, no model in which the premises are true and the conclusion false). We express this fact by saying that the tree method is *sound* with respect to validity.[1] Given (C), if an argument is valid, then the tree method will tell you that it is (in the form of all paths closing in any finished tree that begins with the premises and the negation of the conclusion). We express this fact by saying that the tree method is *complete* with respect to validity.

Before proving that the tree method is sound and complete with respect to validity, we might ask why it is necessary to do so. Recall the discussion of analyses and methods in §9.5. Our story about models yields a precise analysis of what such terms as "validity" mean—but models don't give us a method for showing that an argument is valid. Such methods are very useful. Trees are one such method (in the next chapter we look at other methods). A little thought makes it clear that we should not simply assume that our method works: we should prove that it does. That is what we do now. Before proceeding to the proofs, we explain in the following section a particular style of reasoning that is very common in metalogic and is used in both the soundness and completeness proofs.

14.1.1 Proof by Induction

If we want to show that a certain property P holds for every one of a certain group of things, it is often useful—especially when there are infinitely many things in the group—to prove this fact by *induction* (aka *mathematical induction*). Such proofs proceed as follows:

I. Enumeration:
   We assign to each object a number 1, 2, 3, . . .

II. Base case:
   We prove that property P holds for the object(s) numbered 1.

III. Induction step:
   We prove that the property holds for the object(s) numbered $n + 1$, on the assumption that the property holds for all the object(s) numbered 1 through n. This assumption is called the inductive (or induction) hypothesis.

How do these steps establish that every object in question has the property P? By step (III), on the assumption that all objects numbered 1 have the property P, it follows that all objects numbered 2 have the property P. But by step (II), all objects numbered 1 do have the property P. So it follows that all objects numbered 2 have the property P. Now by step (III) again, assuming that all objects numbered 1 and 2 have the property P, it follows that all objects numbered 3 have the property P. But we have already established that all objects numbered 1 and all objects numbered 2 have the property P, so it follows that all objects numbered 3 have the property P. Now by step (III) again, assuming that all objects numbered 1, 2, and 3 have the property P, it follows that all objects numbered 4 have the property P. But we have already established that all objects numbered 1 and all objects numbered 2 and all objects numbered 3 have the property P, so it follows that all objects numbered 4 have the property P. In general, whatever number n we pick, by this style of reasoning we can establish that all objects numbered n have P. But every object has been given some number n—that is step (I)—so it follows that every object has P.

There is a variant form of proof by induction where, in the induction step, we prove that the property holds for object(s) numbered $n + 1$, on the assumption that the property holds for object(s) numbered n (rather than 1 through n). Often we can get by with this weaker inductive hypothesis ("weaker" in that it is implied by, but does not imply, the original inductive hypothesis). Sometimes the terms "strong induction" and "course-of-values induction" are used to indicate induction using the stronger inductive hypothesis; sometimes the term "weak induction" is used to describe induction using the weaker inductive hypothesis.

Another common variation involves numbering the objects from 0 rather than from 1 in step (I) (i.e., 0, 1, 2, 3, . . . rather than 1, 2, 3, . . .). In this case, in step (II) we prove that property P holds for object(s) numbered 0, and in step (III) the (strong) inductive hypothesis assumes that P holds for all object(s) numbered 0 through n.

The key to a successful inductive proof often lies in step (I)—in finding a way of assigning numbers to the objects under consideration that facilitates establishing steps (II) and (III). When the objects under consideration are wffs—when we want to show that all of some group of wffs have a certain property—one way of assigning numbers that is often very useful is to assign to each wff the number of logical operators it contains. So atomic wffs (e.g., $Pa, b = c$) are assigned the number 0; wffs with one connective or quantifier (e.g., $(Pa \lor Rb)$, $\neg b = c$, $\forall x Rx$) are assigned the number 1; and so on. The number of logical operators contained in a wff α is often called the *complexity* of α.[2] A proof by induction in which the objects in question are wffs assigned numbers in step (I) according to their complexity is often called a *proof by induction on complexity of formulas*. Such proofs are common in logic; we shall see one in §14.1.3.

14.1.1.1 EXERCISES

What is the complexity of each of the following wffs?

1. Fa

2. $(Hx \to \forall x(Fx \to Gx))$

3. $\forall x x = x$

4. $\forall x \exists y \neg Rxy$

5. $\neg \forall x a \neq x$

6. $\forall x(Fx \to \exists y Rxy)$

7. $(\forall x a = x \land \neg \exists x a \neq x)$

8. $(Fa \land (Fa \land (Fa \land (Fa \land (Fa \land Fa)))))$

9. $\forall x(Fx \to \forall x(Fx \to \forall x(Fx \to \forall x(Fx \to \forall x(Fx \to Fx)))))$

10. $(((\neg \exists x(\neg Fx \lor Gx) \land a \neq b) \to \neg Fa) \lor (\neg \exists x(\neg Fx \lor Gx) \lor \neg Fa))$

14.1.2 Soundness

We want to show:

(S)   If all paths close in a tree that starts from propositions $\alpha_1, \ldots, \alpha_n$, then there is no model in which $\alpha_1, \ldots, \alpha_n$ are all true.

We shall show (S) by showing the contrapositive: if there is a model in which $\alpha_1, \ldots, \alpha_n$ are all true, then there must be an open path in any tree that starts from $\alpha_1, \ldots, \alpha_n$.[3] We show the contrapositive by induction on the stages of constructing any such tree. We can think of the process of constructing a tree starting from $\alpha_1, \ldots, \alpha_n$ as follows. At stage 0, one writes up the initial wffs $\alpha_1, \ldots, \alpha_n$ and then checks for closure, closing the path if necessary. At stage 1, one applies a first tree rule[4] and then checks for closure, closing any paths as necessary. At stage 2, one applies a second tree rule and then checks for closure; and so on. At some point, there may be no more rules to apply (one—but not the only—way in which this could happen is if every path has closed): the tree is finished and finite.[5] Alternatively, the process continues forever: the tree is infinite.

Note that in the above account, there is no restriction on the order in which rules may be applied: our aim is to show that if there is a model in which $\alpha_1, \ldots, \alpha_n$ are all true, then there is no way of constructing a tree that starts with $\alpha_1, \ldots, \alpha_n$ such that all paths close.

Consider an example to illustrate the general idea that a tree starting from $\alpha_1, \ldots, \alpha_n$ can be thought of as being constructed in a series of stages. Suppose we begin our tree with $\exists x F x$, $\exists x G x$ and $\neg \exists x (F x \wedge G x)$. At stage 0 the tree looks like:

$$\exists x F x$$
$$\exists x G x$$
$$\neg \exists x (F x \wedge G x)$$

At stage 1, the tree looks like:[6]

$$\exists x F x$$
$$\exists x G x$$
$$\neg \exists x (F x \wedge G x) \ \checkmark$$
$$\forall x \neg (F x \wedge G x)$$

Stage 2:

$$\exists x F x \ \checkmark \ a$$
$$\exists x G x$$
$$\neg \exists x (F x \wedge G x) \ \checkmark$$
$$\forall x \neg (F x \wedge G x)$$
$$F a$$

Stage 3:

$$\exists x F x \ \checkmark \ a$$
$$\exists x G x \ \checkmark \ b$$
$$\neg \exists x (F x \wedge G x) \ \checkmark$$
$$\forall x \neg (F x \wedge G x)$$
$$F a$$
$$G b$$

Stage 4:

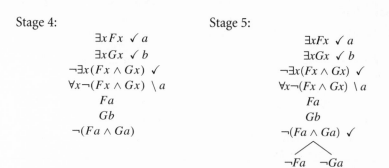

Stage 5:

$\exists x Fx$ ✓ a
$\exists x Gx$ ✓ b
$\neg\exists x(Fx \wedge Gx)$ ✓
$\forall x\neg(Fx \wedge Gx) \setminus a$
Fa
Gb
$\neg(Fa \wedge Ga)$ ✓
$\neg Fa \quad \neg Ga$
       ×

Stage 6:

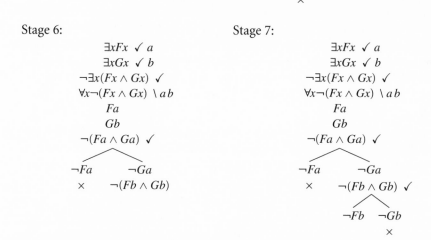

$\exists x Fx$ ✓ a
$\exists x Gx$ ✓ b
$\neg\exists x(Fx \wedge Gx)$ ✓
$\forall x\neg(Fx \wedge Gx) \setminus a\,b$
Fa
Gb
$\neg(Fa \wedge Ga)$ ✓
$\neg Fa \qquad \neg Ga$
  × $\qquad \neg(Fb \wedge Gb)$

Stage 7:

$\exists x Fx$ ✓ a
$\exists x Gx$ ✓ b
$\neg\exists x(Fx \wedge Gx)$ ✓
$\forall x\neg(Fx \wedge Gx) \setminus a\,b$
Fa
Gb
$\neg(Fa \wedge Ga)$ ✓
$\neg Fa \qquad \neg Ga$
  × $\qquad \neg(Fb \wedge Gb)$ ✓
$\qquad\qquad \neg Fb \quad \neg Gb$
                  ×

This tree is now finished. For convenience, we shall speak of stages 8, 9, 10, . . .
of the construction of this tree: it is just that nothing happens at these stages.
That is, after stage 7, the tree remains the same through all subsequent stages.
This way of speaking is convenient, because we want to be able to generalize
about all trees, regardless of whether they are finite or infinite. Thus, we need
to be able to speak of "stage n" of the construction of any tree for any n. The
mark of an infinite tree, then, is not that there are infinitely many stages in
its construction, but that it changes (propositions are added) at every one of
these stages.

§

Having now introduced the idea of numbering the stages of construction of
any tree, we turn to the first major part of the proof of (S). But first we establish
some terminology. A path in a tree will be said to be *satisfiable* if there is a
model in which every proposition on that path is true. We prove by induction
on stages that, assuming that there is a model in which $\alpha_1, \ldots, \alpha_n$ are all true,

any tree starting from the propositions $\alpha_1, \ldots, \alpha_n$ has at least one satisfiable path at every stage n of its construction. We have already seen how to number the stages of construction of any tree—that is step (I) in our inductive proof. This brings us to step (II)—the base case: at stage 0, the tree has a satisfiable path. This claim is immediate, given the assumption that there is a model in which $\alpha_1, \ldots, \alpha_n$ are all true. At stage 0, the tree has only one path, and the only formulas on it are $\alpha_1, \ldots, \alpha_n$. Now for step (III)—the induction step: if the tree has a satisfiable path at stage n of its construction, then it has a satisfiable path at stage $n + 1$. There are two cases to consider. (i) Nothing happens at stage $n + 1$: the tree is already finished at stage n. In this case the result is immediate. (ii) The tree changes at stage $n + 1$. In this case the result holds because (as discussed, for example, in §10.1—and see further Exercises 14.1.2.1 below) the tree rules all *preserve truth*. More precisely, suppose we are applying some rule at the bottom of a path p. Our nonbranching rules, which extend p to p$'$, all have this property:

> If there is a model in which every proposition on p is true, then there is a model in which every proposition on p$'$ is true

and our branching rules, which will create two paths q and r, all have this property:

> If there is a model in which every proposition on p is true, then there is a model in which every proposition on q is true, or there is a model in which every proposition on r is true, or both

We now know that if there is a model in which $\alpha_1, \ldots, \alpha_n$ are all true, then at every stage n of its construction, any tree starting from $\alpha_1, \ldots, \alpha_n$ has a satisfiable path (i.e., a path such that there is a model in which every proposition on that path is true). It follows that at every stage n of its construction, every such tree has an open path. For a path closes only if it contains either (i) a wff and its negation or (ii) a wff of the form $\underline{a} \neq \underline{a}$. In both these cases, however, there cannot be a model in which every wff on the path is true, because (i) there is no model in which both a wff and its negation are true, and (ii) there is no model in which a wff of the form $\underline{a} \neq \underline{a}$ is true.

We want to show that if there is a model in which $\alpha_1, \ldots, \alpha_n$ are all true, then there is an open path in any tree that starts from $\alpha_1, \ldots, \alpha_n$ (i.e., the contrapositive of (S)). We are not quite there yet. What we currently have is: if there is a model in which $\alpha_1, \ldots, \alpha_n$ are all true, then at every stage n of its construction, any tree starting from $\alpha_1, \ldots, \alpha_n$ has an open path. In theory, this still allows the possibility that an infinite tree might have no open path; that is, although it has an open path at every stage of its construction, after an infinite amount of time the finished infinite tree might have no open path. There are, in principle, two ways in which this might happen: (i) the tree has infinite paths, and they are all closed or (ii) the tree has no infinite paths but has infinitely many finite paths, and they are all closed. However, both possibilities were ruled out in §10.3.7: no tree has an infinite closed path, and every tree that grows forever has an infinite path. Thus, the case is closed—the contrapositive of (S) (and hence (S) itself) is established: if there is a model in which $\alpha_1, \ldots, \alpha_n$ are all true, then there is an open path in any tree (finite or infinite) that starts from $\alpha_1, \ldots, \alpha_n$.

14.1.2.1 EXERCISES
In §10.1 we showed that the tree rules for (negated and unnegated) disjunction and the quantifiers are truth-preserving (in the precise sense spelled out in §14.1.2), and in §13.4 we showed that the tree rule SI is truth-preserving. Complete the soundness proof by showing that the remaining tree rules are truth-preserving:

1. Unnegated conjunction.
2. Negated conjunction.
3. Unnegated conditional.
4. Negated conditional.

5. Unnegated biconditional.
6. Negated biconditional.
7. Negated negation.

14.1.3 Completeness
We want to show:

(C)   If there is no model in which propositions $\alpha_1, \ldots, \alpha_n$ are all true, then all paths close in every finished tree that starts from $\alpha_1, \ldots, \alpha_n$.

We shall prove (C) by showing the contrapositive: if there is an open path in a finished tree that begins with $\alpha_1, \ldots, \alpha_n$, then there is a model in which $\alpha_1, \ldots, \alpha_n$ are all true.

In §13.4.2 we described how to read off a model from an open saturated path. What we prove now is that when we read off a model in this way, every wff on the saturated path from which the model is read off is true in that model. For convenience, we refer to the path from which we are reading off the model as p and the model being read off as $\mathfrak{M}$.[7]

We want to prove something about every wff on p; we do so by induction on complexity of formulas. That is, step (I) of our inductive proof consists of assigning to each wff on p the number that represents its complexity (recall §14.1.1).

Step (II) is the base case: we show that all wffs on p numbered 0 are true in $\mathfrak{M}$. These wffs are atomic wffs. There are two cases to consider: (i) wffs of the form $\underline{F^n a_1} \ldots \underline{a_n}$, where $\underline{F^n}$ is some predicate other than the identity predicate and (ii) wffs of the form $\underline{a} = \underline{b}$. Model $\mathfrak{M}$ is designed precisely to make all these wffs true: those of form (i) are true because in step (3) of reading off $\mathfrak{M}$ (recall §13.4.2), for every standalone atomic wff $\underline{F^n a_1} \ldots \underline{a_n}$ appearing on p, we put into the extension of the n-place predicate $\underline{F^n}$ the ordered n-tuple consisting of the referents of the names $\underline{a_1}$ through $\underline{a_n}$ in that order; those of form (ii) are true because in step (2) of reading off $\mathfrak{M}$ (recall §13.4.2), when we encountered a wff $\underline{a} = \underline{b}$ on p, we made the referents of $\underline{a}$ and $\underline{b}$ the same.

Step (III) is the induction step: we show that all wffs on p of complexity $n+1$ are true in $\mathfrak{M}$, assuming that all wffs on p of complexity 0 through n are true in $\mathfrak{M}$. From here we proceed by cases. We are considering a wff of complexity $n + 1$. For convenience, we refer to this wff as γ. Its main operator could be any of our connectives or quantifiers, so we consider each case in turn.

Conjunction. γ is of the form $(\alpha \wedge \beta)$; that is, its main operator is conjunction. Then p also contains α and β (because p must be saturated: we are given that the tree is finished and that p is open, and in a finished tree, every path is either closed or saturated). The complexities of α and β are less than the complexity of $(\alpha \wedge \beta)$, so by the induction hypothesis α and β are true in $\mathfrak{M}$. So by the rule governing the truth of conjunctions in models,[8] $(\alpha \wedge \beta)$ is also true in $\mathfrak{M}$.

Disjunction. γ is of the form $(\alpha \vee \beta)$. Then p also contains either α or β (because p is saturated). These are of lesser complexity than $(\alpha \vee \beta)$, so by the induction hypothesis, whichever of them is on p is true in $\mathfrak{M}$; hence by the rule governing the truth of disjunctions in models, $(\alpha \vee \beta)$ is also true in $\mathfrak{M}$.

Existential quantifier. γ is of the form $\exists \underline{x} \alpha(\underline{x})$. Then p also contains $\alpha(\underline{a}/\underline{x})$, for some name $\underline{a}$ that does not appear on p before this occurrence of $\alpha(\underline{a}/\underline{x})$. The complexity of $\alpha(\underline{a}/\underline{x})$ is less than that of $\exists \underline{x} \alpha(\underline{x})$, so by the induction hypothesis $\alpha(\underline{a}/\underline{x})$ is true in $\mathfrak{M}$. But then the following argument shows that $\exists \underline{x} \alpha(\underline{x})$ is also true in $\mathfrak{M}$. By the rule governing the truth of existentially quantified wffs in models, $\exists \underline{x} \alpha(\underline{x})$ is true in $\mathfrak{M}$ iff there is at least one object o in the domain of $\mathfrak{M}$ such that $\alpha(\underline{b}/\underline{x})$ is true on $\mathfrak{M}_o^b$, where $\underline{b}$ is some name not assigned a referent on $\mathfrak{M}$, and $\mathfrak{M}_o^b$ is a model just like $\mathfrak{M}$ except that in it the name $\underline{b}$ is assigned the referent o. There is at least one such object o: the object that is the referent of $\underline{a}$ on $\mathfrak{M}$.

Universal quantifier. γ is of the form $\forall \underline{x} \alpha(\underline{x})$. Then (by the requirements on saturation relating to the tree rule for the universal quantifier) p also contains $\alpha(\underline{a}/\underline{x})$ for every name $\underline{a}$ that appears on p, and there must be at least one such name. The complexity of each $\alpha(\underline{a}/\underline{x})$ is less than that of $\forall \underline{x} \alpha(\underline{x})$, so by the induction hypothesis each $\alpha(\underline{a}/\underline{x})$ is true in $\mathfrak{M}$. Now note that, given the way models are read off paths, there is no object in the domain of $\mathfrak{M}$ that is not the referent in $\mathfrak{M}$ of some name appearing on p, because in step (1) of reading off $\mathfrak{M}$ (recall §13.4.2), we put one object into the domain for each name that appears on p and then assign the first of these objects as the referent of the first name, the second as the referent of the second name, and so on. Furthermore, in step (2), if (in light of any identity statements on p) we change the referent of some name $\underline{b}$ so that it is the same as the referent of some other name $\underline{a}$, then we remove the object that was the referent of $\underline{b}$ from the domain. Thus, the following argument shows that $\forall \underline{x} \alpha(\underline{x})$ is true in $\mathfrak{M}$. By the rule governing the truth of universally quantified wffs in models, $\forall \underline{x} \alpha(\underline{x})$ is true in $\mathfrak{M}$ iff for every object o in the domain of $\mathfrak{M}$, $\alpha(\underline{b}/\underline{x})$ is true in $\mathfrak{M}_o^{\underline{b}}$, where $\underline{b}$ is some name not assigned a referent in $\mathfrak{M}$, and $\mathfrak{M}_o^{\underline{b}}$ is a model just like $\mathfrak{M}$ except that in it the name $\underline{b}$ is assigned the referent o. But we know that $\alpha(\underline{b}/\underline{x})$ is true in $\mathfrak{M}_o^{\underline{b}}$ for every o in the domain of $\mathfrak{M}$, because for each such o there is at least one corresponding wff $\alpha(\underline{a}/\underline{x})$ on p—where $\underline{a}$ refers to o in $\mathfrak{M}$—and every such $\alpha(\underline{a}/\underline{x})$ is true in $\mathfrak{M}$.

Negation. γ is of the form $\neg \alpha$. Here we need to consider all possible forms of the negand α:

1. (i) α is an atomic wff of the form $\underline{F^n}\underline{a_1} \ldots \underline{a_n}$, where $\underline{F^n}$ is some predicate other than the identity predicate. Now $\underline{F^n}\underline{a_1} \ldots \underline{a_n}$ cannot appear by itself on p, for then p would close. But then $\underline{F^n}\underline{a_1} \ldots \underline{a_n}$ must be false in $\mathfrak{M}$, because we put the n-tuple $\langle$referent-of-$\underline{a_1}$, $\ldots$, referent-of-$\underline{a_n}\rangle$ into the extension of $\underline{F^n}$ in $\mathfrak{M}$ iff $\underline{F^n}\underline{a_1} \ldots \underline{a_n}$ appears on p.[9] Hence, by the rule governing the truth of negations in models, $\neg \underline{F^n}\underline{a_1} \ldots \underline{a_n}$ is true in $\mathfrak{M}$.

   (ii) α is an atomic wff of the form $\underline{a} = \underline{b}$. Now $\underline{a} = \underline{b}$ cannot appear by itself on p, because then p would close. But then $\underline{a} = \underline{b}$ must be false in $\mathfrak{M}$, because we set the referents of $\underline{a}$ and $\underline{b}$ to the same object iff $\underline{a} = \underline{b}$ appears on p.[10] Hence, by the rule governing the truth of negations in models, $\neg \underline{a} = \underline{b}$ is true in $\mathfrak{M}$.

2. α is of the form $\neg \beta$; that is, its main operator is negation. So the formula $\neg \alpha$ we are considering is of the form $\neg\neg \beta$. Then β also occurs on p. The complexity of β is less than that of $\neg\neg\beta$, so by the induction hypothesis β is true in $\mathfrak{M}$. So $\neg\neg\beta$ is also true in $\mathfrak{M}$.

3. α is of the form $(\beta \vee \delta)$; that is, its main operator is disjunction. So the formula $\neg \alpha$ we are considering is of the form $\neg(\beta \vee \delta)$. Then $\neg\beta$ and $\neg\delta$ also occur on p. The complexities of these wffs are less than that of $\neg(\beta \vee \delta)$, so by the induction hypothesis $\neg\beta$ and $\neg\delta$ are true in $\mathfrak{M}$. So $\neg(\beta \vee \delta)$ is also true in $\mathfrak{M}$.

4. α is of the form $\forall \underline{x}\beta$; that is, its main operator is the universal quantifier. So the formula $\neg \alpha$ we are considering is of the form $\neg\forall \underline{x}\beta$. Then $\exists \underline{x}\neg\beta$ also occurs on p. By the clause above covering the case of wffs on p whose main operator is the existential quantifier, $\exists \underline{x}\neg\beta$ is true in $\mathfrak{M}$. So by the

reasoning in §10.1.2 (which establishes that $\neg\forall\underline{x}\beta$ and $\exists\underline{x}\neg\beta$ are true and false in the same models), $\neg\forall\underline{x}\beta$ is also true in $\mathfrak{M}$.

5. α is of the form $(\beta \wedge \delta)$. See Exercises 14.1.3.1, question 1.

6. α is of the form $(\beta \rightarrow \delta)$. See Exercises 14.1.3.1, question 2.

7. α is of the form $(\beta \leftrightarrow \delta)$. See Exercises 14.1.3.1, question 3.

8. α is of the form $\exists\underline{x}\beta$. See Exercises 14.1.3.1, question 4.

Conditional. γ is of the form $(\alpha \rightarrow \beta)$. Then p also contains either $\neg\alpha$ or β. (i) Suppose p contains β. The complexity of β is less than that of $(\alpha \rightarrow \beta)$, so by the induction hypothesis β is true in $\mathfrak{M}$; hence, $(\alpha \rightarrow \beta)$ is also true in $\mathfrak{M}$. (ii) Suppose p contains $\neg\alpha$. The complexity of $\neg\alpha$ is not necessarily less than that of $(\alpha \rightarrow \beta)$: if β is an atomic wff (i.e., it has complexity 0), then $\neg\alpha$ and $(\alpha \rightarrow \beta)$ have the same complexity. So we consider two cases: (a) β is not atomic, so the complexity of $\neg\alpha$ is less than that of $(\alpha \rightarrow \beta)$, so by the induction hypothesis $\neg\alpha$ is true in $\mathfrak{M}$; hence, α is false in $\mathfrak{M}$; hence, $(\alpha \rightarrow \beta)$ is true in $\mathfrak{M}$. (b) β is atomic, so the complexity of $\neg\alpha$ is the same as that of $(\alpha \rightarrow \beta)$. Our induction hypothesis is that all formulas in p with complexity less than that of $(\alpha \rightarrow \beta)$ are true in $\mathfrak{M}$. Given that the complexity of $\neg\alpha$ is the same as that of $(\alpha \rightarrow \beta)$, this hypothesis asserts that all formulas in p with complexity less than that of $\neg\alpha$ are also true in $\mathfrak{M}$. Because $\neg\alpha$ is in p (we are still in case (ii)), by the reasoning in the clause(s) for negation above, it follows that $\neg\alpha$ is true in $\mathfrak{M}$. Hence, α is false in $\mathfrak{M}$, and so $(\alpha \rightarrow \beta)$ is true in $\mathfrak{M}$.

Biconditional. See Exercises 14.1.3.1, question 5.

Claim (C) is now established, via its contrapositive: if there is an open path p in a finished tree that begins with $\alpha_1, \ldots, \alpha_n$, then there is a model $\mathfrak{M}$ in which every formula on p is true. Hence, in particular, $\alpha_1, \ldots, \alpha_n$ are all true in $\mathfrak{M}$, because the initial formulas in a tree lie on every path through the tree.

§

Note that the completeness result as presented here does not provide a guarantee that if you start with (say) an argument that is in fact valid and begin constructing a tree starting from the premises and the negation of the conclusion, then your tree will eventually close. The completeness result tells us only that (in this situation) every finished tree is closed—and as we have seen in §10.3.1, there are, for some choices of starting propositions, ways of constructing trees that lead to infinite paths that are not saturated. Nothing in the completeness result itself guarantees that when you start constructing a tree, you will not hit on one of these poor orderings of rule applications. That is, although the completeness result refers to finished trees, it does not show how to construct finished trees—how to avoid infinite but unfinished trees.

For that, we need to turn somewhere else: to the sort of systematic procedure for building trees given in §10.3.5.[11] When we build trees in accordance with such a procedure, we have a guarantee that the result (perhaps after an infinite amount of time) will be a finished tree. Thus, completeness plus such a systematic tree-building procedure provides a guarantee that if you start with (say) an argument that is in fact valid and build a tree following this procedure starting from the premises and the negation of the conclusion, then your tree will eventually close. Furthermore, note that because every infinite tree has an infinite path and there are no infinite closed paths (§10.3.7), a closed tree is always finite. Thus, if you start with an argument that is in fact valid and start building a tree in accordance with a systematic procedure that guarantees finished trees, then you will always have a closed tree after a finite amount of time. We return to this point below.

14.1.3.1 EXERCISES
Fill in the remaining cases in step (III) of the completeness proof.

1. γ is of the form $\neg\alpha$, and α's main operator is conjunction.

2. γ is of the form $\neg\alpha$, and α's main operator is the conditional.

3. γ is of the form $\neg\alpha$, and α's main operator is the biconditional.

4. γ is of the form $\neg\alpha$, and α's main operator is the existential quantifier.

5. γ's main operator is the biconditional.

14.2 Decidability and Undecidability
The idea that our method of assessing arguments for validity should be foolproof encompasses two parts: the method should be mechanical (able to be followed in a straightforward, routine way, without recourse to intuition or imagination), and it should always give the right answer. In §14.1 we partially addressed the second part: we showed that if the tree method indicates that an argument is valid, then the argument is valid (soundness); and that if an argument is valid, then the tree method will indicate that it is, after a finite amount of time (completeness, together with a systematic procedure for constructing finished trees). In this section we turn to the first part.[12]

Recall the notion of an effective procedure (mentioned in Chapter 1, n. 29). A procedure is effective if it can be encapsulated in a finite set of instructions, to be followed in a specified order, where each instruction is:

1. mechanical (no ingenuity or insight is required to carry it out—a computer could be programmed to do it);

2. deterministic (it involves no random devices, e.g., coin tosses); and

3. finitely achievable (only a finite amount of time is required to complete it).

For example, think of the familiar procedure for adding two numbers. Write the numbers down, one above the other, aligned at the right. Look up the two rightmost digits in the addition tables for numbers 0–9. If the answer is a one-digit number, write it down underneath the rightmost two digits; if it is a two-digit number, write down its right digit and carry the left digit (i.e., write it above the second-rightmost digits of the original numbers). Move to the second-rightmost digits and repeat (more or less: it won't quite be a simple repeat if there is a carried digit to add as well), and so on. When there are no digits left to process, the answer will be written under the original two numbers. I have just sketched the procedure here, to jog your memory, but evidently it could be written out in complete detail, resulting in a finite set of instructions to be followed in a particular order, where each instruction is mechanical, deterministic, and finitely achievable. (Note that the addition tables for numbers 0–9 can be included as part of these instructions.)

Note two points. First, because each step of an effective procedure is deterministic and the order in which the steps are to be followed is specified as part of the procedure, two different people following the same effective procedure will always get the same result. Second, in an effective procedure the order in which the instructions are to be followed may include loops. Thus, although each instruction must be finitely achievable, an effective procedure as a whole might run for an infinite amount of time. For example, the following is an effective procedure for writing an infinite string of alternating 1s and 0s:

1. Write 1; go to step (2).

2. Write 0; go to step (1).

Let's now consider the tree method for testing an argument for validity. We write down the premises and the negation of the conclusion of the argument to be tested. We then apply tree rules. When the tree is finished, we check whether all paths are closed. If so, the argument is valid; if not, it is invalid.

Is this an effective procedure? Well, it involves a finite number of instructions (there are only finitely many tree rules), but we have allowed that the rules can be followed in any order one pleases. To obtain an effective procedure, we need to specify an order in which the rules are to be followed. This can be done via a systematic procedure for building trees of the sort described in §10.3.5—a procedure that tells us exactly which rule to apply at each stage of construction. For the remainder of this section, when we talk of the "tree method," we include such a systematic tree-building procedure.

Each step of the tree method is mechanical, or at least it can be made so, if we add more detail (in the way that each step of the procedure for adding two numbers can be made mechanical). For example, no ingenuity or insight is required to apply a tree rule or to check a path for closure.

Given the way we originally presented the tree rules, it was not the case that each step was deterministic. For example, we said to apply the rule for the unnegated existential quantifier with a new name but did not specify which name. Thus, two persons following the same rule might construct different trees, if they pick different new names. However, the systematic tree-building procedure removes this indeterminacy: for example, for the rule for the unnegated existential quantifier, the procedure specifies that we are to use the alphabetically first name that does not occur on the path.

Finally, each step of the tree method is finitely achievable: applying a tree rule involves writing down at most finitely many things; checking for closure at any point requires checking through the finitely many entries in the tree at that point; and so on. Of course the method as a whole may in some cases run forever and generate an infinite tree, but as already discussed, this does not prevent the method from counting as an effective procedure.

The tree method, then, constitutes an effective procedure. In this respect, it is unlike, say, the methods taught in school geometry. Suppose we are given a geometric diagram with certain information in it (certain angle sizes, certain lengths) and asked whether two angles η and θ are equal. We are taught how to set out a proof properly but are given no mechanical method to follow to find the proof in the first place. We just have to look at the diagram and think and try various tactics until the answer strikes us. With trees, in contrast, we can just start applying the tree rules mechanically.

§

It might seem, then, that the tree method is foolproof: it is an effective procedure, and it is sound and complete. Yet there is a catch. We want a mechanical method that always yields the correct answer. We have a mechanical method, and its answers are always correct (if all paths close, the argument is valid [soundness]; if a finished tree has an open path, the argument is invalid [the contrapositive of completeness]). However, the method does not always yield an answer in a finite amount of time. Suppose we are given an argument that (as a matter of fact, although we might not know this yet) is valid. Then the tree method will yield a (correct) answer in a finite amount of time: all paths will close, which establishes that the argument is valid. But suppose we are given an argument that (as a matter of fact, although we might not know this yet) is not valid. Then one of two things might happen. First, the finished tree might be finite. Then, as above, the tree method will yield a (correct) answer in a finite amount of time: the tree will be finished, at least one path will be open, and this will establish that the argument is invalid. The second possibility, however, is that the finished tree might be infinite. In this case the tree method does not yield an answer in a finite amount of time. In a sense the tree method yields the correct answer here, but it takes an infinite amount of time to do so. (In another sense, what it yields—an infinite tree—is not a legitimate answer at all, because it is infinitely long. At any rate, it is not a *proof* of invalidity, in the way that a finite closed tree is a proof of validity. We discuss this issue in §14.3.)

To clarify the situation further, some terminology will be helpful. A *positive test* for a property is an effective procedure that can be applied to an object, and if (and only if) the object does have the property, then the test will tell us that it does (i.e., say Yes) after some finite amount of time. A *negative test* for a property is an effective procedure that can be applied to an object, and if (and only if) the object does not have the property, then the test will tell us that it doesn't (i.e., say No) after some finite amount of time.[13] A *decision procedure* for a property is an effective procedure that can be applied to an object and that will, after some finite amount of time, yield a (correct) answer as to whether this object has the property (Yes if it does, No if it doesn't). A positive test and a negative test for a property together provide a decision procedure for the property. The steps of the decision procedure are obtained by interleaving the steps of the positive and negative tests: steps 1, 2, 3, . . . of the positive test become steps 1, 3, 5, . . . of the decision procedure, while steps 1, 2, 3, . . . of the negative test become steps 2, 4, 6, . . . of the decision procedure. Now when we apply the decision procedure to an object, if the object does have the property, that fact will be established at some odd-numbered step of the decision procedure (i.e. by some step of the positive test), and if it does not have the property, that fact will be established at some even-numbered step (i.e. by some step of the negative test). Either way, we will know, after some finite amount of time, whether the object has the property. The *decision problem* for a property is said to be *solvable* iff there exists a decision procedure for that property (and it is *solved* when we actually know at least one such decision procedure).[14]

The property we are concerned with here is validity. The objects that may or may not possess this property are arguments. (In §14.3 we consider other logical properties, e.g., logical truth and equivalence. The objects that may or may not possess these properties are, respectively, propositions and pairs of propositions.)

The tree method is a positive test for validity. If we are given an argument that, as a matter of fact, does possess the property of being valid, then the tree method will tell us this in a finite amount of time: all paths will close, and we will know that the argument is valid. (Recall from the end of §14.1.3 that a closed tree is always finite.) The tree method is not, however, a negative test for validity. When applied to an argument that, as a matter of fact, does not possess the property of being valid, the tree method will sometimes establish that it is invalid in a finite amount of time, but it will not always do so—because some invalid arguments generate infinite trees.[15]

So the tree method is not a decision procedure for validity. Is there some other method we could employ that would do better? At this point it will be useful to consider our logical systems PL, MPL, and GPL separately. First, consider PL. In this case, the tree method is a decision procedure, because there are no infinite PL trees (infinite trees emerged only when we moved to predicate logic). The truth table method is also a decision procedure (or at least it can be made to be one, if we add enough detail to each step to make it purely mechanical and add rules specifying the precise order in which the steps are to be carried out). So the decision problem for validity of arguments in propositional logic is solved.

Second, consider MPL. We can have infinite trees in MPL, so the tree method is not a decision procedure for validity of arguments in MPL. However, as a matter of fact, the decision problem for MPL is solvable: there are decision procedures for validity in MPL.[16] Indeed, we can extend the tree method to yield such a decision procedure. The only way that an MPL tree can continue forever is if it contains a formula beginning with a universal quantifier that has within its scope either an existential quantifier or a negated universal quantifier. (Not every tree with such a formula in it continues forever but every infinite tree has such a formula in it.) However, there is an effective procedure that, given any formula of MPL, generates an equivalent formula with the following form (known as $\exists^*\forall^*$ form), where α contains no quantifiers:[17]

$$\exists \underline{x} \exists \underline{y} \ldots \forall \underline{z} \forall \underline{w} \ldots \alpha$$

That is, it has all its existential quantifiers (if any) in front, then all its universal quantifiers (if any), followed by everything else (atomic wffs and connectives). So if we supplement our tree method with this additional procedure, which allows us to cross out any formula in our tree that is not in $\exists^*\forall^*$ form and replace it with an equivalent formula that is in $\exists^*\forall^*$ form, then our trees will never be infinite—and so we will have a decision procedure for validity.

Third, consider GPL. The additional procedure we mentioned in the case of MPL—the one that converts each formula in the tree to an equivalent formula in $\exists^*\forall^*$ form—will not work in GPL: it is not true in general predicate logic, as opposed to monadic predicate logic, that every formula is equivalent to some formula in $\exists^*\forall^*$ form. What is true is that every formula is equivalent to some formula in prenex normal form (§12.5.3). Indeed, there is an effective procedure for putting any formula into prenex normal form (i.e., finding an equivalent formula in that form). But there is no guarantee that we can find an equivalent formula in prenex normal form in which, furthermore, all

existential quantifiers precede all universal quantifiers—that is, a formula in
∃*∀* form. Consider, for example, the following two formulas:

$$\forall x \exists y (Fx \land Gy) \tag{14.1}$$

$$\forall x \exists y Rxy \tag{14.2}$$

Formula (14.1) is equivalent to $(\forall x Fx \land \exists y Gy)$ (recall §12.5) and to
$\exists y \forall x (Fx \land Gy)$, which is in ∃*∀* form. However, (14.2) is not equivalent
to $\exists y \forall x Rxy$ (recall §12.1.7) or to any other formula in ∃*∀* form.

If we cannot supplement our tree method for GPL with a procedure that will
exclude infinite trees, perhaps we can do something else. In §10.3, we began
producing a tree to determine whether the wff $\forall x \exists y (Fx \land Gy)$ is satisfiable.
After a finite amount of time spent developing the tree we determined that
the tree would indeed remain open, no matter what we did and concluded
that the wff is satisfiable (§10.3.1). The idea now is to try to write up a set of
rules—an effective procedure—that we can follow to determine whether any
unfinished tree will be finite or infinite when finished. It turns out, however,
that there can be no such set of rules. This conclusion is not at all obvious—
in fact, on first encounter, it is puzzling. But it is a consequence of the fact that
the decision problem for validity in general predicate logic is not solvable; that
is, there is no decision procedure for validity in GPL. This extraordinary fact—
one of the key results of twentieth-century logic—was proved independently
in the 1930s by Alan Turing in Cambridge and Alonzo Church in Princeton.[18]
Proving this fact—known as the *undecidability of first-order logic*—is beyond
the scope of this book.[19] But note that it follows from this fact that there
can be no effective procedure of the sort we just imagined: one that tells us
whether a given unfinished tree will—when extended in accordance with our
systematic tree-building procedure—go on forever. Because if there were such
a procedure, then it, together with the tree method, would yield a decision
procedure for validity in GPL as follows. Given an argument, we write up
its premises and the negation of the conclusion; we then run the imagined
procedure to determine whether the finished tree will be infinite. If it will be
infinite, we know the argument is invalid; if it will be finite, we then construct
the tree to find out whether the argument is valid. None of this is to deny
that sometimes we can see—after a finite amount of time and with absolute
certainty—that a given tree will be infinite when finished. The point is that we
cannot be seeing this by following a single effective procedure that could be
applied to any unfinished tree and would always yield a correct answer.

In sum, the tree method of testing an argument for validity is an effective
procedure, and it provides a positive test for validity. Once we move beyond
MPL, however, the tree method does not provide a negative test for validity.[20]
In its defense, however, no other method can do any better: there can be no
negative test for validity in GPL, because it is known that there is no decision

procedure for validity in GPL—and a positive test (which we already have) together with a negative test would yield a decision procedure.

14.3 Other Logical Properties

We have discussed the extent to which trees provide a foolproof method of assessing arguments for validity. But we have also used trees for other purposes: testing for logical truth, equivalence, and so on. In this section we consider the situation with respect to these other logical properties.

Recall the distinction between a-properties and s-properties (originally drawn in §5.7 in terms of truth table rows rather than models). The presence of an s-property can, in principle, be established by citing a single model; the presence of an a-property cannot be so established:

A-property	S-property
Validity	Invalidity
Logical truth	Non-logicaltruth
Equivalence	Inequivalence
Unsatisfiability	Satisfiability

To show that an argument is invalid, it suffices to come up with a single model in which the premises are true and the conclusion false, whereas no single model could, by itself, establish that an argument is valid. To show that a proposition is a non-logicaltruth, it suffices to come up with a single model in which the proposition is false, whereas no single model could, by itself, establish that a proposition is a logical truth. Similar remarks apply to inequivalence/equivalence and satisfiability/unsatisfiability.

In the table, the property on the left is just the property something of the relevant sort has if it does not have the property on the right, and vice versa. Thus, checking for the absence of an a-property is the same as checking for the presence of the corresponding s-property, and vice versa. So the absence of any a-property can, in principle, be established by citing a single model; the absence of an s-property cannot be so established.

The a-properties are all interdefinable (and similarly for the s-properties). If we start with the notion of unsatisfiability (of a set of propositions), a valid argument $\alpha_1, \ldots, \alpha_n / \therefore \beta$ is one where the set $\{\alpha_1, \ldots, \alpha_n, \neg\beta\}$ is unsatisfiable; a logical truth is a proposition α where the set $\{\neg\alpha\}$ is unsatisfiable; two propositions α and β are equivalent iff the sets $\{\alpha, \neg\beta\}$ and $\{\neg\alpha, \beta\}$ are unsatisfiable. Starting with the notion of validity, we can define unsatisfiability as follows: a set is unsatisfiable iff there is some proposition in it whose negation follows logically from the other propositions in the set (i.e., the set $\{\alpha_1, \ldots, \alpha_n\}$ is unsatisfiable iff there is some α_i such that

$\alpha_1, \ldots, \alpha_{i-1}, \alpha_{i+1}, \ldots \alpha_n / \therefore \neg\alpha_i$ is a valid argument). Having defined unsatisfiability, we can proceed as above to define the other notions. Starting with the notion of logical truth, we can define validity as follows: the argument $\alpha_1, \ldots, \alpha_n / \therefore \beta$ is valid iff $(\alpha_1 \wedge \ldots \wedge \alpha_n) \to \beta$ is a logical truth. Having defined validity, we can proceed as above to define the other notions. Starting with the notion of equivalence, we can define logical truth as follows: α is a logical truth iff it is equivalent to $a = a$ (or any other known logical truth). Having defined logical truth, we can proceed as above to define the other notions.[21]

Where P is any of our logical properties (a- or s-properties), a system of proof is *sound* with respect to property P iff when there is a proof in the system that some object has P, that object really does have P. A system of proof is *complete* with respect to property P iff when some object has property P, there is a proof in the system that it has P.[22] Now, with respect to which properties in our table is the system of tree proofs sound, and with respect to which properties is it complete? Jumping ahead, the answer is that it is sound with respect to all of them; it is complete with respect to all a-properties and none of the s-properties. But before we can establish this answer, we need to be more precise about what a proof is.

14.3.1 Proofs

Intuitively, a proof that something is the case establishes beyond doubt that it is the case. Thus, a proof that X (or that not X) ends any argument as to whether or not X: if something does not end such an argument once and for all, then even though it might be good evidence for or against X, it isn't a proof that X (or that not X). If a proof that X is to end any argument as to whether or not X, then there should not be any doubt that it is a proof that X: otherwise, the argument will shift to whether it is a genuine proof. In logic, we make this idea precise as follows (a proof in the precise sense we are about to explain is often called a *formal* proof). First, there must be a specified set of symbols from which proofs may be constructed. (These will be the symbols of the logical language, together perhaps with some additional symbols, e.g., the lines and crosses in tree proofs.) Any finite array of these proof symbols will then be a candidate for the title of "proof"—it may or may not actually be a proof, but it is at least in the running to be one (unlike something that is not even composed of the right symbols). Second, there must be a decision procedure for determining whether a candidate proof that something is the case really is a proof that that thing is the case. That is, there must be an effective procedure which, given any candidate proof as input, will yield an answer one way or the other (either "yes it is a proof that X" or "no it is not a proof that X") in a finite amount of time. This makes precise the idea that if something is a proof that X, then there should not be any doubt that it is (and furthermore, if it is not, then there should not be any doubt that it is not): we can just apply the effective procedure to check whether it is a genuine proof.

One upshot of the foregoing is that proofs must be finite. This requirement is intuitively correct: something cannot end an argument if it itself never ends. It is also necessary if there is to be a decision procedure for checking whether any proof candidate is a genuine proof. For suppose we did allow infinite proofs. Then the proof-testing procedure, when fed this proof as input, would run forever (because the input is infinite), and therefore fail to yield the correct verdict "yes, this is a proof" in a finite amount of time. Thus, it would not be a decision procedure.

14.3.2 Tree Proofs

In light of these general considerations about proofs, let's consider our system of tree proofs. As we will see, the system provides proofs of the presence of s-properties and proofs of the presence of a-properties. (In this respect, the tree system is unlike two of the other three major kinds of proof system— natural deduction and axiomatic systems—to be discussed in Chapter 15. Those systems do not provide any proofs of the presence of s-properties— or in other words, of the absence of a-properties: they provide proofs only of the presence of a-properties.) Let's start with validity (an a-property) and invalidity (its corresponding s-property).

A finite closed tree beginning with $\alpha_1, \ldots, \alpha_n, \neg\beta$ is a proof that the argument $\alpha_1, \ldots, \alpha_n/\therefore \beta$ has the property of being valid. First, there is a decision procedure for whether any given candidate tree proof is a finite closed tree beginning with $\alpha_1, \ldots, \alpha_n, \neg\beta$. For we could, in principle, write out an effective procedure (or program a computer) to determine—given as input any finite array of the symbols used to make trees (logical symbols, lines, crosses, etc.)— whether this array is a correctly formed tree beginning with $\alpha_1, \ldots, \alpha_n, \neg\beta$ in which every path is closed. The procedure would need to check that

1. the initial entries are $\alpha_1, \ldots, \alpha_n$ and $\neg\beta$;

2. every entry after the initial entries follows from an earlier entry or entries by one of the tree rules—that is, that the tree-building rules (of which there are only finitely many) have been applied correctly;

3. the path-closing rules have been applied correctly (any path that should close is closed with a cross; any path closed with a cross should indeed be closed); and

4. every path has a cross at the bottom.

Second, by (S) (§14.1.2), if such a tree exists, then the argument $\alpha_1, \ldots,$ $\alpha_n /\therefore \beta$ is valid. Thus, a finite closed tree beginning with $\alpha_1, \ldots, \alpha_n, \neg\beta$ constitutes a proof that the argument $\alpha_1, \ldots, \alpha_n /\therefore \beta$ has the property of being valid.

Similarly, a finite finished tree with an open path, beginning with $\alpha_1, \ldots,$ $\alpha_n, \neg\beta$, is a proof that the argument $\alpha_1, \ldots, \alpha_n /\therefore \beta$ has the property of being invalid. First, there is a decision procedure for whether any given candidate tree proof is a finite finished tree with an open path, beginning with $\alpha_1, \ldots, \alpha_n, \neg\beta$. For we could, in principle, write out an effective procedure (or program a computer) to determine—given as input any finite array of the symbols used to make trees—whether this array is a correctly formed tree beginning with $\alpha_1, \ldots, \alpha_n, \neg\beta$ in which every path is closed or saturated, and in which some path is open. The procedure would need to check that

1. the initial entries are $\alpha_1, \ldots, \alpha_n$ and $\neg\beta$;

2. every entry after the initial entries follows from an earlier entry or entries by one of the tree rules—that is, that the tree-building rules (of which there are only finitely many) have been applied correctly;

3. the path-closing rules have been applied correctly (any path that should close is closed with a cross; any path closed with a cross should indeed be closed);

4. every path that does not have a cross at the bottom is saturated; and

5. at least one path does not have a cross at the bottom.

Second, by the contrapositive of (C) (§14.1.3), if such a tree exists, then the argument $\alpha_1, \ldots, \alpha_n /\therefore \beta$ is invalid. Thus, a finite finished tree with an open path, beginning with $\alpha_1, \ldots, \alpha_n, \neg\beta$, constitutes a proof that the argument $\alpha_1, \ldots, \alpha_n /\therefore \beta$ has the property of being invalid.

So far so good. However, an infinite finished tree with an open path, beginning with $\alpha_1, \ldots, \alpha_n, \neg\beta$, is not a proof that the argument $\alpha_1, \ldots, \alpha_n /\therefore \beta$ has the property of being invalid. For although, by the contrapositive of (C), if such a tree exists, the argument really is invalid—nevertheless, such a tree, being infinite, does not constitute a proof.

Similar comments apply to the other pairs of properties—for example, unsatisfiability and satisfiability. A closed tree beginning with $\alpha_1, \ldots, \alpha_n$ is a proof that the set $\alpha_1, \ldots, \alpha_n$ has the property of being unsatisfiable. A finite finished tree with an open path, beginning with $\alpha_1, \ldots, \alpha_n$ is a proof that the set $\alpha_1, \ldots, \alpha_n$ has the property of being satisfiable. However, an infinite finished tree with an open path, beginning with $\alpha_1, \ldots, \alpha_n$ is not a proof that the set $\alpha_1, \ldots, \alpha_n$ has the property of being satisfiable (even though, by the contrapositive of (C), if such a tree exists, the set is satisfiable).

14.3.3 Soundness and Completeness . . .

In light of the foregoing discussions of what a proof is in general—and of which kinds of trees constitute proofs of which kinds of facts—let us return to the questions of whether the system of tree proofs is sound and complete with respect to other a-properties (apart from validity) and whether it is sound and complete with respect to any s-properties.

Our proofs of (S) and (C) in §14.1 established that trees are sound and complete with respect to validity. If an argument is valid, there is a proof that it is (i.e., a closed tree starting with the premises and the negation of the conclusion), which is completeness with respect to validity. And if there is a proof that an argument is valid, the argument really is valid, which is soundness with respect to validity. But our proofs of (S) and (C) also establish much more: they establish that trees are sound and complete with respect to all other a-properties as well. Recall what we proved:

(S)   If all paths close in a tree that starts from propositions $\alpha_1, \ldots, \alpha_n$, then there is no model in which $\alpha_1, \ldots, \alpha_n$ are all true.

(C)   If there is no model in which propositions $\alpha_1, \ldots, \alpha_n$ are all true, then all paths close in every finished tree that starts from $\alpha_1, \ldots, \alpha_n$.

Now consider the property of logical truth. A proof that α is a logical truth is a closed tree beginning with $\neg\alpha$. If the tree system provides such a proof, then by (S), there is no model in which $\neg\alpha$ is true; that is, α is true in every model—it is a logical truth. Thus, the tree method is sound with respect to logical truth. Conversely, if α is a logical truth, then there is no model in which $\neg\alpha$ is true— so by (C), all paths will close in a finished tree beginning with $\neg\alpha$—that is, there is a tree proof that α is a logical truth (i.e., a closed tree beginning with $\neg\alpha$). Thus, the tree method is complete with respect to logical truth.[23] Similar reasoning applies to equivalence and unsatisfiability: the tree method is sound and complete with respect to these properties, as well as with respect to validity and logical truth.

What about the s-properties? It follows from the contrapositive of (C) that trees are sound with respect to the s-properties. If there is a tree proof that an argument is invalid—a finished finite tree with an open path that begins with the premises and the negation of the conclusion—then by the contrapositive of (C), the argument really is invalid (there is a model in which the premises and the negation of the conclusion are all true). If there is a tree proof that a proposition is a non-logicaltruth—a finished finite tree with an open path, beginning with the negation of the proposition—then by the contrapositive of (C), the proposition really is a non-logicaltruth (there is a model in which the negation of the proposition is true). Similarly for tree proofs of inequivalence and satisfiability.

What about completeness with respect to the s-properties? First, it does not follow from the contrapositive of (S) that trees are complete with respect to the s-properties. Suppose that an argument $\alpha_1, \ldots, \alpha_n / \therefore \beta$ is invalid. What follows from the contrapositive of (S) is:

It is not the case that all paths close in a tree that starts from $\alpha_1, \ldots, \alpha_n$ and $\neg\beta$

But this statement does not mean there will be a proof that the argument is invalid, that is, a finite finished tree with an open path, starting from $\alpha_1, \ldots, \alpha_n$ and $\neg\beta$. We know the finished tree will have an open path, but there is no guarantee it will be finite. And an infinite tree is not a proof. Similar comments apply to non-logicaltruth, inequivalence, and satisfiability.

So it does not follow from the contrapositive of (S) that trees are complete with respect to the s-properties—and in fact, trees are not complete with respect to these properties. We know that some invalid arguments generate infinite finished trees. Infinite trees are not proofs. So there are some invalid arguments for which there is no tree proof that they are invalid. That is, the system of tree proofs is not complete with respect to the property of invalidity. Similarly, some satisfiable sets generate infinite finished trees. Again, infinite trees are not proofs. So there are some satisfiable sets of propositions for which there is no tree proof that they are satisfiable. That is, the system of tree proofs is not complete with respect to the property of satisfiability. Likewise for inequivalence and non-logicaltruth.[24]

14.3.4 . . . and Positive Tests

So the system of tree proofs is sound with respect to all s-properties and complete with respect to none of them. It is interesting to note, however, that no other proof system could possibly do any better, because a sound and complete proof procedure for invalidity would yield a negative test for validity—and this is something we know cannot exist (§14.2). (Likewise, a sound and complete proof procedure for any of the other s-properties in our table in §14.3 would yield a negative test for its corresponding a-property—and that, via the interdefinability of the a-properties, would yield a negative test for validity.) Let us see why this is so. The key step is:

(P)   A system of proof that is sound and complete with respect to property P (where P is any a- or s-property) yields a positive test for P.

We shall show why (P) is true shortly. For now, note that a positive test for any property in the table in §14.3 is, immediately, a negative test for its corresponding property on the other side of the table. For example, a positive test for satisfiability is a negative test for unsatisfiability (because a set is satisfiable iff it is not unsatisfiable), and a positive test for invalidity is a negative test for validity. Thus, by (P), a proof procedure that was sound and complete with respect to invalidity would yield a positive test for invalidity, and that would yield a negative test for validity. We know there can be no negative test for validity; hence, we know there can be no proof procedure that is sound and complete with respect to invalidity.

Let us see, then, why (P) is true. A proof in some system that some object has some property (e.g., a tree proof that some argument is valid, or a tree proof that some set of propositions is satisfiable) is a finite array of proof symbols. As discussed in §14.3.1, there must (in principle) be a decision procedure for the property of "being a proof in the system that object x has property P" (for any x of the sort that might possess P—e.g., any argument, if P is validity or invalidity; or any set of propositions, if P is satisfiability or unsatisfiability). That is, there must be an effective procedure that, when given as input an arbitrary finite array of proof symbols, will in a finite amount of time return the (correct) verdict "yes, it is a proof that x has P" or "no, it is not a proof that x has P" for arbitrary x. Now suppose that the system is sound and complete with respect to P: for any x that possesses the property P, there is a proof in the system that x has P (completeness); and when there is a proof in the system that x has P, x really does have P (soundness). Then a positive test for P is as follows.

1. Given an object x, start generating, in some predefined order, all possible finite arrays of proof symbols. It may require some ingenuity to figure out an order in which to generate them, such that no array is permanently left off the list, but it will always be possible, provided that the logical language and the system of proof have been set up in a minimally reasonable way.[25]

2. Each time you generate an array of proof symbols in accordance with step (1), use it as input to the decision procedure for the property of "being a proof in the system that x has P." If x does have P, then eventually you must get to a proof that x has P (because the system is complete with respect to P), and at this point the decision procedure will return the verdict "yes, this is a proof that x has P." Now you can conclude "yes, x has P."

This procedure is a positive test for P: you will conclude that x has P only if x does have P (by soundness: if there is a proof that x has P, then x does have P), and if x does have P then you will conclude that it does after a finite amount of time (by completeness, there will be a proof that x has P, and so you will find it after some finite amount of time).

§

Note that (P) is completely general: any system of proof that is sound and complete with respect to any property P yields a positive test for P. Given an x, which we are testing for being P, we just perform a brute force search for a proof that P holds for x; that is, we search through every possible finite array of proof symbols. By completeness, if x has P, then we shall find a proof that it does, and by soundness, if we find such a proof, x has P. Thus, this procedure provides a positive test for P. Note, however, that in the tree system, if we want to know (say) whether an argument is valid, we can search for a proof in a more intelligent—but still effective (i.e., mechanical)—way. In fact, this is just what a systematic tree-building procedure is (i.e., a procedure of the sort discussed in §10.3.5, which ensures finished, although not necessarily finite, trees): an intelligent but still effective method of searching for a proof that an argument is valid. We can also think of it as a search for a proof that the argument is invalid (as trees provide proofs of a-properties and s-properties, we can think of it either way). The search may succeed—that is, terminate with a finished tree—in one of two different ways: it may terminate with a (finite) closed tree—a proof of validity, or it may terminate with a finished finite tree with an open path—a poof of invalidity. The third possibility is that the search never terminates: it continues forever, building an infinite tree. In this case, the search yields no proof of validity or invalidity. After an infinite amount of time, the search will generate a finished tree, but an infinite tree is not a proof.

The point is a general one: it does not apply only to validity. Suppose you want to know whether a set of propositions is satisfiable. You write up the propositions and begin constructing a tree in accordance with a systematic procedure for producing finished trees. One of three things may happen. (i) The search terminates in a proof of satisfiability: a finished finite tree with an open path. (ii) The search terminates in a proof of unsatisfiability: a closed tree. (iii) The search never terminates: you continue building the tree forever. That the tree system involves an intelligent but still effective method of searching for proofs—whether of validity, unsatisfiability, logical truth, equivalence, or their corresponding s-properties—is one of the highly attractive features of the tree method.

§

In sum, the situation regarding the other a-properties is the same as the situation regarding validity: the tree method of testing for the presence of these properties is an effective procedure, and it provides a positive test for each property. Once we move beyond MPL, however, there can be no negative tests for the a-properties. For we know that there cannot be a negative test for validity, and via the interdefinability of the a-properties, a negative test for any a-property would yield a negative test for validity. Thus, there cannot be any proof procedure that is sound and complete for any s-property, because a sound and complete proof procedure for any s-property would yield a positive test for that s-property, and that would yield a negative test for its corresponding a-property. The tree method is sound with respect to the s-properties: this follows from the contrapositive of (C). Therefore, it is not complete with respect to any s-property. Trees do provide proofs of the presence of s-properties, such as invalidity (in the form of finished finite trees with open paths). However, the system of tree proofs is not—and no system can be—complete with respect to the s-properties.

14.4 Expressive Power

We wanted a method of assessing arguments for validity that is both foolproof and general. Having now discussed the extent to which the tree method is foolproof, we turn to the question of generality. When we test an argument given in natural language for validity, we begin by translating the argument into our logical language. When we speak of a method of assessing arguments for validity that is general, what we are really talking about is the expressive resources of the logical language together with its model theory. Thus, the issue of generality concerns our logical languages and their associated systems of model theory, rather than their associated systems of tree proofs.

We gradually increased the expressive power of our logical language, from propositional logic (PL) to monadic predicate logic (MPL) to general predicate logic (GPL) to general predicate logic with identity (GPLI). We also considered some further additions to the language: a definite description operator (GPLID, §13.6.2) and function symbols (GPLIF, §13.7). The generality question can be formulated as: can any argument—that is, any proposition—be represented in GPLI? Or rather, can it be represented in a good or at least reasonable way? Any proposition at all can be represented even in PL—as a sentence letter, but obviously this representation will not, in general, be a good one. Let's begin by considering some examples.

(1) The proposition $2 + 2 = 4$. In GPLIF we represent this proposition (using the glossary of §13.7.1) as:

$$s(a_2, a_2) = a_4 \qquad (14.3)$$

If we follow the procedure of §13.7.3, the corresponding wff of GPLI is:[26]

$$\exists x (Sa_2 a_2 x \wedge x = a_4) \wedge \forall x_1 \forall x_2 \exists y \forall z (Sx_1 x_2 z \leftrightarrow z = y) \qquad (14.4)$$

Although (14.4) could be simplified somewhat, the result would still be considerably more complex than (14.3).

(2) The proposition expressed by an utterance, at 11:44:00 a.m. on Monday, 11 July 2011, of "Ned has not yet been to see his doctor, but he will go." We could represent this proposition in GPLI as:

a: 11:44:00 a.m. on Monday, 11 July 2011[27]
d: Ned's doctor
n: Ned
Tx: x is a moment of time
Pxy: x is prior to y
$Vxyz$: x goes to see y at z

$$\neg \exists x (Tx \wedge Pxa \wedge Vndx) \wedge \exists x (Tx \wedge Pax \wedge Vndx)$$

Note that this representation involves quantifiers that range over moments of time (considered as entities) and names that refer to such moments of time. It also involves representing "Ned goes to see his doctor" using a three-place relation V, which involves argument positions for Ned and his doctor, and a third argument position for a moment of time.

The major alternative way of representing such claims in a logical language is to augment the language with new one-place connectives: G (which can be read as "it will always be the case that;" compare the way that $\neg$ can be read as "it is not the case that"), F ("it will at some time be the case that"), H ("it has always been the case that"), and P ("it has at some time been the case that"). If we add these connectives to PL—giving us the language of propositional *tense logic*—"Ned has not yet been to see his doctor, but he will go" can then be represented in either of the following ways (using the glossary N: Ned goes to see his doctor):

$$\neg PN \wedge FN$$
$$H\neg N \wedge FN$$

As the new connectives are part of the logical vocabulary, we also need to augment the semantics. This task turns out not be simple because the new connectives are not truth functional, and so we cannot simply assign each one a truth table—something more radical is called for.[28]

(3) So far we have contrasted ways of representing claims in GPLI with ways of representing them in logics with a different *syntax*. Now consider the claim "Bertrand is tall." We can represent this claim in GPLI as Tb (using the obvious glossary). In every model, T will be assigned a subset of the domain as extension, and Tb will be true or false. One might object that assigning a sharply defined subset of objects as the extension of "tall" does not do justice to its vagueness—to the fact that there is no sharp division between tall and nontall persons. One might therefore think that although the syntax of GPLI is adequate to the representation of "Bertrand is tall," the semantics is not. Rather, we should have a semantics wherein predicates may be assigned

nonsharply defined collections as their extensions—for example, *fuzzy* sets of objects.[29]

(4) Given a predicate P, we saw in §13.5 how to translate "there are exactly two Ps," "there are exactly three Ps," and so on. One form of quantification that we cannot express in GPLI is "there are finitely many Ps." That is, we cannot form a wff (or even a set of wffs) such that for every model in which that wff (or all wffs in that set) is true, the extension of P is a finite set. (Note that infinite disjunctions are not wffs in GPLI. Thus, we cannot express "there are finitely many Ps" in GPLI as the disjunction of "there are exactly n Ps" for every finite n.) There are extensions of GPLI, however, in which this idea can be expressed.

In light of these examples, let's return to the question of generality. There are some propositions that cannot be represented adequately in GPLI (e.g., example (4)), and other propositions (e.g., examples (2) and (3)) for which the issue of whether their representations in GPLI are better than their representations in certain other logical systems is highly controversial. Nevertheless, GPLI—aka (first-order, or restricted, or lower) *predicate calculus* (with identity), *quantification theory* (with identity), or simply *classical logic*—is a canonical logical system. This is because it has a particularly nice balance of properties. Its expressive power is not limitless, but it is very high (or at least high enough for very many purposes), and, in general, we do not acquire greater expressive power in a logic without some corresponding trade-off. For example, when we move from MPL to GPL, we gain much more expressive power, but we lose the property of decidability. Similarly, when we move from GPLI to certain of its possible extensions or alternatives, we lose certain properties—for example, in some of them there is not even a positive test for validity, let alone a negative test. At this point, we are not in a position to appreciate fully the merits of classical logic—its particular balance of expressive power and other properties (e.g., admitting sound and complete proof procedures). To appreciate these merits fully, one needs to know about the rest of the core metalogical properties of classical logic, and about other logical systems that possess different combinations of features. Exploring these areas—mathematical logic (which includes the study of the metalogical properties of classical logic) and nonclassical logic (which includes the study of various extensions of and alternatives to classical logic)—is beyond the scope of this book. Suffice it to say here that although GPLI cannot do everything and do it better than any other logical system, GPLI is a very attractive system, and one of its merits is its high level of expressive power. Still, there are also other attractive logical systems, some of which have greater expressive power, and some of which have other merits. Classical logic should not, then, be seen as a monopoly. But it is—for good reasons—a central reference point, relative to which other logical systems are inevitably compared.

15

Other Methods of Proof

In §9.5 we contrasted precise analyses of logical properties (e.g., validity) with methods for showing that a given object possesses or does not possess one of these properties (e.g., that a given argument is valid or is not valid). In the case of propositional logic, we looked at two methods of proof: truth tables and trees. In the case of predicate logic, we have so far examined only one method: trees. But there are many other proof methods that have been developed, and in this chapter we look at the three most commonly used among them: axiomatic proof, natural deduction, and sequent calculus.[1]

Before proceeding further, it will be useful to flag the difference between particular methods of proof and styles of proof method. We discussed the notion of a *formal proof* in §14.3.1. A particular method of proof is a set of rules governing the production of some specific kind of formal proofs. Because it is part of the very idea of a formal proof that there should be a decision procedure for whether a given proof candidate really is a formal proof (of such-and-such in a given system), particular proof methods must be extremely precise: the fine details matter crucially, if there is to be a decision procedure for being a proof in the system. From another point of view, however, small differences in details between one proof system and another are not always significant: sometimes they can be seen as different particular ways of doing much the same thing. Thus, it is natural to group particular methods of proof into families or *styles* of proof method. A proof in one particular system is not, in general, a proof in any other particular system, because the rules of each system have to be so precise. This particularity holds even between proof systems in the same family. However, the differences from one family to another are even greater. They are not mere differences of detail; the basic underlying idea behind proofs in two systems from different families might be quite different, even if they are ultimately proofs of the same thing (e.g., that some argument is valid).

The four most common broad families or styles of proof system are tableau proof, axiomatic proof, natural deduction, and sequent calculus. We have looked at one particular method in the tableau style: the tree method. There are other particular methods in the tableau family.[2] For example, in the method of *Beth tableaux*, we write down two columns of wffs: one on the left side of the page and one on the right side. In the left column we write wffs that are supposed to be true, and in the right column we write wffs that are supposed to be false. So to begin testing an argument from premises $\alpha_1, \ldots, \alpha_n$ to conclusion β for validity, we start by writing $\alpha_1, \ldots, \alpha_n$ in the left column and β (without any negation sign out the front) in the right column. Now, suppose we come across a wff of the form $(\gamma \rightarrow \delta)$ in the right column; we then write γ in the left column and δ in the right column (because if $(\gamma \rightarrow \delta)$ is false, then γ is true and δ false). Or suppose we encounter a wff of the form $(\gamma \vee \delta)$ in the left column; we then split the column into two halves and write γ on one side and δ on the other (because if $(\gamma \vee \delta)$ is true, then either γ is true, or δ is true), and so on. The analogue of finding α and $\neg\alpha$ in the same path—which causes the path to close in one of our tree proofs—is finding α in both the left and right columns. This particular method of proof is not exactly the same as our tree method, but it is recognizably similar in certain fundamental ways. Hence, both are classified as (different) specific methods of the same (tableau) style.[3]

In the following sections, we look at specific examples of each of the three other major families of proof methods—axiomatic proof, natural deduction, and sequent calculus—while indicating some of the scope for variation among the members of each family.[4]

15.1 Axiomatic Systems

Some trees provide information about validity: those starting from some formulas followed by a negation. Some trees provide information about logical truth: those starting from a negation. Some trees yield information about equivalence: those starting from a negated biconditional. But all (finished) trees yield information about satisfiability: if the tree closes, the set containing the initial formulas in the tree is unsatisfiable; if it does not close, the set is satisfiable. Thus, it is natural to say that the principal notion of tree proofs is that of the satisfiability of a set of propositions. That is, the primary information that a tree yields—and tree rules are constructed precisely so that trees will yield this information—is whether there is any model in which the propositions written at the top of the tree are all true (i.e., whether the set containing these propositions is satisfiable). Other information (e.g., whether a given argument is valid or a certain proposition is a logical truth) can then be obtained by careful use of trees (an argument is valid if the set containing its premises and negated conclusion is unsatisfiable, a proposition is a logical truth if the set containing its negation is unsatisfiable, etc.).

In axiomatic proof systems (aka *Hilbert* or *Hilbert-Frege* style systems) the primary notion is that of a proposition being a logical truth. So there is a double contrast here with the primary notion in tree proofs. First, in an axiomatic proof we are concerned with a single proposition, not a set of propositions. Second, we are concerned with whether this proposition is a logical truth (true in all models) rather than satisfiable (true in some model). The basic idea behind proving that a proposition is a logical truth in an axiomatic proof system is as follows. The system has two kinds of basic ingredient: *axioms* and *rules of inference*. Axioms are wffs. Rules of inference are rules or procedures that take a certain number of wffs as input and specify a wff as output (which particular wff is given as output depends on which particular wffs are supplied as input). An axiomatic proof is then a list (sequence) of wffs, where every wff in the list is either an axiom or the output of one of the rules of inference when supplied as input some wffs appearing earlier in the list. A proof as just defined is a proof of a particular proposition α if α is the last line of the proof (i.e., the last wff in the list of wffs constituting the proof). If there is a proof of α in some axiomatic system A, then α is a theorem of system A, or in symbols, $\vdash_A \alpha$. The symbol $\vdash$ is called the "single turnstile" or "proof-theoretic turnstile."[5] The symbol $\vDash$ is the "double turnstile" or "semantic turnstile." The expression $\vDash \alpha$ means that α is a logical truth (true in all models). That system A is sound (with respect to logical truth) is therefore expressed as: if $\vdash_A \alpha$, then $\vDash \alpha$. That system A is complete (with respect to logical truth) is expressed as: if $\vDash \alpha$, then $\vdash_A \alpha$.

For an axiomatic proof system to be sound, it is necessary and sufficient that two conditions be met: the axioms are logical truths, and the rules are logicaltruth-preserving (i.e., when all their inputs are logical truths, their outputs are logical truths). In this case, we can readily see why a proof of α establishes that α is a logical truth. The proof is a sequence of wffs, each of which must be a logical truth. (We can establish this claim by induction. The first step is an axiom; hence, it is a logical truth. Now assume steps 1 through n are logical truths—this is the inductive hypothesis. Step $n + 1$ is either an axiom—and hence a logical truth—or follows from earlier steps, all of which are by hypothesis logical truths, by a logicaltruth-preserving rule—and hence is a logical truth.) In particular, the last step α is thus a logical truth.

Let's look at some concrete examples of axiomatic proof systems. To make the presentation easier to follow, we begin—as we did with trees—by restricting ourselves to propositional logic and then look at what further axioms and rules need to be added to handle predicate logic and identity. Figure 15.1

Axioms:

(A1) $\alpha \to (\beta \to \alpha)$

(A2) $(\alpha \to (\beta \to \gamma)) \to ((\alpha \to \beta) \to (\alpha \to \gamma))$

(A3) $(\neg\beta \to \neg\alpha) \to ((\neg\beta \to \alpha) \to \beta)$

Rule (MP):

α

$(\alpha \to \beta)$

▶ β

Figure 15.1. System A_1.

shows an axiomatic proof system A_1 for propositional logic [Mendelson, 1987, 29]. When presenting rules of inference, we mark the output of the rule with a triangle (▶). The modus ponens rule (MP) is sometimes called the rule of *detachment*. Note the use of wff variables in the axioms and rule. Axioms stated using wff variables in this way are called axiom *schemas*. The idea is that any instance of any of the axiom schemas—any wff obtained by replacing wff variables with actual wffs (in the way discussed in §5.2)—may be written down at any point in an axiomatic proof. (The schema itself may not be written down in a proof, because a proof is a sequence of actual wffs, not of logical forms.)[6] Likewise, the rule licenses writing down any wff β, provided that there is some wff α such that both α and $(\alpha \to \beta)$ already appear (in either order) in the list.

Figure 15.2 shows a proof of $(\neg P \to P) \to P$ in system A_1.[7] So $(\neg P \to P) \to P$ is a theorem of A_1; that is, $\vdash_{A_1} (\neg P \to P) \to P$. Note that the numbers down the left, and the annotations down the right, are not part of the proof proper: the proof is simply the sequence of wffs in the middle. The numbers and annotations make the proof easier to follow, but they are not essential. Even without them, it would be possible to write an effective procedure (or program a computer) to check whether a given list of wffs

1. $\neg P \to [(\neg P \to \neg P) \to \neg P]$ (A1)
2. $\{\neg P \to [(\neg P \to \neg P) \to \neg P]\} \to$
    $\{[\neg P \to (\neg P \to \neg P)] \to (\neg P \to \neg P)\}$ (A2)
3. $[\neg P \to (\neg P \to \neg P)] \to (\neg P \to \neg P)$ 1, 2 (MP)
4. $\neg P \to (\neg P \to \neg P)$ (A1)
5. $\neg P \to \neg P$ 3, 4 (MP)
6. $(\neg P \to \neg P) \to [(\neg P \to P) \to P]$ (A3)
7. $(\neg P \to P) \to P$ 5, 6 (MP)

Figure 15.2. A proof in system A_1.

is a genuine proof. For each wff α in the list, the computer has to check only finitely many things—the wffs that appear before α in the list and the three axiom schemas—to check whether α is an instance of one of the axiom schemas or results from earlier wffs by application of (MP).

§

So far so good, but clearly there are logical truths that cannot be proved in A_1 as presented. For example, we cannot prove $P \vee \neg P$, because none of our axioms deals with $\vee$. This brings us to an important point. To keep a proof system as simple as possible (to minimize the number of axioms and rules), it is very common to confine it to a restricted portion of the full language PL. We saw in question 1(i) of Exercises 6.6.3 that $\{\rightarrow, \neg\}$ is a functionally complete set of connectives. Thus, if our axioms allow us to prove all logical truths involving only the connectives $\rightarrow$ and $\neg$, that is, in a sense, enough: for any proposition α involving other connectives, there is an equivalent proposition α' involving only $\rightarrow$ and $\neg$. If α is a logical truth, then so is α' (because α and α' are equivalent), and so we can prove α' in our system. All we need is to supplement our axiom system with definitions of the other connectives in PL in terms of the connectives featured in our axioms. In the case of A_1, we add the following definitions:

- $(\alpha \wedge \beta) := \neg(\alpha \rightarrow \neg\beta)$
- $(\alpha \vee \beta) := (\neg\alpha \rightarrow \beta)$
- $(\alpha \leftrightarrow \beta) := \neg((\alpha \rightarrow \beta) \rightarrow \neg(\beta \rightarrow \alpha))$

Now, to show that $P \vee \neg P$ is a logical truth, we first define out $\vee$, giving $\neg P \rightarrow \neg P$, and then prove the latter in A_1. In fact, the first five lines of the proof in Figure 15.2 constitute a proof of $\neg P \rightarrow \neg P$. This observation illustrates an interesting point about axiomatic proof systems: any initial part of a proof is itself a proof.[8]

The alternative to defining out the other connectives in the way just indicated is to add further axioms that enable us to prove logical truths involving these connectives. For example, Figure 15.3 shows a second axiomatic proof system, A_2, where $\wedge$ and $\vee$, as well as $\rightarrow$ and $\neg$, figure in the axioms [Kleene, 1952, p. 82].[9]

§

Let's turn now to predicate logic and identity. We need some axioms and rules for the quantifiers and for the identity predicate (which is part of the logical vocabulary), or for at least one of the quantifiers, because in keeping with the strategy examined above, we can define the other quantifier in terms

Axioms:

(A1) $\alpha \to (\beta \to \alpha)$

(A2') $(\alpha \to \beta) \to ((\alpha \to (\beta \to \gamma)) \to (\alpha \to \gamma))$

(A3') $\alpha \to (\beta \to (\alpha \wedge \beta))$

(A4') $(\alpha \wedge \beta) \to \alpha$

(A5') $(\alpha \wedge \beta) \to \beta$

(A6') $\alpha \to (\alpha \vee \beta)$

(A7') $\beta \to (\alpha \vee \beta)$

(A8') $(\alpha \to \gamma) \to ((\beta \to \gamma) \to ((\alpha \vee \beta) \to \gamma))$

(A9') $(\alpha \to \beta) \to ((\alpha \to \neg\beta) \to \neg\alpha)$

(A10') $\neg\neg\alpha \to \alpha$

Rule: (MP)

Figure 15.3. System A_2.

of negation and the quantifier for which we have axioms and rules, via the following equivalences:[10]

$$\exists \underline{x}\alpha \quad \text{is equivalent to} \quad \neg\forall\underline{x}\neg\alpha$$

$$\forall \underline{x}\alpha \quad \text{is equivalent to} \quad \neg\exists\underline{x}\neg\alpha$$

First, let us introduce some terminology. Recall (§9.3) that we use $\alpha(\underline{x})$ to stand for an arbitrary wff that may or may not contain free $\underline{x}$ but certainly has no free variables other than $\underline{x}$. We now use $\alpha[\underline{x}]$ (with square brackets instead of parentheses) to indicate a wff that may or may not contain free $\underline{x}$ and may or may not contain free variables other than $\underline{x}$. We use $\alpha[\underline{t}/\underline{x}]$ to indicate the result of replacing all free occurrences of $\underline{x}$ in $\alpha[\underline{x}]$ with the term $\underline{t}$. In this context, a *term* is a name or variable.[11] We say that $\underline{t}$ is *free for* $\underline{x}$ in $\alpha[\underline{x}]$ if either (i) $\underline{t}$ is a name or (ii) $\underline{t}$ is a variable $\underline{y}$, and $\underline{y}$ is free for $\underline{x}$ in $\alpha[\underline{x}]$ in the sense defined in Chapter 13, n. 6—that is, no free occurrence of $\underline{x}$ in $\alpha[\underline{x}]$ lies in the scope of a quantifier containing the variable $\underline{y}$. We use $\alpha[\underline{y}//\underline{x}]$ to indicate the result of replacing some (not necessarily all) free occurrences of $\underline{x}$ in $\alpha[\underline{x}]$ by $\underline{y}$, where $\underline{y}$ is free for $\underline{x}$ in $\alpha[\underline{x}]$. (Compare the terminology $\alpha(\underline{b}//\underline{a})$ introduced in §13.4.)

Now, here are some axioms and a rule for the universal quantifier; we call the system resulting from adding them to A_1 (see Figure 15.1) system $A_1^\forall$:

Axioms:

(A4) $\forall\underline{x}\alpha[\underline{x}] \to \alpha[\underline{t}/\underline{x}]$, where $\underline{t}$ is free for $\underline{x}$ in $\alpha[\underline{x}]$

(A5) $\forall\underline{x}(\alpha \to \beta) \to (\alpha \to \forall\underline{x}\beta)$, where α contains no free $\underline{x}$

Rule (Gen):

α

▶ $\forall\underline{x}\alpha$

The restrictions on (A4) and (A5) are there to prevent us being able to prove things in $A_1^\forall$ that are not logical truths (compare the restriction on the tree rule for the existential quantifier, i.e., the requirement that we use a new name). For identity, adding the following axioms to $A_1^\forall$ yields the system $A_1^{\forall=}$:

(A6) $\forall \underline{x}\,\underline{x} = \underline{x}$
(A7) $\underline{x} = \underline{y} \rightarrow (\alpha[\underline{x}] \rightarrow \alpha[\underline{y}/\!/\underline{x}])$

$$\S$$

We have looked at just a few examples of axiomatic systems out of very many that exist in the literature.[12] Two of the main ways in which these systems differ from one another are the following. First, the number of axioms and rules varies. We have already seen variation in axiom numbers between A_1 and A_2. As for rules, $A_1^\forall$, for example, has two, whereas the axiomatic system for predicate logic in Quine [1951] has just modus ponens, and the axiomatic system for predicate logic in Shoenfield [1967] has five rules. Second, there are three main styles for the presentation of axioms. One is via axiom schemas; we have seen this style above. In the second style, each axiom is a specific wff, not a schema. The power provided by schemas is then attained instead by having an extra rule—a rule of *substitution:* one may infer from a wff any wff obtained from it by replacing certain of its parts by other parts in specified ways. For example, one may infer $(Q \vee R) \vee \neg(Q \vee R)$ from $P \vee \neg P$ by substituting $(Q \vee R)$ for P. In the case of propositional logic, substitution rules can be stated quite simply; in the case of predicate logic, substitution rules become more tricky to state. The third style does not present specific wffs or even specific schemas as axioms, but simply says (for example) that any propositional logical truth is an axiom. (By propositional logical truth, I mean a logical truth whose main operator is a connective, as opposed to a quantifier.) This style of axiom does not threaten the basic requirement that it should be possible to decide mechanically whether a given list of propositions is a legitimate proof, because propositional logic is decidable (§14.2).

15.1.1 Derivations from Assumptions

We have seen how to use an axiomatic proof system to establish that a wff is a logical truth. How can one establish that an argument is valid? Given an argument $\alpha_1, \ldots, \alpha_n /\therefore \beta$, let the *corresponding conditional* be $(\alpha_1 \wedge \ldots \wedge \alpha_n) \rightarrow \beta$. One way to establish that an argument is valid is to establish that its corresponding conditional is a logical truth.[13] Another way is to allow *assumptions* in axiomatic systems. Where Γ is a set of wffs, we say that a *derivation from assumptions in Γ* in axiomatic system A is a sequence of wffs, each of which is (i) an axiom of A, (ii) a member of Γ, or (iii) follows from earlier

$$
\begin{array}{lll}
1. & P \to Q & A \\
2. & Q \to R & A \\
3. & (Q \to R) \to (P \to (Q \to R)) & \text{(A1)} \\
4. & P \to (Q \to R) & 2, 3 \ (\text{MP}) \\
5. & (P \to (Q \to R)) \to ((P \to Q) \to (P \to R)) & \text{(A2)} \\
6. & (P \to Q) \to (P \to R) & 4, 5 \ (\text{MP}) \\
7. & P \to R & 1, 6 \ (\text{MP})
\end{array}
$$

Figure 15.4. A derivation from assumptions in system A_1.

wffs in the sequence by a rule of A.[14] Figure 15.4 is an example of a derivation from assumptions in system A_1 ("A" is short for "assumption"). The assumptions here are $P \to Q$ and $Q \to R$. We now extend our $\vdash$ notation to allow $\vdash$ to be written between a list of wffs and a wff. (Previously $\vdash$ could only be written to the left of a wff.) Where we can derive β from assumptions $\alpha_1, \ldots, \alpha_n$ in system A, we write $\alpha_1, \ldots, \alpha_n \vdash_A \beta$.[15] A derivation from no assumptions is simply a proof in our old sense, so the original use of the $\vdash$ notation is now a special case of the new use. The derivation in Figure 15.4 establishes that $P \to Q, Q \to R \vdash_{A_1} P \to R$. We likewise extend our $\vDash$ notation: $\alpha_1, \ldots, \alpha_n \vDash \beta$ means that β is a logical consequence of $\alpha_1, \ldots, \alpha_n$; that is, there is no model in which $\alpha_1, \ldots, \alpha_n$ are all true and β is false. (So again, the old use is a special case of the new use: $\vDash \beta$ means that there is no model in which β is false.) Now we can say that a system A of axiomatic proof *with assumptions* is sound (with respect to validity) just in case: if $\alpha_1, \ldots, \alpha_n \vdash_A \beta$, then $\alpha_1, \ldots, \alpha_n \vDash \beta$. It is complete (with respect to validity) just in case: if $\alpha_1, \ldots, \alpha_n \vDash \beta$, then $\alpha_1, \ldots, \alpha_n \vdash_A \beta$.

In an axiomatic proof, every line is a logical truth (assuming the system is sound). In a derivation from assumptions, this is not the case. When we write in α as an assumption, we are not supposing that α is a logical truth; we are simply supposing, for the sake of argument, that α is true and then seeing what else follows. So the idea is that every line in the derivation must be true in a model $\mathfrak{M}$, given that all the assumptions are true in $\mathfrak{M}$. For a system to be sound, each of its axioms must therefore be a logical truth (axioms can appear in any derivation, no matter what the assumptions—even in derivations with no assumptions—and they must be true in every model in which all the assumptions are true; so, they must be true in every model),[16] and its rules must be truth-preserving. That is, the rules must be such that for any model $\mathfrak{M}$, if the inputs to the rule are true in $\mathfrak{M}$, then the output is true in $\mathfrak{M}$. This condition is subtly different from the requirement that rules be logicaltruth-preserving: the latter requirement says that if the inputs are true in every model, then the output must be too.[17] We can see, then, how deriving

β from assumptions $\alpha_1, \ldots, \alpha_n$ in a sound system shows that the argument $\alpha_1, \ldots, \alpha_n/\therefore \beta$ is valid: it establishes that in any model in which $\alpha_1, \ldots, \alpha_n$ are all true, β is true too.

We said that the primary notion of tree proofs is that of the satisfiability of a set of propositions, and that the primary notion of a system of axiomatic proof (i.e., without assumptions) is that of a proposition being a logical truth. In a system of axiomatic derivation (i.e., where assumptions are allowed), the prinicipal notion is that of the validity of an argument: the argument whose premises are the assumptions of our derivation and whose conclusion is the last line of the derivation.

15.1.1.1 THE DEDUCTION THEOREM

We have mentioned two strategies for establishing the validity of an argument: prove the corresponding conditional (i.e., derive it from no assumptions) or assume the premises and then derive the conclusion. Now in fact, deriving conditionals is often a rather lengthy process, which can be shortened significantly by assuming the antecedent and deriving the consequent. Recall our derivation of $P \to R$ in Figure 15.4. Had we instead assumed P and derived R, the derivation would have been simpler (Figure 15.5). Fine—but how does the derivation in Figure 15.5 help us establish the conditional $P \to R$? Well, it helps us if we are working in a system for which we can prove the *deduction theorem*:

If $\alpha_1, \ldots, \alpha_n, \beta \vdash \gamma$, then $\alpha_1, \ldots, \alpha_n \vdash \beta \to \gamma$

A_1 is such a system (see below). The deduction theorem says that if there is a derivation of one sort (of γ, from assumptions $\alpha_1, \ldots, \alpha_n$ and β), then there exists a derivation of another sort (of $\beta \to \gamma$, from assumptions $\alpha_1, \ldots, \alpha_n$). So given the deduction theorem for A_1 and our derivation in A_1 of R from assumptions $P \to Q$, $Q \to R$, and P (Figure 15.5), we know—even if we have no such derivation before us—that there is a derivation in A_1 of $P \to R$ from assumptions $P \to Q$ and $Q \to R$, and so we can conclude $P \to Q, Q \to R \vdash_{A_1} P \to R$.

1.	$P \to Q$	A
2.	$Q \to R$	A
3.	P	A
4.	Q	1, 3 (MP)
5.	R	2, 4 (MP)

Figure 15.5. A derivation from assumptions in system A_1.

How do we establish the deduction theorem for a system? The strategy is as follows. We assume that we have a derivation of γ from assumptions $\alpha_1, \ldots, \alpha_n$ and β, and we want to construct a derivation of $\beta \to \gamma$ from assumptions $\alpha_1, \ldots, \alpha_n$. What we do first is add "$\beta \to$" to the front of every wff in our derivation of γ; we call the result the "prefixed list." Note that the last line of the prefixed list is $\beta \to \gamma$. We now show that we can add steps to the prefixed list in such a way that it becomes a legitimate derivation from assumptions $\alpha_1, \ldots, \alpha_n$. We show this by induction on the length of the prefixed list. Here we illustrate for the case of A_1.

Base case. The first line of the prefixed list is $\beta \to \alpha$, for some α. Because this α is the first line of our original derivation in A_1 from assumptions $\alpha_1, \ldots, \alpha_n$ and β, there are only three possibilities. (i) The formula α is an axiom of A_1. In this case we insert the following lines in our prefixed list (above the line $\beta \to \alpha$):

1. α Axiom of A_1
2. $\alpha \to (\beta \to \alpha)$ (A1)

Now $\beta \to \alpha$ follows from these two lines by (MP), and so the first three lines of the prefixed list are now a legitimate derivation of $\beta \to \alpha$. (ii) The formula α is one of $\alpha_1, \ldots, \alpha_n$. This case is handled in the same way as the previous case. This time, α is not an axiom of A_1, but it is one of $\alpha_1, \ldots, \alpha_n$, so the result of expanding our prefixed list in the way indicated will be— as desired—a legitimate derivation of $\beta \to \alpha$ from assumptions $\alpha_1, \ldots, \alpha_n$. (iii) The formula α is β. In this case the first line of our prefixed list is $\beta \to \beta$. Now look at the first five lines of the proof in Figure 15.2: if we put in β in place of $\neg P$, we would have a legitimate proof of $\beta \to \beta$. We insert the first four lines of this proof of $\beta \to \beta$ in our prefixed list (above the line $\beta \to \beta$), and so the first five lines of the prefixed list are now a legitimate derivation of $\beta \to \beta$.

Induction. Suppose that lines 1 through n of the prefixed list have now had lines inserted before them, so as to render the result a legitimate derivation of line n.[18] We want to show that extra lines can now be inserted before line $n + 1$ to render the result a legitimate derivation of that line. Line $n + 1$ of the prefixed list is $\beta \to \alpha$, for some α. Because this α is line $n + 1$ of our original derivation in A_1 from assumptions $\alpha_1, \ldots, \alpha_n$ and β, there are four possibilities regarding it. Three of them—that α is an axiom of A_1, that α is one of $\alpha_1, \ldots, \alpha_n$, and that α is β—are handled in the same way as in the base case. The fourth option is that α follows from earlier steps δ and $\delta \to \alpha$ in the original derivation by (MP). In this case the prefixed list—and hence our derivation of line n (which we assume to exist, by the inductive hypothesis)—must contain $\beta \rightarrow \delta$ and $\beta \rightarrow (\delta \rightarrow \alpha)$. Then we need only insert the following lines above line $n + 1$:

$(\beta \rightarrow (\delta \rightarrow \alpha)) \rightarrow ((\beta \rightarrow \delta) \rightarrow (\beta \rightarrow \alpha))$ (A2)
$(\beta \rightarrow \delta) \rightarrow (\beta \rightarrow \alpha)$ (MP)

Now line $n + 1$—that is, $\beta \rightarrow \alpha$—follows by (MP).

Note that the deduction theorem does not hold in every axiomatic system: whether the above sort of proof can be carried through successfully depends on the particular axioms and rules of the system. We have seen that the deduction theorem holds in A_1. It also holds in A_2 by virtually identical reasoning. In $A_1^{\forall=}$, however, it holds in a restricted form: if there is a derivation of γ from assumptions $\alpha_1, \ldots, \alpha_n$ and β in which there is no application of (Gen) using a variable that is free in β, then there is a derivation of $\beta \rightarrow \gamma$ from assumptions $\alpha_1, \ldots, \alpha_n$.[19]

15.1.2 Formal and Informal Proofs

By a *formal proof* in a given axiomatic system we shall mean an axiomatic proof or derivation as defined above: a sequence of wffs, each of which is (i) an axiom, (ii) the output of one of the rules of inference when supplied as input some wffs appearing earlier in the sequence, or (iii) (in the case of derivations only) a member of the given set of assumptions. When working with axiomatic systems, it is often convenient to show that a formal proof can be given, without actually giving it. By an *informal proof* we shall mean a piece of reasoning that is not itself a formal proof but establishes that a formal proof exists.[20]

Let's consider some examples. Taken as a whole, the reasoning in Figure 15.6 is not a formal proof. Lines 1–5 on their own constitute a formal proof in system A_1, but then lines 6 and 7 have a different status. These lines contain the symbol $\vdash$, which is not a symbol of the logical language and hence never appears inside a formal proof.[21] Rather, $\vdash$ is a symbol we use when talking about a system of axiomatic proof. If we have a formal proof with last line P in, for example, system A_1, then we can conclude "P is provable in system A_1," and we abbreviate this claim as $\vdash_{A_1} P$. Thus, in the informal proof in Figure 15.6, we work within the axiomatic proof system until line 5, and then we step outside it in steps 6 and 7 and make claims about what is provable in the system. Step 6 is justified by the existence of the formal proof comprising steps 1–5. Step 7 then follows from step 6 and the deduction theorem (abbreviated as DT in the proof).

Figure 15.7 shows a second example of an informal proof. Note line 6. The first five lines of the proof in Figure 15.2 constitute a formal proof of

$$
\begin{array}{lll}
1. & P \to Q & \text{A} \\
2. & Q \to R & \text{A} \\
3. & P & \text{A} \\
4. & Q & 1,3\ (\text{MP}) \\
5. & R & 2,4\ (\text{MP}) \\
6. & P \to Q, Q \to R, P \vdash R & 1\text{--}5 \\
7. & P \to Q, Q \to R \vdash P \to R & 6, \text{DT}
\end{array}
$$

Figure 15.6. An informal proof in system A_1.

$$
\begin{array}{lll}
1. & \neg\neg P & \text{A} \\
2. & \neg\neg P \to (\neg P \to \neg\neg P) & (\text{A1}) \\
3. & (\neg P \to \neg\neg P) \to ((\neg P \to \neg P) \to P) & (\text{A3}) \\
4. & \neg P \to \neg\neg P & 1,2\ (\text{MP}) \\
5. & (\neg P \to \neg P) \to P & 3,4\ (\text{MP}) \\
6. & \neg P \to \neg P & \text{lines 1--5 of proof in Figure 15.2} \\
7. & P & 5,6\ (\text{MP})
\end{array}
$$

Figure 15.7. An informal proof in system A_1.

$$
\begin{array}{lll}
1. & P \to Q & \text{A} \\
2. & \neg\neg P & \text{A} \\
3. & \neg\neg P \to P & \text{proof in Figure 15.7, DT} \\
4. & P & 2,3\ (\text{MP}) \\
5. & Q & 1,4\ (\text{MP}) \\
6. & P \to Q, \neg\neg P \vdash Q & 1\text{--}5 \\
7. & P \to Q \vdash \neg\neg P \to Q & 6, \text{DT}
\end{array}
$$

Figure 15.8. An informal proof in system A_1.

$\neg P \to \neg P$. As we now know such a proof exists, we can enter $\neg P \to \neg P$ in our informal proof in Figure 15.7. If we want to transform this informal proof into a formal proof, we need to insert all five lines of the proof of $\neg P \to \neg P$, not just the final line.

Figure 15.8 shows a third example of an informal proof. Note line 3. The proof in Figure 15.7 begins with the assumption $\neg\neg P$ and ends with P. It therefore establishes that $\neg\neg P \vdash P$. From this and the deduction theorem, it follows that $\vdash \neg\neg P \to P$. So in the proof in Figure 15.8, we can write in $\neg\neg P \to P$ at line 3. To make the informal proof in Figure 15.8 into a formal proof, we should need to insert all the lines of the proof of $\neg\neg P \to P$, not just the final line. We do not know what these lines are, but we do know that they exist, and when producing an informal proof, that suffices.

$$
\begin{array}{lll}
1. & Q & A \\
2. & Q \rightarrow (P \rightarrow Q) & \text{(A1)} \\
3. & P \rightarrow Q & 1, 2 \text{ (MP)} \\
4. & \neg\neg P \rightarrow Q & \text{3, line 7 of proof in Figure 15.8} \\
5. & Q \rightarrow (\neg\neg P \rightarrow Q) & 1\text{--}4, \text{DT}
\end{array}
$$

Figure 15.9. An informal proof in system A_1.

Figure 15.9 shows a final example of an informal proof. Note line 4. From line 7 of the proof in Figure 15.8, we know that we can derive $\neg\neg P \rightarrow Q$ from $P \rightarrow Q$. But in the proof in Figure 15.9, we already have $P \rightarrow Q$ at line 3. So at line 4 we may enter $\neg\neg P \rightarrow Q$. To fill out the informal proof in Figure 15.9 and make it a formal proof, we need to insert all lines of the derivation of $\neg\neg P \rightarrow Q$ from $P \rightarrow Q$, not just the final line. Once again, we do not know what these lines are, but we do know that they exist, and when we are producing an informal proof, that is sufficient.

As the foregoing examples illustrate, informal proofs may differ from formal proofs in one or both of two ways. First, they may omit some steps. That is, every line of the informal proof is the sort of thing that could appear as a line in a formal proof, but there are not enough of these lines to make up a (complete) formal proof. Second, informal proofs may contain lines including symbols such as $\vdash$, which never appear inside formal proofs. Such symbols are used only when we are talking about what can be proved in a given system—not when producing formal proofs in that system.

15.1.3 Soundness and Open Wffs

The way to show that an axiomatic proof/derivation system is sound is to show that its axioms are logical truths and its rules are logicaltruth-/truth-preserving. That's all very well for the systems for propositional logic, but we cannot possibly show this for $A_1^\forall$, because in that system, we can prove wffs with free variables. For example, $\forall x P x \rightarrow P y$ is an instance of (A4), and hence has a one-line proof. Yet our semantics assigns truth values only to closed wffs—those with no free variables. So our axiomatic system allows us to prove something that our semantic framework does not recognize as true or false in any model, and hence certainly does not recognize as a logical truth (i.e., true in every model). This problem never arose with tree proofs, because only closed wffs appear in trees. There are axiomatic systems that likewise allow only closed wffs to appear in derivations, for example, the system of Quine [1951] mentioned in §15.1. However, there are also ways of making sense of systems, such as $A_1^\forall$, that allow derivations of open wffs. As already stated, we know that such a system cannot be sound, as we defined soundness above:

If $\alpha_1, \ldots, \alpha_n \vdash_A \beta$, then $\alpha_1, \ldots, \alpha_n \vDash \beta$

because given that the system allows us to prove an open wff, it could be sound only if that open wff were true on all models—and open wffs are never true. So what we must do is replace the requirement of soundness with some other notion that serves as well. We shall discuss two options here: *closure-soundness* and *sowndness*.

§

First we discuss closure-soundness. The *universal closure* (or just "closure" for short) $[\![\alpha]\!]$ of a wff α is the result of prefixing α with one universal quantifier $\forall \underline{x}$ for each variable $\underline{x}$ that has a free occurrence in α. So if α is closed—contains no free variables—its universal closure $[\![\alpha]\!]$ is simply α itself (no free variables, so no quantifiers prefixed). If α contains free occurrences of x and y (and of no other variables), then its universal closure is $\forall x \forall y \alpha$, and so on.[22] Note that whether α is open or closed, $[\![\alpha]\!]$ is always closed.

Now we say that system A is *closure-sound* just in case:

If $\alpha_1, \ldots, \alpha_n \vdash_A \beta$, then $[\![\alpha_1]\!], \ldots, [\![\alpha_n]\!] \vDash [\![\beta]\!]$

The basic idea is this. We allow open wffs in derivations, for the sake of convenience, but we know that open wffs cannot be true. So when interpreting a derivation—extracting information from it about what wffs are logical truths, which arguments are valid, and so on—we regard any open wff in the derivation as standing proxy for its universal closure. So if we have a proof of an open wff α, we regard this proof as telling us not that α is a logical truth, but that its universal closure $[\![\alpha]\!]$ is a logical truth; when we write an open wff in a derivation as an assumption, we are assuming that its closure is true (in some model), and so on. Now to show that an axiomatic system is closure-sound, we need to show (i) that the closure of each axiom is a logical truth and (ii) that for each rule, if the closures of all inputs are true, then the closure of the output is true.

§

We turn now to the second option: sowndness. Sowndness is defined in terms of a new notion, *trewth*, which is itself defined in terms of another notion, *satisfaction*.[23] The notion of satisfaction applies to open and closed wffs alike. Where a closed wff is true or false relative to one thing—a model—a wff is satisfied or unsatisfied relative to two things: a model and a value assignment on that model. A value assignment $\mathfrak{v}$ on a model $\mathfrak{M}$ is just like an assignment of referents to names, except that it assigns values to variables: each variable is assigned as value a particular object in the domain of the model. We use $\mathfrak{M}^{\mathfrak{v}}$ to denote a model $\mathfrak{M}$ together with a value assignment $\mathfrak{v}$ on $\mathfrak{M}$.

Recall that a term is a name or variable. Where $\underline{t}$ is a term, $\mathfrak{M}$ is a model, and $\mathfrak{v}$ is a value assignment on $\mathfrak{M}$, let $[\underline{t}]_{\mathfrak{M}^{\mathfrak{v}}}$ be the referent of $\underline{t}$ in $\mathfrak{M}$ (in case $\underline{t}$ is a name) or the value assigned to $\underline{t}$ by $\mathfrak{v}$ (in case $\underline{t}$ is a variable).

The notion of satisfaction relative to a model and a value assignment on that model is now defined as follows; like the definition of truth in a model in §12.2.1.2, the definition has one clause for each type of wff in the language:

1. $\underline{P^n t_1} \ldots t_n$ is satisfied relative to $\mathfrak{M}^{\mathfrak{v}}$ iff the ordered n-tuple $\langle [\underline{t_1}]_{\mathfrak{M}^{\mathfrak{v}}}, \ldots, [\underline{t_n}]_{\mathfrak{M}^{\mathfrak{v}}} \rangle$ is in the extension in $\mathfrak{M}$ of $\underline{P^n}$.

2. $\neg \alpha$ is satisfied relative to $\mathfrak{M}^{\mathfrak{v}}$ iff α is unsatisfied relative to $\mathfrak{M}^{\mathfrak{v}}$.[24]

3. $(\alpha \wedge \beta)$ is satisfied relative to $\mathfrak{M}^{\mathfrak{v}}$ iff α and β are both satisfied relative to $\mathfrak{M}^{\mathfrak{v}}$.

4. $(\alpha \vee \beta)$ is satisfied relative to $\mathfrak{M}^{\mathfrak{v}}$ iff one or both of α and β is satisfied relative to $\mathfrak{M}^{\mathfrak{v}}$.

5. $(\alpha \to \beta)$ is satisfied relative to $\mathfrak{M}^{\mathfrak{v}}$ iff α is unsatisfied relative to $\mathfrak{M}^{\mathfrak{v}}$ or β is satisfied relative to $\mathfrak{M}^{\mathfrak{v}}$ (or both).

6. $(\alpha \leftrightarrow \beta)$ is satisfied relative to $\mathfrak{M}^{\mathfrak{v}}$ iff α and β are both satisfied, or are both unsatisfied, relative to $\mathfrak{M}^{\mathfrak{v}}$.

7. $\forall \underline{x} \alpha$ is satisfied relative to $\mathfrak{M}^{\mathfrak{v}}$ iff α is satisfied relative to $\mathfrak{M}^{\mathfrak{v}'}$ for every value assignment $\mathfrak{v}'$ on $\mathfrak{M}$ that differs from $\mathfrak{v}$ at most in what it assigns to $\underline{x}$.

8. $\exists \underline{x} \alpha$ is satisfied relative to $\mathfrak{M}^{\mathfrak{v}}$ iff α is satisfied relative to $\mathfrak{M}^{\mathfrak{v}'}$ for some value assignment $\mathfrak{v}'$ on $\mathfrak{M}$ that differs from $\mathfrak{v}$ at most in what it assigns to $\underline{x}$.

We now define trewth as follows. We say that a wff is *trew* in a model if it is satisfied relative to (that model and) every value assignment on that model. It is *fawlse* in a model if it is unsatisfied relative to (that model and) every value assignment on that model. Note that whereas a wff is satisfied or unsatisfied relative to two things—a model and a value assignment on that model—a wff is trew or fawlse relative to one thing—a model. So trewth is just like truth in this respect, even though the former, but not the latter, is defined via the notion of satisfaction.

If a wff α has no free variables, then what particular values $\mathfrak{v}$ assigns is irrelevant to whether α is satisfied relative to $\mathfrak{M}^{\mathfrak{v}}$: what $\mathfrak{M}$ assigns is all that matters. We can see this by considering each clause in turn. Consider clause (1). For atomic wffs, if $\underline{P^n t_1} \ldots t_n$ is closed—that is, $t_1, \ldots, t_n$ are all names—then what it takes for $\underline{P^n t_1} \ldots t_n$ to be satisfied relative to $\mathfrak{M}^\mathfrak{v}$ is exactly what it takes for $\underline{P^n t_1} \ldots t_n$ to be true relative to $\mathfrak{M}$: the ordered n-tuple consisting of the referents in $\mathfrak{M}$ of t_1 through t_n must be in the extension in $\mathfrak{M}$ of $\underline{P^n}$. Clauses (2)–(6) can be considered together. If the particular values $\mathfrak{v}$ assigns are irrelevant to whether α is satisfied relative to $\mathfrak{M}^\mathfrak{v}$, then it is clear from clause (2) that they are irrelevant to whether $\neg\alpha$ is satisfied relative to $\mathfrak{M}^\mathfrak{v}$; similarly for clauses (3)–(6). Now consider clause (7). If $\forall x \alpha$ is closed—that is, α can be represented as $\alpha(\underline{x})$—then what it takes for $\forall x \alpha$ to be satisfied relative to $\mathfrak{M}^\mathfrak{v}$ is exactly what it takes for $\forall \underline{x} \alpha(\underline{x})$ to be true relative to $\mathfrak{M}$: α will be satisfied relative to $\mathfrak{M}^{\mathfrak{v}'}$ for every value assignment $\mathfrak{v}'$ on $\mathfrak{M}$ that differs from $\mathfrak{v}$ at most in what it assigns to $\underline{x}$ just in case for every object o in the domain of $\mathfrak{M}$, $\alpha(\underline{a}/\underline{x})$ is true in $\mathfrak{M}_o^a$. Similar comments apply to clause (8).

Thus, a quick way (for someone who already understands the notion of truth) to conceptualize a closed wff being satisfied relative to $\mathfrak{M}^\mathfrak{v}$ is that the wff is true relative to $\mathfrak{M}$. Furthermore, a closed wff will be (un)satisfied relative to one value assignment on a model just in case it is (un)satisfied relative to all value assignments on that model. Hence, a closed wff is trew in a model just in case it is true in that model: trewth and truth are coextensive among closed wffs.

Some additional notation is useful here. We use $\alpha(\underline{x}, \underline{y}, \ldots)$ to indicate a wff that does have free occurrences of $\underline{x}, \underline{y}, \ldots$ and does not have free occurrences of any other variable. We use $\alpha(\underline{a}/\underline{x}, \underline{b}/\underline{y}, \ldots)$ to indicate the wff that results from $\alpha(\underline{x}, \underline{y}, \ldots)$ by replacing each free occurrence of $\underline{x}$ by $\underline{a}$, each free occurrence of $\underline{y}$ by $\underline{b}$, and so on. Now, a quick way to conceptualize an open wff $\alpha(\underline{x}, \underline{y}, \ldots)$ being satisfied relative to $\mathfrak{M}^\mathfrak{v}$ is that, where $\underline{a}, \underline{b}, \ldots$ are names not assigned referents in $\mathfrak{M}$, $\alpha(\underline{a}/\underline{x}, \underline{b}/\underline{y}, \ldots)$ is true relative to the model $\mathfrak{M}'$ just like $\mathfrak{M}$ except that it assigns as referent to $\underline{a}$ what $\mathfrak{v}$ assigns as value to $\underline{x}$, as referent to $\underline{b}$ what $\mathfrak{v}$ assigns as value to $\underline{y}$, and so on. In other words, think of free variables as names, and of a model plus value assignment as an extended model that assigns those names referents; satisfaction is then simply truth relative to the extended model.

§

So much for the definitions of satisfaction and trewth. We come now to the key point: an open wff can be trew on a model. Consider the wff Px and the following model:

Domain: {Bill, Ben, Alice, Mary}
Extension of P: {Bill, Ben}

Relative to a value assignment on this model that assigns Bill as the value of x, Px is satisfied; relative to an assignment that assigns Alice as the value of x, Px is unsatisfied. So Px is neither trew (satisfied relative to all assignments) nor fawlse (unsatisfied relative to all assignments) in this model. But consider the wff $\forall x\, Px \rightarrow Py$. The antecedent is false in this model; hence, by what we said above, the antecedent is unsatisfied relative to every value assignment on this model, and so the whole conditional is satisfied relative to every value assignment un this model. Hence, the conditional—an open wff—is trew in this model.

Indeed, it is trew in every model. What we just said goes for any model in which the antecedent is false. For a model in which the antecedent is true— that is, in which everything in the domain is in the extension of P—the consequent Py is satisfied no matter what object is assigned as the value of y, and so the whole conditional is satisfied relative to every value assignment. Hence, $\forall x\, Px \rightarrow Py$ is a logical trewth (trew on every model).

Other analogues of our key semantic notions can likewise be defined in terms of trewth and fawlsity: just as logical trewth is trewth in every model, so a conclusion is a *logical conseqwence* of some premises just in case there is no model in which the premises are trew and the conclusion fawlse, and so on.

Now return to the problem of what property to require in a system that allows us to derive open wffs, given that we cannot require that it be sound. We require that it be *sownd*, where a system A is sownd just in case:

If $\alpha_1, \ldots, \alpha_n \vdash_A \beta$, then β is a logical conseqwence of $\alpha_1, \ldots, \alpha_n$

To show that an axiomatic system is sownd, we need to show that its axioms are all logical trewths and its rules are all trewth-preserving.

Note that the second approach to the problem of finding a suitable substitute for soundness for systems that allow derivations of open wffs ultimately comes to the same thing as the first approach. For an open wff $\alpha(\underline{x})$ is trew in a model just in case it is satisfied by every value assignment on that model. That is, in terms of our intuitive gloss, just in case, treating $\underline{x}$ as a name, $\alpha(\underline{x})$ is true in every extension of the model that assigns a referent to $\underline{x}$. But that, as we have also seen, is precisely what it takes for the closure of $\alpha(\underline{x})$ to be true in the model in question.[25]

15.1.4 Completeness

We have indicated strategies for showing that an axiomatic system is sound/ closure-sound/sownd. We now indicate a strategy for showing that an axiomatic system is complete. We want to show that if β is a logical consequence of $\alpha_1, \ldots, \alpha_n$, then β is derivable from assumptions $\alpha_1, \ldots, \alpha_n$. In proving completeness for trees—if β is a logical consequence of $\alpha_1, \ldots, \alpha_n$, then a finished tree beginning with $\alpha_1, \ldots, \alpha_n$ and $\neg\beta$ closes—we showed the contrapositive: if a finished tree remains open, then β is not a logical consequence of $\alpha_1, \ldots, \alpha_n$. Here too, we aim to establish the contrapositive: if β is not derivable from assumptions $\alpha_1, \ldots, \alpha_n$, then β is not a logical consequence of $\alpha_1, \ldots, \alpha_n$.[26]

Now think about what happens when we try to show using trees that $\alpha_1, \ldots, \alpha_n / \therefore \beta$ is valid, when in fact it is not valid. The attempt leaves us with something valuable: a saturated open path. It is valuable because we can read off from it a model in which the premises are true and the conclusion false—and this model plays a key role in the completeness proof (§14.1.3). In the case of an axiomatic system, however, when we try to derive β from assumptions $\alpha_1, \ldots, \alpha_n$ when in fact β is not a logical consequence of $\alpha_1, \ldots, \alpha_n$, we are left with nothing. We simply fail to find a derivation, and that's it: we get nothing useful, such as a saturated open path, for our efforts. So in proving completeness for an axiomatic system, first we play catch-up, to get us to the stage of having something (call it X for now) that will play the role of a saturated open path. From there we proceed as in the case of trees: we construct a model from X and then show that in this model, $\alpha_1, \ldots, \alpha_n$ are true and β is false.

Different completeness proofs for different systems will construct different Xs (e.g., maximal consistent sets of wffs), but we can illustrate the point in a way that will make it easier to understand—easier, that is, for those who have already seen the completeness proof for trees—by supposing that the X we construct is a *saturated consistent set* of wffs containing $\alpha_1, \ldots, \alpha_n$ and $\neg\beta$. We explain the notions of a *consistent* set and a *saturated* set in turn. A saturated consistent set is then simply one that is saturated and consistent.

A set Γ of wffs is consistent relative to axiomatic system A—or A-consistent—if there is no wff α such that one can both derive α in system A from assumptions in Γ and derive $\neg\alpha$ in system A from assumptions in Γ. When it is obvious from context which proof system A is meant, we may just refer to consistent sets (instead of A-consistent sets).

To explain the notion of a saturated set, we first introduce the notion of an *uncrossed tree*. An uncrossed tree is simply a tree in which we never close any paths: we just keep on applying rules until all paths are saturated, without ever checking for closure. So in an uncrossed tree, a path might have α in it, and then later $\neg\alpha$ is added, but we do not close the path and stop applying rules: we keep right on going. Now, a set Γ of wffs is *saturated* if there is a saturated path in an uncrossed tree such that Γ contains all and only wffs appearing on that path. For example, consider a tree beginning with $(A \lor B) \land \neg(A \lor B)$. If we check for closure, we add $(A \lor B)$ and $\neg(A \lor B)$ and then close the path:

$$(A \lor B) \land \neg(A \lor B) \checkmark$$
$$(A \lor B)$$
$$\neg(A \lor B)$$
$$\times$$

However, the set $\{(A \lor B) \land \neg(A \lor B), (A \lor B), \neg(A \lor B)\}$ is not saturated. Rather, we need to suppose that we go on applying rules as long as we can, forgetting about closing paths. So we add $\neg A$ and $\neg B$ and then add a branch with A on one side and B on the other:

$$(A \lor B) \land \neg(A \lor B) \checkmark$$
$$(A \lor B) \checkmark$$
$$\neg(A \lor B) \checkmark$$
$$\neg A$$
$$\neg B$$

$$A \qquad B$$

Now there are no more rules that can be applied. We have two saturated paths, giving two saturated sets: $\{(A \lor B) \land \neg(A \lor B), (A \lor B), \neg(A \lor B), \neg A, \neg B, A\}$ and $\{(A \lor B) \land \neg(A \lor B), (A \lor B), \neg(A \lor B), \neg A, \neg B, B\}$. So if a saturated set contains $(\alpha \lor \beta)$, then it also contains α or β; if it contains $\forall \underline{x} \alpha(\underline{x})$, then it also contains $\alpha(\underline{a}/\underline{x})$ for every name $\underline{a}$ that occurs in any wff in the set, and so on.

$$\S$$

Our strategy for proving completeness is now to show the following (where $\alpha_1, \ldots, \alpha_n \nvdash_A \beta$ means that there is no derivation in system A of β from assumptions $\alpha_1, \ldots, \alpha_n$):

(A) If $\alpha_1, \ldots, \alpha_n \nvdash_A \beta$, then there is a saturated A-consistent set of wffs containing $\alpha_1, \ldots, \alpha_n$ and $\neg \beta$.

This is the catch-up step; from here, we just link in with the completeness proof for trees. For note that if a set Γ is A-consistent, then it cannot contain both α and $\neg\alpha$, for any wff α. (If it did, then there would be one-line derivations of α and of $\neg\alpha$ from assumptions in Γ.)[27] But then our saturated consistent set of wffs is just like a saturated open path, and we know how to read off a model from such a path (set). In addition, we know (from the completeness proof for trees) how to prove that every wff on the path (in the set) is true in that model. Hence, in particular, $\alpha_1, \ldots, \alpha_n$ and $\neg\beta$ are true in the model; hence, $\alpha_1, \ldots, \alpha_n$ are true, and β is false. And that is exactly what we need to show to establish completeness: if $\alpha_1, \ldots, \alpha_n \nvdash_A \beta$, then there is a model in which $\alpha_1, \ldots, \alpha_n$ are true, and β is false.

It only remains, then, to establish (A). We need to show that there is a set with three properties: (i) it contains $\alpha_1, \ldots, \alpha_n$ and $\neg\beta$, (ii) it is saturated, and (iii) it is A-consistent. Suppose we write $\alpha_1, \ldots, \alpha_n$ and $\neg\beta$ at the top of a tree and then apply rules—without crossing any paths—until every path in the tree is saturated (there may be some infinite paths). (For the remainder of this section, "tree" means "uncrossed tree.") As every path in this tree is saturated and contains $\alpha_1, \ldots, \alpha_n$ and $\neg\beta$, properties (i) and (ii) will hold if we take as our set the wffs on some path in the tree. That just leaves property (iii) to consider. What we need to show is:

(B)   If $\alpha_1, \ldots, \alpha_n \nvdash_A \beta$, then any tree starting with $\alpha_1, \ldots, \alpha_n$ and $\neg\beta$ has at least one A-consistent path.

(For brevity, we say that a *path* is A-consistent when the set of all wffs on the path is A-consistent.) Establishing (B) completes the proof of (A): if there is an A-consistent path through our tree, then there is a saturated A-consistent set of wffs containing $\alpha_1, \ldots, \alpha_n$ and $\neg\beta$ (i.e., the set of wffs on this path).

We establish (B) by proving three claims:

(i) The initial tree (i.e., at stage 0—recall §14.1.2), which contains just $\alpha_1, \ldots, \alpha_n$ and $\neg\beta$, has only one path, which is A-consistent. For suppose otherwise: suppose there is some α such that $\alpha_1, \ldots, \alpha_n, \neg\beta \vdash_A \alpha$ and $\alpha_1, \ldots, \alpha_n, \neg\beta \vdash_A \neg\alpha$. We now show how to turn these derivations into a derivation of β from assumptions $\alpha_1, \ldots, \alpha_n$.[28]

(ii) The tree rules all preserve A-consistency. More precisely, suppose we are applying some rule at the bottom of a path p. Our nonbranching rules, which will extend p to p′, all have this property:

If p is A-consistent, then p′ is A-consistent

and our branching rules, which will create two paths q and r, all have this property:

If p is A-consistent, then either q is A-consistent, or r is A-consistent, or both

We establish these properties by considering each tree rule in turn. For example, take the rule for unnegated conjunction. We want to show that if $\Gamma, \alpha \wedge \beta, \alpha, \beta \vdash_A \gamma$ and $\Gamma, \alpha \wedge \beta, \alpha, \beta \vdash_A \neg\gamma$, then $\Gamma, \alpha \wedge \beta \vdash_A \gamma$ and $\Gamma, \alpha \wedge \beta \vdash_A \neg\gamma$. This will be easy to show, as long as $\alpha \wedge \beta \vdash_A \alpha$ and $\alpha \wedge \beta \vdash_A \beta$.

It follows from (i) and (ii) that at every stage n of its construction, any tree starting with $\alpha_1, \ldots, \alpha_n$ and $\neg\beta$ has at least one A-consistent path. To complete the proof of (B)—which applies to any tree, not just any finite tree—we need to show:

(iii) If every stage n in the construction of an infinite path is A-consistent, then the infinite path itself is A-consistent (i.e., A-consistency cannot vanish only at infinity).[29] So suppose we have an infinite path that is not A-consistent. Then we have derivations of α and $\neg\alpha$ from assumptions in this path. But every derivation is a finite list of wffs, involving at most finitely many assumptions. So there must be a stage n in the construction of our infinite path at which all the assumptions in both derivations have appeared in the path; but then at this stage n, the path is not A-consistent.

§

We conclude our discussion of axiomatic systems by mentioning some of their main advantages and disadvantages. The principal disadvantages of axiomatic systems are as follows. Formal proofs and derivations can be very long; they can also be very difficult to find (unlike the tree method, axiomatic systems do not come with a built-in effective procedure for finding proofs; recall §14.3.4). In addition, when an argument is not valid, the attempt to prove that it is valid yields nothing, as opposed to something useful, such as an open path (unlike trees, axiomatic systems provide no proofs of invalidity or other s-properties; recall §14.3.2). So if our concern is to find out whether a certain proposition is a logical truth, or whether a certain argument is valid, an axiomatic system will not in general be the best choice of proof method.

Axiomatic systems are, however, well suited to certain metalogical projects. Derivations have an especially simple structure: they are finite sequences of wffs. Sound and complete axiomatic systems, then, give us a particularly tractable handle on the relation of logical consequence.

Axiomatic systems are also the standard format for the presentation of axiomatic theories (compare §11.3). An axiomatic theory may be obtained from an axiomatic logical system simply by adding some extra nonlogical axioms— statements that, intuitively, characterize the subject matter of the theory in question. When thinking in this way, it is also common to start with a logical language that contains only logical vocabulary (i.e., its signature is the empty set) and then regard a theory as bringing with it not only its own nonlogical axioms but also any nonlogical vocabulary featured in them. For example, the theory of *linear orders* has the following nonlogical axioms (and one nonlogical predicate, R):[30]

$\forall x\, Rxx$	reflexivity
$\forall x \forall y \forall z((Rxy \wedge Ryz) \rightarrow Rxz)$	transitivity
$\forall x \forall y ((Rxy \wedge Ryx) \rightarrow x = y)$	antisymmetry
$\forall x \forall y (Rxy \vee Ryx)$	connectedness

They characterize the subject matter of the theory (linear orders) in the sense that if we ask "what is a linear order?," the answer is "any model that makes true all the axioms." So, for example, the set of natural numbers ordered in the usual way is a linear order (all the axioms are true in a model with a domain consisting of the set of natural numbers and $\langle x, y \rangle$ in the extension of R just in case $x \le y$), and the set of towns on the Hume Highway ordered by distance from Melbourne is a linear order (all the axioms are true in a model with a domain consisting of the set of towns on the Hume Highway and $\langle x, y \rangle$ in the extension of R just in case x is at least as close as y to Melbourne). In just the way that axiomatic logical systems give us a tractable handle on the logical consequence relation, axiomatizing a theory—encapsulating it in some nonlogical axioms, which are added to a base axiomatic proof system for pure logic—gives us a tractable handle on the class of models in which the theory is true.

15.1.5 Exercises

1. Show the following in A_1 by producing formal proofs.
   (i) $\neg P \to Q, \neg P \vdash Q$
   (ii) $P \vdash \neg Q \to P$
   (iii) $\neg Q \vdash (\neg P \to Q) \to P$
   (iv) $\vdash P \to P$
   (v) $\neg(P \to \neg Q) \vdash Q$
   (vi) $P, \neg P \vdash Q$
   (vii) $P \wedge Q \vdash (P \to \neg Q) \to \neg(P \to \neg Q)$

2. Show the following in A_1 by producing formal or informal proofs.
   (i) $\vdash \neg(P \to \neg Q) \to Q$
   (ii) $\vdash P \to (P \vee Q)$
   (iii) $\vdash ((P \to Q) \to (P \to R)) \to (P \to (Q \to R))$
   (iv) $\vdash (P \to Q) \to (\neg Q \to \neg P)$
   (v) $P \to Q, P \to \neg Q \vdash \neg P$
   (vi) $P \to Q, \neg Q \to P \vdash Q$
   (vii) $\vdash (P \to (Q \to R)) \to (Q \to (P \to R))$

3. Show the following in A_2 by producing formal or informal proofs.
   (i) $\vdash P \to \neg\neg P$
   (ii) $P \to \neg P \vdash \neg P$
   (iii) $P \to Q \vdash \neg Q \to \neg P$
   (iv) $\vdash \neg Q \to (Q \to P)$
   (v) $P \wedge Q \vdash P \to Q$
   (vi) $\neg Q \vdash (P \vee Q) \to P$
   (vii) $\neg P \wedge \neg Q \vdash \neg(P \vee Q)$
   (viii) $\neg(P \vee Q) \vdash \neg P \wedge \neg Q$
   (ix) $\vdash \neg(P \wedge \neg P)$
   (x) $\vdash (P \wedge \neg P) \to Q$
   (xi) $\vdash P \leftrightarrow P$
   (xii) $\vdash P \to (\neg P \to Q)$

4. Show the following in $A_1^{\forall =}$ by producing formal or informal proofs.
   (i) $\forall x(Fx \to Gx), Fa \vdash Ga$

(ii) $\forall x F x \vdash \forall x (Gx \lor Fx)$

(iii) $\forall x \forall y (Rxy \to Ryx), Rab \vdash Rba$

(iv) $\exists x F x \to \neg Ga \vdash Ga \to \forall x \neg F x$

(v) $\vdash Fa \to \exists x F x$

(vi) $Fa, a = b \vdash Fb$

(vii) $\forall x \forall y x = y \vdash a = b$

(viii) $a = b, a = c \vdash c = b$

(ix) $\vdash a = b \to b = a$

(x) $Fa, \neg Fb \vdash \neg a = b$

(xi) $\neg b = a, \forall x (\neg F x \to x = a) \vdash Fb$

(xii) $\vdash \forall x F x \to \forall y F y$

5. Explain why the original unrestricted deduction theorem does not hold in $A_1^{\forall=}$ and why the restricted version stated at the end of §15.1.1.1 does hold.

15.2 Natural Deduction

Natural deduction systems are superficially similar to axiomatic systems that allow derivations from assumptions, but there are fundamental differences between the two kinds of proof system. The most crucial difference is that although both kinds of system allow assumptions to feature in derivations, only in natural deduction systems may assumptions be *discharged*. To see what this means, consider the deduction theorem in an axiomatic system (e.g., system A_1). Consider the derivation in Figure 15.5, which establishes $P \to Q, Q \to R, P \vdash_{A_1} R$. The deduction theorem allows us to conclude $P \to Q, Q \to R \vdash_{A_1} P \to R$. That is, it allows us to conclude that there is a derivation in A_1 of $P \to R$ (from assumptions $P \to Q$ and $Q \to R$), but it does not give us such a derivation. This is crucially important: the deduction theorem does not allow us to write in $P \to R$ as the next line at the end of the derivation in Figure 15.5; it just tells us that there is a derivation with last line $P \to R$.[31] The deduction theorem does not indicate what such a derivation looks like (although the proof of the deduction theorem does this)—it just establishes that such a derivation exists in the abstract.

Now a thought along the following lines might occur to you. A perfectly good way of showing that the conditional $P \to R$ is true (given assumptions $P \to Q$ and $Q \to R$) is precisely to assume P (as well as $P \to Q$ and $Q \to R$) and then derive R. That is precisely how we establish the truth of conditionals in ordinary reasoning: we assume the antecedent and then derive the consequent. (There are many examples of this procedure in this book. For example, in the completeness proof in §14.1.3, we want to establish the conditional "if there is an open path in a finished tree that begins with $\alpha_1, \ldots, \alpha_n$, then there is a model in which $\alpha_1, \ldots, \alpha_n$ are all true." So we assume that the antecedent is true, and then show, given this assumption, that the consequent is true.) So a formal system of proof that reflects our ordinary reasoning practice—a *natural* deduction system—would allow us to do precisely what the deduction theorem does not allow: to write in the conditional $P \rightarrow R$ as the next line in our derivation, after deriving R from the assumption P. The idea is that the way we establish a conditional is precisely by deriving its consequent from its antecedent. Once that is done, we actually have established the conditional in that derivation. So we can write in the conditional as the next line in that derivation, rather than simply concluding that there must be some other derivation in which the conditional is the last line.

Now think about what happens to the assumption P after we derive R from it and then conclude—on the basis of this derivation—the conditional $P \rightarrow R$. The derivation of R depends on the assumption that P, but the conclusion $P \rightarrow R$ does not. We do not conclude $P \rightarrow R$ given the assumption that P. We conclude R given the assumption that P, and then from this we conclude $P \rightarrow R$ (i.e., we conclude $P \rightarrow R$ precisely on the basis of having derived R on the assumption that P: that derivation itself is the reasoning establishing the conditional). So the assumption P is *discharged*. The intermediate conclusion R depends on this assumption, but the conclusion $P \rightarrow R$ does not.

So the first characteristic of natural deduction proof methods is that they not only allow assumptions but also have a system for keeping track of what conclusions depend on what assumptions—a method for keeping track of when each assumption is in force (i.e., when the reasoning is proceeding only given that assumption) and when it has been discharged.

The second characteristic of natural deduction systems is that they typically have few axioms and many rules of inference. In fact, canonical natural deduction systems have no axioms, and two rules of inference for each logical operator: an *introduction* rule and an *elimination* rule.

§

We can best explain these two features by introducing a particular natural deduction system. In this system, when we make an assumption, we write it in the top section of a box, separated from the bottom section of the box by a line. For example, here we assume $P \rightarrow Q$:

We start a new box when we make an assumption. So if we later want to make another assumption, we have to enclose it in a new box. For example, here we initially assume $P \to Q$, and then as the next step of our proof we assume $Q \to R$:

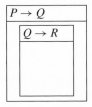

A wff or a box is *in* a box b if it is immediately enclosed in b, that is, enclosed in b and not also enclosed in any box that is enclosed in b. A wff or a box is *inside* a box b if it is enclosed in b at any depth: whether immediately in it, or enclosed in a box that is in it, and so on. So in our previous example, if we call the outer box a and the inner box b, $P \to Q$ is both in and inside box a, and it is not in or inside box b; $Q \to R$ is inside but not in box a, and it is both in and inside box b; box a is not in or inside box a or box b; box b is both in and inside box a; and box b is not in or inside box b.

We said that any natural deduction system needs a way of keeping track of when assumptions are in force and when they have been discharged. This is the point of the boxes in the present system. An assumption is in force everywhere inside the box it is in. An assumption is discharged when we close the box it is in: when we move outside a box, the assumption written at the top of that box is no longer in force.

Now we need to introduce the rules of inference of the system. As before, we begin by restricting our attention to propositional logic. Figure 15.10 shows a system of natural deduction rules for propositional logic [Bergmann et al., 2009, pp. 160–239]; we refer to this system as N_1. Note that in some cases the input to the rule is a single wff; for example, given α as input, the rule of $\vee$-introduction gives $\alpha \vee \beta$ (or $\beta \vee \alpha$) as output. In some cases the input is two wffs; for example, given α and β as input (in either order), the rule of $\wedge$-introduction gives $\alpha \wedge \beta$ as output. In some cases the input is a *subproof*, contained in its own box; for example, given a subproof whose assumption (i.e., the first entry in the box, above the line) is α and whose last entry is β, the rule of $\to$ introduction gives $\alpha \to \beta$ as output (note that this output is written outside the box, not inside it). Finally, in some cases the input is a combination of wffs and subproofs; for example, given a wff $\alpha \vee \beta$ and two subproofs, one of which has assumption α and last entry γ and the other of which has assumption β and last entry γ, the rule of $\vee$-elimination gives γ as output. Rules that take subproofs as inputs allow us to discharge assumptions. For when the rule is applied, the output is written outside the box; when we move out of a box, the assumption at the top of that box is no longer in force.

Connective	Introduction rule	Elimination rule
$\rightarrow$	$\begin{array}{\|l} \alpha \\ \vdots \\ \beta \end{array}$ ▶ $\alpha \rightarrow \beta$	α $\alpha \rightarrow \beta$ ▶ β
$\wedge$	α β ▶ $\alpha \wedge \beta$	$\alpha \wedge \beta$ ▶ α (or β)
$\neg$	$\begin{array}{\|l} \alpha \\ \vdots \\ \beta \\ \neg\beta \end{array}$ ▶ $\neg\alpha$	$\begin{array}{\|l} \neg\alpha \\ \vdots \\ \beta \\ \neg\beta \end{array}$ ▶ α
$\vee$	α ▶ $\alpha \vee \beta$ (or $\beta \vee \alpha$)	$\alpha \vee \beta$ $\begin{array}{\|l} \alpha \\ \vdots \\ \gamma \end{array}$ $\begin{array}{\|l} \beta \\ \vdots \\ \gamma \end{array}$ ▶ γ

Figure 15.10. Natural deduction rules for system N_1.

Figure 15.11 shows an example of a natural deduction proof. To facilitate writing, we draw in only the left sides of boxes, and only the left ends of the horizontal lines under assumptions.[32] To facilitate reading, we number the lines of the proof on the left and annotate them on the right to indicate where they come from. In these annotations, subproof inputs are indicated by a range of numbers; for example, 2–5 indicates the subproof whose assumption is the wff on line 2 and whose last entry is the wff on line 5. We do not need to annotate assumptions (e.g., by "A"): the fact that a wff occurs at the top of a box and has a line immediately under it already indicates clearly that it is an assumption. Introduction rules are indicated by the connective followed by

$$
\begin{array}{lll}
1 & A \vee (B \wedge C) & \\
2 & \quad A & \\
3 & \quad A \vee B & 2\ (\vee I) \\
4 & \quad A \vee C & 2\ (\vee I) \\
5 & \quad (A \vee B) \wedge (A \vee C) & 3, 4\ (\wedge I) \\
6 & \quad B \wedge C & \\
7 & \quad B & 6\ (\wedge E) \\
8 & \quad C & 6\ (\wedge E) \\
9 & \quad A \vee B & 7\ (\vee I) \\
10 & \quad A \vee C & 8\ (\vee I) \\
11 & \quad (A \vee B) \wedge (A \vee C) & 9, 10\ (\wedge I) \\
12 & (A \vee B) \wedge (A \vee C) & 1, 2\text{–}5, 6\text{–}11\ (\wedge E)
\end{array}
$$

Figure 15.11. A proof in system N_1.

$$
\begin{array}{lll}
1 & A & \\
2 & \quad B & \\
3 & \quad A & 1\ (\mathrm{RI}) \\
4 & \quad B \to A & 2\text{–}3\ (\to I) \\
5 & A \to (B \to A) & 1\text{–}4\ (\to I)
\end{array}
$$

Figure 15.12. A proof in system N_1.

I (e.g., $(\vee I)$); elimination rules are indicated by the connective followed by E (e.g., $(\wedge E)$).

The proof in Figure 15.11 establishes $A \vee (B \wedge C) \vdash_{N_1} (A \vee B) \wedge (A \vee C)$. In general, a natural deduction proof establishes $\alpha_1, \ldots, \alpha_n \vdash \beta$ when β is the last line of the proof, and $\alpha_1, \ldots, \alpha_n$ are all the assumptions that, as of that last line, have not been discharged. There may be one such assumption (as in the proof in Figure 15.11), more than one, or none. Figure 15.12 shows an example of a proof with no undischarged assumptions. It also illustrates the new rule *repetition inward* (RI), which is discussed below. Note that the final line of this proof occurs outside all boxes: by the time we reach the final line, every box has been closed; that is, every assumption has been discharged. This proof establishes $\vdash_{N_1} A \to (B \to A)$.

What about the rule (RI), which is applied at line 3 of the proof? At line 1, we assume A (starting a new box—call it box 1). At line 2, we assume B (starting a second box—call it box 2). Now to close box 2 and conclude $B \to A$ using the rule $(\to I)$, we have to be able to derive A within box 2. But when we are in box 2, we are still inside box 1 (box 2 is in box 1), so the assumption A is still in play. So we can trivially "derive" A within box 2, because A is something we are already assuming. The rule (RI) just makes this explicit. It allows us to repeat any wff in a proof inside any box in which that wff appears. (It does

1	A	
2	$(A \wedge B) \rightarrow C$	
3	$A \rightarrow (B \vee C)$	
4	$B \vee C$	1, 3 ($\rightarrow E$)
5	B	
6	$A \wedge B$	1, 5 ($\wedge I$)
7	C	2, 6 ($\rightarrow E$)
8	C	
9	C	8 (RI)
10	C	4, 5–7, 8–9 ($\vee E$)

Figure 15.13. A proof in system N_1.

not allow a wff to be brought outside a box: repetition can only occur inward.) Unlike the other rules, (RI) is not a substantive rule of inference but is merely a bookkeeping rule: it simply makes explicit at a certain stage of a proof that a certain assumption is indeed in play at that stage.

Figure 15.13 shows a third example of a natural deduction proof. This proof establishes $A, (A \wedge B) \rightarrow C, A \rightarrow (B \vee C) \vdash_{N_1} C$.

The system N_1 does not contain rules for $\leftrightarrow$. With regard to such additional connectives, we have the same choices in natural deduction systems as we had in axiomatic systems: we can supplement our rules of inference with definitions of the connectives that do not feature in the rules in terms of connectives that do, or we can add additional rules (typically, an introduction rule and an elimination rule for each additional connective).

§

We saw that there is not just one possible set of axioms and rules for propositional or predicate logic. There are various different axiomatic systems—different combinations of axioms and rules—that are sound and complete with respect to logical truth and/or validity. The situation is the same in natural deduction. Systems may differ, for example, concerning (i) which connectives feature in the rules and (ii) which particular rules are used. Let's look at some examples. Consider the rules in Figure 15.14; names for these rules are shown in parentheses.[33] Let N_1^- be the set of rules of our original system N_1 (shown in Figure 15.10) without the two negation rules ($\neg I$) and ($\neg E$). Then we can define the following systems:

- N_2 is N_1^- plus ($\neg I'$), ($\neg E'$), ($\neg\neg I$), and ($\neg\neg E$);
- N_3 is N_1^- plus ($\bot E$) and (TND);
- N_4 is N_1^- plus ($\bot E$) and (NCD); and
- N_5 is N_1^- plus ($\bot E$) and (RAA).

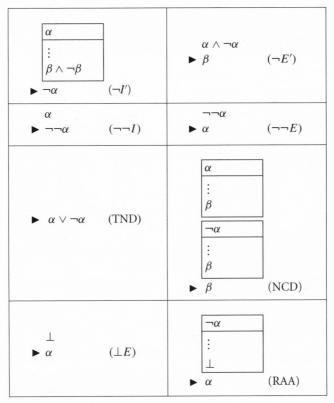

Figure 15.14. More natural deduction rules.

In systems N_3, N_4, and N_5, $\perp$ is a primitive symbol of the system, and $\neg$ is defined in terms of $\perp$ and $\rightarrow$, as in §6.6:

- $\neg\alpha := \alpha \rightarrow \perp$

So in N_3, for example, (TND) becomes $\alpha \vee (\alpha \rightarrow \perp)$ when the negation is defined out.

We said earlier that canonical natural deduction systems have no axioms, and two rules of inference—an introduction rule and an elimination rule—for each logical operator. We see now that not all natural deduction systems fit this pattern. System N_2 does not have just two rules for each connective: $\wedge$ features in the rules $(\neg I')$ and $(\neg E')$, as well as in $(\wedge I)$ and $(\wedge E)$. And N_3 does not fit the model of having no axioms, because the rule (TND) has no inputs and hence is simply an axiom—it allows us to write an instance of $\alpha \vee \neg\alpha$ at any point in a proof.

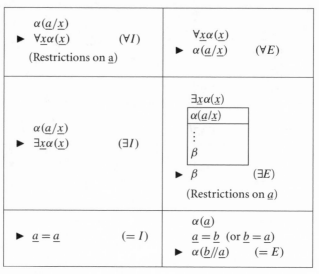

$\alpha(\underline{a}/\underline{x})$		$\forall \underline{x}\alpha(\underline{x})$	
$\blacktriangleright \ \forall \underline{x}\alpha(\underline{x})$ $(\forall I)$		$\blacktriangleright \ \alpha(\underline{a}/\underline{x})$ $(\forall E)$	
(Restrictions on $\underline{a}$)			

Figure 15.15. Natural deduction rules for quantifiers and identity.

We turn now to predicate logic. Figure 15.15 shows rules for the quantifiers and for identity; adding them to N_1, for example, yields the system $N_1^{\forall\exists=}$. As was the case with trees and axiomatic systems, we need to impose some restrictions on the quantifier rules to avoid being able to prove arguments/propositions that are not in fact valid/logically true. For ($\forall I$), $\underline{a}$ must not occur in any assumption undischarged at the point we write the output of the rule, and $\underline{a}$ must not occur in that output (i.e., in $\forall \underline{x}\alpha(\underline{x})$). For ($\exists E$), $\underline{a}$ must not occur in any assumption undischarged at the point we write the output of the rule, and $\underline{a}$ must not occur in that output (i.e., in β), and it must not occur in the input $\exists \underline{x}\alpha(\underline{x})$. Figure 15.16 shows a proof in this system; the proof establishes that $\neg\exists x(Fx \wedge \neg Gx) \vdash_{N_1^{\forall\exists=}} \forall x(Fx \rightarrow Gx)$.

15.2.1 Soundness and Completeness

The primary notion of tree proofs is the satisfiability of a set of propositions, the primary notion of a system of axiomatic proof (i.e., without assumptions) is a proposition being a logical truth, and that of a system of axiomatic derivation (i.e., where assumptions are allowed) is the validity of an argument (the argument whose premises are the assumptions of the derivation and whose conclusion is the last line of the derivation). Natural deduction proofs are like axiomatic derivations from assumptions in this respect: their principal notion is the validity of the argument whose conclusion is the last

$$
\begin{array}{ll}
1 \quad \neg\exists x(Fx \land \neg Gx) & \\
2 \quad\quad Fa & \\
3 \quad\quad\quad \neg Ga & \\
4 \quad\quad\quad\quad Fa \land \neg Ga & 2, 3 \; (\land I) \\
5 \quad\quad\quad\quad \exists x(Fx \land \neg Gx) & 4 \; (\exists I) \\
6 \quad\quad\quad\quad \neg\exists x(Fx \land \neg Gx) & 1 \; (\text{RI}) \\
7 \quad\quad\quad Ga & 3\text{--}6 \; (\neg E) \\
8 \quad\quad Fa \to Ga & 2\text{--}7 \; (\to I) \\
9 \quad \forall x(Fx \to Gx) & 8 \; (\forall I)
\end{array}
$$

Figure 15.16. A proof in system $N_1^{\forall\exists=}$.

line of the proof and whose premises are all the assumptions that remain undischarged as of that last line. Of course, although the notion of validity is foremost, natural deduction systems can still be used to answer other questions of interest: α is a logical truth if we can prove it with no (undischarged) assumptions; a set Γ of wffs is unsatisfiable if we can prove both α and $\neg\alpha$ from assumptions in Γ (for some wff α); two wffs α and β are equivalent if we can both prove α from the assumption that β and prove β from the assumption that α. However, like axiomatic systems—and unlike tree systems—natural deduction systems do not provide proofs of the presence of s-properties (e.g., invalidity); in other words, they do not provide proofs of the absence of a-properties (e.g., validity). If one tries to prove β on the assumption that α, when in fact β is not a logical consequence of α, one will never end up with a proof that β does not follow from α: one will simply end up with no proof at all. (In a tree system, in contrast, one might end up with a proof that β does not follow from α: a finite finished tree with an open path.)[34]

To show that a natural deduction system is complete with respect to validity, we can follow the strategy used in §15.1.4 for axiomatic systems. To show that a natural deduction system is sound, however, we cannot proceed by trying to show that each of its axioms (if it has any) is a logical truth, and that each of its rules is truth-preserving (in the sense that for any model $\mathfrak{M}$, if the inputs to the rule are all true in $\mathfrak{M}$, then the output is true in $\mathfrak{M}$). For some rules take subproofs as inputs, and a subproof is not the kind of thing that can be true or false in a model. What we do, then, is show by induction that every line n of a natural deduction proof has the following property: if all the assumptions in the proof that are undischarged as of line n are true in a model $\mathfrak{M}$, then line n is true in that model. The base case concerns the first line in a proof. This line must be either (i) an assumption α or (ii) an axiom (if the system allows axioms). Of course α is true in any model in which it is true, so case (i) is trivial; as long as the axioms are logical truths, case (ii) is equally straightforward. For the inductive step, we consider each possibility in turn regarding the origin of line n: it is an assumption; it is an axiom; it is the output of some rule. Let's consider one example: line n is the output of $(\rightarrow I)$:

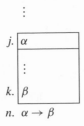

Let us use Γ_i to denote the set of assumptions undischarged as of line i. Now the part of the proof just shown might be nested within any number of boxes. So we do not know exactly what assumptions are undischarged as of line n. What we do know, however, is that Γ_n contains everything Γ_k contains except perhaps α, because the assumption of α at line j is discharged when we write $\alpha \rightarrow \beta$ at line n on the basis of rule $(\rightarrow I)$.[35] The inductive hypothesis tells us that $\Gamma_k \vDash \beta$. Because the only thing Γ_k could contain that Γ_n does not is α, it follows that $\Gamma_n \cup \{\alpha\} \vDash \beta$, where $\Gamma_n \cup \{\alpha\}$ is the set of wffs containing everything in Γ_n and (also) α.[36] But if β is true in every model in which α and every wff in Γ_n are true, then $\alpha \rightarrow \beta$ is true in every model in which every wff in Γ_n is true, because the only way $\alpha \rightarrow \beta$ can be false is if α is true and β is false. And that is precisely our desired result: $\Gamma_n \vDash \alpha \rightarrow \beta$.

As with axiomatic systems, there are systems of natural deduction that allow open wffs to appear in proofs. Comments analogous to those made in §15.1.3 apply concerning the interpretation of such proofs.

15.2.2 Boxes, Lists, and Stacks

The key characteristic of natural deduction proof methods is that they allow assumptions to be discharged, and so a natural deduction system requires a method for keeping track of when assumptions are in play and when they have been discharged. Boxes are only one such method.[37] Two other methods in common use are *lists* and *stacks*.

In the list method, we write a proof as a flat list of wffs, as in axiomatic proofs (in contrast to a nested list, as in the box method). However, in addition to the line numbers and annotations, we have an additional column showing the *dependency set* for each line of the proof.[38] The dependency set of a line n—written to the left of its line number—is a set of numbers: it contains the line numbers of assumptions on which line n depends. When presenting rules for such a system, we not only need to say what output each rule yields for given inputs, we also must specify how the dependency set of the output is

{1}	1.	$A \to (B \to C)$	A
{2}	2.	B	A
{3}	3.	A	A
{1, 3}	4.	$B \to C$	1, 3 $(\to E)$
{1, 2, 3}	5.	C	2, 4 $(\to E)$
{1, 2}	6.	$A \to C$	3, 5 $(\to I)$
{1}	7.	$B \to (A \to C)$	2, 6 $(\to I)$

Figure 15.17. A list-style natural deduction proof.

derived from the dependency sets of its inputs. For example, here is a rule for $\to$ elimination:

Γ	$n.$	α	
Δ	$m.$	$\alpha \to \beta$	
$\Gamma \cup \Delta$	$k.$	β	$n, m \ (\to E)$

In this rule n, m, and k are line numbers; n and m may come in either order; k comes after them both. On the left of the line numbers are dependency sets. The idea is, when we conclude β from α and $\alpha \to \beta$, the conclusion depends on everything on which the two inputs depend: no assumptions get discharged. Contrast the rule for $\to$ introduction:

{n}	$n.$	α	A
$\Delta \cup \{n\}$	$m.$	β	
Δ	$k.$	$\alpha \to \beta$	$n, m \ (\to I)$

Here, n comes before m (because m depends on n—see on), and k comes after them both. The idea is as follows. We assume α and derive β on the basis of this assumption. The fact that β is derived on the basis of the assumption that α is made clear by the dependency set for line m (β's line) containing n (α's line number). Of course, β may also depend on earlier lines as well: that is the point of the set Δ (it contains the numbers of all lines apart from α's line on which β depends). So β depends on α. But when we then conclude $\alpha \to \beta$— on the basis of having derived β on the assumption that α—the conclusion $\alpha \to \beta$ does not depend on the assumption of α at line n: that assumption gets discharged. So the dependency set of line k ($\alpha \to \beta$'s line) does not include n (α's line): it includes only whatever other lines β's line depends on (i.e., the lines in Δ). Figure 15.17 show a proof illustrating the use of these rules.

Note that a new assumption depends only on itself. This highlights the important point that the set of assumptions on which a given line n depends (in list-style natural deduction proofs) cannot be equated with the set of assumptions that are undischarged as of line n (in box-style natural deduction proofs).

For example, suppose we make two assumptions in a row. In a list proof the second assumption depends only on itself, whereas in a box proof the first assumption is still in play at the time of making the second assumption. In fact, the idea of an assumption being in play for a while (viz., as long as we are inside the box it is at the top of) and then (perhaps) being discharged (when that box is closed) does not pertain to list-style natural deduction systems. Instead, it is replaced by the idea that a line may depend on some assumptions but not others. So in a list proof, the "scope" of an assumption—the area where it is in force—is not a connected region (like the interior of a box): it is the (possibly disjointed) group of lines that depend on that assumption. For example, in Figure 15.17, the scope of the assumption of B at line 2 is lines 2, 5, and 6 (these are the lines which have line 2 in their dependency set). This difference between box- and list-style proofs has significance for the interpretation of proofs. The idea behind a box proof is that each line is a logical consequence of the set of assumptions that are undischarged as of that line. The idea behind a list proof is that each line is a logical consequence of the set of assumptions on which it depends.

A point related to the one just noted is that there are no subproofs in list-style natural deduction proofs. In box-style natural deduction proofs, rules can take as inputs wffs (represented in annotations as numbers), subproofs (represented in annotations as ranges of numbers), or both. In list-style natural deduction proofs, the inputs of rules are always wffs, represented in annotations as numbers. The guiding idea, that in (say) $\rightarrow$ introduction we conclude $\alpha \rightarrow \beta$ on the basis of having derived β from α, shows up in box-style natural deduction in the fact that $(\rightarrow I)$ takes a subproof—which proceeds from α as assumption to β as conclusion—as input. In list-style natural deduction, $(\rightarrow I)$ takes as input simply the wffs α and β, but the guiding idea still shows up in the requirement that the rule can be applied only when β's line includes α's line in its dependency set.

$$\S$$

The third commonly used style of natural deduction proof is the stack style.[39] Proofs in this style are written as layers of wffs, with horizontal lines separating the inputs of rules from their outputs. They have one wff at the bottom—the conclusion of the proof—and grow bigger as we move up the page. Assumptions are represented as topmost wffs in the stack: wffs with nothing above them. Assumptions may (of course) be discharged; when an assumption is discharged, we draw square brackets around it. We can see which assumptions a wff α in the stack depends on by tracing down from the assumptions (topmost wffs) to α: if we can get from an assumption β to α by moving down only (i.e., without moving sideways or up at any point), then α depends on β—unless of course β has already been discharged by the time we reach α. An example will

$$\frac{[A]_1 \quad A \to (B \to C)}{B \to C}(\to E)$$

$$\frac{\dfrac{B \to C \quad [B]_2}{C}(\to E)}{\dfrac{A \to C}{B \to (A \to C)}(\to I)_1}(\to I)_2$$

Figure 15.18. A stack-style natural deduction proof.

help make these ideas clear. We go through the example presented in list style in Figure 15.17, presenting it this time in stack style. First, here are the rules for → elimination and introduction:

$$\frac{\alpha \quad \alpha \to \beta}{\beta}(\to E) \qquad \begin{array}{c} [\alpha]_n \\ \vdots \\ \dfrac{\beta}{\alpha \to \beta}(\to I)_n \end{array}$$

Note that the assumption α is discharged—placed in square brackets—when we apply the rule $(\to I)$. The numerical subscript n on the square brackets is matched by a subscript on the annotation showing which rule has been applied: the subscripts show exactly which application of which rule results in the discharge of a particular assumption. Figure 15.18 shows our proof re-presented in stack style. Note that the assumption A is discharged at the first application of $(\to I)$. So the step C, for example, depends on this assumption, but then this assumption is discharged, and lower steps do not depend on it. The step $B \to C$ also depends on the assumption of A, but it does not depend on the assumption of B, because one cannot get from the B assumption to $B \to C$ by going only down: one would have to go sideways. The final step depends only on $A \to (B \to C)$: although we can move from the A assumption down to the final step, by the time we get there, that assumption has been discharged; similarly for the B assumption. The proof therefore establishes $A \to (B \to C) \vdash B \to (A \to C)$. In general, a proof with last line α establishes $\Gamma \vdash \alpha$, where Γ contains all assumptions that remain undischarged at the end of the proof.[40]

§

We conclude our discussion of natural deduction systems by mentioning some of their main advantages and disadvantages. Like axiomatic systems—and unlike trees—natural deduction systems do not provide proofs of invalidity or other s-properties. If we try to prove α on the assumption that β, when in fact α is not a logical consequence of β, we do not end up with something useful, such as a saturated open path: we simply end up with nothing.

One important advantage of natural deduction systems is that the structure of formal proofs in them closely mirrors the kinds of informal proofs typically found in mathematics and logic books. One consequence is that finding proofs in natural deduction systems is typically easier than finding proofs in axiomatic systems. Of course it is not easier than finding proofs in tree systems, where we have an effective proof-search procedure—and in fact it can still be hard to find natural deduction proofs in practice. (Introductory books that focus on natural deduction typically discuss heuristics for finding proofs of wffs of given forms. For example, to prove a conditional, try assuming the antecedent and then deriving the consequent.)

The structure of natural deduction proofs is more complex than the structure of axiomatic proofs. Although this is a disadvantage from one point of view—natural deduction proofs do not give us such a simple handle on the relation of logical consequence—from another point of view it makes natural deduction proofs intrinsically interesting objects of study, and considerable attention is paid to them in the area of *proof theory* (the study of formal proofs and formal proof systems).

15.2.3 Exercises

1. Show the following in N_1.

   (i) $\vdash (\neg P \rightarrow P) \rightarrow P$

   (ii) $A \rightarrow C, B \rightarrow C, A \vee B \vdash C$

   (iii) $\vdash \neg\neg P \rightarrow P$

   (iv) $\neg(A \vee B) \vdash \neg A \wedge \neg B$

   (v) $A, \neg A \vdash B$

   (vi) $A \rightarrow B, B \rightarrow C \vdash A \rightarrow C$

   (vii) $P \rightarrow Q \vdash \neg Q \rightarrow \neg P$

   (viii) $A \vee B, \neg A \vdash B$

   (ix) $P \rightarrow R, Q \rightarrow R, P \vee Q \vdash R$

   (x) $P \rightarrow Q \vdash \neg(P \wedge \neg Q)$

2. Establish each of the following in each of the systems N_2 through N_5.

   (i) $\vdash A \vee \neg A$

   (ii) $A \wedge \neg A \vdash B$

   (iii) $\vdash \neg\neg A \rightarrow A$

   (iv) $\vdash \neg(A \wedge \neg A)$

3. Show the following in $N_1^{\forall\exists=}$.

   (i) $\vdash \forall x(Fx \rightarrow Fx)$

   (ii) $\exists x(Fx \wedge Gx) \vdash \exists x Fx \wedge \exists x Gx$

   (iii) $\forall x(Fx \rightarrow Gx), \neg\exists x Gx \vdash \neg\exists x Fx$

   (iv) $\forall x(Fx \rightarrow x = a) \vdash Fb \rightarrow a = b$

   (v) $\forall x \forall y x = y, Raa \vdash \forall x \forall y Rxy$

   (vi) $\vdash \forall x Rxx \rightarrow \forall x \exists y Rxy$

   (vii) $\vdash \exists x Fx \rightarrow \neg\forall x \neg Fx$

   (viii) $\neg\exists x Fx \vdash \forall x \neg Fx$

(ix) $\forall x x = a \vdash b = c$

(x) $\vdash \forall x \forall y ((Fx \land \neg Fy) \to \neg x = y)$

4. (i) Reformulate the rules of system N_1 in list style. Re-present your answers to question 1 above as proofs in the list style.

(ii) Reformulate the rules of system N_1 in stack style. Re-present your answers to question 1 above as proofs in the stack style.

5. State natural deduction rules (i.e., introduction and elimination rules) for $\leftrightarrow$.

15.3 Sequent Calculus

In all the proof methods we have looked at so far, the basic objects that appear in proofs are wffs. The final proof method we shall look at—sequent calculus—differs from the others in this respect: in sequent calculus, the basic objects that appear in proofs are *sequents*. A sequent looks like:

$$\Gamma \Rightarrow \Delta$$

where Γ and Δ are sets of wffs. The set Γ is called the left side (or antecedent) of the sequent, and Δ is the right side (or succedent). We say that a sequent *holds* in a model $\mathfrak{M}$ just in case the following condition is satisfied:

If all wffs on the left side are true in $\mathfrak{M}$, then some wff on the right side is true in $\mathfrak{M}$.

It may be easier to think about this in reverse: a sequent does not hold in a model when all wffs on its left side are true and all wffs on its right side are false; otherwise (i.e., when some wff on the left side is false, or some wff on the right side is true, or both) it does hold. And here is a third way of thinking about sequents holding, which can also be useful: the sequent $\{\alpha_1, \ldots, \alpha_n\} \Rightarrow \{\beta_1, \ldots, \beta_m\}$ holds in a model just in case the corresponding conditional $(\alpha_1 \land \ldots \land \alpha_n) \to (\beta_1 \lor \ldots \lor \beta_m)$—whose antecedent is the conjunction of the wffs on the sequent's left side and whose consequent is the disjunction of the wffs on the sequent's right side—is true in that model.[41]

In a system of proof where wffs are the basic objects, the aim is that the last line of any proof should be logically true.[42] In a system of proof where sequents are the basic objects, the aim is that the last line of any proof should hold logically; that is, it should hold in every model.

We can define other concepts of interest in terms of the concept of a sequent holding logically. For example,

The argument $\alpha_1, \ldots, \alpha_n /\therefore \beta$ is valid just in case the sequent $\{\alpha_1, \ldots, \alpha_n\} \Rightarrow \{\beta\}$ holds logically.

The reasoning behind this statement is as follows. The sequent holds logically just in case in every model in which all wffs in $\{\alpha_1, \ldots, \alpha_n\}$ are true, some wff in $\{\beta\}$ is true. But β is the only wff in $\{\beta\}$, so to say that some wff in $\{\beta\}$ is true is simply to say that β is true. So we can rephrase as follows: the sequent holds logically just in case in every model in which all of $\alpha_1, \ldots, \alpha_n$ are true, β is true. That is exactly what is required for the argument $\alpha_1, \ldots, \alpha_n / \therefore \beta$ to be valid.

Consider a second example:

α is a logical truth just in case $\emptyset \Rightarrow \{\alpha\}$ holds logically.

The reasoning behind this statement is as follows. The sequent holds logically just in case in every model in which all wffs in $\emptyset$ are true, some wff in $\{\alpha\}$ is true. There are no wffs in $\emptyset$, and recall (Exercises 9.4.3, question 5(i)) that "all Fs are Gs" is true when there are no Fs, so the condition "all wffs in $\emptyset$ are true in $\mathfrak{M}$" obtains for every model $\mathfrak{M}$. Thus, the sequent holds logically just in case in every model, some wff in $\{\alpha\}$ is true—that is, α is true. That is exactly what is required for α to be a logical truth.

A third example is:

The set Γ of wffs is unsatisfiable just in case $\Gamma \Rightarrow \emptyset$ holds logically.

The reasoning behind this statement is as follows. The sequent holds logically just in case in every model in which all wffs in Γ are true, some wff in $\emptyset$ is true. There are no wffs in $\emptyset$, and "some Fs are Gs" is false when there are no Fs, so the condition "some wff in $\emptyset$ is true in $\mathfrak{M}$" obtains for no model $\mathfrak{M}$. Thus, the sequent holds logically just in case there is no model in which all wffs in Γ are true. That is exactly what is required for Γ to be unsatisfiable.

§

The goal, then, is to set up a system in which we can prove all and only those sequents that hold logically. Restricting ourselves initially to propositional logic, Figure 15.19 presents rules for one such system, which we call S_1. Let's think through why each of these rules is *hold-preserving*: if the input sequent(s) hold in a model, then the output sequent holds in that model too. The first rule has no inputs, so it is an axiom. It allows us to write $\{\alpha\} \Rightarrow \{\alpha\}$ anywhere in a sequent proof. Obviously any such sequent holds in every model: if every wff on the left side is true—that is, if α is true (α being the only wff on the left side)—then some wff on the right side is true—that is, α is true (α being the only wff on the right side). Or think about it this way: the conditional corresponding to the sequent $\{\alpha\} \Rightarrow \{\alpha\}$ is $\alpha \to \alpha$, which is true in every model.

Axiom	$\{\alpha\} \Rightarrow \{\alpha\}$
Thinning	$\dfrac{\Gamma \Rightarrow \Delta}{\Theta \cup \Gamma \Rightarrow \Delta \cup \Lambda}\text{(Th)}$

Connective	Introduction on left	Introduction on right
$\rightarrow$	$\dfrac{\Gamma \Rightarrow \Delta \cup \{\alpha\} \quad \{\beta\} \cup \Gamma \Rightarrow \Delta}{\{\alpha \rightarrow \beta\} \cup \Gamma \Rightarrow \Delta}(\rightarrow\Rightarrow)$	$\dfrac{\{\alpha\} \cup \Gamma \Rightarrow \Delta \cup \{\beta\}}{\Gamma \Rightarrow \Delta \cup \{\alpha \rightarrow \beta\}}(\Rightarrow\rightarrow)$
$\wedge$	$\dfrac{\{\alpha, \beta\} \cup \Gamma \Rightarrow \Delta}{\{\alpha \wedge \beta\} \cup \Gamma \Rightarrow \Delta}(\wedge\Rightarrow)$	$\dfrac{\Gamma \Rightarrow \Delta \cup \{\alpha\} \quad \Gamma \Rightarrow \Delta \cup \{\beta\}}{\Gamma \Rightarrow \Delta \cup \{\alpha \wedge \beta\}}(\Rightarrow\wedge)$
$\neg$	$\dfrac{\Gamma \Rightarrow \Delta \cup \{\alpha\}}{\{\neg\alpha\} \cup \Gamma \Rightarrow \Delta}(\neg\Rightarrow)$	$\dfrac{\{\alpha\} \cup \Gamma \Rightarrow \Delta}{\Gamma \Rightarrow \Delta \cup \{\neg\alpha\}}(\Rightarrow\neg)$
$\vee$	$\dfrac{\{\alpha\} \cup \Gamma \Rightarrow \Delta \quad \{\beta\} \cup \Gamma \Rightarrow \Delta}{\{\alpha \vee \beta\} \cup \Gamma \Rightarrow \Delta}(\vee\Rightarrow)$	$\dfrac{\Gamma \Rightarrow \Delta \cup \{\alpha, \beta\}}{\Gamma \Rightarrow \Delta \cup \{\alpha \vee \beta\}}(\Rightarrow\vee)$

Figure 15.19. Sequent calculus S_1.

The Thinning rule (aka Weakening) is equally obvious: expanding (i.e., adding wffs to) the left or right side of a sequent that holds in a model will always result in a sequent that also holds in that model, because if every wff in the expanded left side holds, then a fortiori every wff in the original unexpanded left side holds. But then, given the input to the rule, some wff in the original unexpanded right side holds, so a fortiori some wff in the expanded right side holds.

The remaining rules come in pairs: two rules for each logical operator. One rule tells us how to derive a sequent with the connective on its left side; the other tells us how to derive a sequent with the connective on its right side. The easiest way to see that each of these rules is hold-preserving is to read it from the bottom up: suppose the output does not hold, and then show that in that case, at least one of the inputs must also not hold. In fact, when we read the rules this way, it is easy to see that they correspond precisely to our tree rules: the left introduction rule for a given connective is just like the unnegated tree rule for that connective; the right one is just like the negated tree rule for that connective.

For example, consider the rules for the conditional. Ignore Γ and Δ— they are just whatever other wffs are in the left and right side of the sequent, besides the conditional $\alpha \rightarrow \beta$ and its components α and β—and just focus on $\alpha \rightarrow \beta$, α, and β. Look at the left introduction rule, and read it from the bottom up. Suppose the output sequent does not hold; that is, every wff on its left side is true and every wff on its right side is false. So in particular, $\alpha \rightarrow \beta$, which is on the left side, is true. Then the rule tells us (reading from the bottom up) that at least one of the input sequents does not hold. The first input has α on the right side, so if it does not hold, α is false. The second input has β on the left side, so if it does not hold, β is true. So in sum, the rule says: if $\alpha \rightarrow \beta$ is true, then either α is false or β is true (or both). That is exactly what the tree rule for unnegated conditional says: if $\alpha \rightarrow \beta$ is true, then either $\neg\alpha$ is true—that is, α is false—or β is true.

Now look at the right introduction rule for $\rightarrow$, and again read it from the bottom up. Suppose the output sequent does not hold; that is, every wff on its left side is true and every wff on its right side is false. So in particular, $\alpha \rightarrow \beta$, which is on the right side, is false. Then the rule tells us (reading from the bottom up) that the input sequent does not hold. The input has α on the left side and β on the right side, so if it does not hold, α is true and β is false. So the rule says: if $\alpha \rightarrow \beta$ is false, then α is true and β is false. That is exactly what the tree rule for negated conditional says: if $\neg(\alpha \rightarrow \beta)$ is true (i.e., $\alpha \rightarrow \beta$ is false), then α is true and $\neg\beta$ is true (i.e., β is false).

If one works through the sequent rules for the other connectives, one can see that they too correspond to the tree rules and so are hold-preserving for the same reasons that the tree rules are truth-preserving.

§

Figure 15.20 gives an example of a proof in S_1. The proof establishes $\vdash_{S_1} \{(A \wedge B) \vee \neg(A \rightarrow B)\} \Rightarrow \{C \rightarrow A\}$. We have set out the proof in the form of a stack (recall §15.2.2). The proof could also be set out in list form, as in Figure 15.21. The advantage of setting out proofs as stacks is that it leads to a natural method of finding proofs. The method works from the bottom up: we write the sequent we wish to prove at the bottom of the page. We now suppose that it does not hold, and consider what must then be the case, and we write the answer above the original sequent. The answer depends on what are the main connectives of the wffs on the left and right sides of the original sequent. For example, if the sequent has on its left side a wff whose main connective is $\vee$, then the rule ($\vee \Rightarrow$) tells us that if this sequent does not hold, then at least one of two other sequents must not hold: one with the left disjunct on its left side, and one with the right disjunct on its left side. For another example, if the sequent has on its right side a wff whose main connective is $\neg$, then the rule ($\Rightarrow \neg$) tells us that if this sequent does not hold, then another sequent must not hold: one with the negand on its left side. And so on. What we are doing, of course, is perfectly analogous to building a tree, only upside down (recall the correspondence between sequent rules and tree rules). In particular, the process has this feature: the wffs written down as we go up the page become simpler. For the sequent rules introduce connectives (on the left or the right), so when we apply them in reverse, in our current method for finding proofs, connectives are eliminated. Eventually, we obtain sequents whose left and right sides contain wffs with no connectives. At this point, these topmost sequents might be of one of two sorts: (i) some wff α is on both the left

$$
\cfrac{
\cfrac{
\cfrac{\{A\}\Rightarrow\{A\}}{\{A,B,C\}\Rightarrow\{A\}}\ (\text{Th})
}{\{(A\land B),C\}\Rightarrow\{A\}}\ (\land\Rightarrow)
\qquad
\cfrac{
\cfrac{
\cfrac{
\cfrac{\{A\}\Rightarrow\{A\}}{\{C,A\}\Rightarrow\{A,B\}}\ (\text{Th})
}{\{C\}\Rightarrow\{A,A\to B\}}\ (\Rightarrow\to)
}{\{\neg(A\to B),C\}\Rightarrow\{A\}}\ (\neg\Rightarrow)
}{}
}{
\cfrac{\{(A\land B)\lor\neg(A\to B),C\}\Rightarrow\{A\}}{\{(A\land B)\lor\neg(A\to B)\}\Rightarrow\{C\to A\}}\ (\Rightarrow\to)
}\ (\lor\Rightarrow)
$$

Figure 15.20. A proof in S_1.

1. $\{A\} \Rightarrow \{A\}$ Axiom
2. $\{A,B,C\} \Rightarrow \{A\}$ 1 (Th)
3. $\{(A\land B),C\} \Rightarrow \{A\}$ 2 ($\land\Rightarrow$)
4. $\{C,A\} \Rightarrow \{A,B\}$ 1 (Th)
5. $\{C\} \Rightarrow \{A,A\to B\}$ 4 ($\Rightarrow\to$)
6. $\{\neg(A\to B),C\} \Rightarrow \{A\}$ 5 ($\neg\Rightarrow$)
7. $\{(A\land B)\lor\neg(A\to B),C\} \Rightarrow \{A\}$ 3, 6 ($\lor\Rightarrow$)
8. $\{(A\land B)\lor\neg(A\to B)\} \Rightarrow \{C\to A\}$ 7 ($\Rightarrow\to$)

Figure 15.21. The proof of Figure 15.20 in list form.

and right sides or (ii) no wff is on both sides. (In trees the analogue of situation (i) is a path containing α and $\neg\alpha$; the analogue of situation (ii) is an open finished path.) A sequent of type (i) holds logically: if every wff on the left (including α) is true, then some wff on the right (namely, α) is true. Such sequents can be proved by Thinning from the axiom $\{\alpha\} \Rightarrow \{\alpha\}$. In contrast, a sequent of type (ii) does not hold logically and cannot be proven. So now we are in the following situation: if all topmost wffs are of type (i), we add axioms and Thinning steps above them, and we now have a proof of the initial sequent at the bottom. If even one topmost wff is of type (ii), then there can be no such proof: the initial sequent at the bottom does not hold logically.

Let's look at a couple of examples of this method for finding proofs. First, we can see the proof in Figure 15.20 as having been arrived at via this method. We begin by writing down the sequent at the bottom. The left side contains one wff, whose main connective is $\lor$, and the right side contains one wff, whose main connective is $\to$. As in the case of trees, we begin with the latter, because it involves no branching. (Remember, left sequent rules are like tree rules for unnegated connectives, and right sequent rules are like tree rules for negated connectives. The tree rule for unnegated $\lor$ branches; the tree rule for negated $\to$ does not branch.) Now we are at the sequent that is one up from the bottom of the stack. The only compound wff now is on the left side; its main connective is $\lor$. Applying the relevant rule, the stack forks (in the upward direction). On the left side, we have a sequent whose left side contains a wff whose main connective is $\land$. Applying the relevant rule leads to a sequent

$$\dfrac{\dfrac{\{B\}\Rightarrow\{A\} \qquad \{B\}\Rightarrow\{A\}}{\{A \to B,\, B\}\Rightarrow\{A\}}\ (\to \Rightarrow)}{\{A \to B\}\Rightarrow\{B \to A\}}\ (\Rightarrow \to)$$

Figure 15.22. Unsuccessful search
for a proof in S_1.

of type (i): it has A on the left and right sides. So we add the axiom $\{A\} \Rightarrow \{A\}$ at the top of this branch, and it is finished. Going back to the right side of the fork, we work up it in a similar fashion and eventually reach another type (i) sequent. Thus, all branches lead to type (i) sequents, and so our method finds us a proof of the sequent at the bottom of the stack.

Now let's look at an example where the sequent we set out to prove does not hold logically, and the method (of constructing stacks from the bottom up) does not yield a proof. Consider Figure 15.22. We start at the bottom with $\{A \to B\} \Rightarrow \{B \to A\}$. Working first on the conditional on the right gives us the first line up from the bottom. Working on the conditional on the left side of this sequent then leads to a branching of the stack. As it happens, both sides of the branch contain the same sequent, $\{B\} \Rightarrow \{A\}$.[43] This sequent is of type (ii): it features no logical operators, and no wff appears on both its left and right sides. So in this case our method does not yield a proof—but it does yield something useful: a counterexample. Just as in the case of trees with open paths, for stacks with one or more type (ii) topmost sequents, we can read off a counterexample. We can read it off directly from the type (ii) sequent: the countermodel is a model that makes every wff on the left side true and every wff on the right side false. In this case, then, the countermodel makes B true and A false. We can easily verify that in such a model, every wff on the left side of our target sequent (i.e., just $A \to B$) is true and every wff on the right side (i.e., just $B \to A$) false—and so the sequent does not hold.

The system S_1 does not contain rules for $\leftrightarrow$. With regard to such additional connectives, we have the same choices in sequent calculus as we had for axiomatic systems and natural deduction: we can supplement the rules of inference with definitions of the connectives that do not feature in the rules in terms of connectives that do, or we can add additional rules for the additional connectives.

§

Turning now to predicate logic, Figure 15.23 shows rules for the quantifiers and for identity; adding them to S_1 yields the system $S_1^{\forall\exists=}$. Let's consider the quantifier rules first. As with the rules for the connectives, there are two equivalent ways to read them: from top to bottom (the rules should be such that for any model in which the upper sequent holds, the lower sequent holds)

Quantifier	Introduction on left	Introduction on right
∀	$$\frac{\{\alpha(\underline{a}/\underline{x}),\ \forall\underline{x}\alpha(\underline{x})\}\cup\Gamma\Rightarrow\Delta}{\{\forall\underline{x}\alpha(\underline{x})\}\cup\Gamma\Rightarrow\Delta}(\forall\Rightarrow)$$	$$\frac{\Gamma\Rightarrow\Delta\cup\{\alpha(\underline{a}/\underline{x})\}}{\Gamma\Rightarrow\Delta\cup\{\forall\underline{x}\alpha(\underline{x})\}}(\Rightarrow\forall)$$ ($\underline{a}$ nowhere in lower sequent)
∃	$$\frac{\{\alpha(\underline{a}/\underline{x})\}\cup\Gamma\Rightarrow\Delta}{\{\exists\underline{x}\alpha(\underline{x})\}\cup\Gamma\Rightarrow\Delta}(\exists\Rightarrow)$$ ($\underline{a}$ nowhere in lower sequent)	$$\frac{\Gamma\Rightarrow\Delta\cup\{\exists\underline{x}\alpha(\underline{x}),\ \alpha(\underline{a}/\underline{x})\}}{\Gamma\Rightarrow\Delta\cup\{\exists\underline{x}\alpha(\underline{x})\}}(\Rightarrow\exists)$$

	Identity
Axiom	$\emptyset\Rightarrow\{\underline{a}=\underline{a}\}$
SI left	$$\frac{\{\alpha(\underline{b}/\!/\underline{a}),\ \underline{a}=\underline{b},\ \alpha(\underline{a})\}\cup\Gamma\Rightarrow\Delta}{\{\underline{a}=\underline{b},\ \alpha(\underline{a})\}\cup\Gamma\Rightarrow\Delta}\ (SI\Rightarrow)$$
SI right	$$\frac{\{\underline{a}=\underline{b}\}\cup\Gamma\Rightarrow\Delta\cup\{\alpha(\underline{a}),\ \alpha(\underline{b}/\!/\underline{a})\}}{\{\underline{a}=\underline{b}\}\cup\Gamma\Rightarrow\Delta\cup\{\alpha(\underline{a})\}}\ (\Rightarrow SI)$$

Figure 15.23. Sequent calculus rules for quantifiers and identity.

or from bottom to top (the rules should be such that for any model in which the lower sequent does not hold, the upper sequent does not hold). When we search for proofs in accordance with the method outlined above, we start by writing the target sequent at the bottom of the page, and we work upward—so we think of the rules in the second way. When read from bottom to top in this way, sequent rules correspond precisely to tree rules: left introduction rules to rules for unnegated operators; right introduction rules to rules for negated operators.

So ($\forall\Rightarrow$) and ($\exists\Rightarrow$) correspond to the tree rules for unnegated quantifiers. In particular, two points of analogy are worth mentioning. First, in the rule ($\forall\Rightarrow$) (read from bottom to top) the quantified formula is retained in the sequent, alongside its instance; whereas in the rule ($\exists\Rightarrow$) (read from bottom to top) the quantified formula is dropped from the sequent, and only its instance appears. This corresponds to the fact that when applying the tree rule to an existentially quantified formula, we check off the formula—we never come back and apply the rule again to get another instance of the same formula—whereas when applying the tree rule to a universally quantified formula, we do not check off the formula and so can obtain another instance of it. Second, there is no restriction on the name used in the rule ($\forall\Rightarrow$), but there is a restriction on the name used in ($\exists\Rightarrow$).

The right introduction rules ($\Rightarrow\forall$) and ($\Rightarrow\exists$) correspond to the tree rules for negated quantifiers—although the correspondence is not as direct as in the case of the left introduction rules. Consider the existential quantifier first. The

$$\frac{\{\forall \underline{x} \neg \alpha(\underline{x})\} \cup \Gamma \Rightarrow \Delta}{\Gamma \Rightarrow \Delta \cup \{\exists \underline{x} \alpha(\underline{x})\}} \ (\Rightarrow \exists')$$

Figure 15.24. The rule ($\Rightarrow \exists'$).

$$\frac{\cfrac{\cfrac{\cfrac{\Gamma \Rightarrow \Delta \cup \{\exists \underline{x} \underline{\alpha}(\underline{x}), \alpha(\underline{a}/\underline{x})\}}{\{\forall \underline{x} \neg \alpha(\underline{x})\} \cup \Gamma \Rightarrow \Delta \cup \{\alpha(\underline{a}/\underline{x})\}} \ (\forall \Rightarrow')}{\{\neg \alpha(\underline{a}/\underline{x}), \forall \underline{x} \neg \alpha(\underline{x})\} \cup \Gamma \Rightarrow \Delta} \ (\neg \Rightarrow)}{\{\forall \underline{x} \neg \alpha(\underline{x})\} \cup \Gamma \Rightarrow \Delta} \ (\forall \Rightarrow)}{\Gamma \Rightarrow \Delta \cup \{\exists \underline{x} \alpha(\underline{x})\}} \ (\Rightarrow \exists')$$

Figure 15.25. Obtaining the result of ($\Rightarrow \exists$) using ($\Rightarrow \exists'$).

tree rule converts $\neg \exists \underline{x} \alpha(\underline{x})$ to $\forall \underline{x} \neg \alpha(\underline{x})$. The basic idea here is that if $\exists \underline{x} \alpha(\underline{x})$ is false, then $\forall \underline{x} \neg \alpha(\underline{x})$ is true (if it is false that something is F, then it is true that everything is non-F). A sequent rule that directly corresponds to this is given in Figure 15.24 (note the prime symbol $'$ in the name of the rule, to distinguish it from the rule ($\Rightarrow \exists$) given in Figure 15.23). Remember, when reading sequent rules from bottom to top, we suppose that every wff on the left side of the lower sequent is true and every wff on the right side is false, and then we see what follows from these assumptions: whatever must be true goes on the left side of the upper sequent, and whatever must be false goes on the right side. So for the rule given in Figure 15.24, the idea is that if $\exists \underline{x} \alpha(\underline{x})$ is false (note that this wff is on the right side of the lower sequent), then $\forall \underline{x} \neg \alpha(\underline{x})$ is true (note that this wff is on the left side of the upper sequent). If we now apply ($\forall \Rightarrow$), we obtain $\neg \alpha(\underline{a}/\underline{x})$ on the left side; if we then apply ($\neg \Rightarrow$), we get $\alpha(\underline{a}/\underline{x})$ on the right side. Finally, if we apply a new rule ($\forall \Rightarrow'$), which reverses ($\Rightarrow \exists'$), the result is as shown in Figure 15.25. The rule ($\Rightarrow \exists$) compresses all these steps into one, moving (upward) directly from $\exists \underline{x} \alpha(\underline{x})$ on the right side to $\alpha(\underline{a}/\underline{x})$ on the right side. (As in the case of ($\forall \Rightarrow$), the quantified formula itself is also retained where it is in the sequent—this time, on the right side— as we may want to apply the rule again to that formula.) Note that this rule also makes perfectly good sense in its own right (not just as a compression of other rules): if "something is F" is false, then it is false that a is F, whatever a is. Note also that the rule ($\Rightarrow \exists$), unlike ($\Rightarrow \exists'$), does not involve operators other than $\exists$.

Similar comments apply to ($\Rightarrow \forall$). We can view it as a compression of a rule ($\Rightarrow \forall'$), which corresponds directly to the tree rule, followed by ($\exists \Rightarrow$) (which is where the restriction on a enters), and then followed by ($\neg \Rightarrow$)—see Figure 15.26. The rule ($\Rightarrow \forall$) also makes sense in its own right: if "everything is F" is false, then there must be something—call it a, but make sure you haven't

$$\frac{\Gamma \Rightarrow \Delta \cup \{\alpha(\underline{a}/\underline{x})\}}{\{\neg\alpha(\underline{a}/\underline{x})\} \cup \Gamma \Rightarrow \Delta} \ (\neg \Rightarrow)$$
$$\frac{\{\exists \underline{x}\neg\alpha(\underline{x})\} \cup \Gamma \Rightarrow \Delta}{\Gamma \Rightarrow \Delta \cup \{\forall \underline{x}\alpha(\underline{x})\}} \ (\exists \Rightarrow)$$
$$(\Rightarrow \forall')$$

Figure 15.26. Obtaining the result of
($\Rightarrow \forall$) using ($\Rightarrow \forall'$).

already attributed any other properties to a (i.e., make a a new name)—such that it is false that a is F.

§

Now let's consider the rules for identity (Figure 15.23). Recall that α is a logical truth just in case $\emptyset \Rightarrow \{\alpha\}$ holds logically. The statement $\underline{a} = \underline{a}$ is indeed a logical truth, so the axiom holds logically. Hence, read from the top down, it is indeed appropriate to begin a sequent proof with this axiom. Read from the bottom up, the axiom corresponds precisely to the tree rule allowing us to close a path when we encounter $\underline{a} \neq \underline{a}$. If we arrive (moving upward) at a sequent with $\underline{a} = \underline{a}$ on its right side, $\underline{a} = \underline{a}$ must be false if the sequent is not to hold. This can, of course, never happen. Accordingly, the axiom allows us to stop developing this branch of the stack: we just add the axiom (by Thinning) and then stop.

As for the SI rules, they are exactly like the tree rule (SI), except that we now have two versions: one for the case where $\underline{a} = \underline{b}$ is true and $\alpha(\underline{a})$ is true (i.e., appears on the left) and another for the case where $\underline{a} = \underline{b}$ is true and $\alpha(\underline{a})$ is false (i.e., appears on the right). Note that in the SI rules (read from bottom to top), the formulas to which the rules are applied—$\underline{a} = \underline{b}$ and $\alpha(\underline{a})$—are retained in the sequent (in their original position, left or right) when the rule is applied. This corresponds to the fact that in trees we do not check off formulas when applying SI: rather, these formulas are still available for subsequent use.

Figure 15.27 shows a proof in the system $S_1^{\forall\exists=}$. This proof establishes:

$$\vdash_{S_1^{\forall\exists=}} \{\exists x Fx, \exists y Gy, \forall x \forall y x = y\} \Rightarrow \{\exists x (Fx \wedge Gx)\}$$

Reading from bottom to top, note the use of SI to obtain the formula Ga, which already appears on the right side of a sequent, onto the left side as well; this then allows us to reach the axiom $\{Ga\} \Rightarrow \{Ga\}$ via Thinning.

Figure 15.28 shows an unsuccessful search for a proof of the sequent $\{\exists x Fx, \exists y Gy\} \Rightarrow \{\exists x (Fx \wedge Gx)\}$. The stack has three branches. The left and right branches top out in axioms. The central branch tops out in the sequent $\{Fa, Gb\} \Rightarrow \{\exists x (Fx \wedge Gx), Ga, Fb\}$. This sequent is not an axiom, nor does it follow from an axiom by Thinning. Furthermore, the only nonatomic wff in

$$\{Ga\} \Rightarrow \{Ga\} \quad \text{(Th)}$$
$$\{Ga, Fa, Gb, a=b, \forall y\,a=y, \forall x\forall y\,yx=y\} \Rightarrow \{\exists x(Fx \land Gx), Ga\} \quad \text{(SI} \Rightarrow)$$
$$\{Fa, Gb, a=b, \forall y\,a=y, \forall x\forall y\,yx=y\} \Rightarrow \{\exists x(Fx \land Gx), Ga\} \quad (\forall \Rightarrow)$$
$$\{Fa, Gb, \forall y\,a=y, \forall x\forall y\,yx=y\} \Rightarrow \{\exists x(Fx \land Gx), Ga\} \quad (\forall \Rightarrow)$$
$$\{Fa, Gb, \forall x\forall y\,yx=y\} \Rightarrow \{\exists x(Fx \land Gx), Ga\} \quad (\land \Rightarrow)$$

$$\{Fa\} \Rightarrow \{Fa\} \quad \text{(Th)}$$
$$\{Fa, Gb, \forall x\forall y\,yx=y\} \Rightarrow \{\exists x(Fx \land Gx), Fa\}$$
$$\{Fa, Gb, \forall x\forall y\,yx=y\} \Rightarrow \{\exists x(Fx \land Gx), Fa \land Ga\} \quad (\Rightarrow \exists)$$
$$\{Fa, Gb, \forall x\forall y\,yx=y\} \Rightarrow \{\exists x(Fx \land Gx)\} \quad (\exists \Rightarrow)$$
$$\{Fa, \exists yGy, \forall x\forall y\,yx=y\} \Rightarrow \{\exists x(Fx \land Gx)\} \quad (\exists \Rightarrow)$$
$$\{\exists xFx, \exists yGy, \forall x\forall y\,yx=y\} \Rightarrow \{\exists x(Fx \land Gx)\}$$

Figure 15.27. A proof in $S_1^{\forall\exists=}$.

$$\{Gb\} \Rightarrow \{Gb\} \quad \text{(Th)}$$
$$\{Fa, Gb\} \Rightarrow \{\exists x(Fx \land Gx), Ga, Gb\} \quad (\Rightarrow \land)$$
$$\{Fa, Gb\} \Rightarrow \{\exists x(Fx \land Gx), Ga, Fb\}$$
$$\{Fa, Gb\} \Rightarrow \{\exists x(Fx \land Gx), Ga, Fb \land Gb\} \quad (\Rightarrow \exists)$$
$$\{Fa, Gb\} \Rightarrow \{\exists x(Fx \land Gx), Ga\} \quad (\Rightarrow \exists)$$

$$\{Fa\} \Rightarrow \{Fa\} \quad \text{(Th)}$$
$$\{Fa, Gb\} \Rightarrow \{\exists x(Fx \land Gx), Fa\}$$
$$\{Fa, Gb\} \Rightarrow \{\exists x(Fx \land Gx), Fa \land Ga\} \quad (\Rightarrow \exists)$$
$$\{Fa, Gb\} \Rightarrow \{\exists x(Fx \land Gx)\} \quad (\exists \Rightarrow)$$
$$\{Fa, \exists yGy\} \Rightarrow \{\exists x(Fx \land Gx)\} \quad (\exists \Rightarrow)$$
$$\{\exists xFx, \exists yGy\} \Rightarrow \{\exists x(Fx \land Gx)\}$$

Figure 15.28. Unsuccessful search for a proof in $S_1^{\forall\exists=}$.

this sequent is $\exists x(Fx \wedge Gx)$, which appears on the right side—and we have already applied ($\Rightarrow \exists$) (in reverse, building up the stack from the bottom) for every name that appears in the sequent (a and b). So there is nothing more we can do: the search for a proof has terminated.

However, this situation is not analogous to that in axiomatic or natural deduction systems when we fail to find a proof; instead, it is like having an open path in a finished finite tree. That is, we do not simply lack a proof that the sequent holds logically; we can read off from the stack a model in which the sequent we were trying to prove does not hold. We can read off the model from the topmost sequent in the branch that does not top out in an axiom. Just as when reading off a model from an open path, we look at atomic wffs in the path that appear as entire formulas, and hence are supposed to be true,[44] so too, when reading off a model from a sequent, we look at atomic wffs on its *left* side, that is, at wffs that are supposed to be true. In the present example Fa and Gb are on the left side, so we have two objects in the domain—one as the referent of a, and one as the referent of b—and the extension of F contains the referent of a (to make Fa true), and the extension of G contains the referent of b (to make Gb true):

Domain: $\{1, 2\}$
Referents: $a: 1 \quad b: 2$
Extensions: $F: \{1\} \quad G: \{2\}$

It is easy to verify that in this model, both the wffs on the left side of the sequent we wanted (but failed) to prove are true (i.e., $\exists x\, Fx$ and $\exists y\, Gy$), while the wff on the right side (i.e., $\exists x(Fx \wedge Gx)$) is false—hence, this sequent does not hold.

Of course, once we move from propositional to predicate logic, just as trees may be infinite, so too the search for a sequent proof may not terminate.

15.3.1 Soundness and Completeness

A sequent calculus is sound (with respect to the property of sequents of holding logically) if every provable sequent holds logically. We could establish soundness by a strategy mirroring that used in the soundness proof for trees (§14.1.2). However, there is a more direct way, because a sequent proof, when read from the top down, is just like an axiomatic proof: it proceeds from axioms, by rules of inference, down to the target sequent at the bottom. So to establish soundness, we just need to establish that the axioms hold logically and that the rules preserve the property of holding logically (i.e., if the inputs to a rule hold logically, so does the output, reading the rule from top to bottom). This is obvious for the axioms and the Thinning rule. For the other rules, the easiest way to establish the result is to look at the rules from the bottom up and show that if the lower sequent does not hold in some model, then the upper sequent (or at least one of them, if there is more than one) does not hold in some model. (The desired result then follows: if the inputs to a rule hold in every model, so does the output.) In each case, showing this involves essentially the same reasoning as that involved in showing that the corresponding tree rule is truth-preserving.

As with axiomatic and natural deduction systems, there are versions of sequent calculus that allow open wffs to appear in (sequents in) proofs; see, for example, Kleene [1952, pp. 440–48]. Comments analogous to those made in §15.1.3 apply concerning the interpretation of such proofs.

A sequent calculus is complete (with respect to the property of sequents of holding logically) if every sequent that holds logically is provable. We can establish completeness by a strategy mirroring that used in the completeness proof for trees (§14.1.3). Here, in outline, are the steps:

(1) Let's call a stack of the sort obtained when searching for a proof of a sequent S from the bottom up a "search stack for S." Our first step is to define the notion of a *fully developed* search stack (this is the analogue of a finished tree): every branch either tops out in an axiom (analogous to a closed path) or is such that every rule that can usefully be applied (in reverse, from bottom to top) has been applied (analogous to a finished path). Note that a fully developed search stack—like a finished tree—might be infinite.

(2) We show that if there is a branch in a fully developed search stack for S that does not top out in an axiom (either because it tops out in a nonaxiom—analogous to a finite saturated open path, or because it goes up forever—analogous to an infinite path), then there is a model in which S does not hold. Completeness follows immediately: if S holds in every model, then every branch in a fully developed search stack for S must top out in an axiom; that is (looking at the search stack from the top down), there is a proof of S.

To establish step (2), we proceed as follows:

(2a) We show how to read off a model from any branch in a fully developed search stack that does not top out in an axiom. Recall the way we read off a model from a saturated open path by looking at unnegated atomic formulas in the path. We read off a model from a branch in exactly the same way, taking as our starting point all and only those unnegated atomic formulas that are on the left side of any sequent in the branch. (An unnegated atomic formula on the right side of a sequent is the analogue of a negated atomic formula in a tree.)

(2b) We assume (for the purposes of establishing step (2)) the antecedent of that step: there is a branch p in a fully developed search stack for S that does not top out in an axiom. We can read off a model $\mathfrak{M}$ from p as in step (2a). We now show:

- Every wff on the left side of any sequent on p is true in $\mathfrak{M}$.

- Every wff on the right side of any sequent on p is false in $\mathfrak{M}$.

Each of these claims is proved by an induction on complexity of formulas. The cases in the induction for the right side are like the subcases for negation in the induction used to prove completeness for trees; those for the left side are like the cases for other kinds of wffs (i.e., not negations) in the induction used to prove completeness for trees. It now follows, in particular, that every formula on the left side of S is true in $\mathfrak{M}$ and every formula on the right side of S is false in $\mathfrak{M}$; that is, S does not hold in $\mathfrak{M}$. So step (2) is established: if there is a branch p in a fully developed search stack for S that does not top out in an axiom, then there is a model in which S does not hold.

15.3.2 Variants

15.3.2.1 CUT AND ITS ELIMINATION

In addition to rules more or less like those of S_1, Gentzen [1935] discusses the following rule, called Cut:

$$\frac{\Gamma \Rightarrow \Delta \cup \{\alpha\} \qquad \{\alpha\} \cup \Theta \Rightarrow \Lambda}{\Gamma \cup \Theta \Rightarrow \Delta \cup \Lambda} \text{ (Cut)}$$

Gentzen then shows that the Cut rule is inessential, in the sense that anything that can be proved with it can also be proved without it. Here's a quick way of seeing that this must be the case. First, Cut is hold-preserving. (Suppose the lower sequent $\Gamma \cup \Theta \Rightarrow \Delta \cup \Lambda$ does not hold in some model, so all wffs in Γ and Θ are true in that model, and all wffs in Δ and Λ are false. Now α is either true or false: in the former case, the input sequent $\{\alpha\} \cup \Theta \Rightarrow \Lambda$ does not hold; in the latter case, the other input sequent $\Gamma \Rightarrow \Delta \cup \{\alpha\}$ does not hold. So for any model in which both input sequents hold, the output sequent must hold too.) Thus, adding Cut to a sound system will not allow us to prove any sequents that do not hold logically. But if our original system (without Cut) was also complete, then we could already prove in it all sequents that do hold logically. So, adding Cut does not allow us to prove anything we could not already prove (given that the original system was sound and complete).

This proof that Cut is eliminable is nonconstructive. It shows that for any sequent proof that uses Cut, there must be a proof (of the same sequent) that does not use Cut, but it does not give us any idea what the Cut-free proof looks like or how to find it. Contrast the proof of the deduction theorem in §15.1.1.1. The theorem tells us that if there is a derivation of γ from assumptions $\alpha_1, \ldots, \alpha_n$ and β, then there exists a derivation of $\beta \rightarrow \gamma$ from assumptions $\alpha_1, \ldots, \alpha_n$. The theorem itself does not say anything about what these derivations might look like—but the proof we sketched does. The proof is *constructive*: it sets out a method that, given as input a derivation of γ from assumptions $\alpha_1, \ldots, \alpha_n$ and β, allows us to construct a derivation of $\beta \rightarrow \gamma$ from assumptions $\alpha_1, \ldots, \alpha_n$. Gentzen gave a constructive proof that Cut is eliminable: a proof based on a method for transforming a proof that uses Cut into one that does not. He calls the result stating that any proof that uses Cut can be transformed into one that does not the *Hauptsatz*.

Unlike ours, Gentzen's proof of Cut elimination does not depend on a prior proof that the original system of sequent proofs (without Cut) is sound and complete. In fact, Cut elimination can be used as part of a strategy to establish completeness, given a prior proof of the completeness of a suitable natural deduction system. This is because adding Cut allows the sequent system to mirror natural deduction proofs (we'll see how this works in §15.3.2.2). So we can then reason as follows: the natural deduction system is complete; anything provable in the natural deduction system is provable in the sequent system with Cut (the mirroring result); anything provable in the sequent system with Cut is provable in the sequent system without Cut (Cut elimination); so the sequent system without Cut is complete.

15.3.2.2 INTRODUCTION ON THE LEFT AND ELIMINATION ON THE RIGHT

The sequent rules introduced above were designed to mirror the tree rules introduced earlier in this book. What would happen if we started instead with natural deduction rules—say, those of system N_1—and modeled our sequent rules on them? In some cases we would end up with exactly the sequent rule we already have, in other cases with a slightly different rule, and in yet other cases with a completely different rule. To translate a natural deduction rule into a sequent rule, let's read a sequent $\Gamma \Rightarrow \{\alpha\}$ as meaning that α can be derived from assumptions in Γ. Now let us look at the three types of case. Consider, for instance, the natural deduction rule $(\rightarrow I)$. It says that we can conclude $\alpha \rightarrow \beta$, given a derivation of β from the assumption α. Translated into sequent form, this rule becomes:

$$\frac{\{\alpha\} \Rightarrow \{\beta\}}{\Rightarrow \{\alpha \rightarrow \beta\}}$$

which is perfectly analogous to our sequent rule $(\Rightarrow\rightarrow)$.[45] Next, consider the natural deduction rule $(\neg I)$. It says that we can conclude $\neg\alpha$, given a derivation of β and $\neg\beta$ from the assumption α. Translated into sequent form, this rule becomes:

$$\frac{\{\alpha\} \Rightarrow \{\beta, \neg\beta\}}{\Rightarrow \{\neg\alpha\}}$$

This is not perfectly analogous to our sequent rule ($\Rightarrow \neg$), because it includes $\{\beta, \neg\beta\}$ on the right side of the input sequent—but it is at least somewhat similar. Finally, however, consider the natural deduction elimination rules, say, the rule ($\rightarrow E$), which says that we can conclude β, given α and $\alpha \rightarrow \beta$. Translated into sequent form, it becomes:

$$\frac{\Rightarrow \{\alpha\} \qquad \Rightarrow \{\alpha \rightarrow \beta\}}{\Rightarrow \{\beta\}}$$

which is nothing like the sequent rule ($\rightarrow \Rightarrow$). The relationship between natural deduction and sequent calculus, then, is that natural deduction rules that eliminate operators on the right are replaced by sequent rules that introduce operators on the left. The big advantage of having all the rules take the form of introduction rules is that it makes possible the method, discussed earlier, of finding proofs by working from the bottom up: the wffs written down as we go up the page become simpler, and so eventually we reach sequents whose left and right sides contain wffs with no connectives, and the search terminates.[46]

We said above that adding Cut allows the sequent system to mirror natural deduction proofs. What we meant is that rules that eliminate on the right can be simulated by rules that introduce on the left together with Cut. Consider, for example, the case of $\rightarrow$ elimination. The following proof uses ($\rightarrow \Rightarrow$) (which introduces $\rightarrow$ on the left) together with Cut to achieve the effects of the rule given most recently above (which eliminates $\rightarrow$ on the right):[47]

$$\frac{\dfrac{\dfrac{\Rightarrow\{\alpha\}}{\Rightarrow\{\alpha, \beta\}}\,(\text{Th}) \qquad \{\beta\}\Rightarrow\{\beta\}}{\{\alpha \rightarrow \beta\}\Rightarrow\{\beta\}}\,(\rightarrow\Rightarrow) \qquad \Rightarrow\{\alpha \rightarrow \beta\}}{\Rightarrow\{\beta\}}\,(\text{Cut})$$

15.3.2.3 STRUCTURAL RULES

In our sequents, the left and right sides are sets of wffs. In Gentzen's original presentation, the left and right sides are (finite) sequences of wffs.[48] This distinction makes a significant difference to sequent calculus. Both $\{\alpha\}$ and $\{\alpha, \alpha\}$ are (two ways of writing) the same set—the one containing just the wff α, so $\{\alpha\} \cup \Gamma \Rightarrow \Delta$ and $\{\alpha, \alpha\} \cup \Gamma \Rightarrow \Delta$ are just (two expressions for) the same sequent. In contrast, $\langle\alpha\rangle$ and $\langle\alpha, \alpha\rangle$ are two different sequences, and so $\langle\alpha\rangle^\frown\Gamma \Rightarrow \Delta$ and $\langle\alpha, \alpha\rangle^\frown\Gamma \Rightarrow \Delta$ are different sequents.[49] Of course, these two different sequents are logically equivalent, because whether a wff α appears at all in the left or the right side of a sequent is relevant to whether all wffs on the left side and some wff on the right side are true in a model; but if α does appear (on a given side), then it does not make any further difference to this question whether it appears only once or multiple times on that side. Thus, we need new rules of inference to derive one sequent from the other. To move from $\langle \alpha, \alpha \rangle^\frown \Gamma \Rightarrow \Delta$ to $\langle \alpha \rangle^\frown \Gamma \Rightarrow \Delta$, we use Contraction:

Contraction on left	Contraction on right
$\dfrac{\langle \alpha, \alpha \rangle^\frown \Gamma \Rightarrow \Delta}{\langle \alpha \rangle^\frown \Gamma \Rightarrow \Delta}$	$\dfrac{\Gamma \Rightarrow \Delta^\frown \langle \alpha, \alpha \rangle}{\Gamma \Rightarrow \Delta^\frown \langle \alpha \rangle}$

To go the other way, we use Thinning (here reformulated in terms of sequences rather than sets and separated into two rules, one for the left side and one for the right):

Thinning on left	Thinning on right
$\dfrac{\Gamma \Rightarrow \Delta}{\langle \alpha \rangle^\frown \Gamma \Rightarrow \Delta}$	$\dfrac{\Gamma \Rightarrow \Delta}{\Gamma \Rightarrow \Delta^\frown \langle \alpha \rangle}$

Gentzen calls rules like these—which, unlike the left and right introduction rules, "refer [not] to logical symbols, but merely to the structure of the sequents" [Gentzen, 1935, 82]—*structural* rules. In addition to Contraction and Thinning, his sequent calculus has structural rules of Interchange:

Interchange on left	Interchange on right
$\dfrac{\Theta^\frown \langle \alpha, \beta \rangle^\frown \Gamma \Rightarrow \Delta}{\Theta^\frown \langle \beta, \alpha \rangle^\frown \Gamma \Rightarrow \Delta}$	$\dfrac{\Gamma \Rightarrow \Delta^\frown \langle \alpha, \beta \rangle^\frown \Theta}{\Gamma \Rightarrow \Delta^\frown \langle \beta, \alpha \rangle^\frown \Theta}$

When the left and right sides of sequents are sets, not sequences, we get the effects of Contraction and Interchange for free. To illustrate this point for the case of Interchange on the left: when sequents involve sets, we do not need a rule allowing us to derive $\Theta \cup \{\beta, \alpha\} \cup \Gamma \Rightarrow \Delta$ from $\Theta \cup \{\alpha, \beta\} \cup \Gamma \Rightarrow \Delta$, because $\Theta \cup \{\alpha, \beta\} \cup \Gamma$ and $\Theta \cup \{\beta, \alpha\} \cup \Gamma$ are simply (two ways of writing) the same set, and hence $\Theta \cup \{\alpha, \beta\} \cup \Gamma \Rightarrow \Delta$ and $\Theta \cup \{\beta, \alpha\} \cup \Gamma \Rightarrow \Delta$ are just (two ways of writing) the same sequent.

A third option is to have the left and right sides of sequents be *multisets*. We can think of a set as being obtained from a sequence by ignoring both ordering and repetition. A multiset ignores ordering but not repetition. That is, a multiset is a collection of objects together with a record of how many times each object occurs in the collection.[50] When sequents employ multisets, we get the effects of Interchange, but not Contraction, for free.

§

We conclude our discussion of sequent calculus by mentioning some of its main advantages and disadvantages. Like trees—and unlike axiomatic and natural deduction systems—sequent calculi, when combined with the method of searching for sequent proofs by working from the bottom up, (i) offer an effective procedure for finding sequent proofs (where proofs exist; i.e., where the sequent at the bottom does hold logically), and (ii) provide proofs of the property of sequents of not holding logically (an s-property).[51] Trees have the advantage of requiring less paper and ink (because the same wffs are not written down repeatedly, as they are in sequent proofs), but sequent proofs, like axiomatic proofs, can be written out as flat sequences (of sequents). At the same time—especially when the left and right sides of sequents are taken to be sequences (not sets)—sequent proofs exhibit a structural richness that makes them intrinsically interesting objects of study, and a great deal of attention is paid to them in proof theory.

15.3.3 Exercises

1. Define the following notions in terms of sequents.

   (i) The proposition α is:
      (a) a contradiction
      (b) satisfiable

   (ii) Propositions α and β are:
      (a) jointly satisfiable
      (b) equivalent

2. Redo some of Exercises 7.3.1.1 and 7.3.2.1 using the sequent calculus S_1 instead of trees.

3. Redo some of Exercises 10.2.2, 12.3.1, and 13.4.3 using the sequent calculus $S_1^{\forall\exists=}$ instead of trees.

4. State sequent rules (i.e., left and right introduction rules) for $\leftrightarrow$.

5. State a (new) tree rule that is the analogue of Cut.

16

Set Theory

This chapter—more in the nature of an appendix—explains basic concepts from set theory, some of which have been employed earlier in this book; it is not a full introduction to the field of set theory.

16.1 Sets

A *set* is a collection of objects. These objects are said to be *members* or *elements* of the set, and the set is said to *contain* these objects.

If we are in a position to name all elements of a set, we can name the set itself by putting braces ("{" and "}") around them. For example, we denote the set containing the numbers 1, 2, and 3 as {1, 2, 3} and the set containing Alice, Bob, and Carol as {Alice, Bob, Carol}. If we cannot name all elements of a set, we might do one of two things. If the elements come in some known order, we can name the first few of them and then write an ellipsis ("..."). For example, we denote the set of all positive integers as {1, 2, 3, ...} and the set of all even positive integers as {2, 4, 6, ...}. Alternatively, we can state a condition C that is satisfied by all and only the elements of the set, and we then denote the set as $\{x : C\}$ (or $\{x | C\}$). For example, the set of all red things is denoted $\{x : x$ is red$\}$ (read as "the set of all x such that x is red"), and the set of all even numbers is denoted $\{x : x$ is even$\}$ (read as "the set of all x such that x is even").

We use the symbol $\in$ (epsilon) to denote membership, as in $1 \in \{1, 2, 3\}$ and Alice $\in$ {Alice, Bob, Carol}. To say that something is not a member of a set, we use the symbol $\notin$, as in $4 \notin \{1, 2, 3\}$ and Dave $\notin$ {Alice, Bob, Carol}. The symbol $\in$ is a two-place relation symbol, but as with =, we write it in between its arguments (as in $x \in S$), not in front of them. The expression $x \notin S$ can be seen as an abbreviation for $\neg x \in S$.

When asked to picture the set containing, say, Alice and Bob, many people will simply picture Alice and Bob standing side by side. This isn't the best way to think of sets. Alice and Bob are the members of the set containing Alice

Alice   Bob

Set containing Alice and Bob

Figure 16.1. Alice, Bob, and the set that contains them.

and Bob, but the set itself is a third thing, distinct from its two members. So we should picture the situation as in Figure 16.1, where the arrows indicate membership (i.e., the thing at the tail of an arrow is a member of the thing at the head of that arrow). This is the guiding idea behind set theory: to treat a collection of objects—that is, a set—as an object in its own right. Set theory is then the theory of these objects—of sets. As Georg Cantor—the founder of set theory—put it: a set is a *many* or *multiplicity* that can be conceived of as *one* or *single*.[1] Note that—unlike its members, Alice and Bob—the set containing Alice and Bob is not visible or tangible. For this reason sets are often referred to as *abstract* objects.

There is a set called the *empty set* or *null set,* symbolized by ∅, which has no elements. This may sound odd. A set is supposed to be a collection of things— but we cannot collect together nothing! So how can there be a set containing no things? Actually, the idea makes perfect sense, once we think of it in the right way—that is, once we remember to think of sets as objects, distinct from their members, with membership indicated by arrows (as in Figure 16.1). We then picture the empty set (i.e., the set with no members) as a dot—an object, a thing, just like all other sets—that simply has no arrows pointing to it.

16.1.1 Extensionality

Suppose we have some kind of thing: Ps. We make a first choice of a P—call it x. We make a second choice of a P (maybe a different thing from our first choice, or maybe we have chosen the same thing a second time)—call it y. An *identity condition* for Ps determines whether $x = y$; that is, whether we chose the same thing twice or chose two different things, for any choices x and y. Sets have a very simple identity condition: for any sets x and y, x and y are identical (i.e., $x = y$) iff every member of x is a member of y, and vice versa. This property of sets—that they are individuated by their members; that if "two" sets have exactly the same members, then they are in fact one and the same set—is known as *extensionality.*

Here are some examples:

$$\{1, 2\} = \{2, 1\}$$

The set on the left has two elements (1 and 2), and each of them is a member of the set on the right. The set on the right has two elements (2 and 1), and each of them is a member of the set on the left. Thus, every member of the set on the left is a member of the set on the right, and vice versa, so they are two different ways of writing the same set. When we name a set by listing its members with braces around them, the order in which we write the elements of the set within the braces does not matter.

$$\{1\} = \{1, 1\}$$

The set on the left has one element (1), and it is a member of the set on the right. The set on the right has just one element (1)—we have simply named this element twice when writing the set on the right—and it is a member of the set on the left. Thus, every member of the set on the left is a member of the set on the right, and vice versa, so they are two different ways of writing the same set. When we name a set by listing its members with braces around them, it makes no difference whether we write a given element once or multiple times: the only significant thing is whether a certain object is named as an element at all.

$$\{4\} = \{2 + 2\}$$

The expressions "$2 + 2$" and "4" pick out the same number: thus, the only element of the set on the left is a member of the set on the right, and vice versa. Note here that even though extensionality fixes the facts as to whether set x is identical to set y, for any sets x and y, it need not always enable us to see whether sets x and y are identical. For example, because $2 + 2$ and 4 are the same number, extensionality fixes that the set $\{4\}$ is the same object as the set $\{2 + 2\}$. However, if someone does not know that $2 + 2 = 4$, then simply knowing the principle of extensionality will not enable him to see that $\{4\}$ and $\{2 + 2\}$ (described thus) are the same set.

$$\{2, 4, 6, \ldots\} = \{x : x \text{ is an even positive integer}\}$$

Again, the expressions on the left and right of the identity sign are just two different ways of writing the same set.

Properties—in contrast with sets—are *intensional*. Consider a property, say, the property of redness. The set of all things that possess a property is often called the *extension* of the property; thus, the set containing all and only red things is the extension of the property of redness.[2] Now two distinct properties might be possessed by exactly the same objects; that is, they might have the same extension. For example, the property of being a human being is not (intuitively) the same as the property of being a featherless biped, but both properties have the same extension (i.e., all humans are featherless bipeds and vice versa). Thus, we say that properties are intensional, as opposed to extensional: knowing that properties P and Q are possessed by the same objects does not allow you to conclude that properties P and Q are identical, whereas knowing that sets S and T contain the same objects does allow you to conclude that S and T are identical. So "being possessed by the same objects" is not the identity condition for properties (whereas "containing the same objects" is the identity condition for sets). In fact there is no obviously correct precise identity condition for properties. Certain cases might be clear enough—such as the featherless biped example—but there is no widely accepted theory spelling out a general precise identity condition for properties. One of the advantages of working with sets—rather than properties—is their crystal clear identity condition (i.e., extensionality).

16.1.2 Subsets

A set S is a subset of a set T—in symbols, $S \subseteq T$—iff every member of S is a member of T:

$$S \subseteq T \text{ iff } \forall x (x \in S \rightarrow x \in T) \tag{16.1}$$

Note that this definition leaves open whether or not $S = T$: that depends upon whether there is anything in T that is not in S. If there is nothing in T that is not in S (i.e., if $T \subseteq S$ as well as $S \subseteq T$), then $S = T$. This is just the principle of extensionality phrased in a new way. If there is something in T that is not in S (i.e., $S \subseteq T$ but not $T \subseteq S$), then S is a *proper* subset of T, symbolized by $S \subsetneq T$.[3] Note that every set is (trivially) a subset of itself, but no set is a proper subset of itself.

The null set is a subset of every set. Given any set T, it is automatically true—because $\emptyset$ has no members—that every member of $\emptyset$ is a member of T. Recall (Exercises 9.4.3, question 5(i)) that "all Fs are Gs" is true when there are no Fs. Similarly, because $x \in \emptyset$ is false for every x, the following comes out true no matter what set T is:

$$\forall x (x \in \emptyset \rightarrow x \in T)$$

But this is just the condition required for $\emptyset$ to be a subset of T; hence, for all T, $\emptyset \subseteq T$.

We can now see that the empty set is unique; that is, there is only one empty set (there are not two different sets, each of which has no members). For suppose there were two empty sets, a and b. For the reasons just given, $a \subseteq b$ and $b \subseteq a$—but then, by extensionality, $a = b$.

A set containing just one element—for example, $\{3\}$—is a *singleton* or *unit set*.

Note that 1 is an *element* of the set {1, 2, 3} but is not a subset of it, whereas {1} is a subset of the set {1, 2, 3} but is not an element of it. Sometimes we are given a set S and we want to consider a set of subsets of S. For example, suppose we have the set $S = \{1, 2, 3, 4\}$, and we want to consider the set S_2 of all two-membered subsets of this set:

$$S_2 = \{\{1, 2\}, \{1, 3\}, \{1, 4\}, \{2, 3\}, \{2, 4\}, \{3, 4\}\}$$

(Because $\{2, 3\} = \{3, 2\}$, we do not list $\{3, 2\}$ separately. Similarly for $\{2, 1\}$ etc.) Note that:

$$\{1, 2\} \subseteq S$$
$$\{1, 2\} \in S_2$$

That is, an element of S_2 is a subset of S.

One very important set of subsets of any set S is the *power set* of S—the set of *all* subsets of S—symbolized by $\wp S$:

$$\wp S = \{x : x \subseteq S\}$$

For example, for $S = \{1, 2, 3\}$,

$$\wp S = \{\emptyset, \{1\}, \{2\}, \{3\}, \{1, 2\}, \{1, 3\}, \{2, 3\}, \{1, 2, 3\}\}$$

16.1.3 Operations on Sets

The *union* of two sets S and T, denoted $S \cup T$, contains everything in either S or T (or both):

$$S \cup T = \{x : x \in S \lor x \in T\}$$

or visually:

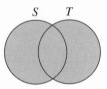

Here, the left circle represents the set S (i.e., think of the members of S as the things within this circle; note that these elements of S are not shown in the picture); the right circle represents the set T; the union of S and T is shaded gray.

The *intersection* of two sets S and T, denoted $S \cap T$, contains everything which is in both S and T:

$$S \cap T = \{x : x \in S \land x \in T\}$$

or visually:

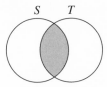

Here, the intersection of S and T is shaded gray.

Two sets S and T are *disjoint* if they have no members in common; that is, if $S \cap T = \emptyset$:

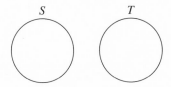

Often when dealing with some sets, it is useful to consider them as subsets of some background set (e.g., the background set might be the domain of some model). The *complement* of a set S, denoted S', is the set of all things that are *not* in S.[4] Here it is important that we are restricting ourselves to the contents of some background set: S' contains everything in the background set that is not in S, not everything at all that is not in S:

$$S' = \{x : \neg x \in S\}$$

or visually:

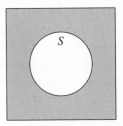

Here, the square represents the background set; the circle represents the set S; the complement of S is shaded gray.

The set-theoretic *difference* of two sets S and T (taken in that order), denoted $S \setminus T$, is the set of things in S but not in T:

$$S \setminus T = \{x : x \in S \wedge \neg x \in T\}$$

or visually:

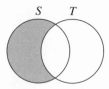

Here, the shaded area is $S \setminus T$. The set $S \setminus T$ is also known as the *relative complement* of T in S. Note that if we think of S and T as subsets of a background set U, then $S \setminus T = S \cap T'$, and $S' = U \setminus S$.[5]

Note that, for any sets S and T, $S \cup T = T \cup S$ and $S \cap T = T \cap S$.[6] It is not the case, however, that for any sets S and T, $S \setminus T = T \setminus S$. Compare the following picture of $T \setminus S$ to the previous picture of $S \setminus T$:

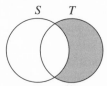

Of course, if $S = T$ then $S \setminus T = T \setminus S = \emptyset$.[7]

There is an evident parallel between the set-theoretic operations of complement, union, and intersection and the logical operations of negation, disjunction, and conjunction, respectively: the complement of S contains all objects *not* in S; the union of S and T contains all objects in S *or* in T; the intersection of S and T contains all objects in S *and* in T. Recall (§6.6) that every possible two-place connective can be defined in terms of $\neg$, $\vee$, and $\wedge$. Similarly, suppose we have two sets, S and T, that are subsets of a background set U. Suppose we want to specify a third subset, V, such that for any object x in U, whether x is in V is completely determined by whether x is in S and whether x is in T. Then, any such V can be defined in terms of S and T and the operations of complement, union, and intersection. We have already seen an example of this: $S \setminus T = S \cap T'$. Here is a second example. The *symmetric difference* of two sets S and T, denoted $S \triangle T$, contains everything that is in exactly one of S and T:

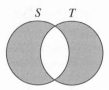

This set may be defined in any of the following ways:

$$S \triangle T = (S \cup T) \setminus (S \cap T)$$
$$S \triangle T = (S \setminus T) \cup (T \setminus S)$$
$$S \triangle T = (S \cup T) \cap (S \cap T)'$$

The third is a direct definition in terms of S and T and the operations of complement, union, and intersection. The first two reduce to such definitions when we define out the relative complement operation in these terms. Note that, unlike the set-theoretic difference operation, the symmetric difference operation is symmetric (hence its name); that is, for any sets S and T, $S \triangle T = T \triangle S$.

You may notice that the symmetric difference operation is the set-theoretic analogue of exclusive disjunction (§6.4). That is, we could specify the symmetric difference of S and T as:

$$S \triangle T = \{x : x \in S \veebar x \in T\}$$

If we take any other two-place connective, we can likewise obtain a corresponding operation on sets. For example, corresponding to the conditional, we could specify an operation $\overset{s}{\to}$ on sets as follows (we put an "s" on top of the arrow symbol to indicate that this new operation takes sets as arguments, whereas the conditional $\to$ connects wffs):

$$S \overset{s}{\to} T = \{x : x \in S \to x \in T\}$$

Remembering that $\alpha \to \beta$ is equivalent to $\neg \alpha \vee \beta$ and to $\neg(\alpha \wedge \neg \beta)$, the set $S \overset{s}{\to} T$ could be defined in either of the following ways:

$$S \overset{s}{\to} T = S' \cup T$$
$$S \overset{s}{\to} T = (S \cap T')'$$

As you can see by comparing the following picture of $S \overset{s}{\to} T$ with the earlier picture of $S \setminus T$, $S \overset{s}{\to} T = (S \setminus T)'$.

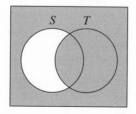

To take a second example, corresponding to the biconditional, we could specify an operation $\overset{s}{\leftrightarrow}$ on sets as:

$$S \overset{s}{\leftrightarrow} T = \{x : x \in S \leftrightarrow x \in T\}$$

Remembering that $\alpha \leftrightarrow \beta$ is equivalent to $(\alpha \wedge \beta) \vee (\neg\alpha \wedge \neg\beta)$ and to $\neg((\alpha \vee \beta) \wedge \neg(\alpha \wedge \beta))$, the set $S \overset{s}{\leftrightarrow} T$ could be defined in either of the following ways:

$$S \overset{s}{\leftrightarrow} T = (S \cap T) \cup (S' \cap T')$$

$$S \overset{s}{\leftrightarrow} T = ((S \cup T) \cap (S \cap T)')'$$

As you can see by comparing the following picture of $S \overset{s}{\leftrightarrow} T$ with the earlier one of $S \Delta T$, $S \overset{s}{\leftrightarrow} T = (S \Delta T)'$. Also, $S \overset{s}{\leftrightarrow} T = (S \overset{s}{\to} T) \cap (T \overset{s}{\to} S)$. You can see this identity by looking at the picture of $S \overset{s}{\to} T$, imagining a picture of $T \overset{s}{\to} S$, and comparing them with the following picture of $S \overset{s}{\leftrightarrow} T$, or by noting that $\alpha \leftrightarrow \beta$ is equivalent to $(\alpha \to \beta) \wedge (\beta \to \alpha)$.

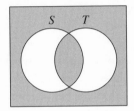

16.1.4 What Sets Exist?

An intuitively appealing principle is that every property has an extension: for any property, there is a set of objects that have that property. (It may be the empty set, but that is still a set.) We can make this idea more precise by replacing the notion of "property" with that of a condition specifiable in a particular formal language. Let's take the fragment of GPLI including no nonlogical symbols (no names, and no predicates apart from =) and add the set-theoretic symbol $\in$ (a two-place predicate). Call the resulting language GPLI with Set Membership (GPLIS). An open formula $\alpha(x)$ of GPLIS—which contains free occurrences of the variable x—can be thought of as a condition that objects may or may not satisfy. Now the more precise version of the intuitive thought is that for any such condition $\alpha(x)$, there exists a set containing all and only the objects satisfying the condition—that is, the set:

$$\{x : \alpha(x)\}$$

Note that the empty set can be specified in this way by giving a condition $\alpha(x)$ in GPLIS:

$$\emptyset = \{x : \neg x = x\}$$

Because $\forall x\, x = x$ is logically true, no object satisfies the condition $\neg x = x$; hence, the set of all and only the objects that satisfy this condition is the empty set. Assuming that sets S and T have been specified in this way—that is, that we have introduced "S" as a name for a certain set specified by some condition and "T" as a name for a certain set specified by some condition—the sets S', $S \cup T$, $S \cap T$, and so on can also be specified in this way. That is precisely how we did specify them in §16.1.3: with conditions stated using only logical symbols of GPLI and the new symbol $\in$ (and the names "S" and "T").

Let's return to the precisified version of the intuitive thought. It is known as the principle of *unrestricted comprehension* (or "unlimited comprehension"):

For any wff $\alpha(x)$ in GPLIS containing one or more free occurrences of x, there exists a set:

$$\{x : \alpha(x)\}$$

The term *naïve set theory* is often used for the theory of sets that takes extensionality and unrestricted comprehension as its basic principles. Unrestricted comprehension determines which sets exist; extensionality determines when sets x and y are one and the same set. Frege [1964, p. 105] took as an axiom (Basic Law V) in his later formal system a principle that implies both a version of unrestricted comprehension and extensionality. However—as Russell [1902] pointed out to Frege in a now-famous letter, we can derive a contradiction from the principle of unrestricted comprehension. Let $\alpha(x)$ be the formula $\neg x \in x$. Then the principle yields a set $\{x : \neg x \in x\}$. Call this set R (the Russell set). By pure logic, either $R \in R$ or $\neg R \in R$. Suppose the former: then $\neg R \in R$ (because the condition required for R to be in R is $\neg R \in R$). Suppose the latter: then it is not the case that $\neg R \in R$ (again because the condition required for R to be in R is $\neg R \in R$, so if R is not in R, it must be that the condition is not satisfied); that is, $R \in R$. Thus, we have $R \in R \vee \neg R \in R$, $R \in R \rightarrow \neg R \in R$ and $\neg R \in R \rightarrow R \in R$. From these, the contradiction $R \in R \wedge \neg R \in R$ follows by pure logic. We have derived a contradiction ($R \in R \wedge \neg R \in R$) from the principle of unrestricted comprehension. This is *Russell's Paradox*.

We therefore need a new theory about which sets exist: unrestricted comprehension will not do. A common picture nowadays concerning which sets exist is the *iterative conception of set*. In this view, sets are built up in stages. A set S can only be built at stage x if all members of S already exist as of stage x. In particular, a set that contains sets as members can only be built at stage x if these member sets were built at some stage prior to x.

We start building sets at stage 0. At this stage—as we have not yet built any sets—all we have available to put in the sets we are building are objects that are not sets; these are called *urelements*. There may be no urelements; as we shall see, we can still build plenty of sets in this case. At stage 0 we can always build the empty set. If there are no urelements, this is the only set we can build. If there is one urelement, a, we can build the sets $\emptyset$ and $\{a\}$. If there are two urelements, a and b, the possible sets are $\emptyset$, $\{a\}$, $\{b\}$, and $\{a, b\}$; and so on if there are more urelements.

At stage 1, we can build any set containing urelements or sets built at stage 0, that is, any set whose members are already available at the beginning of stage 1. If there are no urelements, we can build $\emptyset$ and $\{\emptyset\}$. (Note that $\emptyset$ was already built at stage 0. At every stage, we can always build again everything built at any earlier stage. In general, when talking about the stage at which a set is formed, we mean the earliest stage at which it is formed.) If there is one urelement, a, then at stage 1 we can build the following eight sets:

$$\emptyset$$

$$\{a\} \qquad \{\emptyset\} \qquad \{\{a\}\}$$
$$\{a, \emptyset\} \qquad \{a, \{a\}\} \qquad \{\emptyset, \{a\}\}$$
$$\{a, \emptyset, \{a\}\}$$

(Two of these—$\emptyset$ and $\{a\}$—were already built at stage 0.) If there are more urelements, we can build even more sets at this stage.

At stage 2, we can build any set containing urelements, sets built at stage 0, or sets built at stage 1, that is, any set whose members are already available at the beginning of stage 2. If there are no urelements, we can build the following four sets:

$$\emptyset$$

$$\{\emptyset\} \qquad \{\{\emptyset\}\}$$
$$\{\emptyset, \{\emptyset\}\}$$

(The empty set $\emptyset$ was already built at stage 0 and at stage 1; $\{\emptyset\}$ was already built at stage 1.) If there is one urelement, a, then at stage 2 we have nine objects available to put into sets: a, and the eight sets built at stage 1 (the two sets built at stage 0 were also built at stage 1, so we do not count them again). Thus, we can build $2^9 = 512$ sets (too many to show here). If we have more urelements, we can build even more.

The progression of stages never stops: indeed, it extends to *transfinite* stages. Thus, it is not just that there is a stage n for every finite n: after all these finite stages (infinitely many of them), there is another stage, stage ω. At this stage, we form sets whose members may be any urelement (if there are any), or any set formed at any earlier stage $(1, 2, 3, \ldots)$. Next we have a stage $\omega + 1$, at which we form sets whose members may be any urelement (if there are any), or any set formed at any earlier stage $(1, 2, 3, \ldots, \omega)$; and so on, through stages $\omega + 2$, $\omega + 3$, . . . , $\omega + \omega (= \omega.2)$, $\omega.2 + 1$, $\omega.2 + 2$, $\omega.2 + 3$, . . . , $\omega.2 + \omega (= \omega.3)$, . . . , $\omega.\omega$, ...

Sets built up in this way from no urelements are called *pure* sets. They can be arranged into a hierarchy—known as the *cumulative* or *iterative* hierarchy—according to the stage at which they are (first) formed. All the usual objects considered in mathematics can be identified with sets in the cumulative hierarchy. For example, the natural numbers 0, 1, 2, . . . can be identified with the sets $\emptyset$, $\{\emptyset\}$, $\{\emptyset, \{\emptyset\}\}$, . . . (note that each set in the sequence contains all the earlier sets in the sequence). At the same time, certain problematic sets are not built at any stage—and so they do not exist at all, in this conception. For example, there is no Russell set. For note that no set in the cumulative hierarchy is a member of itself: a set S can only have as members things that have already been formed prior to the stage at which S is formed; so for S to contain itself, S would have to be formed at some stage prior to the stage at which S is formed—which is impossible. Thus, the set of all sets that are not members of themselves would simply be the set of all sets in the cumulative hierarchy. But there is no such set. For if there were, it would have to be formed at some stage—and then it would not contain the sets formed at subsequent stages (remember, the progression of stages never ends).

The iterative conception thus provides a theory about what sets exist that yields enough sets for mathematics and promises to avoid contradictions, such as Russell's paradox. Of course, the theory—as we have presented it here—is not precise. Greater precision may be attained by formulating axioms that are true in the cumulative hierarchy and then working directly from the axioms; this is known as *axiomatic set theory*.[8]

16.2 Ordered Pairs and Ordered *n*-tuples

Roughly speaking, an *ordered pair* consists of two objects, given in a particular order: one first, the other second. The ordered pair consisting of Alice first and Bob second is represented as ⟨Alice, Bob⟩ or (Alice, Bob). An *ordered triple* consists of three objects, given in a particular order. The ordered triple consisting of Alice first, Bob second and Carol third is represented as ⟨Alice, Bob, Carol⟩ or (Alice, Bob, Carol). In general, an *ordered n-tuple* (or just an *n*-tuple, for short) consists of *n* objects in a particular order. The ordered *n*-tuple consisting of Alice first, Bob second, . . . , and Carol in *n*th position is represented as ⟨Alice, Bob, . . . , Carol⟩ or (Alice, Bob, . . . , Carol). "Ordered pair" is then just another term for an ordered 2-tuple, and "ordered triple" is another term for an ordered 3-tuple.

I said "roughly speaking" because in fact an ordered pair does not have to comprise two different objects, an ordered triple does not have to comprise three different objects, and so on. For example, ⟨1, 1⟩, ⟨Alice, Alice⟩, and

⟨Bob, Bob⟩ are perfectly good ordered pairs. Here we have just one object (in each case) that occupies both positions in the pair. Thus, we should think of an ordered pair not as "two objects" given in a certain order, but as an abstract ranking or ordering with two positions, first and second: a stipulation of a first object and a second object (which may or may not be the same object). There is, in general, no reason why Alice (or any other individual) should not be ranked first *and* second. For example, suppose that some children are working out an ordering of who gets to go on the swing. If Alice has been sick in bed for a week and has just rejoined the group, the children might deem that not only should she have first go, she should have two goes in a row. Thus, she occupies positions one and two in the ordering. The idea is not that she is standing behind herself in a queue: that she is both first and second in line. That is impossible. Rather, the ordering—in which she occupies both first and second position—is an abstract thing.

The same point applies to ordered triples, and indeed to ordered n-tuples in general. Thus, the following are all perfectly good ordered triples, and they are all different triples:

$$\langle 1, 2, 3 \rangle \quad \langle 1, 2, 1 \rangle \quad \langle 1, 2, 2 \rangle \quad \langle 3, 2, 3 \rangle \quad \langle 1, 1, 1 \rangle \quad \langle 3, 3, 3 \rangle \quad \langle 2, 2, 1 \rangle$$

In general, there must be at least one, and at most n, distinct objects in an ordered n-tuple. At one extreme we have the same object occupying all positions; at the other extreme we have different objects in every position.

We saw that for sets, the order in which one writes the members is irrelevant; for example, $\{1, 2\} = \{2, 1\}$, and $\{1, 2, 3\} = \{2, 1, 3\}$. For ordered n-tuples, this is not the case: $\langle 1, 2 \rangle \neq \langle 2, 1 \rangle$ and $\langle 1, 2, 3 \rangle \neq \langle 2, 1, 3 \rangle$. We also saw that $\{1, 1\}$ is just another way of writing $\{1\}$, $\{1, 1, 2, 2\}$ is just another way of writing $\{1, 2\}$, and so on. For ordered n-tuples, this is not the case: $\langle 1, 1 \rangle \neq \langle 1 \rangle$ and $\langle 1, 1, 2, 2 \rangle \neq \langle 1, 2 \rangle$. The n-tuple $\langle 1, 1 \rangle$ is an ordered pair with 1 in both positions (first and second); $\langle 1 \rangle$ is an ordered 1-tuple with 1 in its first (and only) position. Similar remarks apply to $\langle 1, 1, 2, 2 \rangle$ and $\langle 1, 2 \rangle$.

For any object and any set, there are only two possibilities: the object is either in the set, or it isn't. So, a is in the set $\{a, c\}$, b isn't, and c is. If we write something like $\{a, a, c\}$, we have just written the same set as before—the one that has a and c in it, and nothing else—only in a more long-winded way. We can write a twice, but a can't be in the set twice: it is either in, or it isn't—there are no different grades or ways of being in a set. For an object and an ordered n-tuple, however, the question is not simply whether the object is in the n-tuple. The question is: where in the n-tuple is the object? The following are therefore three different n-tuples:

$$\langle a, c \rangle \quad \langle a, a \rangle \quad \langle a, a, c \rangle$$

The first is a 2-tuple (i.e., an ordered pair) in which a appears in first position, c appears in second position, and no other object appears. The second is also a 2-tuple, but this time, a appears twice—in first and second positions—and no other object appears. The third is a 3-tuple (i.e., an ordered triple), in which a appears in first and second positions, c appears in third position, and no other object appears.

For any sets S and T, their *Cartesian product* $S \times T$ is the set of all ordered pairs whose first member is an element of S and whose second member is an element of T. For example, if $S = \{1, 2\}$ and $T = \{3, 4\}$, then

$$S \times T = \{\langle 1, 3 \rangle, \langle 1, 4 \rangle, \langle 2, 3 \rangle, \langle 2, 4 \rangle\}$$

Where S and T are the same set, the Cartesian product $S \times S$ is denoted S^2. For example, if $S = \{1, 2, 3\}$, then

$$S^2 = \{\langle 1, 1 \rangle, \langle 1, 2 \rangle, \langle 1, 3 \rangle, \langle 2, 1 \rangle, \langle 2, 2 \rangle, \langle 2, 3 \rangle, \langle 3, 1 \rangle, \langle 3, 2 \rangle, \langle 3, 3 \rangle\}$$

The set of all ordered triples of elements of S is denoted S^3, and in general the set of all ordered n-tuples of elements of S is denoted S^n. For example, if $S = \{1, 2\}$, then

$$S^3 = \{\langle 1, 1, 1 \rangle, \langle 1, 1, 2 \rangle, \langle 1, 2, 1 \rangle, \langle 1, 2, 2 \rangle, \langle 2, 1, 1 \rangle, \langle 2, 1, 2 \rangle, \langle 2, 2, 1 \rangle, \langle 2, 2, 2 \rangle\}$$

Note that the rows in the matrix of a truth table for a proposition (or collection of propositions) containing n basic propositions are precisely the ordered n-tuples in $\{T, F\}^n$, where $\{T, F\}$ is the set of truth values. (In each row of the matrix, the first entry is the truth value of the first basic proposition, the second entry is the truth value of the second basic proposition, . . . , and the final—nth—entry is the truth value of the nth basic proposition. The rows cover all possible assignments of values to these propositions—that is, all possible n-tuples of values.)

16.2.1 Reduction to Sets

Ordered pairs do not have to be thought of as a new kind of primitive entity: they can be identified with sets of a certain sort. This can be done in various ways; the now-standard approach is due to Kuratowski [1921, 171]:[9]

$$\langle a, b \rangle = \{\{a, b\}, \{a\}\}$$

The essential thing about an ordered pair is that it specifies which object comes first and which comes second. In other words, the identity condition for ordered pairs is: if we have an ordered pair x and an ordered pair y, they are one and the same ordered pair iff x's first object is the same as y's first object and x's second object is the same as y's second object. In symbols:

$$\langle x, y \rangle = \langle z, w \rangle \leftrightarrow (x = z \wedge y = w)$$

The key aspect of a reduction of ordered pairs to sets is that this identity condition should then follow from the identity condition (i.e., extensionality) for the sets to which $\langle x, y \rangle$ and $\langle z, w \rangle$ are reduced (i.e., here, $\{\{x, y\}, \{x\}\}$ and $\{\{z, w\}, \{z\}\}$). That is, it should follow from extensionality that:

$$\{\{x, y\}, \{x\}\} = \{\{z, w\}, \{z\}\} \leftrightarrow (x = z \wedge y = w)$$

The right-to-left direction holds trivially. For the left-to-right direction, suppose that $\{\{x, y\}, \{x\}\} = \{\{z, w\}, \{z\}\}$ (call this identity A). We want to show that $x = z$ and $y = w$. There are two cases to consider:

(i) $x = y$. In this case, $\{x, y\} = \{x, x\} = \{x\}$, so $\{\{x, y\}, \{x\}\} = \{\{x\}, \{x\}\} = \{\{x\}\}$. So A becomes $\{\{x\}\} = \{\{z, w\}, \{z\}\}$, from which it follows, by extensionality, that both $\{z, w\}$ and $\{z\}$ are in $\{\{x\}\}$; that is, $\{z, w\} = \{x\}$, and $\{z\} = \{x\}$. By extensionality the former yields $z = x$ (and so $x = z$) and $w = x$; from $x = y$ and $w = x$ we get $y = w$.

(ii) $x \neq y$. Hence, $\{x, y\}$ is a two-membered set, so $\{x, y\} \neq \{x\}$ (as $\{x\}$ is a one-membered set, and by extensionality a two-membered set cannot be identical to a one-membered set), and so $\{\{x, y\}, \{x\}\}$ is a two-membered set. Hence, given A, $\{\{z, w\}, \{z\}\}$ must also have two members, so $z \neq w$. Furthermore, one of the members of $\{\{z, w\}, \{z\}\}$ must be $\{x, y\}$, and the other must be $\{x\}$. As $\{x, y\}$ and $\{z, w\}$ are both two-membered and $\{x\}$ and $\{z\}$ are one-membered, (a) $\{x, y\} = \{z, w\}$, and (b) $\{x\} = \{z\}$. From (b), $x = z$. From (a), and $x \neq y$ and $z \neq w$ and $x = z$, it follows that $y = w$.

Other reductions would also work—for example, we could say that $\langle a, b \rangle = \{\{a, b\}, \{b\}\}$. Not anything would work, however—for example, if we said that $\langle a, b \rangle = \{\{a\}, \{b\}\}$ then it would turn out that $\langle a, b \rangle = \langle b, a \rangle$ (even when $a \neq b$).

What about ordered n-tuples, where n is a number other than 2? An ordered 1-tuple $\langle x \rangle$ can simply be identified with the set $\{x\}$. An ordered triple $\langle x, y, z \rangle$ can be identified with the ordered pair $\langle \langle x, y \rangle, z \rangle$. Note that the first member of this ordered pair is itself an ordered pair. An ordered 4-tuple $\langle x, y, z, w \rangle$ can then be identified with the ordered pair $\langle \langle x, y, z \rangle, w \rangle$. Note that the first member of this ordered pair is an ordered triple. Given that we have seen how to reduce an ordered triple to ordered pairs, this representation shows how to reduce an ordered 4-tuple to ordered pairs. In general, we can reduce the ordered $(n + 1)$-tuple $\langle x_1, \ldots, x_n, y \rangle$ to the ordered pair $\langle \langle x_1, \ldots, x_n \rangle, y \rangle$, and thus all ordered n-tuples ($n > 2$) may ultimately be reduced to ordered pairs—which, as we have seen, may be reduced to sets.[10]

A second approach to ordered n-tuples, for $n > 2$, is to view an ordered n-tuple as a *sequence* of length n—in the precise sense of "sequence" introduced in §16.5. As we shall see, a sequence in this sense is a certain sort of function, and a function may be seen as a certain sort of set of ordered pairs. Thus, it would be circular to identify ordered pairs with sequences of length 2. However, once we identify ordered pairs with sets in the way discussed above, we are then free to identify ordered n-tuples, for $n > 2$, with sequences of length n.

16.3 Relations

An n-place relation is a condition that an n-tuple of objects may or may not satisfy; thus, we think of it as a set of n-tuples. For example, consider the relation "x is a brother of y." Let's say Bill is a brother of Ben, and vice versa; Bill is a brother of Carol, but not vice versa; and Ben is a brother of Carol, but not vice versa. Then we can think of this relation as the following set of ordered pairs:

$$\{\langle \text{Bill, Ben}\rangle, \langle \text{Ben, Bill}\rangle, \langle \text{Bill, Carol}\rangle, \langle \text{Ben, Carol}\rangle\}$$

A 2-place relation is also called a *binary* relation; a 3-place relation is also called a *ternary* relation.

Often we want to be quite specific about the sets from which the elements of the ordered n-tuples in a relation (a set of n-tuples) are drawn. We say that a binary relation *from* a set S *to* a set T is a subset of $S \times T$, that is, a set of ordered pairs whose first elements are in S and whose second elements are in T. Where S and T are the same set, a binary relation from S to T—that is, from S to itself—is also called a binary relation *on* S. A binary relation on S is a subset of S^2. Similarly, a ternary relation on S is a subset of S^3 (i.e., a set of ordered triples of elements of S), and in general an n-place relation on S is a subset of S^n.

There are various properties that a binary relation R on S may have. For example,

Reflexivity: for every x in S, $\langle x, x\rangle \in R$. That is, the relation holds between every object x and itself.

Irreflexivity: for every x in S, $\langle x, x\rangle \notin R$. That is, the relation holds between no object x and itself.

Transitivity: for every x, y, and z in S, if $\langle x, y\rangle \in R$ and $\langle y, z\rangle \in R$, then $\langle x, z\rangle \in R$. That is, if the relation holds between x and y and between y and z, then it holds between x and z.

Symmetry: for every x and y in S, if $\langle x, y\rangle \in R$, then $\langle y, x\rangle \in R$. That is, if the relation holds between x and y in one order, then it holds between them in the other order as well.

Antisymmetry: for every x and y in S, if $\langle x, y\rangle \in R$ and $\langle y, x\rangle \in R$, then $x = y$. That is, the only case in which the relation holds between x and y in both directions is the case where x and y are one and the same object.[11]

Asymmetry: for every x and y in S, if $\langle x, y \rangle \in R$ then $\langle y, x \rangle \notin R$. That is, if the relation holds between x and y in one direction, then it does not hold in the other direction.[12]

Connectedness: for every x and y in S such that $x \neq y$, either $\langle x, y \rangle \in R$ or $\langle y, x \rangle \in R$ (or both). That is, for any distinct objects x and y, the relation holds between them in at least one direction.[13]

Relations having certain groups of these properties are important in certain contexts and hence have been given special names. Three examples of such relations are equivalence relations, partial orders, and linear orders.

R is an *equivalence relation* if it is reflexive, symmetric, and transitive. Note that if R is an equivalence relation, then it divides S into subsets—*equivalence classes*—with the following features: every member of S is in exactly one equivalence class (i.e., the equivalence classes are nonoverlapping and between them they cover all of S; i.e., they constitute a *partition* of S); for any x and y in S (including the case $x = y$), $\langle x, y \rangle \in R$ iff x and y are in the same equivalence class. The identity relation on any set S is an equivalence relation; each equivalence class contains exactly one object. The relation of logical equivalence on the set of wffs of PL is an equivalence relation; if an equivalence class contains a wff α, then it also contains all and only the wffs that are logically equivalent to α.

R is a *partial order* if it is reflexive, transitive, and antisymmetric. It is a *strict* partial order if it is irreflexive and transitive (it follows that it must also be asymmetric). R is a (strict) *linear order* if it is a (strict) partial order that is also connected. The relation $\leq$ on the natural numbers is a linear order (and hence also a partial order); the relation $<$ on the natural numbers is a strict linear order (and hence also a strict partial order). For any set S, the relation $\subseteq$ on $\wp S$ is a partial order (but not in general a linear order);[14] the relation $\subsetneq$ on $\wp S$ is a strict partial order (but not in general a strict linear order). Note that given any partial order, if we remove all pairs $\langle x, x \rangle$, the result will be a *strict* partial order; given any strict partial order, if we *add* all pairs $\langle x, x \rangle$ (for all x in S), the result will be a partial order. An analogous result holds for linear orders and strict linear orders.

16.4 Functions

A *function* (aka map, mapping, operation) f from a set S to a set T, written:[15]

$$f : S \to T$$

assigns particular objects in T to objects in S. S is called the *domain* of the function and T the *codomain*. The essential feature of a function is that it never assigns more than one object in T to any given object in S. If x is a member of

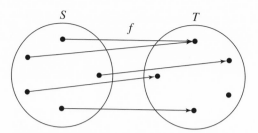

Figure 16.2. Picturing a function as a collection of arrows.

S, $f(x)$ is the object in T that the function f assigns to x. We say that $f(x)$ is the *value* or *output* of the function f for the *argument* or *input* x, or it is the value *at* x; we also say x is *sent to* $f(x)$, that $f(x)$ is *hit by* x, or that $f(x)$ is the *image* of x under f. Note that S and T may be the same set. In this case we call a function from S to T—that is, from S to itself—a function *on* S.

A function $f : S \rightarrow T$ is commonly identified with the set of ordered pairs $\langle x, f(x) \rangle$, where x is an object in S that is sent to some object in T by f, and $f(x)$ is the object in T to which x is sent. For example, consider the *successor* function on the set of natural numbers, which, given a number as input, yields as output the *next* number in the sequence of natural numbers. Represented as a set of ordered pairs, it is:

$$\{\langle 0, 1 \rangle, \langle 1, 2 \rangle, \langle 2, 3 \rangle, \ldots\}$$

The crucial feature of a function—that it never assigns more than one object in T to any given object in S—emerges here as the requirement that no element of S appears more than once as the first element of an ordered pair in the set.

Another useful way to picture a function $f : S \rightarrow T$ is as a collection of arrows pointing from objects x in S to objects $f(x)$ in T (Figure 16.2). Binary relations can also usefully be pictured as collections of arrows. In this depiction, functions are distinguished from relations in general by the requirement on functions that no object has more than one arrow departing from it.

As with relations, there are various properties which a function $f : S \rightarrow T$ may have. For example:

A function $f : S \rightarrow T$ is said to be *total* if it satisfies the condition that every member of S is sent to some member of T. A function that is not total is called *partial*. Such a function assigns nothing to some member(s) of S. In the representation of a function as a set of ordered pairs, to say that $x \in S$ is assigned no value by the partial function $f : S \rightarrow T$ means that x does not appear as the first element of any ordered pair in the set; in the representation of a function as a collection of arrows, it means that x has no arrow leading from it.[16]

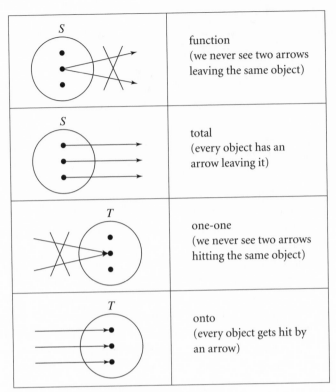

S	function (we never see two arrows leaving the same object)
S	total (every object has an arrow leaving it)
T	one-one (we never see two arrows hitting the same object)
T	onto (every object gets hit by an arrow)

Figure 16.3. Kinds of function from S to T.

A function $f : S \rightarrow T$ is said to be *onto* (aka surjective, a surjection) if it satisfies the condition that every member of T is hit at least once; *one-one* (aka one-to-one, into, injective, an injection) if no member of T is hit more than once; and a *correspondence* (aka bijective, a bijection) if it is total, onto, and one-one. (See Figure 16.3. Note that the top property in the table, unlike the three below it, is a sine qua non for functions: if a subset of $S \times T$ does not possess this property, then it is not a function. Also, do not be misled by the picture of an onto function: a function can be onto without being one-one.)

Note that if (as discussed above) we identify a function f with the set of all ordered pairs $\langle x, y \rangle$ such that $f(x) = y$, then the following identity condition for functions holds: $f = g$ iff f assigns values to all and only the objects to which g assigns values, and for all such objects x, $f(x) = g(x)$. This condition follows from the identity condition for sets (extensionality) together with the identity condition for ordered pairs given in §16.2.1 (which itself follows from extensionality, if we identify ordered pairs with sets in the way discussed in §16.2.1).

So far we have considered functions that take a single object as argument and assign to it an object as value. What about functions, such as addition or multiplication, that take two objects as arguments and assign to them an object as value? (These are called *binary* functions.) In general, what about functions that take three, four, or in general n objects as arguments? One common way of conceiving of such functions, which brings them within the framework articulated above for one-place functions, is to conceive of an apparently n-place function from S to T as a (one-place) function from S^n to T. That is, it is a one-place function that takes as input an n-tuple of objects. (An n-tuple, like a set, is considered to be a single object.) So, for example, the addition function, which we normally think of as taking two numbers as input, may be thought of as taking a single input: an ordered pair of numbers.

16.4.1 Operations on Functions

Given a function $f : S \rightarrow T$, we can invert the function: switch the first and second members of each ordered pair (make each arrow point the opposite way). If the result of this process is a function (from T to S), this resulting function is called the *inverse* function of f and is denoted by f^{-1}. If the result is not a function, we say f^{-1} does not exist. (Of course, the set of switched-around ordered pairs always exists: it's just that it might not be a function: f^{-1} names the inverse function, if it exists.) It's not too hard to see that the condition required for the set of switched-around ordered pairs to be a function is that f is one-one. Furthermore, provided f^{-1} exists:

- f^{-1} is one-one (because f is a function).
- If f is total, then f^{-1} is onto.
- If f is onto, then f^{-1} is total.

To see why these statements are true, it is helpful to recall Figure 16.3.

Given a function $f : S \rightarrow T$ and a function $g : T \rightarrow U$, the *composite function* $g \circ f$ (read as "g after f") from S to U is defined thus: for every x in S, $(g \circ f)(x) = g(f(x))$. The idea here is that we first apply f to the input x (a member of the set S) and then apply g to the result (i.e., to the output of f for input x, which is a member of T). In terms of arrows, the composite function is found by taking each f arrow from an object x in S to an object y in T and extending it so that it hits whatever object z in U the g arrow from y hits. (If there is no g arrow from y, then in the composite function there is no arrow from x.) Think through why the following must be true:

- If f and g are both total, so is $g \circ f$.
- If f and g are both onto, so is $g \circ f$.

- If f and g are both one-one, so is $g \circ f$.

- If f and g are both bijections, so is $g \circ f$.

16.4.2 Characteristic Function of a Set

Given a subset S of a background set U, the *characteristic* (or indicator) function of S is a total function $\mathbf{I}_S : U \to \{0, 1\}$ defined as follows. For all x in U:

$$\mathbf{I}_S(x) = \begin{cases} 1 & \text{if } x \in S \\ 0 & \text{if } x \notin S \end{cases}$$

We can think of the characteristic function as answering "yes" (1) or "no" (0), for every object in U, to the question whether that object is in S.

Instead of the set $\{0, 1\}$, we might take the set $\{T, F\}$ of truth values as the codomain of the characteristic function (with T being "yes" and F being "no"). Conversely, it is also common to take $\{0, 1\}$ as the set of truth values: that is, to use 1 everywhere we have used T and 0 everywhere we have used F (e.g., in truth tables).

Think through why the following are true for any subsets S and T of a background set U.

For every $x \in U$, $\qquad \mathbf{I}_{S \cup T}(x) = \max\{\mathbf{I}_S(x), \mathbf{I}_T(x)\}$
$$= \mathbf{I}_S(x) + \mathbf{I}_T(x) - [\mathbf{I}_S(x) \times \mathbf{I}_T(x)]$$

Note here that where x and y are numbers, $\max\{x, y\}$ is the greater of x and y; if $x = y$, then $\max\{x, y\} = x$.

For every $x \in U$, $\qquad \mathbf{I}_{S \cap T}(x) = \min\{\mathbf{I}_S(x), \mathbf{I}_T(x)\}$
$$= \mathbf{I}_S(x) \times \mathbf{I}_T(x)$$

Note here that where x and y are numbers, $\min\{x, y\}$ is the lesser of x and y; if $x = y$, then $\min\{x, y\} = x$.

For every $x \in U$, $\qquad \mathbf{I}_{S'}(x) = 1 - \mathbf{I}_S(x)$

$S \subseteq T$ iff for every $x \in U$, $\quad \mathbf{I}_S(x) \leq \mathbf{I}_T(x)$

For every $\langle x, y \rangle \in U^2$, $\quad \mathbf{I}_{S \times T}(\langle x, y \rangle) = \mathbf{I}_S(x) \times \mathbf{I}_T(y)$

In relation to the last of these facts, note that $S \times T$ is a subset of U^2, so the characteristic function of $S \times T$ is a function from U^2 to $\{0, 1\}$.

16.5 Sequences

Whereas a set is a collection of objects, a sequence is a collection of objects given in a particular order: first, second, third, and so on—either up to nth (for a finite sequence of length n), or forever (for an infinite sequence). Intuitively, the idea of a finite sequence of length n of members of a set S is just the idea of an ordered n-tuple of members of S under a new name. The idea of an infinite sequence of members of S, however, is something new.

It is standard to cash out the intuitive idea of a sequence (finite or infinite) in the following precise way. Consider the set $\mathbb{Z}^+ = \{1, 2, 3, \ldots\}$ of positive integers. For each $n \in \mathbb{Z}^+$, there is an *initial segment* $\mathbb{Z}_n^+$ of $\mathbb{Z}^+$ containing all and only the numbers up to and including n. In order of increasing size, these initial segments are $\mathbb{Z}_1^+ = \{1\}$, $\mathbb{Z}_2^+ = \{1, 2\}$, $\mathbb{Z}_3^+ = \{1, 2, 3\}$, and so on. A finite sequence of length n of members of the set S is a total function from $\mathbb{Z}_n^+$ to S. An infinite sequence of members of the set S is a total function from $\mathbb{Z}^+$ to S.[17]

Note how this formal definition captures the intuitive idea. The first object in the sequence is the value of the function (with which the sequence is identified) for input 1; the second object in the sequence is the value of the function for input 2; and so on. The process continues either up to the nth and final object in the sequence (in the case of a finite sequence, whose domain is $\mathbb{Z}_n^+$) or forever (in the case of an infinite sequence). For an infinite sequence, the inputs to the function never run out (its domain is $\mathbb{Z}^+$) and so, because the function is total, there is an ith entry in the sequence for every i.

A sequence may involve repetitions: there is no requirement that the function (with which the sequence is identified) be one-one, so the same object may appear at multiple positions. Thus, even if there is only one thing in S, we can have a sequence of any length of members of S: it will just have that same object in every position. (Given that the function must be total, however, we cannot have a sequence of any length of members of the empty set.)

Suppose we take as S the set containing the first seven letters of the alphabet:

$$S = \{a, b, c, d, e, f, g\}$$

Here are some examples of sequences of members of S.

$$f(1) = a, \ f(2) = b, \ f(3) = c, \ f(4) = d, \ f(5) = e, \ f(6) = f, \ f(7) = g$$

f is a sequence of length 7; its domain is $\mathbb{Z}_7^+$. We can also write this sequence as $\langle a, b, c, d, e, f, g \rangle$ or (a, b, c, d, e, f, g). In this notation, the first object shown is the first object in the sequence (the value of f for input 1), the second object shown is the second object in the sequence (the value of f for input 2), and so on.

$$g(1) = c$$

g is a sequence of length 1; its domain is $\mathbb{Z}_1^+$. We can also write this sequence as $\langle c \rangle$ or (c).

$$h(1) = a, \ h(2) = b, \ h(3) = a, \ h(4) = b, \ h(5) = a, \ h(6) = b, \ldots$$

h is an infinite sequence; its domain is $\mathbb{Z}^+$. We can also write this sequence as $\langle a, b, a, b, a, b, \ldots \rangle$ or $(a, b, a, b, a, b, \ldots)$.

Two finite sequences f and g may be *concatenated*; that is, the elements of f (in order) placed before the elements of g (in order), so as to form a new sequence whose length is that of f plus that of g. Concatenation is represented using the symbol $\frown$. Thus, $\langle a, b \rangle \frown \langle a, b \rangle = \langle a, b, a, b \rangle$, $\langle a \rangle \frown \langle a, b, c \rangle = \langle a, a, b, c \rangle$, and so on. More formally, concatenation is a binary operation on sequences, defined as follows. Where f and g are sequences of lengths m and n, respectively, of members of S; that is, $f : \mathbb{Z}_m^+ \to S$ and $g : \mathbb{Z}_n^+ \to S$:

$$(f \frown g)(i) = \begin{cases} f(i) & \text{for } 1 \leq i \leq m \\ g(i - m) & \text{for } m + 1 \leq i \leq m + n \end{cases}$$

Note how this definition specifies the sequence (function) $f \frown g$ by specifying which object is in each position i of the sequence (i.e., which object the function assigns as value for input i). For i such that this definition does not specify what is in position i of $f \frown g$ (i.e., does not specify a value for the function $f \frown g$ for input i), we are to understand that $f \frown g$ has no position i (meaning that $f \frown g$ is a total function from some set that does not include i—as opposed to a partial function from some set that does include i). It then follows from the definition that $f \frown g$ is of length $m + n$ (i.e., it is a total function from $\mathbb{Z}_{m+n}^+$ to S).

Given this definition, it can be shown that for any sequences f, g, and h

$$f \frown (g \frown h) = (f \frown g) \frown h$$

Hence, we are free to omit parentheses, as in $f \frown g \frown h$.

16.6 Multisets

As mentioned in §15.3.2.3, we can think of a set as being obtained from a sequence by ignoring both ordering and repetitions. A *multiset* ignores ordering but not repetition. That is, a multiset is a collection of objects together with a record of how many times each object occurs in the collection.

More formally, a multiset S, all of whose elements are members of a background set U, may be thought of as a total function from U to the set $\mathbb{N} = \{0, 1, 2, 3, \ldots\}$ of natural numbers. (Note that $\mathbb{N}$, unlike $\mathbb{Z}^+$, includes 0.) The number assigned to each object x in U indicates how many times x occurs in S. This idea is a generalization of the notion of characteristic function (§16.4.2). The characteristic function of a normal set S has only two possible values for any input x: 0 ("x is not in S") or 1 ("x is in S"). The characteristic function of the multiset S has infinitely many possible values: 0 ("x occurs zero times in S"), 1 ("x occurs once in S"), 2 ("x occurs twice in S"), and so on.

For example, suppose we take as the background set U the set containing the first seven letters of the alphabet:

$$U = \{a, b, c, d, e, f, g\}$$

Here are some examples of multisets of members of U.

$$f(a) = 3, f(b) = 2, f(c) = 1, f(d) = 0, f(e) = 0, f(f) = 0, f(g) = 0$$

We can also write this multiset as $[a, a, a, b, b, c]$.

$$f(a) = 2, f(b) = 2, f(c) = 2, f(d) = 2, f(e) = 2, f(f) = 2, f(g) = 2$$

We can also write this multiset as $[a, a, b, b, c, c, d, d, e, e, f, f, g, g]$.

$$f(a) = 0, f(b) = 0, f(c) = 0, f(d) = 0, f(e) = 0, f(f) = 0, f(g) = 0$$

We can also write this multiset as $[\ ]$. It is the *empty* multiset on U.

Note that $[a, a, b] \neq [a, b]$, and $[a, a, b] = [a, b, a]$. If we identify multisets with functions in the way indicated above, then these facts follow from the identity condition on functions given in §16.4. The multiset $[a, a, b]$ is a function that assigns 2 to a, and $[a, b]$ is a function that assigns 1 to a, so they are different functions. In contrast, $[a, a, b]$ is a function that assigns 2 to a and 1 to b, and $[a, b, a]$ is a function that assigns 2 to a and 1 to b, so they are the same function. (We assume here that the domain of these two functions is the same.) Thus, as indicated at the outset, multisets (unlike sequences) ignore ordering of elements, but (unlike sets) they do not ignore repetition of elements.

We can define operations on, and relations between, multisets by mimicking certain facts about characteristic functions of normal sets. For example, recall from §16.4.2 that

$$I_{S \cap T}(x) = \min\{I_S(x), I_T(x)\}$$

If we take the Is here to be multiset functions—which take values in $\mathbb{N}$, not $\{0, 1\}$—then we can take this formula to *define* the intersection of multisets S and T. For example, the intersection of $[a, a, b]$ and $[a, b, c]$ will then be $[a, b]$. (Here a occurs once in the intersection, because 1 is the minimum value assigned to a by $[a, a, b]$ and $[a, b, c]$; the former assigns it 2 and the latter 1. And c occurs no times in the intersection, because 0 is the minimum value assigned to c by $[a, a, b]$ and $[a, b, c]$; the former assigns it 0 and the latter 1. Similar points apply to b.)[18] To take a second example, recall from §16.4.2 that

$$S \subseteq T \text{ iff for every } x \in U, \quad I_S(x) \leq I_T(x)$$

If we once again take the Is here to be multiset functions, then this formula can define the subset relation between multisets. The multiset $[a, b]$ is a subset of

[a, a, b], because the value assigned to a by the former is less than or equal to the value assigned to a by the latter, and similarly for b. In contrast, [a, a, b] is not a subset of [a, b, b], because the value assigned to a by the former is greater than the value assigned to a by the latter.[19]

16.7 Syntax

Let us return now to specifications of the syntax of our various logical languages and try to get a clearer understanding of them. We'll take as an example the syntax of GPL (§12.1.3); the same essential points apply to PL, GPLI, and the others.

The presentation of the syntax comes in two main parts. First, we give the symbols of the language: names a, b, c, . . .; variables x, y, z, . . .; predicates A^1, B^1, . . ., A^2, B^2, . . .; connectives $\neg$, $\wedge$, $\vee$, $\rightarrow$, and $\leftrightarrow$; quantifier symbols $\forall$ and $\exists$; and parentheses (and). Second, we specify the wffs: where $\underline{P^n}$ is any n-place predicate and $t_1 \ldots t_n$ are any names and/or variables, $\underline{P^n} t_1 \ldots t_n$ is a wff; where α and β are wffs and $\underline{x}$ is a variable, $\neg\alpha$, $(\alpha \wedge \beta)$, $(\alpha \vee \beta)$, $(\alpha \rightarrow \beta)$, $(\alpha \leftrightarrow \beta)$, $\forall \underline{x}\alpha$ and $\exists \underline{x}\alpha$ are wffs.

We should understand this presentation as follows. Each symbol is a particular object, and each wff is a finite sequence of these objects. The first part of the definition gives us a set S of objects (the symbols). Given S, we may consider the set S^* of all finite sequences of members of S. The second part of the definition then specifies a particular subset W of S^*: the wffs. It first tells us (in the clause for atomic wffs) that any sequence of length $n + 1$ that has an n-place predicate in first position and n names and/or variables in the remaining positions is in W.[20] It then specifies that for any sequences in W, certain other sequences formed from them (and from length-1 sequences of certain of the basic symbols) by concatenation are also in W. For example, if α is a sequence in W, then the sequence $\langle\neg\rangle^\frown\alpha$ is also in W. (Note that concatenation is defined on sequences, so we cannot concatenate α directly with the symbol $\neg$: we have to concatenate it with the length-1 sequence $\langle\neg\rangle$ whose only entry is the symbol $\neg$.) If α and β are sequences in W, then the sequence $\langle(\rangle^\frown\alpha^\frown\langle\wedge\rangle^\frown\beta^\frown\langle)\rangle$ is also in W. If α is a sequence in W, and $\underline{x}$ is any one of the variable symbols, then $\langle\forall\rangle^\frown\langle\underline{x}\rangle^\frown\alpha$ is in W,[21] and so on.

Note that the syntax does not stipulate what the symbols of the language look like. In a sense, it does not tell us which objects they are. What the specification of the symbols really amounts to is as follows:

- There is a certain object—the negation symbol. When I write something of the same shape as:

$$\neg$$

it is to be understood that I am picking out this negation object.

- There are certain objects—the variable symbols. When I write something of the same shape as:

$$x$$

it is to be understood that I am picking out the first of these objects. When I write something of the same shape as:

$$y$$

it is to be understood that I am picking out the second of these objects, and so on.

- There is a certain object—the universal quantifier symbol. When I write something of the same shape as:

$$\forall$$

it is to be understood that I am picking out this universal quantifier object.

Similar statements hold for the other symbols. The symbols themselves—the actual objects, as opposed to the ink shapes we use to pick them out—might be abstract objects, for example, pure sets. In that case, they have no shapes at all. They might be physical objects, in which case they have shapes, but the negation object might not actually look like the ink shape "$\neg$" we use to pick it out. The convention is that when I write something with the shape of "$\neg$," I pick out the negation object; this does not mean that the negation object itself has this shape. (Consider the following analogy. When you blow your whistle—or any whistle that sounds just like it—Rover comes. This does not mean that Rover himself sounds like the whistle: Rover may make no noise—or a completely different noise, such as a bark or a snuffle.)

So the first part of the syntax (the part listing the symbols) states that there are certain objects, and it also (implicitly) sets down a convention for picking out these objects using ink marks of certain shapes. The second part then specifies which sequences of these objects are wffs. It also implicitly sets down a convention, which is that when we write the shape that picks out symbol x immediately to the left of the shape that picks out symbol y, the resulting bigger shape (comprising those two shapes next to each other) is to pick out the sequence that is the concatenation of the length-1 sequence whose only entry is x with the length-1 sequence whose only entry is y. The convention is actually a bit more complex than that, because it also involves the use of wff variables. It would be an interesting exercise to write out the convention in full—but the result would be far less comprehensible than the specification of the syntax as given in §12.1.3. That is, of course, why we actually present the syntax in that simpler way. The point now is to clarify what that presentation of the syntax is really doing. Wffs are not lines of ink marks: they are abstract objects—sequences of basic symbols. (Even if the symbols are not abstract objects, sequences of them are: they are functions from initial segments of $\mathbb{Z}^+$ to the set S of symbol objects.) These symbols are particular objects, and there is only one of each: one negation symbol, one first variable, one second variable, and so on. When we write $\neg\neg A^2xx$, we use two ink marks of the shape "$\neg$" and two of the shape "x," but both of the former pick out the same object (the one and only negation object) and both of the latter pick out the same object (the first variable object). The whole shape "$\neg\neg A^2xx$" picks out the length-5 sequence whose entries are:

1. the negation object,

2. the negation object (i.e., the same object that is in first position),

3. the first two-place predicate object,

4. the first variable object, and

5. the first variable object (i.e., the same object that is in fourth position).

Note that an abbreviation is just an extension of the conventions that associate certain ink shapes with certain wffs (sequences of symbol objects). The presentation of the syntax establishes the convention that the ink shape "$(P^1a \land P^1b)$" picks out a particular sequence of symbols. When we introduce the abbreviation that omits outermost parentheses, we are simply extending this convention in such a way that the ink shape "$P^1a \land P^1b$" will pick out the same sequence of symbols that the ink shape "$(P^1a \land P^1b)$" picks out.

16.7.1 Models

We have been using S for the set of symbols of the logical language. Let's use S' to denote the subset of S that contains the nonlogical symbols. (In Chapter 9, n. 6 we mentioned that S', thus defined, is the *signature* of the logical language.)

In light of the foregoing discussion, we can now also clarify what a *model* is. We said that a model comprises a domain, together with a specification of a referent for each name and an extension for each predicate. The domain is a set D of objects. We can now see that the rest of the model is a total function from S'—which is a set of objects (symbols)—to objects of the appropriate sorts. The members of S' are names, one-place predicates, two-place predicates, and so on. Names are sent to members of D by the function (i.e., the value of a name in a model is an object in the domain); one-place predicates are sent to members of $\wp D$ (i.e., the value of a one-place predicate in a model is a subset of the domain); and n-place predicates for $n > 1$ are sent to members of $\wp(D^n)$ (i.e., the value of an n-place predicate in a model is a set of n-tuples of members of the domain).

16.7.2 Definitions of Logical Operators

We mentioned in Chapter 15, n. 8 that there are two quite different ways of interpreting the definition of one logical operator in terms of others, for example, $(\alpha \wedge \beta) := \neg(\alpha \to \neg\beta)$, or $\exists \underline{x}\alpha := \neg\forall \underline{x}\neg\alpha$. We are now in a position to explain these two ways. I'll present the discussion in terms of the first example—in the context of propositional logic—but the point is general.

Recall the context: we have a proof apparatus (e.g., a system of axioms and rules) that mentions only certain connectives, say $\neg$ and $\to$. To prove tautologies stated using other connectives, (e.g., $\neg(P \wedge \neg P)$), we first define out these other connectives (in this case $\wedge$) in terms of $\neg$ and $\to$ (see the definition above). We then prove the resulting formula—in this case, $\neg\neg(P \to \neg\neg P)$.

At this point we need a preliminary definition. The language PL was defined in §2.5. Imagine a definition of a language (call it PL*) that is completely analogous except that the only connectives mentioned are $\neg$ and $\to$: the other connectives of PL ($\wedge$, $\vee$, and $\leftrightarrow$) are not symbols of PL*, and so there are no wffs of PL* featuring these symbols. That is, the set of symbols of PL* is a proper subset of the set of symbols of PL: there are objects in the latter that are not in the former.

The first way of understanding the process of defining out $\neg(P \wedge \neg P)$ as $\neg\neg(P \to \neg\neg P)$ is as follows. Our logical language is PL*. When we give the syntax for PL*, we introduce the convention that ink shapes like "$\neg\alpha$" and "$(\alpha \to \beta)$" pick out certain sequences of symbol objects. When we now introduce the definition $(\alpha \wedge \beta) := \neg(\alpha \to \neg\beta)$, we are extending the convention, so that ink shapes like "$(\alpha \wedge \beta)$" will pick out the same sequences of symbols that shapes like "$\neg(\alpha \to \neg\beta)$" pick out. Thus, the definition allows us to use new ink shapes in a meaningful way. It gives us a new kind of handle with which to manipulate the logical language PL*. It is thus exactly the same in character as the abbreviation that allows us to omit outermost parentheses.

The second way of understanding the process of defining out $\neg(P \wedge \neg P)$ as $\neg\neg(P \to \neg\neg P)$ is as follows. Our logical language is PL, not PL*. So the language contains a conjunction object, and we could always use ink shapes like "$(\alpha \wedge \beta)$" right from the start: the presentation of the syntax for PL implicitly introduces conventions governing what sequences these shapes pick out, as discussed in §16.7. However, our proof apparatus gives as outputs (i.e., proved wffs) only sequences that do not contain the objects $\wedge$, $\vee$, or $\leftrightarrow$ at any position. As we said in §15.1 (and subsequently in the same chapter), we extend the proof apparatus so that it also outputs (some) wffs for symbols (i.e., the ones that are in fact tautologies)—for axioms and/or rules that feature $\wedge$, $\vee$, and $\leftrightarrow$. F ing the alternative, which is to leave the proof ap such definitions as $(\alpha \wedge \beta) := \neg(\alpha \to \neg\beta)$. We n tions as follows. If we want to prove a wff of a kind prove (a wff involving $\wedge$, $\vee$, or $\leftrightarrow$), we must first find an equivalent wff of a kind the proof apparatus does handle and then prove it. (Note that if α and β are equivalent, then if the proof system proves that α is a tautology, it follows that β is a tautology, because something equivalent to a tautology is itself a tautology.) Such definitions as $(\alpha \wedge \beta) := \neg(\alpha \to \neg\beta)$ (in this second way of understanding them) specify how to find such equivalent wffs. (The process of replacing any occurrence of $\wedge$ in a formula, using an equivalence such as $(\alpha \wedge \beta) := \neg(\alpha \to \neg\beta)$, is illustrated in §6.6.) They thus have the same character as the equivalences in §12.5 and §12.5.3, which enable us to find a prenex equivalent of any given formula.

16.7.3 Operations on Wffs

As discussed in §3.5, the terms "negation," "conjunction," "conditional," and so on can be used to refer to three different types of objects. We illustrate with the case of conjunction, but the point is general. The term "conjunction" can be thought of as picking out:

1. a connective: a symbol in the logical language—a particular object;

2. a compound proposition: a wff—a sequence of symbol objects whose main connective is "conjunction" in sense (1) (each such sequence may be called a "conjunction"); or

3. a truth function: the function from $\{T, F\}^2$ to $\{T, F\}$, which sends $\langle T, T \rangle$ to T and all other inputs to F.

We can now see that there is a fourth kind of object that the term "conjunction" can be used to pick out: a binary function on the set of wffs, which, given wffs α and β as input (in that order) returns the wff $(\alpha \wedge \beta)$ as output. (In other words, given sequences α and β as input, it gives as output the sequence $\langle () ^\frown \alpha ^\frown \langle \wedge \rangle ^\frown \beta ^\frown () \rangle$.) Note that the output of this function is always a conjunction in sense (2) above.

We can now interpret the syntax specification "when α and β are wffs, $(\alpha \wedge \beta)$ is a wff" as stating that the set W of wffs is *closed* under the operation of conjunction (in this fourth sense of conjunction). That is, for any two objects (sequences) in W, the output of this function when fed those two objects as input (in either order) is also in W.

We can also now see that when constructing a wff of PL as in §2.5.3, we reach it, starting from basic propositions by (i) feeding these basic propositions (which are symbol objects, not sequences) as inputs to the clause stating that length-1 sequences of basic propositions are wffs (see n. 20) and then (ii) feeding the outputs of stage (i) as inputs to the functions on sequences just discussed (i.e., conjunction, negation, etc., in the fourth senses of these terms). We then repeat stage (ii), using the outputs of any earlier stages as inputs, until desired wff (sequence) is attained.

NOTES

Chapter 1: Propositions and Arguments

1. For example, the opening sentence of the classic Jevons [1870] is "logic may be most briefly defined as the Science of Reasoning." Similar formulations occur right across the wide range of modern introductions to logic, from the mathematically oriented Mendelson [1987], which opens "one of the most popular definitions of logic is that it is the analysis of methods of reasoning," to the philosophically and linguistically oriented Gamut [1991a], which opens "logic, one might say, is the science of reasoning."

2. That is, we do not mean something done by people wearing lab coats and safety glasses. There is a narrower usage of the term "science," by which it means something like the systematic study of the structure and behavior of the physical and natural world carried out through observation and experiment—and a broader usage, by which it means something like the systematic pursuit of knowledge. I am using "science" in the broader of these two senses.

3. Our usage of the term "proposition" is a technical one—but it is related to one of the multiple ordinary meanings of this term. Ordinarily, "proposition" can mean a number of things—for example, an offer of terms for a transaction, a suggested scheme or plan of action, or a statement that expresses an opinion. Our technical usage is related to (but not the same as—see §1.2.2) the last-mentioned of these ordinary meanings. This sort of situation—where we take an ordinary term and give it a technical meaning related to one of its ordinary uses—is very common. (E.g., consider the term "body" as used in physics. The systematic study of the motions of objects and the forces that affect these motions is called "mechanics," and the term "body" is used for the objects of this science: *bodies*, in this technical sense, are those things which can move and are subject to forces. This is a technical usage of the term "body," but it is abstracted from one of the ordinary meanings of the term.)

4. Doesn't "open the door!" represent the door as being shut? No: if the door is already open, saying "open the door!" is inappropriate, but it isn't false.

5. As explained in the Preface, some parts of this book cover core material, and some parts cover additional material which will be of interest to some readers. The Preface gives details concerning which parts of the book are core material, and which of the noncore parts might be relevant to a given reader, depending upon her interests. This is

the first of the noncore sections. This note will not be repeated in subsequent noncore sections.

6. Instead of talking of what the *sentence* says when uttered in a certain context, one might prefer to talk of what a *speaker* says by uttering the sentence in a certain context. That is, one might think that sentences do not say things: speakers do (by uttering sentences). As far as what follows is concerned, it makes no difference whether we think of sentences or speakers as making claims, and so I shall use both formulations interchangeably. It is the claims themselves (i.e., the propositions) in which we shall be interested.

7. This distinction is originally due to Peirce [1906, para. 537].

8. For further discussion of the notion *sequence* involved here, see §16.5 and §16.7.

9. Tokens of a type need to be distinguished from *occurrences* of a type. Suppose that we are talking about opening lines of novels, and we note that the word "was" occurs eleven times—or has eleven occurrences—in the opening sentence of Dickens's *A Tale of Two Cities*. What are we counting? Not word types: the eleven occurrences are all of the single word type "was." Not word tokens: we are not talking about a particular printed copy of the novel, counting tokens of "was"—we are talking about the sentence type of which the opening lines of countless printed editions of the novel are tokens (even if all printed copies of the book were destroyed, our claim would still be true); thus, we are not counting tokens of "was"—for tokens are physical objects (e.g., strings of ink marks), and there are none of these in the picture when we are talking about the sentence type. So what are we counting? Well, the idea is as follows. A sentence type is a sequence of word types (in the particular sense of "sequence" explained in §16.5), and the same word type may appear at multiple points in the sequence. For example, the opening sentence of *A Tale of Two Cities* is a sequence of 119 words—and the word "was" (i.e., the single word type "was"—an abstract object) occupies positions 2, 8, 14, 20, 26, and so on in the sequence: eleven positions in all. When we say that "was" occurs eleven times in this sentence, what we are counting is the number of positions in the sequence that are occupied by the word type "was." Note that when we produce a token of the sentence type, there is a token of "was" for each occurrence of the type "was" in the sentence type: thus, in a printed copy of *A Tale of Two Cities*, there will be eleven different tokens of "was" on the opening page, before the first full stop. In the sentence type itself, however—which is an abstract object—there are no tokens of the word type "was": there are eleven occurrences of this word type.

10. A note on terminology. In ordinary usage, an "utterance" could be either the action of saying something or the spoken words produced by this action; likewise, an "inscription" could be either the action of inscribing something or the inscribed words produced by this action. In keeping with much of the literature on these matters, I shall use "utterance" and "inscription" for the token word or sentence produced (not for the act of producing it), and furthermore I shall ignore the ordinary restriction of "utterance" to spoken words and of "inscription" to written words, instead using both terms simply as synonyms of "token." Likewise, I ignore the ordinary restriction of "speaker" to someone who produces spoken words: by "speaker" I simply mean a producer of tokens.

11. However, if two persons make claims, and it turns out that there cannot be a situation in which what one of them says is true while what the other says is false, this does *not* automatically mean that they say the same thing (make the same claim about

the world or express one and the same proposition). It might be that they express two different propositions that are *equivalent* (cf. §4.3). (Compare a situation in which you are trying to determine whether the person walking in the door is the same person who walked out a minute ago. If the person who walked out was six feet tall, and the person who is walking in is five feet tall, you know they are different persons. But if the person walking in has the same height as the person who walked out, this does not automatically mean it is the very same person: they might be different persons who have the same height.)

12. The sentence "I am hungry" is obviously one that can be used to state different propositions on different occasions—for it contains a word ("I") that picks out a different person, depending on who utters the sentence. ("I" refers to me when I utter the sentence, to you when you utter the sentence, and so on). Word types that pick out different things depending on the context of utterance are *indexicals*. Examples include "I," "you," "now," "yesterday," and "here." As we have just seen, if someone uses a sentence type containing an indexical to make a claim about the world, it is no good trying to identify the claim he makes—the proposition he expresses— with the sentence type that he utters: for the same sentence type could be used on another occasion to make a quite different claim about the world. But can we identify propositions with sentence types that do not contain any indexicals? That will not work either. Consider the sentence "it is snowing." It does not contain any (obvious) indexicals. Yet it behaves in the same way as the sentence "it is snowing here now," which contains two indexicals ("here" and "now"): when uttered in London at 11 pm on 4 March 1901 it makes the claim that it is snowing in London at 11 pm on 4 March 1901; when uttered in Hobart at 9 a.m. on 2 November 1854 it makes the claim that it is snowing in Hobart at 9 a.m. on 2 November 1854; and so on. Now contrast "it is snowing" with "snow falls in Sydney, Australia, at 10:55 a.m. (local time) on 4 April 2011." The former sentence does not specify, in itself, a time or a place that it talks about: generally speaking, it can be used to make a claim about any time or place, by uttering it at that time in that place. The second sentence, in contrast, is fully specific: it includes a specification of the place and time it talks about. As a consequence, no matter where or when the sentence is uttered, it makes the same claim about the world. So can we identify propositions with such fully specific sentence types? To make good on this proposal, we should of course need to say precisely what it takes for a sentence to be fully specific, and this may well prove difficult. (The notion of a fully specific sentence is related to, but not the same as, the notion of *eternal* sentences: "sentences that stay forever true, or forever false, independently of any special circumstances under which they happen to be uttered or written" [Quine, 1986, 13].) In any case, there is a more fundamental problem for this proposal. Let us suppose that John, who speaks only English, says "snow falls in Sydney, Australia at 10:55 a.m. on 4 April 2011," while Johann, who speaks only German, says "Schnee fällt um 10:55 a.m. am 4 April 2011 in Sydney, Australien." Note that John's sentence is a correct translation of Johann's sentence into English and Johann's sentence is a correct translation of John's sentence into German. John and Johann utter different fully specific sentence types: one a sentence in English, one in German. Yet (it seems obvious) they make the same claim about the world: they express the same proposition. Two different sentences, one proposition: so we cannot identify the proposition with both sentences. We could identify it with just one of the sentences—say, the English one—but this would be

arbitrary, and it would also have the strange consequence that the claim Johann makes about the world is a sentence in English: a language he does not speak or understand. Thus, we cannot happily identify propositions with fully specific sentence types.

13. If we have two distinct objects B and C, then we cannot say of an object A both that it is the same thing as B and that it is the same thing as C—for if that were so, then this one object A would at the same time be two different objects, B and C, which is impossible. (E.g., given that your mother and father are different persons, and that "the prime minister of New Zealand" picks out a single individual, it cannot be the case that the prime minister of New Zealand is your mother *and* that the prime minister of New Zealand is your father.) See Chapter 13.

14. For a more detailed discussion, see, for example, Cartwright [1987].

15. If any: it is of course an open possibility that some combinations of sentence, speaker, and context do not determine any proposition at all. It is also possible that some combinations of sentence, speaker, and context determine multiple propositions—that is, that by uttering a certain sentence in a specific context one might simultaneously make multiple claims about the world.

16. The proper home of these controversies is philosophy of language, where they can be found under headings including "semantics versus pragmatics" and "minimalism versus contextualism."

17. We noted earlier (n. 3) that our usage of the term "proposition" is a technical one, related to but distinct from one of the multiple ordinary meanings of this term. To prevent confusion that might otherwise arise when the reader consults other works, it is also worth noting that even within philosophy and logic, the term "proposition" has been used in a number of different technical senses. Some of the most common of these are as follows (we shall discuss the question of what a "declarative sentence" is in a moment): (1) A proposition is what is said by an utterance of a declarative sentence in a context: it is a claim about how things are—it represents the world as being some way. (2) A proposition is the information content of an utterance of a declarative sentence in a context. (3) A proposition is the literal meaning of a declarative sentence type. (4) A proposition is that which is in common between synonymous declarative sentences—that is, that single thing which each of the various synonymous sentences expresses. There are various views about how these notions relate to one another (e.g., whether some of them amount to different ways of phrasing the same essential idea), and also about how they relate to various other notions in the literature—most notably Frege's notion of a Thought (*Gedanke*) [Frege, 1892, 1918–19]—which, although introduced using terms other than "proposition," are clearly related in some way to one or more of the above notions. A couple of further factors add to the terminological complexity. First, some writers (often those who think of propositions in terms of sense (1) above) use "statement" as a synonym for "proposition," while others contrast statements and propositions. Among the latter, there are further distinctions between those who use "statement" as a synonym for "declarative sentence" (see below), those who use "statement" for the act of uttering a declarative sentence (recall n. 10), and those (often the ones who think of propositions in terms of sense (4) above) for whom statements are rather like (but not exactly the same as) propositions in sense (1) above. Second, those who employ the notion of a *declarative* sentence need to say what such a thing is. Often a declarative sentence is defined as one that makes a statement—which takes us back to the previous point—but the notion is also sometimes defined in other

ways, for example: "A *declarative sentence* of English is defined to be a grammatical English sentence which can be put in place of '*x*' in 'Is it true that *x*?' so as to yield a grammatical English question" [Hodges, 1977, 19]. The task of explaining all these notions in detail and then sorting out the relationships among them is a vast one—but it is not a task that we wish to take on in this book. The purpose of the present note is simply to alert the reader to the complexity of the situation with regard to the term "proposition." When this term is encountered elsewhere, it must not be assumed that it is being used in the technical sense in which we use it in this book.

18. For discussion—and quotations from Sextus Empiricus, Samuel Taylor Coleridge, and others—see Anderson and Belnap [1975, §25.1].

19. We have just given the term "NTP" two slightly different uses. Sometimes we shall use "NTP" as a label for a property that arguments might have (the property of necessary truth-preservation) and sometimes as a label for arguments with this property (i.e., those which are necessarily truth-preserving). It will always be clear from the context what is meant in any given case.

20. A kelpie is a particular breed of dog (a sheepdog with smooth coat and upright ears).

21. We use the terms "form" and "structure" interchangeably.

22. It would be unusual for a boy to be named "Susan," but no doubt it has happened. For the sake of argument, however, let us suppose that it is impossible for a male to be named "Susan."

23. If the glass contained no H_2O (i.e., the conclusion were false), then the glass could not contain water (i.e., the premise would have to be false) for water is just H_2O.

24. The situation regarding validity is thus exactly the same as the situation regarding propositions (§1.2.2): in advance of our study of logic, we set out a rough guiding idea; a precise account is then one of the goals of our subsequent study.

25. The notes in the quotation are mine, not Tarski's.

26. This is the idea that the argument should be NTP.

27. This is the idea that the argument should be NTP by virtue of its form.

28. That is, (1) NTP, (2) guaranteed by form.

29. More precisely, what we want is an effective procedure for determining validity that always yields the correct answer. A procedure is said to be "effective" if it can be encapsulated in a finite set of instructions, to be followed in a specified order, where each instruction is (1) mechanical (no ingenuity or insight is required to carry it out—a computer could be programmed to do it); (2) deterministic (it involves no random devices, e.g., coin tosses); and (3) finitely achievable (only a finite amount of time is required to complete it). For further discussion, see §14.2.

30. Inductive reasoning in this sense should not be confused with reasoning by *mathematical induction:* the latter is a form of deductive reasoning that will be discussed in §14.1.1.

31. As we shall see, there are certain special cases where logic does tell us that a particular proposition is true or false—for it turns out that the laws of truth ensure that certain propositions must be true no matter what and that certain other propositions must be false no matter what. Hence, there are certain arguments—involving these special kinds of propositions—such that logic does tell us that they are, or are not, sound. That is why I said that logic has very little—as opposed to nothing—to say about soundness.

32. Although I have given a brief definition of the notion, I do not expect it to be clear at this point what it means for a connective to be truth functional. This will become clear as we proceed and see some examples. But it is important to state in advance that we shall be looking at connectives of a particular sort—namely, the truth-functional ones. Otherwise, our selection of connectives below might seem arbitrary and unmotivated. (This is another point where those who say that logic is the science of reasoning face difficulties. If logic is the science of reasoning, why focus on truth-functional connectives, when they are far from the only connectives that figure in ordinary reasoning? If we regard logic as the science of truth, however, then it is obvious why truth-functional connectives are of the first importance: these connectives are concerned only with the truth or falsity of the propositions they are connecting.)

33. A note on terminology: In grammar, the term "conjunction" is used as a general term for what we call "connectives"—whereas in logic, "conjunction" is used as a name for one particular connective.

34. The same issue arises in Exercises 1.6.4.1. We regard (1) "if that's pistachio ice cream, it doesn't taste the way it should" as a conditional with antecedent "that is pistachio ice cream" (A) and consequent "that does not taste the way it should." The consequent is itself the negation of "that tastes the way it should" (B). So (1) is formed from A and B using negation and conditional. Now consider (2): "that tastes the way it should only if it isn't pistachio ice cream." We regard this as a conditional whose antecedent is B and whose consequent is the negation of A. So (2) is also formed from A and B using negation and conditional. But (1) and (2) are different propositions, because although they have the same ingredients, these ingredients are put together in different ways: (1) is "if A, then not B," and (2) is "if B, then not A." However, as we shall see later, (1) and (2) are equivalent.

Chapter 2: The Language of Propositional Logic

1. Of course, for other purposes—e.g., everyday communication—English is an excellent vehicle for making claims about the world. Compare Frege's comment in the Preface to the work in which he first introduced his symbolic logical language:

> I believe that I can best make the relation of my ideography to ordinary language clear if I compare it to that which the microscope has to the eye. Because of the range of its possible uses and the versatility with which it can adapt to the most diverse circumstances, the eye is far superior to the microscope. . . . But, as soon as scientific goals demand great sharpness of resolution, the eye proves to be insufficient. The microscope, on the other hand, is perfectly suited to precisely such goals, but that is just why it is useless for all others. [Frege, 1879, 6]

2. I say "languages" because later we introduce further languages in addition to PL.

3. We never have a glossary that pairs two different sentence letters on the left with the same proposition on the right.

4. Normally we would read this expression as "not P" rather than "neg P." Sometimes we need to refer to the symbol ¬ itself, in which case it is useful to have the name "neg" rather than having to say, for example, "the negation sign." Mostly, however, we do not use the names of the connective symbols: we read out these symbols using words in English that express the same connective.

5. Again, normally we would read this as "P and Q" rather than "P caret Q."

6. Parentheses are suppressed here to avoid excess clutter (see §2.5.4). For a further set of alternatives, see §2.5.5. Note that the third option for conjunction is not a misprint: the symbol for conjunction has not accidentally been left out. Rather, the idea is that there is no symbol for conjunction: the conjunction of P and Q is represented by concatenating P and Q, that is, by writing Q immediately after P. Compare the way multiplication can be written as $x \times y$, $x \cdot y$, or simply xy.

7. Nevertheless, it is worth noting that certain symbols have nice features. For example, using $\vee$ and $\wedge$—symbols that are inversions of one another—for disjunction and conjunction draws attention to the fact that these two connectives are related in a fundamental way (they are *duals*—see §6.6). It also calls attention to the analogies between disjunction and the notion of the *union* of two sets—symbolized $\cup$—and between conjunction and the notion of the *intersection* of two sets—symbolized $\cap$. (These notions are explained in §16.1.3.) Likewise, using $\rightarrow$ and $\leftrightarrow$ for conditional and biconditional reminds us of the relationship between the biconditional $A \leftrightarrow B$ and the two conditionals $A \rightarrow B$ and $B \rightarrow A$ (as discussed in §1.6.5, the biconditional is equivalent to the conjunction of the two conditionals). (Note that $\leftarrow$ is not a symbol in our logical language: the conditional with B as antecedent and A as consequent must be written as $B \rightarrow A$; it cannot be written as $A \leftarrow B$.)

8. The same point applies to basic propositions. We have symbolized them using capital letters—or more specifically, capital Roman letters in italics (A, B, C, ...). Some other books use capital Roman letters in sans serif (A, B, C, ...), or lowercased Roman letters in italics (p, q, r, ...) or in sans serif (p, q, r, ...), or capital Greek letters (Ξ, Π, Φ, Ψ)—and so on. We have said that if we need additional basic propositions, we can add numerical subscripts to the letters (A_2, A_3, ..., B_2, B_3, ...). Some books use numerical superscripts (A^2, A^3, ..., B^2, B^3, ...), or a prime symbol $'$, which may be repeated any number of times (p', p'', ..., q', q'', ...)—and so on. As in the case of connectives, making a choice of symbols—and sticking to it consistently—is important; what choice we make is not nearly so important.

9. Wff variables are also known as *metavariables* (or *metalinguistic variables*) in the literature. The idea behind this terminology is as follows. We noted that α, β, and so on are not new symbols of PL: they are symbols we use in talking about PL. When we are talking about a language, a distinction is often made between the language we are talking about—the *object language*—and the language in which the discussion (of the object language) is carried out, that is, the language used for the discussion— the *metalanguage*. When we use α, β, and so on to talk about propositions of PL, PL is the object language, and the symbols α and β are part of the metalanguage used to talk about PL. Hence, the term "metavariable"—for a variable that is part of the metalanguage.

10. This use of "argument" has nothing to do with our earlier use of the term: these are simply two quite different uses of the same word. Whenever we use the term "argument" in this book, the sense in which we mean it will be clear from context.

11. The sort of ambiguity I have in mind here is explained in §2.5.4.

12. Furthermore, there is never any uncertainty regarding the arguments of the main connective. Thus, every nonbasic wff is either of the form $\neg\alpha$ for unique α (i.e., the formula has to be read as a negation—there is no choice of main connective—and it has to be read as a negation of α—there is no choice as to the argument of the negation sign) or of the form $(\alpha * \beta)$ for unique α and β, where $*$ is a unique choice from among

our two-place connectives (i.e., the formula has to be read as having exactly one two-place connectives as its main connective—there is no choice of main connective—and there is no choice as to the arguments of this connective: they have to be α and β, in that order). This important property of wffs is known as *unique readability*. Note that a consequence of unique readability is that every wff can be decomposed (down to its simplest components: basic propositions and connectives) in essentially just one way: every wff divides into a unique main connective together with its uniquely specified argument(s); each argument is itself a wff (it is a subformula of the original wff) and so itself divides into a unique main connective (of that subformula) together with its uniquely specified argument(s); and so on down to basic propositions. (We say "essentially" just one way, because, as we have seen, in constructing a wff there are sometimes multiple possible choices for the order in which certain steps are performed: but these choices ultimately make no difference, in the sense that every acceptable construction yields the same target wff and the same subformulas along the way—it's just that these subformulas are written in different orders in different constructions).

13. Exactly what is going on when we introduce abbreviations of this sort is explained in §16.7.

14. "The principle of my notation is to write the functors before the arguments. In this way I can avoid brackets. This symbolism without brackets, which I invented and have employed in my logical papers since 1929 . . ." [Łukasiewicz, 1957, 78]. Łukasiewicz used the following symbols for the connectives: N for $\neg$, K for $\wedge$, A for $\vee$, C for $\rightarrow$, and E for $\leftrightarrow$. (Obviously he did not also use capital Roman letters for basic propositions! Recall n. 8.)

15. xy is x with y appended at the right-hand end (not x multiplied by y).

Chapter 3: Semantics of Propositional Logic

1. It is also common in the literature to symbolize truth as 1 and falsity as 0. On bivalence: we said in Chapter 1 that a proposition is a claim about how things are—it represents the world as being some way. It is true if things are the way it represents them to be, and otherwise it is false. There are some utterances, however, that appear to make claims about the world, but are such that there seems to be no sharp division between ways the world might be that would make the claim true and ways that would make it false. For example, if I say "Bob is tall," there are ways things could be that would clearly make my claim true (Bob's height being six feet and four inches), and ways things could be that would clearly make my claim false (Bob's height being four feet), but there seems to be no sharp division between the two kinds of case. (Just think: when exactly, in the process of growing up, did Bob become tall?) This is the problem of *vagueness*. Note that it is different from the issue of *context sensitivity*. Suppose I say "Bill Bradley is tall." If we are engaged in a discussion of current and former basketball players, my claim would seem to be false, because Bill Bradley is below the average height of current and former basketball players. If we are engaged in a discussion of past presidential candidates, my claim would seem to be true, because Bill Bradley is among the tallest of past presidential candidates. It seems that in the first context, "tall" excludes persons who are not of a height significantly greater than the average height of current and former basketball players, while in the second context "tall" excludes persons who are not of a height significantly greater than the average height of past presidential candidates. In other words, "tall" is context sensitive: who counts as tall depends on the

context. Now this sort of context sensitivity is different from vagueness—for vagueness emerges within a fixed context of the sort just considered. For example, it seems that there is no sharp division between the tall basketball players and the nontall ones. There are different accounts of vagueness in the literature. Options concerning what to say about vague utterances, such as "Bob is tall," include the following: (i) the utterance expresses a single proposition, which is either true or false—although we have no way of knowing which; (ii) the utterance simultaneously expresses a number of different propositions, some of which are true and the rest of which are false; (iii) the utterance expresses a single proposition, which is neither true nor false (it has no truth value); and (iv) the utterance expresses a single proposition, which is neither true nor false (it has a truth value other than T or F). Thus, some accounts of vagueness are compatible with the assumption that each proposition is either true or false—i.e., bivalence— and some are not. A proper discussion of these issues is beyond the scope of this book, which seeks to introduce classical logic, of which bivalence is a fundamental assumption. For an introduction to the issues—and an argument for the view that an accurate theory of vagueness must in fact involve additional truth values, apart from T and F (and hence must involve moving beyond classical logic)—see Smith [2008].

2. When we refer to the rows in this way, we do not count the header row: so row 1 is the first row after the header row, row 2 is the row after that, and so on.

3. The clauses referred to in the third column are those of §2.5 (as in the constructions of wffs in §2.5.3). The term "tv" is short for "truth value," and "tt" is short for "truth table."

4. This section makes use of the notions of *set* and *function;* these notions are explained in §16.1 and §16.4. In §16.7.3 we shall see that there is also a fourth kind of entity that such terms as "negation," "conjunction," and "conditional" can be used to denote.

5. These are not all the one-place and two-place truth functions: they are just some arbitrarily chosen truth functions, taken as examples to illustrate the discussion to follow. It will become clear in §6.6 exactly how many one-place and two-place truth functions there are.

6. Conjunction is sometimes known as *logical product* and disjunction as *logical sum.* If you look at the truth functions associated with these connectives—and write 1 in place of T and 0 in place of F—you can see why: the value of the conjunction function, for inputs x and y, is $x \times y$; the value of the disjunction function is $x \dot{+} y$. ($\dot{+}$ is a capped version of addition, whose maximum value is 1. Thus, $0 \dot{+} 0 = 0 + 0 = 0$, $0 \dot{+} 1 = 0 + 1 = 1$ and $1 \dot{+} 0 = 1 + 0 = 1$; but although $1 + 1 = 2$, $1 \dot{+} 1 = 1$. The reason for capping addition in this way is to ensure that the result of applying this operation to a pair of truth values is always a truth value—i.e., 0 or 1.)

Chapter 4: Uses of Truth Tables

1. Throughout this book I use "scenario" in a special sense: as an abbreviation for "way of making propositions true or false." (The notion of a possible way of making propositions true or false plays an important role in what follows, so it is convenient to have a shorter term for it: "possible scenario.")

2. Note the lack of a space in the latter term. We do not call it a "nonlogical truth," because this would suggest that it is a truth, just not a logical one. In contrast, a nontautology need not be true in the actual row or indeed in any row: a contradiction

is one kind of nontautology. We do not call it a "logical nontruth," because this term would suggest something that is always false—a logical falsehood. In contrast, the mark of a nontautology is simply that it is not the case that it is true in every row: a contradiction is just one kind of nontautology; another kind is a proposition that is true in some rows and false in others.

3. There is a variant usage of "contingent" in which a contingent proposition is one that is true in some rows and false in others; thus, the contingent propositions—in this sense—are the ones that are both satisfiable and nontautologies: the central region in the diagram in Figure 4.1. There is no mention of the actual row in this definition: truth tables provide a foolproof test of contingency in this variant sense.

4. See §16.1 for a more detailed introduction to the notion of set.

5. The fact that the first conjunct is false is enough to make the whole conjunction false, so we need not work out the value of the second conjunct.

6. There are nonclassical logics called *relevance logics* (aka *relevant logics*), which are motivated in part by the thought that such arguments as $S/\therefore (G \to G)$ and $S, \neg S/\therefore G$ should not be counted as valid, because the premises are not relevant to the conclusion. See, for example, Anderson and Belnap [1975].

Chapter 5: Logical Form

1. That is why, in describing the truth table test for argument forms, I spoke of rows in which the premises or conclusion of an argument form "have a T" or "have an F"— rather than of situations in which they are true or false.

2. Or at least any number that is a power of 2—recall §3.3.

3. We also discussed two other notions: that of two propositions being contradictories and that of two propositions being contraries. These are both compound notions: two propositions are contradictories if they are jointly unsatisfiable and their negations are jointly unsatisfiable; two propositions are contraries if they are jointly unsatisfiable and their negations are jointly satisfiable. Here we discuss only the components of these compound notions. (A similar point applies to the variant sense of 'contingent' mentioned in n. 3 of Chapter 4. A proposition is contingent in this sense if it is both satisfiable and a nontautology—or equivalently, both it and its negation are satisfiable.)

4. The "s" stands for "some" and the "a" for "all."

Chapter 6: Connectives: Translation and Adequacy

1. Note that we are interested in assessing utterances, not in assessing speakers. Suppose a speaker produces an utterance that is not (in the given circumstances) a good one. This does not automatically mean that the speaker is to be blamed: a mark against an utterance is not the same thing as a mark against the speaker who produced it. This sort of distinction—between assessing the thing produced and assessing the producer—is quite general: it does not apply only when the thing produced is an utterance. For example, someone who produces a bad piece of pottery may deserve praise, if it is his first try at the wheel; someone who tells some tourists that the best way to reach a certain lookout is by taking a certain trail gives bad advice if the trail turns out to be blocked by a fallen tree—but she could not be blamed for giving this advice if the trail she indicated would indeed have been the best route had it not been for the fallen tree, and if there was no reason for her to think the tree would be there; someone who steps on your foot and injures it does a bad thing (injuring your foot)

but cannot be blamed for doing it, if it was a genuine accident and in no way due to carelessness.

2. Identifying implicatures and distinguishing them from what is said and from what is implied was Grice's distinctive contribution; he also coined the term "implicature."

3. In contrast, what is implied are those things that follow from the assumption that what is said is true. As we saw above, one can say something true but still not speak correctly. In general, therefore, one will implicate things that one does not imply: things will follow from the assumption that one speaks correctly that do not follow from the assumption that one speaks the truth. Conversely, one may imply things that one does not implicate. The Maxim of Quality says that one should try to make one's contribution one that is true: one should not say what one believes to be false; one should not say something for which one lacks adequate evidence. So, if we assume someone is speaking correctly—and, in particular, conforming to the Maxim of Quality—it follows that she believes that what she says is true. It does not, however, follow that what she says is true (she may be mistaken). Hence, things may follow from the assumption that what one says is true that do not follow from the assumption that one speaks correctly.

4. Note that this information is again an implicature. What she says is that she will have a second lunch. She does not say, or imply, that she would like to have the lunch you are offering—but she does implicate this.

5. Stated more carefully, what I mean here is the following: "Necessarily, if James is a human being, then James is mortal" apparently expresses a proposition of the form $*\alpha$, where $*$ is the one-place connective expressed by "necessarily," and α is the proposition expressed by "if James is a human being, then James is mortal." Similar comments apply to the other examples.

6. If there is a single such connective. If not, we take some combination of connectives of PL that yields the desired truth table.

7. In the future, for the sake of readability, material of the sort placed in parentheses in this sentence will generally be taken for granted rather than being stated explicitly.

8. If it is possible for what is said by one utterance to be true while what is said by another utterance is false, then the two utterances cannot be saying the same thing (i.e., expressing the same proposition). Hence, they cannot be translated in the same way: recall that the translation of an utterance into PL is a representation of the proposition expressed by that utterance.

9. Note that this is a conventional, as opposed to conversational, implicature: it stems from a particular norm of correct use attached to the word "but."

10. Burgess [2009, 91] gives another reason in favor of viewing "most poor people are not honest" as an implicature—rather than a third conjunct—of "she was poor but honest":

> If it were such a conjunct, the suggestion that there is a contrast [between being poor and being honest] would go away as soon as assertion is replaced by questioning or denial. But it does not. Anyone who takes offense at "she's poor but honest" on the grounds that the rich are at least as likely to be dishonest as the poor will equally take offense at "is she poor but honest?" and "she isn't poor but honest."

11. I say "partially," because it is not "but" alone that is expressing the conditional: it is "but" used together with "never" in this particular way.

12. "Albert took off his shoes and then went inside" cannot be translated as $S \wedge W$, because it is sufficient for the truth of the latter that "Albert took off his shoes" and "Albert went inside" are true, whereas it is necessary for the truth of the former that the time at which Albert took off his shoes precedes the time at which Albert went inside. In fact, if we treat "and then" as a two-place connective, it cannot be translated into PL at all, because it is not truth functional: settling the truth values of A and B does not determine whether A happened before B. The two main options for treating such claims as "Albert took off his shoes and then went inside" in logic are (i) to translate into the language of classical *predicate* logic, where the proposition will be represented as having a more complex form than $\alpha * \beta$, or (ii) to translate into the language of *tense logic*, which is nonclassical. For further details, see §14.4.

13. Compare Grice [1989, 47–49]. More precisely, this argument is one instance of a general argumentative strategy, and it is the general strategy—rather than this particular instance of it—that is known as "Grice's Razor."

14. Of course, in one sense there are as many kinds of conditional sentence as you like: those that have been uttered on a Monday, those that contain eleven words, those that mention ice cream, and so on. What we mean when we say that there are two different kinds of conditional in English is that conditionals of these two sorts must be treated differently from the logical point of view. That there are (in this sense) two kinds of conditionals in English is the orthodox view—but a nonnegligible number of thinkers reject this view.

15. The most popular theories of counterfactuals employ logics that go beyond the classical logic presented in this book. For an introduction, see Burgess [2009] or Priest [2008].

16. I mean here no other possible truth table for a two-place connective—not just none of the other truth tables we have encountered so far (those for conjunction, disjunction, etc.). In §6.6 we shall see that there are sixteen such possible truth tables.

17. Remember that we are talking about truth here, not assertibility. In many contexts, "if it is raining, it is raining" is not an appropriate or interesting thing to say—but it could hardly be said to be false.

18. Given our assumption of bivalence (introduced at the beginning of Chapter 3), any proposition that is not true is false.

19. Recall from §4.1.3 that when we speak in this way of a proposition of PL being true, we mean that it has the value T in the actual row of its truth table.

20. The foregoing defense of the translation of the indicative conditional as $\rightarrow$ in the face of the problematic examples comes more or less from Grice [1989, essay 4; see especially pp. 61–62]. The issue of whether indicative conditionals are correctly translated using $\rightarrow$ is probably the most controversial of all the issues surrounding translation from English into PL, and a vast amount has been written about it. What we have presented are just the opening moves from a long, ongoing debate. For a detailed introduction to the issues, see Bennett [2003]; here we indicate a few further landmarks. One idea that has found wide support is *Adams's Thesis*: the degree to which the conditional "if A then B" is assertible (by a speaker S) equals S's conditional subjective probability of B given A [Adams, 1965]. (To explain the notion of *conditional* probability: the probability of drawing an ace from a shuffled deck is 4/52. But what if you have already drawn one card—and not returned it—and are drawing a second card? If you drew a non-ace the first time, the probability is 4/51. If you drew an ace

the first time, the probability is 3/51. Thus, the conditional probability of drawing an ace given that you drew a non-ace is 4/51; the conditional probability of drawing an ace given that you drew an ace is 3/51. In general, the conditional probability of B given A is denoted $P(B/A)$. Now let us explain the notion of *subjective* probability. It is a widely held view that beliefs need not be all-or-nothing: they can be weaker or stronger; they can come in degrees. For those who hold such a view, it is common to model an agent's degrees of belief as probabilities. When probabilities are viewed in this way—as a measure of an agent's degrees of belief—they are called "subjective probabilities.") Defenders of the idea that indicative conditionals have the same truth conditions as material conditionals have sought a story that explains why Adams's Thesis is true. That is, the story takes as input (i) the idea that "if A then B" is true iff A is false or B is true (or both) and (ii) a theory about correctness of utterances; it then yields as output Adams's Thesis. Lewis [1976] tells such a story, where ingredient (ii) is simply Grice's conversational maxims. In contrast, Jackson [1979, 1987] adds to (ii) a special norm governing the correctness of utterances of indicative conditionals. The norm is that one should assert "if A then B" only if one's confidence in $A \to B$ is *robust* with respect to A: that is, one would not abandon belief in $A \to B$ were one to discover that A. Thus, where Lewis—and the Gricean story told in the text above— would explain the phenomena (e.g., the intuitive incorrectness of certain conditionals that are true when interpreted as material conditionals) in terms of conversational implicatures, Jackson would explain them in terms of conventional implicatures. For a number of reasons, Jackson's approach has found greater favor among those who argue that it is correct to translate indicative conditionals as $\to$ (indeed Lewis [1986, 105, n. 6] abandons his earlier view in favor of Jackson's). Among those opposed to the view that indicative conditionals have the same truth conditions as material conditionals, the major positions defended in the literature are (i) that indicative conditionals are nontruth-functional connectives (e.g., Stalnaker [1968]) or (ii) that indicative conditionals do not have truth conditions at all (e.g., Edgington [1986]). In the latter view, "if A then B" does not express a proposition: it does not make a claim about the world and so is not the sort of thing that is true or false.

21. Alternative symbols for the same notion include $\not\equiv$, $\overline{\vee}$, $\oplus$, $\nleftrightarrow$, and XOR.

22. As Gamut [1991a, 200] also note, a similar comment applies to the following example from Tarski [1946, 21]:

> If . . . a child has asked to be taken on a hike in the morning and to a theater in the afternoon, and we reply: *no, we are going on a hike or we are going to the theater,* then our usage of the word "*or*" is obviously of the [exclusive] kind since we intend to comply with only one of the two requests.

The correct translation here (using the glossary H: We are going on a hike; T: We are going to the theater) is $\neg(H \wedge T) \wedge (H \vee T)$, so the "or" here is translated as $\vee$. The key point is the presence of the initial "no": it is translated as $\neg(H \wedge T)$—that is, as stating "no: we are not going on a hike and going to the theater." It thus plays the same role in this example as "but not both" plays in the example given in the text above.

23. "Or, conj. 1," [OED Online, March 2011].

24. The reasoning here is similar to that we went through in §6.3.2, when we showed that to be in a position to assert $A \to B$, one must not believe $\neg A$ or B.

25. Cases of this sort also raise the issue of whether there is something wrong with the entire PL framework, given that it deems possible a scenario in which "you roll a 3"

and "you roll a 4" are both true—that is, it countenances a truth table row in which both these propositions are true—when it quite clearly seems impossible for a die to come up showing both 3 and 4. In fact there is no problem here: see the discussion in Chapter 11.

26. For a critique of some other supposed examples of exclusive disjunction in English, see Barrett and Stenner [1971].

27. Recall §5.7. If we apply the truth table test for equivalence to the logical forms $(\alpha \to \beta)$ and $(\neg\alpha \lor \beta)$, we see that they have the same value in every row; that is, they are equivalent*. It follows that any instance of $(\alpha \to \beta)$ is equivalent to the corresponding instance of $(\neg\alpha \lor \beta)$.

28. The reason is as follows. When we calculate the truth value of γ, the contribution of the subformula α is complete once it has supplied a truth value as input to the subsequent calculation. If we replace α by an equivalent formula β—that is, one that supplies the same truth value as α in all situations—then the subsequent calculation will not be affected by the replacement.

29. Note that by "first," "second," and so on I simply mean first (second, etc.) in our ordering of the columns in the second table above—which is arbitrary. So there is no deep sense in which the connective $\textcircled{1}_1$ comes before the connective $\textcircled{1}_2$.

30. There are no obvious examples of three-place connectives in English—but we can imagine introducing some. The film *Wayne's World* popularized the use of a trailing "not" to express negation, as in "I'm having a good time . . . not." We can imagine a two-place version of the connective ("A, B, . . . not"), a three-place version ("A, B, C, . . . not"), and so on. We would of course need to specify the truth conditions of these connectives—for example, whether "A, B, . . . not" denies both A and B (i.e., has the same truth table as $(\neg A \land \neg B)$) or just denies that they are both true (i.e., has the same truth table as $\neg(A \land B)$). Church [1956, 129ff.] discusses a three-place connective $[p, q, r]$ whose truth table is the same as that of $(q \to p) \land (\neg q \to r)$. Church [1956, 129, n. 203] writes that "a convenient oral reading of '$[p, q, r]$' is 'p or r according as q or not q.'" Another possible reading would be "if q then p, otherwise r," or again "p if q, else r." However, none of these English constructions is naturally interpreted as involving a three-place connective (Church was not suggesting otherwise): they are most naturally translated as $(q \to p) \land (\neg q \to r)$.

31. Note that this truth table is just a randomly chosen example. There is no special reason I chose this particular truth table. I just need some truth table to use as an example, to illustrate the general method—a method that can be applied to any truth table.

32. Recall our precise definition of what it takes for the connective $*$ to be definable in terms of the connectives $\dagger_1, \ldots, \dagger_n$: for any formula γ containing one or more occurrences of $*$, there is a formula δ that contains no occurrences of $*$ but may contain $\dagger_1, \ldots, \dagger_n$, and is equivalent to γ. Note that the defining formula may contain occurrences of $\dagger_1, \ldots, \dagger_n$; it need not contain them all. The crucial point is simply that it does not contain $*$.

33. Again, this is a randomly chosen example to illustrate the general method: there is no special significance to this table.

34. Other common symbols for this connective are $\uparrow$ and NAND.

Chapter 7: Trees for Propositional Logic

1. We should not get overly excited about the speed of trees. First, although trees are faster than truth tables for many typical everyday logic problems, there are also cases for which trees are slower than truth tables [D'Agostino, 1992]. For example, once you have learned how to construct trees in this chapter, come back and test whether the following formula is satisfiable, both by tree and by truth table: $(A \vee B \vee C) \wedge (A \vee B \vee \neg C) \wedge (A \vee \neg B \vee C) \wedge (A \vee \neg B \vee \neg C) \wedge (\neg A \vee B \vee C) \wedge (\neg A \vee B \vee \neg C) \wedge (\neg A \vee \neg B \vee C) \wedge (\neg A \vee \neg B \vee \neg C)$. How many rows does your truth table have—and how many branches does your tree have? Second, a problem is *intractable* if one or more effective procedures for solving it exist, but these procedures all require so much time (or space) to complete that they cannot be used successfully in practice. One idea that has found wide support is the view (often attributed to Cobham [1964] and/or Edmonds [1965]) that a problem is *tractable* iff it is in the complexity class **P**: that is (roughly—for a proper introduction to the issues touched on in this note, see Sipser [2006]), there is a procedure for solving it whose running time is bounded by a polynomial function of the length of the input to the procedure. The running time of the truth table procedure for testing whether a given formula is satisfiable is not bounded by a polynomial function of the length of the formula being tested—and neither is the running time of the tree method. Thus, the tree method is not so fast that its existence establishes that the satisfiability problem (i.e., the problem of deciding whether a formula of propositional logic is satisfiable) is tractable. (If there were a procedure for solving the satisfiability problem in polynomial time, then—because this problem is **NP**-complete—it would follow that **P** = **NP**. Whether **P** = **NP** is "one of the greatest unsolved problems in theoretical computer science and contemporary mathematics" [Sipser, 2006, 270].)

2. More precisely, if the input proposition is of the form $\neg\alpha$, then it is not $\neg$ that is eliminated, but the main connective of α.

3. More precisely, in some cases it is only required that some outputs must be true, assuming that the input is true.

4. More precisely, we may have several such groups, and we know that if the original propositions at the top of the tree are all true, then there must be at least one group such that all propositions in that group are true.

5. There are three rows of its truth table in which $(\alpha \vee \beta)$ is true—the row in which α and β are true, the row in which α is true and β is false, and the row in which α is false and β is true—so you may wonder why the rule is not as follows:

$$(\alpha \vee \beta)$$

$$\begin{array}{ccc} \alpha & \alpha & \neg\alpha \\ \beta & \neg\beta & \beta \end{array}$$

Well, we could have a tree system with rules like this—but our rules are simpler, and they do the job (as we shall see in §14.1). In the alternative rule just given, the three branches are jointly exhaustive (i.e., between them, they cover all the ways in which $(\alpha \vee \beta)$ could be true) and also mutually exclusive (i.e., it is impossible for all the propositions on two different branches to be true). In contrast, the branches of our tree rules are always jointly exhaustive (recall the second of the two essential features of tree rules mentioned in the opening part of this chapter) but not necessarily mutually exclusive.

6. Or perhaps we should say it gets us too far: it would make our trees go on forever, as we apply the rule to the output of the previous application of the rule ad infinitum.

7. We do not apply rules to propositions on paths that have already been closed: see §7.2.4.

8. To avoid confusion, we should note why we impose this requirement. It is not because it makes any deep difference at this stage: our trees might be longer if we waited until the end (after all rules had been applied) before checking which paths close, but they would still yield the same results. However, in predicate logic, we shall see that sometimes trees can go on forever. In this new context, the requirement that one check for closure at each step (rather than waiting until the end—which may never come) plays an important role. (In particular, it plays a crucial role in the proof of the soundness of the tree method in §14.1.2, via its role in the discussion in §10.3.7, where we show that a path cannot close at infinity.) We impose the requirement now—in the context of propositional logic, where it makes no real difference—just to get into a habit that will be important later.

9. A more precise statement of what the tree rules ensure is given in §10.1, in the context of predicate logic.

10. Indeed, an open path represents an assignment on which all propositions on that path are true—not just the ones at the top, which are on every path through the tree. In practice, however, it is often only the propositions we start with that are of interest.

11. Recall the second of the two essential features of tree rules mentioned in the opening part of this chapter and n. 5.

12. This also explains why we deem the methods introduced above for handling unparenthesized strings of ∨s or ∧s to be unofficial abbreviations, rather than adding them to the official rules: the less official rules we have, the easier it is to prove things about all (official) trees.

Chapter 8: The Language of Monadic Predicate Logic

1. Recall that in the case of propositional logic, a possible scenario—a possible way of making propositions true or false—is a truth table row. A truth table row is determined by an assignment of truth values to basic propositions; the truth tables for the connectives then determine the truth value of every compound proposition in every truth table row.

2. A note on terminology: Something is *simple* if it has no parts. A proposition is *basic* if it has no propositions as parts. In Part 1, we treated basic propositions as if they were simple. Now we move beyond this simplification: that is, we look at the parts of basic propositions, at their internal structure. So we no longer treat basic propositions as simple—but they are still basic.

3. It is not essential that we throw out the simple symbols for basic propositions: although we shall not do so, it would be possible to retain them alongside the new symbols for components of basic propositions. We mention a particular way of doing this in §12.1.2.

4. There are two reasons for treating monadic predicate logic separately, before turning to general (polyadic) predicate logic. First, the learning curve is flattened if the material is presented in stages rather than all at once. Second, the approach makes it clear that predicate logic is not a monolithic whole but has a modular structure. This is useful both for later studies in logic and in introductory logic itself: for example, it is enlightening to see that simply introducing many-place predicates, while keeping

the quantifiers the same as in monadic predicate logic, vastly increases the expressive power of the language.

5. Note that here we are not bringing back the symbols for basic propositions that we had in PL. We are re-using the uppercased letters for a completely different purpose. Thus, as we shall see, $(A \lor B)$ for example is not a well-formed formula of MPL—for in MPL (unlike in PL), A and B are not wffs (they are only parts of wffs), and to form a wff using $\lor$, we need to put the latter symbol between two wffs.

6. That is, the novel.

7. Section 2.2.1 is listed in the Preface as noncore material. To understand the basic point of the present section, you do not need to have read §2.2.1. However, if you want a deeper understanding of the points made here—and you did not read §2.2.1—go back and read it now.

8. Word types that pick out different things depending on the context of utterance are called "indexicals" (see Chapter 1, n. 12).

9. It is often thought that predicates, as well as singular terms, can be context-sensitive. Recall the example from Chapter 3, n. 1: if I say "Bill Bradley is tall" in the context of a discussion of current and former basketball players, my claim would seem to be false; if I say the same sentence in the context of a discussion of past presidential candidates, my claim would seem to be true. Suppose that on each occasion I express an atomic proposition. I am talking about the same individual both times—so if I utter different propositions (one true, one false), it must be because I am attributing different properties to this individual on the two occasions. If that is what is going on, then the expression "is tall" is context sensitive, and we have to translate its two occurrences as different predicates of MPL, for example:

T: is tall (for a basketball player)
U: is tall (for a presidential candidate)

If we also have the glossary entry b: Bill Bradley, then the two propositions come out in MPL as Tb and Ub.

10. If you look at other logic books, you will find that other symbols are sometimes used for the quantifiers. Alternatives to $\forall x$ include $(\forall x)$ (note the parentheses, which are not present in our symbolism), (x), (Ax), Λx, $\bigwedge x$, and Πx. Alternatives to $\exists x$ include $(\exists x)$ (note the parentheses), (Ex), Vx, $\bigvee x$, and Σx.

11. "Spondulix" is the name of a famous gold nugget, found in 1872.

12. The notion of the *scope* of a quantifier is explained in detail in §8.4.4.

13. Or the set of persons who signed up for today's excursion, or the set of persons on the tour who are staying in this hotel, and so on—which set, exactly, will depend on the context.

14. In other examples, it might be other maxims that generate the implicature—for example, the Maxim of Relation. If the guide says "let's wait a minute before we start—not everyone is ready," the unrestricted claim that not everyone in the whole world is ready is true. Presumably, however, it is not relevant in the circumstances. Hence we shall infer that what the guide is actually trying to contribute is some relevant piece of information, such as that not everyone on the tour is ready.

15. This does not mean that the English has to contain corresponding predicates—only that it has to contain corresponding expressions. In the case of "everyone" and "someone" (as opposed to "everything" and "something"), we take the expression

"one" (as opposed to "thing") to correspond to the predicate "is a person." Thus, we translate "everyone is special" as $\forall x(Px \rightarrow Sx)$, not as $\forall x\, Sx$.

16. In §13.6.2 and §13.7.1 we will see that there can—in languages richer than MPL—be more complex kinds of terms.

17. The underlining is explained in §8.4.2.

18. We refer to the first line of clause (3ii)—the one featuring ¬—as clause (3ii¬), the second line—the one featuring ∧—as clause (3ii∧), and so on.

19. In practice, it is often possible to omit the underlining on syntactic variables without causing any confusion (because it is obvious from the context that the particular symbol one writes is serving as an exemplar of all symbols of its kind). This is, in fact, one of the advantages of this symbolism.

20. Some books use an alternative terminology, according to which the variable *in* a quantifier is neither free nor bound. Using this terminology, the second two occurrences of x in $\forall x(Rx \rightarrow Qx)$ are bound (by the quantifier $\forall x$), while the first (the one in the quantifier $\forall x$) is neither free nor bound.

21. In the literature, closed wffs—as opposed to open wffs—are often called "sentences." We shall not adopt this terminology in this book.

Chapter 9: Semantics of Monadic Predicate Logic

1. In the literature, models are also referred to as "interpretations," "structures," and "model structures." When the term "interpretation" is employed, the term "model" is then sometimes used in a different sense (i.e., not as a synonym for "interpretation"), according to which a model of a set of wffs is an interpretation in which all those wffs are true.

2. See §16.1.2 for an explanation of the notion "subset."

3. Is there a model in which the name a refers to Santa Claus, to the number 3, or to beauty (considered as an abstract object)? We make no rulings on these matters here. Our only requirement on what can be in the domain of a model is this: anything can go in; "mere nothings" cannot. Suppose someone says, "consider a model whose domain contains Santa Claus, Bugs Bunny, and Aristotle." Now with each of these expressions ("Santa Claus," "Bugs Bunny," and "Aristotle"), the person may have picked out something, or she may have failed to pick out anything at all. In the former case, there's no problem. In the latter case, her attempt to specify a model has gone astray, in this sense: if "Santa Claus," singles out nothing at all, then when she says that the domain is to include "Santa Claus," nothing is actually added to the domain of the model. So, in talking about models, we assume only that the members of the domain are objects or things of some sort. We make no rulings on (i) which words in English pick out things (as opposed to failing to pick out anything at all), or (ii) what kinds of things exist (and hence are available to go in the domains of models). Topic (i) involves questions in the *philosophy of language*—for example, does "Santa Claus" refer to something (a fictional entity, an abstract object, a guy in a suit at the shopping mall) or does it fail to refer to anything at all? Topic (ii) involves questions for *metaphysics*—for example, assuming "Aristotle" (as uttered now) picks out some thing (rather than failing to pick out anything at all), what kind of thing is it: the real flesh and blood Aristotle, or an abstract object (e.g., a collection of properties that Aristotle alone possessed)? None of these questions are our concern here. We assume only that when we specify models, the names that we use to do so

do indeed select "things" in some sense. (If you think that some of the examples of models given in this book are specified using English expressions that in fact fail to pick out anything at all, then you should simply substitute different examples in their place.)

Although it is beyond the scope of this book to explain the following points (for explanations, see e.g., Boolos et al. [2007, Chapter 12]), it is worth mentioning that from a purely logical point of view, we can focus solely on models whose domains contain either all the natural numbers $\{0, 1, 2, \ldots\}$ or some initial segment of them $\{0, 1, 2, \ldots, n\}$ (and furthermore, these domains can be thought of as purely set-theoretic entities, i.e., as sets in the iterative hierarchy; see §16.1.4). This is so because of two results: the *Löwenheim-Skolem theorem*, which states that if a proposition is true in some model (i.e., satisfiable), then it is true in some model with a countable domain; and the *isomorphism lemma*, which states that if a proposition is true in a model $\mathfrak{M}$, then it is true in any model that is isomorphic to $\mathfrak{M}$.

4. Although it is a requirement on models that each name be assigned a referent, it is not a requirement that different names get different referents. So the only general requirement on domains is that they have at least one member. In a model with fewer objects in the domain than there are names to be assigned referents, some names will have the same referent; in a model with only one object in the domain, all names will refer to that one object.

It should be noted that the reason given in the text as to why the domain must be nonempty is deliberately oversimplified: the true story is more complex. Below we shall see that not every model has to assign a referent to every name in the full language MPL: we countenance models of fragments of the language. We also countenance fragments containing no names (only predicates). So why can't models of these fragments have domains with nothing in them? Well, every model must determine a truth value for every proposition made up from logical vocabulary together with those items of nonlogical vocabulary that are assigned values in that model. So, for example, a model that assigns an extension to P must determine a truth value for $\exists x\, Px$ and $\forall x\, Px$. The story that we tell (in §9.3) about how quantified propositions are assigned truth values in models makes essential use of the idea of assigning values to certain new names (ones not assigned values on the original model). For these new names to be assigned values, there must be at least one object in the domain of the original model—even if that model itself assigns values to *no* names. (The situation actually becomes more complex. In §15.1.3 we look at a different account of how quantified propositions are assigned truth values in models: one which does not make use of the idea of assigning values to certain new names. However, it does make use of the idea of assigning values to variables. These values are drawn from the domain of the model. So again, for the account to work, the original model needs to have at least one thing in its domain, so that each variable can be assigned a value.) Note that there are nonclassical logics that relax our requirements on models: *free logics* drop the requirement that every name must have a referent drawn from the domain of the model; *inclusive* (aka *empty*, or *universally free*) logics drop this requirement, and the requirement that the domain be nonempty (for further details, see, e.g., Bencivenga [2002] and Lehmann [2002]).

5. It is thought that the Big Bang occurred about 13 billion years ago.

6. The set of nonlogical symbols in a fragment is the *signature* of that fragment.

7. Where σ is the signature of a fragment, a model that assigns referents/extensions to all and only the names/predicates in that fragment (i.e., in σ) is said to be of signature σ.

8. In Chapter 13, we look at the logical language GPLI, which includes an identity predicate. This predicate is part of the logical vocabulary. Thus, there are fragments of GPLI with no nonlogical symbols.

9. The distinction between the full language and fragments thereof applies also to PL. In PL, to obtain fragments containing propositions, we need to include at least one basic proposition. When we were translating into PL, we used fragments of the full language (in each case, the fragment containing just those basic propositions featured in our glossary); likewise, our truth tables were all for fragments of the full language (in each case, the fragment containing just those basic propositions that appear in the matrix).

10. In §15.1.3 we discuss a different way of proceeding, according to which some open wffs can have truth values.

11. That is, the set of positive integers.

12. That is, the set of odd numbers.

13. That is, the set of even numbers.

14. As already mentioned, there is an alternative way of treating the truth conditions of quantified formulas, which uses the notion of an assignment of values to variables. We discuss it in §15.1.3. The alternative treatment is probably more common in logic textbooks—although the treatment to be given here can be found in such canonical works as Boolos et al. [2007]. My reason for giving the following treatment precedence is that it maintains a clear conceptual distinction between the semantic functions of names (singular terms) and variables—and (a not unrelated point) it is easier for newcomers to grasp. See also Chapter 15, n. 25.

15. What happens to our procedure of considering a new name—one not already assigned a referent on $\mathfrak{M}$—in the case where $\mathfrak{M}$ already assigns a referent to every name in the full language MPL? Well, we could add an extra stock of names—say, $a', a'', a''', \ldots$—reserved for the purpose of evaluating quantified propositions.

16. Except in the special case where the domain contains expressions of English (or some other language).

17. I owe this analogy (used originally in a different context) to Sybille Smith.

18. That is, the set of prime numbers.

19. That is, every model that assigns referents/extensions to all the names and predicates featured in the argument. Recall (§9.1) that if a model does not assign a referent/extension to some name or predicate in a proposition, then that proposition has no truth value in that model.

20. A couple of terminological points: (i) the term "tautology" is usually restricted to formulas of propositional logic that are logically true, and (ii) it is quite common to call a wff that is true on all models a "valid formula," or simply "valid."

21. For reasons mentioned in n. 3, the facts about validity do not actually depend sensitively on the facts about what sets exist. As long as we have available all the sets $\{0, 1, 2, \ldots, n\}$ (for finite n) and the set $\{0, 1, 2, \ldots\}$, the facts about which arguments are valid will not change if we add additional sets. For if an argument has a countermodel whose domain is one of the original sets, then a fortiori it has a countermodel among the expanded range of models. Conversely, if an argument has no counter-

model whose domain is one of the original sets, then it cannot have a countermodel among the expanded range of models: if it has a countermodel with an uncountable domain, then it has a countermodel with a countable domain (Löwenheim-Skolem); and if it has a countermodel with a countable domain, then it has a countermodel whose domain is one of the original sets (isomorphism).

22. Here (and in corresponding places below) I assume without loss of generality that *a* (or whatever name symbol is used) is not assigned a referent in $\mathfrak{M}$. That is, you can view *a* here as a proxy for the first name alphabetically that is not assigned a referent in $\mathfrak{M}$.

Chapter 10: Trees for Monadic Predicate Logic

1. In Chapter 7, we said that tree rules should have a second feature as well: the output propositions should be simpler than the input proposition—in particular, the main operator of the input should be eliminated. We return to this point after the rules for the quantifiers have been presented.

2. Reasoning in this sort of way is especially common in mathematics.

3. The principle that the truth of a formula involving a name depends on the name's referent, not on what name it is, is nicely expressed by Juliet in the famous speech in *Romeo and Juliet* in which she says "What's in a name? that which we call a rose/ By any other name would smell as sweet;/ So Romeo would, were he not Romeo call'd,/ Retain that dear perfection which he owes/ Without that title." Note that we are saying that on a given model, a formula involving *a* will have the same truth value as any formula obtained from it by replacing some or all of the *a*s with *b*s, provided that *a* and *b* have the same referent on that model. This is quite compatible with the fact that, for example, $Fa \rightarrow Fa$ is logically true, whereas $Fa \rightarrow Fb$ is not. In a model in which *a* and *b* have the same referent, $Fa \rightarrow Fa$ and $Fa \rightarrow Fb$ have the same truth value. There are, however, models in which *a* and *b* do not have the same referent—and in some of these models, $Fa \rightarrow Fb$ is false. In every model, however, $Fa \rightarrow Fa$ is true— because in any given model, the two occurrences of *a* in $Fa \rightarrow Fa$ must always have the same referent.

4. Recall n. 1. We can now see the extent to which the rules for the quantifiers have the feature that they eliminate the quantifiers—and the extent to which they do not. The rules for the negated quantifiers do not eliminate the quantifier—but they switch the quantifier from existential to universal or vice versa and put it in front, where the rule for the unnegated quantifier of the relevant sort can operate on it. So the question becomes: do the rules for the unnegated quantifiers eliminate the quantifier? The rule for the unnegated existential quantifier does indeed eliminate the quantifier. At first glance, it might seem that the rule for the negated universal quantifier does too: but the appearance is misleading. For the original formula is not checked off: it remains in play, and the rule for the universal quantifier can potentially be applied to it again. Thus, its universal quantifier is not actually eliminated from the path. As we shall see (§10.3), this means that in predicate logic—unlike in propositional logic—trees need not always terminate; that is, they may continue forever. This fact turns out to have a rather deep significance (§14.2).

5. In §7.2.5, we imposed this closure-checking requirement on trees for propositional logic, but in n. 8 of that section we noted that it would not actually make any difference if we waited until the tree was finished before closing paths. Now—in the

context of predicate logic—the closure-checking requirement takes on real importance. As mentioned in n. 4, trees for predicate logic need not always terminate—in which case we cannot wait until the tree is "finished" before closing paths.

6. The "first" in "first name" refers to the alphabetical ordering of our name symbols, not to the order in which the names appear in the path. We could do it the latter way, but the former is easier to keep track of in general.

7. See Jeffrey [2006, Supplement B, pp. 151–55] for a description of the method.

8. That is, α is of one of the forms $\neg\neg\beta$, $(\beta * \gamma)$, or $\neg(\beta * \gamma)$, where $*$ is $\vee$, $\wedge$, $\rightarrow$, or $\leftrightarrow$.

9. That is, α is of one of the forms $\neg\exists\underline{x}\beta(\underline{x})$ or $\neg\forall\underline{x}\beta(\underline{x})$.

10. That is, α is of the form $\exists\underline{x}\beta(\underline{x})$.

11. We actually need to specify exactly what we mean by "alphabetically first" here—for example, is a_2 before or after b? Let's specify that the alphabetical ordering of the names is: $a, b, c, \ldots, t, a_2, \ldots, t_2, a_3, \ldots, t_3, a_4, \ldots$.

12. That is, α is of the form $\forall\underline{x}\beta(\underline{x})$.

13. For example, if α is $\forall x Fx$, α lies on an open path, and somewhere on this path the name b appears (in some formula), then we add Fb at the bottom of the path, unless Fb already appears somewhere on this path, in which case we do not write it again.

14. Note that as you work through step (1), new propositions may be added to the tree. These will always be added below the proposition you are currently visiting, so their addresses will come later. You visit them later, in order; that is, you do not only visit propositions that were already in the tree when you started step (1). Note, however, that you never backtrack: you never revisit—within the same iteration of step (1)—a proposition you have already visited on that round.

15. That is, make another round of visiting all propositions in the tree, once each, in order of address, and dealing with each one in accordance with the instructions given in step (1).

16. Recall the two examples of infinite unfinished trees discussed earlier: the one in §10.3.1, where we repeatedly applied the universal quantifier rule to $\forall x\exists y(Fx \wedge Gy)$ (with a new name each time) and never applied the conjunction rule to $(Fa \wedge \neg Fa)$ (which would close the path immediately) and the one in §10.3.4, where we extended the tree in accordance with the pattern $1a$, $1b$, $1c$, $\ldots$ and so never applied the universal quantifier rule to proposition (2). The procedure just given ensures that these problems never happen: the procedure requires you to visit every proposition in the tree on each iteration of step (1). It therefore ensures that no propositions are permanently overlooked.

17. More precisely, there cannot be such a procedure that applies to trees in GPL as well as in MPL. We shall discuss this issue in more detail in §14.2.

18. The reasoning proceeds in exactly the same way if $\neg\delta$ comes first.

19. At this stage, of course, we are not assuming that it has any infinitely long path: that is what we want to show. We are assuming only that it has infinitely many entries, arranged in some way.

20. One form of *König's Lemma* says that an infinite tree in which each entry has only a finite number of immediate descendants must have an infinite path. This is a generalization of what we have just shown, which is that an infinite tree of our sort—in which each entry has at most two immediate descendants—must have an infinite

path. König's Lemma can be proven by a simple generalization of the reasoning given in the text.

Chapter 11: Models, Propositions, and Ways the World Could Be

1. No doubt there are other possible ways of giving content to wffs, but these are the ones that are commonly employed. Although they are all in common use, it is very uncommon for a clear distinction to be drawn among the three methods. In fact, I am not aware of any prior discussion that tries to clarify the methods in the way presented in this chapter.

2. We do not mean here that if, in those imagined circumstances, someone were to utter the words "Mount Everest is tall," what they said would be false. We are talking about the proposition expressed by some actual utterance of "Mount Everest is tall," and we are saying that this proposition (not the sentence actually used to express it), while true given the way the world actually is, would be false were the world different in certain ways. In the imagined circumstances, speakers might use an entirely different language—one in which "is tall" has a quite different meaning from its actual one—or there might be no language users at all. None of this affects what we are saying: we are not imagining the words "Mount Everest is tall" being spoken in these imagined circumstances. Instead we are talking about the proposition expressed by some actual utterance of these words, and considering whether the way it claims the world to be is the way the world would be in the imagined circumstances.

3. "Possible world" is the standard term, but use of this term can be distracting, if not misleading—it has connotations that go far beyond anything we are assuming about wws. See also n. 21.

4. The notion of a *function* is explained in §16.4.

5. We here assume *compositionality* of content (aka *Frege's Principle*): the content of a proposition is determined by the contents of its parts, together with their mode of composition (i.e., the way the proposition is formed from those parts).

6. The term "intension" and the essential idea behind this definition (although not its exact details) are from Carnap [1956].

7. Often the intension of a name is called an "individual concept," the intension of a predicate is called a "property," and the intension of a closed wff is called a "proposition." We shall not adopt these terms here (although we return to this use of "proposition" in §11.4).

8. There are cases—involving made-up words, for example—where (expressions that behave grammatically like) names and predicates have no content. There are other, more problematic cases, where names and predicates seem to have content, but this content is not sufficient to determine an intension—at least, not if intensions are thought of as total functions from wws to values. (The notion of a total—as opposed to partial—function is explained in §16.4.) For example, there are cases involving vague predicates: it might seem that there are wws relative to which the proposition expressed by some actual utterance of "Bill Bradley is tall" is neither true nor false—because of the facts, according to those wws, concerning the (relative) height of Bill Bradley (here the content of the predicate seems not to determine a total function from wws to extensions, where extensions are precise sets of objects). For another example, it might seem that there are wws relative to which the proposition expressed by some actual utterance of "Bill Bradley is a professional basketball player" is neither true nor false—because according to those wws, the man we call "Bill Bradley" was never born (here

the content of the name seems not to determine a total function from wws to objects). We have already mentioned vague predicates in Chapter 3, n. 1; we return to the issue of singular terms that seem to lack a referent (relative to some wws) in §13.6.3.

9. Sometimes we also speak of the content of an *utterance* (of some sentence in a context). By this we mean the proposition expressed by that utterance—which itself has a content, in the (different) sense of content just explained.

10. Well, they must at least determine intensions—but in keeping with our simplifying assumption, we take them just to be intensions.

11. I am supposing that a ww specifies which non-sets (urelements) exist. Given the urelements specified by a ww, a hierarchy of sets is then specified in the way discussed in §16.1.4. The set-theoretic story—the recipe for generating the hierarchy—does not vary from ww to ww: only the initial set of urelements varies. The domain of the model generated by a ww together with some intensions is then a set in the hierarchy built up from the urelements specified by that ww; in the simplest case, it is just the set containing all and only the urelements. (Note that if we took a ww to specify that all the sets in the hierarchy exist, then we could not have a model whose domain is the set containing all the things specified to exist by that ww: for, as discussed in §16.1.4, there is no set of all sets in the hierarchy.)

12. We assume throughout that there is a fixed collection of wws, representing all the ways the world could be.

13. The analogue of the actual model in the case of propositional logic is the actual row (§4.1.3).

14. Well, generally speaking. Of course, logical truths are true in all models and logical falsehoods are true in no models.

15. An axiom system that does fix its models up to isomorphism is said to be *categorical*.

16. Of course, there are models that are different from these four but are isomorphic to one of them. For example, the following model is isomorphic to the first of our earlier models—it arises from it by switching 1 for Alice:

Domain: {Alice}
Extensions: A: {Alice} B: ∅ C: {Alice}

17. In the philosophical literature, this definition is usually phrased as follows: a proposition is a set of possible worlds. The two definitions are interchangeable, given that "possible worlds" and "wws" are terms for the same things (recall n. 3) and that sets go hand in hand with characteristic functions (see §16.4.2): a set of wws determines a function from wws to truth values (the function that assigns True to all wws in the set and False to all wws not in the set) and vice versa.

18. The notion of an equivalence relation is explained in §16.3.

19. In the philosophy of language, there is talk of Fregean propositions as opposed to Russellian (or singular) propositions. Propositions in our sixth sense are a version of Fregean propositions; those in our seventh sense are a version of Russellian propositions.

To make these models of propositions fully coherent, we need to replace logical symbols with something that stands in relation to them as intensions/values stand in relation to nonlogical symbols (otherwise, our propositions are a strange mix of symbols and intensions/values). But we have not countenanced values for the logical vocabulary. Our approach has been to treat these symbols *syncategorematically:* we show how to assign values to closed wffs involving these symbols without assigning values to the logical symbols themselves. So if logical symbols were to be assigned values—that is, if they were to be treated *categorematically*—what would these values be? (Once we have values, intensions are then simply functions from wws to these values.) In the case of connectives, one simple answer is: truth functions (§3.5). In the case of quantifiers, a simple answer is: the value of a quantifier is a function from subsets of the domain to truth values. Specifically, the universal quantifier picks out that function that sends the entire domain to True and all other subsets to False; the existential quantifier picks out that function that sends the empty set to False and all other subsets to True. (Note that if we regard P as picking out a subset of the domain, then $\forall x\, Px$ will then be true just in case P picks out the entire domain, while $\exists x\, Px$ will then be true just in case P picks out a nonempty subset of the domain.) For further details of this kind of approach, see, for example, Gamut [1991b].

20. Recall the intuitive idea: a proposition represents the world as being a certain way; it is true if the world is that way and otherwise false. Our wws are just the ways the world could be that feature in this intuitive idea.

21. It is wws in this sense that are called "possible worlds" in the philosophical literature. (Recall n. 3.)

22. For more details on intensional logics, see, for example, Gamut [1991b], Hughes and Cresswell [1996].

23. That validity implies NTP is to be expected, given that validity is supposed to be NTP by virtue of form, that is, a special sort of NTP.

24. Some people distinguish *logical* and *metaphysical* possibility in the following sort of way: they think that there is a big set of possible worlds—the logically possible worlds—in which pretty much anything can happen (e.g. red things can be colourless) and then think of what I have conceived of as the set of *all* possible worlds (wws) as a subset of this big set—the metaphysically possible worlds. The view presented in this book is rather different. First, there is just one set of possible worlds (wws), representing all the ways the world could be. What we do have, however, is a distinction between all *models* and ww-models (relative to a given set of intensions). Second, I have not introduced any notion of "logical" possibility, as opposed to the notion of possibility introduced above (a proposition—closed wff under a glossary—is possibly true if it is true in some ww-model). What we do have, however, is the notion of *satisfiability*: a proposition—closed wff (intensions are irrelevant here)—is satisfiable if it is true on some model.

25. A word of clarification is in order about the idea that logical truths are true by virtue of their form (and that valid arguments are NTP by virtue of their form, and so on). This idea does not mean that there is a special way of generating truth values for logical truths that takes as input only the form of the proposition, not the values of its components. There is no special "way of making true" for logical truths: there is just one set of rules for making propositions true—summarized in §9.4.2—and these rules apply to all propositions, logical truths, and non-logicaltruths alike. (For example, consider a model in which the referents of a and b are in the extension of R. What makes $Ra \lor \neg Ra$ true in this model is exactly what makes $Ra \lor \neg Rb$ true in this model: the disjunction is true because its first disjunct is true; the first disjunct, which is an atomic proposition, is in turn true because the referent of the name is in the extension of the predicate.) What is special about logical truths is that their structure

determines that when these rules are applied, the result will always be true, no matter what the values are of the components of the proposition. Nevertheless, in every model the truth value of the proposition comes from the values of its components, via the standard rules.

26. There is an area of logic (*modal logic*) in which the notions of necessity and possibility are studied. (For an introduction, see, e.g., Hughes and Cresswell [1996].) In modal logic, we enrich the logical language with two one-place connectives: $\Box$, which intuitively means "necessarily," and $\Diamond$, which intuitively means "possibly." A model of the extended language—a modal model—comprises a set of possible worlds together with a two-place accessibility relation on this set, and an assignment of a referent to each name at each world and an extension to each predicate at each world. Propositions without $\Box$ or $\Diamond$ in them are assigned truth values at worlds in much the way as in models in predicate logic. (There is some extra complexity regarding the quantifiers: we can regard each world in the model as having its own domain, or we can think of the modal model as having just one domain for all worlds in the model.) As for propositions with $\Box$ or $\Diamond$ in them, $\Box\alpha$ is true at a world w just in case α is true at every world accessible from w, and $\Diamond\alpha$ is true at w just in case α is true at some world accessible from w. Now even in modal logic, we do not (in general) find out whether particular propositions are necessarily true. In predicate logic, we study logical truth—not actual truth (truth in the actual model). Similarly, modal logic studies the logical truth of formulas of the modal language—that is, it asks which formulas are true in all modal models. It does not offer any way of determining which modal model is the actual one (and which world in that model is the actual world). Thus, it does not offer us any way of finding out whether some formula $\Box\alpha$ actually is true or whether the formula α is necessarily true (α will be necessarily true just in case $\Box\alpha$ is true in the actual world of the actual modal model).

27. Up to isomorphism; this qualification will henceforth be left implicit.

Chapter 12: General Predicate Logic

1. We mentioned in Chapter 8, n. 3, that we do not have to throw away sentence letters when moving from propositional logic to predicate logic: we can retain them, alongside the symbols for predicates and names. One way of doing this is to allow *zero-place* predicates: P^0, Q^0, R^0, ... An n-place predicate, when followed by n names, makes a wff. Thus, a zero-place predicate by itself makes a wff. Hence, zero-place predicates function like sentence letters. Note that we do not actually have zero-place predicates in GPL (the full syntax of which is given in §12.1.3), but we could have had them if desired. Recall the discussion at the end of §2.2.1: in applications of logic, ignoring structure irrelevant for one's particular purposes can sometimes be useful. Thus, it might be convenient to be able to represent a complex proposition (e.g., the one expressed by "Bill and Ben are friends") using a simple symbol (say, P^0) in contexts where the structure of this proposition is irrelevant to the purposes at hand. In this book, however—where we are introducing logic—we shall not have cause to do this sort of thing, and so we shall not have need for zero-place predicates.

2. We shall see the point of this exception in Chapter 13.

3. In §6.2.2 we encountered examples of *phrasal* conjunction, such as "Bill and Ben are brothers." This example could be read as saying simply that Bill is a brother (i.e., he has a sibling) and Ben is a brother, or it could be read as saying that Bill and Ben are brothers of one another—and we promised a translation of the second reading into

GPL that would be more illuminating than the translation into PL (where this claim came out as a basic proposition). Using the glossary:

l: Bill

n: Ben

Bxy: x is a brother of *y*

we translate as *Bln* ∧ *Bnl* (or equivalently, *Bnl* ∧ *Bln*). Note that all two-place predicates in GPL express what we might call *directed* relations. The proposition *Rab* says that relation *R* holds between *a* and *b* in that order: from *a* to *b*, as it were. (What this means will become fully clear in §12.2 when we look at the semantics of GPL and see that the value of a two-place predicate is an *ordered pair* of objects.) Thus, we translate the claim that Bill and Ben are brothers (i.e., of one another—Bill is a brother of Ben and Ben is a brother of Bill) as a conjunction of two directed relational claims. See also §12.4.

4. I put "different" in parentheses here, because the point I have just been making is that any two-place predicate is always different from any one-place predicate. So if "tall" is translated by a one-place predicate, and "is taller than" is translated by a two-place predicate, it follows immediately that they are translated by different predicates.

5. It is important that *x* be replaced with a variable that does not already occur in the wff we are considering (in this case, a variable other than *y*). The proposition ∃*y*∀*yLyy* is *not* equivalent to ∃*x*∀*yLxy*.

6. Given n. 5, it is important that these replacements occur simultaneously. That is, we do not first replace the *x*s by *y*s, resulting in ∃*y*∀*yLyy*, and then replace the *y*s by *x*s, resulting in ∃*x*∀*xLxx*. Neither ∃*y*∀*yLyy* nor ∃*x*∀*xLxx* is equivalent to the original proposition ∃*x*∀*yLxy*.

7. Read "himself" here as gender-neutral—that is, the claim is that no one self-admires.

8. Read "himself" here as gender-neutral—that is, the claim is that Dave admires anyone who doesn't self-admire.

9. Parentheses are often used instead of angle brackets to indicate ordered pairs, that is, (Alice, Bob). This point about notation also applies to the general notion of an ordered *n*-tuple (introduced below).

10. For further discussion of ordered pairs, see §16.2.

11. There need not be *n* distinct objects in an ordered *n*-tuple: one object may appear at more than one position. There must be at least one object, and at most *n* objects. Note that we sometimes refer to ordered *n*-tuples simply as *n*-tuples.

12. For further discussion of ordered *n*-tuples, see §16.2.

13. Clause (3) talks about wffs in general; recall that by "proposition" we mean a closed wff.

14. That is, the set of prime numbers.

15. That is, the set of all pairs ⟨*x*, *y*⟩ such that *x* is less than *y*. A more compact way of writing this set is {⟨*x*, *y*⟩ : *x* < *y*}. See §16.1 for an explanation of this kind of notation for sets.

16. Remember that an intension is a function from wws to values. So the intension of an *n*-place predicate is a function from wws to sets of *n*-tuples.

17. The foregoing points were already illustrated in Exercises 12.3.1, questions (3i) and (3ii). The argument "Alice is older than Bill, and Bill is older than Carol, so Alice must be older than Carol" is invalid. If we add as a premise "anyone older than

someone is older than everyone whom that someone is older than"—the translation of which into GPL is a postulate for "older than" analogous to our second postulate for "taller than" in the text above—then the result is valid.

18. This is a venerable, and still popular, view about belief—but it is also controversial. The relevant debates can be found in the philosophical literature under headings including "propositional attitudes" and "content of belief."

19. Recall (§2.2.1, §8.2.2) that we face no such problems in the logical language itself—because our logical languages are not context-sensitive: there is never any question whether (for example) the two occurrences of a (or of T) in $Ta \rightarrow Ta$ pick out the same thing.

20. There are extensions of classical predicate logic in which there are more kinds of symbol: in which, for example, predicates can be constructed out of simpler components, in a way analogous to the way in which the complex expression "walks slowly" is constructed in English from the simpler expressions "walks" and "slowly." These richer logical languages are especially useful in linguistics. For an introduction, see for example, Dowty et al. [1981] and Gamut [1991b].

21. Here we assume the fact that if γ_1 is equivalent to γ_2, and δ_1 is equivalent to δ_2, then $\gamma_1 \wedge \delta_1$ is equivalent to $\gamma_2 \wedge \delta_2$.

22. There is also a second issue: (12.5) is an open wff; hence it is meaningless to say it is equivalent to anything: our definition of equivalence in §9.5 applies only to propositions, that is, closed wffs. We can avoid this problem by defining the notion of equivalence in a more general way: one that applies to open wffs as well as closed wffs, but gives exactly the same results for closed wffs as our existing definition. The definition is as follows [Boolos and Jeffrey, 1989, 108]. For any wffs α and β, α is equivalent to β just in case α^* and β^* have the same truth value in every model (i.e., are equivalent in our original sense), where α^* and β^* result from α and β by uniformly substituting new names $\underline{a_1, \ldots, a_n}$ (i.e., names that do not occur in α or β) for all free variables $x_1, \ldots, x_n$, respectively.

23. Here we assume the fact that if γ is equivalent to δ, then $\exists x \gamma$ is equivalent to $\exists x \delta$.

Chapter 13: Identity

1. For example Parfit [1987, 201]: "There are two kinds of sameness, or identity. I and my Replica are *qualitatively identical,* or exactly alike. But we may not be *numerically identical,* or one and the same person."

2. We return to the final two—"there are two dogs" and "there are between ten and twenty dogs"—in §13.5.

3. Claim (7) would certainly be an odd thing to say, if Mark Twain were not a novelist. But would it be false in this case? Is the information that Mark Twain is a novelist implied by claim (7), or is it an implicature (recall §6.1)? In general, in this book we have tended to favor weaker translations: ones that do not imply things that could reasonably be regarded as implicatures. We follow that pattern here: Nt ("Mark Twain is a novelist") does not follow logically from the translation of claim (7) given in the text. Note that GPLI is perfectly capable of representing the stronger claim "Mark Twain is a novelist, and he is taller than some other novelist," which quite clearly includes as part of what is said (not merely as an implicature) the information that Mark Twain is a novelist. This claim is translated as $Nt \wedge \exists x((Nx \wedge \neg I^2xt) \wedge Ttx)$.

Those who think that claim (7) implies—rather than merely implicates—that Mark Twain is a novelist will take the latter to be its correct translation.

4. Here again (cf. n. 3) we take it as an implicature that Mark Twain is not taller than Samuel Langhorne Clemens: $\neg Tms$ does not follow logically from our translation. GPLI is, however, perfectly capable of representing the stronger claim "Mark Twain is taller than everyone except Samuel Langhorne Clemens, and he is not taller than Samuel Langhorne Clemens." Similar comments apply in subsequent examples.

5. Many books introduce $=$ as the official symbol for identity—rather than (as here) an informal abbreviation of the official symbol (which is I^2). My reason for introducing I^2 as the official symbol is to make clear that, from the point of view of syntax, the identity predicate is simply a two-place predicate like any other (a fact that is obscured if, right from the start, we write "x is identical to y" in a completely different way from that in which we write "x is taller than y;" i.e., as $x = y$ and Txy, respectively). But from the point of view of semantics and of proofs (trees), the identity predicate will be treated differently from all other predicates, because it is part of the logical vocabulary. It therefore makes sense to write it differently from other predicates, to make its special status salient. (Furthermore, identity in our logical sense is precisely what the familiar symbol $=$ means in arithmetic, as in $2 + 2 = 4$. Thus, it is natural to use this familiar symbol in logic as a symbol for identity.) Having I^2 as the official symbol and $=$ as an informal abbreviation is an attempt to give each of these conflicting impulses its due.

6. To say that $\underline{y}$ is free for $\underline{x}$ in $\alpha(\underline{x})$ means that if we replaced all free occurrences of $\underline{x}$ in $\alpha(\underline{x})$ by occurrences of $\underline{y}$, these occurrences of $\underline{y}$ (i.e., the ones we put in place of free occurrences of $\underline{x}$) would all be free. In other words, no free occurrence of $\underline{x}$ in $\alpha(\underline{x})$ lies within the scope of a quantifier that contains the variable $\underline{y}$. Examples: (i) y is not free for x in $\forall y Rxy$: if we substitute y for all free occurrences of x in $\forall y Rxy$, we get $\forall y Ryy$, in which the occurrence of y that we put in place of the free occurrence of x is bound. (ii) z is free for x in $\forall y Rxy$: if we substitute z for all free occurrences of x in $\forall y Rxy$, we get $\forall y Rzy$, in which the occurrence of z that we put in place of the free occurrence of x is free. In general, $\underline{y}$ is always free for $\underline{x}$ in $\alpha(\underline{x})$ if $\underline{y}$ is a variable that does not occur in $\alpha(\underline{x})$. (iii) y is free for x in $(\exists y Ty \wedge Tx)$: if we substitute y for all free occurrences of x in $(\exists y Ty \wedge Tx)$, we get $(\exists y Ty \wedge Ty)$, in which the occurrence of y that we put in place of the free occurrence of x is free. To be sure, there are other occurrences of y in this formula that are bound—but this does not matter: the point is that all occurrences of y that we put in place of free occurrences of x are free (in this case there is only one such occurrence of y).

7. That is, is or is not in certain extensions, and is or is not the referent of certain names—which ones, exactly, depends on what $\alpha(\underline{a})$ says. For example, if $\alpha(a)$ is $(Pa \rightarrow Rab)$, then a model in which $\alpha(a)$ is true is one in which the referent of a is not in the extension of P, or the pair consisting of the referent of a followed by the referent of b is in the extension of R; whereas if $\alpha(a)$ is $(Pa \vee \exists x Rax)$, then a model in which $\alpha(a)$ is true is one in which the referent of a is in the extension of P, or the referent of a is in the first position of some pair in the extension of R; and so on.

8. For example, if $\alpha(b /\!/ a)$ is $Pb \rightarrow Rab$, then a model in which $\alpha(b /\!/ a)$ is true is one in which the referent of b is not in the extension of P, or the pair consisting of the referent of a followed by the referent of b is in the extension of R.

9. In this application of SI, line 12 is $\alpha(a)$, line 10 is $a = b$, and line 13 is $\alpha(b /\!/ a)$.

10. In general, it is fine to have a model in which some objects in the domain are not the referent of any name. However, in the special case of models read off from open paths, we need to avoid this sort of situation. Otherwise, our procedure for putting objects into the extensions of predicates might yield models in which some formulas on the path are false. For example, suppose that our path contains $\forall x Gx$, and it also contains the names a, b, and c (and no other names). Then, by the requirement on saturation related to universally quantified formulas, it must contain the formulas Ga, Gb, and Gc. Suppose the path also contains $a = c$: so when reading off a model, we make a and c refer to 1 and b refer to 2. But suppose we leave the object 3—the object that was the referent of c, before we made the referent of c the same as the referent of a—in the domain, that is, the domain is $\{1, 2, 3\}$. Notice what goes wrong. We put into the extension of G the referent of each name that occurs after G in a standalone atomic formula: in this case, the referents of a, b, and c. So the extension of G is $\{1, 2\}$. But the domain of the model is $\{1, 2, 3\}$. So $\forall x Gx$ is false in this model. But we want the model that we read off from a saturated open path to be one in which every formula on the path is true. Hence, when we make c refer to what a refers to, we also need to strike out the original referent of c (object 3) from the domain.

11. Note that $\{a\}$, $\{a, a\}$, and $\{a, a, a\}$ are just three ways of writing the same set—the set containing a, that $\{a, b\}$ and $\{a, a, b, b\}$ are just two ways of writing the same set—the set containing a and b, and so on. For ordered n-tuples, however—as opposed to sets—the situation is quite different: $\langle a, a \rangle$ is an ordered pair with a in both first and second place. And $\langle a, a, a \rangle$ is something quite different: an ordered *triple* with a in first, second and third place. For further discussion, see §16.1 and §16.2.

12. Given that the symmetry of identity is a logical law (§13.3), we do not have to say separately that $x \neq y$ and $y \neq x$: we need say only one of these, and the other follows automatically. Also, we do not want nonidentity statements in our formula with the same variable on both sides (e.g., $x \neq x$) because these are logically false. That is why we need one nonidentity statement for each nonordered pairing of the variables in the formula (i.e., one for each set containing two of these variables), not one for each ordered pair of variables. For further discussion of the distinction between two-membered sets and ordered pairs, see §16.2.

13. Thus there are $\binom{n}{2}$ nonidentity statements. The formula $\binom{n}{2}$—read as "n choose 2"—represents the number of nonordered pairs of n things; that is, the number of two-element subsets of a set of size n. Note that $\binom{n}{2} = 1 + 2 + \ldots + (n - 1)$.

14. Thus, there are $\binom{n+1}{2}$ identity statements.

Each of these translations is equivalent to one beginning with a negation followed by $n + 1$ existential quantifiers: (13.5) is equivalent to $\neg \exists x \exists y (Dx \wedge Dy \wedge x \neq y)$, (13.6) is equivalent to $\neg \exists x \exists y \exists z (Dx \wedge Dy \wedge Dz \wedge x \neq y \wedge x \neq z \wedge y \neq z)$, and so on.

15. That is, $\binom{n}{2}$ nonidentity statements.

16. Recall that this notion was defined in n. 6.

17. See Russell [1905] and Whitehead and Russell [1910, pp. 181–95].

18. Alternatively, we could translate the uniqueness assumption ("there is exactly one inventor of Post-it notes") in the first way discussed in §13.5 (i.e., as the conjunction of "there is at least one inventor of Post-it notes" and "there is at most one inventor of Post-it notes"): $\exists x Ix \wedge \forall x \forall y ((Ix \wedge Iy) \rightarrow x = y)$. Then we could translate the whole claim "the inventor of Post-it notes is rich" either as $\exists x Ix \wedge \forall x \forall y ((Ix \wedge Iy) \rightarrow x = y) \wedge \exists x (Ix \wedge Rx)$ or as $\exists x Ix \wedge \forall x \forall y ((Ix \wedge Iy) \rightarrow x = y) \wedge \forall x (Ix \rightarrow Rx)$. The

former adds to the uniqueness assumption the further claim that some inventor of Post-it notes is rich; the latter instead adds the claim that all inventors of Post-it notes are rich. In the context of the uniqueness assumption, both claims come to the same thing: these two translations are equivalent—and each is equivalent to the original translation given in the text. A fourth equivalent translation is $\exists x(Ix \wedge \forall y(Iy \rightarrow x = y) \wedge Rx)$; a fifth is $\exists x \forall y((Iy \leftrightarrow y = x) \wedge Rx)$.

19. Furthermore, the former part can itself be seen as involving two parts: an existence condition, which claims that there is at least one inventor of Post-it notes; and a solitude condition, which claims that there is at most one inventor of Post-it notes.

20. In some books, ι (i.e., the Greek letter iota itself) is used instead.

21. We also need to extend the system of tree proofs, but we do not discuss this here.

22. That is, the value of $\iota \underline{x}\alpha(\underline{x})$ in a model $\mathfrak{M}$ is the unique object o in the domain of $\mathfrak{M}$ such that $\alpha(\underline{a}/\underline{x})$ is true in $\mathfrak{M}_o^a$, where $\underline{a}$ is some name not assigned a referent in $\mathfrak{M}$, and $\mathfrak{M}_o^a$ is a model just like $\mathfrak{M}$ except that in it the name $\underline{a}$ is assigned the referent o.

23. That is, the one and only object o in the domain such that the ordered pair $\langle o, \text{the-referent-of-}s \rangle$ is in the extension of S.

24. See Frege [1892, p. 170, n. 13] and Frege [1964, pp. 49–51, §11]. Compare also Carnap [1956, pp. 35–39, §8].

25. After developing this treatment, I came across a different, but related proposal in Quine [1982, pp. 274–77, §43].

26. More precisely, we translate expressions that would be closed definite descriptions in GPLID as names. Expressions that would be open definite descriptions in GPLID may be treated using *function symbols* (§13.7).

27. Once a replaces x, the initial quantifier $\exists x$ becomes vacuous and so can be removed, giving $\forall y(Iy \leftrightarrow y = a)$. The ys here can then be uniformly replaced with xs, giving the uniqueness postulate as presented above.

28. Of course, we can also be more specific: we can deny just the existence part of the uniqueness assumption (there is at least one inventor of Post-it notes) or just the solitude part (there is at most one inventor of Post-it notes).

29. More precisely, what needs to be true is the version of the uniqueness assumption that involves an existential quantifier, rather than the name that translates the definite description. For example, suppose the description is "the inventor of Post-it notes," and suppose we translate this description as a. Then what needs to be true is not $\forall x(Ix \leftrightarrow x = a)$, but $\exists x \forall y(Iy \leftrightarrow y = x)$. For the former cannot be true—that is, true in the actual model—when the intension of a sends the actual ww to no referent at all; that is, when there is no actual model. So what we want to do is set aside the name a and just consider the intension of I. Now consider the actual model of the fragment containing I. If $\exists x \forall y(Iy \leftrightarrow y = x)$ is true in this model, then there will indeed be an actual model of the expanded fragment that also includes a. The idea is that this is the sort of check we should go through before using a—before using a definite description.

30. We should drop the name a (retreat to a smaller fragment; withdraw the glossary entry for a) and deny $\exists x \forall y(Iy \leftrightarrow y = x)$: we should not deny $\forall x(Ix \leftrightarrow x = a)$, because the latter still involves a. (Recall the previous footnote, and the discussion in the text preceding n. 28, of different ways of denying claims made using definite descriptions.)

31. Precisely what this means will be made clear in §13.7.1.

32. We mentioned in Chapter 12, n. 1 that zero-place predicates could play the role of sentence letters. Likewise, zero-place function symbols could play the role of names.

33. For the distinction between total and partial functions, see §16.4.

34. The problem actually affects the function symbols f and m in the above example as well. True, all persons have exactly one father and exactly one mother—if we interpret "mother" and "father" in the biological sense; but not everything in the world has a mother and father—for example, my first car has neither a father nor a mother. Note that the following is not a simple fix to the issue: "Let the value of a function symbol on a model be a partial function." This solution is certainly possible—it is just not a simple one: it leads to issues similar to those we face if we allow $\imath x \alpha(x)$ to lack a referent in some models. As mentioned at the end of §13.6.2, there are several ways to proceed, but they all lead outside standard classical logic and hence are beyond the scope of this book.

35. For details, see, for example, Jeffrey [2006, pp. 85–98].

36. Compare Boolos et al. [2007, pp. 255–57].

37. In the special case where no wff in Γ contains any function symbols, $\Gamma' = \Gamma$.

38. Note that we mean "equivalent" here in the sense of Chapter 12, n. 22.

39. What we mean here is that if we replace all free variables in $\underline{f}(t_1, \ldots, t_n) = \underline{x}$ and $\underline{R}t_1 \ldots t_n \underline{x}$ by new names, then the former is true in any model just like $\mathfrak{M}$ except that it assigns referents to the new names iff the latter is true in the corresponding model just like $\mathfrak{M}'$ except that it assigns those same referents to the new names.

40. Recall the point noted in §13.7.2: the value of an n-place function is similar to the value of an $(n + 1)$-place relation, but is not exactly the same. The value of an $(n + 1)$-place relation can be any set of ordered $(n + 1)$-tuples of members of the domain. The value of an n-place function, in contrast, cannot be just any set of ordered $(n + 1)$-tuples of members of the domain: it must be one that contains exactly one $(n + 1)$-tuple x' for each n-tuple x of members of the domain, where the first n entries of x' constitute x. That the extension of each $\underline{R}$ is a set of $(n + 1)$-tuples of this special sort is precisely what the truth of its associated postulate ensures.

41. That is, $\{\langle 1, 2 \rangle, \langle 1, 3 \rangle, \langle 2, 3 \rangle, \langle 1, 4 \rangle, \langle 2, 4 \rangle, \langle 3, 4 \rangle, \langle 1, 5 \rangle, \langle 2, 5 \rangle, \langle 3, 5 \rangle, \langle 4, 5 \rangle, \ldots\}$.

42. That is, $\{\langle 1, 1 \rangle, \langle 2, 4 \rangle, \langle 3, 9 \rangle, \langle 4, 16 \rangle, \ldots\}$.

43. That is, $\{\langle 1, 1, 2 \rangle, \langle 2, 1, 3 \rangle, \langle 2, 2, 4 \rangle, \langle 1, 2, 3 \rangle, \langle 3, 1, 4 \rangle, \langle 3, 2, 5 \rangle, \langle 3, 3, 6 \rangle, \langle 2, 3, 5 \rangle, \langle 1, 3, 4 \rangle, \langle 4, 1, 5 \rangle, \ldots\}$.

44. That is, $\{\langle 1, 1, 1 \rangle, \langle 2, 1, 2 \rangle, \langle 2, 2, 4 \rangle, \langle 1, 2, 2 \rangle, \langle 3, 1, 3 \rangle, \langle 3, 2, 6 \rangle, \langle 3, 3, 9 \rangle, \langle 2, 3, 6 \rangle, \langle 1, 3, 3 \rangle, \langle 4, 1, 4 \rangle, \ldots\}$.

Chapter 14: Metatheory

1. The term "sound" is used here in a new sense, different from the sense in which it was used earlier in the book. Confusion can be avoided by noting that the two senses of the term apply to different things. An argument is said to be sound if it is valid and its premises are true (§1.5). The tree method is said to be sound (with respect to validity) because if it tells you that an argument is valid, the argument really is valid.

2. We have said that the complexity $C(\alpha)$ of a wff α is the number of logical operators that α contains. Equivalently, we can define $C(\alpha)$ as follows (note that this definition has one clause for each clause in the definition of a wff, thereby ensuring that it assigns a complexity to every wff):

(i) where α is atomic, $C(\alpha) = 0$;

(ii) $C(\neg\alpha) = C(\forall \underline{x}\alpha) = C(\exists \underline{x}\alpha) = C(\alpha) + 1$;

(iii) $C((\alpha \wedge \beta)) = C((\alpha \vee \beta)) = C((\alpha \to \beta)) = C((\alpha \leftrightarrow \beta)) = C(\alpha) + C(\beta) + 1$.

Note that the identity symbol is part of the logical vocabulary, but it is not an operator (i.e., a connective or a quantifier) it is a predicate. So $a = b$, $x = y$, and so on are atomic wffs and have complexity 0; $a \neq b$, $x \neq y$, and so on are abbreviations of $\neg a = b$, $\neg x = y$, and so on and have complexity 1.

3. A conditional $\alpha \to \beta$ is equivalent to its contrapositive $\neg\beta \to \neg\alpha$. Thus, (S) follows immediately once its contrapositive is established. Do not confuse "contrapositive" and "converse." The converse of the conditional $\alpha \to \beta$ is $\beta \to \alpha$. In general, these are not equivalent.

4. Applying this rule may involve—depending on the particulars of the rule applied and the proposition(s) to which it is applied—writing down some new proposition(s) and/or marking some proposition with a check mark, backslash, and/or a name.

5. It may even happen at stage 0, if the tree closes immediately, or if the initial set of formulas contains no formula to which any tree rule can be applied.

6. That is, stage 1 looks like this for one way of constructing a tree starting with $\exists x F x$, $\exists x G x$, and $\neg\exists x(F x \wedge G x)$. Of course, there are other ways in which a tree could be constructed from these propositions—remember that we are placing no restrictions on the order in which rules may be applied—and for some of these other ways, stage 1 is different from what is shown here. The point at present is simply that however one constructs a tree, the construction can be seen as progressing through a series of stages.

7. When we first described how to read off a model from an open path in §10.2.1, we said that the domain can be any set of objects. Where there are n names on the path, we write the domain as $\{1, \ldots, n\}$, and we assign object 1 as the referent of the first name on the path, object 2 as the referent of the second name on the path, and so on (modulo any trimming in light of identity statements on the path). But it may occur to you that there is an issue here in relation to our present proof of (C). Given only the assumption that there is an open path in a finished tree that begins with $\alpha_1, \ldots, \alpha_n$, we want to establish that there is a model in which $\alpha_1, \ldots, \alpha_n$ are all true. But if all we are allowed to assume is that there is an open path, then it seems that we cannot assume that any objects exist at all—so we cannot assume that we have anything to put in the domain, and hence our model building never gets going. But hang on a minute: if we have an open path, then we do know that some things exist; that is, the wffs on the path, and the symbols that make them up. So we can let our domain comprise name symbols that appear on our path: the first name symbol on the path will then refer to itself in our model, the second name symbol will refer to itself, and so on (modulo any trimming).

8. That is, rule (3) in §12.2.1.2. Other references below to rules governing the truth of wffs (with such-and-such main operator) in models refer to other rules in §12.2.1.2.

9. Suppose a path contains just $R c d$, $a = c$, and $b = d$. Then a model read off from this path in accordance with the procedure of §13.4.2 has a domain containing two objects, 1 and 2; it assigns 1 as the referent of a and c and 2 as the referent of b and d; and it assigns $\{\langle 1, 2 \rangle\}$ as the extension of R. So the n-tuple $\langle$referent-of-a, referent-of-$b\rangle$

is in the extension of R, even though Rab does not appear in our path—contrary to the claim in the text. But this sort of counterexample to our claim is irrelevant in the present context; because it turns on the fact that the path in the example we have just considered is not saturated. To saturate it, we need to apply SI three times, adding Rad, Rcb, and Rab to the path (recall §13.4.1), and then Rab does appear in the path.

10. Again, you might think that a counterexample is provided by a path containing just $a = b$ and $b = c$: in a model read off from this path, a and c have the same referent, even though $a = c$ does not appear on the path. Again, however, this path is not saturated: SI allows us to add $a = c$ to it.

11. The procedure given in §10.3.5 now needs to be updated to take into account the new tree rules for identity. I leave this task as a challenge; if you have problems with it, see Jeffrey [2006, 77].

12. In §4.1, we said that the first step in determining whether an argument is valid is to translate it into the logical language, if the argument is given in English. The process of translation is certainly not mechanical. What we are interested in here is whether the process of testing the validity of an argument that is already in the logical language is mechanical.

13. Failing to say Yes is not to be equated with saying No, and vice versa. Think of Yes as a green light and No as a red light. The green light not coming on is not the same as the red light coming on, and vice versa.

14. When we say a decision procedure "exists," we do not mean that we necessarily know what it is: we mean that it exists in the abstract.

15. Think of Yes (valid)—a green light—as a closed tree, and No (not valid)—a red light—as a finished tree with an open path. When a tree is infinite, neither light comes on in a finite amount of time.

16. For details, see Börger et al. [1997, pp. 249–57].

17. See Partee et al. [1990, pp. 229–30].

18. Strictly speaking, what each proved is that there is no effective procedure for deciding validity in GPL, given a certain precise analysis of effective procedure.

19. For a proof, see, for example, Boolos et al. [2007, pp. 126–36].

20. In fact it does not, by itself, provide such a test in MPL; however, it can be supplemented to yield such a test in MPL, but not in GPL.

21. Throughout this book, we have taken an argument to have any finite number of premises, and when we have spoken of sets of propositions being satisfiable or unsatisfiable, we have been assuming that these sets are finite. The concepts of a set Γ of propositions being satisfiable or unsatisfiable, and of a proposition α being a logical consequence of a set Γ of propositions, can be generalized to the case where Γ is an infinite set, but the issues which then arise lie beyond the scope of this book. Notable among these issues is the fact that first-order logic is *compact*: if every finite subset of a (possibly infinite) set Γ of propositions is satisfiable, then Γ is satisfiable. For a proof and discussion of this fact, see, for example, Boolos et al. [2007, pp. 137–65].

22. By "some object" here we mean some object of the sort appropriate to P: an argument, where P is validity; a proposition, where P is logical truth; and so on.

23. What we have called "completeness with respect to logical truth" is often called "weak completeness;" what we have called "completeness with respect to validity" is sometimes called "strong completeness."

24. Note that a tree indicates that something has an s-property by having an open path (when the tree is finished—and we can then read off from this path a model that establishes the s-property), whereas a tree indicates that something has an a-property by having all paths closed—and recall that closed trees are always finite (§14.1.3), but finished trees with open paths may be infinite.

25. Here is a simple example. Imagine that proofs are written out as plain text without any punctuation apart from spaces between words: so the proof symbols are just the twenty-six letters of the alphabet, plus the space; and an array of these symbols is just a sequence of symbols. Think of the space as a twenty-seventh letter of the alphabet—symbolized by "$\llcorner$." Then we can generate all possible finite sequences of proof symbols by first writing out the one-symbol sequences in alphabetical order: a, b, c, . . . , x, y, z, $\llcorner$; then the two-symbol sequences in alphabetical order: aa, ab, ac, . . . , $\llcorner$y, $\llcorner$z, $\llcorner\llcorner$; and so on. Any possible sequence of these proof symbols will eventually be reached in this way. In the case of tree proofs—where there are more symbols, which may be arranged in more complex ways (two-dimensional arrays instead of one-dimensional sequences)—thinking up a procedure for generating every finite array of tree-proof symbols, one after the other, is trickier, but it is possible. At this point, recall §2.5.6. The point made there about PL applies also to our subsequent logical languages.

26. In the terminology of §13.7.3, where (14.3) is γ, (14.4) is γ^{**} conjoined with the postulate for S, S being the three-place relation introduced to replace the two-place function symbol s.

27. That is, the moment of time.

28. For details, see, for example, Burgess [2009, pp. 13–39]. Similar issues arise with respect to modal claims, such as "Bob is neither a vet nor a dog; he could have been a vet, but he could not have been a dog." We can represent these in GPLI by quantifying over and referring to wws and by adding an argument place for a ww to each predicate. Or we can augment the logical language with new connectives—modal operators—giving us a *modal* logic. See Chapter 11, n. 26.

29. For details, see, for example, Smith [2008].

Chapter 15: Other Methods of Proof

1. This chapter is written for readers who are already familiar with the material covered earlier in this book. This book does not offer multiple first routes into logic for the beginner: a route via trees, a route via natural deduction, and so on. It offers one such route—which goes via trees—and then in this chapter provides an overview of the other major proof methods for those who already have an understanding of logic via trees.

2. In its ordinary meaning in English, a *tableau*—plural *tableaux*—is an arrangement of objects representing a scene or story.

3. For the details of Beth tableaux, see Beth [1955]. Beth and Hintikka invented the tableau style of proof independently at the same time; see also Hintikka [1955]. The term "semantic tableau" is due to Beth. Tree proofs of the simpler sort presented in this book—one-sided tableaux—are due to Smullyan; his major work on the subject is Smullyan [1995] (first edition, 1968). Trees in this style (including a treatment of identity) were made popular by Jeffrey [2006] (first edition, 1967). The tree rules presented in this book are the same as Jeffrey's.

4. The four kinds of proof system examined in this book are canonical, but they are far from the only kinds. For example, other kinds of proof—notably *resolution*

[Robinson, 1965]—are common in the field of *automated theorem proving,* where it is *computers* that construct the proofs.

5. In a context where it is obvious, or does not matter, which proof system is in play—or in which we wish to speak generally about various proof systems, rather than about just one of them—we may omit the subscript on the turnstile, writing simply $\vdash \alpha$. See also n. 15.

6. Note also that, for convenience, we have omitted outermost parentheses—but strictly speaking, they should be there. (In future we shall leave such notes as this one implicit.)

7. The expression P here is a wff of PL, the language of propositional logic. Because we have temporarily switched back from predicate to propositional logic, capital letters now represent wffs again, not predicates.

8. There are actually two quite different ways of interpreting the process of defining some connectives in terms of others in the way just indicated. For a discussion, see §16.7.2.

9. The biconditional $\leftrightarrow$ does not appear and so would have to be defined out, or else yet further axioms added.

10. You can establish each equivalence by the kind of reasoning used in §10.1.1 to show that $\neg \exists \underline{x} \alpha(\underline{x})$ and $\forall \underline{x} \neg \alpha(\underline{x})$ are equivalent and in §10.1.2 to show that $\neg \forall \underline{x} \alpha(\underline{x})$ and $\exists \underline{x} \neg \alpha(\underline{x})$ are equivalent.

11. In GPLID (§13.6.2) and GPLIF (§13.7.1) there are complex terms; but here we are just talking about GPLI.

12. See Prior [1962, pp. 301–17] for a catalog of axiom systems (up to 1960). Note that Prior uses Polish notation (§2.5.5).

13. The conditional is true unless the antecedent is true (which requires that each of $\alpha_1, \ldots, \alpha_n$ be true) and β is false. So the conditional is a logical truth if this situation never occurs. But that is precisely what is required for the argument to be valid.

14. Recall (§2.4) that we use lowercased Greek letters α (alpha), β (beta), γ (gamma), and δ (delta) to stand for arbitrary wffs. We use the uppercased Greek letters Γ (gamma), Δ (delta), Θ (theta), and Λ (lambda) to stand for arbitrary sets of wffs.

15. We may also say that $\alpha_1, \ldots, \alpha_n \vdash \beta$ holds in system A. (The distinction here is between saying that $\alpha_1, \ldots, \alpha_n \vdash_A \beta$ [note the subscript A on the turnstile] holds [without qualification], and saying that $\alpha_1, \ldots, \alpha_n \vdash \beta$ [note the plain turnstile, with no subscript] holds in system A.) This formulation is especially convenient when we wish to compare different systems.

16. More subtly, for axiom schemas, each instance of an axiom schema must be a logical truth. We can establish this claim by showing that the axiom schema is a logicaltruth* (compare the discussion of the notion of a tautology* in §5.7).

17. The difference, then, is between "in each model, preserving truth (in that model)" and "preserving truth-in-all-models."

18. Line numbers always refer to the prefixed list, before extra lines are inserted. So by "line n" here I mean the wff on the nth line of the prefixed list before any extra lines are inserted. Of course, after extra lines have been inserted it is on a higher-numbered line.

19. See also Exercises 15.1.5, question 5. In fact a version of the deduction theorem with a weaker restriction also holds in $A_1^{\forall=}$, but the weaker restriction is complicated

to state (see Mendelson [1987, p. 59]) and is irrelevant to the present point, which is simply that the deduction theorem does not hold in its fully general form in $A_1^{\forall=}$, but it does hold in a restricted form.

20. By "exists" here we mean exists in the abstract: the point is precisely to show that a formal proof could be produced without actually producing one.

21. Recall that a formal proof is a sequence of wffs, and wffs contain only symbols of the logical language.

22. This definition of universal closure does not specify a unique wff as the universal closure, for we have not specified the order in which the universal quantifiers are to be prefixed. This will not matter for our purposes. If it did matter, we could easily specify an ordering of the variables in the language and then say that the added quantifiers in the universal closure must appear in order of the variables in them.

23. In other works, what I call "trewth" is just called "truth;" what I call "sowndness" is just called "soundness;" and so on. That is, the "w" words—"trewth" and words defined in terms of it, such as "sowndness" and others to be introduced below—are not standard: they are unique to this book. However, the notions I refer to using these words—notions defined below—are perfectly standard. I have two reasons for using new terms for standard notions. The first is that the notion of truth in a model (as defined earlier in this book—see, e.g., §12.2.1.2) is not defined in the same way as trewth in a model (to be introduced below). Given their different definitions, it is potentially confusing to label both these notions with the same word. As we shall see, the two notions end up coinciding to a certain extent, so ultimately it will not make much difference if we call them both by the same name, but doing so from the outset is potentially confusing. The second reason is that if we are going to apply the ordinary term "truth" to some precisely defined formal notion, then it would be a good idea if that formal notion were in some sense a precise spelling-out or analysis of the ordinary intuitive notion of truth, and as I explain in n. 25, I do not think that the notion of trewth can be understood in this way.

24. If a wff is not satisfied relative to $\mathfrak{M}^v$, we say that it is *unsatisfied* relative to $\mathfrak{M}^v$.

25. I return now to my second reason (mentioned in n. 23) for refraining from calling trewth "truth," which is that the notion of trewth cannot be seen as a precise spelling-out or analysis of the intuitive notion of truth. The reason is simple: open wffs can be trew, but the analogues of open wffs in English (what you get if you translate an open wff back into English, using some glossary) do not express propositions— they make no claim about the world—and cannot be regarded as true or false (recall §8.4.5). Thus, the precise notion is too inclusive: there are things that are trew that cannot be regarded as (intuitively) true (and similarly for fawlsity). So trewth does not correspond to the ordinary notion of truth.

What trewth does correspond to, it seems to me, is the notion of something that would be true (in the intuitive sense) whatever its free variables denoted, if its free variables were regarded as singular terms. That is why trewth coincides with (intuitive) truth for closed wffs: wffs that have no free variables. For open wffs, however, the notions come apart: an open wff that would be true no matter what (i.e., is such that if it were converted into a proposition—a closed wff—by turning its free variables into names, then it would be true no matter what those names denoted) is not actually true (intuitively) as it stands (with free occurrences of variables in it), just as an unfinished manuscript by a famous writer does not actually have an interesting conclusion (because it has no conclusion at all), even if it is true that no matter how she had finished it, the conclusion would have been interesting.

Some authors use the term "true" where I have used "trew" (i.e., they say that a wff is true in a model iff it is satisfied in that model relative to every value assignment on that model). Others use the term "true" slightly differently: they restrict it to closed wffs but define it in the same way (i.e., they say that a closed wff is true in a model iff it is satisfied in that model relative to every value assignment on that model; but even if an open wff has this property, the term "true" is not applied to it). The latter terminological move makes no difference to my point. For the property these authors call "truth" in closed wffs is one that open wffs can also have. My point is that, because open wffs can possess it, this property cannot be "truth" in the intuitive sense. Declining to call an open wff "true" when it has this property does not take away from the fact that one has defined a property that open wffs can have. My point is that because open wffs can also have this property, possessing it does not make something (not even a closed wff) true in the ordinary sense.

So, I claim, the notion of trewth (satisfaction relative to all value assignments) does not provide an analysis of the intuitive notion of truth. But that is not to say that we should abandon it—it is only to say that we should understand it correctly. In fact, we certainly should not abandon it: trewth and satisfaction are useful notions. This is precisely because satisfaction is well defined (relative to a given model and variable assignment) for all wffs, open and closed. The notion of satisfaction has uses throughout logic, and not only in situations where we have proof systems that allow open wffs. Even closed wffs have open wffs as subformulas, and often it is convenient to be able to say things that apply to wffs and their subformulas alike.

26. Throughout the following, we assume that $\alpha_1, \ldots, \alpha_n$ and β are closed. This assumption is not necessary, but it makes for a simpler presentation.

27. Likewise, if a set Γ is A-consistent, then it cannot contain $\underline{a} \neq \underline{a}$, for any name $\underline{a}$, because any adequate axiomatic system A for identity will allow $\underline{a} = \underline{a}$ to be proved, for any name $\underline{a}$.

28. The details of this will depend on the axioms and rules of A, but here's one possibility. If the deduction theorem holds for A, then we have $\alpha_1, \ldots, \alpha_n \vdash_A \neg\beta \to \alpha$ and $\alpha_1, \ldots, \alpha_n \vdash_A \neg\beta \to \neg\alpha$. If we can prove the logical truth $(\neg\beta \to \alpha) \to ((\neg\beta \to \neg\alpha) \to \beta)$ in A, then if (MP) is a rule of A, we have $\alpha_1, \ldots, \alpha_n \vdash_A \beta$.

29. We are assuming here that if a tree is infinite (i.e., it grows at stage n for every n), then it has an infinite path; this result was established in §10.3.7.

30. Recall that $=$ is part of the logical vocabulary. On linear orders, see also §16.3.

31. Recall the discussion of the informal proof in Figure 15.6. Although we may write in the extra steps 6 and 7 at the end of our derivation, what results is not then a derivation in system A_1: it is a hybrid of a formal derivation (steps 1–5) with two extra lines (6 and 7) that are outside system A_1 and indicate what may be proved in system A_1. Furthermore, line 7 is not $P \to R$: it is $P \to Q, Q \to R \vdash_{A_1} P \to R$, which says precisely that there is a derivation in A_1 whose last line is $P \to R$.

32. This footnote is for readers who already have a knowledge of the literature, who might otherwise misunderstand what I am doing at this point. The proof in Figure 15.11 looks (at first glance) like the proofs in Fitch [1952], which employ *scope lines*. Kalish et al. [1980], in contrast, present natural deduction proofs using *boxes*.

The proofs in the two books just cited are not mere notational variants of one another: some of the inference rules are different. Thus, readers who already have a knowledge of the literature might get the mistaken impression that at this point I am switching proof systems: from one like that in Kalish et al. [1980] to one like that in Fitch [1952]. I am, however, doing no such thing. I am not changing the proof system at this point: I am simply saying that we may draw boxes in a quicker way, that is, without showing all their lines in full. There is just one proof system in play (at the moment—we shall consider others below), and it involves boxes. However, for convenience—just as we omit outermost parentheses—we will omit some of the lines that make up a box: the top line, the bottom line, the right line, and most of the line under the assumption. What is left may look like something new (a scope line) but it is in fact just the left side of a box.

33. "TND" is from the Latin "tertium non datur"; this rule is also commonly known as the principle of excluded middle. "NCD" stands for "nonconstructive dilemma," and "RAA" for "reductio ad absurdum." The rule $(\neg E')$ is sometimes known as "ex falso quodlibet," which means "from a falsehood, [infer] whatever you like."

34. I say "might," because the finished tree might be infinite, and hence not a proof.

35. I say "except perhaps α," because there may be another assumption of α earlier in the proof, which is still in play. So Γ_n may contain α—but we cannot assume that it does.

36. The symbol $\cup$ represents the *union* of two sets. Given two sets Γ and Δ, $\Gamma \cup \Delta$ is the set containing everything in Γ and everything in Δ and nothing else. So, for example, $\{1, 2, 3\} \cup \{4, 5, 6\} = \{1, 2, 3, 4, 5, 6\}$. For further discussion, see §16.1.3. Note that $\Gamma \vDash \beta$ is another way of writing $\gamma_1, \ldots, \gamma_n \vDash \beta$, where $\gamma_1, \ldots, \gamma_n$ are the members of Γ.

37. The box method was invented by Jaśkowski [1934]. See also the books mentioned in n. 32.

38. The list method in this form was developed by Suppes [1957]; a different form of the list method was originally invented by Jaśkowski [1934]. Here we discuss only the rules for the conditional; for a complete presentation of a natural deduction system of this style—including the other connectives, the quantifiers, and identity—see Lemmon [1965].

39. This style of natural deduction proof was invented by Gentzen [1935]. It is usually called the "tree" style of natural deduction proof, but I avoid the term "tree" here, because using it might lead to confusion between this style of natural deduction proof and the tree proofs used earlier in this book.

40. For a complete presentation of a natural deduction system of this style, including the other connectives, the quantifiers, and identity, see van Dalen [2004].

41. Sequent calculus was invented by Gentzen [1935]. His stated aim was to come up with a system that—like the original axiomatic systems examined in §15.1 (before we introduced the idea of allowing assumptions in derivations)—does not allow assumptions, but that divides the rules of inference into an introduction rule and an elimination rule for each logical operator (as in natural deduction systems). Gentzen notes that the most obvious way of eliminating assumptions in natural deduction proofs would be to take such a proof, and wherever we find a formula α that depends on earlier assumptions $\beta_1, \ldots, \beta_n$, replace it with $(\beta_1 \wedge \ldots \wedge \beta_n) \to \alpha$. However, this then makes the operators $\wedge$ and $\to$ feature in (almost) all rules, and so we lose the desired

feature that each operator should appear only in its own introduction and elimination rules. Gentzen's solution was to replace the wff $(\beta_1 \wedge \ldots \wedge \beta_n) \to \alpha$ with the sequent $\{\beta_1, \ldots, \beta_n\} \Rightarrow \{\alpha\}$, where the latter has the same intuitive meaning as the former; that is, the sequent holds just in case its corresponding conditional is true.

42. If assumptions are allowed, then the aim is that the last line should be true in any model in which all the (undischarged) assumptions are true; that is, the argument whose premises are those assumptions and whose conclusion is the last line should be valid.

43. Note that we write simply $\{B\} \Rightarrow \{A\}$ on the left branch, not $\{B\} \Rightarrow \{A, A\}$, and likewise $\{B\} \Rightarrow \{A\}$ on the right branch, not $\{B, B\} \Rightarrow \{A\}$. This is because a set either contains something, or it does not: a set cannot contain the same thing twice. So $\{B, B\}$ is just another—more long-winded—way of writing the set $\{B\}$ (i.e., the set containing the wff B and nothing else). For further discussion, see §16.1.1.

44. We do not look, for example, at negated atomic formulas (i.e., atomic formulas that are supposed to be false).

45. To increase readability, I omit auxiliary sets of wffs Γ and Δ on the left and right.

46. In predicate logic, of course, this is not the case: we can have an infinite search for a sequent proof, just as we can have infinite trees.

47. The proof also makes use of Thinning and the axiom $\{\beta\} \Rightarrow \{\beta\}$.

48. The notion of a sequence is explained in §16.5.

49. The symbol $\frown$ represents concatenation of sequences; see §16.5 for an explanation of this notion. Note also that we have hitherto used Γ and Δ to represent sets of wffs. In this last sentence, we use them to represent sequences of wffs. It will always be clear from the context whether capital Greek letters are being used to represent sequences or sets.

50. The notion of a multiset is explained in more detail in §16.6.

51. Note that a terminated failed systematic search for a proof that a sequent holds logically constitutes a proof that it does not hold logically (of course, as with trees, the search might not terminate).

Chapter 16: Set Theory

1. "Unter einer 'Mannigfaltigkeit' oder 'Menge' verstehe ich nämlich allgemein jedes Viele, welches sich als Eines denken läßt" [Cantor, 1932, 204].

2. This usage is not the same as—but clearly related to—the usage of "extension" to mean the value of a predicate.

3. Some works use the symbol $\subset$ to indicate proper subset (and use $\subseteq$ in the way we do here), but others use $\subset$ to mean exactly what we mean by $\subseteq$.

4. Sometimes $\bar{S}$ or S^c is written instead of S'.

5. Sometimes $S - T$ is written instead of $S \setminus T$; sometimes the former notation is restricted to contexts where $T \subseteq S$.

6. Consider the definitions of union and intersection. For any x, $x \in S \cup T$ iff $x \in S \vee x \in T$, and $x \in T \cup S$ iff $x \in T \vee x \in S$. But $\alpha \vee \beta$ and $\beta \vee \alpha$ are equivalent, so $x \in S \cup T$ iff $x \in T \cup S$—hence, $S \cup T = T \cup S$. Likewise, for any x, $x \in S \cap T$ iff $x \in S \wedge x \in T$, and $x \in T \cap S$ iff $x \in T \wedge x \in S$. But $\alpha \wedge \beta$ and $\beta \wedge \alpha$ are equivalent, so $x \in S \cap T$ iff $x \in T \cap S$—hence, $S \cap T = T \cap S$.

7. Consider the definition of set-theoretic difference. For any x, $x \in S \setminus T$ iff $x \in S \wedge \neg x \in T$, and $x \in T \setminus S$ iff $x \in T \wedge \neg x \in S$. In general, $\alpha \wedge \neg \beta$ is not equivalent

to $\beta \wedge \neg\alpha$, so it is not in general the case that $x \in S \setminus T$ iff $x \in T \setminus S$—hence, in general $S \setminus T \neq T \setminus S$. However, when α and β are equivalent, $\alpha \wedge \neg\beta$ is equivalent to $\beta \wedge \neg\alpha$: both are equivalent to the contradiction $\alpha \wedge \neg\alpha$. This corresponds to the fact that when $S = T$ (i.e., $x \in S$ iff $x \in T$), $S \setminus T = T \setminus S = \emptyset$.

8. There are various systems of axiomatic set theory. Not all of them feature axioms that are true in the cumulative hierarchy. However, what is generally considered to be the standard set of axioms for set theory—ZFC (Zermelo-Fraenkel set theory with the axiom of Choice)—does: see Boolos [1971], Shoenfield [1977], and Devlin [1993, pp. 29–65].

9. For the history of early reductions of ordered pairs to sets, see van Heijenoort [1967, 224].

10. Of course, there are other equally good options; for example, we could reduce the ordered $(n + 1)$-tuple $\langle x, y_1, \ldots, y_n \rangle$ to the ordered pair $\langle x, \langle y_1, \ldots, y_n \rangle \rangle$.

11. In this case, "both" directions are really one and the same. If $x = y$, then R holding between x and y in that order, and R holding between x and y in the other order, are just the same thing: R holding between x and x. While there are two ordered pairs containing both the objects 1 and 2 (i.e., $\langle 1, 2 \rangle$ and $\langle 2, 1 \rangle$), there is just one ordered pair containing the object 1 (i.e., $\langle 1, 1 \rangle$). This follows from the identity condition for ordered pairs discussed in §16.2.1.

12. Given what we said in n. 11, evidently a relation that is asymmetric must also be irreflexive.

13. This condition says nothing about the case $x = y$: all the different possibilities— $\langle x, x \rangle \in R$ for all x (reflexivity), $\langle x, x \rangle \in R$ for no x (irreflexivity), $\langle x, x \rangle \in R$ for some but not all x (neither reflexive nor irreflexive)—are compatible with connectedness.

14. That is, a partial order on $\wp S$, not on S.

15. This use of the arrow symbol has nothing to do with our use of this symbol for the conditional: these are simply two different uses of the same symbol. This phenomenon—where the same term or symbol means different things in different contexts—is common in logic and mathematics.

16. Readers coming from certain backgrounds might not be used to thinking of partial functions as functions at all. They might take a "function" from S to T to mean a subset of $S \times T$, where every element of S appears *exactly* once as the first element of an ordered pair in the set. Here—and this is standard in logic—we take a function from S to T to be a subset of $S \times T$, where every element of S appears *at most* once as the first element of an ordered pair in the set. If, in addition, every element of S appears once as the first element of an ordered pair in the set, it is a total function; if not, it is a partial function—but we still count it as a function. Partial functions arise naturally at many points in logic.

17. It is also useful in some contexts to countenance the *empty* sequence of members of S: the sequence with no entries, which has length zero (no positions). In the sense in which we have just defined finite and infinite sequences, the empty sequence is neither a finite sequence nor an infinite sequence (it is not a total function from any initial segment—as we defined "initial segment"—of $\mathbb{Z}^+$ to S, nor is it a total function from $\mathbb{Z}^+$ to S). We shall not consider the empty sequence further here, but note that if we did wish to include it when we spoke of "all sequences of members of S" (which, as mentioned, is useful in some contexts), we would need to alter or augment our existing definition of a sequence to include it.

18. If we chose instead to take the other fact about characteristic functions of intersections stated in §16.4.2 as our starting point—that is, $I_{S \cap T}(x) = I_S(x) \times I_T(x)$—then we would obtain a very different notion of intersection of multisets: one according to which the intersection of a multiset that contains a twice and a multiset that contains a five times contains a ten times. Likewise, in the case of union, it is more natural to take the first fact stated in §16.4.2 as our starting point—that is, $I_{S \cup T}(x) = \max\{I_S(x), I_T(x)\}$.

19. The notion of complement of multisets is a bit more subtle. For a start, the fact about characteristic functions of complements stated in §16.4.2—that is, $I_{S'}(x) = 1 - I_S(x)$—is not much help when I may take values greater than 1. For a discussion, see Hickman [1980]. For more details about multisets, see, for example, Syropoulos [2001].

20. In the case of PL, the corresponding clause says "any basic proposition is a wff." This clause tells us that for any basic proposition x in S, the length-1 sequence $\langle x \rangle$, which has x in its only position, is in W.

21. Again, because concatenation is defined on sequences, we cannot concatenate α directly with the symbols $\forall$ and $\underline{x}$: we have to concatenate α with the length-1 sequences $\langle \forall \rangle$ and $\langle \underline{x} \rangle$.

REFERENCES

Adams, Ernest. The logic of conditionals. *Inquiry* 8:166–97, 1965.

Anderson, Alan Ross, and Nuel D. Belnap. *Entailment: The Logic of Relevance and Necessity*, volume I. Princeton University Press, Princeton, N.J., 1975.

Aristotle. *Metaphysics*, c. 350 BC-a. In Jonathan Barnes, editor, *The Complete Works of Aristotle: The Revised Oxford Translation*, volume 2 (Princeton University Press, Princeton, N.J., 1984).

———. *Prior Analytics*, c.350 BC-b. In Jonathan Barnes, editor, *The Complete Works of Aristotle: The Revised Oxford Translation*, volume 1 (Princeton University Press, Princeton, N.J., 1984).

Austin, J. L. Ifs and cans. In J. O. Urmson and G. J. Warnock, editors, *Philosophical Papers*, pp. 205–32. Clarendon Press, Oxford, second edition, 1970.

Barrett, Robert B., and Alfred J. Stenner. The myth of the exclusive "or." *Mind* 80:116–21, 1971.

Bencivenga, Ermanno. Free logics. In D. M. Gabbay and F. Guenthner, editors, *Handbook of Philosophical Logic*, volume 5, pp. 147–96. Kluwer, Dordrecht, second edition, 2002.

Bennett, Jonathan. *A Philosophical Guide to Conditionals*. Clarendon Press, Oxford, 2003.

Bergmann, Merrie, James Moor, and Jack Nelson. *The Logic Book*. McGraw-Hill, Boston, fifth edition, 2009.

Beth, Evert W. Semantic entailment and formal derivability. *Mededelingen der Koninklijke Nederlandse Akademie van Wetenschappen, Afd. Letterkunde*, Nieuwe Reeks 18:309–42, 1955.

Boolos, George S. The iterative conception of set. *Journal of Philosophy* 68:215–31, 1971.

Boolos, George S., and Richard C. Jeffrey. *Computability and Logic*. Cambridge University Press, Cambridge, third edition, 1989.

Boolos, George S., John P. Burgess, and Richard C. Jeffrey. *Computability and Logic*. Cambridge University Press, Cambridge, fifth edition, 2007.

Börger, Egon, Erich Grädel, and Yuri Gurevich. *The Classical Decision Problem*. Springer, Berlin, 1997.

Burgess, John P. *Philosophical Logic*. Princeton University Press, Princeton, N.J., 2009.

Cantor, Georg. *Gesammelte Abhandlungen*. Julius Springer, Berlin, 1932.

Carnap, Rudolf. *Meaning and Necessity: A Study in Semantics and Modal Logic*. University of Chicago Press, Chicago, enlarged edition, 1956.

Cartwright, Richard. Propositions. In *Philosophical Essays*, pp. 33–53. MIT Press, Cambridge, Mass., 1987.

Church, Alonzo. *Introduction to Mathematical Logic*. Princeton University Press, Princeton, N.J., revised enlarged edition, 1956.

Cobham, Alan. The intrinsic computational difficulty of functions. In Y. Bar-Hillel, editor, *Proceedings of the 1964 Congress for Logic, Mathematics, and Philosophy of Science*, pp. 24–30. North-Holland, Amsterdam, 1964.

D'Agostino, Marcello. Are tableaux an improvement on truth-tables? Cut-free proofs and bivalence. *Journal of Logic, Language, and Information* 1:235–52, 1992.

Davis, Martin D., Ron Sigal, and Elaine J. Weyuker. *Computability, Complexity, and Languages: Fundamentals of Theoretical Computer Science*. Morgan Kaufmann, San Francisco, second edition, 1994.

Devlin, Keith. *The Joy of Sets: Fundamentals of Contemporary Set Theory*. Springer, New York, second edition, 1993.

Dowty, David R., Robert E. Wall, and Stanley Peters. *Introduction to Montague Semantics*. D. Reidel, Dordrecht, 1981.

Edgington, Dorothy. Do conditionals have truth-conditions? 1986. In Frank Jackson, editor, *Conditionals*, pp. 176–201 Oxford University Press, Oxford, 1991.

Edmonds, Jack. Paths, trees, and flowers. *Canadian Journal of Mathematics* 17:449–67, 1965.

Enderton, Herbert B. *A Mathematical Introduction to Logic*. Academic Press, San Diego, second edition, 2001.

Fitch, Frederic Brenton. *Symbolic Logic: An Introduction*. Ronald Press, New York, 1952.

Frege, Gottlob. Begriffsschrift, a formula language, modeled upon that of arithmetic, for pure thought, 1879. In Jean van Heijenoort, editor, *From Frege to Gödel: A Source Book in Mathematical Logic, 1879–1931*, pp. 1–82 (Harvard University Press, Cambridge, Mass., 1967).

———. On sense and meaning, 1892. In Gottlob Frege [edited by Brian McGuinness, translated by Max Black, V. H. Dudman, Peter Geach, Hans Kaal, E.-H. W. Kluge, Brian McGuinness, and R. H. Stoothof.] *Collected Papers on Mathematics, Logic, and Philosophy*, pp. 157–77 (Basil Blackwell, Oxford, 1984).

———. Logical investigations, Part I: Thoughts, 1918–19. In Gottlob Frege [edited by Brian McGuinness, translated by Max Black, V. H. Dudman, Peter Geach, Hans Kaal, E.-H. W. Kluge, Brian McGuinness, and R. H. Stoothof.] *Collected Papers on Mathematics, Logic, and Philosophy*, pp. 351–72 (Basil Blackwell, Oxford, 1984).

———. [Edited and translated by Montgomery Furth.] *The Basic Laws of Arithmetic: Exposition of the System*. University of California Press, Berkeley, 1964. Originally published in German as *Grundgesetze der Arithmetik* in 1893 (volume I) and 1903 (volume II).

Gamut, L.T.F. *Logic, Language, and Meaning*, volume I: *Introduction to Logic*. University of Chicago Press, Chicago, 1991a.

———. *Logic, Language, and Meaning*, volume II: *Intensional Logic and Logical Grammar*. University of Chicago Press, Chicago, 1991b.

Gentzen, Gerhard. Investigations into logical deduction, 1935. In M. E. Szabo, editor, *The Collected Papers of Gerhard Gentzen*, pp. 68–131. North-Holland, Amsterdam, 1969.

Grice, Paul. *Studies in the Way of Words*. Harvard University Press, Cambridge, Mass., 1989.

Haack, Susan. *Philosophy of Logics*. Cambridge University Press, Cambridge, 1978.

Heim, Irene, and Angelika Kratzer. *Semantics in Generative Grammar*. Blackwell, Malden, Mass., 1998.

Hickman, J. L. A note on the concept of multiset. *Bulletin of the Australian Mathematical Society* 22:211–17, 1980.

Hintikka, K. Jaakko J. Form and content in quantification theory. *Acta Philosophica Fennica* 8:7–55, 1955.

Hodges, Wilfrid. *Logic*. Penguin, London, 1977.

Hrbacek, Karel, and Thomas Jech. *Introduction to Set Theory*. Marcel Dekker, New York, third edition, 1999.

Hughes, G. E., and M. J. Cresswell. *A New Introduction to Modal Logic*. Routledge, London, 1996.

Hughes, R.I.G., editor. *A Philosophical Companion to First-Order Logic*. Hackett, Indianapolis, Ind., 1993.

Jackson, Frank. On assertion and indicative conditionals, 1979. In Frank Jackson, editor, *Conditionals*, pp. 111–35. Oxford University Press, Oxford, 1991.

———. *Conditionals*. Basil Blackwell, Oxford, 1987.

———. Introduction, 1991. In Frank Jackson, editor, *Conditionals*, pp. 1–7. Oxford University Press, Oxford, 1991.

Jaśkowski, Stanisław. On the rules of suppositions in formal logic, 1934. In Storrs McCall, editor, *Polish Logic: 1920–1939*, pp. 232–58 (Clarendon Press, Oxford, 1967).

Jeffrey, Richard. [Edited, with a new supplement, by John P. Burgess.] *Formal Logic: Its Scope and Limits*. Hackett, Indianapolis, Ind., fourth edition, 2006.

Jevons, William Stanley. *Elementary Lessons in Logic*. Macmillan, London, 1870.

Kalish, Donald, Richard Montague, and Gary Mar. *Logic: Techniques of Formal Reasoning*. Harcourt Brace Jovanovich, San Diego, second edition, 1980.

Kleene, Stephen Cole. *Introduction to Metamathematics*. D. Van Nostrand, Princeton, N.J., 1952.

Kuratowski, Casimir. Sur la notion de l'ordre dans la théorie des ensembles. *Fundamenta Mathematicae* 2:161–71, 1921.

Lehmann, Scott. More free logic. In D. M. Gabbay and F. Guenthner, editors, *Handbook of Philosophical Logic*, volume 5, pp. 197–259. Kluwer, Dordrecht, 2nd edition, 2002.

Lemmon, E. J. *Beginning Logic*. Nelson, London, 1965.

Lewis, David. Probabilities of conditionals and conditional probabilities, 1976. In Frank Jackson, editor, *Conditionals*, pp. 76–101. Oxford University Press, Oxford, 1991.

———. Probabilities of conditionals and conditional probabilities II, 1986. In Frank Jackson, editor, *Conditionals*, pp. 102–110. Oxford University Press, Oxford, 1991.

Łukasiewicz, Jan. *Aristotle's Syllogistic from the Standpoint of Modern Formal Logic.* Clarendon Press, Oxford, second enlarged edition, 1957.

Mendelson, Elliott. *Introduction to Mathematical Logic.* Wadsworth and Brooks/Cole, Pacific Grove, Calif., third edition, 1987.

Parfit, Derek. *Reasons and Persons.* Clarendon Press, Oxford, corrected edition, 1987.

Partee, Barbara H., Alice Ter Meulen, and Robert E. Wall. *Mathematical Methods in Linguistics.* Kluwer, Dordrecht, 1990.

Peirce, Charles Sanders. The fixation of belief, 1877. In Charles Hartshorne and Paul Weiss, editors, *The Collected Papers of Charles Sanders Peirce*, volume 5: *Pragmatism and Pragmaticism*, book II, paper IV (Harvard University Press, Cambridge, Mass., 1934).

———. Prolegomena to an apology for pragmaticism, 1906. In Charles Hartshorne and Paul Weiss, editors, *The Collected Papers of Charles Sanders Peirce*, volume 4: *The Simplest Mathematics*, book II, chapter 6 (Harvard University Press, Cambridge, Mass., 1933).

Plato. *Cratylus*, c. 360 BC. In Edith Hamilton and Huntington Cairns, editors, *The Collected Dialogues of Plato* (Pantheon Books, New York, 1963).

Priest, Graham. *An Introduction to Non-Classical Logic: From Ifs to Is.* Cambridge University Press, Cambridge, second edition, 2008.

Prior, A. N. *Formal Logic.* Clarendon Press, Oxford, second edition, 1962.

Quine, Willard Van Orman. *Mathematical Logic.* Harper and Row, New York, revised edition, 1951.

———. *Methods of Logic.* Harvard University Press, Cambridge, Mass., fourth edition, 1982.

———. *Philosophy of Logic.* Harvard University Press, Cambridge, Mass., second edition, 1986.

Robinson, J. A. A machine-oriented logic based on the resolution principle. *Journal of the Association for Computing Machinery* 12:23–41, 1965.

Russell, Bertrand. Letter to Frege, 1902. In Jean van Heijenoort, editor, *From Frege to Gödel: A Source Book in Mathematical Logic, 1879–1931*, pp. 124–25 (Harvard University Press, Cambridge, Mass., 1967).

———. On denoting. *Mind* 14:479–93, 1905.

Shoenfield, Joseph R. *Mathematical Logic.* Addison-Wesley, Reading, Mass., 1967.

———. Axioms of set theory. In Jon Barwise, editor, *Handbook of Mathematical Logic*, pp. 321–44. Elsevier, Amsterdam, 1977.

Sipser, Michael. *Introduction to the Theory of Computation.* Thomson, Boston, second edition, 2006.

Smith, Nicholas J.J. *Vagueness and Degrees of Truth.* Oxford University Press, Oxford, 2008.

Smullyan, Raymond M. *First-Order Logic*. Dover, New York, corrected edition, 1995.

Stalnaker, Robert. A theory of conditionals, 1968. In Frank Jackson, editor, *Conditionals*, pp. 28–45. Oxford University Press, Oxford, 1991.

Suppes, Patrick. *Introduction to Logic*. D. Van Nostrand, Princeton, N.J., 1957.

Syropoulos, Apostolos. Mathematics of multisets. In Cristian S. Calude, Gheorghe Păun, Grzegorz Rozenberg, and Arto Salomaa, editors, *Multiset Processing: Mathematical, Computer Science, and Molecular Computing Points of View*, pp. 347–58. Springer, Berlin, 2001.

Tarski, Alfred. On the concept of logical consequence, 1936. In Alfred Tarski [translated by J. H. Woodger] *Logic, Semantics, Metamathematics: Papers from 1923 to 1938*, pp. 409–20 (Clarendon Press, Oxford, 1956).

———. *Introduction to Logic and to the Methodology of Deductive Sciences*. Oxford University Press, New York, second revised edition, 1946.

van Dalen, Dirk. *Logic and Structure*. Springer, Berlin, fourth edition, 2004.

van Heijenoort, Jean, editor. *From Frege to Gödel: A Source Book in Mathematical Logic, 1879–1931*. Harvard University Press, Cambridge, Mass., 1967.

Whitehead, Alfred North, and Bertrand Russell. *Principia Mathematica*, volume I. Cambridge University Press, Cambridge, 1910.

INDEX

prenex, 296–297, 372
probability
  conditional, 478–479n20
  subjective, 478–479n20
problem
  intractable, 481n1
  tractable, 481n1
procedure
  for constructing trees, 235–237,
    367–369, 373, 381, 500n11
  decision (*See* decision, procedure)
  effective, 19, 159, 237, 368–369,
    471n29, 500n18 (*See also*
    tree, method, whether it is an
    effective procedure)
product
  Cartesian, 451
  logical, 475n6
proof, 371, 375–376
  axiomatic (*See* axiomatic proof)
  box, 408–409, 416, 504–505n32,
    505n37
  constructive, 434
  cut-free, 433
  formal, 375, 385, 395–397
  informal, 395–397
  list style (*See also* axiomatic proof)
    natural deduction, 416–418, 505n38
    sequent calculus, 424–425, 437
  method, 358, 385–386
  natural deduction (*See* natural
    deduction proof system)
  nonconstructive, 433–434
  search, 381, 405, 420, 424–426, 431,
    437, 506n51 (*See also* search,
    stack)
  sequent (*See* sequent, calculus)
  stack style
    natural deduction, 418–419, 505n39
    sequent calculus, 424–426 (*See also*
    search, stack)
  style, 385–386
  symbol, 375
  system, 386
  theory, 420, 437
property, 168, 191, 266, 440–441, 489n7
proposition, 10, 187–188, 195–196,

267, 289–291, 337, 470n17,
477n8, 489n7, 503–504n25. *See
also* constant, propositional;
parameter, propositional; wff,
closed
  atomic, 168, 191–192
  basic, 24, 32–33, 164, 166, 168, 473n8,
    482n2
  coarse-grained, 257
  compound, 24, 51–53
  definition of
    intuitive, 5, 242–243, 491n20
    precise, 253–256
    pluralism with regard to, 256–257
  fine-grained, 257
  versus formula, 35
  Fregean, 490n19
  versus nonproposition, 4–5, 121–122
  Russellian, 490n19
  versus sentence, 6–7, 8–9, 32, 33–34,
    170–171, 292
  way of making true or false, 63, 146,
    163, 189–191, 192–193, 206,
    211, 475n1

quantification. *See also* quantifier
  theory, 384
quantifier, 167, 173, 184, 186
  alternative symbols for, 483n10
  equivalences, 293–297
  existential, 173, 175
    tree rule, 214–215
      need for a new name, 216–217
    tree rule for negated, 214
    ways of expressing, 173
  moving, 293–297
  multiple, 271–274
  numerical, 321–325, 384
  restricted, 177–180
    pragmatic approach, 178–180
    semantic approach, 179–180
  scope, 178, 186–187
  symbol, 184
  translating into MPL, 174–177
  universal, 173, 174
    tree rule, 217–219
    tree rule for negated, 214